THE
URBAN PATTERN

SIXTH EDITION

THE URBAN PATTERN

SIXTH EDITION

SIMON EISNER   ARTHUR GALLION   STANLEY EISNER

VNR VAN NOSTRAND REINHOLD
New York

Printed in the United States of America

Van Nostrand Reinhold
115 Fifth Avenue
New York, New York 10003

Chapman and Hall
2-6 Boundary Row
London SE1 8HN, England

Thomas Nelson Australia
102 Dodds Street
South Melbourne 3205
Victoria, Australia

Nelson Canada
1120 Birchmount Road
Scarborough, Ontario MIK 5G4, Canada

16 15 14 13 12 11 10 9 8 7 6 5 4 3 2 1

Library of Congress Cataloging-in-Publication Data

Eisner, Simon.
    The urban pattern : city planning and design. — 6th ed. / Simon
  Eisner, Stanley A. Eisner, Arthur B. Gallion.
       p.   cm.
     Rev. ed. of: The urban pattern / Arthur B. Gallion, Simon Eisner.
  5th   ed. c1986
     Includes bibliographical references (p.
  and index.
    ISBN 0-442-00752-3
    1 . City planning.   I. Eisner, Stanley A.   II. Gallion, Arthur B.
  III. Gallion, Arthur B.   Urban pattern. IV. Title.
  NA9031.E38   1992
  711' .4--dc20   91-44990
                                                         CIP

To Arthur B. Gallion 1902–1978

Arthur Gallion loved and respected the people of this world. He traveled to many lands and observed the basic goodness of all he met. As an educator, he devoted much of his life to the betterment of young seekers of knowledge. He expressed concern for honesty among those who determine the character of the environment. His enthusiasm and critical dialogues inspired and motivated all who knew him.

Development of this Sixth edition of *The Urban Pattern* without the creative contributions of Arthur Gallion has been a lonely task.

Simon Eisner
and
Stanley A. Eisner

CONTENTS

No one can fail to observe that, despite the marvels of human inventive genius and the material comforts enjoyed by some, the spiritual and cultural lives of many people in the modern world are still impoverished. All the thought and money that have been devoted to planning have not substantially improved the total environment. The authors of this book do not presume that planning will solve all of the ills of the urban community or in itself be adequate to preserve or conserve our natural resources, even though major advances have been made in the years since the first edition was published. Without continued creative planning and active implementation, however, we will not be able to begin to achieve an environment conducive to the good life to which we aspire.

The sixth edition of *The Urban Pattern* has been designed for students and for persons active in professional offices, as well as for individuals and organizations interested in the political and social sciences, the environment, and urban planning practices. We hope that the book and the concepts contained herein will encourage readers to fulfill their professional potential and expand their abilities to better serve the public they represent, consistent with the highest ethical standards. The reorganization and additions to the book are a response to the changes that have taken place in recent years in the comprehensive planning and urban design profession and should be of interest to both novice and professional.

The current thrust for comprehensiveness by the planning profession, in response to numerous rulings and decisions by the courts, has broadened the horizons and responsibilities of persons in or entering the field.

No longer concerned only with land use regulation, professionals must now be increasingly involved in related fields. The "comprehensive planner" must blend many related individuals in the complicated and often conflicting interests of urban living.

The sixth edition of *The Urban Pattern* responds to many of these new opportunities and concerns. It focuses on areas where innovation and experimentation affect the public and private sectors, notably the crisis in housing availability. It also examines growth management regulations, which some communities require as they begin to feel the stress of growth without the substantial economic base required to support the needs and demands of new residents.

The environment within and around urban areas has been expanded with respect to the increasing concern for health and security in those urban areas subject to careless treatment of resources. Environmental impacts are cited as well as the current method of determining the extent of potential problems and some of the efforts essential to mitigate them. The role of geography in determining the location and nature of urban centers is explored as well.

The problems confronting the increasing number of aging persons are of paramount importance to planners both in the United States and abroad. Materials dealing with housing programs for the elderly in many nations are included. Planning for public health is also discussed.

Policy planning, the current emphasis of many university programs in urban planning, is reviewed with reference to the policy statement of the American Planning Association.

Materials dealing with areas of exposure to dangerous natural phenomena have been expanded, as have data on the disposition of dangerous waste.

The chapter dealing with implementation has been greatly expanded as well; it now includes the role of zoning, land subdivision, capital improvements, installation and maintenance of infrastructure, and available financial resources and methods.

The planning process is delineated and the various persons and groups involved are cited. The relationship between the public and private sectors is described, and the potential struggles between the regulators and regulated are illustrated. Additional examples of new towns, satellite towns, and villages are viewed. National capitals are part of the expanded chapter dealing with these important facilities in several parts of the world. Additional material on art in the cities, urban design, and historical preservation and conservation is included.

ACKNOWLEDGMENT

We extend our special thanks to Shelley Eisner for her contributions and valuable assistance in the production of this book and to the many persons who improved the text by their critiques and suggestions.

The authors are grateful to the many individuals and organizations who have, with excerpts from their articles and lectures, contributed materially to the expanded contents of this sixth edition and to the many who were responsible for prior contributions. Their thought and writings have given depth and richness to this book.

Special thanks to the staff of Van Nostrand Reinhold, especially Wendy Lochner, whose courtesy, encouragement, and consideration added to the pleasure of preparing this revised manuscript.

Simon Eisner, AICP
Stanley A. Eisner, AICP, AEP.

PART 1

KNOWLEDGE

THE BASIS
FOR PLANNING

The People, Yes.
Out of what is their change
from chaos to order
and chaos again?

—Carl Sandburg

CHAPTER 1

ENVIRODYNAMICS

HUMANS LIVING IN HARMONY WITH NATURE

Never since the beginning of time did anything happen without being conditioned by its environment. At each stage in the millions of years of existence of this planet, the environment conditioned the activities and development of the earth and the animals and plants that lived on it. As the molten surfaces cooled and deteriorated under the impact of rain, volcanoes, wind, heat, and ice, the creatures and plant life responded with growth and development, evolving from one form to another as the conditions dictated. It was only after time, years without number, since there were no clocks other than changes in the seasons to identify or define a calendar, that humans developed to the stage where they could bend some of the natural forces to their will, and then only for short periods when the natural forces again ran their own course. In ancient times those animals and plants that lived in harmony with their environment survived through change and evolution.

Over 4,100 years ago a Neolithic people built a remarkable monument on the Salisbury Plain in what is now southern England. As an engineering feat alone, Stonehenge stands as one of the wonders of the world. But a recent discovery has revealed that it served not only as a temple, but as an astronomical computer.

We know very little about the life of the people who built Stonehenge. But one thing that has become increasingly evident is that they were far more sophisticated than was previously believed. Even though they worked only with Stone Age technology, they built a monument which apparently acted as an astronomical clock. With Stonehenge they could predict eclipses, the exact days of the solstices, the long-term cycles of the moon and sun, and other important heavenly events. They could begin to understand that the universe had order and how it worked.

THE ENVIRON-MENT

Stonehenge, England.

The need to understand the workings of the universe is very ancient in the species. One might even say that it is instinctual, that it is part of what makes us human.

A leap of forty-one centuries and we find ourselves still confronted with the same questions that drove the prehistoric Britons to build Stonehenge. How does the universe work? How did it begin? Will it ever end?[1]

Habitat

Humans, too, have changed their form, occupations, habitat, and choice of food. As the hunter, a migrant in order to survive, left cave or the makeshift portable precursor to the tent, the tepee, and built the first stone and mud homes, the food eaten changed from slain birds, mammals, and fish to grains. The hunter became a farmer learning to save grain to plant for next year's food supply. Once in a fixed location, the human next had the task of providing for the defense of the family and joined with other families to form the first community where the participants shared in the planting, harvesting, and storing of food for the time between crops. So, the first of the elements of civilization were manifested: living peacefully in a group to work cooperatively and provide mutual protection.

NATURAL DESTRUCTIVE FORCES

Decisions as to where human habitation should occur have been made without concern for the natural forces that might adversely affect life and development. Some of the natural forces are predictable. We know that there will be forces on the land and from the sky that will endanger humans; the unknown is the time when those natural events will occur. In planning urban communities or parts of communities, the habitation of known dangerous areas must be avoided and urbanism should be developed where risks are minimal.

---

1. Lockheed Company and *Smithsonian* Magazine, September 1989.

It is not difficult to craft a scenario on the original form of the planet earth as a sphere covered entirely with water and ice. The core of the planet is a molten mass that formed gases that pressured the outer rim of the core and were expelled into the atmosphere. Afterward great explosions occurred, forming undersea volcanoes that gradually extended out of the water and created the first land-masses. As the eruptions continued, all over the globe, the mountains became islands, then continents. Thus we find, today, the world as we know and map it.

Evidence to substantiate this scenario is to be found in all parts of the world. The monster volcano Krakatoa, lying between Sumatra and Java; Vesuvius, lying south of Naples, Italy, which in one of its many eruptions destroyed both Pompeii and Herculaneum; and Mt. Etna, on Sicily, the largest active volcano in the Mediterranean Sea, are all examples of the widespread distribution of this form of earth-changing activity.

The Ring of Fire, along the Pacific coast of North and South America, discloses a series of great volcanoes, extending from the northernmost part of Alaska to Tierra del Fuego at the base of South America. The ring includes, among many others, Mt. McKinley in Alaska; Mt. Baker, Mt. Rainier, and Mt. St. Helens in Washington; Mt. Hood in Oregon; and Mt. Shasta and Mt. Lassen in California. Farther to the south, in Mexico, Popocatepetl and Ixtacihuatl cast their giant shadows over Mexico City. In addition, Crater Lake in Oregon and Lake Tahoe in California are both the calderas of great volcanoes. Other volcanic evidence is found in the great lava flows at the Craters of the Moon in Idaho and over thousands of acres of Idaho, Montana, and other western states.

The Hawaiian Islands and many other islands in the Pacific Ocean are the exposed tops of massive undersea volcanoes. At the present time, the very live volcano on the Big Island of Hawaii, Kilauea, continues to erupt, with molten lava destroying everything before it as it moves toward the sea, enlarging the size of the island. Sister volcanoes lie dormant, possibly awaiting their time. In this case, as at the base of Mt. Vesuvius in Italy, people have rebuilt their homes without

Volcanoes

Volcano at rest—part of the Ring of Fire—Mt. Shasta, California.

understanding the dangers to which they and their families are continuously exposed.

In most cases, earthquakes precede eruptions. Flight from the area after the eruption begins is quite often too late as fear and panic result in death and injury.

Earthquakes and Tsunamis

Of all the natural forces that have created havoc among the people of the earth, the great earthquakes must rank at the top of the list. Coming without warning, these massive movements of the earth have a destructive force of tremendous magnitude. Although predictions have been made, very few have yet been of value in preventing the destruction and loss of life that have been associated with the movement of the tectonic plates that the earth's landmasses comprise. The loss of life can be very great where the construction in cities has been slipshod. One instance can illustrate the extent of the impact of an earthquake on people and their communities:

> In 23 seconds, at 3:42 a.m. on July 28, 1976, an earthquake officially announced to be at 7.8 magnitude on the Richter Scale totally demolished Tangshan, China, an industrial city of one million people. The quake, which also affected the cities of Tianjin and Beijing, left a death toll of 240,000 with a great many more injured.[2]

Tsunamis, great walls of water spawned by undersea earthquakes or violent quakes near the waterfront, have done great damage to ocean front cities such as Hilo, Hawaii, and Crescent City, California.

WATER SHAPES THE ENVIRON-MENT
___
Too Much Water—Flooding

Humans have been aware of the power of water for centuries. The Egyptians knew what the Nile River could do as the floods swept across the Nile Valley. They reaped the harvests grown in the silt deposited by the floods and understood the relationships among water, fertility of the soil, and food.

Ever since the biblical story about Noah's Ark humans have recorded the history and menace of floods. One of the great disasters, among many others all over the world, occurred in 1889 at Johnstown, Pennsylvania, where more than twenty-two hundred persons died. One of the natural forces to be wary of is flooding.

Areas for urbanization should be located outside floodplains. They should avoid the bottom of steep canyons, where flash floods may destroy everything in their path. Danger of subsidence and structural failure is related to high water tables.

Two flooding tragedies were related to the failure of dams; both occurred in the western United States. In the first an earthen dam was created by a massive landslide (near Jackson, Wyoming). Slide Lake, as it was appropriately called, was formed. It was enjoyed as a recreation facility until the day that the earth in the dam became saturated and the pressure of the water behind it washed away the temporary obstruction. As the water flooded the valley below, the small village of Kelley was destroyed.

Not so lucky were the people in the vicinity of Los Angeles when on the morning of March 12, 1926, the St. Francis Dam, built by the city's Department of Water and Power, broke, emptying the reservoir impounded behind it. The water flowed through the Santa Paula Valley and out into the Pacific Ocean, killing 450 people and causing tremendous property damage. In the investigations that fol-

___
2. Zhu Yuchao, "Tangshan Earthquakes," *China Reconstructs,* China Welfare Institute, Peking, China, March 1986.

San Andreas earthquake fault at the Carizzo Plain, northern California. (BAREPP Photo.)

St. Francis Dam after collapse and the tragic flood that swept all before it on the way through the Santa Paula Valley to the Pacific Ocean (below).

lowed, the dam failure was attributed to inaccurate geological data, which did not disclose the faulty character of the rock on the side of the dam where it failed until after water seepage was discovered.

The state of Texas has always been thought of in terms of excess. Everything has to be bigger, just as Texas is big. Thus we find that when natural forces play havoc with a state, Texas seems to be the recipient of the dramatic events. Droughts appear to plague the state every decade; the worst, in 1953–1957, in many ways was more severe than the Dust Bowl in the Midwest in the 1930s. The semiarid western areas of the United States have also been subject to periodic droughts. By 1991, the California drought had already lasted almost 6 years. Water rationing was proposed and watering of lawns was restricted or forbidden in many areas.

Too Little Water— Drought

WIND

Several well-defined areas are, more than others, subject to severe windstorms in the form of tornadoes, hurricanes, cyclones, and similar forces. There are no means of preventing these natural phenomena; even the best of structures are subject to failures under the trying conditions. Storm cellars and masonry construction appear to be the best safeguards for human life in these exposed areas.

Tornadoes and Cyclones

Tornadoes are a combination of wind and torrential rain; cyclones are tornadoes with great spirals or plumes of wind that sweep across the plains of Kansas and other midwestern states and cause great amounts of damage and often considerable loss of life. Where flimsy structures such as motor homes or factory-built homes are used extensively, these homes are shredded into splinters. Many of the more substantial dwellings have storm cellars to protect the residents. The worst natural disaster in American history occurred at Galveston, Texas, on September 8, 1900, when a tornado and floods caused eight thousand deaths and tremendous property damage. The tornado that descended on Wichita Falls, Texas, in 1979 developed a track almost two miles wide and ten miles long and caused many deaths and almost a half billion dollars in property damage.

Even more recently, on April 30, 1991, a cyclone swept in from the Bay of Bengal and onto the low-lying area adjacent to the sea, devastating Bangladesh and drowning more than 125,000 persons while the 20-foot wall of water carried countless thousands to their death. Property damage was so widespread that the land looked like a junkyard of splintered rubble. To understand what causes people to concentrate in such dangerous areas facing recurrent storms is to know that the fertility of the soil permits high agricultural yield, producing much needed food, and in poverty-stricken countries, people just do not learn from history.

Hurricanes On September 10–18, 1988, Hurricane Gilbert rolled across the tropical Atlantic Ocean, Caribbean Sea, and Gulf of Mexico and onto Yucatan. It was the worst hurricane ever recorded. The maximum speed of the wind was 185 miles per hour. When the storm abated, more than three hundred people were dead. Property damage exceeded $2 billion in Jamaica and Mexico and $50 million in the United States. Twenty-nine Texas tornadoes were the result of Gilbert. Total estimated damage was $5 billion.

Typhoons Typhoons usually hit the Orient; Hong Kong and the China coast seem to get them every year. They, like tornadoes, are usually formed at sea and sweep across the adjacent coastline with winds exceeding 100 miles per hour and heavy rain. The following is a report of Typhoon Dot, which struck Hong Kong on October 13, 1964, with devastating force, while the author was in Singapore:

> The typhoon, which roared past the British Crown Colony early in the day with fringe winds of 120 mph, left a trail of casualties and widespread damage. The fifth typhoon of the year to brush Hong Kong, "DOT" had taken a toll of about 15 dead, 40 injured and eight missing. The missing included three persons trapped in a house which collapsed on nearby Pingchau Island.

> "DOT" left nearly 13 inches of rain on the Crown Colony in a 24 hour period, causing serious flooding in the low-lying rural areas and also in the business section of Hong Kong and Kowloon. Widespread landslides and fallen trees blocked many roads in the City and in suburban areas. Sea and land transport came to a standstill.

> The storm made thousands homeless and people were still being evacuated to higher ground early today.

From a structural standpoint it is interesting to note that the bamboo scaffolding that was erected to assist in the construction of high-rise buildings in the downtown area of Kowloon (on the mainland) withstood the brunt of the storm while the steel members holding signs and other structures were twisted and broken.

EROSION

Erosion of the soil is erosion of life. If we don't care for the soil, it will not take care of us.

In the past 50 years, as a result of careless destruction of the forests and the overuse of agricultural lands, 50 percent of the nation's topsoil has been destroyed by erosion. Conservationists believe that without careful treatment the remaining topsoil, the fertile basis for all plant life, will disappear within the next 50 years.

LIGHTNING

Many of the worst forest fires have been the result of lightning strikes, including the great devastation in Yellowstone Park in September 1988. Many people are killed each year all over the world as the result of lightning strikes, one of nature's most fearful phenomena. The displays are, when observed from a distance, beautiful and awesome and as yet relatively unpredictable.

There are several critical areas, insofar as climatic conditions are concerned, because of the impact of temperature on human settlements. These areas lie at the polar regions, north of the 60th and south of the 45th parallels, and to some degree in the torrid equatorial region. One finds few large human settlements in the frigid areas, while life in the very hot areas must be conditioned to permit humans to live in relative comfort. Building construction and air-conditioning have made both extremes in weather tolerable, but they depend on high building costs and use of great amounts of energy for heating and cooling.

CLIMATIC EXTREMES

Temperature inversions are directly related to the incidence of smog. This occurs in any area where the inversion is coupled with high concentration of contaminants from industrial development and intense use of automobiles. This condition is a health hazard and sensitive people are endangered.

TEMPERA-TURE INVERSIONS

Humans, too, have had a hand in changing the structure of the earth. They have changed forests to grasslands and then, through overgrazing and other misuse, turned the grasslands into the great deserts such as the Sahara. Humans have also rerouted great rivers to provide irrigation in one area while turning the lakes and seas that depended on those rivers as the source of their replenishment into barren areas and salt flats.

HUMAN IMPACT ON THE ENVIRON-MENT: SHORT-TERM GAINS, LONG-TERM DANGERS

Humans have also changed the form and nature of many of the animals that reside with them on the planet, domesticating them; witness the Laplanders' converting the reindeer to domestic herds. These northern people have also changed the form of their own movement, from walking and running to skiing and then to driving gasoline-powered snowmobiles.

In the relatively few years that humans have inhabited the earth they have done more to alter the balance in the environment than all of the millenniums before their arrival. They have seriously altered the thin ozone blanket that protects human life on earth from the dangerous ultraviolet rays of the sun, with consequences yet undetermined.

The danger of urban life is the subject of much human thought. Mere exposure to traffic and smog has deadly consequences. Violent crime challenges the lives of innocent urban residents every day. Where intensive living arrangements place pressures on people, the result is tragic.

Humans in An Urban Environment

Some criteria should be established to govern decisions on the location of urban settlements:

Criteria for Settlements

- Settlements should be located where the threat of natural forces, be they seismic or wildfires, are minimal and then only when construction safety standards are adequate to assure maximum protection of both life and property.
- Access routes to areas of safety should be identified and all residents should be constantly advised of how and when to take advantage of them.
- People should be educated in how to live with potential danger to minimize the impact when such an event occurs.
- Communications systems must be available to warn people in time to react effectively.
- Relief programs should be in place before the dangers become apparent.
- Open areas such as parks, agricultural spaces and other spaces where humans

are not concentrated should be sought for use as safe havens when required by emergencies.

- Reduction in population densities in areas subject to danger, whether the threat is immediate or at an unknown time in the future, should be planned.

Destruction of the Rain Forests

While flying to Rio de Janeiro, the author saw great wild fires raging in the dark below. Later we learned that we were witnessing the demolition of thousands of acres of the world's precious protection of the air that we breathe and of the ozone layer that prevents the problems that arise from radiation exposure and the temperature increases related to the warming of the earth (the greenhouse effect).

In 1978 a group of American planners witnessed the construction of the Amazonia Project. They traveled from Brazilia to Belem by air and then along the dusty road into the area that was being opened up to settlement. Surrounded by torrid heat, dust, and mosquitoes, they saw the wooden structures of the new settlements being built by the Brazilian farmers simultaneously destroyed by the termites. Although the government's proposed development was well intended, providing opportunities for the local migrant population to gain a livelihood by involving them in agriculture, the fertility of the shallow topsoil lacked the basis for sustained production of even the food necessary for their own survival, especially in light of the fact that the normal foods of the native tribes were destroyed along with the forests.

In the meantime, in addition to the burning, many of the precious big trees are being felled each day to produce lumber required for homes and furniture and paper. Many trees that have taken 200 years or more to grow to their monumental stature come down in 5 minutes with the action of the chain saw. As the price of lumber increases, an area greater than that of Switzerland is cleared. One does not have to go to Brazil to see how, along with the big trees, all the land around them is "clear-cut" to produce food and move the products more easily to market. In the states of Oregon, Washington, and Montana there is evidence of bald spots in the midst of forested areas, spots created by the mad scramble to obtain rapid "farm to market" products.

Owls or Jobs?

Forest industry stories would have us believe in the oversimplification that saving the forests is a struggle between saving trees and owls and creating jobs. Sustained yield through selective cutting, preserving the basic structure of the forest, should be emphasized to protect both ecological systems and long-term employment.

DAMS

The art of dam building developed with time until today we can observe some of the great miracles of construction, such as Hoover Dam in Nevada and Grand Coulee Dam in Washington.

Some of the more recent dams are major engineering achievements that display the power of humans to harness nature, sometimes with grave consequences. In Egypt, the Aswan High Dam was built during the 1960s with the assistance of engineers from the Soviet Union. It created a great lake behind the concrete structure and thus controlled the Nile River, preventing it from flooding the area between the dam and the Mediterranean Sea. It also flooded the area where the temple of Isis at Philae and the superb Temple at Abu Simbel were located. Great artistic and historical monuments, sculpted in 1388–1322 B.C., were saved by moving them to high grounds out of the reach of the lake. The engineering involved was a splendid example of the skilled work of the participants in the project.

In the meantime, the anticipated consequences of the retaining of the water of the Nile, preventing it from flooding the area below, kept it from depositing the fertile silt that before the dam had swept down the stream every rainy season. New means of fertilizing the crop areas were necessary, introducing use of chemical fertilizers.

One of the more recent ventures into dam building is Gezhouba Dam on the Chang Jiang (Yangtze) River, lying just below the three almost vertical gorges that confine the river before it flows out onto the plain that opens this part of China to the sea. The dam has been constructed for the generation of power badly needed to fuel Chinese industry. It will, of course, create a lake of tremendous proportions behind its concrete walls. It will also control the flooding of the lowlands below it while it piles up silt that will, in not many years, create problems both behind the dam as its capacity is reduced and in the areas below the dam as fertile silt is lost. To understand the enormity of this problem, one must stand at the edge of the river during the dry season and realize that the level seems to be a hundred feet or more below the main part of Chungking.

While building the dam, the engineers had to take into account that the river was navigable from Chungking to Shanghai; thus locks were constructed to lower boats approximately 72 feet so that they might continue to carry cargo and passengers to and from Chungking to the downriver ports. It can be observed, however, that at flood stage it is necessary to carry both cargo and passengers from the upper area to the level below the dam since the locks became inoperative.

Another mighty dam, the largest to date, has been constructed across the Parana river, on the border of Paraguay and Brazil. The Itapu (Itaqui) Dam has taken 7 years to construct. It contains enough concrete to provide housing for 4 million people. It will be possible to generate enough electricity to meet the needs of all of the people of Paraguay and the two largest cities in Brazil, Rio de Janeiro and Sao Paulo. It will produce electricity for the next 300 years.

However, as in many other projects of this scale, there are down sides to the venture, for more than forty-four thousand people will be displaced as the land behind the dam is flooded. In addition, the food supply grown on the late site will be lost, creating further pressure on the limited supplies available to the people of the area. One of the positive aspects of the planning program is the planting of 1 million trees along the edges of the lake to prevent silting, keep the water clear, and permit planting of fish.

The following is an account of another dam and its construction and relation to its settings.

Massive Dam Project in Anatolia

"On the western edge of the brown, rolling steppe of southeastern Turkey, the blue-green waters of the Euphrates surge into a giant reservoir behind one of the world's largest dams. It is named for the father of modern Turkey, Mustafa Kemal Ataturk. Upriver, two other big dams, the Keban and the Karakaya, stretch across deep river gorges in the southeastern flank of the Taurus Mountains. The once-quiet valleys resonate with a sizzling and crackling. It is electricity, coursing through power lines carried on lofty towers to far-off Anatolian towns.

This is one of three dams, the first of 22 to be built on the Tigris and Euphrates river systems, as part of the Turkish government's Guneydogu Anadolu Project (Southeastern Anatolia Project), or GAP. The plan is to revitalize six Turkish provinces by transforming nearly 30,000 square miles of arid and semiarid land, an area larger than Belgium, Holland and Luxembourg combined, into the breadbasket of the Middle East. But it will do so at a fearful cultural cost. The first three dams alone are submerging hundreds of archaeological sites, many dating from prehistoric times.[3]

Plans to Protect the Physical Environment

In *Portrait of the Earth,* the following world conservation strategy is prescribed as the basis for a planned approach to the preservation of the environment:[4]

- One, do not exploit resources to the end that would destroy them.
- Two, do not interfere with the natural process in the sky, the green surfaces, the sea and the forests.
- Three, preserve the diversity of life because we depend on it for our food. We know so little about the forms of life on earth that we have no moral right to destroy any of it. Continued survival rests in our hands.

Our Many Other Environments

When the word *environment* is flashed across the headlines of the daily press or the news programs on TV, one immediately conjures up the vision of radicals who are out to save the whale, the horned frog, the bighorn sheep, the peregrine falcon, or the giant sequoia (redwood). Seldom does the public consider the wide range that the word implies, including the following:

Economic Environment. Can plans be financed? Are world economic conditions stable and are interest rates at a level that would permit funding of a proposed program, or are people reluctant to invest?

Political Environment. Are the people in power politically interested in a program? Are party members secure in the program's ability to get them reelected? Is the program supported by the public, the press, the power structure in the community? Can financial support be obtained from friendly sources for the project, and is it important to their political security and advancement?

Even seemingly unrelated events, such as political stability and economic growth of other countries, can influence the price of food on our dinner table. We must realize that we are world citizens and, therefore, the world environment is also our environment.

Social Environment. Is the proposed plan or project in the best social interest of the majority of the people of the community? How does one know? What of the minority interest? How are the two divergent interests melded into a humanistic fabric? Does the program improve the cultural opportunities of a broad spectrum of the population? Does it improve the health and overall welfare of the poor and homeless? Does it increase opportunities of those needing improved educational programs? Does it raise the standard of living for all people?

The new demand to meet the social and physical needs of the aging population in urban settlements causes changes in how we build our environment: the types of specially designed facilities that are required to serve the "graying of America."

---

3. Diana Raines Ward, *Smithsonian* Magazine, Smithsonian Society, Washington, D.C., August 1990.

4. Based on the program by David Attenborough, BBC London, July 26, 1990.

Humans create new environments, large cities where people live within the congested canyons imposed on the earth. Humans create great artificial environments within the massive temples and shrines called "high-rise buildings," where artificial light and air are provided to keep the occupants alive and working. They approach their homes under the ground (subways) and take elevators to their cubicles, where in the sacred sanctum the hallway air is filled with the perfume of neighbors' cabbage and tobacco smoke. One wonders whether the great powers above look at these creations of humans as part of the divine scheme?

Built Environments

The Visual Environment The impact on our senses of the world around us includes the signs and billboards, the neon lights that flash before our eyes, the rundown neighborhoods, the unkempt streets, the blinding smog and smoke, the hodgepodge of an incompatible unplanned mixture of land uses, the excessive traffic and congestion and the noise associated with it. These are all part of the personal intimate environment, and they condition the way that we think and act.

Little-Considered Environments

Planning should overcome many of these obnoxious characteristics of our environment. This implies a maximum of participation by people who care about their communities and action by political powers to allocate funds to clean up the mess in an orderly, timely way.

There are instances where glitter and glitz are a way of life and the wild array of big signs, flashing lights, slot machines, and loud music seems as normal as soft sounds or sweet music do at a symphony concert. Las Vegas and Hong Kong and Kowloon are prime candidates for the honkytonk prize, but this ambience makes them look and sound like the artificial showplaces that they are. To line every major street and highway with replicas of this extravaganza is, on the face of it, unbecoming to the communities in which most of us live.

The element of time in the planning of development is as critical as any other factor in the process. Where political action is involved or public support is essential, the timing environment can be decisive and at the very heart of resulting action. One instance stands out to illustrate the significance of the timing environment. In California, in 1990, the state elections presented the public with proposals to spend hundreds of millions of dollars for all sorts of activities intended for the public interest and welfare. Although there were differences of opinion about the appropriateness, cost effectiveness, or current need of the activities, the defeat of the measures was related to other factors:

THE ENVIRON-MENTAL TIME MACHINE

Fear among the public of spending in the aftermath of the savings and loan scandal and the economic threat to many small investors. The increases in taxes to cover the losses deeply concerned a great number of people.

The increasing national debt and the dual threats of inflation and bankruptcy.

The continued discussion of the trade imbalance and the undermining of the world economy.

The threat of an impending recession or depression, which loomed large in the mind of working people faced with layoffs and loss of income.

The rising prices at the supermarket, which made for second looks at expenditures for items that could not be placed on the dinner table.

And on the horizon in the Middle East, the danger of war and its consequences.

In a word, bond issues are doomed not exclusively by their content but by increased expense at an inappropriate time. Thus timing can be a major factor in voter response.

Facing the Dangers in the Natural Environment: Knowledge Can Ensure Safety

Where can we live safely? It seems that in one form or another humans face danger from the caprices of natural forces: an earthquake or a volcanic eruption, a windstorm or a flood. In addition, fire storms may be produced by both nature and human beings. What can we do to mitigate the constant threats to life and resources—where to run, how to escape, when to react?

We must recognize that humans are relatively slow to respond to dangerous situations, since stability has many real advantages, such as employment, family ties and commitment, lack of real knowledge of the significance of the potential danger, and a frightening sense of security that they are not individually subject to danger. Also, the belief that pending problem may not really occur at all.

HAZARD PLANNING: WHOSE RESPONSI-BILITY?

It is difficult to predict natural events that cause danger to humans and their property. These events are often the result of a course of action initiated by the people themselves. The potential dangers are thus a consequence of actions taken in the face of known, unstable conditions with the hope and expectation that, if and when catastrophic events occur, those responsible will somehow escape the consequences. However, plans must be made to safeguard human lives in such instances and to care for them after tragedies occur. Wesley Marx, a writer on marine and environmental affairs, states:

> Traditionally, the jurisdiction that has the power to avoid hazardous development through land-use and building controls also happens to be the one with the strongest incentives to risk disaster: the city or county. The local government profits from allowing people to occupy hazardous areas: the property tax base expands. A community in an upper watershed has very little motivation to control land uses—such as mining—whose siltloads can intensify flood hazards in downstream communities.[5]

George Mader, a planning consultant in Portola Valley, California, had this to say on the subject of planning for hazard mitigation:

> Land use planning is an important coordinating device for dealing with seismic hazard mitigation. Strides have been made in this field in recent years. We are doing a better job. We still, however, flounder considerably in selling our ideas to decision-makers. Better prediction will improve our own work and our ability to convey critical information to legislators as to the risks involved in taking or not taking mitigation actions.[6]

CONCERN FOR THE TOTAL ENVIRON-MENT

Halting efforts are being made in all parts of the world to check the undisciplined exploitation of nature. Sometimes the freedom to abuse continues in the guise of the costs involved in making the changes needed to ameliorate the problems. This is particularly true in the areas of pollution and wasted energy. The long-term effects of our negligence have not been clearly determined.

---

5. "Disaster Planning," *California Tomorrow*, Summer 1978.

6. George Mader, AICP, *California Planner*, March 1980.

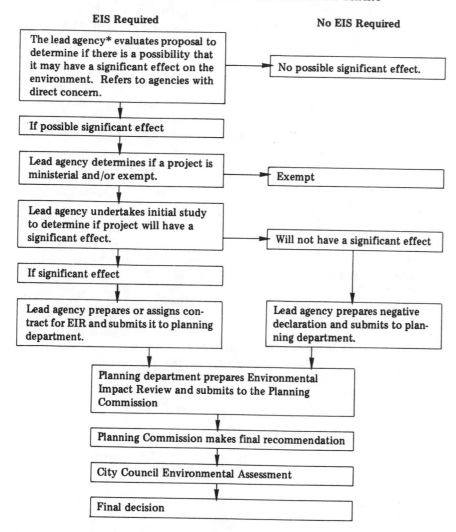

ENVIRONMENTAL ASSESSMENT PROCESS FLOW CHART

EIS Required   **No EIS Required**

The lead agency* evaluates proposal to determine if there is a possibility that it may have a significant effect on the environment. Refers to agencies with direct concern.

No possible significant effect.

If possible significant effect

Lead agency determines if a project is ministerial and/or exempt.

Exempt

Lead agency undertakes initial study to determine if project will have a significant effect.

Will not have a significant effect

If significant effect

Lead agency prepares or assigns contract for EIR and submits it to planning department.

Lead agency prepares negative declaration and submits to planning department.

Planning department prepares Environmental Impact Review and submits to the Planning Commission

Planning Commission makes final recommendation

City Council Environmental Assessment

Final decision

*In the majority of cases the planning department is likely to be the lead agency. In some cases, however, the lead agency might be a federal government agency.

The environment has little to do with the political boundaries established by the individual communities or nations that we find all over the world. Development of a meaningful environmental impact assessment requires a broad-range environmental impact report (EIR), including all of the elements that would be found in the study of at least a region or metropolitan area. Unfortunately the political entity needed to finance and develop the environmental basis for judgment is often absent.

At present each community assesses its own area and the overlapping areas that fall into other jurisdictions. The cost of the individual studies can be monumental.

Regional studies of all the elements of the environment—physical, social, and economic—should be prepared and the findings computerized in both mapped and statistical forms. Such a study was prepared in 1981 for the Coachella Valley in California, covering large portions of the unincorporated area and the seven

IMPACT STUDIES

cities contained in the subregion. Basic environmental data were then available for any projects proposed in any part of the study area. Unfortunately, the political support and the funds needed to keep the data current were withdrawn, and the monumental project was abandoned.

These impact studies should become basic in the search for the "good city." One must be knowledgeable about the needs of the people and the delicate balance with nature that must be preserved and respected. The total ecological environment must become the vehicle for the transformation of the inherited earth that thinking people hope that it will someday become. No approach to the good city is possible without a conscious effort to respect the environment, locally and regionally.

Use of Environmental Impact Reports

In order to achieve the objectives set forth in this act the State Legislature finds and declares that the following policy shall apply to the use of environmental impact reports prepared pursuant to this division:

(a) The purpose of an environmental impact report is to identify the significant effects of a project on the environment, to identify alternatives to the project, and to indicate the manner in which those significant effects can be mitigated or avoided.

(b) Each public agency shall mitigate or avoid the significant effects on the environment of projects it approves or carries out whenever it is feasible to do so.

(c) In the event that economic, social, or other conditions make it infeasible to mitigate one or more significant effects of a project on the environment, such project may nonetheless be approved or carried out at the discretion of a public agency, provided that the project is otherwise permissible under applicable laws and regulations.[7]

ENVIRON-MENTAL IMPACT REPORT (EIR) PROCESS, A CASE STUDY

A case in the San Joaquin valley of California provides a full range of the issues involved in a proposed land development and the subsequent assessment of potential social, physical, and financial threats to the environment.

A local property owner proposed creating a large urban development on land in an unincorporated area adjacent and contiguous to an urbanized municipality. He employed a consultant to prepare a subdivision plan for 400 plus acres of land, a portion of his entire holding. The plan was prepared with the assistance and guidance of the staff of the adjoining city, and conformed to all local design standards. The proposal was then taken to the Local Agency Formation Commission (LAFCO), a county agency concerned with annexations and the creation of new cities. In this instance LAFCO was concerned with the impact that the proposed urban development would have on the remaining agricultural land, the major land use and economic base of the county. LAFCO found that the subject land was a logical extension to existing urban development in the city and thus would not be an invasion into the heart of the agricultural land. LAFCO recommended approval of the annexation.

The next step was presentation of the plans to the city with a request that it proceed to annex the property. In conformity with state and local laws, the city required an EIR prior to any action and so informed the property owners. They then employed a planning/engineering firm to prepare the required studies and make appropriate recommendations based on research and cooperative submis-

---

7. The California Environmental Quality Act, Chapter 1514, Statutes of 1984.

sions from all concerned agencies and boards involved in providing services to the proposed development. The EIR was to include all of the environmental problems associated with both the land and the proposed plans for development. The report would recommend what alternatives might be appropriate and what mitigating actions might be taken to overcome the adverse impacts on the local environment. The consultants would present their findings to the planning department and then to the planning commission, which would hold public hearings prior to any action on the proposed annexation. Following the planning commission hearings the case would be submitted to the city council (the legislative body) for public hearings and final disposition of the case.

In this case study, disclosures in the EIR indicated that the current sewage disposal plant serving the local area was overloaded and could not be expected to accept additional sewage, especially from the approximately 500 dwellings that were proposed for the site. In order to service the site the owners would have to build a new sewage treatment plant or cause to be installed a "dry sewerage system" in the streets and require septic tanks for each dwelling, provided that the soil conditions and water table permitted. In addition the EIR reported that the local public school system was incapable of handling additional students and that a new site and facility would have to be ready for the children from the new development.

In light of the EIR the planning commission and city council recommended that the developer postpone his request for annexation until the adverse environmental impacts could be mitigated.

The alternatives evaluated included the continued agricultural use of the property or allowing the land to remain fallow until such time as the developer and others looking to utilize adjacent property could band together and economically provide the services required for sound urban development.

CHAPTER 2

ECOSPHERE

ECOLOGY Ecology involves the mutual relations among organisms and between them and their environments and with social studies of the spatial distribution of population in reference to material and social causes and effects.

Study of the ecological processes and interactions within urban areas and between human settlements and the surrounding natural systems that support them constitutes the ecology of urban development. It is concerned with the analysis of the total urban system as well as its various elements. President Carlos Salinas De Gortari, President of Mexico stated: "If we don't address the issue of global ecology, we won't have to worry about other issues."[1]

Ecology, according to *Encyclopedia Americana,* is that phase of biology that considers plants and animals as they exist in nature, and studies their interdependence, and the relation of each kind and individual to its environment. It is the study of the actions and interactions of living things, and their reactions toward external influences. Although there always have been observers of organic nature, and collectors and recorders of facts—the material for the generalizations of biology—this information has for the most part consisted of isolated facts only slightly correlated with the circumstances surrounding each case. It has rarely been studied in the light shed by other sciences, as chemistry, meteorology, geology, etc., on the physical processes attending growth, individual success and group-development in nature. It is in this wide, synthetic method that ecologists seek to work, including in any problem all the influences that combine to produce and modify an animal or a given

---

1. *Smithsonian* Magazine, July 1990, p. 44.

fauna, and thus to account for its existence and peculiarities in the place where it is found. Ecology, then, is more than merely a study of life-history, or of habit and behavior, for it seeks to ascertain and interpret the causes of, and reason for, observed facts by gaining a knowledge of the complex influences to which the animal or plant in question is exposed, and the nature of its reactions.

It is only within recent years that this field of study has been recognized in its full value, and scientifically utilized, but the very illuminating results obtained have converted to it many naturalists who were at first openly skeptical of its practical value.[2]

Desertification, the process of transforming productive lands into veritable deserts, directly affects millions of people living in arid and semiarid ecosystems worldwide. Agricultural lands are reduced; water resources are depleted, and under extreme conditions, livestock and people become threatened with malnutrition or starvation. Desertification can occur naturally or through droughts coupled with overgrazing and the overharvest of woody plants for fuel wood. Desertification can be an affliction not only of poor nations, whose people may have no choice but to overharvest desert plants for fodder and fuel, but, also in rich nations as well.[3]

Arid and Semiarid Ecosystems and Desertification

Some experts consider landscape ecology "the science of patches." Seen from the air, any broad area of land appears as a mosaic, with patches of land in dozens of uses—croplands, pastures, wooded groves, grasslands, roads, river corridors, and towns. This newest ecological specialty, landscape ecology, deals with such questions as

Landscape Ecology

> How can the patterns of the mosaic best be described?
>
> How did the different patches and patterns come about?
>
> What maintains the patterns, and what is their fate likely to be under a variety of uses?
>
> How do the patterns affect processes that extend across whole landscapes?

In a broader sense landscape ecology seeks to give people who make decisions on the uses of land an understanding of the connections between natural and social systems in the landscape.[4]

No more dramatic example of the implications of ecological relationships exists than the vanishing wetlands. The impact of human disregard of the natural relationships between one part of the environment and other significant parts can disrupt the lives of a wide range of living creatures that are totally dependent on a balanced system.

VANISHING WETLANDS AND RECOVERY

Natural Waste Treatment

At one time there were more than 220 million acres of wetlands in the continental United States; more than half are gone. Of the 4 million acres of wetlands in the prehistoric Central Valley (of California), about 300,000 acres exist today.

Wetlands are nature's kidneys—thriving in the rich nutrients that overwhelm streams. They also protect shorelines, recharge groundwater, moderate flooding and climate, and provide essential habitat to, among others, 187 endangered species.

---

2. From the *Encyclopedia Americana,* 1948 Edition. Copyright 1948 by Grolier Incorporated. Reprinted by permission.

3. Council on Environmental Quality, *12th Annual Report* (Washington, D.C.: U.S. Government Printing Office, 1989)

4. University of California, Davis Extension Catalogue, October 1990.

After more than 200 years of diking, draining and filling swamps—much of it encouraged by government programs called reclamation—marshes are now being recreated throughout the nation, for example in cities such as Martinez, Santa Rosa and Sacramento, California, to do precisely what they did before. But at least as kidneys, they are coming back an acre at a time.

Arcata and Eureka on the north coast, Gustine in the valley and Hayward in the Bay Area—communities throughout California are turning to wetlands as an affordable way to meet ever tightening water-quality standards. They are using wetlands to reduce the pollutants carried by storm run-off draining into streams and bays, and as a way to get rid of something that never runs short no matter how long the drought—wastewater.

If there is an indefatigable voice of optimism in this debate it comes from Picayune, Mississippi, from inventor Bill Wolverton. As a NASA engineer, Wolverton was given one of the less glamorous jobs: if man ever lives on the Moon or Mars, what should be done with the sewage? That led him to a solution that has found a home in the equally challenging environment of earth.

Septic tanks collect the solids, which are consumed by anaerobic organisms. The wastewater is then dispersed either into marshes or highly refined wetlands—rock gardens really, with plants like canna lilies to take up the water and nutrients.

If heavy metals are a problem, Wolverton said, the plants could be harvested, dehydrated in a clay-lined pit, and the metals recycled. He's trying it now. He also sees the vegetation as a source of biomass that will help solve the nation's energy problems when it gets tired of importing oil. No room for marshes in Manhattan? He suggests high-rise gardens—sewage in, cut flowers out. "I have no doubt this is what is going to happen," said Wolverton, who relishes the low-technology in the projects he designs. Our waste may be our greatest asset.[5]

---

5. Excerpts from Jim Mayer, "Making the Most of Waste," *Sacramento Bee*, 1991, Copyright, The Sacramento Bee 1991.

CHAPTER 3

RESOURCES

President Theodore Roosevelt, in 1908, stated: "The wise use of all of our natural resources, which are our national resources as well, is the great material question of today. I have asked you to come together now because of the enormous consumption of these resources, and the threat of imminent exhaustion of some of them, due to reckless and wasteful use. . . ."

Although the subject of resources could fill a book of its own, it is important that this brief encounter with the supports of life on this planet be explored to open doors for additional thought on the subject. We cannot live without most of these resources; therefore, it is essential that we become familiar with at least some of them.

Where We're Going . . .

The environmental activity during the 1970's climaxed a century of gradually increasing public and private consciousness of environmental quality. By the 1970's, it seemed that because public owned natural resources had been undervalued by all parties using them, they rapidly were losing their value to both present and future generations. Far more environmental legislation was passed in that decade than in any similar period, as the nation faced the short-term and long-term economic and social implications of environmental deterioration.

Prior value judgments on the optimal use of public lands in the West were made when this country enjoyed ample supplies of inexpensive liquid fuels produced both domestically and in foreign countries. That situation has changed dramatically during the past decade. Because international political instability poses a threat to the

THE ENVIRONMENT AND NATURAL RESOURCES

U.S. economic and social system, the value of domestically owned energy resources has increased sharply. Today, the federal government owns a large part of these domestic energy resources, which include oil, natural gas, coal, oil shale, and tar sands. During the coming decade the nation should be reevaluating its prescribed uses for public resources in the context of a radically altered energy situation. The relative value of clean air, scenic vistas, agricultural water use, and pristine wilderness areas will be weighed against the economic and national security value of domestic mineral and energy supplies. As in the past, conflicts between competing uses will be decided in the political arena, as the issues are debated by the Congress, within the Administration, by special interest groups, and private citizens.

This kind of thinking should extend to environmental standards, control technologies, natural resource user fees, compliance alternatives, and the definition of environmental problems themselves. The air quality standard for particulate should be reassessed in light of the widely varied effects of different sizes of airborne particles. Alternative methods of human water disposal, especially those that use substantially less potable water, should be considered. The benefits of controlling "non-point" sources of water pollution (such as runoff from farms and cities) should be balanced against the benefits accrued from continuing to tighten controls on "point" sources (such as waste treatment plant discharges) which have been the prior focus of water quality regulations. All the various users of public lands, whether logging or energy companies, recreationists, campers, or ranchers, should pay user fees commensurate with the value received. This reevaluation of the nation's environmental problems and the public's responses should, as appropriate, lead to changes in current standards and regulations. More important, it should lead to a more efficient and equitable use of the nation's natural resources.[1]

NATURAL RESOURCE EVOLUTION

Certain resources, such as water and air, seemed to exist in such quantities that no matter what people did to them they were able to absorb the contaminants and remain viable for human use. Only in recent years have we seen what pollution can do to these resources and what impact abuses can have on health and welfare. Those who perpetrate the abuses tend to resist changes that may cause them economic hardship. The cost in human suffering as a consequence of the continuation of the pollution is discounted because of the difficulty of directly linking pollutants to disease in many cases. Cancer and heart disease that appear related to industrial activities are considered part of the "facts of life" in essential production.

Although environmentalists and ecologists have been energetically pointing out the dangers to the population associated with pollution and abuse of the wilderness areas and many of our other essential natural resources, few have been concerned with the use and abuse of land in urban and rural areas.

National Resources Planning Act

The resource planning agency (RPA) process is a continuing one. Every 5 years, the secretary of agriculture is to prepare a long-range program. The president then transmits the program, together with a statement of policy, to the Congress to be used in framing budget requests. The Congress can approve, revise, modify, or disapprove this statement of policy. Year-to-year funding, however, is provided through the annual presidential budget and congressional appropriations process.

Forest Service activities during the year 1980 did not always fall within the high and low range goals identified in the first (1975) RPA program. For example, recreational use of the National Forests (as measured by visitor days) in the year

1. Council on Environmental Quality, *12th Annual Report* (Washington, D.C.: U.S. Government Printing Office, 1991).

1980 was substantially above the RPA high level projection. By contrast, Forest Service progress in improving fish and wildlife habitat, grazing, timber sales, and soil and water resources was below RPA projections.

In December 1980, Congress amended the President's Statement of Policy which transmitted the 1980 Program to Congress. The congressional resolution endorsed a program emphasizing the highest levels of goods and services. The congressional revision stated that the recommendations of the past Administration might not be sufficient to meet the stated goals in some areas such as range, watershed, timber, and state and private forestry cooperation.

More specifically, for timber, the revision implied the necessity for the United States to become a net exporter of wood products by the year 2030. To do this might require bringing most commercial timber lands to 90 percent of their potential level of growth, consistent with the provisions of the National Forest Management Act of 1976 on federal lands. With respect to grazing, the revision indicated that rangelands should be maintained and enhanced, including their water and other resource values. The goal will be to provide annually 310 million animal unit-months of forage by the year 2030, along with other benefits.[2]

OUR PRIME RESOURCES—PEOPLE, LAND, WATER, AND AIR

Urban places are more than a collection of buildings and open space, more than a transportation system and the services that are essential to preserve and promote health and safety. All of these physical characteristics mean little without the people that give them life and meaning. Without planning, the contribution of the human mind, addressed and dedicated to human welfare, our prime resource and the future of civilization itself are at stake.

The people of the world and the land they live on are our prime resources. All of planning is intended to improve their welfare and provide an environment within which the pursuit of happiness and the maintenance of health can be enjoyed. Whatever the rules that become the policies of the planning process, we must never lose sight of the prime objective, (protection of the health, safety, and general welfare of the residents of this planet.)

Population prognosticators expect the total world population to increase by more than 30 percent by the year 2000. Land fit for cultivation will increase by only around 5 percent during that time—so farmers will be forced to use many more chemicals, artificial fertilizers, and pesticides to provide food for a burgeoning population. In the United States the amount of farmland is being reduced by one million acres each year.

Population Data

The United States Bureau of the Census produces not only decennial estimates of the population and social and economic structure but periodic special census data collected on a random-sampling basis for communities requesting this information. In addition, numerous banks and other local economic institutions collect and publish data on their own communities. Regional planning organizations such as councils of governments collect and analyze both growth and distribution of population in the areas under their jurisdictions, and state employment development departments deal with employment statistics and job referrals.

The 1980 Census of Population and Housing contains a mass of statistical data that are valuable to planners in the preparation of comprehensive plans for their communities. Briefly, the information deals with age distribution, family status,

2. Council on Environmental Quality, *12th Annual Report* (Washington, D.C.: U.S. Government Printing Office, 1981), 150–51.

nativity, language, education, and commuting practices. Additional important statistics on income and poverty, the labor force, and general social and economic characteristics are also collected, listed by the nation as a whole and by various statistical areas, including cities and census tracts.

Housing information, furnished with the same degree of detail, includes general housing statistics, structural characteristics, fuel, financial information on dwelling units, and data on the characteristics of housing for specific racial groups and persons of Hispanic origin.

Public Health and Safety

In ancient times the tragedy of epidemics aroused rulers to improve the physical environment. Primitive though they were, there were efforts to provide drainage and distribute water in the cities of Crete and the Indus Valley. It was not until the cholera plague of the Middle Ages had violently reduced the urban population in Europe that sanitary sewer connections and water distribution were provided as public services.

Measures for the public health and safety were extended during the nineteenth century. The first system of water supply by gravity flow was installed in Boston in 1652. By 1820 pumping systems were in general use and methods for the disposal and treatment of sewage were improved. Extensive street paving permitted effective cleaning, and storm sewers augmented the sanitary equipment. Urban hygiene in the factory town did not lag for lack of facilities. It was simply outstripped and nullified by overpopulation and the intensity of land use.

Need for Health Planning

The planning of both public and private health services ranks close to the provision of reasonable shelter in all of the industrialized nations, regardless of their social or economic philosophies. A considerable number of activities fall within the network dealing with the prevention and control of disease and the care to be provided for the afflicted.

Facilities for care and treatment of persons vary from the intensive care units in large urban medical complexes to the clinics and first aid stations that serve as first contact points in dealing with minor illness or accidents. In addition, there are paramedic services in large urban areas and field medics (barefoot doctors in China) in rural areas. Further convalescent homes take the pressure from hospitals when patients require less intensive care than that provided by hospitals.

Health planning is a critical professional activity since in many nations the services are part of a social security system, such as Medicare and Medicaid in the United States or the Health Services in Great Britain. Payment for private health services is either totally or partially covered by insurance programs sponsored by large private insurance companies. Many states have health planning agencies whose responsibility it is to oversee the location and distribution of hospitals and convalescent homes in relation to the presumed needs in a given area. All of the techniques of planning are involved in this process.

LAND

Fertile land exists in some parts of the world where nature has woven a pattern of vegetable and mineral substances, which over millions of years, has created a thin surface capable of supporting vegetable growth, the food supply for the people. Natural disasters such as dust storms have moved this thin surface from one area to another especially following human abuses involving destruction of forests and grasses through clearcutting and overgrazing. The use of chemical fertilizers has in recent years been a costly effort to replace the natural fertility of the land.

Much attention is given to land-use planning, both urban and rural. Practically every city and county has developed a land-use plan, in one form or another. Most of the detailed land-use planning, however, has taken place in urban areas where comprehensive plans and zoning regulations are implemented.

WATER

Water is a critical resource in many countries. Without water little of life can survive. Excessive water at a given time can threaten life, land, crops, and habitation in general, especially in low-lying areas or where there is little vegetation to hold the rains and help the percolation process, taking the water into the underground reservoirs.

Water has always been subject to the most intensive planning of all natural resources. Great aqueducts were constructed by the Romans thousands of years ago to transport water from storage basins where rainfall was adequate to areas of population concentration. Great dams and reservoirs were planned and constructed to store and regulate the flow of water, diverting it from areas where it was abundant to those where agriculture and urbanism required a steady supply.

The conservation planning of water resources, especially in arid or semiarid locations, is essential to the continuity of human survival in these locations. Conservation and reuse of water from the effluent produced by sewage have become a matter of concern by local residents. The following excerpt summarizes the situation and key issues with regard to water resources in the United States.

Water Resources [3]

The 1980–81 and 1988–90 winter droughts throughout the West and Midwest focused widespread public attention once again on the nation's water resources. The drought followed dry conditions in previous years and led to speculation that cyclical dry weather is adversely affecting the West. Many eastern areas of the country also have been affected in recent years by dry conditions.

Since the early years of this century, at least 20 major national water assessments have been conducted by governmental and private organizations. The most recent was the U.S. Water Resources Council's Second National Water Assessment in 1978 which covers the period 1975–2000.

According to this report, total freshwater withdrawals (physical removal of water from surface and groundwater sources) amounted to about 350 billion gallons per day (bgd) in 1975, of which 96 (bgd) was consumed (i.e., not returned to the source of withdrawal because of evaporation or incorporation into products).

Adoption of more efficient water use technology and abandonment of irrigation agriculture in some areas subject to ground water overdraft could effect a slight decline in water withdrawals by the year 2000. Nevertheless, consumption of water in the year 2000 is projected to increase from 96 billion gallons per day to 135 billion gallons per day.

Although analysts expect that the total amount of available water in the whole of the United States in 2000 will exceed total water consumption, such aggregated figures can mask serious and growing water deficits in wide areas, especially in the

---

3. Council on Environmental Quality, *12th Annual Report* (Washington, D.C.: U.S. Government Printing Office, 1991).

West. In this area, overdrafting of ground water, as well as limited availability of surface water, is already apparent. Thus, water resource issues are likely to remain a prominent concern for the foreseeable future.

Strategies to address water resource problems often take years or decades to implement fully. A key issue in resolving regional problems is whether previous assessments have provided sufficiently accurate and reliable information upon which to base water resource policies. A recent Library of Congress study, based in part on interviews with key water resource professionals representing government, academia, and private consulting firms, concluded that "most past assessments have been limited in scope, based on incomplete or questionable data, or have been suggestive of findings that were not really produced." The consensus was that a continuing process for annual assessment and appraisal of key priorities and problems is essential if water assessments are to be useful in guiding policy. Those interviewed also agreed on the need for greater state and local involvement in the assessment process.

Water Planning

To prevent a water-supply crisis in the twenty-first century, water development and management policies must change. The reform of water pricing is crucial. The state must use its currently developed supplies of water more efficiently instead of encouraging overuse and cultivation of marginal land by subsidizing water prices and constantly expanding its energy-hungry system of water delivery. It must also take into account environmental values, such as the need to preserve wilderness, wildlife, and wetlands. The following planning policies have been suggested:

- Reforming the pricing of state and federal water supplies so as to encourage efficient use and eliminate large price disparities.
- Creating a "water market" by changing laws and practices to permit holders of water rights to sell or trade their surplus water, thereby increasing the effective supply; guaranteeing provision for "unprofitable" uses such as the maintenance of fisheries and recreation.
- Management of state groundwater reserves for sustained yield; state delineation of natural groundwater basins; and the establishment of a basin wide district for the management of ground and surface water.
- Conserving water. Pricing water at its real cost will encourage it; all water agencies must promote it. Shifting away from water-intensive crops and using new technologies for precise irrigation can save as much as a third of the water used in agriculture. Setting municipal water rates to penalize waste, legalizing secondary uses (such as irrigating gardens with kitchen graywater), and reviving such old-fashioned economies as rainwater cisterns and nighttime sprinkling can save water in urban areas.[4]

Desalinization of Sea Water

The process of desalinization of sea water was developed to a high degree in the 1980s. Many of the cruise ships plying the seas used this process to provide potable water for their passengers. In the early 1990s the American armed forces of approximately 500,000 persons living in the desert of Saudi Arabia were being provided desalinized water to the tune of millions of gallons a day. There is no doubt that the cost is greater than collecting rain, but the technique is there to be used in the desert and severe drought emergencies.

It should be noted that one of the counties in Northern California is placing a bond issue before its residents in 1991 asking economic support for the development of a desalinization system to serve the needs in case of recurrent droughts,

---

4. Alfred Heller (ed.), "Cry California," *California Tomorrow*, 1980.

such as those that plagued the area during the years 1984–1991, when water rationing had to be applied.

Before the 1940s hardly anyone was concerned about the purity of the air that we breathe. True, there were some incidents in Europe, in which industrial waste, generated with the industrial revolution and the widespread use of coal as the principal fuel, produced pollution problems. However, other than in the Pittsburgh area of the United States, where for years smoke and contaminants from steel and other industries darkened the skies, there appeared to be little concern about pollution. Even in Pittsburgh the air condition was associated with the prosperity of the steel industry, and efforts to control it were linked with the price of steel and competition in the world market. It was at that time tolerated as a necessary evil demanded by economic considerations.

The word *smog* was invented in the Los Angeles area to describe the pollution generated by local industry, the intensive use of the gasoline-driven automobiles, and the private incineration of rubbish. With the severe conditions that became a danger to the health of the residents of a community that prided itself on being a health resort, studies of the conditions that contributed to the incidence of smog began.

Meteorologists described the temperature inversion that trapped the air in basins like Los Angeles. Nothing short of a change in the natural conditions, bringing fresh air into the area, would improve the conditions that led to the concentrations of smoke and fog from which smog derived its name. Planning then must occur at the other end of the spectrum: the producers of the industrial wastes discharged into the atmosphere must be regulated to assure a minimal level of discharge when the atmospheric conditions indicated that an inversion condition was imminent. The Air Pollution Control Board was created to monitor conditions and regulate the industries that were the participants in the pollution problems.

Other air pollutants in the Midwest, along the Canadian-American border, in the form of gases from coal-fired power plants (mainly sulfur oxides [SO_x] and nitrogen oxides [NO_x]), were converted in the atmosphere to "acid rain" when combined with water vapor in the clouds and sunlight. The poisoning of the lakes, streams, and soil in the vicinity of the producers of these pollutants caused international problems between two otherwise friendly nations. Planning for the reduction of the dangerous pollutants became a matter of international necessity.

Gases from solid waste disposal areas have stirred residents in the vicinity of acid pits and other disposal areas for dangerous wastes. Efforts to clean up and detoxify the areas became a matter of national importance and involved actions and planning at the highest levels of government. Association of exposure in these areas with the causes of cancer and other medical ailments was instrumental in the efforts to plan for future handling of solid wastes in a manner and location that would not endanger human life.

The Council on Environmental Quality provides the following description of local and national efforts to protect air quality:

> During the last 25 years, and particularly in the past decade, the United States has made a concerted and successful effort to deal with many of its air pollution problems. New laws, regulations, procedures, policies, and court decisions on air pol-

AIR RESOURCES

National Efforts to Protect Air Quality

lution controls have been implemented. Control technologies have been developed and installed on facilities throughout the country. There has been a noticeable improvement in air quality. Emissions of common substances (such as particles, carbon monoxide, sulfur oxides, and hydrocarbons), which when released in sufficient quantity may threaten human health, have been notably reduced. Air quality has improved in most urban areas. In others, the air quality has remained steady even though the area's population and economies have grown.

Air pollution is not new. The waste products that come from heating, cooking, producing goods, mechanized transportation, and burning wastes have been considered a necessary by-product of our efforts to survive and progress. Air pollutants also come from natural sources. Windblown dust from the soil, tree pollen, and volcanoes are sources of particulate—sometimes to levels that far exceed air quality standards.

Except in a few isolated instances, air pollution was not regarded as a problem for much of human history because overall population was small and dispersed. Problems became more noticeable as the Earth's population grew, gathered in large cities, and used fuel (without controls) in manufacturing, commerce, and transportation. Photographs of the 19th century industrial centers in England and Europe, for example, show smoke-blackened skies and tarnished buildings.

As this nation grew, some American industrial cities began to experience similar circumstances. Chicago and Cincinnati established smoke-control laws in 1881, and 23 of the 28 largest cities had passed laws by 1912. At the time, however, most of these cities found it difficult to enforce such laws, and few major steps were taken until after World War II. One successful example was the strict smoke-control law enacted in East Chicago, Illinois, in 1948. In the Pittsburgh area, during the late 1950's and early 1960's, officials of Allegheny County and the steel industry resolved to correct the area's severe air quality problems.

The Clean Air Act amendments of 1977, the most recent changes in the law, incorporated a requirement for preventing the significant deterioration of air quality in areas where air is already cleaner than required by the national ambient air quality standards (NAAQS). It is important to understand how stringent these standards are. By law, a "primary" standard for each air pollutant covered by a NAAQS must be set low enough to protect the most sensitive segment of the population against identifiable adverse health effects. The primary health standard must incorporate an adequate margin of safety. Furthermore, a "secondary" standard must be set which protects against identifiable adverse welfare effects on vegetation and materials whether or not such vegetation or material exists in the area where the standard is being applied.[5]

ECONOMIC RESOURCES

The economic resources of an area vary widely with the location in terms of natural resources and the availability and ability of humans to transform these resources into finished products for human consumption. Industrial employment, however, is but one part of the economic strength of a community: the transportation, sale, and exchange of commodities constitute major functions of the service element of the economic base. More persons work in service industries than in manufacturing the products they handle, especially in current times, when automation has turned to the computer to replace human hands.

Need for Economic Planning

We simply must begin to consider the distant future in our economic planning. Any enterprise that depends on fouling the nest and expending principal will fail in time: pollution equals waste equals bad long-term management. Deregulation is simply a demand that the whole of society absorb the inevitable costs of pollution. At

5. Council on Environmental Quality, *12th Annual Report* (Washington, D.C.: U.S. Government Printing Office, 1982), 21–22.

present, even without deregulation, ecological disaster, spawned by the present style of human habitation in California, goes on apace: Our chances of maintaining the present level of air quality are tenuous at best; toxic wastes are not yet dealt with at the source, as a production rather than a disposal problem; water delivery on demand threatens wild rivers and estuarine water quality, fosters sprawl, and salts the earth; bad forestry practices destroy watersheds; and the reduction of biological diversity resulting from accelerating species extinction is doubtless undermining the resilience of the entire biosphere.

These system-wide problems are life-endangering: Whether or not they are still newsworthy, they must be solved. They affect the life of the land, our lives, and the lives of generations to come. They are a direct outcome of our benighted self-interest and our earlier ignorance of how eco-systems function.[6]

FOREST RESOURCES

If property is planned and managed, the forests that play such a critical part in our economic system could last forever, for they are a replaceable resource. Used for so many purposes, ranging from home building to paper products, wood is critical to individuals, corporations, and government.

Major lumbering industries are, for their own welfare, involved in reforestation, planting new growth where they have harvested timber. Ecologists have been critical of some of the activities of those firms that have denuded the land of trees by clear cutting and have destroyed the young growth with the mature, leaving the soil open to erosion and ultimate flooding of the lowlands.

National forest management by the federal government is intended to require firms leasing acreage for purposes of timber harvesting to reforest the land leased, while making economic use of the products growing on nationally owned land. Great areas of western America fall under the control of the National Forest Service, the Bureau of Land Management, and other federal agencies.

So much of the nation's wealth in forest land has been totally destroyed in the past that only through careful planning can the future be secured for generations to come.

CROP RESOURCES

As our environmental problems grow, plant life, and the animal life dependent on it, will be in ever-increasing danger.

Among the most important biological resources are the wild relatives of crop plants. Unfortunately, many of these plants and others of potential use that occur in the United States and elsewhere are in danger of extinction. The wild relatives of crop plants provide important genetic material for crop breeding to increase yields, improve quality, widen adaptation, add vigor, provide new modes of reproduction, and confer a number of other desirable characteristics, including resistance to diseases and pests. One recent and highly publicized discovery is the perennial wild maize, *Zea diploperennis,* which is known only in a few small areas in Jalisco, Mexico. Scientists have speculated that this plant may be used to develop a perennial corn, and recent research has shown it to be immune to four of the seven major viruses which attack field and sweet corn. There is great potential for using this and other wild maizes to improve the disease resistance and productivity of corn.

A recent draft report, prepared for the International Board of Plant Genetic Resources, calls for an international program to ensure the conservation of wild rela-

6. Alfred Heller (ed.), "Cry California," *California Tomorrow, Fall/Winter 1981.*

tives of crop plants. The report argues that conservation of the natural habitats of these plants is the chief means by which these resources can be conserved and identifies taxa for which reserves should be established. These include plants native to the United States that are insufficiently represented in U.S. parks and reserves.[7]

MINERAL RESOURCES

Most minerals are classified as a diminishing resource. Once found, extracted, smelted, formed, and used, they are no longer a resource. Even with the efforts to recycle some of the minerals, mostly steel, aluminum, and copper, the amount absorbed in the development of urban communities and industrial activities makes these minerals a diminishing resource.

PETROLEUM

Petroleum was discovered in America at Titusville, Pennsylvania, in 1859, and since then the extraction of petroleum has taken place in all parts of the world, from California, Louisiana, Mississippi, Oklahoma, Texas, and Alaska to Venezuela; the offshore areas of Europe to the Persian Gulf, where the vast supplies exist in Saudi Arabia, Kuwait, and Iran; and farther to the north, in the former Soviet Union. Despite all of these reserves, the supply of petroleum, even with recovery programs, is an ever-diminishing resource that may not last beyond the middle of the twenty-first century.

Secretary of the Interior Hodel recommended to the Congress that 750 million acres of Pacific seacoast be made available for oil exploration and extraction.

The danger of damaging the coastal ecology and the impact on fish and other wildlife were glossed over in spite of the damaging effect of the oil spills off the coast of Santa Barbara in 1967, the 10.9 million gallons of crude oil that covered the sea and shoreline of Prince William Sound in Alaska in March 1989, and the 0.5 million gallons that flowed onto the shore at Galveston, Texas, in July 1990 —all this in the name of providing fuel for gas guzzling automobiles when the loose restrictions were reduced by the current national administration, in the name of international economic competition and profit through deregulation.

When oil is extracted, it passes through the following processes on the path from well to exhaust:

>Explorations
>
>Drilling and extraction
>
>Transportation to the refineries, by pipeline, by ships of tremendous size and capacity, by trucks and rail cars
>
>Refining and cracking of the crude oil for many uses, in addition to fuel
>
>Storage in great tanks at the refinery
>
>Delivery to and use at a distribution terminal
>
>Transportation to the marketplace for public use as energy for transportation, industry, and heating
>
>Disposal of waste by-products, with inherent smog, ozone destruction, and related health risks

The solution to the threat of scarcity of oil resources includes the following:

7. Council on Environmental Quality, *12th Annual Report* (Washington, D.C.: U.S. Government Printing Office, 1981).

- Development and use of alternate forms of fuel that are not environmentally dangerous
- More efficient use of all forms of energy
- Design of vehicles and machines to use energy more efficiently and by these actions reduce impact on the ozone layer and eliminate smog and associated health dangers

Humankind has made a selective attack on ores and minerals, as the following excerpt eloquently explains.

In addition to possessing characteristics that will make him a remarkably fine index fossil, man through his works has attained a geological significance that is altogether out of proportion to the shortness of the period in which he has been the dominant form of life on the globe or to the length of time he is likely to survive if some current trends persist. As a geologic agent, man has already made a notable mark on the earth and left rather a distinctive record, for he has been peculiarly active in a number of ways that have had no counterpart in any other age in the history of the planet.

One of his most sharply directed efforts in this capacity has been his attack on those relatively scarce geologic bodies known as ore deposits. With remarkable selectivity he has sought for these local concentrations of specific elements wherever he has been able to reach them in the crust of the earth, and for the past few centuries he has been most energetically digging them out as promptly as he could find.

This procedure, in a geologic sense at least, has been a most sudden one, for it did not attain any importance whatever until the current industrial civilization developed. It is really less than a couple of hundred years old, and yet it has become a phenomenon that is one of the unique features of the age.

The bulk of the raw materials needed for the machines and tools and for the structures, chemicals, and power, without which modern industry and the life it supports could not survive, comes from ore or mineral deposits or from organic accumulations formed in the remote past. In a very real sense they are a geologic heritage, which we are spending freely and enjoying thoroughly, and without which human life on earth would have necessarily been organized on a very different and less elaborate basis. Once gone, these accumulations of metallic and other useful minerals cannot be replaced in any period of time significant to the human race. The destruction of these rare and valuable deposits and the dissipation of the elements contained in them are geologic changes of truly profound character which can be attributed almost entirely to man's very special and increasing need under current conditions for the materials obtained from them.

Metals and minerals are the "vitamins" of modern industry, as the National City Bank of New York put it recently. Some, such as copper, lead, zinc, and aluminum, as well as steel, are needed in huge tonnages, whereas others are required only in very small amounts for some special function. Germanium is a critical element in transistors, which are revolutionizing communications, but only a minute fraction of an ounce is needed in each instrument. In contrast, wire and cable consumed nearly 800,000 tons of copper in 1954. Without alloy steels dependent on elements such as nickel, manganese, chromium, molybdenum, and vanadium, modern engines and soaring structures would be impossible. And another metal-god serves us well in another very special capacity by providing some measure of international support to the depreciating paper dollar.

To meet the insistent and growing demand for these essential metals and minerals, the whole world is being searched for the deposits from which they are derived. Whenever found, these restricted geologic bodies are being exploited with ever increasing skill and on scales that are becoming grander and grander. The consumption of these basic resources has now become so great—and is expanding at such a rate—that their adequacy in relation to the mounting requirements must be most carefully reviewed in any serious appraisal of means by which the multiplying masses of human beings in all parts of the earth will be able to support themselves. It is most surely a factor that has to be taken into account in any forecast of the course that competent and ambitious nations or races are likely to take in the centuries ahead.

The distribution of ores and minerals has had a profound effect on the migration of peoples and on the settlement of particular lands. It has been a dominant element in the growth of states in which possession or content of such deposits has led to the creation of vast industrial enterprises. Exploitation of these resources has resulted in new patterns of life in many old regions, and their exhaustion in some places has forced adjustment of a far-reaching sort that at times have had disturbing consequences.[8]

New explorations under the seas will provide, at considerable additional cost, some of these essential products, but even then the amount mined will not add much to the total inventory.

The world's most valuable known supply of manganese nodules lies three miles deep in the international waters of the Pacific Ocean between Central America and Hawaii. Rich in strategic metals, these fist-sized nodules are being explored and analyzed by five international industrial consortia, four of which include U.S. companies. The metals—manganese, copper, nickel, and cobalt—are essential for the production of steel, aircraft engines, alloys, and other industrial materials. The United States currently imports large quantities of these metals, including virtually all of its cobalt and manganese. Zambia and Zaire provide most of the world's cobalt. By the end of the century, the Soviet Union and South Africa are expected to control virtually all the world's manganese resources.[9]

In the past great pressure was exerted to encourage the exploration and mining of mineral resources. They were considered an inexhaustible horn of plenty, to be taken from the earth without fear or concern for the future. In the latter part of the twentieth century, however, the need for husbanding the diminishing supply of minerals has caused more careful use, including substitution of alternative materials such as paper and plastics where the purpose permitted.

ENERGY NEEDS—THE HIGH-TECH REVOLUTION

The development of "high-technology" industrial production in the latter half of the twentieth century has caused and is causing as great a change in the economic and social system as the industrial revolution, with many of the same consequences. The development of miniature circuits on plastic chips introduced robot- and computer-controlled production, causing great changes in the requirement for labor in many industries. The need for planning, starting with the education and retraining of great numbers of displaced workers, is of paramount importance if a reasonable level of employment and economic stability is to be achieved. This can only be accomplished through understanding the nature of the problems and planning and producing techniques that will provide a wider base of support for the millions of families impacted by this revolution.

Will high-tech industries require exotic new forms of energy to power the mechanical components that will replace human energy? Will Orwell's *1984* predictions be realized, making a fictional treatise reality? What will become of cheap labor supplies in the third world countries when the button pushers relegate human energy to oblivion?

---

8. Excerpts from Donald A. McLaughlin, in *Man's Role in Changing the Face of the Earth*, ed. W. L. Thomas, (Chicago: University of Chicago Press, 1956), 851–52.

9. Council on Environmental Quality, *12th Annual Report* (Washington, D.C.: U.S. Government Printing Office, 1981).

Some of the newer forms of energy are already providing a growing number of industrially developed nations with electrical energy from sources other than the traditional ones, water, coal, gas, and petroleum. For each of the new forms of energy opportunities and problems must be resolved to make them economically and physically viable and socially acceptable.

ENERGY TYPES

From the earliest times people have sought and devised means for developing alternative types of energy to replace brute force. The wheel reduced human energy requirements in agriculture, industry, and transportation. Fire produced both heat and light and thus added to both the preservation of peace and the conduct of war.

The earth, seas, and sun have given humans the basic resources. Knowledge about their use has opened the windows to protection of the health and welfare of countless generations by providing food and shelter. Only recently have people come to realize that someday soon it may be necessary to search for alternative sources of energy to maintain life on this planet.

Hydroelectric Power

Water use as a means of providing power goes back in the pages of history to the time when the water wheel was utilized to mill grain and turn the wheels of small industrial plants. Water power for the generation of electrical energy was a factor in the first turbines developed during the nineteenth century and has in the twentieth century been a major source of electrical service. Great inertial systems of transmission of electricity have made it possible to transport this form of energy over long distances from the points of generation to the areas of the world where other means of energy are limited.

Energy from the Sky

Many forms of energy are generated from the sun and moon, and perhaps from other neighbors in our solar system. When sunlight falls on leaves of green plants, it causes a chemical reaction called photosynthesis that enables plants to grow and produce food and fiber on which humans depend. When sunlight falls onto a strip of silicone, some of the solar energy is absorbed within the atomic structure of the silicone, producing a charge of electrical energy.

Energy from outer space in many forms is being experimented with by present-day scientists, including wind-powered turbines, passive solar collectors, solar furnaces (which capture the rays of the sun in great series of reflective mirrors and transmit this light to a collector that uses them to heat oil and generate electrical current), solar ponds, and photovoltaic collector cells. All are related to the sun as the basic source of energy.

Wind Farms: Harvesting Wind Power

One of the oldest energy sources is the wind. In Holland and in many other parts of Europe windmills have done society's work in performing tasks requiring more than human strength. In recent years wind has again received attention as a source of electrical energy production.

Wind generated over the cool Pacific Ocean waters flows through the passes that separate the coastal areas from the hot, arid deserts that extend from Canada to the Mexican border and beyond. In these passes the wind constitutes a resource that can and does already generate electrical energy. As one travels from the Sacramento Valley to the San Francisco Bay area, traveling through Altamont Pass, wind farms have been established and are currently supplying electrical energy. Additional wind farms are located at the mouth of San Gorgonio Pass,

Windmills on the island of Mallorca in the Mediterranean Sea (right).

Windmills in the Netherlands, an efficient way to create energy (bottom).

just to the northwest of Palm Springs, and in the windy areas of the desert just east of the pass in the Tehachapi area, south and east of Bakersfield. State and federal tax laws have been designed to support alternative energy resources and thus provide attractive economic advantages to persons interested in entering this new field.

A considerable amount of research and planning is involved in the location of the wind farms. There must be adequate open space and an absence of obstructions that would deflect the wind or the sun, which is the source of the differences in temperature that make the wind farms operate.

GEOTHERMAL ENERGY

The search for alternate sources of energy has led to the exploration and exploitation of geothermal areas where superheated water rises to the surface of the earth through vents that discharge the water and steam into the air, in the form of hot springs and geysers. At Rotorua, New Zealand, and in other locations, the geysers have been harnessed to produce a considerable supply of electrical energy for local use. Other areas located in Northern California and along the southern shore of the Salton Sea in Southern California are likewise being explored for their geothermal energy potential.

SOLAR ENERGY

Solar energy in passive systems has been used in tropical and semitropical areas for a considerable period of time. Many buildings in Jerusalem had passive systems on their roofs as far back as the 1960s. This system involves a solar collector and a storage tank for the heated water. The system must be supplemented with an alternate heating system for those times of the year when the sun does not produce the energy because of fog or general overcast.

In the search for energy, solar energy has an excellent future when the costs are lowered to within the reach of a greater number of people.

Solar Energy Ponds

Solar energy is also being generated in the solar pond developed by the state of Israel along the bank of the Dead Sea. Here the highly saline water of the Dead Sea is being used, together with less saline water from the Mediterranean Sea, to produce a salt differential that, together with the rays of the sun, forms the basis

Wind farm in Altamont Pass in Northern California, one of the many efforts to add to the supply of clean energy.

for the production of electrical current to supply at least part of the needs of the community of Masada.

On December 16, 1978, the Papago village of Schuchuli became the first community in the world to rely entirely on solar energy for its power needs. Schuchuli is located on the western edge of the 2.7 million-acre Papago Reservation in southwestern Arizona. The village's fifteen families (ninety-five people) live 17 miles from the nearest electric utility power source. Before the installation of the photovoltaic system the community was served by a diesel-powered pump that provided water and kerosene lamps and candles that generated light.

First Solar Community

Solar access as a component of comprehensive planning for urban development will become increasingly important, especially in those states where the potential for use of solar energy is an important element of the total energy system. The following extract is an example of planning in the state of California.

Solar Access Planning

Why Plan for Solar Access?

A plan is an integrated set of objectives and policies developed by a community to guide its future growth and development. It represents options and alternatives that have been chosen to meet future needs and desires of the community. However, under the state planning and zoning laws, all communities are required to adopt comprehensive plans, and one of the best ways to protect solar access as a local option is to incorporate a concern for solar access into the regular planning procedure. This is important for a number of reasons.

First, planning is absolutely necessary to support the regulations that will be required to protect solar access. Communities can consider two approaches to solar access planning: either existing general plan elements can support solar access and solar energy objectives, or the adoption of a new general plan element can be considered. Either of these would fulfill the planning aspect of local solar access regulations.

Because all local regulations must be consistent with adopted comprehensive plans under California law, it may be necessary to address solar access within the plan if a community is considering adopting specific regulations to promote solar access. The recently passed California Solar Rights Act allows communities to consider solar access in approving tentative subdivision maps, but even this consideration depends on the subdivision map complying with adopted comprehensive plans. If a community is going to exercise its authority under the Solar Rights Act in reviewing subdivisions for solar access, then it may wish to adopt a solar access plan component to support the regulatory standards it desires to impose on proposed developments requiring tentative map approval. By planning for solar access, a community can be assured that its regulatory standards are appropriate for its solar energy and solar access needs, as well as legally defensible under state laws.

There are five general steps in the solar access planning process:

1. Gather preliminary information about solar access and solar energy use. (Optional)
2. Analyze existing solar access and problems of shading.
3. Consider and make a decision about possible levels of solar access desired for the community.
4. Consider how solar access policies and goals may conflict with other community planning objectives.
5. Draft policies on solar access and integrate them into existing policies and plans.[10]

NUCLEAR ENERGY

Nuclear power, developed in many parts of the world, has become the most controversial source of energy as its dangers are contemplated and the disposal of waste and the dismantling of plants become subjects of both health and financial concerns. The cost of the power generated, therefore, would appear uneconomic.

All of the energy alternatives being explored, including nuclear energy, are still adding but a minimum amount of the energy needs of the industrial communities of the twentieth century, and all will have to be planned for to meet the increasing demands, all over the world, in the twenty-first century and later.

Energy policy analysis and planning, in both the public and private sectors of the national economy, are among the most important tasks of our times if we are to have this essential resource continuously available when needed.

METHANE GAS RECOVERY— ENERGY FROM WASTE

The city of Modesto, California, in 1972 considered the use of a purified digester to recover methane gas from by-products of waste water treatment. Processed methane, essentially a natural gas, is produced by the bacteria in the digester unit of the plant. A new purification process was developed, and the city has tested the gas for 4 years in an eight-car test fleet of automobiles. In 1982, after successful testing, the city installed a full-scale system capable of providing fuel for two hundred city vehicles.

A new plant was opened in the Puente Hills of Southern California in spring 1984; it will produce enough methane gas to generate electricity to serve more than five thousand homes. In the future the capacity of the plant will increase to serve more than ten times the number of residences and, in a few years, will recoup the investment associated with the development of the installation. The plant was developed with public funds, the energy being sold to a private utility company for local distribution.

NATURAL GAS

Natural gas, as part of the petroleum extraction process, is widely used in residential and commercial projects. It is also being used for the propulsion of com-

---

10. California Energy Commission, *Solar Access, A Guidebook for California Communities*, March 1980, Sacramento, Calif.

mercial automobiles in some areas for homes and motor vehicles but is limited by the storage capacity for motor vehicles.

With the realization of the limited sources of energy came the concern for planning the conservation of the known resources. There is no doubt that planning must be at the core of protection. The scope of the explorations must cover not only the use of the resources but the alternate means of using them. Thus we find exploration in the sphere of building design to limit the need for energy demands during extremes of both heat and cold. New concepts of utilizing the sun and the earth to reduce energy demands are presented as an approach to community building. The architect Solari has been exploring earth-integrated housing for a number of years in the torrid areas of Arizona. Forms of shelter that presumably protect occupants from nuclear fallout have also been an approach to using the earth itself as a means of surviving. The following extracts provide a synopsis of the past and a look at the future.

Conservation of Energy

Fuelish Hopes [11]

As to the likelihood of our developing unconventional new sources of energy, our prognostications have been even more misguided. *Fortune* magazine (to pick an unfortunate example) ten years ago published an article on "The Coming Hydrogen Economy," which conjured up visions of huge nuclear reactors, floating on platforms in the ocean, producing immense supplies of burnable hydrogen gas by electrolyzing seawater. Pumped ashore in flexible, leak-proof pipelines, the gaseous hydrogen would be stored in underground tanks or pressure-cooled into liquid for convenient transportation to waiting customers. *Fortune* foresaw the possibility of hydrogen-cooled and hydrogen-driven generating plants, trucks, buses, ships, trains—even automobiles.

In the midst of the Arab oil embargo of 1973–74, the United States government eagerly endorsed the rapid development of nuclear-fueled electric plants. But within three years, the related problems of cost and safety had brought the production of nuclear reactors virtually to a stop. Economic forecasters now doubt that nuclear power will provide more energy to the United States in the 1990s than it does today.

By 1979, synthetic fuel had become the miracle on the horizon. President Carter proposed that the country spend $88 billion on a crash program to develop "Synfuels." Congress cut the budget by three quarters. The catch phrase "alternative energy" meanwhile came into our political vocabulary—portmanteau for an assortment of old-fashioned and new-fangled remedies. Every "alternative"—solar batteries, tidal turbines, geothermal dynamos, photovoltaic cells, biomass generators, windmills, methane from decomposing garbage, heat differentials in saltwater ponds, and petroleum substitutes extracted from seaweed, wood chips, straw, or desert weeds—attracted an enthusiastic cult.

The concluding opinion of two professors who made an energy study at the Harvard Business School in 1979 was clouded by gloom: "The United States simply cannot rely on any substantially increased overall output from conventional energy sources," said the report of Robert Stobaugh and Daniel Yergin. "Only coal can be counted on for additional supply over the next decade. And it is possible that the increase in coal production will be offset by a decrease in the total combined output from domestic oil, gas and nuclear power. Synthetic fuels can only begin to make a very modest contribution by 1990." The only hope, Stobaugh and Yergin said, was in rapid development of renewable energy sources and in great improvements in energy efficiency.

---

11. Alfred Heller and Samuel Wood, *California Tomorrow, California 200—The Next Frontier*, Summer 1982.

It Can Be Done![12]

The events taking place in the Middle East demonstrate the significance of actions taken by Pacific Gas and Electric since the oil embargo of 1973–74 to reduce our dependence on foreign oil.

We do not anticipate any shortage of electricity or natural gas, or any immediate impact on customer bills, as a result of the current Middle East crises. The relatively small amount of oil we use comes primarily from the Far East.

The company once relied on oil to see it through dry years when hydroelectric power was greatly reduced. In the drought years of 1976–79, about 28.8 million barrels of oil were used each year to generate electricity. In contrast, during the drought years of 1986–89, the company's average annual use of oil was only 2.9 million barrels—a decrease of 90 percent.

This impressive reduction was made possible by:

* energy conservation practiced by our customers;
* operating our Diablo Canyon nuclear power plant safely, efficiently and productively, saving the equivalent of 23 million barrels of oil a year;
* switching from oil to natural gas in our power plants, because of the greater availability of natural gas, and because it is cleaner and less costly than oil;
* buying more electricity from independent producers who use wind, solar, hydro, geothermal, waste-to-energy, cogeneration and natural gas to generate electric power; and
* working in a regulatory environment that enables and encourages these developments.

PG&E has become one of the nation's foremost utilities in energy conservation and in using and developing renewable and alternative energy sources. The company already buys more wind-generated electricity than any other utility in the world, and is a leader in developing solar energy.

As the company continues its efforts in these areas, however, it will also be stressing the importance of energy efficiency. It is estimated that PG&E customers will need 3,300 additional megawatts of power by the end of the decade—and the company's plan is to meet 2,500 megawatts of that total through energy efficiency and load management improvements. That's enough energy to serve the needs of 2.5 million people, and will save the equivalent of about 11 million barrels of oil per year. As a result, PG&E's programs are helping to meet two of the nation's most important objectives: improving environment and achieving energy security.

PROGRESS Late in 1990 Congress passed and President Bush signed the Clean Air Act of 1990. The legislation was deemed by the president to be the greatest effort to improve air conditions in all of history. Interestingly, the effective date for achieving the goals is in the future, some as much as 20 years from the date of passage of the bill. The question that must appear in the minds of concerned people is, Will the increases in population; the proliferation of automobiles, whose production levels seem to parallel that of rabbits; the addition of industries and other activities affecting the quality of atmosphere outstrip the gains proposed by the new law? It is understandable that there must be time to permit industry to find the ways to change their operations and provide the equipment to meet the new standards, but implementation should ensure the progress that is the intent of the law. The following extract brings the discussion of federal legislation up to the actions of the 101st Congress.

---

12. Report to stockholders of Pacific Gas and Electric Company, October 25, 1990.

The 101st Congress ended in late October after a session that provided both good news and bad news for the environment. In the ongoing battle to protect Americans' health and environment from pollution, Congress passed two long awaited improvements—an historical new Clean Air Act and a substantial improvement of oil spill liability law.

On the other hand, Congress rejected a proposal to give states more authority over the clean up of contaminated facilities operated by the Departments of Defense and Energy.

Environmentalists made some progress in their continuing efforts to protect America's endangered wild lands. Congress granted new protection for various wilderness areas around the country, including Alaska's Tongass National Forest. However, Congress failed to provide permanent protection for the California desert and other proposed areas.

In the way of good news, though, Congress turned back efforts to open the Arctic National Wildlife Refuge in Alaska to oil and gas development. Congress also refused to accelerate the logging of ancient forests in the Pacific Northwest and California.

Environmentalists' efforts to reduce global warming, air pollution, and the nation's dependence on foreign oil took a blow when Congress failed to require automakers to improve automobile fuel efficiency.

Great Lakes

Congress passed new legislation that will accelerate the Environmental Protection Agency's cleanup plans for 31 toxic "hot spots" around the Great Lakes ecosystem. The new law also moves states to set higher water quality standards, with an ultimate goal of zero discharge.

This new law incorporates an existing agreement between the United States and Canada to protect the Great Lakes. The bill will also aid cleanup of Long Island Sound, Lake Champlain, and the highly polluted Onondaga Lake.

Environmentalists are expected to push for legislation in the next Congress that would expedite the cleanup of contaminated sediments in coastal areas, including the Great Lakes.[13]

The 101st Congress and the Environment

---

13. Southern Sierra Club, *Southern Sierran*, December 1990, Los Angeles, Calif.

PART 2

URBANISM IS BORN

*Sir, if you wish to have
a just notion of the magnitude
of this city, you must not be satisfied
with seeing its great streets and squares,
but must survey the innumerable
little lanes and courts.*

-Samuel Johnson

CHAPTER 4

THE DAWN OF URBANISM

The simplest definition of *urbanism* or an *urban area* might be the confederation or union of neighboring clans resorting to a center used as a common meeting place for worship, protection, and the like; hence, the political or sovereign body formed by such a community.

An urban area can also be defined as a composite of cells, neighborhoods, or communities where people work together for the common good. The types of urban areas can vary as greatly as the variety of activities performed there: the means of production and the kinds of goods, trade, transportation, the delivery of goods and services, or a combination of all of these activities.

According to a third definition, urban areas are those locations where there is opportunity for a diversified living environment and diverse life-styles. People live, work, and enjoy themselves in social and cultural relationships provided by the proximities of an urban area.

Urban areas can be simple or complex. They can have a rural flavor or that of an industrial workshop. They can be peaceful or filled with all types of conflict. They can be small and easy to maintain, or gargantuan and filled with strife and economic problems.

Cities have circulation systems that unite the different areas and provide routes for transporting commodities from the farms and elsewhere to the city's distribution centers. In large cities, several kinds of transportation and transit are often available.

Cities have many obvious faults in terms of their services to people. They can be overcrowded, contain large amounts of substandard housing, be centers of unemployment, and have corrupt governments. Taxation tends to be high and services less than adequate. However, even with all of these faults, cities are here to stay. The charge to planners at all levels, public and private, is to find ways to make these essential elements in our social system work better, more efficiently, and thus to make our cities more desirable places in which to live.

FROM THE CAVE TO THE VILLAGE

Contrary to popular belief, urbanism did not begin when people left the cave. It probably started in the caves themselves, where the people gathered for protection against the elements or for defense against rival tribes.

Lewis Mumford states:

> Though permanent villages date only from the Neolithic times, the habit of resorting to caves for the collective performance of magical ceremonies seems to date back to an earlier period; and whole communities, living in caves and the hollowed-out walls of rock, have survived in widely scattered areas down to the present. The outline of the city as both an outward form and inward pattern of life might be found in such ancient assemblages.[1]

These places of communal living gave way to the village. The village was a by-product of the development of agriculture in areas where there was an adequate water supply and fertile soil. Many of these earliest villages arose adjacent to what are now the Mediterranean Sea and the Nile, Tigris, and Euphrates rivers. Mumford holds that the so-called urban areas thus newly created and their rural hinterlands were part of an interlaced whole essential to the sustenance of human and animal life, which in turn promoted agricultural production.

Many early villages were located on sites that offered some natural protection, sites such as elevated terrain, islands, and peninsulas. Otherwise artificial defenses had to be built, and villages would be surrounded by barricades or moats, for example. One of the earliest known villages was built on pilings in a Swiss lake.

People have always been gregarious beings. They have sought companionship and devised group activities and entertainment. The village was also an appropriate sanctuary for the altar of their deity, a meeting place for assembly, and a center for trade. As the environment became increasingly populated, urbanization resulted.

As communities have taken on added functions and have grown, the care of fertile land has become to some extent ignored. Lands still used for agriculture have been infused with so many artificial fertilizers that the soil has become the vehicle for these chemicals. These fertilizers are the main nutrients for fruit and vegetable crops rather than the soil's natural nutrients. Concern for the protection of fertile soils has been slow to develop, but increasing attention is now being focused on conservation worldwide. Sometimes the concern is expressed locally as well. Some Native American communities, for example, have opposed urban development on their reservations, favoring instead the protection of their land and culture despite the greater cash return that might result from urbanization.

1. "The Natural History of Urbanizations," in *Man's Role in Changing the Face of the Earth,* ed. William L. Thomas, Jr., (Chicago, Ill., University of Chicago Press, 1956).

A village near Stutgart, Germany. *A cluster of homes forming a small center of population in a predominantly agricultural area.*

The large community, as opposed to the village, came about as the result of the growth of crops and the breeding of stock on a more permanent basis than before. The production of hard grains that could be stored from year to year offered stability, since it provided insurance against starvation. Urban areas became known for the type of food they could conserve—wheat and rye in the European areas, rice in the Orient. The ability to preserve food made it possible to diversify into other activities.

With the development of a diversified economy not totally dependent on food production, it became possible to attract people into a labor pool, thus providing employment in a variety of forms. This in turn brought about the enlargement of villages or hamlets into towns and cities, which operated on different political and economic bases than had been possible in the simpler forms.

Newly created cities retained many of the physical and social characteristics of the earlier urban areas. Even today the food supply of many agricultural centers is located in the fields that surround them. Urban centers like these have had little reason to grow beyond the limited size that their basic needs have dictated.

Although many changes have taken place in some rural areas, great parts of the world's developing countries still live primitively as far as their economy and standards of living are concerned. The native populations wrest what food they can from poor land, constantly remaining on the verge of starvation. Recent events in Ethiopia are a horrifying illustration of this condition.

The People's Republic of China made its greatest step forward when it freed itself from the danger of famine. The primary planning goal in that nation is still a large-scale commitment to agriculture. A tremendous amount of labor has been allocated to that end because of the current lack of mechanical equipment.

THE NATURE OF CITIES

The word *city* implies a large concentration of people in a given geographic area who support themselves on a fairly permanent basis from the economic activities of that area. The city can be a center of industry, trade, education, or government or involve all these activities. This diversity of opportunity attracts people from rural areas to the cities.

Thus we find that cities tend to become big if their economic base is broad. The smaller cities are usually satellites that depend on larger cities to sustain their economic life. For example, central cities have multiple functions, whereas the suburban "bedroom" communities surrounding them mainly serve the purpose of housing the more affluent members of the work force.

CHAPTER 5

LOCATION AND TYPES OF URBANISM

Historically, natural factors played an important part in the development and growth of urban areas. The danger of fire and flood, extreme climatic conditions, the possibility of earthquakes and volcanic eruptions, lack of natural resources or fertile soils—all influenced decisions either to settle in a given area or to move to a more favorable site. The larger early urban areas, with some exceptions, are found where the climate is relatively moderate. Few of any great size are located north of the sixtieth or south of the forty-fifth parallel. This does not mean that there are no great temperature extremes within these boundaries. The torrid Sahara Desert and the frigid winter of parts of Canada, the United States, and the Soviet Union lie within this so-called temperate zone. However, the climate is habitable for major parts of the year so that life can exist or even flourish.

Geographic studies indicate that urban areas seldom form where the topography is steep. Some cities are located at high altitudes, but the slope of the land is relatively level. For example, Denver, Colorado, and Mexico City are more than 5,000 feet above sea level, but the terrain at these sites is relatively flat. It is only recently, with the invention of earthmoving equipment like the bulldozer, that steep areas have been leveled to permit urban development.

The accessibility of other important places usually determines the location of larger cities. Thus most of the largest cities of the world can be found on or near major waterways. New York, Seattle, Boston, Rio de Janeiro, and Chicago illustrate this principle. Some of these cities serve as transportation terminals;

THE INFLUENCE OF GEOGRAPHY

others, such as Chicago and Kansas City, are crossing points for networks of internal transportation. The geographic study of cities also takes into account the relationships among people, types of housing, population densities and concentration, rates of growth, and impact of growth on the land and all other resources.

Impact on the Natural Environment

Urbanism brings about many changes in the surrounding environment. Buildings occupying formerly open land, pavements on streets, and smoke from factories can alter the climate. Sometimes the unintended change is dramatic. The construction of a simple irrigation canal from the Colorado River to the fertile Imperial Valley of California brought about the formation of the Salton Sea in 1905 after a heavy rainfall in the upper reaches of the river. Thus a body of water about 40 miles long and 10 miles wide exists today where in 1904 there was only desert land.

Recent ventures into the Alaskan wilderness may have long-term adverse effects on the cycles of human and animal life there. Where once a perfect balance in nature existed, today the advances of "southern civilization" has replaced the dogsled with the gasoline-powered automobile. The once-limited paths and roads that did not disturb the permafrost have been replaced by trenches cut by the many heavy vehicles. The migration pattern of the caribou and other large animals may be disrupted by the hundreds of miles of the oil pipeline. Each incident may not be critical to the survival of the Alaskan Inuit, but the sum of these changes may cause change as great as those that created the Sahara Desert.

The future presents all humanity—not just those living in urban areas—with the problem of coping with the consequences of technological change. The use and disposal of nuclear power and wastes, the filling of the skies and waters with pollutants, even the artificial inducing of rain with iodides: such elements may not only change the microclimate but ultimately affect the habitability of our planet.

POLITICAL AND SOCIAL ORGANIZATION

Society has been forged in the crucible of natural forces. Because communities are part of nature, people have suffered from many of the evils they have inflicted on the environment. They have faced the necessity to improve economic security, correct social maladjustments, discard mass superstitions, or resist seizure of power by autocrats bent upon personal glory and self-aggrandizement. The conflicts have created varying degrees of pressure upon humankind under a variety of circumstances.

The village brought something new to the lives of primitive people: the need for mutual responsibility and cooperation. Various social and political organizations emerged as a direct result.

People did not adjust easily to the self-discipline that community life requires. Personal rivalry flared within the village, and the most powerful individual assumed the role of tribal leader. Rivalry between villages often resulted in armed conflict. Several villages might come under the domination of the victorious tribe with that tribe's leader rising to the position of ruler. In time, empires were created and rulers took the titles of king and emperor.

What distinguishes the early city from the primitive village is its higher degree of political and social organization. The more sophisticated social structure allows people to live together in relative peace. Social, economic, and political organization is essential to the growth and development of a city. The history of China, from the time of the Qin dynasty (221–206 B.C.) to the present, vividly illustrates this progression.

As a result of the more advanced social structure, bold aesthetic changes took place. Temples and other structures of the ruling group became permanent. Tremendous amounts of energy were expended to produce great edifices, such as palaces and cathedrals, which became a source of pride to the public and the seat of power for its rulers. In the meantime, most of the people lived as slave labor in mud huts or worse where none of the basic amenities existed or even basic needs were met. Such situations still exist in many parts of the world today, where great numbers of people live in slums, *favellas,* and *barrios,* many of which are in or adjacent to urban areas.

EVOLUTION OF PHYSICAL FORM

Sensitive to the surge between oppression and justice, the physical form of cities has been shaped by the economic, social, and political forces of society. The degree to which freedom or slavery has dominated human life, the manner in which war has been waged, the instruments of destruction and defense, the tools for peaceful pursuits and the way they have been used, the consideration, neglect, or disdain people have shown their fellows, all account for the kind of cities people have built for themselves. The effect of these factors on urban development in the past may help guide us in charting future enterprises in city building.

Historians have attempted to isolate and codify the variations in the patterns of cities, but their development almost precludes such classification. Adjectives like *organic* and *inorganic, irregular* and *geometrical, magical* and *mystical, formal* and *informal, medieval* and *classic,* often obscure rather than clarify the distinctions or describe a form without the substance.

Two basic urban forms are discernible in the past: the walled town and the open city. Within these basic forms a wide variety of patterns was woven, each form and design shaped by the character of society at the time.

Neither the presence nor the absence of a particular form affixed upon a people or a period is a conclusive expression of that society. It is rather the manner in which the forms have been manipulated and the purpose for which they have been devised that give significance to the physical patterns of cities. Within these various patterns similar social, economic, and political habits and customs may be found.

Few cities in which great cultures thrived began with a plan. They developed by a process of accretion—the growth was irregular, responsive to changes in the habits of people, and dynamic in character. They began as free cities settled voluntarily. Their external form, their physical pattern, was introduced according to the structure of the land itself or the manner in which the land was apportioned among the inhabitants. Colonial cities founded by great states were given a formal pattern determined in advance by a ruling authority. Privileged landowners divided their land for allocation to settlers, the plots being generally identical in form and character.

With the ebb and flow of civilization irregular and geometrical patterns have been grafted one upon the other. Villages that grew into cities because of geographic, economic, or social advantages may show evidence of geometrical patterns superimposed on original irregular ones, or an informal and irregular system may have been grafted onto a city with an original gridiron pattern. Cities have been subjected to the process of continuous remodeling through the ages, and the variety of their forms is the result of the particular force or forces that were dominant during the successive periods of their history. Motives of city builders are reflected in the designs they have stamped on their portions of a city.

We are accustomed to measuring a civilization by the monuments it produces. Certain cultural characteristics are revealed by these structures, but it is not enough to observe the monuments alone. If the characteristics of a civilization are to be discerned, attention cannot be confined to the rulers: the affairs of the people must be observed. The city is not the palace, the temple, or a collection of art objects. The city means all of the people who inhabit it, the entire collection of the houses the people live in, the places in which they work, the streets they traverse, and the shops and markets in which they trade. To separate the palace from the dwellings of the populace is like removing a phrase from its context. When related to the lives of the people, the palace may provide quite a different interpretation than when observed as an isolated monument.

More than the great and impressive structures, the common dwellings of the people mark the culture of cities. Civilization is not measured by creations and inventions alone, but by the extent to which the people share the benefits these make possible. Progress is not properly gauged by the comparison of an aboriginal village with a modern city; it is more accurately appraised by the degree to which the people participate in the advantages of each. Standards of quality are relative, and it is the contrast between the environment of the privileged and that of the poor that provides the yardstick to measure the freedom and happiness enjoyed by the people in any given period.

Historically there is a lag between moments of great social ideals and the structures that reflect them. Institutions of social and political justice or oppression gather momentum that carries beyond the zenith of their influence. The substance of these institutions, the freedom they have nurtured or denied, may have altered or vanished by the time the physical structure of the urban environment they engendered is finally completed. Frequently the powerful human forces that produced a city have begun to change or disappear, but the physical form of the city has seldom if ever been modified. An environment that emerged from a society of high ideals may then become the dramatic scene of its decline.

Stability, a status quo of human institutions, in the sense of a consistency of human conduct over a more or less long period, does not long endure. Civilization has not remained static for any protracted period. Humanity must continuously have new cultural food on which to nourish, or it decays. During periods when social and political institutions were molded to the welfare of the people, they provided the very climate of freedom that permitted humanity to forge and wield the tools of oppression, inequality, and injustice. We observe these trends in early villages, in ancient cities, in medieval cities, and during the baroque period—and there is evidence of their presence in our cities of today.

URBAN COMMUNITIES

From earliest times, each urban community has fulfilled a special purpose in the social and economic structure. They have all had particular functions to perform, some singular and others multiple. Thus can be found the following types:

The Crossroad. This is the simplest form of community, expanding or contracting as traders travel from one area to another. It is a place for rest, food, and exchange of merchandise and ideas. The location can be at some transportation terminal, such as a river or a seaport.

The Primary Agricultural Community. This is the service area for rural activities. Essentials for agricultural activities are acquired here, and here the harvest is taken for shipment to processors and ultimately to its consumers.

The Commercial City. The business ventures, the exchanges, the dealings in commodities take place here. A wide range of goods is available from which the consumer may select.

The Industrial City. Raw or partly processed materials are turned into finished goods here, for a shipment to the marketplaces of the world.

The Transportation City. Such a city is located at the center of the transportation web, where goods are taken from far-off places to be distributed to other far-off places.

The Recreational City. Because of their climate or other special offerings, such cities attract large numbers of people for other than business-related or work-related purposes. Examples include health resorts, gambling centers, and sports and scenic areas.

Educational Cities. A major educational institution or group of institutions constitutes the primary functions of the urban area. Examples of such places are Claremont, California; Davis, California; and Princeton, New Jersey.

Mining Communities. Here the extraction of minerals forms the economic base. Diamond-mining communities in South Africa are of this type, as are towns in coal-mining areas.

Retirement Communities. These include cities where the principal export capital comes from income and pensions. The communities in the Sun Belt of the United States are examples.

Governmental Centers. Centers of governmental activity, where the principal employer is the government.

Combination (Regional) Cities. A few cities perform all or many of the functions listed. They are therefore larger and more complex than any of the individual types of communities.

CHAPTER 6

CITIES OF ANCIENT LANDS

Early civilization spread along the fertile valleys where food, water, and transportation possibilities were at hand. A series of great and small empires rose, waged wars, and fell. Supremacy shifted from one kingdom to another, each adding its contribution to the evolution of the civilized world. One characteristic was shared by every one of these civilizations: All possessions of the kingdom, the land, and its benefits were subject to the will of the ruling monarchs and their appointed emissaries. The rulers were generally considered deities, and their representatives transmitted the orders of a god to be obeyed.

EGYPT AND OTHERS

In Egypt the lives of the people were dedicated to the pharaoh. The towns they built in the third millennium B.C., erected on the reigning pharaoh's order, housed the slaves and artisans engaged in building the great pyramids—the tombs of royalty and nobility. Resembling huge barracks, the cells of sun-dried brick were crowded about common courtyards. Narrow lanes served as open drainage sewers as well as common passageways. Walls surrounded the towns. Ancient Egypt was large and mighty enough to be fearless, so these walls were probably built primarily for protection against seasonal floods rather than against invading enemy armies.

Concurrent with the building of the pyramids, permanent towns of sun-baked brick arose along the Indus Valley. In Mohenjo-Daro and Harrapa the streets were arranged in a regular pattern, and, as in Egypt, the dwellings were compactly built about interior courts. Building heights were established in proportion to the width of streets, one and two stories predominating. Sanitation was of a relatively high order; a system of underground sewers extended through the towns, and there is evidence that disposal lines were connected to the dwellings. But all trace of the civilization that produced these cities has apparently vanished, and it remains a matter of conjecture whether the peoples who occupied them influenced the city building of the Near East in subsequent centuries.

In the second millennium B.C. Egyptian pharaohs built temple cities on the banks of the Nile. Monumental avenues, colossal temple plazas, and tombs cut from rock remain as mute testimony to the luxurious life of the nobility in Memphis, Thebes, and Tel-el-Amarna. But few snatches of recorded history remain to describe the city of the people. Time and the elements have washed away the clay huts and "tenements" in which the people dwelled. The dramatic Avenue of the Sphinxes in Thebes and the broad temple enclosure (a third of a mile wide and a half-mile long) in Tel-el-Amarna tell a vivid story of powerful aristocrats, whereas historians must piece together fragmentary remains of people's homes to conclude that slums spread about the towns.

A series of empires rose in Mesopotamia, and once-humble villages along the valley of the Tigris and Euphrates rivers became monumental cities of the kings. Each was heavily fortified to resist the siege of many enemies. The stately palace-temple dominated the city, and the people lived in the dual shadows of slavery and superstitious religion. Economic hardship added to their burden. A skilled artisan in ancient Sumeria could obtain housing for 5 or 6 percent of his income,

Egyptian Pharaoh. (*British Museum, London.*)

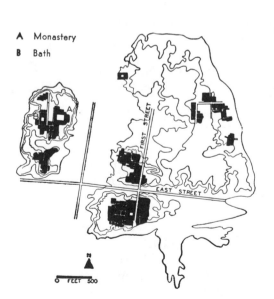

A Monastery
B Bath

Mohenjo-Daro. *Excavations at Mohenjo-Daro in the Indus Valley have revealed the remains of a large city built about 3000 B.C. It is apparent that a relatively advanced civilization flourished in this city. Houses ranged in size from two rooms to mansions with numerous rooms. The map shows the archaeologist's assumption that a major street ran in the north-south (First Street) and east-west (East Street) directions. Areas shown in black have been excavated and indicate the intricate plan of narrow roads. Buildings were of masonry, streets were paved, and considerable evidence of sewer drainage from dwellings has been uncovered. The principle buildings excavated are a public bath and a monastery (right).*

King Solomon's temple and citadel, Jerusalem, c. 900 B.C. *The splendor of the temples and palaces of the kings contrasts with the congested dwellings of the populace. (Restoration by Dr. John Wesley Kelchner.)*

but the poorest dwelling cost unskilled workers as much as 30 or 40 percent of their subsistence allowance.[1]

Out of the slums of thriving imperial cities were carved triumphal avenues connecting magnificent city gates. King Sennacherib built his temples and palaces in seventh-century Nineveh. The Greek historian Herodotus described the vivid spectacle of the processional avenues, great walls, monumental gates, and hanging gardens of Nebuchadnezzar's palace in Babylon during the sixth and fifth centuries B.C. He also told that behind the avenues were the narrow streets lined with the three- and four-story dwellings of the populace. Laid in a regular pattern at right angles to each other, the houses of the people were crowded together.

Seeking to improve the lot of the common people, King Hammurabi of Babylon in approximately 1800 B.C. set up a system of laws, among the greatest in the ancient world. Now called the Hammurabi Code, among other things it set out regulations governing the building of structures, their first recorded appearance. Harsh punishment was meted out to irresponsible builders. For example, if the wall of a building should fall and kill the occupant's son, the life of the builder's son would be sacrificed in retaliation.

CITIES OF THE AEGEAN

A more enlightened society appears to have arisen in the islands of the Aegean Sea. The reigning kings were apparently not deified as they were in eastern lands. In contrast to the austere detachment of royal palaces in Mesopotamia, the palaces here served as the centers of Aegean life and culture.

These early cities of the Aegean were irregular in form. Meandering streets followed the rugged topography of the sites. The streets were narrow lanes but were paved with stone. Excavations have revealed highly developed systems of water supply, sanitation, and drainage for the palace and many of the houses. Most dwellings were one story in height, and, although densely built, the towns did not reach the great size and congestion that were apparent in cities of the Near East.

---

1. Albert Bemis and John Burchard, *The Evolving House,* vol. 1 of *A History of the Home* (Cambridge, Mass.: MIT Press, 1933-36).

Beijing was founded in the eighth century B.C. in approximately its present location. The capital of the People's Republic of China, it is located in the northern part of the North China Plain. It has an area of more than 6,175 square miles and a population exceeding 8 million people. Geographically, Beijing occupies about the same position in China that New York does in North America, both being near the fortieth parallel and enjoying the same climatic conditions in the spring and fall. Unlike New York, however, Beijing does not have direct access to an important river or to the seacoast. The present city plan originated in the eleventh century A.D. The Grand Canal, which at one time provided access to the sea, no longer serves that purpose.

Beijing today retains the same general layout it had in the Ming dynasty (1368–1644), square and symmetrical. In the center of the city is the group of palaces called the Forbidden City—so named because the common people were forbidden to enter there. To the south of the Forbidden City is the Imperial Palace, Tiananmen, with a circumference of 5 miles. A 4,940 acre area outside the Imperial City is the "Inner City"; it was constructed in 1397. The rectangular part of the city to the south is the Outer (or Chinese) City.

The Inner City is crisscrossed with main streets intersected by lanes called *hutongs*. These *hutongs* are traditionally the homesites for many artists and artisans, as well as shops that provide for local residents' everyday needs.

Lukang, the old port town in Changua County, is the site where the Chinese people and culture first appeared on Taiwan:[2] With the silting up of its harbor, the shipping of rice, hemp, and deerskin from the port ceased. Today's Lukang, whose name means "deer-port," is a town of 70,000 people with a total area of

BEIJING AND LUKANG

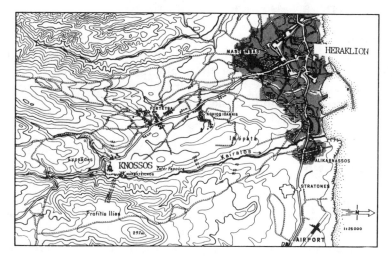

Knossos. *Knossos was the capital of the mythological King Minos of Crete, considered the founder of the Minoan civilization that flourished over 3,000 years ago. Knossos was one of the greatest cities of the ancient world; its population at the height of its splendor was in the range of 100,000. One of the earliest and largest communities, it was famous for great beauty and grandeur. Because of the natural protection offered by its site, Knossos was not surrounded by walls. The people enjoyed free access to the sea and entered into trade with other lands. On the mainland of Greece, however, cities needed the protection of ramparts; the cities of Tiryns and Mycenae were heavily fortified. (Source: Knossos, CHR Mathiouvoussis, Athens, 1974.)*

2. Nien-Ting Chang, "Lukang, an Old Port Town in Taiwan," unpublished paper, UCLA.

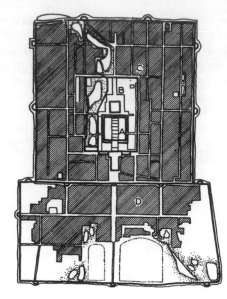

A Forbidden City
B Imperial City
C Tartar City
D Chinese City

Beijing (Peking). *Within each of the cells surrounded by streets in the sketch is a maze of narrow minor roads, also laid out in rectilinear form.*

about 15,000 acres. It is a backwater town, but it has one quality few other places in Taiwan can boast of: a human and intimate scale.

Crooked streets characterize Lukang. It is an easily walkable community, with visible signs of old China frequently evident, such as the ancient temples and the shops in which artisans worked and musicians performed. The commercial area is located along the line of the main street, as are the two major temples. Beyond the residential section is the agricultural area with its large farmhouses and fish ponds. Small factories are also located outside the town.

The north-south and east-west streets that divided the ancient town into blocks performed the function of social control. Each block was surrounded by walls that formed a self-contained area. Traditional Chinese architecture expressed the belief that people and the space they occupy were meant to be in harmony. This concept is crucial to understanding the Chinese city.

NATIVE AMERICAN COMMUNITIES

In the Southwest we have the oldest continuous record of human habitation on the continent outside Mexico. By the middle of the sixteenth century, most of the Native American tribes were living where they are now, or nearby. Some were settled in permanent villages where strong tribal organization and a rich ceremonial life gave them unity and purpose. Because much of the land was in desert or mountain country unwanted for white settlement, the southwestern native peoples were not hustled off to far-away reservations. The many tribes who live on this rugged and beautiful land share a vision of life, a felt sense of continuity with a tradition that has survived years of foreign domination.

The evidence is everywhere, in potsherds and pit houses that go back hundreds of years, in petroglyphs and chipped stone tools fashioned millennia ago. Pottery making and cultivation of corn, beans, and squash had come up to the Southwest from Mexico centuries before the dawn of Christianity. By the beginning of the Christian era, three cultures were forming in the Southwest: the Hohokam, the Mogollon, and the Pueblo.

The Hohokam had grown up along the Salt and Gila rivers in southern Arizona, a land that can be most inhospitable. They adapted well to their seared landscape, constructing a system of irrigation canals that remains their most impressive legacy.

The Mogollon culture centered in the rugged mountains of western New Mexico and eastern Arizona. The Mimbres people, who represent the culture's highest development, created the finest pottery designs of any Native Americans north of Mexico. By the present millennium—before the passing of the Hohokam—the Mimbres had been absorbed by another culture to the north, one that survives today after hundreds of years in the same ancient homeland.

This heritage of the past groups many people who speak different languages and dialects. They live in villages of multistoried houses that are responsible for the name they now bear. The conquistadors called the tribes Pueblos, the Spanish word for "towns." The Pueblo culture reached a climax in the Four Corners area, where Colorado and Utah meet Arizona and New Mexico, from the tenth through the thirteenth century. Then flourished the architectural wonders of Canyon de Chelly and Mesa Verde: penthouses of stone and masonry clinging to cliffs like swallows' nests.[3]

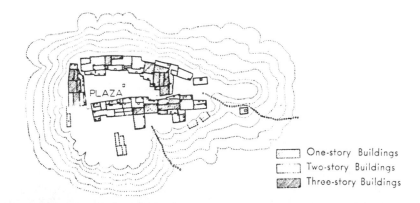

One-story Buildings
Two-story Buildings
Three-story Buildings

Hopi Pueblo, Shupolovi. *The Hopi village of Shupolovi was the organization of a clan or group of clans who built their villages for protection from their enemies. An agrarian people, they formed a society that was communal in political organization. Perched atop the mesas of northern Arizona the people sought their scant water supply at lower levels, where they carefully tilled small plots of level land.*

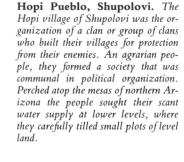

Cliff dwelling at Mesa Verde National Park. *Four corner area, Colorado.*

3. Adapted from *The World of the American Indian* (Washington, D.C.: National Geographic Society, © The National Geographic Society, 1974).

CHAPTER 7

THE CLASSIC CITY

THE GREEKS On the mainland of Greece the shepherds from the north mingled with the Aegean peoples of the rising city-states and gradually were absorbed within that culture. The wealthy landowning noble class rose to power, and during the eighth century B.C. this group appropriated much of the influence previously exercised by the kings. The palace citadel disappeared, and temples dedicated to the gods of the Greeks replaced them on the elevated section of the cities, the acropolis. The nobles assumed the power of kings, dominated the cities, and oppressed the peasant classes. A merchant middle class emerged. Feuds between this new economic group and the city-dwelling nobles forced the selection of a common leader of the popular classes, and in the seventh century the Tyrants of Athens came into power by usurping the existing legal authority.

Although they were themselves of the noble class, the tyrants maintained their leadership by the support of the common people. The large estates of the nobles were redistributed among the people, and a strong landholding farmer class developed. Under the successive leadership of Solon, Pisistratus, and Clisthenes, the principle of law as a basis of social conduct evolved. The political organization of the community was given a new form: a government of laws determined by the people.

During the fifth century B.C., with the inspired leadership of Pericles, democracy and a high order of morality took root among the Athenian citizenship. Political education was extended by way of free speech and assembly. Magistrates were elected to execute the laws, and public service was vested with dignity. Sovereignty of the people was assured and protected by a body of laws to which all agreed and all were subject. The deep sense of individual responsibility was expressed in the vow taken by all male Athenian citizens:

> I will not dishonor these sacred arms; I will not abandon my comrade in battle; I will fight for my gods and my hearth singlehanded or with my companions. I will not leave my country smaller, but I will leave it greater and stronger than I received it. I will obey the commands which the magistrates in their wisdom shall give me. I will submit to the existing laws and to those that the people shall unanimously make; if anyone shall attempt to overthrow these laws or disobey them, I will not suffer it, but will fight for them, whether singlehanded or with my fellows. I will respect the worship of my fathers.

Inspired by the political genius of Pericles, the democracy of Athens in the fourth century B.C. could be said to have acquired a soul. It required wise citizenship to retain this quality, and such philosophers as Socrates strove to cultivate the requisite wisdom and intelligence. Although Socrates sometimes disapproved of the laws and thought some of them bad, he insisted upon the obligation of the citizenry to abide by them until they were revised. Although Demosthenes came somewhat later, esteem for the law was perhaps best expressed in the words of that great orator:

Athenian Democracy

> The whole life of men, whether they inhabit a great city or a small, is ordered by nature and the laws. Whilst nature is lawless and varies with individuals, the laws are a common possession, controlled, identical for all. . . . They desire the just, the beautiful, the useful. It is that which they seek; once discovered it is that which is created into a principle equal for all and unvarying; it is that which is called law.

The Athenian democracy of the fifth century B.C. has been described this way:

> . . . as the exercise of sovereignty by free and equal citizens under the aegis of law. The law, which protects the citizens one against the other, defends also the rights of the individual against the power of the State and the interests of the State against the excesses of individualism. Before the last years of the fifth century there is no sign that liberty has degenerated into anarchy or license, nor is the principle of equality carried so far as to entail the denial of the existence of mental inequalities.[1]

Democracy in the age of Pericles produced that inherent dignity of the individual born of free speech, a sense of unity with one's fellow human beings, and a full

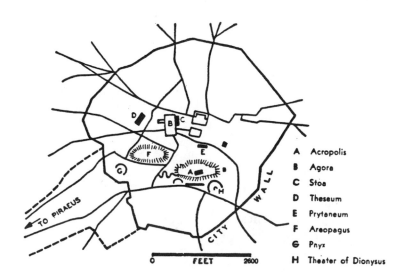

A Acropolis
B Agora
C Stoa
D Theseum
E Prytaneum
F Areopagus
G Pnyx
H Theater of Dionysus

Ancient Athens.

The Acropolis, Athens. *The temple, rather than the palace of the rulers, dominated the ancient Hellenic city. Among its other uses, it added a meeting place for political assembly of the people—the pnyx—to the urban pattern. As the power of kings diminished and democracy expanded, the houses of the people and the community facilities established for their use assumed greater importance in the city plan. (Trans World Airways photo.)*

opportunity for participation in affairs of the community. The Athenian citizen experienced the exhilaration of freedom and accepted the challenge of responsibility it thrust on him with honor and with pride. The discovery of freedom gave impetus to the search for truth as honest people desire it. Philosophy was nurtured, and there were no depths that the wise and intelligent were afraid to plumb. Reason was encouraged, logic invited, and science investigated. There was no truth that might be discovered and remain undisclosed. Inspired by this atmosphere and its freedom of the spirit, it is no wonder great philosophy was born; only in freedom can such greatness appear and be cultivated. This was the culture that produced Socrates, Plato, and Aristotle.

The affinity between freedom and spiritual values was symbolized in the temples built on the acropolis. In them was reflected the exalted stature of democratic man. Some four centuries later another philosopher, this one from Bethlehem, was to recreate the spiritual values demonstrated by the Greeks at the height of their democracy.

The Humble City

During the early years of Athenian democracy, the Greek city was a maze of wandering unpaved lanes, lacking drainage and sanitation. Water was carried from local wells. Waste was disposed of in the streets. There were no palaces and, with the exception of the temples, public buildings were few and simple. The common assembly place was the *pnyx,* an open-air podium where the citizens met to consider and discuss affairs of state. The agora or marketplace, the center of urban activity, was irregular in form. There was little distinction between the dwellings of the well-to-do citizen and less privileged individuals. The few rooms that the house comprised were grouped about an interior court behind a windowless facade that faced one of the randomly placed streets. Most towns were surrounded by protective walls.

For the Greek citizen the temple was the symbol of his democratic way of life, the equality of men. On the temples he lavished all his creative energies, and in them we find a refinement of line and beauty of form that expressed the dignity and humility of the Athenian. In later and less happy days Demosthenes reflected upon this period. "These edifices," he said,

---

1. Gustave Glotz, *The Greek City and Its Institutions* (London: Routledge & Kegan Paul, 1929).

The Parthenon. *Located on the Acropolis, overlooking the city of Athens, Greece, the temple stands as evidence of the sophistication and architectural skill of the ancient Greeks. It is a tribute to the goddess of wisdom and protector of the city.*

Sculptures from the pediment of the Parthenon, known as the Elgin Marbles—also on page 62. (British Museum, London.)

which their administrations have given us, their decorations of our temples and the offerings deposited in them, are so numerous that all efforts of posterity cannot exceed them. Then in private life, so exemplary was their moderation, their adherence to the ancient manners so scrupulously exact, that, if any of you discovered the house of Aristides or Miltiades, or any of the illustrious men of those times, he must know that it was not distinguished by the least extraordinary splendor.[2]

Hippodamus

It was natural that an atmosphere of philosophical inquiry should impel a search for order in the city. It was a topic that engaged the attention of teacher-philosophers and politicians alike. In the latter part of the fifth century B.C. an architect from Miletus named Hippodamus advanced positive theories of the art and science of city planning. He has been credited with the origination of the gridiron street system. This is not entirely accurate, however. A semblance of geometrical form had been present in early towns of Egypt, Mesopotamia, and the Indus Valley, and a formal rectangular pattern was used in part in the rebuilding of some earlier Greek cities after their destruction by the Persians in the sixth century. Hippodamus nevertheless vigorously applied the gridiron pattern to obtain a rational arrangement of buildings and circulation.

The city plan was conceived as a design to serve all the people. The individual dwelling was the common denominator. Blocks were shaped to provide appropriate orientation for the dwellings within them. The functional uses of buildings and public spaces were recognized in the arrangement of streets. They provided for the circulation of people and vehicles without interference with the orientation of dwellings or the assembly of people in the marketplace.

Superimposing the rigid geometrical form of the Hippodamian street system upon the rugged topography of the sites occupied by most Greek cities created numerous streets so steep they could be negotiated only with steps. Since the movement of people was almost entirely on foot, this did not present the problem it might today, although there were probably some puffing Grecians who reached the top of a long climb to attend a political meeting in the assembly hall. The principal traffic streets, however, were placed to allow the circulation of the few horsedrawn vehicles that entered the town.

---

2. Ibid., 302.

Sculptures from the pediment of the Parthenon, known as the Elgin Marbles. (British Museum, London.)

PUBLIC SPACE IN GREEK CITIES

The expanding affairs of government required appropriate facilities. The agora was the center of business and political life, and about it were lined the shops and market booths. Accessible from the agora square but not facing it were the assembly hall *(ecclesiasteron)*, council hall *(bouleuterion)*, and council chamber *(prytaneum)*.

The agora was usually located in the approximate center of the town plan, with the major east-west and north-south streets leading to it. It was designed to accommodate all the citizens who would have business in the marketplace or would attend public functions in the adjacent public buildings. The open space enclosed by the agora occupied about 5 percent of the city area; the dimensions were approximately one-fifth of the width and breadth of the town itself.

The agora was geometrical in form. Square or rectangular open spaces were surrounded by colonnaded porticoes sheltering the buildings about the square. This arrangement was meant to prevent interference of the movement of people across the open space with that of those who assembled for trade and business in the market. Streets generally terminated at the agora rather than crossing it, as the open space was reserved primarily for pedestrian traffic and circulation.

Common open space in Greek cities was largely confined to enclosures in public buildings. Because the city was small, the citydweller was never far from the open countryside around the town. Olive groves flourished outside the walls, and it was here that the philosophers founded the academy and the lyceum. In these quiet groves they met their pupils and set the pattern for later institutions of higher learning. From such academies came the world's first university, the Library of Alexandria in Egypt.

Evidence of attention to building regulations is recorded in the chronicles of various Athenian writers. There is reference to laws restricting buildings from encroachment upon the streets and prohibitions against projection of upper floors beyond the first floor walls. These are forerunners of the present-day notions of "rights-of-way." Windows were not permitted to open directly onto the street, and water drains were not allowed to empty into the street. Though primitive when judged by the standards acceptable today, the early Greek town plans demonstrated a conscious effort to improve the environment for the whole people, the final test of genuine civic responsibility.

It was in the cities founded by the city-states on the shores of the Mediterranean that the planning theories of Hippodamus found their fullest expression. It is recorded that Hippodamus himself planned Piraeus, the port city of Athens, as well as Thurii and Rhodes. The old established cities were remodeled in parts, the agoras assuming a more orderly form as new buildings were erected for public affairs, but the newer cities had the benefit of planning before settlement. Although they were founded by a mother city-state, they enjoyed a degree of political autonomy, becoming a part of the confederation of Greek cities that the Athenian "empire" comprised.

In their houses the Greeks sought quiet privacy. Most of the social contacts and all business affairs were carried on outside the homes. Small merchants frequently had shops adjacent to their houses, but business and politics were generally conducted in and adjacent to the agora. Sports and recreation were concentrated in the gymnasium, drama and festivals in the theater. Feasts and other celebrations seldom took place in the private dwelling. A small altar was usual in the home, but religious exercises and worship occurred in the temple precincts. Consequently the house was unpretentious in its appointments, and, as previously mentioned, there was little distinction among the dwellings in the town. A display of affluence was not consistent with the tenets of Greek democracy in the fifth century.

PRIVATE SPACE: THE DWELLINGS

The temple of Apollo, where a priestess would render the oracles to those who would know the future. Located at Delphi, Greece, the temple stands on high ground surrounded by high mountains.

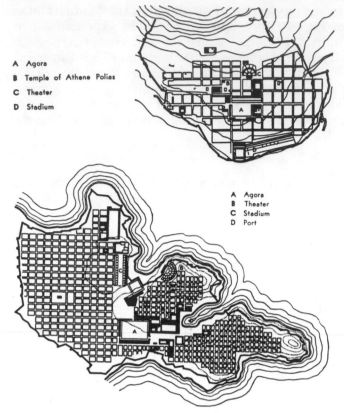

A Agora
B Temple of Athene Polias
C Theater
D Stadium

A Agora
B Theater
C Stadium
D Port

Priene and Miletus. *These cities demonstrate the Hippodamian plan as it developed toward the end of the Hellenic period. The agora occupies the approximate geographical center of the town. About it are the temple shrines, public buildings, and shops. The dwelling blocks are planned to provide the appropriate orientation of houses. Recreation and entertainment facilities are provided in the gymnasium, stadium, and theater. The contours of the site indicate that some of the streets were very steep, steps being frequently required, but the main streets connecting the gates and the agora were generally placed so that beasts of burden and carts could traverse them readily.*

Early houses were enclosed about a central hearth. A hole in the roof allowed the smoke to escape and also permitted collection of rainwater in the cistern. Terra cotta braziers supplemented the hearth as a source of heat in the larger houses. In late Hellenic towns sanitation was improved by the paving of streets and the installation of underground drains beneath dwellings. The town maintained reservoirs, but there was no water distribution system. With the improvement of drainage, however, an increasing number of homes had private baths. Sanitary disposal of sewage was apparently not provided for, and the portable latrine and private cesspool continued in use.

Care in planning the dwelling was no less because of its simplicity; on the contrary, as the center of family life, the home was the focus of attention, from the proper arrangement of rooms to the relation to the site, from builders and philosophers alike.

The climate created an emphasis upon the orientation of the dwelling. The maximum amount of sunshine inside the dwelling was desirable in the winter months, and heat could be conserved if the rooms were shielded from the cold north winds. Conversely, the heat of summer was relieved when the direct rays of the sun were excluded. These criteria were satisfied in the plan of the Greek house.

The principal rooms faced to the south, opening on the private courtyard. A colonnade projecting from the rooms was tall enough to permit the warming low rays of the winter sun to enter and sheltered them from the high hot rays of the summer sun. The north wall of the house was punctured with only a few small windows. This type of plan was used in practically all dwellings in the town, whether the street entrance was on the north, south, east, or west.

Chroniclers of the period referred to the importance of proper orientation. Aristotle wrote, "For the well-being and health . . . the homesteads should be airy in summer and sunny in winter. A homestead possessing these qualities would be longer than it is deep; and the main front would face south." According to Xenophon in his *Memorabilia*, Socrates applied the following reasoning to the dwelling arrangement:

> When one builds a house must he not see to it that it be as pleasant and convenient as possible? And pleasant is to be cool in summer, but warm in winter. In those houses, then, that look toward the south, the winter sun shines down into the *paestades* [court portico] while in summer, passing high above our heads and over our roofs, it throws them in shadow.

The effect of these criteria was a planning system that sprang from the elements of the individual unit—the home—applied uniformly throughout the town plan. This consistent treatment is unique in urban planning; it does not recur for 2,400 years, when a similar relation between the dwelling and the site was recognized in the vast housing program in Europe after the First World War.

WHAT IS A CITY?

The Greeks and Romans distinguished a city from a town, which was a mere assemblage of people living together under municipal law. The city was an independent community or state possessing sovereign authority; it included any portion of the surrounding territory whose inhabitants had the rights of citizenship but excluded conquered or dependent territories.

In current times a population center is deemed to be a city if it has a full complement of public facilities and services and contains a substantial population and employment base to provide economic and social facilities for its residents. In many areas the terms *town* and *city* are interchangeable, as size and cultural history determined which name is applied. Small communities with populations below 50,000 are called towns; any community with a larger population is a city. Population centers of less than 500 are considered villages. As is the case with the Greek and Roman definition, each city, town, or village must have a governing body and laws and regulations to govern the residents and the activities of businesses and industries operating within their political boundaries.

A classic example of the current usage of the terms may be found in Columbia, Maryland, where their New Town is divided physically into groups of villages. In this case, the villages are not independent entities with basic governmental powers of their own, although they may have resident associations to determine local policies and activities.

THE SIZE OF CITIES

In the fifth and fourth centuries B.C. the citizen population of Athens was some 40,000; when slaves and foreigners were included, total population jumped to between 100,000 and 150,000. Most Greek cities, however, were relatively small. Only about three towns exceeded 10,000 persons during the thriving Hellenic period. Hippodamus theorized that this was an appropriate size for cities, and Plato later concluded the range should be between 5,000 and 10,000. It was customary to dispatch about 10,000 people from the mother city-state to settle a colonial town. The descriptions of the glorious metropolis with its teeming millions are undoubtedly exaggerations of the actual number who dwelt in urban communities in ancient times. The metropolis as we know it today is of comparatively recent origin.

A number of factors influenced the size of a city and the population it could support. The food and water supply was a primary consideration. The tools for cultivating the soil, the means for transporting the products, and the source and methods for distributing the water supply established limits on the urban population that could be accommodated in a single group. As long as people depended upon the primitive hand plow, the horse cart, and gravity flow of water, it was not feasible to gather in great numbers and maintain adequate standards of urban hygiene. Hellenic towns relied primarily on local watercourses, wells, and springs, but supplemental supply was sometimes available through conduits from more remote sources in higher surrounding hills.

THE GREEK CITY'S DECLINE

It cannot be assumed that political affairs always ran smoothly in the age of Pericles. The teachings of the Sophists were disturbing some of the well-established customs. In addition, a little man by the name of Socrates subjected many of the prevailing habits to severe questioning. He insisted on inquiry and application of reason to the activities of men. He raised questions about the existence of the gods. He desired that the individual should cultivate an insight into truth, that he should become neither stronger than the state nor subservient to it.

There were some good democrats who believed Socrates was wrong in raising these questions; they had suffered from uprisings of the oligarchy and feared lest the faith in democracy be weakened. They brought charges against Socrates for heresy and for subversion of the youth of Athens. There were those who loved this wise man whose only ambition was the quest for truth. They appealed to him to flee his accusers, as was the custom, but Socrates would not. He had suggested changes in the habits of men that would improve their lot, and if these were unlawful he would remain to face the consequences of the people's judgment as expressed in the law. Found guilty, he was sentenced to die, and in 399 B.C. he drank the poison hemlock.

The lesson of Socrates has been repeated in history. Human institutions must change or decay, grow or wither. Socrates showed a way for people to command their destiny by seeking truth. He strove to improve the institutions that they might better serve the people, and for this his contemporaries found him guilty of treason. Greater confidence in the strength of democracy would not have caused him to be so accused; greater confidence might have saved democracy itself.

During the fourth century B.C. there was evidence of growing indifference toward the responsibility of government. Accustomed to liberty, the people were taking it for granted, and they were inclined to allow affairs to run themselves. Freedom guaranteed by democracy was coming to mean that "the people has the right to do what it pleases." In the words of Demosthenes, some people were "even building private houses whose magnificence surpasses that of certain public buildings."

Well-to-do citizens spent more of their time in their country villas, whereas the common people found the difficulty of earning a living more absorbing than participation in public affairs. The middle class was disappearing, and a wide gap was growing between those with money and those without it. Plato and Aristotle saw a degeneration of the democracy of Pericles. They perceived a growing abuse of individual liberty and became increasingly critical of democracy itself. Other philosophers were gripped with cynicism while maintaining the fight for democracy.

Glotz describes the alarming developments of this period:

> In Greece as a whole there existed almost everywhere a glaring contrast between the equality promised by the constitution and the inequality created by social and economic conditions.

> The power of money was spreading and corrupting morality. . . . Agriculture was commercialized to such an extent that by progressive eviction of small peasants and the concentration of estates in the same hands the system of large estates was recreated. Rhetoricians, advocates, and artists, who had formerly reckoned it a dishonor to commercialize their talent, now felt no scruples in selling their goods as dearly as possible. Everything could be bought, everything had its price, and wealth was the measure of social values. By gain and by extravagance fortunes were made and unmade with equal rapidity. Those who had money rushed into pleasure-seeking and sought every occasion for gross displays of luxury. The newly rich were cocks of the walk. Men speculated and rushed after money in order to build and furnish magnificent houses, to display fine weapons, to offer to the women of their family and to courtesans jewels, priceless robes, and rare perfumes, to place before eminent guests and fashionable parasites fine wines and dishes prepared by a famous chef, or to commission some popular sculptor to carve their bust.

> What happened to public affairs when "love of money left no one the smallest space in which to deal with other things, to such an extent that the mind of each citizen, passionately absorbed in this one purpose, could attend to no other business than the gain of each day" (Plato). Politics also was a business concern; the most honest worked for a class, the others sought for themselves alone the profits of power and barely concealed their venality. We are dealing with a time when "riches and rich men being held in honor virtue and honest men are at a discount," when "no one can become rich quickly if he remains honest" (Plato). Were these merely the capricious outbursts of a philosopher in love with the ideal or of a character in a comedy? Listen to the terrible words uttered before a tribunal: "Those who, citizens by right of birth, hold the opinion that their country extends wherever their interests are, these obviously are people who will desert the public good in order to run after their personal gain, since for them it is not the city which is their country, but their fortune."[3]

The struggle between democracy and oligarchy was renewed; the Athenian orator Isocrates sums up the growing conflict between the widely separated issues:

> Instead of securing general conditions of well-being by means of mutual understanding, the antisocial spirit has reached such a pitch that the wealthy would rather throw their money into the sea than relieve the lot of the indigent, while the very poorest of the poor would get less from appropriating to their own use the property of the rich than from depriving them of it.

The Peloponnesian Wars weakened Athens financially, and corrupt politicians began to gnaw at the moral fiber of the people. Athens became easy prey for a conqueror and succumbed to the Macedonian armies of Alexander the Great. But the essential qualities of wisdom, logic, and reason; the sensitive, aesthetic character of democratic days, had sunk its roots deep into the soil of Athens. The Greeks were conquered by mighty armies, but their culture dominated the con-

The Hellenistic City

---

3. Ibid., 311, 312.

queror. Greek influence spread throughout the Mediterranean shores, and the Hellenistic period brought new city building—the planning and architecture patterned after the great works of the Greeks.

Old cities flourished and new cities were founded. Pergamon, Alexandria, Syracuse, and Candahar grew large and populous; the humble quality of the Hellenic city vanished. The city became the scene of luxury, ruddy with the display of empire. Magnificent public buildings—the *odeion,* the treasury, the library, the prison—were added to the agora. The assembly retained its traditional place among these monumental structures, but it remained, as Percy Gardner expressed it in his *The Planning of Hellenistic Cities,* for the citizens "to exercise such functions (a mere show of autonomy) as the real rulers of the country . . . left to them." Baths, *palaestrae,* and stadia were built for entertainment and festivals. Gardens and parks were introduced from the Orient. An entourage of royalty built villas in the urban environs, and distinctions in caste grew more apparent.

Small kings, wealthy families, and ambitious foreigners desirous of acclaim within this frame of monumental splendor bestowed generous gifts on the city. Empty honors were accorded for their beneficence. The great *stoa* at Priene was the gift of a king of Orophernes of Cappadocia. Here, one by the name of Zosimus staged a festive dinner for the whole citizen population of the city in return for receipt of the "dignity of Stephanephorus." According to Pausanias, the bouleuterion at Megalopolis was named after Thersilius who dedicated it, and the donor of the bouleuterion at Elis was one by the name of Lalichmium.[4] Inscriptions bear a quantity of evidence of the surge for popularity through these magnanimous gestures of philanthropy. The genuine character of the Hellenistic city was, in the third and second centuries B.C., degenerating into a hollow form of a decaying social structure.

THE ROMANS

In their early migrations to the Italian peninsula, the Greeks had founded cities. Like other peoples on the shores of the Mediterranean, the Romans drew on the Greek culture planted there. They grafted Hellenic forms onto the irregular patterns of their villages and used these forms for the new towns they founded in the near and far reaches of their broad empire.

The Romans were calculating organizers. They excelled in technical achievement and were skilled engineers and aggressive city builders. But they lacked the philosophy of the Greeks. Preoccupied with conquest, they emphasized administration as their prime business and devised a political organization that has continued to this day. Intense builders with a flair for gargantuan scale, they did not grace their works with the refinement of line and form or the creative spirit of the Athenians. Greek forms were reduced to mechanical formulae that could be readily applied like parts arranged on graph paper.

With inventive genius the Romans solved technical problems created by the congregation of great numbers of people in cities. They developed water supply and distribution, drainage systems, and methods of heating on which the health of the masses depended. The great aqueducts for transport of water over tremendous distances and the underground sewers like Cloaca Maxima were feats of engineering skill and prowess. The great highways paved with stone represented the tireless efforts of intense builders.

---

4. William A. McDonald, *The Political Meeting Places of the Greeks* (Baltimore, Md.: Johns Hopkins University Press, 1943).

The Forum Romanum, Rome, Italy. *The center of political activity and discussions involving the people of Rome and their representatives.*

The Forum Romanum of the Republic had a human scale. Its proportions and form undoubtedly caused the citizen to feel a part of the activity that took place there. Here individual identity was merged with "Rome." The buildings were not so overwhelming in size that they humbled the individual. The common people had their share of hardships, but one can imagine the Gracchi pleading their case in the Senate for an equitable distribution of the land and its benefits. The citizen understood the religion of the temples and was proud of the triumphs of the Roman legions abroad. He could participate in the business affairs of the basilica and perhaps engage in the moneylending enterprise carried on there. He felt himself to be one of the actors in this drama as a Greek had been in his assembly and agora.

This citizen of early Rome saw gracious living like that in Pompeii and Herculaneum or the busy life and fashions of Ostia. He observed distinctions in class among the dwellings but took these for granted in a day when a slave economy was all he had thus far witnessed in history. If the citizen was not blessed with wealth, he could nevertheless indulge himself in the various common forms of entertainment the community offered—the combat in the Colosseum, the drama in the theater, or a festival in the forum.

But the scene changed. World conquest was the ambition of Rome, and the citizen saw great riches flow into his capital. He saw intrigue absorb the military and political leaders, and he saw monuments erected in dedication of great victories and the triumphant entry of generals from abroad.

The Roman citizen saw emperors crowned and saw them build new fora that dwarfed his Forum Romanum. He saw each new forum exceed in size the one that preceded it. The Forum of Augustus was greater than the Forum of Julius Caesar; the Forum of Vespasian matched that of Augustus; and the Forum of

Monuments and Diversion

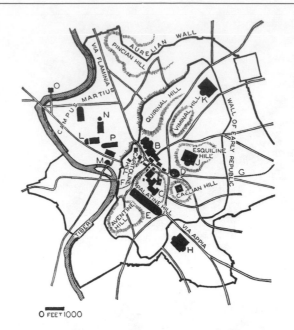

A   Forum Romanum
B   Forum of Emperors
C   Palace of the Emperors
D   Colosseum
E   Circus Maximus
F   Cloaca Maxima
G   Claudian Aqueduct
H   Baths of Caracalla
J   Baths of Trajan
K   Baths of Diocletian
L   Theater of Pompey
M   Theater of Marcellus
N   Pantheon
O   Tomb of Hadrian
P   Circus Flaminius

O FEET 1000

Rome. *The original settlement of Rome lay on the banks of the Tiber near the later Forum Romanum. From this center, protected by the surrounding hills, the city fanned out in all directions. It became the scene for a series of ever-greater projects glorifying the military leaders and emperors. In addition to the temples, fora, and palaces, huge facilities for entertainment were built for diversion of the masses—the baths, colossia, theaters, stadia, and the circus.*

There is no indication that the street system in Rome was other than an irregular pattern typical of great cities which grew by accretion. In contrast to a small city like Pompeii, Rome grew in population, suffered speculation in land and buildings, became congested, and was overrun with slums. Buildings increased in height until Augustus found it necessary to decree a height limit of 70 feet.

A	Forum Romanum	M	Temple of Saturn
B	Comitium	N	Temple of Vespasian
C	Arch of Septimus Severus	O	Rostrum
D	Basilica Julia	P	Curia
E	Temple Castorum	Q	Forum of Julius Caesar
F	Temple Vestae	R	Forum of Augustus
G	Atrium Vestae	S	Forum of Trajan
H	Arch of Augustus	T	Basilica Ulpia
J	Basilica Aemilia	U	Temple of Trajan
K	Temple of Julius Caesar	V	Forum of Nerva
L	Temple of Augustus	W	Palace of Tiberius

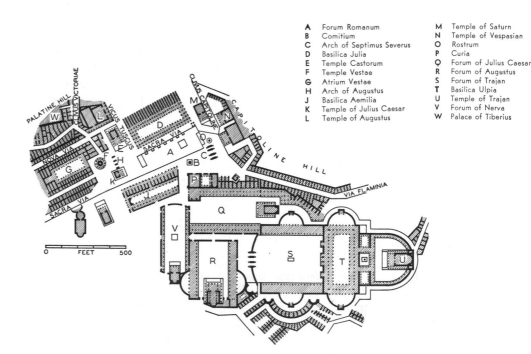

0   FEET   500

The Forum Romanum was the original center of business and political life in the early Republic. In it the triumphant generals built their memorials to the successful military campaigns. In the days of the Empire, the emperors built additional fora, and the total area was a magnificent collection of monumental buildings unparalleled in splendor. About these great public spaces were the innumerable shops and crowded tenements of the people.

The ancient Appian Way, the road that led from Rome to Ostia, on the Mediterranean Sea. (Courtesy of TransWorld Airways.)

Trajan was the most magnificent of all. He saw the Palace of Augustus crown the Palatine and the Golden House of Nero span acres.

The Roman citizen saw institutions of pleasure, rather than culture, built to divert attention from social and economic inequities. He saw the huge Colosseum, where carnal displays and bloody gladiatorial combats were staged for the excitement of a populace that might otherwise have grown restless. He saw the Circus Maximus, where he could join 150,000 fellow citizens to witness the drama of daring chariot races.

The scale of all these structures, the spaces they enclosed, and the architectural fitments with which they were adorned appalled the Roman citizen. It was not the plan of a city that he saw emerging but a series of ever greater monuments to the glory and deification of his rulers. Even the colonial cities followed the form of the military camp.

One can only wonder whether the present civilization with its baseball, football, basketball, automobile racing, and other stadiums is telling us something about ourselves in comparison to the Romans.

Diversion was afforded citizens, but they saw the city grow congested. They saw men, like Crassus, profess to be civic leaders but speculate in the land and build huge tenements. They saw the city crowded with slums to become fuel for disastrous fires. The height of buildings reached six, seven, and eight floors, and Emperor Augustus found it necessary to decree a limit of 70 feet for all tenements. According to the Constantine Regionary Catalog there were 46,602 blocks of apartments and only 1,797 private houses in Rome in the fourth century after Christ.

This Roman citizen saw nobles, returning heroes, and rulers move to great estates and comfortable villas in the country. The empire had grown so broad and so fat

Slums and Decay

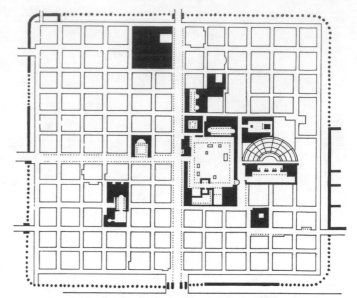

Timgad. *The Pattern of a Roman Camp.*

The Coliseum at Verona, Italy. *It appears that the Romans had almost as many coliseums as Americans today have sports stadiums.*

no enemy could reach them. Luxury and display were imported from the Orient, and the leaders grew soft. The citydweller lived in slums while the affluent enjoyed leisure in the country. No strong and healthy men with convictions remained to defend the empire, and Rome gradually merged with the camp of barbarians from the north. Civilization descended into the Dark Ages.

The lesson of Rome and the cities it built is well stated by Henry Smith Williams:

> During the entire ages of Trajan and the Antonines, a succession of virtuous and philosophic emperors followed each other; the world was in peace; the laws were wise and well administered; riches seemed to increase; each succeeding generation raised palaces more splendid, monuments and public edifices more sumptuous, than the preceding; the senatorial families found their revenues increase; the treasury levied greater imposts. But it is not the mass of wealth, it is on its distributions, that the prosperity of states depends; increasing opulence continued to meet the eye, but men became more miserable; the rural population, formerly active, robust, and energetic, were succeeded by a foreign race, while the inhabitants of towns sank in vice and idleness, or perished in want, amidst the riches they had themselves created.[5]

---

5. The Historian's History of the World (Outlook Company, 1904).

CHAPTER 8

THE MEDIEVAL TOWN

OUT OF THE DARK AGES

By the fifth century after Christ the Roman Empire had crumbled under the weight of its own luxury, pomp, and ceremony. Western civilization declined, trade disintegrated, urban populations to a large degree returned to rural life, and cities shrank in size and importance. The period of social and economic confusion and stagnation called the Dark Ages followed.

Barbaric rulers established city-states and formed the nucleus of future nations. The economy was rooted in agriculture, and the rulers parceled their domains among vassal lords who pledged military support. The people were dependent on the land for their subsistence and entered a state of serfdom under their lords. The feudal system was the new order.

Wars among the rival feudal lords were frequent. Strategic sites were sought for their castles, and within these fortified strongholds the serfs of the surrounding countryside found protection. Through the centuries of the Dark Ages monasteries served as havens of refuge for the oppressed. The church strengthened its position greatly during this period. This influence, combined with the power of the feudal lords, renewed the advantages of communal existence within the protective walls of towns and cities. Invention of the battering ram and catapult increased the danger from enemies, forced the construction of heavier walls, and gave increased impetus for a return to urban life. The countryside was not safe, and fortifications were extended to include the dwellings that clustered about the castle and monastery.

By about the eleventh century the movement to the towns brought a marked revival of trade. Many advantages accrued to the feudal lords—not least because they collected higher taxes and rent for their land in return for protection. Many new towns were founded, and sites of old Roman towns restored. Urban life was encouraged by the lords; they granted charters that secured certain rights and privileges of citizenship to the urban dwellers. This new form of freedom was attractive to those who had lived their lives in serfdom.

In urban areas merchants and craftsmen formed guilds to strengthen their social and economic position. Weavers, butchers, tailors, masons, millers, metalworkers, carpenters, leatherworkers, glassmakers, all established regulations to control their standards of production, maintain their prices, and protect their trade. A new social order was in the making: a wealthy mercantile class was rising to challenge the power of the feudal lords.

A HUMAN SCALE

The scale of the space forms in cities reflects in some measure the degree of participation a people enjoyed in their civic affairs. The agora of the Hellenic city was large enough to accommodate the citizen population; its space was commodious but the city population was small. Size itself was not the aim of Greek city builders; the human scale was a measure of design for their urban environment. A monumental quality was obtained through the juxtaposition of small and large spaces, the contrast between the shape of forms and the rhythm of voids and solids.

The self-reliance of ancient society produced the unity of solid horizontal forms, the positive rhythm of colonnades. Builders in the Middle Ages, less certain of their mortal destiny, directed their vertical forms toward infinity. Released from

Hamlet's castle, Helsingor, Denmark.

**Schonburg Castle, Ober-
wesel, Germany.**

the limitations of the monolithic structure of ancient forms, the heavy walls of
the Roman vault, a greater play of forms was introduced to the medieval town.
The massive forms of the classic city were transformed into the pointed arch and
the flying buttress thrust heavenward to the spiritual unity of Christendom.

There was harmony among these forms, but devices were employed to link the
enclosing frame of the open spaces. The width of streets entering a plaza was
pinched, or the openings were spanned with a portal. Adjacent roads were diverted to spread the effect of their opening entering the square, or they were
joined to enter the plaza as a single opening. Building mass was increased to
compensate for the gap created by two intersecting streets at a corner of the
square. Irregular angles of entering streets distorted the perspective to subdue the
apparent penetration of enclosing walls.

Intimate scale marked the church square and the marketplace of the medieval
town. The great bulk of the cathedral was given scale by the variety of its
structural forms and sculptural interstices. Its great mass was fused with the scale
of the open space. Its size dominated the town—such was the spiritual need of a
people emerging from the Dark Ages—but it was not set apart from its surroundings. It was a part of them, built against other buildings on one or more
sides and becoming an integral part of the enclosing walls. When its size warranted, more than one plaza was created about its dominant features, a facade, a
tower, or a transept.

Sculpture adorned the public spaces, but they were placed so as to prevent interference with the natural circulation about the marketplace.

Serving as the principal water supply, fountains were situated to one side of open
spaces, accessible for use without obstructing circulation. The parts of the urban

form were disposed in a manner natural to their function in the community, and —although this description is not intended to encourage a return to or the adaptation of the "picturesque medieval town" in development of the industrial and commercial city of tomorrow—we might well compare the integral character of the ancient urban forms with the unrelated and useless ornamental centerpieces to which many features of the contemporary urban scene have degenerated.

THE PLAN OF THE TOWN

The early medieval town was dominated by the church or monastery and the castle of the lord. The church plaza became the marketplace and, with citizenship bestowed on the people and merchant and trade guilds established, the town hall and guild hall were built on or adjacent to the market plaza. The commanding position of the cathedral or church gave a singular unity to the town, a unity strengthened by the horizontal envelope of the encircling walls. The castle was surrounded by its own walls as a final protection in the event that an enemy penetrated the main fortifications and entered the city.

Distinction between the town and the country was sharp, and this demarcation and the small size of the city provided ready access to the open countryside in times of peace. To aid in the protection of cities, towns were usually sited on irregular terrain, occupying hilltops or islands. The town was designed to fit the topographic features of the area. Circulation and building spaces were molded to these irregular features and naturally assumed an informal character.

The roads radiated generally from the church plaza and market square to the gates, with secondary lateral roadways connecting them. The irregular pattern was probably consciously devised as a means to confuse enemies in the event that they gained entrance to the town. Although the battering ram and the catapult

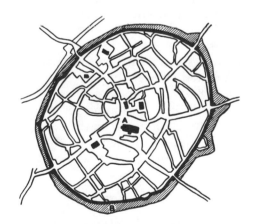

A **Market Square**
B **Castle**
C **Church of Sr. Nazaire**

A **Cathedral Plaza**
B **Moat**

Carcassonne and Noerdlingen. *Medieval cities of the twelfth and thirteenth centuries usually had irregular street patterns and heavy walls. Carcassonne (left) was restored by Viollet-le-Duc in the nineteenth century. In it we see the castle (B) with its own moat and walls, the marketplace (A), and the Church of St. Nazaire (C). The plan of Noerdlingen (right) shows the radial and lateral pattern of irregular roadways, with the church plaza as the principal focal point of the town. The city of the Middle Ages grew within the confines of the walls.*

While the population remained small, there was ample space in the town, but when the number of residents increased, the buildings were packed together more closely and the open spaces filled. Sanitation and water supply did not change, however, and the results were intolerable congestion, lack of hygiene, and pestilence.

A   **Cathedral Square**
B   **Market Square**

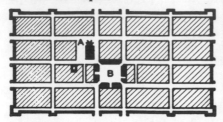

Montpazier. *During the thirteenth and four-teenth centuries colonial cities were founded by young empires to protect their trade and provide military security. The regular plan is a distinct contrast to the informal development of the normal medieval town.*

Air view of the island of Venice, Italy. *The charm of this ancient city includes its canals as a means of interisland transportation and its many architectural and artistic gems as well as its central piazza.*

were instruments for assault upon the heavy fortifications and hot oil poured from the battlements was a means for mass defense, hand-to-hand combat was the principal form of military action. In the maze of wandering streets the advantage rested with the inhabitants against an enemy unfamiliar with the town arrangement.

The entire town was treated with a structural logic that characterized the architectural treatment of the Romanesque and early Gothic buildings. Open spaces —the streets and plaza—developed as integral parts of the sites on which the buildings were erected. With the exception of a few main roads between the gates and the marketplace, streets were used for pedestrian circulation about the town rather than as traffic arteries as we know them today. Wheeled traffic was generally absent from all but the main roadways.

The monks and artisans were sensitive to the form and materials of the buildings they erected. Under their guidance, care was exercised in the placement of and relation between the structures of the town. Buildings assumed a functional character in both form and location. They were not built to be "picturesque"; that quality emerged from the consideration given to such towns centuries later. Beautiful vistas and lovely contrasts were accidents of form and color resulting from the contours of the land and the ingenious selection of the sites for each structure.

DWELLINGS

In part because of the need to conserve heat in the cold climates and also because of the restricted area of the town, houses were built in connected rows along the narrow streets. Open space in which the domestic animals were kept and gardens cultivated was reserved behind these rows. The workshop and kitchen occupied the ground floor. Here the merchants and craftsmen operated their enterprises and produced their goods.

There was little distinction between classes in the population of the early medieval town. The workers and apprentices lived in the homes of their employers. The space for both living and sleeping was on the second floor. Some of the burghers enjoyed separate sleeping rooms, but the accommodations were universally simple and modest in their appointments. The simple plan provided little privacy within the house. The chimney and fireplace replaced the open hearth of the ancient house. Windows were small and covered with crude glass or oiled parchment. Facilities for waste disposal within the dwelling were not usually provided, although some of the houses were equipped with privies. Construction was of masonry or wood frame filled with wattle. As a rule thatch covered the roofs, and the fire hazard eventually caused some towns either to prohibit this type of roofing or to encourage use of fire-resistant materials by offering special privileges for their use. Streets were usually paved and maintained by the owners of the property facing upon them. This may account in part for their narrow width.

UNIVERSITY AND CHURCH

Meditation and study characterized the monastery. It was extended to research by scholars intent on the cultivation of professional skills. Monasteries and the guilds combined to form the university, and here were welcomed those who desired to study in withdrawal from the marketplace. Here also were conducted research and training in law, medicine, and the arts. Universities were assisted by the growing wealth of the merchant class. The universities at Bologna and Paris were founded in the twelfth century and those at Cambridge and Salamanca in the thirteenth century. The churches also established hospitals in which the sick could receive care and treatment not previously available to the people.

The Church of Santa Maria della Salute, on an island across the Grand Canal from Venice.

Life in medieval cities had color, a color visible to all the people. The church provided pageantry and gave drama to the life of every person. It was an institution in which all could participate, giving inspiration and adding a measure of beauty to the existence of the people. It lifted people above baseness and encouraged better deeds. It offered music, meditation, and meaning. The people—merchants, artisans, and peasants—mingled in the marketplace, the guild hall, and the church; a human scale pervaded the informal environment of the city of the people.

The people of the Middle Ages endured innumerable hardships, but in the early towns they did not lose the sense of intermingling. Each person had the feeling of being an active citizen in his community. This attribute of the urban environment—a social well-being—was, however, soon to be dissipated in the eras to come.

The Baptistry at Pisa, Italy.

The bell tower (the Leaning Tower) at Pisa. *Many efforts have been expended to preserve the tower from potential further destruction.*

CHAPTER 9

THE NEOCLASSIC CITY

The number of towns increased rapidly during the Middle Ages, but population remained relatively small. Many had only a few hundred people, and the larger cities seldom exceeded 50,000 inhabitants. The distance across a town seldom exceeded a mile, the physical size being restricted by the girth of the fortifications, water supply, and sanitation. Water was available at the town fountain. There was no sewage disposal, and all drainage was by way of the streets.

As long as the population remained small, the apparent deficiencies presented no serious problem. Communication between towns was slow, facilities for transport were cumbersome, and the necessity for mutual assistance in times of conflict urgent. The towns were built within ready reach of each other. Most were within a day's journey apart and frequently a round trip to a neighboring town could be made on foot in a single day.

World travel and trade, however, brought a concentration of people to centers situated on main crossroads. During the fourteenth century Florence grew from 45,000 to 90,000 people, Paris from 100,000 to 240,000, and Venice to 200,000. Successful merchants consolidated their interests in several towns, and money-lending helped their enterprise. Commerce increased between towns and other countries. The danger of military aggression gradually diminished, the roads became safer, and travel increased.

The mercantile economy expanded, and the power of the feudal lords declined. Ownership of the land gradually shifted to a new variety of noblemen, the

THE RISE OF MERCAN- TILISM AND THE CONCEN- TRATION OF POPULATION

wealthy merchants. At the same time the church accumulated a vast domain, and consequently two privileged classes emerged: the nobles and the clergy. The guilds declined and serfdom disappeared, but the facilities for processing materials and goods—the mills, ovens, presses—came into the possession of the new noble class. The peasants were required to pay tolls of various sorts for the use of any of these facilities. The feudal economy had been rooted in the land, and the new economy was dominated by the possession and control of money.

Congestion and Slums

The growing population brought about a congestion within the cities not present in earlier days. The traditional height of two stories for dwellings changed to three and four stories. The upper floors projected beyond the first floor; roofs often spanned the width of the street. Open space within the interior blocks of dwellings was built up. Population density increased without change in the systems of water supply or sanitation.

Wheeled traffic increased. The narrow streets became congested, dark, and filth-ridden from refuse thrown from dwelling windows. Provision for elimination of waste remained inadequate. The call of *gare de l'eau* was familiar in France and, contracted to the anglicized "gardo loo," it became equally familiar in Edinburgh. Excreta were disposed of in cesspools beneath dwelling floors; there or in the streets it was left in some European cities to ripen for use as fertilizer. Odors from filth in the streets were overcome by keeping windows or shutters closed; ventilation was by way of the chimney only. Because of these conditions, disease spread rapidly in times of epidemic; in the fourteenth century the Black Death, a pestilence of the bubonic plague, took the lives of nearly half the urban population.

During this period the cities reverted to a condition inferior to that of the days of Rome a thousand years before. The manor house of the nobleman grew spacious while the typical dwelling of the poor remained cramped and moved ever higher into the attic. The first sewer was not installed in London until after the Black Death. Water closets were not introduced until the sixteenth century in Spain, France, and England, and it was early in the seventeenth century before water supply was connected to dwellings in London. Fire hazards were prevalent everywhere. A thirteenth-century London ordinance required that slate or tile roofs replace the usual reed and straw as a precautionary measure. It is interesting to note a similar order that appeared in the American colonies at a somewhat later date.

> New Amsterdam, 15 December 1657:
>
> The Director General and Council of New Netherland to All who shall see these presents or hear them read, Greeting! Know ye, that to prevent the misfortunes of conflagrations, the roofs of reeds, the wooden and plastered chimneys have long ago been condemned but nevertheless these orders are obstinately and carelessly neglected by many of the inhabitants. . . . The said Director General and Council have decided it to be necessary, not only to renew their former ordinances, but also to amplify the same to increase the fines. . . .[1]

Overcrowding within the small dwellings of the poorer people further increased the hazards to health and the spread of epidemics. In 1539 an act of Parliament mentioned that "great mischiefs daily grow and increase by reason of pestering houses with divers families, harboring of inmates, and converting great houses into tenements, and erection of new houses."

1. Quoted Straus and Wegg, *Housing Comes of Age* (New York: Oxford University Press, 1938).

Gunpowder was introduced into Europe from China in the fourteenth century, and new techniques of warfare appeared as a consequence. The feudal lords had relied on citizen-soldiers to man the crenellated parapets in time of siege, but the new weapons of attack and defense required larger numbers of soldiers who were better trained and professional. Military engineering became a science. Fortifications were extended, and heavy bastions, moats, and outposts were built. Extension of the area occupied by the fortifications created a "no-man's land," and separation of town and country became more distinct. Open space outside the walls was further removed from the urban dweller. People came to the cities in large numbers to participate in the expanding commercial enterprise and to fill the ranks of professional armies.

The Appearance of Gunpowder

In fifteenth-century France the kings achieved a semblance of national unity. Elsewhere cities remained provincial dukedoms with wealthy merchant families wielding control. It became the ambition of rulers to display their affluence and power by improving their cities. As in most of their intellectual pursuits, they drew on the classic heritage of Rome for this cultural activity. The noble families of Florence, Venice, Rome, and Lombardy proceeded to embellish those cities; the Medicis, Borgias, and Sforzas built themselves new palaces on which were draped the classic motifs. Although the buildings of the medieval town retained the fortress quality characteristic of the Middle Ages, a formalism was grafted to them. The basic form did not change, but the structure was decorated with facades made up of classic elements.

THE RENAISSANCE

The church participated in this movement. The residence of the popes was reestablished in Rome, and work on the Vatican Palace was begun. Pope Julius planned to replace the old basilica of St. Peter with a great church that would become the center of Christendom.

Feverish preoccupation with the arts gripped the merchant princes, churchmen, and the kings. The well-rounded man became the ideal. Practice of the arts became a profession. The apprentice system prepared men to work in a variety of artistic fields. An apprentice to a painter would also work in the shop of a goldsmith; a sculptor would study architecture. Versatility was characteristic of the artists. Leonardo da Vinci practiced all the visual arts and became a planner, military engineer, and inventor as well. Kings, merchant nobles, and popes were patrons of the arts and bid heavily for the services of the growing number of practitioners.

Arts and Architecture

The anonymity of the master builders of medieval towns no longer prevailed in the Renaissance. Robert du Luzarches, William of Sens (Canterbury Cathedral), Geoffrey de Noyes (Lincoln Cathedral), Jean-le-Loup, and Henrico di Gambodia (Milan Cathedral) are seldom recorded in the history of medieval town building, whereas a host of individuals received personal recognition in the Renaissance and later periods. The names of Brunelleschi, Alberti, Bramante, Peruzzi, and Sangallo in Italy, and Bullant, de l'Ormé, and Lescot in France are as well known as their works. Many others achieved world renown; their names were more prominent than those of the patrons who commissioned their works. Mansart, Bullet, Blondel, Lemercier, de Brosse, Le Nôtre, and Percier in France; Bernini, Longhena, Borromini, Palladio, Michelangelo, and Raphael in Italy; Inigo Jones, Christopher Wren, and the Brothers Adam in England were artists who enjoyed the confidence and patronage of popes, kings, and merchants.

Piazza of St. Peter, Rome. *Originally, a narrow winding street led to St. Peter's. The suddenness with which the visitor was thrust into this magnificent open space made the square seem even more beautiful.*

With Paris in mind, the dictator Mussolini ordered that the path to St. Peter's be opened, and so the medieval buildings that had lined the approaches were removed and the axial avenue from the Castle St. Angelo to St. Peter's came into being. (Photograph by Richard Eisner.)

Monarchy and Monumentalism

Formal plazas of the Renaissance were carved out of the medieval town and given monumental scale and form reminiscent of classical antiquity. Exterior space was enclosed with formal facades, and the shapes were modeled like sculptural pieces, isolated from the rest of the city.

The monumental character of the classic had returned to the city. Every form had its centerline, and every space its axis. The structural quality of the Middle

Ages was replaced by a classic sculptural form, modeled symmetrically. The "barbaric" art of medieval cities was forsaken. With haughty disdain Molière called it:

> The rank taste of Gothic monuments,
>
> These odious monsters of the ignorant centuries,
>
> Which the torrents of barbarism spewed forth.

The axis and the strong centerline symbolized the growing concentration of power. Kings of France became monarchs, wealthy merchants in Italy became autocratic dukes, large landowners in England became lord barons, and the popes became benevolent partners of all. Louis XIV of France gave voice to the spirit of the times when he shouted his famous words, *"L'Etat, c'est moi."*

Out of the cramped medieval town were carved formal squares. The modeling of spatial forms absorbed the attention and skills of designers and planners, and classic elements were ingeniously assembled to form the spaces. Michelangelo created the Campodiglio on the Capitoline Hill in Rome, Bernini designed the huge Piazza of St. Peter's, the Piazza di San Marco in Venice was completed, Rainaldi built the twin churches on the Piazza del Popolo, the Place Royale (now Place des Vosges) and Place des Victoires were built in Paris.

Long-range artillery removed the advantage of the old walls for military defense. Louis XIV ordered Vauban, his military engineer, to redesign the defense system. The engineer tore down the walls and built earthwork ramparts beyond the city. Within the leveled space of the old walls boulevards and promenades were laid. The famous Ringstrasse of Vienna occupied the open space left when the walls of that city were demolished. Cities were opening up, and the city of the Middle Ages was being released from its clutter. Transition from the Renaissance to the baroque was in process.

THE BAROQUE CITY

An air of grandeur permeated the courts of kings. Louis XIV ordered Le Nôtre to design the gardens of Versailles. Here was space of unparalleled proportions, scale of incomprehensible size. Here was the conception of a man who, having achieved domination over the lives of men, confidently set about to become the master of nature. The egotism of rulers knew no limitations, nor could it brook a hint of equality; Louis XIV threw the wealthy financier Foucquet into prison for having the temerity to build a château almost as fine as the king's.

In the eighteenth century the baroque city expanded and the dominance of the ruler intensified. The avenues of Versailles focused upon the royal palace, and in Germany the whole cities of Karlsruhe and Mannheim revolved about the palaces and great gardens of the royalty.

Plazas of the seventeenth century had been designed as isolated, enclosed spaces. They were now opened and less confined, as though moved by a desire to recapture the space of the countryside. Design shifted from walled-in architectural forms to extension and expansion of open space. Jules-Hardouin Mansart, one of the architects of Versailles, designed the Place Vendôme with greater dimensions than those of any previous square in Paris. The three squares by Here de Corny in Nancy were connected, the continuity of open space emphasized by colonnades and enhanced by a tree-lined avenue.

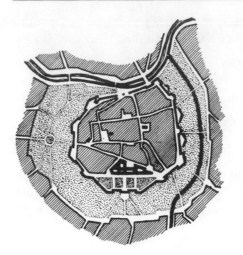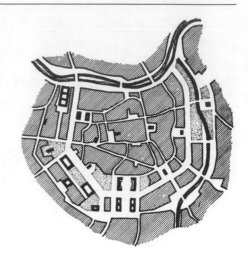

Vienna before 1857 (left). Vienna after 1857 (right). *The effectiveness of the old system of walls, moats, and ramparts for military defense was reduced as long-range artillery greatly improved in the late eighteenth and early nineteenth centuries, and the form of the city underwent drastic alterations. The walls and ramparts were leveled, the moats were filled in, and boulevards were built in the open space, as in the famous Ringstrasse encircling the original town of Vienna. These spaces were gradually built up in response to the ruthless speculation of the late nineteenth century, and open space disappeared from the city.*

Probably the most dramatic example of the new surge to penetrate the city with open space was the Place de la Concorde, designed by Jacques-Ange Gabriel during the reign of Louis XV. In this square, space is almost completely released. It flows from the gardens of the Tuileries and the Louvre on one side into the broad avenue of the Champs-Élysées begun by Louis XIV to connect Paris with his palace at Versailles. The scale is further amplified by the River Seine lying along one side. Across the river is the only group of buildings facing this tremendous square.

Another departure in urban design was the Piazza del Popolo in Rome, designed by Rainaldi and completed by Valadier. A three-dimensional transition of space was obtained with a series of terraces linking the lower level of the square and the gardens of the Pincio Hill above. Continuity replaced the enclosure of open space as the new direction in civic design.

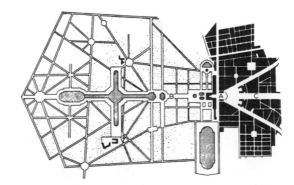

A Palace
B Gardens
C Town

Versailles. *The centerline and the axis symbolized the mighty power of the monarch. Louis XIV ordered the removal of his palace from the congested city of Paris to the open hunting grounds of Versailles, and he ordered the avenues to radiate from his magnificent palace.*

In England the classic revival came later than elsewhere, the Tudor style having absorbed the Renaissance shock. In reaction against the hazards of overhanging upper stories, a 1619 building ordinance decreed that building walls would henceforth be constructed vertically from foundation to roof. Timed with the onrushing wave of classic formalism, this law aided the introduction of the so-called Italian style ushered in by Inigo Jones, its leading exponent.

The landowning class had tempered the rise of monarchy in England, and the monumentalism of the "grand plan" did not quite take root there. Christopher Wren attempted it in his plan for rebuilding London after the fire of 1666. He went so far as to place the stock exchange at the symbolic focal point of his plan instead of the traditional palace or cathedral. Even this acknowledgment of the domination of mercantilism in England was not enough to offset disagreement over the necessary reapportionment of property values destroyed in the fire.

Formalism permeated the English Renaissance, but it was expressed in terms of quiet repose rather than striking grandeur. This quality can be observed in the simple curved building forms facing broad open spaces of the Circus and Royal Crescent in Bath designed by John Wood the Younger. The same quality was built into the undulating surfaces and freely curving forms of Lansdowne Crescent, also in Bath. John Nash carried these curving forms overlooking spacious open parks over into his designs for London's Park Crescent and Regent's Park.

Formalism was unobtrusively introduced in the enclosed squares of London during the eighteenth century. They were intended not as impressive plazas but as places for the quiet relaxation of the area's residents. These simple though formal open spaces were created largely by builders who would be classified today as "speculators": they were in the business of subdividing land and building homes. Many are unknown, as in the case of the builder of Lansdowne Crescent; two builders prominent in London at the time were James Burton and Thomas Cubitt. They and others like them, known and unknown, lent dignity to their profession by the work they performed.

The fine rows of formal dwellings and squares in England; the monumental vistas, royal gardens, and palaces of France; the well-modeled piazzas in Italy, all had been built for the upper classes, the wealthy merchants, and the kings. The lot of the people of lesser means had not substantially improved. It had not been

Behind the Facades

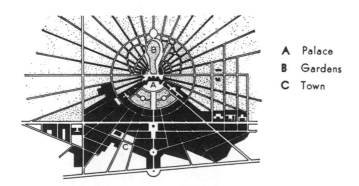

A Palace
B Gardens
C Town

Karlsruhe. *The entire city of Karlsruhe was designed to revolve about and radiate from the prince's palace.*

A   Stock Exchange

B   St. Paul's Cathedral

C   Tower of London

D   London Bridge

E   Old Walls

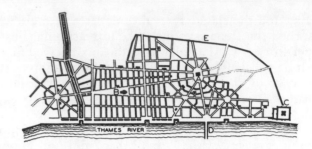

London (Christopher Wren's plan). *After the Great Fire of 1666 Christopher Wren proposed a monumental plan for the rebuilding of London. He conceded the new power dominant in England by placing the stock exchange as the major focal point. But the plan was not accepted; the necessary adjustment of property boundaries and prices could not be resolved.*

the purpose of the designers and builders of the baroque town to engage in reforms. They were concerned with such improvement of the urban environment that would maintain the prestige and glory of those of exalted position. At the same time, the broad avenues provided more than satisfaction of the vanity and ego in despots, more than delightful promenades for the elegant carriages of the aristocrats; they offered a means with which to impress the populace with the power and discipline of marching armies.

Behind the fine facades of the plazas and wide avenues dwelt the congested urban population. The city lacked sanitation, sewers, water distribution, and drainage. Epidemics and pestilence were frequent, and poverty was appalling. A breach was widening between the aristocracy and the masses. The seventeenth-century fratricidal wars of religion and social restlessness were followed by the stamp of the despotic heel and the courtiers. Oppression brought revolutions in the eighteenth century. The baroque city had unfolded its grand open spaces, and they were overlapping upon the people.

CHAPTER 10

COLONIAL EXPANSION IN THE AMERICAS

Aided by the mariner's compass, courageous explorers in the fifteenth and sixteenth centuries extended the net of colonial empires over the face of the globe. At the same time, oppressed people in Europe looked toward the New World, now North America, for relief from their plight. Many colonies in the Americas were settled by pioneers impelled by a burning desire for freedom, religious and otherwise. Far removed from the mother countries and with a whole great land as an ever-widening frontier to the west, many early settlements did not grow to become permanent fortified towns. Although strong forts were established at some early settlements—San Juan, St. Augustine, New Amsterdam—the barricades thrown up as protection from attack by the native people offered no impediment to the development of villages and towns in the way that fortifications had restricted the growth of European medieval cities. The principal occupation was agriculture; the towns were small and all parts were within walking distance of the countryside about them.

The earliest settlement was sometimes irregular and uneven. The Wall Street district of today's Manhattan retains the pattern of its 1660 settlement as New Amsterdam, and in Boston, streets meander about the Common as they did in colonial days. But most of the towns were allocated in advance for the settlers. The people who ventured across the sea to this new land sought opportunities of which they had been deprived in their homeland, and that meant in part the freedom to work their own land.

Towns in New England reflected the modest character of the Puritan. The center was the meeting house on the common, and each family had its own dwelling, however humble. The environment was one of beauty in simplicity—communities of neighbors. Towns in the South were settled by people just as eager to improve their lot, but they reflected the stamp of the English Crown. Class distinctions, although not so obviously expressed as in England, were retained, and formality characterized the life and pattern of the towns.

Mexico

Sculpture of the head of the Rain God Tláloc on the Temple of Quetzalcóatl at the town of Teotihuacán, near Mexico City. *The temple is located in the City of the Gods at the Ciudadela, near the Pyramids to the Moon and Sun and the Temple of the Butterflies. The sculpture is thought to be a Toltec God.*

Williamsburg

In Williamsburg, Virginia, the quiet and formal repose of an English town was transplanted to the new land. Through the beneficence of John D. Rockefeller, Jr., it was restored as recently as 1926 and presents an accurate impression of the early colonial town. Williamsburg was settled in 1632 as Middle Plantation, and in 1693 the College of William and Mary was granted a charter and located there. It became the capital of the Virginia Colony in 1699.

The surveyor, Theodorick Bland, laid out the city with formal axes adapted from the European aristocratic mode. The Duke of Gloucester Street was the main avenue, extending from the college to the capitol building. A green was placed at right angles to this street and terminated at the palace. The town was subdivided into residence lots of one-half acre each. It was a formal plan, but it neither revolved about monumental features nor was overpowered by them. A human scale characterized the environment; the town appeared to exist for the people who lived there rather than for the rulers who dominated it.

THE GRIDIRON APPEARS

Philadelphia

Early Philadelphia may have enjoyed this quality of human scale, but it is not apparent in its plans. The City of Brotherly Love was planned for William Penn in 1682 by the surveyor Thomas Holme. It consisted of a rigid gridiron street pattern extending between the Delaware and Schuylkill rivers. Two main streets, Broad and Market, bisected the plan in each direction and intersected at the public square in the center of the town. A square block was allocated for a park in each quadrant.

The plan had little distinction. Penn expected it to be a town of single houses and shade trees. By the middle of the eighteenth century, however, it was common practice to build the houses from lot line to lot line, and the open spaces were lost within the walls of brick that lined the gridiron streets. Continuous rows of buildings shut off access to the rear of the property, and alleys were cut through the center of the blocks. Then dwellings were built along the alleys, to become the quaint and narrow business and residential streets for which the city is known today.

Savannah

The aristocratic paternalism that characterized the early settlements in the southern colonies was reflected in the plan for Savannah, Georgia. Laid out in 1733 by James Oglethorpe, the plan was a rectilinear street system similar to the gridiron but liberally interspersed with park squares along the avenues. The streets linked these parks and created a continuity of open space when the town was made up of single houses. This pleasing continuity has since been forsaken by the intensive building coverage of the intermediate blocks.

Lansingburgh-on-the-Hudson

Trade and shipping thrived in the North and settlers flocked to the colonies. Landowners opened subdivisions and plotted lots for sale and lease. Rights to pasture and timber on adjacent land were sometimes granted to purchasers of lots in the new towns.

Such a development was Lansingburgh-on-the-Hudson, surveyed by Joseph Blanchard for the landowner Abraham Lansing. This, like many others, was a speculative venture; the plan was a gridiron with a common reserved in the center, as in the New England villages. Profiting from the precedent in Philadelphia, alleys were plotted in the original subdivision.

The gridiron plan adopted for this and similar towns was not only the simplest form to survey; it was also not an unsatisfactory form for the small village. A sense of unity was maintained by the close relation of all dwellings to the town square and to the agricultural land on the outskirts. When this same pattern was

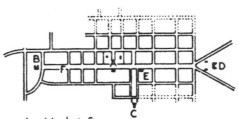

A Market Square
B The Capitol
C Governor's Palace
D College of William and Mary
E Bruton Parish Church
F Duke of Gloucester Street

New Amsterdam. *The Dutch settlement of New Amsterdam was built on the tip of what is now known as Manhattan. The streets established in 1660 near the harbor still exist in their original pattern, among them Lower Broadway (called Breedweg by the Dutch), Broad Street, and Wall Street. The almost medieval irregular street plan and the canal are reminiscent of towns in Holland.*

Williamsburg. *Settled in 1632 as Middle Plantation, the town was renamed Williamsburg and became the capital of Virginia Colony in 1699. It was laid out by the surveyor Theodorick Bland. The main street, Duke of Gloucester Street, was ninety-nine feet wide and extended from the College of William and Mary to the capitol. The land was subdivided in lots about one-half acre in size and held a population of 3,000 to 4,000 people. The spaces are not "grand": they are of human scale. The quiet formality of the community reflects the English influence.*

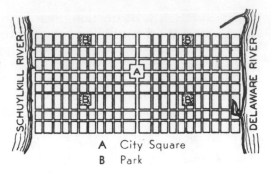

Philadelphia. *William Penn commissioned the surveyor Thomas Holme to lay out the city in 1682. A rigid gridiron plan was adopted. Two major streets crossed in the center of the town and formed a public square. A square-block park was placed in each of the four quadrants. Early dwellings were single-family houses. In the middle of the eighteenth century it became a common practice to build dwellings on the side lot lines, resulting in continuous rows of buildings that cut off access to the rear yards. Alleys were then cut through the center of the blocks. These alleys have since become streets.*

A City Square
B Park

extended endlessly, the monotony of the checkerboard lay heavily upon the town.

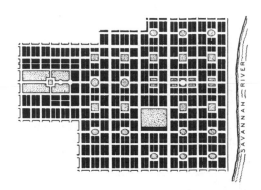

Savannah. *Laid out in 1733 by James Oglethorpe, the Savannah plan was a regular pattern of rectangular streets with park squares liberally spotted in alternate blocks. The plan is similar to that of Philadelphia with a more generous allocation of open spaces.*

THE RADIAL PLAN

A small settlement begun in 1649 on the banks of the Severn River in Maryland received the name of Annapolis in 1694. It was the first city in America to adopt diagonal avenues and circles as its basic plan. It was followed by a more dramatic display, the classic plan for Washington, D.C., by Major Pierre Charles L'Enfant.

Washington, D.C.

After much deliberation about an appropriate location for the capital of this new nation, it was decided to avoid existing urban centers such as New York and Philadelphia. Ambitious for the future of their new country, the founding fathers selected a site along the banks of the Potomac River, removed from the commercial environment of established cities. L'Enfant, a young French designer, was commissioned to prepare a plan for the new capital city. With his background in the baroque atmosphere of Paris and inspired by the spirit of the American cause, it was natural that he should conceive of this new city on a grand scale woven into a pattern of geometrical order. Such a plan appealed to the aristocratic tastes of men like Washington and Jefferson, and it was adopted by them in 1791.

Other Examples

Following the example of their capital, a number of American cities wrapped themselves in the radial plan, that system of diagonal streets overlaid upon a gridiron pattern. Joseph Ellicott, brother of Andrew Ellicott, who surveyed Washington, D.C., planned the city of Buffalo, New York, in 1804. His plan's diagonal streets crossed a gridiron pattern at the central square near the lake waterfront.

After the 1805 Detroit, Michigan, fire, Judge Augustus Brevoort Woodward and Governor William Hull prepared a plan for Detroit in 1807. It was a grand complex elaborated with concentric hexagonal streets and contained most, if not all, the myriad forms used in Washington, D.C. To implement the plan, owners of property destroyed in the fire were ceded larger sites conforming to the new layout. New plans in 1831 and 1853 drew away from the original idea, and, with the exception of a few spots like Grand Circus Square, there is little apparent planned form in the city today.

Among the other cities with diagonal streets were Indianapolis and Madison. Both these cities were based on the gridiron, but diagonals ranged from the center to the four corners of the plan. The center in Indianapolis was an open circle; in Madison the focal point was the Wisconsin state capitol building.

Washington, D.C. *The plan by Pierre Charles L'Enfant, approved by Washington and Jefferson, began a series of city planning projects in which diagonal and radial streets were superimposed on the typical gridiron layout. The city was designed as a huge monumental setting for the federal government of a new nation.*

NEW YORK CITY

In the midst of this wave of radial planning a significant development occurred in New York City. In 1800 the city surveyor and architect Joseph Mangin proposed a plan for extension of the city to the north, which provided for major north-south streets with squares and plazas somewhat reminiscent of those of Washington, D.C. He also suggested a treatment for the waterfront that surrounds Manhattan Island. But Mangin's plan was not adopted.

Instead, in 1811 an official commission prepared a plan. The commission was composed of three members, two of whom were lawyers and landowners and the third a surveyor. They proposed a rigid gridiron street system to be laid over the entire island irrespective of the topography and the extensive waterfront. Only one angular street was retained—Broadway. The position of the commission was quite clear: "Straightsided and right-angled houses," they stated, "are the most cheap to build and the most convenient to live in."[1]

The matter of economy obviously guided the commission in its deliberations and dictated its conclusions. They found that "the price of land is so uncommonly great," and their proposal for retention of open space was indeed frugal. The limit of open area deemed feasible consisted of 69 acres reserved for a military parade ground, 55 acres for a public market, and five small parks.

Assuming that the major traffic would continue to move back and forth between the Hudson and East rivers, the east-west streets, 60 feet in width, were spaced

---

1. Quoted in Turpin Bannister; *Town Planning in New York State,* American Society of Architectural Historians.

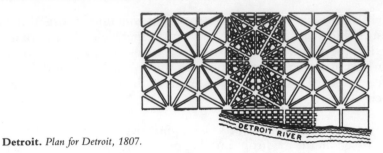

Detroit. *Plan for Detroit, 1807.*

260 feet apart. This extravagance was offset, however, by economy of streets in the opposite direction; north-south streets, 100 feet wide, were spaced at distances ranging from 600 to 900 feet.

The commission's appraisal of traffic flow was hardly accurate, as the precisely reverse direction in growth it has since taken readily attests. Nor did it reflect particular optimism for the future of this great city. But it is the emphasis on economy on the part of the commission that poses the most pertinent issue, because it bears strong resemblance to that practiced in later and less happy days of urban planning.

It will be recalled that Peter Minuit purchased the entire island of Manhattan from the Native Americans in 1626. At that time he paid the astounding sum of 24 dollars. When the commission laid out its plan in 1811, most of the land was still devoted to agriculture. Guided by the economy of a surveyor's rod and chain, the island was mapped in a huge checkerboard. The ultimate cost of fitting the topography, "broken by hills and diversified by watercourses," to this pattern of land subdivision was overlooked, to be sure. The commission obviously expected the city to continue the growth it was then enjoying; they so mapped it for subdivision and sale. The reservation of 30 percent of the land for streets can possibly be explained by the extensive frontage it provided for the sale of lots. But can the omission of ample open space be construed as economy?

Even if the land had been developed with single-family houses on individual lots, the open space in the commission's plan would have been inadequate in the face

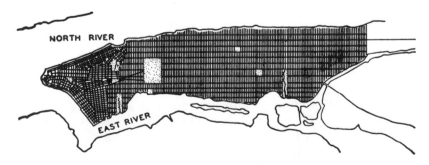

New York City. *After turning down the 1800 proposal of the city surveyor and architect Joseph Mangin, a commission was appointed in 1811 to arrive at a plan. They proposed a rigid gridiron street pattern laid upon the irregular topography of the city. Open space was not generously allocated; a military parade ground of sixty-nine acres, fifty-five acres for a public market, and five small parks were the only open areas provided for in the plan. Despite the "uncommonly great" price of land, explained as the reason for the paucity of open space, the layout of streets can hardly be construed as economical; they occupy only some 30 percent of the land area. This harsh and uncompromising original plan is reflected in the cramped city of today, in which open space has all but completely vanished. It was not until the middle of the nineteenth century that the great Central Park was definitely established in the plan. (United Press International photo.)*

Lower Manhattan from the Statue of Liberty, showing the twin towers of the World Trade Center.

of virtually any future growth. Forty-five years later, in 1856, 840 acres was purchased for Central Park, and it cost the city's taxpayers $5.5 million, an astronomical sum at the time.

This kind of "economy" distorts the planning of our cities today. We are obliged to learn and profit from the experience of New York City. Is it economical to avoid the reservation of open space in the name of practical planning, only to find the land value has become so dear we cannot afford the space when the need is urgent? The value of learning from yesterday is to prepare today for a better tomorrow.

There were those who protested the formlessness of the commissioner's plan. Many agreed with Henry R. Aldrich when he claimed its inspiration was "the great facility which it provides for the gambling in land values and ready purchase and sale of building blocks," which has "wrought incalculable mischief." It was an omen of the fate to befall the American city in subsequent years.

PART 3

THE CITY
IN
TRANSITION

CHAPTER 11

THE INDUSTRIAL REVOLUTION

With the nineteenth century came the dawn of the Industrial Revolution, which can properly be called the Machine Age. Until then all goods had been assembled and produced by hand. Shops were modest and generally located in the home of the proprietor. The number of employees was small, and a close relationship existed between worker and employer, for good or ill.

New and important inventions had occurred throughout history. During the Renaissance the uses of gunpowder expanded, the printing press was invented, and the processing of various materials was greatly improved. Simple hand machinery became more efficient. But in 1769 James Watt invented the steam engine and, with it, mechanical power became independent of direct operation by hand. This power was applied to the workplace, and the production of goods grew. With increased production, trade expanded, the shop moved from the home into separate quarters—the factory—and the distance between employee and employer widened.

With the advent of machines driven by independent power a new era was born. In 1776 Adam Smith set forth his theories of laissez-faire capitalism in his *Wealth of Nations,* and his influence is felt to this day. The number of employees in proportion to owners increased rapidly, and trade unions of workers, in contrast to the medieval guilds of artisans and proprietors, were formed.

The invention of industrial machinery touched off feverish activity; speed of production absorbed the attention of industrial management, and the repetition

FROM HANDCRAFT TO MACHINE

of operations replaced the variety of individual handcraft. Each machine had its job, and each man, woman, or child his or her machine. Factories grew in size and the number of workers increased. The factory was like a magnet, drawing about it an ever-increasing belt of workers' dwellings, schools, and shops. With every new device production per worker jumped; the introduction of what can be called mass production made it possible for more people to have more things than had ever been available to them before.

TRANSPOR-TATION

The industrial system depended upon the movement of raw materials to the factory and finished products to the consumers. Thus the development of transportation was crucial to the period.

Before the invention of the steam engine, goods were hauled in wagons and towed on river barges. Beginning in 1761 the inland waterways of America were linked by a system of canals, and in 1807 Fulton built his steamboat, the *Clermont*. In 1825 the first steam railroad to be used for public transportation began operation in England, and a railroad line was laid in the United States in 1829. Industrial production increased and domestic and foreign commerce expanded. Between 1850 and 1880, export trade from the United States leaped from $17 million to $100 million.

In the crowded city, small horsedrawn carriages trundled people about the streets. The *voiture-omnibus,* a larger vehicle capable of holding several passengers, was introduced to Paris in 1819 and 1831 in New York City as the "horse car".

Traffic congestion paralleled the increase in population density, and in 1867 an elevated cable car was built in New York City to alleviate the density in the streets. A steam train replaced the cable in 1871, but congestion was hardly diminished. By extending their rails beyond the city, the steam railroads offered some relief to city congestion. Suburbs sprang up along their routes, inviting "commuters" who could afford the time and luxury of escape from the city centers on a daily basis.

The electric street railway that ran on rails replaced the horse car in about 1885 and thenceforth became the principal urban transport until fairly recent times. By 1917 there were 80,000 streetcars and 45,000 miles of track in American cities. In 1895 an electric elevated line was installed in Chicago and, shortly thereafter, in New York and Philadelphia. As a result of this readily available mass transportation, the population moved somewhat away from the center to the periphery of the city, but congestion persisted as a result of the street pattern and population increase.

Having failed to untie the knotty problem of traffic and transportation, the electric railway went underground. In 1897 a short line was built in Boston, and the first major subway was started in New York City in 1904. As we are sadly aware today, these developments aided and abetted congestion. The cities spread, population grew, and available transportation only intensified concentration in the urban centers.

When Gottlieb Daimler constructed the first high-speed internal combustion engine in 1885, transportation took a deeper step into the tangle of urban traffic. There were 4 automobiles registered in the United States in 1895; in 1900 there were 8,000; in 1972, 97,000,000; in 1985, an estimated 125,000,000. The automobile split the city open at the seams, and to this day we are frantically trying to hold it together with patches on a wornout fabric.

It is recorded that Leonardo da Vinci tinkered with a toy flying machine as early as the 1400s, but in the nineteenth century human beings finally took themselves to the air in gliders and by 1903 the first motor-driven heavier-than-air machine was invented. In 1927 Charles Lindbergh flew the Atlantic Ocean, and in 1938 Howard Hughes flew around the world in 3 days, 19 hours, eight minutes, and 10 seconds. Today commercial planes travel to every part of the earth, carrying more than three hundred passengers at over 600 miles per hour, and soaring into the stratosphere. How long can the city remain congested?

Civilization has moved at the rate that humans have been able to communicate their ideas. In ancient times messages were carried by a runner. With the invention of the printing press thoughts could be recorded for all to see and read. The introduction of a postal service widened the area and types of communications, but their transmission depended upon a carrier on foot or on horseback.

COMMUNICATIONS

The Industrial Revolution, however, sprang wide the door of inventive genius. By 1850 messages were being ticked off on a telegraph key. Then, on March 10, 1876, Alexander Graham Bell sat in his laboratory and spoke into a gadget. His assistant, listening at the other end of a wire, heard the words "Mr. Watson, come here: I want you." People could talk to each other on the telephone, and the effect of space and time was drastically altered.

By the end of the first quarter of the twentieth century the miracle of radio not only further changed time and space: it exploded them in the face of civilization, and the adjustment to this fundamental change is still far from complete.

With the development of radio, television, and especially the computer in the latter half of the twentieth century, instantaneous contact and the retrieval and transfer of information in fractions of a second are now possible. Satellites in space make it possible to relay messages, verbal and visual, to all parts of the world in a flash. The long-range social and psychological consequences of all these new systems are yet to be determined.

Measures for the public health and safety were extended during the nineteenth century. The first system of water supply, by gravity flow, was installed in Boston in 1652. By 1820 pumping systems were in general use, and methods for the disposal and treatment of sewage improved. The heavy building cover on the land reduced the natural drainage of the city, but extensive street paving permitted effective cleaning, and storm sewers augmented the sanitary equipment.

PUBLIC HEALTH AND SAFETY

Public thoroughfares in towns of the Middle Ages were dark and foreboding lanes. An occasional oil lamp hanging from a corner building was the only light to guide the stranger through the night. The use of artificial gas for lighting began in London in 1812 and by 1840 was in common use in city streetlamps. Electricity began to replace gas for street lighting when the first central generating plant for the distribution of electricity started operating in 1882.

Electricity illuminated the highway and the residential street. It made the "great white ways" that brighten the city of today, but it also brought the gaudy display of signs and advertisements that flash at night and droop hideously by day. With questionable taste they sell the wares of commerce and industry but reduce the visual aspect to that of a cheap bazaar.

Services for the health, safety, and convenience of the urban population advanced further in a period of less than one hundred years than in all previous history. The tremendous progress in this area when opposed to the everyday living and working conditions of the industrial city presents a bewildering contrast. Glorification of the industrial system and the fruits of its newborn activity blinded people to the ruin and havoc spreading across the urban community.

Many of the systems of public health and safety that arose in the nineteenth century still are in use. They are obsolete. Their continued use and the consequent difficulties with sewage and solid waste disposal are reflections of some cities' problems, both economic and political.

CITY AND FACTORY TOWN

The steam railroad extended its rails from the raw products to the factory, and to the cities of consumers all over the land. With its sprawling yards the railroad penetrated the town with a network of tracks. Every amenity of urban life was sacrificed to the requirements of industrial production. The factory with its tentacles of trains and shipping was the heart and nerve center of the city. Railroads and ships joined at the factories, and the waterfront became the industrial core of the city. Port cities on the oceans, lakes, and rivers prospered, drawing to them ships laden with coal and ore to fuel the factories and sending from them shiploads of manufactured goods.

The impact of the Industrial Revolution was first felt in England. The new industrial economy brought with it greater exploitation of the poor and with that the new slums. What could be called mechanical slums, row on row of crowded workers' houses in the shadow of the factory, were added to the traditional slums. The degraded environment of the factory town hung like a cloud over urban life for the next century and a half. Writing in 1865, Dr. Clifford Allbutt described what he saw in England:

> This is no description of a plague-stricken town in the fifteenth century; it is a faint effort to describe the squalor, the deadliness, and the decay of a mass of huts which lies in the town of Leeds, between York Street on the one side and Marsh Lane on the other; a place of "darkness and cruel habitations" which is within a stone's throw of our parish church and where the fever is bred. These dwellings seem for the most part to belong to landlords who take no interest whatever in their well-being. One block perhaps has fallen years ago by inheritance to a gentleman in Lancashire, Devonshire, or anywhere; another to an old lady; a third, perhaps, to an obscure money-lender. Meanwhile, the rotten doors are falling from their hinges, the plaster drops from the walls, the window frames are stuffed with greasy paper or old rags, damp and dung together fester in the doorways, and a cloud of bitterness hangs over all. To one set of houses, appropriately named Golden Square, there is no admission save by alleys or tunnels, which are only fit to lead to dungeons; so that for perhaps half a century or more the winds of heaven have never blown within its courts.

In the new land across the sea there was a vast source of natural resources and an energetic people inspired by a new-won freedom. The Industrial Revolution, unimpeded by traditions, swept across America. Then the echo of events in Europe was heard. As the American economy shifted from agrarian to industrial, the people and the resources were soon to experience the same throes of exploitation and the same struggle for a decent living environment.

SLUMS

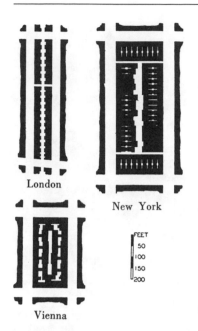

London

New York

FEET
50
100
150
200

Vienna

Among the deplorable slums of the nineteenth-century factory town in England, the two-story row house predominated, stretching in long rows with small backyards and narrow streets. The living environment was dreary and monotonous. Crowding on the European continent, however, was even more severe, as indicated in the outline of a tenement block in Vienna. Built to a height of four and five floors, the block typically contained a double row of dwellings, the interior row facing a narrow interior court on both sides. Although it has been customary to assume that European slums were more crowded than housing in the New World, the tenement block in New York City does not confirm such a notion. The sketch shows a combination of the "railroad" and "dumbbell" tenements, many of which remained in use for decades after they were outlawed in 1901.

The air of American towns became <u>polluted</u> with smoke and grime from the belching chimneys of the new age./Railroads ate into the core of cities, waterfronts were ruined, soot covered the villages, and sewage flowed into streams and rivers and lined the beaches/Buffalo, Chicago, Detroit, St. Louis all devoted their splendid sites on lakes and river waterfronts to the industrial plants, the railroads, and the ships of the new factory system. The land was plotted and advertised as "desirable sites for industry."

Floods of <u>immigration</u> from foreign lands created <u>a need for housing</u> and invited the <u>construction of cheaply built tenements</u>. Into them the newcomers crowded, grateful for someplace to live in this country of promise. <u>Industrial growth in the large centers induced the people to remain in cities rather than migrate to the more healthful environment of rural communities, and the inevitable result was the creation of slums.</u>

The Jungle

There was an exception to the concentration in congested cities. A large supply of labor was needed to obtain the raw products for manufacture, and "company towns" sprang up at mining and lumber sites in various parts of the country. They occupy an infamous place in the annals of American town development. Living in deplorable shacks and shanties, the workers' families were subject to the will of a single employer for their livelihood. Shelter, food, and clothing were available only through the mining or lumber company, and only on terms the company prescribed.

There was a depressing consistency about the factory town of the nineteenth century. It bred mediocrity in every aspect of life; mediocrity at best was its characteristic. Peaks of creative inspiration were few and far between. Monotonous order was an inevitable result of rigid organization of people and things. Here and there a pseudo-gaiety pierced the haze, but it was fluffy with gray frills touched more with half-concealed vulgarity than genuine pleasure. The urban environment, when it was not oppressive and filthy, reflected the bawdy can-can

MID-VICTORIAN MEDIOCRITY AND INHUMANITY

The Industrial Revolution and the nineteenth-century city: Stoke-on-Trent, England.
(British Information Service.)

rather than the graceful waltz. Vast areas of mean dwellings lay under a pall of smoke; an atmosphere of haze hung over the environment. A film of grime and soot covered all, and the wide range from wealth to poverty meant little more culturally than the difference between glut and endless want. The cultural energy of the city was sapped by the gigantism of industrial development.

Proof of the mediocrity and inhumanity of the age can be found among the few who recognized it. William Morris and John Ruskin cried out against it; Charles Dickens wove it into his classic stories; Octavia Hill fought it with vigorous social work. They saw the dulling of the human creative spirit. They perceived it in all its shabbiness, poverty, and grime—the nineteenth-century industrial city.

THE LAST OF THE BAROQUE

In the midst of the orgy of urban expansion, a development of monumental proportions was undertaken in Paris. Sensitive to the restlessness of the working classes, Napoleon III proposed to open broad avenues through the slums in which discontent festered. Besides clearing some of them away in this manner, he was not unmindful of the advantage these open spaces would provide his soldiers in controlling mob violence.

In 1853 Georges-Eugène Haussmann, a baron and bureaucrat in the city administration, was selected to take charge of the huge program. The result was an amazing demonstration of administration and organization. The entire boulevard system of Paris was planned and executed in a period of 17 years and under the most strenuous circumstances. Haussmann was resisted on the one hand by a city council reluctant to appropriate the necessary funds, and on the other hand by bourgeois property owners affected by his broad strokes of planning.

He laid out the new streets in long sweeps that cut through the maze of winding medieval lanes. With these avenues he connected old plazas and created new ones. He laid out the radiating avenues across the open fields from the Place de L'Étoile, the Bois de Boulogne, the monumental Avenue de L'Opéra, and many other grand boulevards. He was aware of the need to design for the traffic of a new industrial age, and the broad avenues opened through the congested districts improved circulation. He had the conception of scale appropriate for the new city: he saw it as a complex wanting unification.

The program engineered by Haussmann was stupendous. It transformed Paris and gave that great city much of its color. A series of masterful projects was executed.

But the tradition of monuments was deeply rooted in the process of city building. It was not long since the revolution against tyranny, and an emperor was again the ruler. The tree-lined avenues and vistas were meant to impress rather than to serve the people.

The time was not ripe for solving the new urban problems. The avenues became continuous streets of ground-floor shops, with dwellings on the upper floors. There was no separation of land uses, as there had been in the earlier London residential developments about Bloomsbury that traffic arteries and shopping streets bypassed. Haussmann's scheme was gargantuan in scale, but it was too late to become an effective monument to the ego of a monarch, and too early to solve the planning of the industrial city. It was the swan song of the baroque city.

Development of Paris

Beginning as a fortified town on a small island in the River Seine, Paris was known as Lutetia by the Romans. At the time of the Norman invasion in the ninth century, the town had expanded beyond the original Ile de la Cité and was fortified on both sides of the Seine. The fortifications were extended by Philip Augustus in the twelfth century. The left or south bank was the principal location for churches and colleges, the commercial center lying on the right bank. The kings made their residence on this bank, and in the fourteenth century Charles V built a wall to contain this growing part of the city more adequately. At the east end of the town was the tower known as the Bastille; at the west end, on the banks of the Seine, was the Louvre, which became the royal palace.

The Louvre was extended in the sixteenth century under Henry II, and the Tuileries gardens were created. The power of the monarch was growing. Henry IV built the Place Royal, and in the seventeenth century Louis XIII had the walls expanded to contain the Tuileries gardens.

During the reign of Louis XIV, the Sun King, Paris grew rapidly and court life extended its influence. Vauban reduced the fortified walls, and the ramparts were transformed into promenades, the first of the *Grands Boulevards*. The Tuileries gardens and the Louvre were enlarged, and the initial stage of the Champs Élysées was built into the "suburbs" to the west. The Place des Victoires and Place Vendôme were built. Monumental quais were created along the Seine. Louis XIV, however, built the great palace and gardens of Versailles and moved his court and residence there.

The city expanded farther under Louis XV. During his reign the Place Louis XV (now the Place de la Concorde), Rue Royale, and Church of the Madeleine were

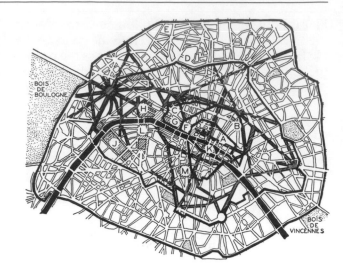

Wall **A**   Built by Philip Augustus, Twelfth century
Wall **B**   Built by Charles V, Fourteenth century
Wall **C**   Built by Louis XIII, Seventeenth century
Wall **D**   Built by Louis XV, Eighteenth century
Wall **E**   Built by Napoleon III, Nineteenth century
   F   The Louvre
   G   The Tuilleries
   H   The Champs Élysées
   J   The Champs de Mars
   K   The Île de la Cité
   L   The Invalides
   M   The Luxembourg

Paris. *The dark-shaded streets are Haussmann's interpolations on earlier forms.*

built. Streets were widened and new avenues built for fine residences. The Champs de Mars was also established. In the latter part of the eighteenth century a new wall was built to contain the growing city.

After the revolution the city's industrial development increased. The city outskirts were built up, and a new wall was built in 1840. Under Napoleon III, the huge program of Baron Haussmann was carried out.

Paris underwent remodeling during the reign of each monarch, but the greatest projects in each period were those along the fringes of the city. The great open spaces that distinguish the city today were developed in advance of the city's expansion, and the walls were extended to include them as the city spread about them. The most expansive spaces in today's city, such as the Champs Élysées, the Place de l'Étoile, and the boulevards radiating out from them, were laid across open fields. The rapid growth of Paris has spread the city in all its suburbs and absorbed many of the open spaces created when the walls of 1840 were leveled in the latter part of the nineteenth century.

The Madelaine, Paris.

CHAPTER 12

THE CITY OF CONTRASTS

It was an ironic paradox that out of the smoke, soot, and grime of the industrial cities, the Columbian Exposition of 1893 in Chicago would be called "White City." The fair would be everything the urban environment was not. Cities were cramped, monotonous, and ugly: the fair would be big, broad, and beautiful. The purpose of the exposition was to demonstrate amply the great new industrial empire and to give it pedigree. What more natural way to accomplish this than by clothing it in the robes of classic form, the style of the great days of the past? Was this not an appropriate cloak for a new era when people could produce more than at any time in history? With this new power they could reproduce classic structures that would surpass those of the emperors. This was an easy conclusion in the late nineteenth century, and it was true.

Daniel Burnham, the exposition's chief architect, uttered the magic words that marked the new era: "Make no small plans." The Ecole des Beaux Arts in Paris was the fountainhead for the designers of this period, and plans had to be big to be beautiful. The fair began a tidal wave of "city planning" and it swept across the United States. Every large city planned to become the "City Beautiful." Burnham was commissioned to prepare a plan for San Francisco after the earthquake and fire of 1906. The Commercial Club of Chicago engaged him for the plan of that city in 1909. He produced one for Manila and Baguio in the Philippines and was an active member of a commission of architects who revised the plan of Washington, D.C.

THE CITY BEAUTIFUL

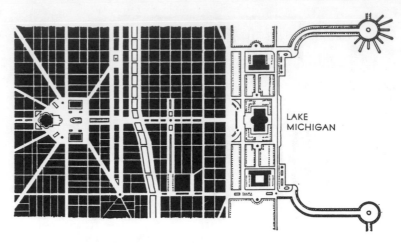

City beautiful plan, central part of the 1909 plan for the city of Chicago, Illinois.

Other cities followed suit. Plans were of colossal scale with monumental proportions. Great plazas and broad avenues, generously punctuated with monuments, were almost a civic obsession. Axes shot off in all directions, terminating with proposed buildings that put the visions of past kings to shame. The City Beautiful was the Grand Plan reincarnate.

Civic centers became a popular theme. Nearly every city had its civic center plan —open space landscaped in the traditional fashion, fountains distributed about plaza and garden, public buildings limited in number only by the size and ambition of the city, topped off with a frosted glass dome terminating a long and broad vista.

All this activity was performed in something of a vacuum; an air of haughty detachment, an isolation from the affairs of people and community, pervaded the planning.

A monument or public building blithely placed in the middle of an important traffic artery suggests the characteristic disregard for the ongoing life of the city. It was as though the planners had determined that the people must adjust themselves to the mighty formal arrangement. It did not occur to them that the entire development of a city was essentially derivative of human needs. The civic center concept was one of removal from the life of the community rather than involvement as a functional entity within it. The grandiose buildings were imposing, not inviting. They held the spellbound citizen at arm's length. They did not fit the city, its life, its habits, or its manners; theirs was an air of disdain rather than dignity.

These projected great structures became so expensive that reality stepped in at last. It was recognized that the citizenry could not afford the sums of money they cost. Some grand gestures were made and executed, but on the whole the lavish plans were destined for respectable storage in the archives of a more modest realized city hall. Most of the planning actually executed had to be remodeled later, usually haphazardly, to fit the requirements of traffic and circulation that were ignored in the original conception.

The seeds of city planning had nevertheless been planted during this period. Planning organizations sprang up in various parts of the country. A town planning board was established in Hartford, Connecticut, in 1907. In 1909 the first National Conference on City Planning was held. This was followed in 1911 with the founding of the National Housing Association. By 1913 there were official planning boards in eighteen cities in the country, and in the same year the Massachusetts state legislature was the first to make city planning a mandatory responsibility of local governments, decreeing that all cities with a population of 10,000 or more were required to establish a planning board.

Meanwhile, the real city was shoving its sprouts through these well-intentioned but fortuitous efforts. The technical know-how required for industrial production had been gained; industry had now become a commercial process. Financing and distribution were the new emphasis. Selling the rapidly produced merchandise and financing the expanding facilities to produce more transformed the system into a financial empire. Problems of production solved, industrial management turned its attention to commercial organization, banking, and national and worldwide trade associations. Commodities and their production gave way to tickertape and figures in a set of books. The businessman—the tycoon of commerce—became the main cog of the new era. Statistics, business cycles, bookkeeping, financing, and the stock market were the stock-in-trade of those who strove for success. Trade in commodities rather than the commodities themselves was what counted now. The city began to bristle with buildings, sheltering acres of floor space for the offices of business.

It was apparent that affairs must be operated on a practical basis. Land cost money, buildings cost money, services cost money, and so did time. Cities must work, the ornamental must be discarded, and only the useful could be tolerated. Such demands required the attention of practical men, not dreamers. A "city beautiful" was well and good, but it was far more important that it pay dividends.

To answer these demands there emerged the "city engineer," the practical man who could make surveys and calculations; determine the necessary size of sewer, water, and drainage systems; lay out rail lines, streets, walks, and roadways. These businesslike qualities instilled confidence in civic and business leaders. Businessmen chose such an individual for the responsibility of planning within established budget limitations. City planning became an engineering process engaging practical men free from dreams.

There was merit in this position; the City Beautiful was not frowned upon; it was simply too expensive, costing more than the problems it was intended to solve. Awed by the monumental dreams, impressed by the vision, community leaders set aside the proposals, not with disrespect. The great designs had simply lost all connection with the needs of the commercial city growing up in the twentieth century. The City Beautiful was a thing apart, detached, unrelated to human affairs. It solved none of the commercial city's problems. Moreover, there was probably some unconscious recoiling from the classic mold into which it would cast the physical environment.

Land took on a new value. First it had been sold as lots; value was later measured in terms of street frontage, a price per front foot. It was now being measured by the square foot. Every square foot of land had monetary value and none could be

CITY PLANNING: THE COMMERCIAL CITY

wasted. The result: building coverage became intense; layer upon layer of floor space was piled onto the land. In the twentieth century, the skyscraper was the dramatic manifestation of the commercial city.

The value attached to every square foot of land for commercial use conflicted with the fine balance between the buildings and open space of classic planning; the classic treatment had made a deep impression. It gave the look of pedigree, which was itself an asset to the business world. In order to capture appearances, remnants of the classic revival were hung upon the facades of buildings. It was a sham, to be sure, but the street thus assumed a stylish front, and the value of land behind the facades was protected. The appearance of dignity was achieved without the loss of a square foot of land.

Monumental Compromise: Washington, D.C.

Washington, D.C., is not a typical American city, but it dramatically displays the contradictions of the twentieth century. The job of government in a great democracy attracted an expanding population to the capital city. With the people came commercial enterprise, and the forces of conflict were set; the commercial city and the classic city were diametrically opposed.

The federal government vigorously attempted to retain the city's original plan. In 1901 the MacMillan Commission was appointed to restore the original character of the L'Enfant plan. Consequently the railroad that had cut across the Mall was removed, and the site for the present Union Station was established. A uniform height limit of future buildings was established. To preserve these and other accomplishments the National Commission of Fine Arts was appointed in 1910 by President Theodore Roosevelt, followed in 1926 by the creation of the National Capital Parks and Planning Commission.

These commissions performed yeoman service to the preservation of the classic city, but that city had changed. A new age had arrived, immature but nonetheless a moving force. Commercialism had descended on Washington, with all its collection of shops, hotels, office and loft buildings, entertainment and residential development, traffic and transportation. The increased value of land and the consequent intensity of development that had overtaken other cities happened in the capital city as well.

Commercial need and enterprise paid respect to the monumental street system originally laid down by squeezing into this framework the features of the new city. Classic facades were again draped upon building fronts, and behind these fronts formless building space was heaped upon the land, just as in other cities.

The contradiction between the classic and the commercial city was clearly apparent. To protect its character of monumental buildings and planning, the government-building area became a reservation necessarily isolated from the remainder of urban development. With the complex separated in this way, uniform building height and style could be maintained and the choice of site, form, and the use of open space could be easily enforced.

The paradox of the city was substantially complete. The plan for the capital of a great democratic government could be executed only by rigidly controlling its form in a preconceived and inflexible mold.

It was falsely assumed that a planning style could be transferred from another age and adapted to a new set of conditions. But great cultures are not recognized by

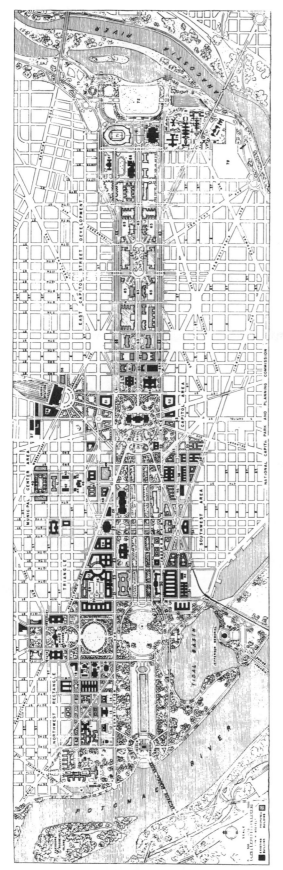

Washington, D.C. *The national capital as envisioned in 1941 by the National Capital Parks and Planning Commission. Washington is a city of monumental compromise between the classic and the commercial. The Capitol is near the center. It is encircled (left and counterclockwise) by the House Office Building, Library of Congress, Supreme Court, and Senate Office Building. To the right is Union Station. The Mall extends from the Capitol to the Washington Monument, from which the Reflecting Pool leads to the Lincoln Memorial.*

their similarities to previous periods but by their special stamp, the distinctive qualities they have contributed to the progress of civilization.

The effect of the false premise upon which the plan of Washington, D.C., has evolved is magnified by the design of the structures themselves, the insistence on classic forms without regard for the required arrangement of interior space. The design of exterior space is equally oblivious to the functional elements of the city. The classic courtyards, their prototypes covered with fine paving or gracious gardens, have in Washington become oil-stained parking lots filled with automobiles. The federal reservation of classic monumentalism is hollow and unnatural; the commercial city, warped into the pattern of its streets, is equally artificial.

THE NEED FOR REGULATION

Laissez-faire took deep root in human affairs as the commercial city formed. But soon it became increasingly apparent that if freedom were to avoid license some order must be established. In practical terms this meant the adoption of rules and regulations that placed certain restraints on laissez-faire.

We have observed that regulations on city building were not new in the annals of history. Hammurabi's were perhaps the first, in 2000 B.C. The Greeks had building regulations as well. The Romans established height limits for tenements. Towns of the Middle Ages adopted various regulations against fire hazards and projecting upper stories.

The sad condition of housing that developed with the factory system in the nineteenth century eventually forced the enactment of many laws to curb abuses. Regulations for light, air, and lot coverage, though lax in enforcement, were accepted for residential buildings. Restrictions regarding commercial and industrial buildings remained rare, however. Commercial structures were permitted to occupy as much as 100 percent of the lot area for the entire height. Steel construction and elevators pushed buildings even higher. Light and air could penetrate on the street frontage only, and these diminished as buildings rose, floor upon floor, into the air. The advent of the skyscraper had made the need for appropriate regulations more and more apparent.

Regulations increased in number and scope during the early part of the twentieth century. Codes establishing standards of construction and mechanical and electrical installations were adopted to protect the public health and safety. Fireproof construction was required where congestion was most acute. Protection was assured for public rights-of-way.

Mixed land uses—the indiscriminate placement of stores and shops in residential areas—induced premature depreciation of land values and disruption of residential neighborhoods. The need to exercise some measure of public control over land use had become pressing.

Zoning Precedents

There was some precedent for zoning in Europe. When town walls in Germany were leveled in the nineteenth century, building regulations designated "belts" in which apartments and single houses could be built about the periphery of the ramparts. Protection from the encroachment of undesirable land uses had been attempted in America as well. Exclusive residential sections in some midwestern cities were planned. Access to homes in these areas was by way of private streets and guarded gates. Block ordinances were framed to restrict improvements to so-called high-class residences. In Boston in 1903 limits were set on building height: 125 feet in the central district and 80 feet elsewhere. In 1909 Los Angeles divided the business area into seven industrial districts; the remainder of the city was declared to be residential.

These cases were hardly more than experimental gestures, but the chaotic growth of cities made it imperative that positive steps be taken to bring some order into the urban pattern. It is a fortunate characteristic of human history that when leadership is needed there is usually someone willing and capable of assuming the responsibility. Such a man was Edward M. Bassett, a New York City attorney. To him goes credit for a public service on behalf of the entire urban population. He undertook a thorough investigation of the power of the people to regulate their own destiny and worked diligently to prepare a legal instrument whereby they could effectively exercise their power to control the use of land in the urban community.

Edward Bassett defined zoning as "the regulation by districts under the police power of the height, bulk, and use of buildings, the use of land, and the density of population." (*Police power* refers to the government's authority to legislate for the protection of the health, safety, and general welfare of citizens.) With this clear-cut purpose, the first comprehensive zoning ordinance in the United States was enacted by New York City in 1916. There is no better testimony to the remarkable thoroughness of Edward Bassett and his colleagues than the subsequent history of zoning in the courts. Challenged a number of times in later years, the principle was upheld in every case.

One of these is particularly significant. It confirmed the democratic foundation of zone planning, and established it as an instrument with which the people could attempt to order the destiny of their cities. In *Euclid v. Amber,* Associate Justice George Sutherland of the U.S. Supreme Court said:

> Until recently urban life was comparatively simple; but with the increase and concentration of population, problems have developed, and constantly are developing, which require additional restrictions in respect to the use and occupation of private lands in communities. Regulations, the wisdom, necessity, and validity of which, as applied to existing conditions, are so apparent that they are now uniformly sustained, a century ago, or even a half century ago, probably would have been rejected as arbitrary and oppressive.[1]

An instrument had been created to control the use of land in urban areas for the first time. It is a technique that protects the general welfare of the people by protecting that of each individual citizen.

Nothing in the nature of zoning confines it to urban development alone. It is essentially a planning device and as such can be applied in any scale and for any land area that requires public control over its use. It has been applied to counties in a manner similar to that of cities, and it has been adapted as a means to conserve natural resources. For example, in 1929 the state of Wisconsin empowered counties to establish districts comprising privately owned lands in which agriculture was excluded and forestry and recreational development encouraged for the public good.

---

1. *Village of Euclid, Ohio, v. Ambler Realty Company*, 272 U.S. 363 (November 22, 1926).

New York City. *New York illustrates the contrasts, conflicts, and chaos of modern commercial centers.*

Zoning is a vital part of the urban machinery, but it can fail through abuse, misuse, and rigid resistance to changes in the urban pattern essential to the general welfare.

Extension of Public Services

The Industrial Revolution changed the city into a metropolis. The urban population became the multitude, and the supply of basic human wants to this multitude required highly organized services. The need for some form of mass transportation via common carriers, building and maintenance of roads, adequate water supply, sewage disposal and drainage, sufficient communications capacity, power and light—all vastly expanded in scope. Their impact on the public health and safety in turn increased accordingly. Thus connected with the public interest, some of these private services were subject to public regulation; others were embraced in public ownership.

Public works to control or harness natural resources for the community at large were not new. We will recall the dikes, reservoirs, and irrigation projects along the Nile of ancient Egypt; the aqueducts, sewers, and roads built by the Romans as public projects. Royalty or the nobility took on this responsibility; it disappeared for a time during the age of feudalism but returned toward the end of the Middle Ages.

In the early history of this country many of the highways were private toll roads. They were later transferred to public ownership and control. The sewage system and drainage were and remained a public responsibility. Other public services, however, are owned and operated as private enterprises. Because of their impact upon the common welfare, their continuity and consistency are essential, and they enjoy a monopoly guaranteed by franchise. These, the public utilities, are subject to regulation by public authority.

The airlines, railroads, buses, and other common carriers; the telephone, telegraph, radio, and television are with some exceptions regulated public utilities. The same is true of electric power, illumination, and gas distribution. The supply of water is generally owned by the public, although there are exceptions.

The social control of utilities is an important factor in the future of urban development. The response of the courts is therefore pertinent to our understanding.

In 1876 Chief Justice of the U.S. Supreme Court Morrison Remick Waite set forth the theory of public interest in private property. The case was that of a grain operator who violated a local statute controlling the rates for storage. The court held that the enterprise was "affected with the public interest" because of public dependence on it and the consequent right of the public to exercise authority over its operations. Justice Waite stated:

> When, therefore, one devotes his property to a use in which the public has an interest, he, in effect, grants to the public an interest in that use, and must submit to be controlled by the public for the common good, to the extent of the interest he has thus created.[2]

Supreme Court Chief Justice William Howard Taft confirmed this position in a later case with the following opinion:

> In a sense, the public is concerned about all lawful business because it contributes to the prosperity and well-being of the people. The public may suffer from high prices or strikes in many trades, but the expression "clothed with the public interest" as applied to a business means more than that the public welfare is affected by the continuity or by the price at which a particular kind of business with a public interest, in the sense of Munn v. Illinois and other cases, must be such as to create a peculiarly close relation between the public and those engaged in it, and raise implications of an affirmative obligation on their part to be reasonable in dealing with the public.[3]

It will be observed that any enterprise engaging in public service assumes a dual obligation: first, to supply all the needs of the public implied by the nature of the service; second, to provide the services at a cost reflecting reasonable but not excessive profit. This status of a public utility—a public service for which it enjoys a monopoly—imposes obligations beyond the scope of the usual private enterprise. Public utilities became an integral part of city planning, and successful development of the city largely depends upon the effectiveness of their operations.

---

2. *Munn v. Illinois,* 94 U.S. 113 (1876).

3. *Charles Wolff Packing Company v. Court of Industrial Relations of the State of Kansas,* 262 U.S. 522 (1923).

CHAPTER 13

SEARCH FOR THE GOOD CITY

THE NEW UTPOIANS

THE SEARCH FOR A DEFINITION

The population of the world is exploding. The rising flood of urbanization is surging outward from the center and engulfing the surrounding countryside. Congestion festers within and eats about the edges. Communications are breaking down. Medical science sustains health and prolongs the lifespan. Famine and pestilence are no longer the levelers of excess population in most of the world. Nuclear war may be. If humans are to live on, the urban pattern they occupy will require major unraveling and reweaving. Much understanding will be required, and the nature of the metropolis will undergo severe examination.

People in all walks of life have raised their voices against the inequities, the ugliness, and the congestion of the city. John Ruskin and William Morris pleaded for craftsmanship, Charles Dickens portrayed the evils of the workhouses, Edward Bellamy in *Looking Backward* warned and predicted, Patrick Geddes in his *Outlook Tower* urged a broader vision, Karl Marx threatened, Robert Owen experimented, Ebenezer Howard reasoned, Jacob Riis exposed.

An early utopian expression, mentioned previously in the discussion of the Columbian Exposition of 1891, was the swan song of Victorian grandeur: "The City Beautiful." Absorbed in the monumental splendor of avenue and plaza, Daniel Burnham reflected the fading era with his famous words:

> *Make no little plans:* they have no magic to stir men's blood and probably will not be realized. Make big plans; aim high in hope and work, remembering that a noble, logical diagram once recorded will never die, but long after we are gone will be a

living thing, asserting itself with ever-growing insistency. Remember that our sons and grandsons are going to do things that would stagger us. Let your watchword be order and your beacon beauty.[1]

This, however, was not typical. Many other social critics turned the light of their analysis on the city, tested the forces of disintegration in the laboratories of their keen minds, and some dared to describe cities people could build when they acquired the will.

Nor were they all cries in the wilderness. Housing, the most appalling testimony to neglect in the urban scene, received attention. Planning agencies were formed; zoning and building laws were enacted. But these efforts remained a step behind the improvement of which society was actually capable; they never quite caught up with technological and scientific progress. The overgrown metropolis fed on its inhabitants, gnawing at the physical, mental, and spiritual fabric of the people. No inhabitant could escape the heavy weight of urban living, regardless of fortune or social status.

The insidious course of urban disintegration had forced an examination of the basic nature of the urban structure, and it was to this task that the new utopians set themselves.

THE SEARCH FOR SPACE

The driving urge has been for release from the cruel congestion that so degrades the individual, a search for space in which individuals may recapture their identity. This quest lends unity to otherwise apparently divergent views of future urban structure.

The persistent expansion about the periphery of the great cities has removed the countryside farther and farther from the urban population. Abandoning the concentric form of the crowded city, in 1882 the Spaniard Soria y Mata propounded the theory of the linear city—*la cuidad linear*. He sought to expand the city along the spine of communication—the highway. Housing and industry stretched along the roadway would thus border a continuous artery that linked existing cities. Raymond Unwin, an English housing pioneer, espoused the cause of satellite communities about the periphery of the city, an idea clearly in the tradition of the garden city. Each community would contain 12,000 to 18,000 people and be small enough to require no vehicular transport within it.

The linear city uses the countryside to contain urbanization along the highway. The garden city and satellite town rely on their relatively small size to maintain a balance between urban development and surrounding open space. Integrating these elements, in 1917 Tony Garnier presented his plans for *la cité industrielle,* the industrial city. His inspiring idea separated the civic center and residential sections from the factory district with a broad buffer zone, a greenbelt, and the highway and railroad traversed this broad space.

In the latter half of the twentieth century many opportunists have become articulate and persuasive. Congestion has inspired a variety of panaceas and some fantastic proposals have been suggested by otherwise practical people. Among the most popular were the concept of the double- and triple-decked street and the doubling up of families in order to provide shelter for economically displaced

1. Quoted in Charles Moore, *Daniel Burnham: Architect, Planner of Cities* (Boston, 1921).

persons. High land cost was so firmly rooted in the urban state of mind that its effect was accepted as the normal course of "land economics." Nevertheless the traffic problem had to be solved, and piling layers of street on each other and increasing density all had the appearance of plausibility. As the roofs of skyscrapers moved upward so did proposals for multiple-level streets.

The idea of double-decked streets stemmed from the New York World's Fair of 1939, where the dramatic proposals by Norman Bel Geddes illustrated the separation of the automobile way and the pedestrian way. These ideas have been adopted in limited form in many cities, with the raised pedestrian "flyway." Urban freeways have been double decked where rights of way were limited, as along the East River in New York and the Alaska Skyway in Seattle.

The doubling up of families, either in individual homes or in backyard garages, has returned to the American scene as the economic plight of elderly people has caused hardships for many. The reduction of lot sizes and the increase in urban densities during the past few years are facts of life in many cities, even those that have had a history of low-density development.

Beneath, on the surface of the earth, darkness pervaded the human environment. A growing apprehension of the light gripped the people. Humankind was building so broad and so high that the more there was light the deeper were the shadows.

The metropolis lay heavily on its inhabitants. The problem of the underprivileged increased, social welfare expanded, and more and more of the tax income was directed to charity, until the advent of "Reaganomics."

The great industrialist Henry Ford said what was in the minds of many people: "Nothing will finally work more effectively to undo the fateful grip which the city has taken upon the people than the destruction of the fictitious land values which the city traditions have set up and maintained."[2] It is rather vexing that he did not suggest how those "fictitious land values" might be "destroyed," but he did point out a major obstacle to the improvement of the urban environment.

All who have protested the congestion and ugliness of the city reveal the anachronism of our industrial age—the inability of society to muster the forces of technological progress in the cause of the improvement and organization of the urban environment. Theories conflict and opinions vary. It is inevitable, and it reflects the enigma of the age. The tremendous advance of science and invention thrusts forward the horns of a dilemma and civilization is perched upon them.

Congestion in the city is not new. It has occurred in all civilizations from the beginning of urbanized existence. The gregarious instincts of individuals are satisfied by the agglomeration of people. Crowds have a natural attraction. The problem of density does not turn about this issue; it hinges on the necessity to maintain a balance between enclosed and open space to accommodate the functions of both.

The drama of the city by day and by night will be enhanced when this balance is achieved. There will be room for people to circulate with convenience and plea-

2. From "Mr. Ford's Page," *The Dearborn Independent*, Dearborn, Michigan, 1922.

sure. The ground level will not be reserved solely as conduits for moving vehicles or storage places for them. The spectacle of the city will be a visual experience from all about—from below as well as from above—when interior and exterior space are in balance.

In 1922 in Paris, the architect Le Corbusier displayed his vision of La Ville Contemporaine. His utopian scheme was a city of magnificent skyscraper towers surrounded by a broad and sweeping open space. The city was a huge park. Sixty-story office buildings accommodating 1,200 people per acre and covering only 5 percent of the ground area were grouped in the heart of the city. The transportation center, railway and airfield, was the hub. Surrounding the skyscrapers was the apartment district, eight-story buildings arranged in zigzag rows with broad open spaces about them, the density of the population 120 persons per acre. Lying about the outskirts were the *cité jardins,* the garden cities of single houses. The city was designed for a population of 3 million.

The beautifully delineated plans and succinct reasoning with which they were described created a sensation, and in 1925 Le Corbusier adapted his Ville Contemporaine to the Plan Voisin for the center of Paris. The contrast with the old city was dramatic, and the architect hammered at his theme, pointing a finger of scorn at the undesirable population density in Paris: an average of 146 persons per acre, and 213 persons in the overcrowded sections.

Le Corbusier followed this conception with his Ville Radieuse, the Radiant City, one of continuous rows of tall buildings woven in zigzag form across landscaped space. A prolific writer and indefatigable reformist, he prepared his visionary schemes for Algiers, Nemours, Antwerp, and Stockholm. The conception and construction of Brasilia were based on his theories. He was enamored of the skyscrapers of America and the energy of the industrial processes. His shock value was tremendous, and those who waved aside his proposals as another wild dream were themselves quite blind to the wilderness that had overtaken the city in which they themselves were trapped.

Le Corbusier

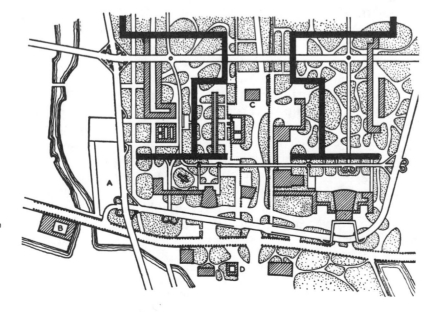

A Railroad Station

B City Hall

C Concert Hall

D Palace

La Ville Radieuse by Le Corbusier. *The plan submitted in the international competition of 1933 for the replanning of Nedre Normalm in Stockholm was an adaptation of Le Corbusier's scheme for continuous staggered rows of high buildings (shown in black) set on piers with broad open space. The plan also makes a distinction between the various types of roadways: the encircling freeway raised above the ground level, the secondary trafficways uninterrupted by the building forms, and the informal system of local traffic and pedestrian ways that likewise circle beneath the buildings, which are open at the ground level. The existing or new proposed low buildings (cross-hatched) are provided settings within landscaped open space.*

THE SEARCH FOR FORM

A brutal quality of the great city is the absence of human scale. The sense of community is obscured by the common grayness of the industrial metropolis. Despite the durability of great cities, they are caving in beneath the mammoth weight piled up at the center. As they spiral upward and outward, the people are forsaking the centers for the suburbs. Satellite bedroom communities all over the Western world cling to the economic lifeline of the existing city, and regions of greatest urban settlement have actually become continuous linear cities. But expanding suburbanization is exhausting the space it was intended to preserve and overextending the cities' public facilities and lines of communication.

Movement to the suburbs is essentially motivated by the search for a more desirable environment. The basic yearning for harmony between the individual and community scale is no less reflected in the suburban sprawl about great cities than in the garden city, the greenbelt, the towers of Le Corbusier, or the British New Towns. The contrast between worn-out, secondhand residential districts and neighborhoods in new subdivisions; between shopping centers and stores without parking on traffic-ridden streets; or the advantages of an industrial park over the disorderly factory district: all suggest the same aspirations that appear in the models of the new utopians. The search is for an organic structure for the city of the industrial and scientific age in which we are destined to live. As we move toward an integration of urban components, the form of a regional city begins to emerge.

The International Congress of Modern Architects (CIAM) posited four basic elements of urban biology: (1) sun, (2) space, (3) vegetation, (4) steel and concrete. Le Corbusier, who assumed a leading role in CIAM, organized the Assembly of Constructors for an Architectural Renovation (ASCORAL) and extended the investigation into the character of the city.

ASCORAL set forth the "Three Human Establishments": the farming unit, the radioconcentric city, and the linear industrial city. The farming unit is the space for agriculture and the villages that serve it; the radioconcentric city is exemplified by the existing urban area from which the theory of concentration evolved. The third human establishment—the linear industrial city—is derived from the ideas of earlier utopians, but it is a new element in Le Corbusier's theories. Leaving the "evils of the sprawling town," the ASCORAL studies move into the country. New industrial communities are placed at intervals along the main arteries of transportation—water, rail, and highway—that connect the existing cities; the latter remain as administrative, commercial, and cultural centers. Factories, called "green" factories because of their proximity to landscaped areas, are placed along the main transportation routes, separated from the residential section by the auto highway and green strips. The residential area includes the horizontal garden town of single houses and a vertical apartment building with its complement of communal facilities. Sports, entertainment, shopping, and office facilities are distributed in this district, and all the facilities of the community are placed within ample open space enhanced with natural verdure.[3]

Thus the image of a regional city unfolds and, with it, the conventions that dominate today's concepts of urban zoning practices are exposed as the stultifying elements they are.

---

3. Les Trois Etablissements Humains, ASCORAL (Paris, Denoel, 1945).

Implicit in the planning postulates of the new utopians is the assumption that land zoned for specific uses will be reserved for those uses. This is presumably the reason for planning, and it is apparent that the effective reorganization of the urban structure depends on acceptance of this assumption. Our present practice of zoning, however, runs quite counter to this; any use is permitted in an industrial zone, while only industry is excluded from a commercial zone and all types of residential uses are permitted therein. As a consequence the only zone actually reserved for its planned use is the single-family district (a premise disputed in the 1980s). Indiscriminate mixture of land uses is a contradiction, inconsistent with the meaning of planning. The means by which it may be corrected are essential to the effective relationships among land uses in the future. The distinction between present trends and the theories of the new utopians would appear less sharp if the chaotic mingling of incompatible uses were replaced by the principle that urban land uses shall conform to the classifications for which they are planned and zoned. This is a rather disarming thesis, since it would reveal excessive overzoning and materially alter prevailing attitudes toward zoned uses for which there is inadequate economic support.

Zoning

As the future decentralized city form emerges, some land will necessarily be withdrawn from intense use, while the intensity of use for other land will increase. The changes should result from planning decisions rather than fortuitous speculation. Under the system of zoning for public control of land use, the potential capacity of land is thereby a function of community determination. Land value thus created by the community should be retained by the community; by the same token, losses in value imposed by the community should be compensated by the community.[4]

THE DENSITY EQUATION

Planned mixture of residential and commercial land uses in a French suburb.

---

4. See the discussion of compensation and betterment in chapter 38.

Taxation based on the densities and intensities of the uses permitted by zoning, the sliding scale ascending from low to high, might provide for more careful zoning and the better use of critical land in both urban and rural areas. It certainly would have an impact on the premature zoning of land with only a long-range speculative prospect and no development plans or infrastructure to serve existing proposals.

The extreme population density to which we have become accustomed is due for critical review. The density equation is compounded by the introduction of factors that serve the mental and spiritual needs of people, the environmental features that enrich the process of living. Such an environment, to be sure, should be the overriding aim of planning in an advanced civilization, but the practical issues compel attention to the density equation.

The balance between floor space occupied by people and the ground space for circulation is among these practical factors. Many cities in the industrial nations must accommodate the transportation vehicles on the streets and provide space for their storage. It might be possible to so regiment people's lives that the freedom of movement afforded by modern motor vehicles could be rigidly curtailed, but the means for such control would hardly be consistent with the doctrine of liberty upon which the West's institutions are founded. The density equation must therefore embrace three practical elements: population in buildings, space for the movement of vehicles on streets, and parking space for the vehicles. A workable urban pattern requires a balance among these elements.

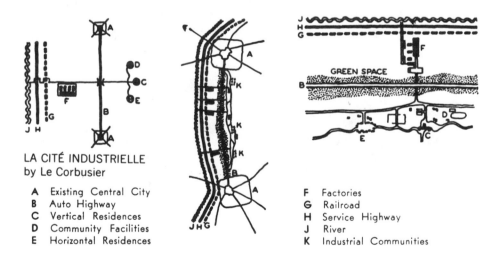

LA CITÉ INDUSTRIELLE
by Le Corbusier

A Existing Central City	**F** Factories
B Auto Highway	**G** Railroad
C Vertical Residences	**H** Service Highway
D Community Facilities	**J** River
E Horizontal Residences	**K** Industrial Communities

La Cité Industrielle by Le Corbusier. *In 1945, under the leadership of Le Corbusier, ASCORAL shifted attention from the existing urban center to a consideration of the basic organization of urban settlement in this industrial age. The group presented a fusion between the concentric form of the garden city and the ribbon form of the linear city. The principal forms of circulation—water, rail, air, and highway—became the arteries along which self-contained industrial cities were distributed. Although it is assumed that open space surrounding these industrial clusters would be maintained, the greenbelt is here used as a buffer between the various and separate land uses: housing, highway, and factories.*

The basic organization is shown in the left-hand sketch, the passenger highway connecting the great existing cities; between it and the river, rail line, and service highway are the groups of "green factories," located in landscaped areas. Opposite are the housing areas, which contain the administrative, shopping, sports, and educational facilities for the immediate population. The existing metropolis remains the principal administrative, commercial, and cultural center.

The sketch at the center indicates the distribution of these industrial "cities" between the great cities, and the one on the right indicates the separation of through traffic and local traffic. Le Corbusier retains the tall building—the vertical residence—for apartments near the civic center and places the community of single-family homes away from this center to permit greater freedom for families.

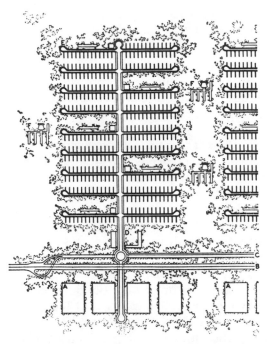

A Industry
B Main Highway
C Local Highway
D Commercial Area
E Residential Area
F Schools in Park Area

Urban reorganization. *Searching for an urban form appropriate to the metropolis of the industrial age, the new utopians have produced some principles that may guide a reorganization of the city of tomorrow. These principles merge the common characteristics of the linear and concentric city forms; they accept the physical properties of the neighborhood unit in favor of the basic needs of the family and regain the prospect for identity of the individual parts of the great city now lost within the dreary grayness of the present metropolis. Because the city form must change if it is to survive, and because it must survive as an integral element of the industrial age, the proposals of the new utopians are essential ingredients of urban thought and action.*

Relationship of residential areas to light industrial and commercial areas, as proposed by Ludwig Hilberseimer.

Human beings have demonstrated a consummate ability to build tremendous structures. The construction of a skyscraper is a remarkable feat, but the high-rise has struck a popular chord by default rather than by design. It is presumed to compensate for high land cost and thus maintain a semblance of economic balance. In reality it induces ever-mounting land prices. Every urban dweller is familiar with the consequence: intolerable congestion.

The attraction of the skyscraper is undeniable. The drama has been eloquently expressed by Le Corbusier. With boundless enthusiasm for the ingenuity, the daring, and the skill of those who made the tall building possible, he expresses a desire for the machine, conditioned air, pushbuttons, and swift elevators that is like a romance with science. Dreaming of his future city from within the medieval context of the European city, he sees the

> tonic spectacle, stimulating, cheering, radiant, which from each office appears through the transparent glass walls leading into space. Space! That response to the aspiration of the human being, that relaxation for breathing and for the beating heart, that outpouring of self in looking far, from a height, over a vast, infinite, unlimited expanse. Every bit of sun and fresh, pure air furnished mechanically. Do you try to maintain the fraud of hypocritical affirmations, to throw discredit on these radiant facts, to argue, to demand the "good old window," open on the stenches of the city and street, the noise, air currents, and the company of flies and mosquitoes? For thirty years I have known the offices of Paris: conversations cut to pieces by the uproar, suffocating atmosphere, the view broken thirty feet away by the wall of houses, dark corners, half-light, etc. . . . Imposters should no longer

deny the gains of our period and by their fright prevent changing from one thing to another, keeping the city or cities in general from going their joyously destined way.[5]

The towers of Manhattan and the gridiron plan are straight and clear to the European eye, the hygiene of plumbing so inviting, the illuminated brilliance by night so thrilling. It is a fascination not reserved to Europeans alone; Americans find it appealing too. Le Corbusier argues concentration versus congestion. He demonstrates that his city will concentrate the people, conserve the daily hours they consume in horizontal travel, and direct this time into productive effort and leisure. He contends that the American skyscraper is too small and proposes a residential population of 6 million on Manhattan, with a density of 400 persons per acre and 88 percent of the ground left free and open. In his City of Tomorrow, the density is 1,200 per acre in 60-story office towers with 95 percent of the land in open space, a "green" city. The concept is magnificent, but it reflects the deception of high buildings, high density, and the actual use of this "open" space.

Structures permitting such densities are not unusual. Several times the density proposed by Le Corbusier is found in the huge apartment buildings of America. The density in his proposed office towers is less than half that of Radio City, and the Empire State Building can accommodate nearly 10,000 people per acre. Concentration is an accomplished fact in the cities of America. The World Trade Center in lower Manhattan exceeds these intensities of use, here presumably compensated by the open space of the adjacent Hudson River. The drama of the high-rise building is heightened by the space about it and the prospect it offers for trees and landscaped gardens. Such space, in which the tensions of the day may be dispelled, has strong appeal in contrast to the cluttered surroundings of the congested city.

But here enters the delusion of high density and open space. When the automobile is reckoned with, a site housing 400 persons per acre becomes not a lovely garden but a parking lot. And the open space for an office building with a density of 1,200 per acre would be a roof garden atop a three- or four-story garage. The balance of the "open" space is in the streets that carry the cars into and out of these storage places. The "green" space, to which we aspire and that offers much promise, actually becomes a pavement for the vehicles of transportation. Complicating the situation further is that preservation of the air space above the ground could be assured only by restricting all buildings to high-rise; low buildings with high density would continue to cover the ground as it is now covered.

The desirability of low density for a residential environment is obvious; it has been demonstrated in all places and for all people on the face of the earth. Low density does not forestall blight, but with the exception of apartment developments with commodious space and enriched facilities, high density has induced blight. A protest against the density of population that our gigantic buildings can accommodate does not deprecate the ingenuity of the builders, but some questions require deliberation and answer if concentration is to be seen as an organic necessity of the future metropolis, among them, is every individual destined to live in an apartment cubicle in a high-rise building?

The city performs a far greater variety of services today than ever before. Its economic theory and practice are more complex. Yet the same forces that have

---

5. Le Corbusier, *When The Cathedrals Were White* (New York, Reynal and Hitchcock, 1947).

made this so are those that now render congestion unnecessary. Science, commerce, and industry have intensified the functions of the city. They have also created the instruments to neutralize its effect. The heavy concentration of people is no longer necessary for the conduct of business or for convenient and comfortable living. Methods of transportation, power, and communications invalidate the crowded concentration we unwittingly accept as a necessary evil of urban existence. Crowding of people and buildings is a negation of every contemporary means of communication and transportation at our command. Congestion denies them the chance to serve to their full capacity.

There is stimulation in great distances seen from the skyscraper. Conditioned air has its advantages. The elevator rising a thousand feet a minute offers rapid vertical transit. But do these render the human desire for a house on its land a phenomenon or a whim? Horizontal space means much to the human being. Contact with the earth is not a choice reserved to the agrarian, the tiller of the soil, alone. There is a sense of freedom, human freedom, in traversing the space of the earth under one's own power—on foot. There is a healthy sensation when interior and exterior space merge into unity, with no more visual separation than a crystal sheet of glass. There is mental freedom and a quiet repose in horizontal space.

That the "economy" of ownership is often a fiction or that people are frequently tenants does not alter the essential desire for horizontal living space. This is not a question of politics, economics, or social reform. It is a matter of human aims, aspirations, desires, and the mental repose in physical reality. It is not a theory of aesthetics, nor is it romantic nonsense that people desire a home and garden. It is not enough to substitute air-conditioned cells in multistory buildings simply because we have the technical know-how to create them.

It is the fundamental desires that beat in the human breast that must shape the city. The skyscraper holds its head aloft with an air of plausibility; it can absorb high land cost and save utilities and transportation time. But it also can create congestion and high land values that nullify its advantages and remove all choice for another form of habitation from the hope of the urban dweller. If we are concerned with economy, it is not the skyscraper that produces it; the skyscraper is not built because it is economical—it is not so. It is built because the cost of land is excessive, and continuing this process without restraint only adds fuel to the flames of urban congestion, blight, and disintegration.

It is significant that whatever the direction taken in the search for a new urban form and however persistent the trend of decentralization, the idea of the city is not forsaken. The complex and diverse functions are reshaped, regrouped, reorganized, but the constituent elements of the city are not abandoned. The commerce, the industry, the cultural institutions on which our society depends for its spiritual and material enrichment are retained. That the inherent advantages of the city have been abused, misused, exploited, or simply allowed to lie dormant does not deny their necessity.

There is a wavering line of continuity springing from the dismal factory town of the nineteenth century through the garden city and the New Towns, the urban "biology" of ASCORAL, and the reorganization of industrial community clusters in the future regional city. The line moves at a tangent to the city we know today, but there is a strong affinity with the decentralization and sprawling

ON COMMON GROUND

suburbs that are drawing the life-blood from the overgrown, overzoned, and congested metropolis. A comparable liberation of space appears in the greenbelt of the New Towns and the London plan by Abercrombie, Frank Lloyd Wright's Broadacre City, and Le Corbusier's towers in green space. It is likewise present in the standards for planned variety in zoning and modern subdivision practice.

A human scale is recovered in the ideas of the new utopians for a planned integration of land uses. The assumption that the metropolis should absorb an unlimited population is challenged by them, and density standards are related to the organic functions of the city. The natural forces operating the great city are forcing the reevaluation of form and structure, a development the new utopias anticipated. Advances in transportation and communication can release us from the previously inexorable destiny of large cities. We can have tall and low buildings, open space, and convenient communication, as well as the amenities consistent with good living. All of this will take place when the density equation and the relation between planning and zoning for land use are taken into account.

In the Orient, as a result of the age of the cities, the design of the buildings, and the life-styles of the people, we find housing densities that have few parallels to those in the United States and Canada. Hong Kong since the 1960s has increased the number of square feet per person from 35 to 50. In China, the current average living space per person is 22 square feet. This density is equivalent to 18 persons in the typical American two-car garage. The plan is to increase the space per person to 54 square feet by 1985, thus allowing only about 7 persons per "garage." This "living space" would not include kitchen or toilet facilities.

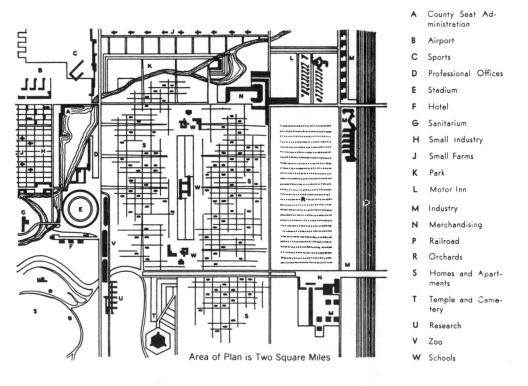

A	County Seat Administration
B	Airport
C	Sports
D	Professional Offices
E	Stadium
F	Hotel
G	Sanitarium
H	Small Industry
J	Small Farms
K	Park
L	Motor Inn
M	Industry
N	Merchandising
P	Railroad
R	Orchards
S	Homes and Apartments
T	Temple and Cemetery
U	Research
V	Zoo
W	Schools

Area of Plan is Two Square Miles

Broadacres by Frank Lloyd Wright. *Essentially a linear city form, Frank Lloyd Wright's proposal distributes industry, commerce, housing, social facilities, and agriculture along the railroad artery and has access to highways. The unit dominating this plan is the minimum one acre of land for each family rather than the neighborhood unit, although the various neighborhood facilities are provided.*

With the cost of land and housing in many of the Western nations soaring out of sight because of the inflation and speculation of the late 1970s and 1980s, the search for an answer to the demand for shelter has initiated the drive to reduce the size of lots and the living space in homes. In the name of providing affordable housing for the people, the theme "smaller is better" is the slogan for the future. Perhaps there will soon be a renewal of the concept that there is something to be gained from overcrowding. No one knows what the consequences of this reversal in direction will be.

As the decade of the 1990s starts we find the emphasis on higher urban center densities stressed in the terms of the environmentalists, using their slogan "STOP SPRAWL; SAVE OUR AGRICULTURE." However, the attraction of less expensive land in the "boondocks" still lures the developers into the open spaces. Seldom do we find the counterdrive for the "good city": the humanistic environment where people feel free to associate with their neighbors and offer the friendship that is inherent in neighborliness. Recently the small low-density coastal city of San Luis Obispo was recognized nationally as a "good city" for the quality of living it offers and the friendliness of its people.

SMALLER IS BETTER?

CHAPTER 14

BETTERMENT OF LIVING CONDITIONS

The depths to which urban communities sank in the nineteenth century (and in which many still remain) is a shameful blot on the world scene. Constructing tenements solely to gouge rents became a profitable enterprise. Excessive building coverage of the land and the crowding of dwellings within the buildings brought about an almost unbelievable population congestion. The population density in London was 265 persons per acre in 1870. In New York City, which then had only one-third London's population, it was 23 percent higher—326 persons per acre.[1]

Standards of land use were lax. The first law to regulate tenement building was passed in New York in 1867, but only faint improvements were forced upon speculators. Planning persisted at a deplorably low level; the "railroad apartment" was typical of the early tenements, and it had no more evil rival in the world. The usual lot was 25 feet wide, with a depth of 100 feet. The building covered as much as 90 percent of the area. The small space remaining at the rear was used for privies, no sanitation being provided within the building. The tenements were five or six stories high, with four apartments on each floor. Only one room in each dwelling enjoyed light and air; all other rooms had no exterior exposure.

---

1. *American Cyclopedia*, 1875, Vol. XII, p. 382.

The unbearable living conditions imposed on the poor did not go unnoticed. A competition was sponsored in 1879 by the *Plumber and Sanitary Engineer* for a "model" tenement. The result was touched with irony. The winning plan by the architect James E. Ware was the prototype of the later accursed "dumbbell" plan, which covered 85 percent of the lot and resorted to a narrow interior light shaft along the property lines. Despite subsequent legislation outlawing both dumbbell and railroad buildings, innumerable remained to afflict the city of New York for several decades of the twentieth century.

THE UTOPIANS

The depressed condition of housing for the poor impressed some nineteenth-century industrial leaders, who recognized that their present privileged state was connected with the masses of workers on whom they directly and indirectly depended; they sensed the problems the deplorable conditions of the poor presented to the future of the industrial economy. As early as 1797 the Society for Bettering the Conditions of the Poor was formed in England, and efforts to relieve the burdens of the working classes pierced the haze all through the nineteenth century. The first half of the century was marked by periodic protests against the "sordidness, filth, and squalor, embroidered with patches of pompous and vulgar hideousness." A number of utopian communities were proposed. One such plan was put forth by Robert Owen.

Owen was the proprietor of a cotton mill at New Lanark in Manchester, England, where he had successfully introduced reforms in the working conditions, hours, and wages for operatives in his plant. Owen saw beyond even these reforms. In 1816 he set forth an unusual plan for a cooperative community that combined industry and agriculture. It was designed to hold about 1,200 people.

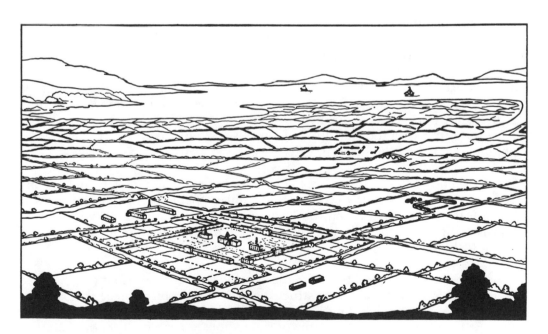

Robert Owen's proposed self-supporting industrial town. *Robert Owen was an English industrialist moved by the deplorable conditions of the ill-housed industrial workers, made worse by increasing unemployment. In 1816 he proposed a plan for a community that, among other things, he believed could become self-supporting and reduce the heavy cost of public relief. Owen further proposed that similar communities be established at appropriate intervals in the countryside. Communal buildings for each were situated in the center of a broad common. About the common were rows of dwellings, and surrounding the dwellings were large gardens. The main road encircled the entire compound, and the factories and workshops were located along the outside boundary of the community. Designed for about 1,200 people, each community was surrounded by an agricultural area of between 1,000 and 1,500 acres to supplement industrial employment.*

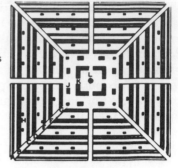

A 1000 houses 20 feet wide   G 120 houses 54 feet wide

B Arcade for workshops   H Schools, baths, dining halls

C 560 houses 28 feet wide   J Public buildings, churches

D Retail shops   K 24 mansions 80 feet wide

E 296 houses 38 feet wide   L Central square

F Winter promenade arcade

J. S. Buckingham's plan of a model town for an associated temperance community of about 10,000 inhabitants. *Proposed in 1849 by the architect J. S. Buckingham, this utopian plan specified a multitude of features within the community. Buckingham recommended that industries using steam engines be situated at least one-half mile from the town. He also suggested that sites be reserved for "suburban villas" in the agricultural land surrounding the town.*

Dwellings were grouped about a large open space in which communal buildings were located. Surrounding the dwellings area were large gardens. This entire area in turn was encircled by a main roadway. On one side of the compound were factories and workshops. Beyond, on all sides, was the agricultural belt, to range in size from 1,000 to 1,500 acres. Owen intended his plan for the use of the unemployed; he assumed that the community would become self-supporting and thereby reduce the heavy cost of public relief.

Another utopian, the English architect J. S. Buckingham, in 1849 published a treatise entitled "National Evils and Practical Remedies," in which he described his plan for a model town for an "Associated Temperance Community of About 10,000 inhabitants." Buckingham adhered to the contemporary distinctions of class. He placed the finer houses near the center of his town and the humbler dwellings and workshops of the working class about the periphery.

Some Genuine Changes

Most utopian proposals were not executed, but they focused attention upon the growing evils of the urban environment. In 1844 the Rochdale Pioneers, a group of English flannel weavers, formed the first consumers' cooperative, and in England the same year the first Royal Commission on Health and Housing was appointed. The first Public Health Act was passed in 1848.

By the middle of the century severe epidemics were spreading over England and the Continent. The wealthy classes could insulate themselves from many undesirable features of urban living, but they were not immune to disease. Spurred by alarm, the rulers of England, France, and Germany caused some model dwellings to be built.

These projects represented two extremes. In the congested urban areas, six- and seven-story tenements were constructed with little improvement in plan and design over previous buildings; they could only decay into more slums with time. At the other extreme, suburbs of single houses were built on the outskirts of the cities. The intention was to encourage home ownership. But the possibility of selling these dwellings at handsome profits removed them from the income group most in need of improved housing. Too expensive for the vast number of low-paid workers, they became no more than middle-class suburbs. There were no solutions in these spurts of activity.

Recognizing the desirability of good housing for their workers and stimulated by the unexecuted proposals of the utopians, industrialists undertook to build model communities. One of the earliest of these towns was Bessbrook, built in 1846 for workers in the linen mills near Newry, Ireland. In 1852 Sir Titus Salt built Saltaire near Bradford, England, for some 3,000 workers in his textile mill. Extensive community facilities were introduced in this development. In 1865 the Krupp family began the first of several model villages in Essen, Germany, for workers in their munitions and iron factories.

George Cadbury, the English chocolate manufacturer, moved his plant from Birmingham to a rural site and began the town of Bourneville in 1879. Originally a company town, this community became an autonomous village in about 1900. Today it contains some 2,000 dwellings. In France, another chocolate manufacturer, M. Menier, built a workers' colony at Noisel-sur-Seine near Paris in 1874. Also in France, similar communities were built by the Anzin Mining company for their workers at Valenciennes, and by M. Schneider et Cie. for the workers at their Creusot Steel Mills near Fontainebleau. Another was developed by the Crespi Cotton Mills near Capriate, Italy, and in 1883 the Van Marken Yeast and Spirit Works put up Agneta Park near Delft, Holland.

In 1886, Lever Brothers, the famous soap manufacturers, built Port Sunlight near Liverpool. Large blocks of the 550-acre site were used as interior gardens and play areas, a forerunner of future planning. Another project foreshadowing subsequent developments was Creswell, built by Percy Houfton in 1895 for his Bolsover Colliery. The community is a hexagon in form, the houses facing inward on the gardens. The cocoa manufacturer Sir Joseph Roundtree commissioned Barry Parker and Raymond Unwin, architects prominent in the emerging new direction of town planning, to build Earswick near York in 1905. This, like Bourneville, was made a community trust.

Some American industrialists sought to improve housing for their workers as well. Among the best known of the community projects is Pullman, Illinois, which was built in 1881 as a permanent town in conjunction with the plant for the manufacture of Pullman sleeping cars.

The model towns of the industrialists were so few that they contributed little to the solution of the real problem of housing in the factory centers. They were

Port Sunlight, England. *Model town by William Hesketh Lever, 1886. The community was the original site of Lever Brothers, Ltd., the soap manufacturers.*

flavored with a paternalism similar to that of the "model" dwellings built by the European rulers at an earlier date. They did demonstrate some planning arrangements from which later communities were to profit, but their rarity emphasized the disparity between the living standards possible for some in the industrial era and the low level to which housing for most had degenerated.

There can be no claim to city planning during this era. The fervor for industrial expansion had blotted out the original plans for cities in America, and only remnants can now be seen. Ambitious proposals remained as diagrams of what might have been. Even the distinction between major and minor arteries established in the early plans, for example, was abandoned in favor of a standard street width of 66 feet.

The gridiron plan of New York City was the early beginning of a sterile urban character that eventually characterized the entire country. The movement westward gripped the early settlers, and with them soon strode the land surveyors. By the time this great trek had moved across the United States the occupied areas of the vast land had been mapped out in a gargantuan gridiron of mile-square sections. The pattern of land division was thoroughly bound in a legal straitjacket of readily recorded deeds. Natural features—rivers, mountains, and valleys—were ignored. Henceforth the grid became the basic pattern of farms, villages, towns, cities, and counties. Desirability of land was measured by its prospects for quick and profitable turnover. Subdivision practices were conveniently designed to enhance these prospects, and the pattern of the future development of cities was fairly sealed in this package of the gridiron plan.

IMPROVEMENT ON THE HORIZON

As the nineteenth century wore on, the British and European governments assumed more and more responsibility for the improvement of the city. Legislation was enacted in Holland to provide for the loan of public funds to "public utility societies" that were engaged in housing, and a similar program began in Stockholm, Sweden, in 1879. The British Housing law of 1890 empowered state and local authorities to condemn land and build dwellings to rent to the working classes. In response to the growing strength of the trade union movement in Germany an 1889 law granted privileges to cooperative housing developments, using funds derived from social insurance inaugurated by Bismarck.

Various measures like these set the stage for the more enlightened era of the next century. Social activism on behalf of decent housing also began and was to extend into the twentieth century as well. Octavia Hill launched her crusade for the underprivileged in London in the late 1800s—a practical program based on the idea that good and consistent management could improve living conditions even in existing tenements.

In the United States, stirred by the gallant efforts of such crusaders as Jacob Riis, a growing protest developed against the congested tenements of the cities. The hideous railroad and dumbbell tenements on 25-foot lots had spread over New York City, but there were feeble signs of reform. As early as 1871 the Boston Co-operative Company began a modest program of rental housing for city workers, and other model dwellings were attempted.

In 1894 the publication of plans for tenements by the architect Ernest Flagg aroused wide interest. These plans provided broader light courts than the standard practice, reduced the length of interior corridors, and improved the exposure of the rooms. A competition for better housing plans was held by the Improved Housing Council in 1896. Flagg won, with a plan requiring a lot 50 feet wide and a structure that accommodated the same number of apartments per floor as the dumbbell plan. The rooms in each apartment were larger, however, and their daylight exposure and arrangement improved.

With this impetus to improve low-cost housing, the Tenements House Committee of the Charity Organization Society conducted a competition in 1899. Among the design requirements were a maximum lot coverage of 70 percent, large light courts, and a given minimum volume of air per occupant within the dwelling. The winning design was submitted by R. Thomas Short.

The 1899 competition spurred renewed efforts for reform and culminated in the passage of the Tenement House Act of 1901, commonly known as the "New Law," in New York City. The act used the standards set in the competition and established the 50-foot lot as subdivision practice.

Progress became more visible as the twentieth century opened. Several organizations formed with the purpose of building better housing for the low-income worker. One of the most notable was the City and Suburban Homes Company of New York. Starting business in 1896 and assisted by Ernest Flagg, it built some 3,500 apartments units. The company's stated purpose is worthy of note: "to offer to capital a safe and permanent investment and at the same time to supply wage earners improved homes at current prices."

In 1879 the Washington Sanitary Improvement Company was established in Washington, D.C., followed by the Washington Sanitary Housing Company. These two organizations built nearly 1,000 apartments for rental to low-income families in the capital city.

The factory system of the Industrial Revolution attracted more and more people to the urban centers. England's rural areas decreased in population from 10,000,000 in 1821 to 9,500,000 in 1936, but cities gained from 4,000,000 to 37,000,000 in the same period. Further changes have occurred since 1936 as rural land has become urbanized. Germany's rural population dropped from 23,000,000 in 1821 to 19,000,000 in 1936, and urban population increased from 2,000,000 to 48,000,000. Between 1800 and 1900 urban population in Europe grew between 300 and 400 percent. At the beginning of the nineteenth century, London had a population of 1,000,000; at the end of the twentieth century it was 9,070,000. During the same period Paris grew from 700,000 to 8,709,000, and Berlin from 172,000 to 4,000,000. The industrial metropolis and congestion became synonymous.

THE MOVEMENT TO THE CITIES

The population of the United States was largely agrarian at the beginning of the nineteenth century. Only about 5 percent of the people lived in towns, and these were small communities. In 1790 there were only two cities with a population as large as 25,000. The inauguration of regular steamship service between Europe and America in 1840 helped to feed the factory system with immigrants seeking the freedom of this land. By the middle of the century 20 percent of the total population lived in cities. From that time onward the acceleration was rapid. By 1960 there were almost 179,300,000 people in the United States. By 1989, the population had increased to 226,500,000—a gain of more than 24 percent in twenty years. The latest statistics indicate that in 1986 the population of the

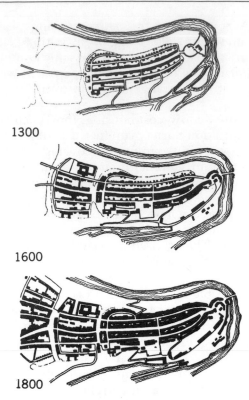

1300

1600

1800

Bern. *The early medieval town had open space within and about it. With the increase in trade and the rise of mercantilism the city form did not change, but open space was lost to building. The methods of water supply, drainage, and waste disposal remained the same as more and more people crowded into the city. Bern has continued to grow in population as have other cities; although it extended its boundaries, the process of congestion has increased the intensity of land use. The current congestion has been made bearable only with the vast improvement in water distribution through the public utilities of gas, electricity, and sewage disposal.*

United States was 247,668,966. Projections to the year 2010 predict that there will be anywhere from 250,910,000 to 282,575,000 U.S. residents.[2]

Population Distribution— Urban and Rural

The 1970 population for urban areas in the United States (the census definition of *urban* includes communities with populations of 2,500 or more) was 149,324,930, compared with 167,050,992 in 1980: an increase of approximately 12 percent. The rural population during the same period grew from 53,886,996 to 59,494,413, an increase of 10.4 percent.[3] Similar increases in the population of the metropolitan areas, which include large cities and their surrounding areas, have occurred in all parts of the world as people have moved from rural areas, adding to the problems in the already overburdened cities.

Patrick Geddes

Urban speculation and its disintegrating effect upon the living environment of man had aroused the consciousness of some prominent spokesmen during the century. The critical voices of eminent men—John Ruskin, Thomas Carlyle, Lord Shaftesbury, Charles Dickens, Friedrich Engels, and Benjamin Disraeli— brought the issues to the fore with the force of their insight and talent.

2. U.S. Dept. of Commerce, Bureau of the Census, *1980 Census of Population. General Population Characteristics. United States Summary* (Washington, D.C.: U.S. Government Printing Office, 1981).

3. U.S. Department of Commerce, Bureau of the Census, *Statistical Abstracts of the United States* (Washington, D.C.: U.S. Government Printing Office, 1984).

Among those who spoke out against the evils at the turn of the century was Patrick Geddes. In 1892 Geddes founded the Outlook Tower in Edinburgh, a center from which he wished to study the whole complex of urban life. He insisted upon a view of all phases of human existence as the base of operations, an integration of physical planning with social and economic improvements.

This principle does not sound unfamiliar today, but it was new when Geddes expressed it. As a contemporary of his said:

> There was a time when it seemed only necessary to shake up into a bottle the German town-extension plan, the Parisian Boulevard and Vista, and the English Garden Village, to produce a mechanical mixture which might be applied indiscriminately and beneficently to every town in this country. Thus it would be "town-planned" according to the most up-to-date notions. Pleasing dream! First shattered by Geddes, emerging from his Outlook Tower in the frozen north, to produce that nightmare of complexity, the Edinburgh Room at the great Town-Planning Exhibition of 1910.

Patrick Geddes gave voice to the necessity for what was later to become regional planning.

Another whose voice rose above the throng was Ebenezer Howard. Disturbed by the depressing ugliness, haphazard growth, and unhealthful conditions of cities, he set forth his ideas in a little book published in 1898 entitled *Tomorrow*. His idea was the garden city.

Howard described a town in which the land would remain in the single ownership of the community. The population would be some 30,000 people in an area of 1,000 acres. The dwellings would be distributed about a large central court, where the public buildings would be located. The shopping center would be on the edge of the town and industries on the outskirts. Surrounding the city would be a permanent belt of agricultural land comprising 5,000 acres.

Unlike the early utopians, Ebenezer Howard saw his idea become a reality before his death in 1928. The Garden City Association was formed in 1899. In 1903 First Garden City, Limited, a limited dividend society, obtained 4,500 acres of land, 34 miles from London and began the city of Letchworth. It contained an agricultural belt of 3,000 acres and was designed for a maximum population of 35,000

The Garden City

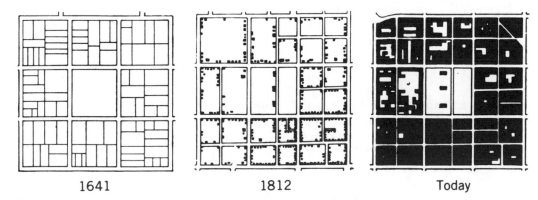

| 1641 | 1812 | Today |

New Haven. *Just as the medieval town became crowded with the increase in trade, the new towns gradually became congested with the development of commercialism. The plan of New Haven shows it as an open residential community until the Industrial Revolution. In the last hundred years, however, the street system has changed only slightly, but the land has been built up until little open space remains.*

at some future date. By 1933 the town had grown to a population of 15,000, had more than 150 shops and 60 industries, and had paid dividends on the invested stock. At a later date a second garden city, Welwyn, was started on a site of 2,400 acres. It was designed for a population of 40,000. In 15 years it had a population of 10,000 and 50 industries.

Just as Ebenezer Howard planned it, the agricultural belt remained a permanent protection for these cities, not a reserve of land for continued expansion of the urban area, which is usually considered the only good use for vacant land on the periphery of cities. The land increases in value as each community grows and prospers, and the community correspondingly prospers that much more.

There is a difference between the usual joint-stock company and Garden City, Limited, which developed Letchworth. The principal object of the latter is to create a town for the benefit of the community. In so doing, the rights of the shareholders to dividends on their stock are limited (5 percent in Garden City, Limited) and profits earned above the dividends are applied to the benefit of the whole community. The company is in a position of public trustee rather than private landlord. It has proved a sound but not a speculative investment. Land for all development purposes is leased for a period of 99 years. The town government consists of an urban district council of fifteen members, elected by the residents; five members retire annually and are eligible for reelection or possible replacement.

Another feature distinguishes Letchworth. Development and growth of the garden city are reversed from the practices of the usual speculative city. Aside from the merits of planning in either type of town, zoning in Letchworth determines the use of specific areas, and only those uses are permitted; for example, only factories and workshops are built in the industrial zones and shops in the commercial zones. In the speculative town, on the other hand, any use of a lesser economic character is permitted in its zoning provisions; dwellings are found in industrial and commercial zones, and these mixed uses are largely responsible for the sad state of the urban environment. The overdeveloped center and under-developed periphery of the speculative town are absent from Letchworth. Open spaces remain for development as the need arises and for use as provided for in the plan.

Of the 1,500 acres of the town located within the surrounding rural belt, the plan allocated 935 acres for residential use, 170 acres for industry, 60 acres for shopping, and the remainder for parks and roads. There are some 4,000 dwellings in Letchworth, of which the Urban District Council has built 1,300 worker's cottages.

THE COMMON DENOMINATOR

The houses families live in form the common denominator of the city; they are the fiber of the city. The link between family dwellings and city building is so close the two are almost synonymous. Industrial and commercial enterprise strengthen the structure of the city, but it is the community of homes that marks the health, even the civilization, of a people.

Haussmann ripped through the slums of Paris with his boulevards, civic centers were planned for American cities, the impressive garb of classic facades was hung on the streets of the commercial city, and zoning was devised as the legal instrument to lend stability to the urban framework. But housing, the manifestation of

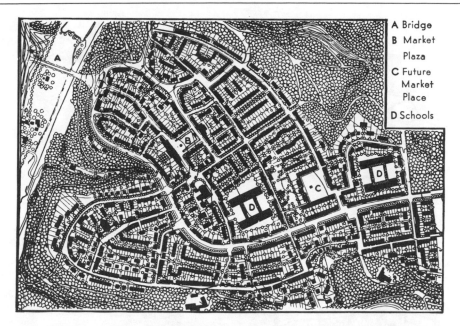

Margarethen-Hohe, Essen, George Metzendorf, architect. *The village of Margarethen-Hohe was developed in 1912 by the Krupp family for workers in the industrial steel plants in Essen. The community was planned for 2,000 to 2,500 dwellings (12,000 to 16,000 population). It illustrates a number of planning features. Surrounded by forest, the principal connection with the city is by way of the bridge (A) on the north boundary. Rather than bisecting the plan in the usual manner, the main traffic street swings around the village and bypasses the market plaza (B). This shopping center and the future principal marketplace (C) are conveniently situated within blocks of dwellings rather than on the periphery. The schools (D) are situated within blocks of dwellings rather than on the traffic roads. The road system is designed to fit the topography of the site but is arranged to avoid through traffic on any but the main roadway. Buildings are generally set back at the road intersections to avoid obstruction of traffic vision at the corners.*

the inner structure of civilization and the culture of people, remained as always the "leftover" in the urban plan.

Had zoning begun early rather than late, the urban predicament might have been much different. It is not exactly practical to plan a city after it has been built. Planning implies a program before an act, but zoning was adopted after the city had taken shape, and zoning could hardly do more than freeze the mixture. There was no chance to prescribe the ingredients before they had been poured together and well stirred. It was inevitable that housing should become the excrescence of urban land use.

City planning was first an urge to improve the aesthetic pattern of the urban environment. Then zoning made of it a statistical exercise and a marathon of prognostication. These movements were necessary and valuable but they did not improve the environment of the people, and that is the purpose of city planning. Housing has thus become the principal instrument to attain that objective. It brings into focus the social, economic, and aesthetic aims and needs of the urban population. It consequently becomes a political responsibility.

After World War I the housing shortage became a major crisis in Europe. Building inactivity through the war years had left the people of all countries with not only a shortage of dwellings but also with monetary systems that, through inflation and war debt, needed transformation. It was essential that governments take a hand.

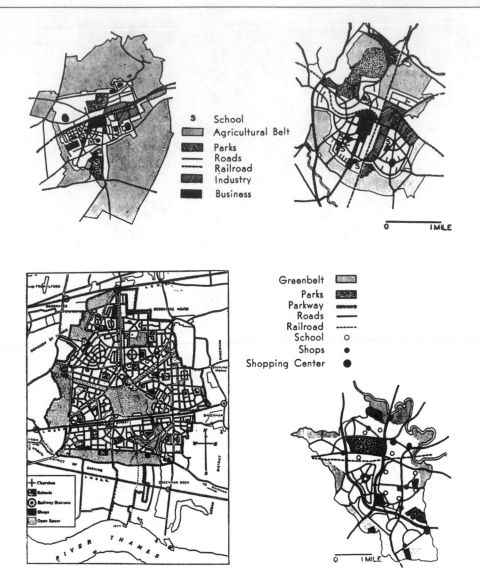

The garden city and the satellite town. *Reflecting the ideas of Ebenezer Howard, the garden city of Letchworth (top, left) was begun near London in 1903; Welwyn (top, right) soon followed. Their initial planning limited the ultimate maximum population. The garden cities were surrounded by agricultural fields, similar to the original proposal by Robert Owen. The satellite towns of Wythenshawe (bottom, right) and Becontree (bottom, left) are similar to the garden cities with the primary exception that the latter are self-contained, each having its own industry, whereas the former are dependent on the larger industrial cities to which they are attached for industrial employment.*

Public policy with respect to housing had made considerable progress in European countries during the nineteenth century. The groundwork for public assistance had been laid. Financial aid was available to private enterprise through public utility societies and trade union cooperatives. Local public authorities were empowered to provide housing for the lowest-income families. The exercise of condemnation by public authorities was an accepted instrument to enforce housing improvement, and cities in a number of countries had acquired large areas of vacant land outlying the built-up city.

The housing program was a reminder that standards of living are more than a load of mechanical equipment surrounded by the walls of a building and covered by a mortgage. The family and its dwelling had been engulfed by the tidal wave of the Industrial Revolution. It emerged from World War I as the primary unit of design in city development.

The record of the program is of historic importance. The performance in each country assumed similar characteristics, but each deserves some attention for the remarkable progress it represents in the total pattern.

CHAPTER 15

IMPROVEMENT IN HOUSING

The environment is composed of many elements, both in the natural setting and in the built sector. All of these factors in total are the world in which we live. In addition to the physical, there are, the social, economic, and political forces that impact upon humans. Combined with the physical, they form the total environment that inspires the responses that take place in the everyday activities of men, women, and children of all ages.

Although the material that follows deals to some degree with the progress in housing, the total environment is considered in evaluating the programs initiated by the several nations of the world.

> Housing may be the sleeper environment issue of the '80s. In the past, environmentalists who advocated slower residential growth were accused of undermining the American dream of owning a single-family home on a quarter-acre lot. Ironically, today that dream is dying, precisely because society has ignored the constraints of natural resources on unplanned home building.[1]

ENGLAND

In response to the Homes for Heroes campaign in England after World War I, the Housing Act of 1919 superseded the 1890 Housing Law. It provided for government subsidies to local authorities for the clearance of slums and building of low-cost housing. During the twenties and early thirties the purposes of this

1. Bruce Stokes, *Sierra Magazine,* September/October 1982.

act were consolidated and extended. Compensation to owners in built-up areas declared ready for clearance was restricted to the market value of the land, and no payment was made for the substandard structures on the site. Standards of occupancy were established to prevent overcrowding of families within dwellings, and local authorities were vested with the police power to order improvements in physically substandard dwellings or their demolition.

The 1890 British housing program had given strong impetus to enactment of the Housing and Town Planning Act of 1909; with subsequent amendments, this became the Town and Country Planning Act of 1932. This was a comprehensive piece of legislation. Local authorities were not only empowered to prepare and enforce plans for the urban area but—typical of the British pride in their rural countryside—the act also provided for the preservation of rural areas and important buildings. It further implemented the cooperative planning for two or more separate political subdivisions, cities and counties, where they required such treatment as a region.

The Housing Act of 1936 brought the relationship of housing, slums, and city planning into clearer focus. Slum clearance was an important phase of the program. The local authority was required to prepare a plan for redevelopment of blighted areas in which these areas were related to the general plan for the city. Such an area may then have been declared suitable for redevelopment, and the authority was empowered to acquire the land in whole or in part and to arrange for its rebuilding by private enterprise or public authority.

The criteria to be met for this declaration were these: at least fifty working-class houses contained in the area; at least one-third of the dwellings overcrowded or physically unfit, congested, or unsatisfactory for renovation; area located suitably to house, in part, industrial workers; and last, redevelopment necessary to establish adequate standards of low-rent housing.

The effectiveness of the British program was demonstrated by performance. According to the Twentieth Annual Report of the Ministry of Health, there were 3,998,366 dwellings built in England between the end of World War I and 1939. Of this number, 2,455,341 were built by private enterprise, 430,481 by private enterprise with some degree of government assistance, and 1,112,544 by local authorities.

Apartment buildings three to five stories in height were considered necessary to restore ample open spaces in the residential plan, but this was contrary to the traditional dwelling. The cottage-and-garden was the type closest to the heart of the English. The most successful housing developments were consequently those in which this type predominated.

Two great projects were undertaken in this period: Becontree, a satellite community for 25,000 families on 2,770 acres near London, and Wythenshawe, adjacent to Manchester.

The Satellite Garden Town

Sir Ernest Simon called Wythenshawe a satellite garden town to distinguish it from garden cities like Letchworth and Welwyn. The satellite garden town and the garden city have similar characteristics: each is a residential area of low density with not more than twelve families per acre, containing factory and shopping areas, parks, schools, other civic buildings, and protective buffers of permanent agricultural belts on the periphery. A garden city, however, is intended to be a self-contained and self-sustaining community, whereas the satellite garden town is situated close to a large city in which the residents of the town may have their places of work and business.

The city council of Manchester appointed a housing committee in 1926 to consider the possibility of relieving the congested slums in the city with a satellite garden town. An estate of about 2,500 acres in single ownership adjacent to the city on the Mersey River was recommended as the site. It was later increased to 5,500 acres, and after some opposition locally and in Parliament the entire area was incorporated in the city in 1920, most of the land being finally purchased at agricultural value. The architect Barry Parker was invited to prepare the plans for the estate. An agricultural belt of 1,000 acres was reserved, and the original estate grounds were retained as a 250-acre park. A golf course of 100 acres was also provided. Two broad parkways that ran through the town connected it with the city. The residential areas that border these parkways were separated from the roadways by an open space 150 feet wide. Side roads gave access to abutting property; the main road was confined to through traffic with limited access. The residential area was 3,000 acres, with a maximum density of 12 houses per acre; 25,000 houses were planned, with an ultimate population of 100,000.

The land on which Wythenshawe is built remains in the ownership of the city of Manchester. Both the city and private developers were allowed to build on the estate. By 1935 a total of about 4,800 dwellings had been completed, of which the city built some 4,600. It was planned that about two-thirds of the residential area would be used for municipal housing and one-third for private housing. About 500 acres was reserved for industrial, commercial, and civic buildings. Both communities are now complete.

Some criticism was leveled at the Manchester city council for extravagance in purchasing a large tract of land and reserving large areas for permanent open space. Sir Ernest Simon, a staunch spokesman for improved housing, defended the policy of the city by comparing it to the usual procedure of land acquisition:

> Let us consider first the question of the bulk purchase of land. The question is whether the City Council has been wise to purchase so large a block of land straight off, or whether it would have been more economical to continue its previous policy of purchasing relatively small plots of land as and when required. It has in fact, since the War [World War I], purchased nearly 2,000 acres at a cost which has been gradually rising, but which must average about £400 an acre. Since then prices have gradually increased. As development has proceeded and as it has become known that the Corporation was in the market for more land, the prices have been put up, and the average price paid for the whole 3,500 acres is perhaps in the neighborhood of about £100 an acre, or a total of say £350,000.

> If at Wythenshawe the Corporation had pursued its old policy, first of all developing main roads and main drainage, then gradually buying pieces of land as they were required for housing and became ripe for building, there is not the least doubt that they would have had to pay a similar average price to that paid in the rest of Manchester; that is to say about £400 an acre.

> The effect of the bulk purchase, therefore, is that the land has been purchased at an average price of £100 per acre as against an average of £400. So far as the 2,000 acres are concerned which are to be used for municipal housing, nobody denies that this land was needed for housing, and that it would, at some time, have had to be bought for that purpose. The economy through buying in bulk has, therefore, been £300 an acre, of a total of £600,000 for the 2,000 acres. Against this savings must, of course, be set the annual loss in owning the land up to the time of development;

say 4 percent for interest charges. This amounts to £8,000 per annum. From this must be deducted the rents receivable from the agricultural land (less cost of management) which would bring the net burden down to a figure of say £6,000 per annum, that is to say, against a total saving of £600,000 there is an annual charge, so long as the land is wholly undeveloped, of £6,000. The period of delay before full development is, of course, uncertain, but if Manchester proceeds with its program of building 3,000 houses a year, most of them being necessarily built at Wythenshawe, the estate will be fully developed in less than ten years. Assuming, however, that twenty years were required, the burden of interest, beginning at £6,000 per annum and gradually falling to nothing, would amount in the whole period to £60,000. The net savings on the housing estate owing to the early purchase would therefore be no less than £540,000.

Let us now turn to consider the 1,500 acres purchased for factories, shops, public buildings, and private enterprise houses. Development is still in its early stages, and no particulars have been published as regards the terms on which this land is being leased for these different purposes. We are informed, however, that the ground rents which are being obtained are such that they represent on the average a capital value of at least £300 per acre above the bare cost of the land. When these 1,500 acres are fully developed there will therefore be a profit on the capitalized value of the land of at least £300 per acre, or £450,000 on the whole area. Against this item also there will be a set-off representing the interest charges during the period of development, which on the assumptions previously made should certainly not exceed £50,000, leaving a net gain of £400,000.

Taking the landlord account as a whole (covering 3,500 acres) we come, therefore, to the following conclusion: that the bulk purchase of 3,500 acres by the Corporation as against the old policy of hand-to-mouth buying of the land required for housing, and not buying any land for other purposes, will, if the estate is fully developed in twenty years or less, show a capital advantage to the Corporation of approximately £1,000,000.

Accusations of extravagance against the City Council for the bulk purchase of land are, therefore, the exact reverse of the truth. The fact is that the City Council has shown a high degree of business foresight in making the purchase, which will ultimately be of great benefit to the ratepayers.

There is only one other aspect of the Wythenshawe development which has been called extravagant: the generous reservation which has been made in the plans for the agricultural belt, parks, parkways, and the preservation of spinneys. Admittedly, the area reserved is an advance on what has previously been done; but the difference between the normal practice of reserving 10 percent of the area for parks, on the one hand, and what has been done at Wythenshawe on the other, is not great. The total expenditure on open spaces in the whole three parishes of Wythenshawe, even if the whole agricultural belt is actually purchased by the City Council, will certainly not reach £200,000; perhaps £50,000 less. But this extra expenditure will make a big difference to the amenity of the estate. Can anybody seriously call this extravagance when it is set off against the £1,000,000 which will be gained on the landlord account?[2]

FRANCE

Cholera epidemics generated some activity in the nineteenth century to correct substandard housing in France, and the threat of mob violence moved Napoleon III to build wide avenues through the slums as a means of control. But it was not until 1894 that serious legislation was enacted. The act passed at that time was similar to the Belgian law of 1889 that made government funds available at low interest rates for houses to be built and sold exclusively to industrial employees.

2. Sir E. D. Simon, *The Rebuilding of Manchester* (New York, Longmans Green, 1935).

In 1912 the Office Public d'Habitations a Bon Marché (Public Office for Low-Cost Housing), an organization of local authorities, was empowered to lend funds for, and to subsidize, low-cost housing. It was augmented several times later, until the Loucheur Act of 1928 concentrated further upon production of housing for low-income families and expanded financing through public authorities and private enterprise. Nearly half the dwellings provided by the Public Office after World War I were concentrated about Paris.

Despite ambitious plans to rebuild the congested slums—the *ilots insalubré*—the housing program in Paris was seriously marred. When the city walls were razed, it was expected that the open space would be reserved and the surrounding slum belt cleared and rebuilt with appropriate planning standards. It was another idle dream. When the fortifications were leveled in 1930, the land was leased to speculative enterprise. In the open space some 20,000 dwellings were crowded into tightly planned tenements eight stories high; the adjacent slums remained.

There were some encouraging developments in the late thirties. The Department of the Seine planned a series of *cités jardins* in the outlying areas of Paris. Literally translated as "garden cities," these developments were designed as satellite garden villages somewhat similar to Wythenshawe in England. In the words of Henri Sellier, administrator of the Housing Office of the Department of the Seine, the *cité jardins* were planned as "essential elements of the city of Greater Paris."

A blow befell the program. Lack of proper arrangements for transportation meant failure for some of the *cité jardins* and near-failure for others. The interesting project at Drancy la Muette remained vacant because transportation was not provided. Chatenay Malabry, planned for 20,000 people, and Plessis Robinson were both partly occupied, but transportation arrangements were not made and neither was successful. All this amply demonstrated the need for cooperation from public utility agencies.

GERMANY

The housing program in France after World War I hardly set a standard to serve as a guide for urban development. The plan for the *cités jardins* about Paris was courageous, but, as indicated, it was not enough for success. Urban development is complex, and provision of the variety of public services required by the residents makes the difference between success and failure.

Certain policies had been well established in Germany before World War I. Public utility societies and trade union cooperatives were recognized as effective instruments in the housing field. State financial aid was an accepted method; during the last half of the nineteenth century Bismarck had inaugurated social insurance, and these funds were a source of housing loans for many years. In addition, local governments had assumed responsibility for the housing of government workers and the financing of public utility societies.

During his tenure of office in 1902, the mayor of Frankfurt obtained passage of a law that permitted the city government to pool private property, rearrange it to conform to the city plan, and redistribute such land for redevelopment. The city was further authorized in this process to retain 40 percent of the land without compensation to the owners for streets, parks, and other public uses. Pursuant to this enactment in Frankfurt, numerous German cities adopted a policy of acquiring outlying vacant land on their periphery. The purpose was protection from the speculation and resulting boom in land prices that inevitably accompanied the rapid increase in urban population.

This policy was fully rewarded after World War I when the need for housing, production which had come to an abrupt halt, became most acute. The cities were then in a position to lease large quantities of these public lands to private and cooperative organizations for the construction of housing without the penalty of excessive land costs. In seventy German towns with more than 50,000 population, more than 6,000 acres of city-owned land was leased between 1926 and the rise of Hitler to power in 1933. Similar policies were adopted in other countries—Austria, Switzerland, Holland, and Denmark; in Czechoslovakia 15,000 acres outlying Prague was made available for housing.

World War I left Germany impoverished. Astronomical inflation demolished the monetary system, an inactive building industry left a serious housing shortage. Intrinsically high financing costs coupled with the inflation rendered it difficult for private enterprise to cope with the housing problem. Although the figures may seem low to Americans, interest on mortgage money had more than doubled, moving from 4 percent to as high as 10 percent. Rents had quadrupled while wages had increased only 50 percent. It became imperative for state and local governments to finance a large part of the housing program.

Property owners had become beneficiaries of the inflation, which had the effect of liquidating all previous mortgages. As a consequence the *Hauszinsteuer* (House Rent Tax) was adopted in 1921. Prewar rents were used as the base for a tax levy ranging from 10 to 50 percent of the rents, and the funds thus derived were used to finance second mortgages at a very low interest rate (generally 1 percent) to compensate for the high cost of first mortgage money. Administered by local government, these funds were loaned to public utility societies and cooperatives for housing. The effectiveness of this policy is evident in the production of some 3 million dwellings between the end of World War I and the rise of Hitler. More than three-quarters of these dwellings received financial aid from the government. The housing problem was not solved, a sufficient supply of dwellings was not provided, and the slums remained, but the program represents a remarkable achievement nonetheless for what it did manage to accomplish.

German cities had suffered the same kind of chaotic growth experienced by other cities on the Continent during the nineteenth century. It was obviously necessary to reconsider land use and planning if the tremendous housing program was to produce a permanent asset to the communities in which it was built. It is a significant contrast with our experience in the United States. Emergencies have been the excuse to postpone urban planning in our country: in the short-lived German Republic the emergency was considered the sound reason to engage in the most serious planning. Despite the shadows cast over that country by Hitler's subsequent rise to power and nazism, the housing program of the decade 1920–30 emerges as an example of an aggressive if immature democracy in action.

The pressing demand for new dwellings gave neither the time nor the funds for a real program to clear the slums; this was necessarily postponed until an adequate supply of dwellings could be built. Two effective means were brought into play in the early twenties: the public utility society (limited dividend company) and the cooperative society. The public utility society, though comparable to the limited dividend company in the United States, was eligible to receive the benefits of several forms of subsidy necessary to implement a large supply of new

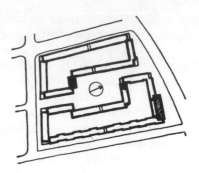

Possmorweg, Hamburg. *Built in 1927–28 by the architectural firm of Schneider, Elingius, and Schramm, Possmorweg is a variation of the "hollow square" planning characteristic of the early housing program in Germany. The large space of the interior courts was a vast improvement over high land coverage, but orientation of the dwellings was compromised. Under the later direction of the city architect Fritz Schumacher, this type of planning was maintained in Hamburg.*

housing. The societies were formed for the purpose of building low-cost housing and, despite careful state supervision, exercised a high degree of initiative and ingenuity in the planning of their projects. The cooperatives, or self-aid societies, were organized largely by trade unions as a means to supply housing for their members. These companies enjoyed privileges similar to those of public utility societies and assumed the same obligations. The effectiveness of these groups is demonstrated by the extensive operations of the three largest, which built 71,000 dwellings up to 1929. These three, known as Dewog, Gagfah, and Heimat, were among some 4,300 cooperative societies in operation.

In addition to large organizations a number of smaller private companies engaged in the program, but they contributed to a much lesser degree than the organizations mentioned. The government created various agencies, under jurisdiction of the several provinces and municipalities, for research in the technical phases of planning, construction, and financing. The results of this research were made available to all private and public organizations in the housing field.

With few exceptions, planning before 1925 had been confined to the usual city blocks. Inadequate building regulations had permitted an excessive density for population and building coverage. The first step away from high density in the postwar program was the arrangement of buildings around the perimeter of the usual city block with a concomitant reduction in coverage within the center of the block. Mainly apartment buildings of three and four stories went up, and the "hollow square" thus formed enclosed recreation and service areas for the tenants. Many large-scale developments were placed on tracts of vacant land. Freedom from the subdivision of the gridiron system led to more informal planning, and the row house was adopted where density was not a prerequisite. Main traffic streets were confined to the periphery of the projects, and internal roads were bordered on each side by a row of dwellings. Apartment houses of three and four stories were included along the marginal areas of the site.

Factors similar to today's hygiene planning were considered. Research led to the consideration of orientation. Sunlight in every room was a rule, and the orientation of all buildings to provide east and west exposure became mandatory. The preferable exposure was west light for living rooms and east light for bedrooms. The attention devoted to the proper orientation for all dwellings at this time is reminiscent of the fifth century B.C. in Greece.

The final step was the relation of the buildings to the streets. Building in parallel lines along each side of a street did not provide equal privacy for living areas or quiet for sleeping rooms. The new site planning produced uniform orientation for all dwellings but did not give them uniform exposure upon the open spaces surrounding the buildings. Instead, all buildings were placed at right angles to the streets. The space between buildings was thereby free of vehicular traffic, although the walks were designed to permit small trucks access and facilitate movement of goods and services. This arrangement provided privacy for all living units, safety for play and recreational areas, and uniform orientation for all dwellings.

Recreation space for children and adults, shops, common meeting rooms, and kindergartens were provided in the housing developments. Laundry facilities were placed on the roof of the two-story buildings of early projects, one-half covered washing space and one-half open drying space. The larger apartment buildings continued this until central heating was adopted and central laundries or "washeries" were built in conjunction. Private gardens were provided to the extent that space permitted but were usually confined to the single-family row houses. Some subsistence plots were included in a few of the large developments.

Strict adherence to this plan produced a rigid uniformity that increased during the late twenties, but it served to overcome some of the traditional inhibitions of the gridiron street system. Some later projects developed in 1931 and 1932 demonstrated a degree of liberation from the earlier regimentation. A more plastic and flexible treatment was emerging, but the progress was interrupted by the political domination of nazism.

Probably the most outstanding example of integrated planning occurred in Frankfurt-am-Main. Ernst May, the chief architect, undertook a comprehensive plan for the entire city in preparation for the housing program. May subscribed to the principle of satellite communities about the periphery of the city. The housing developments were surrounded by permanent open spaces but were planned as part of the city expansion rather than as detached and self-contained garden cities. Frankfurt-am-Main is today considered to be one of the most beautiful cities in Germany.

AUSTRIA

Austria emerged from her period of empire and World War I financially bankrupt. Rampant inflation reduced to a minimum the capacity of private capital to produce housing. Municipal government was forced to take the major role, and Vienna undertook an energetic program. In 1923 the government taxed rents to obtain needed public funds and launched a vigorous program. Approximately a quarter of all revenues from taxes was devoted to housing in 1928.

HOLLAND

At the turn of the century, in 1901, Holland passed an act that required every city with a population of 10,000 or more to prepare a comprehensive town plan in which new areas for housing were to be allocated. Housing standards were to be established by the local authorities, who were responsible for compliance and could exercise the power of condemnation where necessary. Local authorities were also empowered to build low-cost housing. Government funds were made available to public utility societies at low interest rates.

During and after World War I these powers were extended, and the housing program was accelerated. In the ten years after the war some 500,000 dwellings went up. Because careful attention was directed throughout the program to the needs of people of various income levels, it was possible to confine the public housing primarily to the problem of direct slum clearance.

High-rise housing in Rotterdam. *Extensive comprehensive planning was done for many of the large cities after World War II, when urban areas such as Rotterdam were literally destroyed. Rebuilding of that city's town center has resulted in a showplace for the world to enjoy.*

SWITZERLAND

The housing situation in Switzerland after World War I did not present as serious a problem as in European countries because of its stable history and its policies of private finance. Nonetheless it too had a housing shortage after 1918, and local governments rendered financial assistance to cooperatives as encouragement to produce an adequate supply. But the advantages of democratic capitalism had always been more evenly distributed in Switzerland than elsewhere, and the excesses suffered by the poor in many countries had been absent to a marked degree. The result was that this little country had not sunk to such low depths that drastic social action and fundamental economic alteration were required to restore balance.

SWEDEN

Mature policies of land acquisition by cities in the Scandinavian countries resulted in aggressive participation in the supply of housing by private enterprise via the public utility societies and housing cooperatives. Copenhagen in Denmark, Stockholm in Sweden, and Oslo in Norway made outstanding progress in both urban and rural housing. Standards were maintained at a relatively high level. It is estimated that 10 percent of Stockholm's population lived in housing produced by the cooperative societies alone, and a fifth of the people in Copenhagen and Oslo were accommodated in cooperative and public utility housing.

The Industrial Revolution did not reach Swedish cities until electrical power had been developed as a major power source. As a consequence congestion did not afflict Swedish cities to the extent suffered by other cities on the Continent. Decentralization was feasible: electrical power was transmitted to the people, who did not have to congregate at the source. While migration to the cities during the nineteenth century had increased ten- and twenty-fold elsewhere, the increase of population in town and country was stable in Sweden. During the nineteenth century rural population increased from 1 million to 3 million, and urban population increased from 2 million to 4 million.

The central district of Stockholm contained its share of slums, but they did not constitute the relatively large problem that prevailed in other Continental cities. The principal problem in Sweden was overcrowding within dwellings, undoubtedly caused by the rigorous climate and the heating problem it created. More than 40 percent of the families occupied apartments of one and two rooms. Multiple use of space was a design requirement.

Since Sweden remained neutral during World War I, the economy had not only escaped suffering but fared quite well. A shortage of housing occurred because construction had lagged, but the government was in a satisfactory financial position to render all needed assistance to correct it. From 1917 to 1920 municipalities subsidized public utility societies and cooperative groups that were building low-cost housing to the extent of one-third the cost. In 1920 this subsidy was reduced to 15 percent of the cost because of increased wages and resulting capacity to pay higher rents. With stability generally restored by 1923, the subsidies were discontinued. Interest rates on mortgage money were high, and the State Dwelling Loan Fund was set up to make loans for second mortgages at low interest rates to offset the high first mortgage costs.

In the past it was a tradition in Sweden for citizens to have the greatest possible freedom from government aid or interference in the housing market. (Younger Swedes today might well find this unbelievable.) This tradition not only had been strengthened by the vigorous and aggressive cooperative movement but was largely due to it. It became an effective and progressive instrument for the maintenance of democratic procedures and economic freedom. To remove itself from housing operations as much as possible, the government created an independent agency in 1929 to administer the Swedish Housing Loan Fund. This agency made low-interest long-term loans to continue the building of housing for low-income families. The successful operation of cooperatives soon obviated any need for these loans, and financial responsibility was shifted to the cooperative societies. By 1934, 10 percent of the people in Stockholm lived in housing developments sponsored by the cooperative societies.

The cooperatives were of two major types. The SKB (Stockholm Kooperativa Forbundet, or Stockholm Cooperative Society), which produced various consumer goods, built housing primarily for its member employees. The HSB (Hyresgasternas Sparkassa och Byggnadsforening, or Tenant Savings Bank and Building Society) was an organization specifically organized to build dwellings for members of the society, and membership was not restricted to any particular occupation. Careful research in planning was carried on by this society, and the projects it developed introduced advanced techniques in planning, equipment, and community facilities.

Between 1904 and the 1960s, the city of Stockholm purchased 20,000 acres of land surrounding the city. This land was incorporated and planned for "garden suburbs." The city installed streets and utilities and sponsored a program for

Farsta, Sweden. *Housing built on hilly terrain.*

working families to lease lots and build their own dwellings. Loans were available from the municipality for up to 90 percent of the value of each unit. The loans were in the form of materials purchased by the city; the balance, 10 percent, was the owner's contribution in labor. Standard plans for the dwellings, ranging from 700 square feet to 1,000 square feet in floor area, were prepared by the city, and skilled supervision was provided during construction. It was a popular and successful program, offering an opportunity for low-income families to leave the congested slums.

The rebuilding of cities was aided by the Town Planning Act of 1931, which required all urban communities, regardless of size, to prepare a rebuilding plan. All improvements thereafter were obliged to conform to the plan.

In 1935 rehousing slum dwellers by means of rent rebates ranging, according to family size, from 30 percent upward was encouraged. The municipality advanced loans for other forms of housing improvement, such as joint rehabilitation of substandard buildings by owners of contiguous property. Housing for the aged and for single women was also included within the scope of municipal programs.

The methods employed in Sweden to maintain good housing were varied. Public policy was always flexible enough to be adjusted as changing conditions warranted, and private enterprise, through the cooperatives and housing societies, was courageous and astute in its investments.

THE COMMON-WEALTH OF INDEPENDENT REPUBLICS

Since the 1917 Revolution and especially since World War II, planning and housing in the former U.S.S.R. have been treated with vigor. The contrast between prerevolutionary Czarist Russia and the former Soviet Union is apparent. Vast plans for industrial development were made and many were carried out. New cities were built and portions of old cities rebuilt.

There appears to be a distinction, however, between the tremendous activity and Russian standards of construction. The latter does not measure up to expectations suggested by the former. A city plan like that proposed for Stalingrad, a linear city, suggests hopeful prospects for the reorganization of the urban pattern. The extensive executed housing developments, on the other hand, are rife with technical inadequacies and are made up largely of small apartments in multistoried buildings, which offer little to warrant particular attention and leave much to be desired.

It must be said, however, that the quality of the architectural designs appears greatly improved since the 1970s. The buildings nonetheless are even larger than those of earlier planning, seemingly the response to a dedication to bigness for its own sake. The individual apartments continue small, but some flexibility has been provided to satisfy the needs of larger families.

The form of government in the Soviet Union and its economic structure are so different from those of the West that comparisons are ineffective. The political processes, so different from our own, are such an integral part of urban development that experience in planning and its accomplishments cannot be subjected to our reasonable appraisal.

The changes that took place during 1991 leave political, social, and economic conditions in turmoil. For all intents and purposes the Soviet Union, once a union of individual republics, no longer exists. The Balkanization of this great land mass has left the fate of its hundreds of millions of troubled people difficult to forecast.

In this vast, complicated group of 15 separate nations, where local currency has no foreign exchange value, it is difficult to foresee what may happen if the threats of food shortages and lack of reasonable methods of distribution become critical.

INDIA

The current housing situation in India is alarming. About 10 percent of the population is without adequate shelter. With the population ever growing and very little overall economic improvement, the future does not appear encouraging for many millions of people. The need to improve these conditions is imperative if India is to remain a civilized nation.

Professor K. P. Bhattacharjee of Jadavpur University cited these statistics:

> According to a National Building Organization estimate the housing supply shortage in 1971 was 15.6 million units, of which 3.8 million [are] in urban areas and 11.8 million in rural areas; and by 2000 A.D. there would be a shortage of 40 million houses in urban areas. . . . To wipe out this deficit in ten years at least 4 million houses are to be built in a year; the present rate of construction is 400,000 houses only. In rural areas there would be a deficit of 72 million houses.[3]

He recommended the following national housing policies:

> 1) Increase financial allocation in plan outlay; 2) Set up suitable financial lending to intending builders; 3) Prescribe minimum housing standard (in terms of plinth (base) area, materials to be used, and cost) for urban and rural areas; 4) Minimize cost of dwelling units by using indigenous materials and using substitutes for cement and steel; 5) Land price should be kept as low as far as possible and ownership of land should be vested with the Government; land speculation should be discour-

---

3. Professor K. P. Bhattacharjee, architect and city planner, Jadavpur University, Calcutta, India, "Strategy for Housing Development in India during the Decade 1980–1990," paper presented at the thirty-fifth IFHP World Congress, Jerusalem, 1980.

aged; 6) Public housing investment; 7) Research and development of low cost building materials; 8) Dissemination of technical know-how developed in the research organizations of the nation through training of manpower and demonstration projects.[4]

PEOPLE'S REPUBLIC OF CHINA

Cities in all underdeveloped countries face the same problem. The People's Republic of China has a history of both rural and urban slums. The shortage of minimal housing is so great that meeting even basic housing needs will take years. In the cities, a great effort is being made to limit family size to one child. Even in rural areas, where the need for labor is still great, the government has made an effort to limit family size. The government in addition discourages immigration to the cities.

The Chinese consider large cities difficult to manage and poor environments because of high building and population densities. Those who have been to the United States have been quick to cite New York City and its problems as evidence. The relatively undeveloped transportation system still relies heavily on waterways and railroads for long distances and bicycles for short ones. An increase in the number of buses and improved roads have helped, but living near work is still important to the Chinese. And making cities self-sufficient in terms of food supply and consumer goods is also important.

The country is poor but the people do not seem poor. There is none of the squalor usually associated with poverty. People live in what may seem to us cramped quarters with primitive facilities. Although the figures cited on the amount of construction since liberation are impressive, so is the population increase. It is clearly difficult for the nation to keep up with the incredible population growth: less than 550 million at liberation in 1949 to more than a billion in 1988. The housing shortage is constantly cited as a major problem.[5]

Financing housing is accomplished through grants from the central government in Beijing (Peking): grants from the local regional governments; profits made by industry or commerce, including agriculture; and individual savings. The latter approach is, in general, discouraged since it places a drain on the efficient use of material and labor resources.

Before any building program can be initiated there must be a master plan to ensure efficient development. For example, housing and employment centers must be carefully linked so that employees do not have to travel by bicycle more than 30 minutes from home to work.

Planning in the People's Republic is supposed to take place in consultation with the people. The degree to which this actually transpires is uncertain, for most planning decisions seem to be made by the central authorities. Joan Robinson describes it in this way:

> There are several phrases always used in connection with the system of economic planning—"two initiatives, of the top and the bottom"; from the bottom up and from the top down; and leaving leeway, which means allowing room for adjustment as production goes on.[6]

4. Ibid.

5. U.S. City Planners in China, November and December 1980. Martha M. Davis, deputy executive director, New York Department of City Planning. *Urban Planning Update*, an APA Publication, May 1980.

6. *Economic Management in China*, monograph. Modern China Series, no. 4. Anglo-Chinese Educational Institute, 1976.

For example, representatives of the province meet with the planning commission in Beijing to review the various programs the province wishes to propose. The planning commission evaluates these programs and assigns priorities and funds for their implementation.

Robinson delineates the various planning bureaucracies:

> There are various departments concerned in drawing up a provincial plan. The plan for agriculture gives targets for the major crops and for fisheries and forestry. It is also concerned with promoting mechanization.

> The plan for industry gives all major products in quantities and minor ones as a global sum. It makes allowance for trial production of new items.

> There is a plan for communications and transport within the provincial orbit. The plan for commerce covers the volume of purchases of consumer goods to be supplied through the shops and matches the value of sales against total purchasing power.

> The plan for capital construction sets out all major projects and the additional productive capacity that they will provide.

> There is a plan for the labor force and the wage bill, showing the number of new jobs that will be created.

> There are departments concerned with education, culture, and health, dealing with enrollment in schools and colleges and with the medical service, sanitation, and the arts.

> The plan covers the distribution of materials and the products of agriculture and industry.

> Finally, there is a department concerned with finance, dealing with revenue and expenditure and setting targets for reduction of costs of production. This bureaucracy is performing the functions not only of the civil service in the capitalist countries but also of a large part of private business.[7]

Shanghai

All existing cities with an accumulation of uses and infrastructures that are aged beyond their reasonable life expectancy face great problems in planning for the future because of the enormous cost of rehabilitation and redevelopment. Shanghai is no exception; indeed the problems are intensified and multiplied by the conditions that are the result of the extraterritorial rights seized by foreign powers during the nineteenth century.

Shanghai was but a fishing village when Japanese envoys to the Tang court at Xi'an landed there before the tenth century. Under the Yuan (1260–1378) it became a minor cotton spinning and weaving center. By 1800 it was a flourishing port with a population of approximately 50,000. In the middle of the nineteenth century near the end of the Opium War, the Shanghai garrison surrendered to the British in 1842. From that time until the 1949 revolution the city developed as a group of enclaves for foreign interests. These former foreign cities within the city make up the additional complicating aspects of future planning for the most populous city in China.

> There were three cities in Shanghai prior to 1949. They were the International Settlement, the French Concession, and the Chinese City. Each had its own government and exercised exclusive jurisdiction within its own boundaries. The history of the growth of Shanghai's three cities can be found in the history of the expanding China trade of the last half of the nineteenth century. The demand of foreign traders

---

7. Ibid.

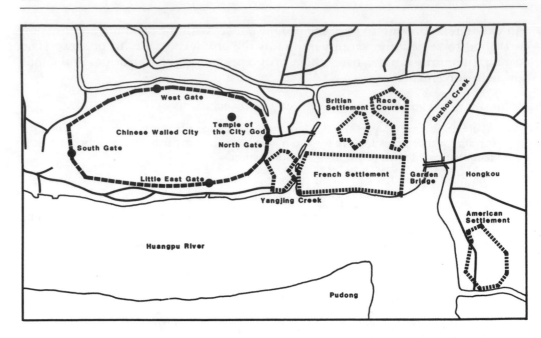

Shanghai, 1853.

that a vast territory with a dense population and strategic locality should not remain closed to the industrialized West led to the opening of Shanghai and other ports in China. The growth of Shanghai and its attainment of the position of key city in China have been due principally to its geographical location as a port of entry to the great and wealthy Yangtze Valley where almost half of China's millions live. During the civil wars and foreign invasions, the two foreign settlements remained undisturbed and came to be islands of safety for the people.[8]

Since all of the elements of the city were distinct entities, the water, sewage, and road systems reflected this separation of authority and were not designed for intercommunity relationships or service. To this day, one of the critical problems facing the city is the coordination of the several communications and servicing systems.

The current population of Shanghai exceeds 11 million. More than 5.4 million of its people live in the congested 58-square-mile urban core. In terms of density this amounts to more than 1,450 persons per acre, exceeded only by the population in the most congested square mile of Hong Kong, considered the most densely populated area of any major city in the world.

Faced with almost impossible demands for housing in all parts of the nation, the People's Republic of China had to make do with the limited space and economic resources inherited from prerevolutionary days. However, although much of the old was permitted to remain, ten industrial towns were constructed in the suburbs around Shanghai. Thirty to seventy kilometers—approximately 18 to 43 miles—away from the central city, these towns have been constructed in keeping with the principles of city planning. They have industrial and residential areas, a road network, commercial centers, greenbelts, railway stations, and social service facilities such as schools, hospitals, and clinics.

Suzhou   The city of Suzhou, located about 75 miles to the east of Shanghai, was settled about 3,000 years ago. It lies astride the Grand Canal, still an important waterway

8. Tsing Tai Chow, master's thesis, University of Southern California, 1950.

for commercial transport. The master plan for the city contains many interesting details, including the development of a new highway system to be built over some of the canals that have, over the years, silted up or become severely polluted and malodorous. However, enough of the canals are to be retained to continue the role of the city as the "Venice of the Far East." The treatment of the banks of the canals with concrete block facings and dredging will make them not only clean but also handsome.

Major landmarks such as pagodas will be protected by keeping competing high buildings outside the line of vision. Major highways will be constructed to a width of 132 feet. The rights-of-way will be landscaped, and pedestrian and bicycle lanes will be provided.

The plan locates amenities such as storytelling houses, libraries, historical museums, stadiums, stage and movie theaters, as well as many smaller features such as special restaurants and candy shops. The ancient Taoist monastery will be preserved and maintained.

Housing located adjacent to the canals will be regulated as to its relationship to the canal, its architectural style, and the color of its exteriors.

The master plan for Beijing is more advanced than those being prepared for other cities. It has been submitted to the state for approval. The plan proposes new development in satellites on the least productive land in agricultural surroundings. Industrial plants are proposed in these satellites, located with reference to prevailing wind directions to reduce pollution in both the local community and the total city. Housing for the workers in the new industrial plants is located near the industries but separated from them by a greenbelt. Transportation needs are reduced by encouraging walking or bicycle riding to places of employment. Traffic arteries bypass the cities to reduce the amount of internal traffic and the congestion that is so often associated with it.

Beijing (Peking)

Beijing. *New housing located where the city wall once existed.*

The Inner City is crisscrossed with main streets that are intersected by *hutongs* (lanes), like squares on a chessboard. Buildings are located about a central court within which all of the residents' large belongings (bicycles, and so on) are kept. These areas are served by narrow lanes.

Since the revolution in 1949, Beijing has undergone many changes. Work to broaden the road around the Forbidden City was started in the 1950s. To ease traffic conditions, the east, west, and north walls of the Imperial City were pulled down and the archways at Tien An Men, Xisi, Dianmen, and Dongsi removed. In recent years, an expressway, the Second Ring Road, was built on the ruins of the old city walls to link the city with its suburbs. Nine overpasses—two triple-decked and seven double-decked—span the expressway. Besides automobile lanes, it has special bicycle lanes for Beijing's some 3 million bicycles.

Underneath the Second Ring Road is China's first subway, built solely with Chinese materials and technology. Since its first stage was completed in 1969, trains carry some 160,000 passengers a day. The second stage of the project was completed in the early 1980s; passengers now number well over 500,000 daily. The circular subway system and the major above-ground roads combine to form a more convenient communication network in the city.

The housing program is integrally related to the new subway system. The high-rise buildings under construction will, when completed, form another type of city wall. Replacing the substandard dwellings in the area, these edifices will have the same visual impact on the city that Tien An Men Square now has: both are dedicated to monumentality.

Located in the heart of Beijing, Tien An Men Square's vast open space of approximately 125 acres can easily accommodate the hundreds of thousands of people who gather here on festivals and holidays and for mass protests.

Temple of prayer for a Bountiful Harvest, Beijing, China.

Terra cotta soldier. *One of the thousands discovered at Sian, China, built under Emperor Qin Shi Huangdi.*

A hutong. *A small street with homes clustered about interior courts.*

HONG KONG

The territory known as Hong Kong is geographically an extension of the People's Republic of China. The crown colony is comprised of Kowloon, the New Territories, Victoria, and other islands. It has, since 1841, been a trade and shipping center in the possession of Great Britain. It is an exciting city for its varied topography, picturesque waterfront (one of the world's great ports) and its energetic people. A center for tourists from all over the world who seek bargain shopping. At least the latter was the case in the 1980s.

Population Size. At mid-1989, the population of Hong Kong was estimated to be 5,761,400, including 47,701 Vietnamese boat people. The population figure included other transients such as visitors and the armed forces. This population resides on 398 square miles of land, an area one-third the size of Rhode Island. A considerable portion of the land is mountainous or used for agriculture and industry.

Over the past 10 years, the population grew at an average annual rate of 1.6 percent. Population in previous decades were estimated as follows:[9]

Year	Total	Average Annual Rate of Increase	Sex Ratio (Males per 1,000 Females)
1949	1,857,000	N.A.	N.A.
1959	2,967,400	4.8	N.A.
1969	3,863,900	2.7	1,016
1979	4,929,700	2.5	1,068
1989	5,761,400	1.6	1,049

Population Density. The population density per square kilometer for the whole territory was 5,335 (14,218 persons per square mile). Mong Kok, with 127,300 people per square kilometer (approximately 4,000 people per acre which is about 10 square feet of land per person) was the most densely populated district.

---

9. *Hong Kong 1985,* (Hong Kong: Hong Kong Information Service, Beaconsfield House, Queen's Road).

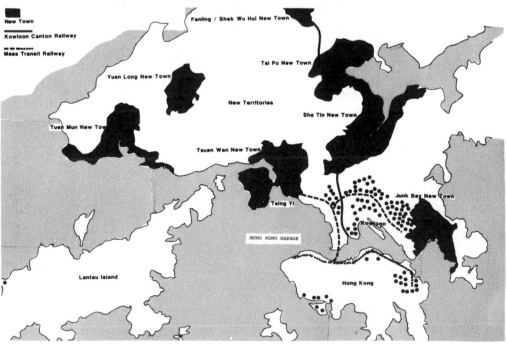

Map of Hong Kong, including Kowloon and the New Territories. *(top) (Courtesy Eno Foundation for Transportation.)* **Map of new town locations, Kowloon and the New Territories, Hong Kong.** *(bottom)*

Resettlement housing (left). *Housing in the central area of Kowloon, constructed to serve as an interim stage in the redevelopment housing program.* **Lek Yuen Estates** *(right). Another estate located in the Sha Tin New Town area. The "flags" are actually clotheslines on poles. This means of clothes drying is common throughout the Orient. (Courtesy of Hong Kong Housing Authority.)*

Population densities are high in parts of the United States, mainly in some of the eastern seaboard cities, but when compared with Kowloon (Hong Kong) the numbers pale.

Housing

Public housing in Hong Kong is managed by the Housing Authority, a statutory body established in 1973 whose executive area, the Housing Department, has a staff of about 6,000. Its purpose was to merge various departments that had previously been responsible for different facets of the task. Aside from planning and construction, the authority is responsible for controlling squatters and for clearing land required for development. It advises the governor on all matters of housing policy.

Hong Kong's public housing program took on a new dimension with plans by the Housing Authority to extend the government's long-term housing strategy by 10 years into 2011.

Construction within the current program continues at a high rate, with over 53,000 flats being completed in 1990; and with greater emphasis being placed on quality, design, and comfort. Nearly three million people, more than half the population, now live in public housing, about 83 percent in rented flats and the rest in their own homes.

Rents charged remain comparatively low, at $28.1 per square meter for the newest urban estates or about one-quarter to one-third of market rates. There is increasing interest in the schemes offered by the authority to purchase flats.

The government provides capital assistance and land for the authority to implement its long-term housing strategy. In the next five years, $35 billion (in 1992, $7.73-Hong Kong equals one US dollar) will be spent on new construction work.

The authority has embarked on a number of major policy initiatives including an examination of the housing needs of the 'sandwich class' and the possibility of

Shek Kip Mei. *This housing estate, located in northern Kowloon, was erected after the great fire of 1953, which left more than 50,000 people homeless. It was one of the first public housing estates built to rehouse many of the refugees fleeing the People's Republic of China after the 1949 revolution. The project has served as a stepping stone from the slums and boat dwellings that sprawled over the hills and waterfronts of the Crown Colony as the population of Hong Kong increased from 600,000 in 1945 to more than 2 million in 1991. (Courtesy of Hong Kong Housing Authority.)*

selling some suitable rental public housing flats to sitting tenants. It also formed an *ad-hoc* committee to review rent policy and allocation standards for public rental housing.

The private non-profit-making Hong Kong Housing Society continued to supplement the provision of public housing through its rental and rural public housing projects, urban renewal scheme, and flats-for-sale scheme. Private sector housing production reached 27,400 units.[10]

Redevelopment. In 1972, a redevelopment program was launched to improve the living environment of some 84,000 families, comprising 240 blocks, which had been built between 1954 and 1964 to house victims of natural disasters and squatters displaced by development clearances. These estates provided only basic accommodation with community and social facilities which were not up to the present standard.

In 1983, the government decided to step up the redevelopment program, so that by 1991 the living conditions of all the remaining tenants could be improved. During 1990, 42 old blocks were evacuated to make way for new buildings, leaving 18 blocks to be redeveloped by 1991. The current five-year rolling redevelopment program for 1991 to 1995 involves 231 blocks accommodating 65,000 families.

10. Ibid.

PART 4

MODERN TRENDS

*Modern trends are sometimes
yesterday's concepts dressed in
new language. Neo-modern is more
of the same, only with panache.*

CHAPTER 16

TWENTIES AND THIRTIES LOOKING TO THE FUTURE

The special attention addressed to the plight of housing in the large urban complexes of the world has led to the formulation of many public programs to help alleviate the horrendous conditions facing residents in the slums and blighted areas. To appreciate the extent of the problem one need only observe housing conditions in the central sectors of Hong Kong, Tokyo, Manila, Shanghai, Rio de Janeiro, and other intensively urbanized places, to say nothing of those in the underdeveloped countries and the rural areas of almost every nation.

The material that follows identifies and traces some of the efforts in the United States, a few of which were begun many years ago by nineteenth-century idealists and benevolent industrialists. It does not by any means cover the wide range of efforts in virtually all modern nations to meet the most pressing of their social responsibilities to the masses of their people who live in conditions that could be described as not fit for animals.

The conditions of shelter are the core of the problem, but the causes are social and economic. Poverty consigns people to these areas. Coupled with lack of education and no opportunity to leave, it creates a situation in which the spirit of the residents becomes dulled to the point of accepting their lot as inevitable.

One of the major gains achieved through the drive for better housing and improved living conditions for the working population has been the concern for site planning and the provision for open space. The green areas required organizations for their maintenance, and apartment rentals for cooperative ownerships were the patterns that emerged. Subsidized developments of single-home parcels where maintenance was the responsibility of the individual occupants were infrequent; when the development consisted of clusters of individual homes, homeowners' associations were created to take care of common areas. The condominiums that developed during the 1970s offered another way of providing for uniform maintenance of grounds and other common-use facilities.

Some 27 million American households, one in three, still rent; in older urban areas, two of three do. Although some rents have not kept pace with inflation, they now exact a higher percentage of renters' incomes than ever before. There have also been some basic shifts in the housing market. Rental housing has been and still is considered hand-me-down housing, left behind in the move to suburbia. During the 1970s, those who could do so moved on to home ownership, leaving behind the poor, elderly, and single people.

Choosing adequate housing amid a wide range of quality and location poses no problems for the wealthy and only minor ones for the upper middle class. The moderate and lower income groups and the poor, on the other hand, face various problems related to their levels of income and social status. Race restrictions have been legally condemned, but there is still the "gentlemen's agreement" that can close the market to those of a color or religion unlike that of the majority in a given location.

It was for the moderate- and lower-income groups that subsidized public housing and rent assistance programs were designed. Many of the programs were established after the two world wars to rehouse those displaced by the destruction of cities and their subsequent reconstruction. New towns were also built in an effort to reduce the pressures on the overpopulated cities.

Critics of such programs noted that the former slum dwellers did not progress to join the mainstream of the middle class. Some critics went so far as to state that subsidizing rents created a situation in which the tenants would avoid improving their economic condition to remain in the public housing. But other problems were as fundamental as the need for money. There were few educational programs to teach those who had lived in slums how to care for their new facilities; further, there was no program to provide for improvement of their economic condition.

WORLD WAR I AND AFTER

During World War I the United States government assumed responsibility for the housing of workers in war industries. Two agencies were created to implement this program: the Housing Division of the Emergency Fleet Corporation and the United States Housing Corporation. The Emergency Fleet Corporation, through loans to shipbuilding companies for the purpose, completed some 9,000 family dwellings and 7,500 single-person accommodations. The United States Housing Corporation planned some 25,000 units in 60 projects but completed about 6,000 family units in 27 projects, none of which was ready for occupancy before the war came to an end.

The services of the most talented professionals in architecture and planning were enlisted for the program. Among the large-scale projects were Yorkship Village in Camden, New Jersey; Atlantic Heights in Portsmouth, New Hampshire; Buchman in Chester, Pennsylvania; Union Gardens in Wilmington, Delaware;

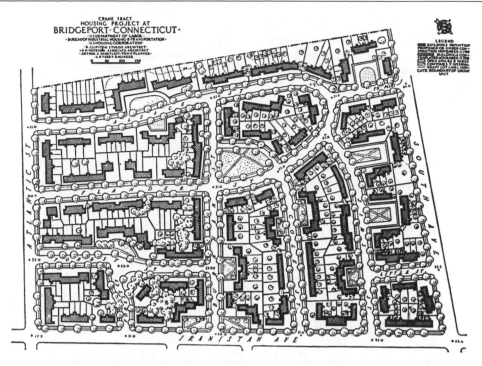

Seaside, Bridgeport, Connecticut. *One of the World War I housing developments undertaken by the federal government, Seaside demonstrated the advantages of large-scale planning. It included flats and single-family residences at a density of about seventeen dwellings per acre.*

and a number of developments in Bridgeport, Connecticut. It was a statutory requirement that projects built by these war agencies be sold immediately upon the end of the war. To make implementation of this provision easier the projects followed the usual general pattern of subdivision, but differences with previous practice were significant. Both superblocks and common open spaces for recreation were absent, but the layout of residential streets and the design of shopping centers presented a decided contrast with what most people had grown accustomed to in their living environment. Most obviously, all dwelling units were only two rooms in depth, in contrast with the narrow, deep building typical of the usual restricted lot in the ordinary urban subdivision. The planning of these projects exerted a strong influence in the decade after the war.

The architect Andrew J. Thomas, who participated in the war program, was active in the postwar period as well. One of his early projects was a large-scale development built in Long Island City, New York, by the Metropolitan Life Insurance Company. Dwelling units were two rooms deep, with stairways serving two dwellings per floor. The units were grouped in a series of U-shaped buildings that covered about 50 percent of the lot area. The open court faced the garden. Although they retained the characteristic narrow space between buildings, these buildings were a vast improvement over the small, enclosed light courts of the traditional single lot.

Thomas carried this simple planning technique further in the development of buildings of various forms, still using a basic unit of two and three dwelling units per stair. The essential contrast with previous planning was the relation of the buildings to the streets. Buildings constructed on the basis of the Tenement House Act of 1901 and before were on a single narrow lot and placed at right

The Garden Apartment

angles to the street: a narrow front and long depth. This forced all but the dwellings on the street front to face into a small courtyard, lightwell, or narrow rear yard. When the restrictions imposed by the narrow lot were removed, large-scale planning permitted the arrangement of buildings with a broad front and shallow depth. The interior of the lot was opened up and the interior court expanded. The result was dwelling units that faced the street in front and an open court in the rear. Such units were henceforth known as garden apartments.

Henry Wright and Clarence Stein

In 1926 the City Housing Corporation of New York built Sunnyside Gardens on a ten-block site in Long Island. Henry Wright and Clarence Stein, the architects, applied the garden apartment principle in a simple perimeter form surrounding an interior garden.

During this period much speculative building was producing the dreary, monotonous rows of cheap and poorly planned single-family houses and apartment buildings that still curse so many of our cities. The architects introduced in Sunnyside the row or group house and the two-story apartment, one dwelling above another with separate private entrances. Ground coverage was less than 30 percent of the lot area. They insisted on the potential of the group house to improve the planning of dwellings and the space about them.

Studies by Henry Wright and Clarence Stein about this time demonstrated the need for a complete analysis of all costs that enter into housing. In practice, planner and architect had been prone to detach their functions from those of management. Wright and Stein made clear that these functions could not be isolated and produce satisfactory housing: that improvement could not be expected unless plan-analysis was merged with experience in the management and maintenance of housing.

The row or group house was not a revolutionary dwelling type. It was prevalent in all Eastern cities. Baltimore and Philadelphia are famous for their row houses with clean, stone entrance stoops. But the architects went one step further: they demonstrated the superiority of dwellings two rooms in depth rather than the tandem arrangement to which the usual row house had degenerated. They showed how the group house improved land planning, in comparison with de-

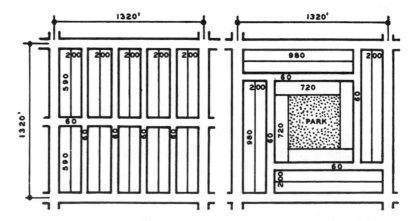

Comparative diagram by Henry Wright illustrates the improvement that a modification in the typical gridiron street and block layout might provide. On the left is the usual street plan, on the right the proposed replanning. With but slight loss of street frontage for subdivision of residential lots (the usual plan has 11,800 lineal feet of streets; the modified plan has 10,720 lineal feet), an interior park is gained and through traffic is eliminated from all interior streets.

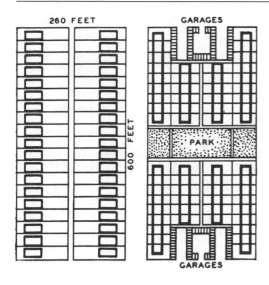

Henry Wright developed his case for the row house with studies like the one for Radburn. The typical block layout with two-story flat buildings facing the street is compared with a revised plan using continuous rows of two-story flat units; the alley is eliminated, garage courts are consolidated at the end of each block, and a park space accessible from all dwellings is gained in the center of the block.

tached units and their wasteful and useless side yards. These architects contributed much to the enlightenment in planning that emerged in the 1920s and early 1930s.

Inspired by the garden city idea, the City Housing Corporation acquired a vacant site in New Jersey within commuting distance of New York City for the community of Radburn. Henry Wright and Clarence Stein introduced the superblock, ranging from 30 to 50 acres in size, here. Through traffic was eliminated from these blocks; traffic streets surrounded rather than traversed the areas. Within them, single-family dwellings were grouped about cul-de-sac (dead-end) roads.

Radburn

Space was allocated for industry, shopping, and apartments, but green space around the town, typical of the English garden cities, was not incorporated in the plan. The houses were oriented in reverse of the conventional placement on the lot. Kitchens and garages faced the road; living rooms and bedrooms turned toward the garden. Pathways provided uninterrupted pedestrian access to a continuous park strip, which led to large common open spaces within the center of the superblock. Underpasses separated pedestrian walks from traffic roadways. The community earned the name of "The Town of the Motor Age."

Radburn's residential character and street access systems have been a prototype of sound community planning in many nations ever since.

Historically, subsidy was a means to encourage the expansion of this country, to push railroads across the land, and to smooth out the peaks and valleys of economic inequalities. It was used whenever necessity dictated. In 1926 it was introduced to housing with passage of the New York Housing Law, which established the State Board of Housing. This act granted the privilege of tax exemption for a 20-year period to limited-dividend companies engaged in providing housing within reach of the lower-middle class. The statutory ceiling on rents was $12.50 per room per month in the borough of Manhattan and $11.00 per room elsewhere. Investment in apartment development was encouraged by this legislation. This was significantly higher (proportionately) in today's dollars. Fourteen proj-

HOUSING AS AN INVESTMENT

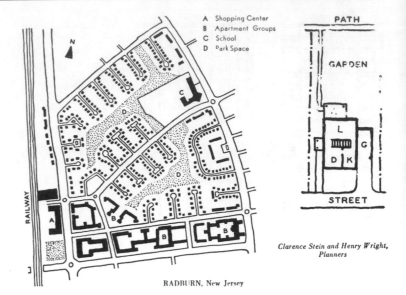

A Shopping Center
B Apartment Groups
C School
D Park Space

Radburn, New Jersey—
Clarence Stein and Henry Wright, planners. The Radburn plan came to be known as the Town of the Motor Age. The cul-de-sac residential streets became service roads rather than trafficways, the house being reversed from the usual plan so that living rooms faced on the rear gardens. Pedestrian paths led to the continuous park space.

RADBURN, New Jersey

Clarence Stein and Henry Wright, Planners

ects, providing a total of nearly 6,000 dwellings, were undertaken in this program. Among the best known were three cooperative developments of the Amalgamated Clothing Workers, which provided 625 apartments for its members. In addition to the Housing Board projects other limited-dividend and semiphilanthropic developments were undertaken in New York. Phipps Houses, Inc., a veteran housing organization, built 344 apartments in four- and six-story walkup and elevator buildings near Sunnyside Gardens. In 1930 John D. Rockefeller, Jr., built the Paul Laurence Dunbar apartments in Harlem, 513 apartments eventually to be acquired by the tenants. About this time the Julius Rosenwald Foundation built the Michigan Boulevard Gardens on the South Side of Chicago, and the Marshall Field Estate built Marshall Field Apartments on the near north side of the city. In Pittsburgh, Chatham Village, built by the Buhl Foundation, was a two-story group house development planned by Henry Wright.

These projects did not produce speculative profits but were sound investments that served a high social purpose as well. Such a purpose is not nourished by irresponsible interests concerned with quick turnover of capital and unlimited profits, nor does it thrive on exploitation and speculation in land, buildings, and people.

The importance of the period we have been discussing is not the quality of planning as a standard to which we aspire today, but rather as a comparison with the unwholesome planning it replaced and the processes that brought it about. Good planning was demonstrated during the twenties and early thirties to be economical planning. Twenty-five years prior, the typical tenement covered 85 percent of a narrow deep lot. More than half the rooms either had no light or peered into dingy lightwells. Open space about the dwelling was either the paved traffic street or a shabby refuse-ridden rear yard. The energetic talents of such architects as Ernest Flagg, Grosvenor Atterbury, Andrew Thomas, Henry Wright, Clarence Stein, and Frederick Ackerman served to bring about a vast change in all this. Land coverage was reduced to 50 percent or less, and space was planned to enhance the environment and provide room for recreation. Careful planning and better interior arrangement of rooms reduced waste space within buildings and eliminated unnecessary corridors and halls. Attention was given to the appropriate size and use of rooms rather than to the greatest number of people that could be loaded on a given site.

Complete disregard for housing standards and desire for profit regardless of the exploitation it entailed had produced high density, excessive land coverage, and decidedly bad housing. The theory that these evils were essentially good business was exploded. Good planning was discovered to be an effective instrument to compete with bad planning. When laws were enacted to curb irresponsible building of slums, the road was cleared for good planning with financial benefits as well as the restoration of positive social values.

The period of activity during the twenties and early thirties did not solve our urban housing ills but did provide a foundation upon which future progress could be continued. Building companies became conscious of the advantages of investment in housing. Large-scale planning opened the opportunity for arranging

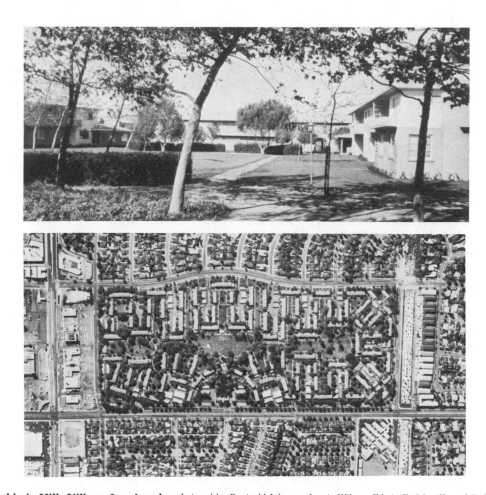

Baldwin Hills Village, Los Angeles, *designed by Reginald Johnson, Lewis Wilson, Edwin E. Merrill, and Robert Alexander, architects. An attractive large-scale rental development of the early 1940s, Baldwin Hills Village consists of 627 dwellings in one- and two-story group houses and flats on an outlying 80-acre tract. The low land price of $2,300 per acre permitted low density—about eight families per acre—and a coverage of only 7.3 percent of the land. An innovative feature of this project is the private patio for about two-thirds of all the dwellings. It will be noticed in the plan that the boulevard along the north (bottom) boundary is separated from the project by a park strip and a service road from which the various garage courts are accessible. Additional parking space is provided by indented parking areas along the service drive and along minor boundary streets. Small playgrounds for children are distributed about the development in addition to the "village green" in the center. The aerial view below reveals that the standards of planning and space in Baldwin Hills Village did not influence the later conventional subdivision of land about the periphery.*

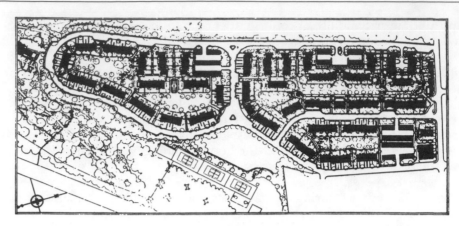

Chatham Village, Pittsburgh, *Ingham and Boyd, architects. A limited-dividend project built as an investment by the Buhl Foundation, Chatham Village was originally planned to include 300 units within reach of the $2,200 to $3,600 per year income group. Henry Wright's plan created a density of about twelve families per acre in two-story group houses. He thus continued to practice and to espouse the cause of the group house on urban land that had not yet reached the increasingly high costs of many other areas.*

buildings on land so that all dwellings were well located. As a permanent investment such factors were important, and good planning was becoming good investment. Good planning built in permanent value.

Charles F. Lewis, director of the Buhl Foundation that built and manages Chatham Village in Pittsburgh, said in 1937:

> Capital is frankly challenged by this unusual opportunity for sound and productive use of its funds.

> Essentially this will be an investment and not a speculative use of capital. . . . No less has it been demonstrated by the so-called limited dividend companies, from Boston in 1871 to Pittsburgh in 1934, that limited dividends pay. I refer you specifically to the remarkable success of the City and Suburban Homes Company of New York, founded in 1896 by Mr. R. Fulton Cutting and associates. After years of operation, in 1933 in the midst of the depression, this company could boast assets of nearly $10,000,000, a surplus of more than $1,380,000, and net earnings of from $263,000 to $445,000 per year through four depression years. Its average annual dividend rate, from 1899 to 1939, was 4.65 percent. Or let us take six noncooperative apartment projects built in New York City under the New York State Housing Board. All have been consistent dividend payers in good times and bad. Or let us take, in the city of Washington, the Washington Sanitary Improvement Company, which with assets of nearly $1,500,000 can boast that from 1897 to 1923 it paid an annual dividend of 5 percent, and from then on, straight through the depression, of 6 percent. Or the Washington Sanitary Housing Company which has paid 5 percent per annum without interruption since 1927. While Chatham Village in Pittsburgh has not yet published earnings statements, those statements when released will give further evidence of the investment soundness of the large-scale housing enterprise on the limited-dividend basis.[1]

THE GREAT DEPRESSION

On the heels of the building boom during the prosperity decade of the twenties came the Crash of 1929 and the decade of the Depression that followed. Financial credit dried up, building stopped abruptly, and unemployment caused wide-

1. Opportunities for Building Rental Properties, Conference on Local Residential Construction, Chamber of Commerce of United States, Washington, D.C., Nov. 17, 1937.

spread privation for millions of families. As the Depression gained momentum, economic and social chaos followed in its wake. Marginal investments in stocks evaporated into thin air. The flood that had been poured into building investments during the craze of the boom was drained off, and ownership changed hands in rapid succession as the level lowered. Homes on farms and in the cities were foreclosed at an alarming rate. Real estate foreclosures jumped from 68,100 in 1926 to 248,700 in 1932.

The state of complete despair made it imperative for the government to act. President Herbert Hoover called his Conference of Home Building and Home Ownership in 1931. Its analysis revealed many of the problems that beset the nation and laid the groundwork for action that ensued in subsequent years. Some twenty-eight states enacted moratoria on mortgage foreclosures in 1931 and 1932. This device relieved the hysteria but only postponed the solution. The Emergency Relief and Construction Act in 1932 created the Reconstruction Finance Corporation, an agency empowered to lend government funds to bolster the faltering economy.

The tide of national collapse forced the government to assume increasing responsibility for the helpless economy and, beginning in 1933 with the election of Franklin Delano Roosevelt, the Congress created a series of agencies in rapid succession. These government actions brought into focus a fact that had been almost unwittingly overlooked: the United States had no inventory of the national welfare, the assets and liabilities of a going concern dealing in democratic enterprise. The blessing of abundant natural resources, the accident of favorable geographic location, and the aggressive enterprise of a free people had brought fortune and a position of world leadership to this country. This achievement, accomplished in so brief a history as our own—then less than 200 years—had blinded the people to the corollary of great industrial and financial empires: the social and economic hardships that filter into the lives of many who make up the society. The Great Depression lifted the veil on this scene and disclosed the gap between fortune and stability. It was apparent that the country must take stock of its resources to measure the future prospects for its enterprise.

The state of the Union was desperate at the beginning of the thirties. At no other time was there a more pressing need for the benefits of city planning than during the years of the Great Depression. Nor could there have been more convincing evidence of its absence. Much lip service had been paid to the cause of planning in previous years, and a small but vocal profession had grown up around this theme. A program for action was imperative, yet cities were unprepared for action when the time was ripe.

The Lack of Coordinated Planning

There was some encouragement in July 1933 when the administrator of public works appointed the National Planning Board. Previously it was customary for separate offices of the government to collect facts appropriate only for their own domain; now these facts would be collated and correlated and thus provide a pattern for appropriate action by the respective agencies. For the first time in the history of this country the advantages of research and analysis of our great natural resources were available for the general welfare.

The National Planning Board became the National Resources Board by executive order of President Roosevelt in June 1934. It was the board's purpose "to prepare and present to the President a program and plan of procedure dealing with the physical, social, governmental, and economic aspects of public policies for the development and use of land, water, and other national resources and such related subjects as may from time to time be referred to the Board by the President.'' The National Resources Committee succeeded the board in 1935. In July 1939 all these functions were transferred to the National Resources Planning Board, which in its turn was discontinued in 1943. Its functions have since been performed by various committees of Congress.

The work of the National Resources Planning Board and its predecessors was directed at issues of national scope, but it was organized on a regional basis. Probably their most significant activity was to encourage planning at local levels and to offer technical assistance to local planning agencies. Regional, state, and city planning were reviewed and organized; comprehensive reports on the state of natural resources were proposed; plans were recommended for appropriate conservation and use; the relative importance of various technological changes and developments was recorded; and valuable data on urban growth and population were assembled.

Despite these gains resistance to planning was considerable at the local level. Cities were unprepared when the Depression struck, the few exceptions emphasizing the general absence of plans. Faced with an immediate opportunity to establish permanent improvements in their environment, the people gave little evidence that they had concerned themselves with the question of their future urban development.

The issues of emergency planning versus sound planning were confused. By the time cities had become aware of their plight, the economic cost of blight, and the social hazard of slums, there was no time to plan. That would have to wait until the Depression had spent itself and prosperity had returned.

Building and maintaining the city constitute a complex and vital problem that requires considerable careful planning. The housing program during the Depression demonstrated the tragic results of its absence. Subdivisions sprawled across the city without a plan for the integration of future urban land use. Such a plan would have become an effective means for improvement of the community welfare. Instead, the public housing program was too frequently interpreted as an opportunity to get rid of some isolated eyesore or festering slum that pricked the civic pride.

Had civic leadership glanced back on the history of city development, it would have been abundantly clear that planning can never wait. The course of human affairs marches steadily on, and the direction of its course is determined by the degree of planning that proceeds it. When goals are set, they can be reached; when they are absent, the urban community drifts like a ship without a compass. Sadly, the goals have not yet been considered, and our cities are still adrift.

Greenbelt Towns   The government did succeed, if moderately, with one of its plans. Beginning in 1935, the Resettlement Administration planned four greenbelt towns. These satellite communities near large cities were inspired by Howard's Garden City idea, but they were not planned as self-contained towns; they were more like dormitory villages, as sources of employment for the residents were in the nearby cities. Each was surrounded by a belt of permanent open space, part of which could be farmed or gardened. A full complement of community facilities was

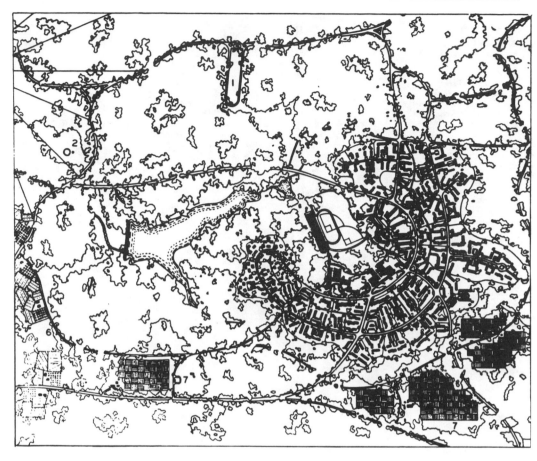

1 Water Tower
2 Disposal Plant and In-
   cinerator
3 Picnic Center and Lake
4 Community Center
5 Store Group
6 Rural Homesteads
7 Allotment Gardens

GREENBELT, Maryland

included in each town: shopping, schools, and recreation space. Three of these towns were actually built: Greenbelt, Maryland; Greenhills, Ohio; and Greendale, Wisconsin. The fourth, Greenbrook, New Jersey, was not built because of legal entanglements.

Greenbelt, Maryland, a development on a 2,100-acre site about 25 minutes' drive from Washington, D.C., includes 712 dwellings in group houses and 288 in apartments, a total of 1,000 units occupying an area of 250 acres. There are 500 garages. The sixteen-room elementary school is also used as a community center. The shopping center includes space for a post office, food stores, a drugstore, a dentist's and a doctor's office, a 600-seat theater, and such services as shoe repair, laundry, tailor, barber, and beauty shops. There are a bus terminal, a garage and repair shop, a fire station, and a gas station. The recreation facilities include an athletic field, picnic grounds, and an artificial lake. The superblock is used, each block containing about 120 dwellings with interior play areas. Underpasses provide continuous pedestrian circulation without the need to cross main roads. The commercial and community center, in the approximate center of the plan, reduces to a minimum the walking distance from all dwellings.

Almost every individual in the city has a home. Some may be rooms in a boardinghouse or a hotel, others fine houses on large estates. Some are slums. Whether the home is a hovel or a mansion, every person should have one. Dwellings

THE REAL CITY

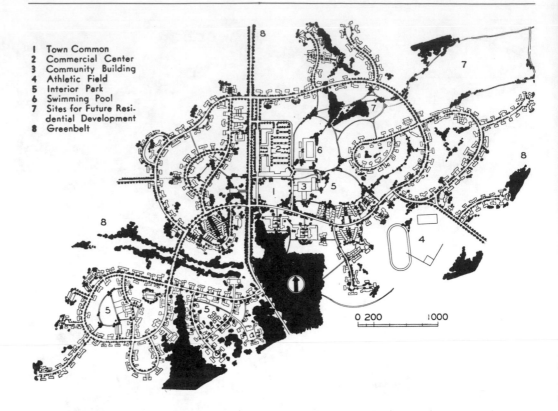

1 Town Common
2 Commercial Center
3 Community Building
4 Athletic Field
5 Interior Park
6 Swimming Pool
7 Sites for Future Residential Development
8 Greenbelt

Green Hills, Ohio. *This development is a satellite of Cincinnati, about 11 miles from the central district. The entire site is 5,930 acres. Planned for 3,000 dwellings, 1,000 comprised the first stage of building. Twenty percent are single- and two-family units, nearly half the units are in group houses containing three to six units per building, the rest—about one-third—are apartments. Garages are available for 17 percent of the dwellings, although space is arranged to provide them for all dwellings if necessary. A total of 168 acres is used for housing, 12 acres for the community center, and 35 acres in roads; 50 acres are for allotment gardens, community parks, and playgrounds. Protective open space occupies about 695 acres. The remaining 4,970 acres in the site are devoted to farms and wooded and wildlife areas. In this, as in Greenbelt, the superblock is the basic element, each averaging about 25 acres and housing between 400 and 500 persons per block. The community center contains the shopping district and the combined grade and high school for 1,000 pupils and auditorium-gymnasium to seat 1,100 people.*

occupy nearly three-quarters of the urban area. The economic equation by which people acquire and maintain a place to live measures the social and physical health of a community. The economics of housing is the base upon which cities rest. It is the foundation on which the social superstructure is built.

If we want to see the real city, we do not confine our view to the great skyscrapers, the shopping promenade, or the park and boulevard. To see the city, we look at the dwellings of the people. We see how people live, their streets of homes, the environment in which they raise their families, the children who will be the fellow-countrymen and countrywomen and neighbors of our children and generations hence.

It is this view that gives us direction toward the city of the future. When we comprehend this aspect of the city, we can more accurately guide the tools with which we shape the urban environment.

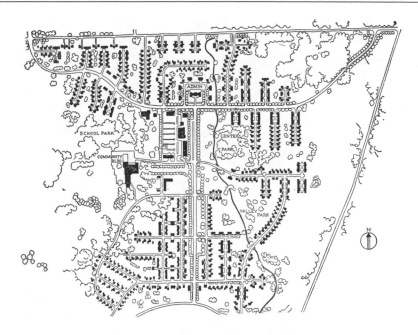

Greendale, Wisconsin. *This site of 3,500 acres is about one-half hour from Milwaukee. Planned for 3,000 units, only 750 dwellings have been built. The single-family detached house predominates, 380 units being of this type, 370 being twin houses. Most dwellings have attached garages. The community center and school and the shopping area at the center of the plan are within one-half mile of all dwellings. Generous park spaces are adjacent to the central part of the town, and permanent open agricultural space surrounds the built-up area.*

Lake Vista Housing Development, New Orleans. *Built in the 1930s on reclaimed land and modeled after Radburn, Lake Vista includes a central neighborhood commercial district and cul-de-sacs with houses that face inward to a central park area with pedestrian walkways lined with trees.*

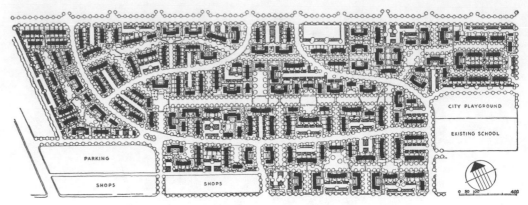

WYVERNWOOD, Los Angeles   *Witmer and Watson, Architects*

This FHA-insured rental project for "white collar" workers is composed of 1,100 two-story apartments on a 72-acre site with a coverage of about 25 per cent of the land area.

INTERLAKEN GARDEN APARTMENTS, Westchester County, New York

Young and Moscowitz, Architects

This project, planned for 3,500 units, is one of the largest approved for FHA insurance. The first stage was 525 dwellings of two stories with a building coverage of only 14 per cent of the land area.

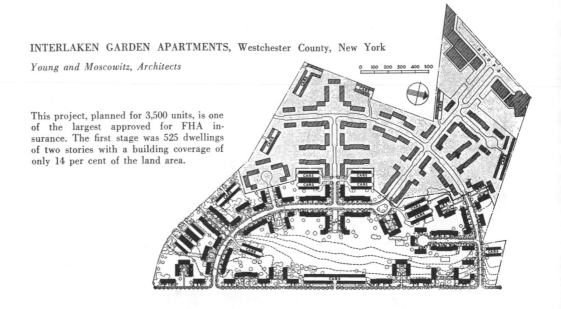

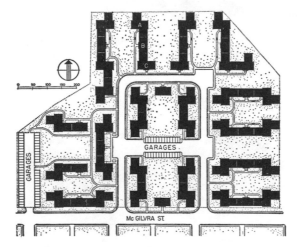

EDGEWATER PARK, Seattle

Graham and Painter, Architects

A 305-dwelling, FHA-insured development on the shore of Lake Washington, it comprises two-story apartments and flats.

Examples of private housing developments constructed during the 1940s at Wyvernwood, Los Angeles; Westchester County, New York; and Seattle, Washington.

CHAPTER 17

WORLD WAR II AND AFTER

Another war came, and a stroke of irony marked the affairs of human conduct. Planning assumed proportions never before conceived in history. With destruction of civilization a grim prospect, the scale of planning was gargantuan, staggering the imagination even now in retrospect. However, all this was planning based on essentially military needs and purposes.

With the ominous spread of Nazi domination in Central Europe and the threat of another world war, in June 1940 Congress enacted the National Defense Bill. Industry turned its attention to the production of war materials, and the Lanham Act authorized funds for housing defense-plant workers. Numerous government agencies entered the housing program. In July 1940, the Office of Housing Coordinator was established to determine and identify areas of acute shortage and to allocate federal funds to the various agencies.

New construction by FHA-insured private enterprise was stepped up, HOLC assisted the conversion of existing facilities, the low-rent program under USHA was stopped, and 100 percent loans were extended to local housing authorities to build defense housing. The Public Buildings Administration, Defense Homes Corporation, and Maritime Commission undertook construction of large-scale permanent government housing, and the Federal Works Agency launched a large program of prefabricated temporary dwellings.

With the attack on Pearl Harbor on December 7, 1941, all the energy of the nation was directed to the successful prosecution of the war. Peacetime and

A NEW ERA BEGINS

177

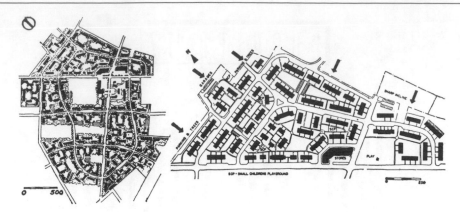

Buckingham, Virginia. *One of the earliest large-scale rental developments undertaken in the FHA program, Buckingham is located just outside Washington, D.C., for white-collar workers in the nation's crowded capital. Designed by Henry Wright, Allen Kamstra, and Albert Lueders, it was planned for 2,000 units on a 100-acre site. The first stage (shown in detail) comprised 622 dwellings on 30 acres. The land cost was twenty-five cents per square foot and permitted low density—about twenty families per acre—with a building coverage of about 20 percent of the land area. Approximately 13 percent of the area is in streets. Dwellings are two-story group houses and flats.*

defense housing were supplanted by a vast program of war housing, and huge plants were constructed to build ships, planes, and armaments. It has been estimated that migration of industrial workers to war jobs created a need for the housing of some 9 million families.

In February 1942, all federal housing agencies were consolidated in the National Housing Agency. The National Housing Act was amended to include Title VI, which provided FHA insurance for 90 percent loans amortized over 25 years, for housing built by operative builders for sale or rent to war workers. The need to conserve materials was critical. The floor area of dwellings and the materials used were rigidly restricted. The Lanham Act was amended to provide for the construction of temporary dwellings by the federal government.

More than 800,000 new dwellings were built and about 200,000 existing units converted by private enterprise, for a total estimated cost of $4 billion. Nearly 550,000 family dwellings and 170,000 dormitory units were built, and 50,000 existing structures converted into family dwellings through the direct operations of the federal government. There were, in addition, about 80,000 stopgap shelters provided in the form of trailers to permit mobility as shifting needs dictated. Building cost, without the conversion of existing units, was some $2 billion.

War work was distributed in all parts of the country, but the most pressing need was in large centers for the tremendous new industrial plants. Individual projects of 4,000 units were built in such places as Willow Run near Detroit; Norfolk, Virginia; Vancouver, Washington; and San Diego and San Francisco, California. The largest single operation was 10,000 dwellings for the Kaiser shipyards at Portland, Oregon.

The influx of great numbers of workers and their families strained every urban service. Housing was not complete without new streets, utilities, parks and playgrounds, theaters, shops and markets, and restaurants. Whole new communities were created in a few months, and war production was sustained.

The war was won. The goal had been clear: the survival of freedom. Planning had guided the production and distribution of goods, materials, food, weapons, and labor. It was necessary and well done.

Thus ended another paradox in the course of human events. While planning for military purposes was winning a great campaign, planning for the peace to come was abandoned. The National Resources Planning Board died during the conflict, and the very planning process with which our institutions were saved in war was denounced as an enemy of freedom. We need to learn from yesterday to prepare today for a better tomorrow.

From 1975 to 1990 the land values in all parts of the country spiraled to new heights. Desert land around Palm Springs, California, subject to wind and erosion damage, was being sold for more than $100,000 an acre. Foreign capital from many nations was pouring into the land market, not only from the oil-rich Middle East but also from Canada, Japan, and Europe. This sharp increase reflected inflation as well as a basic housing shortage. In the Los Angeles–Orange County areas of California a modest home sold for more than $100,000. Jerry-built homes with less than 1,000 square feet of space were selling in the $60,000 to $70,000 range. In some locations, the demand was so great that lotteries were held to award homes, which all too often were then bought by speculators seeking to take advantage of the soaring land values.

Professor Robert A. Brady, formerly of the Economics Department at the University of California at Berkeley, once stated that the depressed economic conditions of the 1930s confirmed the law of physics that holds that "everything that goes up will eventually come down." Perhaps we will soon see a repetition of that 1930s phenomenon.

In the meantime these land costs and interest rates are reflected in the cost of housing, whether as rental rates or as home prices. Because of the high costs, one can readily understand why developers often ask to be allowed to build housing of higher densities than that permitted by comprehensive plans and zoning ordinances. Such requests are difficult to deny when it is claimed, as it often is, that the proportionately smaller profit and consequent higher cost of low-density housing prevent poor people from purchasing decent homes.

This program was designed to help public agencies provide decent, safe, and sanitary housing for low-income families at affordable rents. The Department of Housing and Urban Development (HUD) provided financial and technical assistance to local housing authorities to help them plan, build, and operate low-rent public housing projects. Federal annual contributions covered the debt service of local authority bonds sold to pay for the development or acquisition of public housing. HUD also granted preliminary loans to the local authority for planning and temporary loans for building low-rent housing.

This program was initially intended to eliminate the slums and blighted areas of urban communities. Displacing the residents of these unfortunate areas became most difficult as there were no facilities for rehousing them at rents they could afford. It then became necessary to build public housing on open land. This angered the residents of nearby homes, and protests were launched against the entire program, ultimately reducing the efforts and eliminating many of the

RECENT TRENDS

Public Housing

proposed projects such as the ones at Chavez Ravine and Rose Hills in Los Angeles, California, where 5,000 units were not constructed after land was acquired and plans prepared. Chavez Ravine is now the location of the Los Angeles Dodgers baseball stadium and a sea of offstreet parking.

PLANNING FOR THE ELDERLY

One of the most pressing problems has always been housing for the elderly.[1] This is a worldwide problem, and many nations have taken steps to meet the need. Both public and private solutions have been suggested.

The requirements of the elderly vary greatly. Some are ambulatory, others are infirm, and a wide range exists in between. Special care may be required in addition to a decent living environment.

The ambulatory aged have numerous resources at their disposal. Many have grown children with whom they could live, but often age and other differences make it impossible for the two generations to live together harmoniously. Some elderly have joined large retirement communities. These serve a limited age group, mostly persons over 50 years old who have relatively large financial resources.

The housing of healthy ambulatory persons constitutes today's main challenge in planning for the elderly. The infirm in general are confined to institutional care facilities of one type or another. But decent housing for the ever-increasing number of persons who have contributed to the social and economic well-being of their communities during most of their lives has yet to be accomplished. Our civilization may well be judged by how sympathetically we respond to this segment of the population.

Until the early part of the twentieth century most of the countries of the world relegated the indigent aged to "poor farms." There was no differentiation of their problems from those of the poor. Certainly, little money was spent on resolving the problems of the aged.

The patterns and problems of the aged are similar throughout the industrialized world. The breakup of families for various reasons, whether in rural or urban areas, has left the elderly without any anchor. With the advent of social security, retirement pensions, and welfare programs, families feel even less responsibility for their elders. The elders share this attitude, not wanting to be a burden on their children, opting as far as possible to maintain their independence.

Only after 1920 did there begin to be a recognition of the special needs of the elderly. Since World War II particularly there has been a growing concern for their needs, not the least aspect of which has involved their housing. There is currently, in almost all of the nations of the world, an acceptance of some responsibility of ensuring the welfare of the aging population. During the past 40 years national governments in all countries have passed considerable legislation on behalf of the housing needs of poor elderly persons.

The United States

In 1950 the first National Conference on Aging was held in Washington, D.C., and the problems of the elderly began to assume national importance. In 1961

---

1. This discussion is based in part on an unpublished paper by Sylvia Stern, UCLA, 1978.

President Dwight D. Eisenhower called for another national conference on the subject. More than 2,500 delegates met to define the circumstances, needs, and opportunities of elderly citizens and to find ways to improve their living conditions. The most important conclusion of the 1961 conference will seem obvious: that the problems of housing for the aged are everybody's problem.

In 1976, President Gerald Ford asked Congress to join him in improving government programs servicing the elderly. There was no doubt that the more than 11 percent of the total population that constituted the elderly then needed assistance and that the greatest part of the problem was economic. In 1977, six of ten older Americans had incomes near or below the poverty level. More than 20 percent lived in substandard housing. These same persons were and are faced with inflation and fixed incomes that cannot adjust to the increases in the cost of living.

It seems that the American fascination with bigness runs over into the provision of housing for the elderly. Public or private, the ensemble must be large to be "efficient," even though this so-called efficiency often translates into maximum profit and endless mediocrity. Thus the current public housing facilities for the elderly in the United States, with some exceptions, are in high-rise buildings. These complexes are large enough to make the cost of operating them manageable. The clients are normally persons of the same age bracket and level of health.

The Older Americans Act of 1965 formed the basis of all future housing legislation for the elderly. It established that all older people are entitled to suitable housing independently selected, designed, and located in accordance with their special needs "and available at costs they can afford."

Current Housing Programs

Section 8 of the Housing and Community Development Act of 1974 discussed earlier offered aid to the elderly in its Section 202 in the form of the Senior Citizen Direct Housing Loan. It provides long-term direct federal construction and permanent mortgage loans at below-market interest rates for the construction or substantial rehabilitation of rental housing for the elderly and handicapped. Section 8 is one of the current programs being funded by HUD.

Foster Homes for the Elderly. A specialized service is provided by the Foster Home Program in Bucks County, Pennsylvania.[2] The program is designed for people over sixty who do not need the skilled care of a nursing home but who cannot or should not live alone. It was begun in 1961 by Peggy O'Neill, who developed the program after trying to cope with the problems of a long waiting list at an overcrowded county home for the aged. Many of those in the home, needing only minimal care and supervision, had been institutionalized unnecessarily.

The Foster Home Program started with a grant from the Pennsylvania Department of Labor and Industry. Originally conceived as a way to provide housing for the elderly in a family setting, the program has become an interim care arrangement as much as a housing arrangement.

Unlike house-sharing programs, the Bucks County program is supported by casework services and backup facilities, which are the primary reasons for its success. Caseworkers help their elderly clients with financial matters, make sure they receive any necessary medical and psychiatric attention, and provide ongo-

---

2. Denise P. Frank and Michael J. Frank, *Planning* (The American Society of Planning Officials, 1978), p. 340.

ing counseling. Foster home residents who need skilled care and are financially eligible have priority for admission to the county nursing home.

The Bucks County program benefits not only the elderly but also the community at large and foster care providers as well. The elderly benefit because they remain in the community rather than being institutionalized and segregated. Follow-up contact by caseworkers assures that their arrangements are suitable; a different home is usually found within 2 weeks if irreconcilable conflicts arise or if the elderly person is being given improper care.

Foster home providers benefit, too. Often these individuals are themselves retired or elderly, perhaps "empty-nesters" who provide adult foster care rather than enter the labor market. In addition to the companionship their role provides, they receive supplemental income that can help with home maintenance costs and rising taxes. The fact that the providers know that they are not responsible for all their residents' needs helps make the program work. Their contract requires that they provide only room, board, laundry, and basic supervision.

Last, the Foster Home Program has advantages for the community and the agency that provides the care. The county nursing home is free to serve the elderly who genuinely need skilled care. Furthermore, it is much less expensive to shelter a person in a foster home than in a nursing home.

The International Scene

The European experience provides much that is relevant to the United States.[3]

Consumer housing subsidies in the form of housing allowances, rent rebates, and rent differentials have been an integral part of the European solution. They deal directly with the special hardships of the elderly poor by providing accommodation for the elderly not only through new construction, which necessarily is limited, but also by using existing housing.

Housing production subsidies, amounting to roughly two-thirds of total West European housing subsidies, constitute the main financial thrust of government policy. Some form of production subsidy or incentive is considered essential as long as critical housing shortages exist in general. These subsidies also ensure the construction of an adequate supply of cluster housing, designed specifically for the elderly, that is integrated with neighborhoods with a normal cross section of population. Effective land use planning by the local government has been a further important ingredient in the production approach.

Many areas in Europe of warm climate and beautiful environment, such as the Cote d'Azur, have become popular retirement areas. In towns like Nice more than a quarter of the population is of pensionable age. In Portugal, Spain, Malta, and Cyprus flourishing residential developments are aimed specifically at attracting retirees from northern Europe. This multinational migration, which mainly attracts people who have lived most of their lives in cities, has taken similar forms wherever it has emerged despite the cultural differences of the retired individuals. Indications are that the migration will continue and grow for years; the areas involved must prepare themselves for coping with the special health and social needs resulting from the increasing presence of a population no longer young.

---

3. Sylvia Stern, unpublished paper.

Canada. Since 1946 an estimated 90 percent of all new housing produced specifically for Canada's elderly has been built with the assistance provided by the government's National Housing Act.

The majority of these accommodations have been provided in just the past 20 years, reflecting vastly increased allocations of federal funds for housing and new legislative incentives to stimulate the sponsorship of developments to serve elderly persons and low-income families.

Great Britain. In England the local authority has a statutory duty to review the housing needs of its area from time to time and to provide housing when it is not being provided by private enterprise. Local councils initiate new ideas about housing and often press the minister of housing for supporting legislation. For example, the city of Birmingham petitioned Parliament to obtain powers to pay rent allowances to private tenants long before this idea became part of national policy.

In England there are no income limits on admission to public housing projects; thus there are no means tests that can force a tenant to leave subsequently. The words "the working classes" were deleted from the titles and texts of all housing statutes in 1949. The result is that the tenants of the public housing stock represent a much wider spectrum of the population than in the United States.

American can learn some lessons by example from the British. One may be found at Roehampton, a housing estate within the county of London but outside of the central city. The housing is located within the larger estate in small groups of one-story row houses. There are about twenty units for the elderly in each of the complexes. They are situated in a garden environment, close to an elementary school and the area's shopping facilities. The residents enjoy the friendships that can only be established in small groups and are revivified by the variety of the neighborhood that surrounds them.

Near enough to an elementary school to be aware of the activity of children, but not so close as to be disturbed by them, the residents are thus close enough, yet far away enough from activity. They can visit others, and whenever they wish they can return to the quiet of their homes. They find jobs as babysitters so that they can continue to feel they are useful human beings; the conveniently located stores allow them to shop for themselves and give them as well a place for social contact. All of these aspects contribute to a pleasant and fruitful life.

France. In 1971, the French government set up housing allowances for those over sixty-five or those over sixty unable to work. The purpose was to reduce the rent of a principal home to a level compatible with income. This housing allowance takes the place of the former rental allowance that was subject to the rules of welfare aid. Its purpose was to allow the elderly to remain as long as possible in an independent dwelling adapted to their needs.

Sweden. The Swedish government has an outstanding record, far ahead of that of other nations, in caring for its elderly. The problem was recognized early and remedies attempted in conjunction with other social problems. Sweden has the most extensively organized social service programs of any of the Scandinavian countries. The stated goal is to permit each person handicapped by age or illness to improve within the limits of his or her capacity in order to lead as independent a life as possible.

Roehampton Estates, London. *Housing for the elderly is in the foreground.*

Social services account for 40 percent of Sweden's national budget. Total welfare expenditure amounts to about 20 percent of the country's national income. This is a little above the proportion in other Scandinavian countries and considerably higher than in the United States. Roughly 85 percent of the central government's and 75 percent of the local government's expenditures for social benefits are distributed without a means test.[4]

The Swedes are acutely aware of and responsive to the developing needs of their growing aged population. The national government provides financial support. A person reaching 65 years of age is entitled to an old-age pension, a basic benefit paid to all persons. The sum is index-adjusted and rises with the general cost of living. Approximately half of all pensioners receive supplementary housing allowances in addition.

The support given by local authorities to the elderly is wide ranging. Apart from institutional care and old-age centers, where pensioners live in a hotel environment and enjoy various facilities for recreation and occupation, there is an extensive home care system, upon which the Swedes place great emphasis. Pensioners live in their own homes or apartments until they can no longer care for themselves or their quarters. The country has about 10,000 specially trained workers, 3,400 of whom are on the government's payroll, assisting with services that include visiting and nursing in the home and providing recreational and other activities arranged by the municipality or by private organizations. In 1967 a home nursing allowance was introduced for those requiring special attention and care who would otherwise be entitled to institutional care. The same year successful experiments were begun with occupational therapy in the home. Home helpers, called Samaritans, shop and do other household jobs and try to help break through their patients' sense of loneliness and isolation.

There are numerous housing projects for the elderly, many of which are outstanding in design and amenities offered. The vast majority of housing is cur-

4. John McRae, "Elderly in the Environment—Northern Europe." University of Florida, Gainesville, 1975.

rently constructed by nonprofit building companies, a trend that developed after World War II in all Scandinavian countries. The Swedish National Housing Board finances 90 percent of all housing construction. It provides financial incentives to nonprofit groups, which are eligible for 100 percent loans as opposed to 85 percent loans for private companies.

People's Republic of China. The treatment of the elderly in the People's Republic of China follows traditional lines. The elderly are, in the words of one Chinese guide, "our treasures." They live with and are part of the extended family. Since space in the home is so limited (currently at about 22 square feet per person) the use of space must be carefully planned. All in the family work, so the elders become the managers of the household and the guardians of the very young children, and the linkage that holds the home together.

During the 1980s, and continuing into the 1990s, the plight of the elderly residing in apartments significantly worsened. Property owners, faced with higher taxes, mounting maintenance costs, and other economic problems, raised rents to cover their expenses. Many rent increases were unreasonable, however. The residents had fixed incomes—social security or retirement pensions—which limited their ability to meet the inflated conditions. As the housing market became tighter and the options of the residents fewer, the proportion of their income allocated to rent became excessive to the point that it played havoc with diet and other basic needs. Though there were tenant strikes, there were more often dispossessions: the elderly were evicted from the shelter that they could no longer afford.

As a result, some communities have restricted the conversion of existing buildings, without limiting the construction of new condominiums. The property owners on occasion have assisted residents in obtaining alternative dwellings; municipal housing agencies also have participated in the relocation process. Once moved, however, the elderly find themselves in unfamiliar environments, with little or no ability to adjust to the changed condition of their lives and to the often less desirable housing that their meager income can afford.

Other than units available to the more affluent, few if any of the housing accommodations for the ambulatory elderly were actually designed for their life requirements. In fact, the majority of available accommodations were constructed years ago as general family units. These are old and in many cases too large for the present occupant or occupants, thus wasteful as well. The facilities and amenities available are not designed to meet the needs of the elderly, are often located too far from the dwelling and, without reasonable means of transportation, too difficult for the residents to use conveniently.

The type of building to be developed for housing varies with economic and physical circumstances, with conditions in the urban areas, and the attitude that obtains in each situation. In America, where early pioneers developed the low-intensity towns, as land was almost free for the taking, there developed the notion of the single-family detached home as the dream castle of every family. Development within the larger urban centers, such as New York, Chicago, Baltimore, and Philadelphia, characteristically concentrated high density close to the core where activities were greatest. Just outside these burgeoning core areas, densities tended to fall off to the level seemingly desired by the aspirants of greater living space. One has but to cross the Hudson River or head north along the freeways to find low-density communities where the more affluent find ref-

The Elderly in Rental Apartments

THE HIGH-RISE "SOLUTION"

High-rise Marina Towers, Chicago. *High-rise buildings for both residential and commercial uses, with many floors of parking, where land is scarce and costs are astronomical.*

uge. The really wealthy formed their own compounds in places named Bel Air, Shaker Heights, Newport, Beverly Hills, and the like, where exclusiveness and prestige were the hallmarks of status. No congestion here.

In the world at large, the pattern of congestion in the older portions can be observed. British cities are built up with great densities, and they are matched or exceeded by such places as Shanghai, Calcutta, Hong Kong, Tokyo, Manhattan Island, São Paolo, and Paris. Other cities with smaller populations of approximately 1 million display the same form and structure. High-rise buildings with little or no open space are present in all of them, as are overcrowded streets filled with people and vehicles of all types.

When portions of the older cities have been reconstructed because of war, natural disasters, or reaction against unpleasant and unhealthy conditions prevailing, the forms are more reasonable. However, while providing for some open spaces, the buildings go skyward in order not to reduce the overall densities. The high-rise prevails.

HIGH-RISE BUILDINGS

In general, high-rise residential structure implies more than three stories but more often not fewer than five when economics makes elevators feasible. In practice, however, high-rise has usually meant buildings ranging from ten to fifty stories in height.

Samuel Hurst, former dean of the School of Architecture at the University of Southern California, stated that high-rise buildings were poor places for family living, especially if the family had small children or animals of any kind. In the area of Caracas, Venezuela, public housing was provided in high-rise buildings in the port city of La Guira and residents of the hillside slums were moved into them. After a short period the buildings appeared ready for replacement, and the residents moved out and back to the hillsides, where they had space and could raise chickens, pigs, and flowers in their small personal gardens. The situation in St. Louis, where the high-rise public housing remained largely uninhabited and was finally physically destroyed, is a classic example of the difficulty people have with the barren sterility of high-rise buildings when they are used to living in personalized if poor housing in close-knit communities.

There is no question but that the more affluent, seeking a maximum of security, find high-rise buildings desirable places to live. Several new buildings along Wilshire Boulevard in the Westwood section of Los Angeles advertised high-rise units, condominiums, for sale in the $11 to $15 million range, and they were being purchased in the 1990s.

One of the most controversial items in the housing field in all parts of the United States beginning in the late 1970s and continuing into the 1990s involves apartment rent controls. Faced with inflation and high interest rates, apartment owners in some cases raised rents to an unconscionable rate. In newer apartments occupied by the more affluent, the raises were absorbed as incomes increased. For the lower middle class and the poor, however, the impact was very different. Those with limited incomes could not meet the increases without being adversely affected in terms of diet and other essentials of survival. Protests began, causing responses that found their way into the halls of city and county governments. One community after another adopted rent control laws, fixing the percentage amount that rents could be raised during a specific period (generally related to the cost of living index). In most cases, however, the vacating of an apartment freed the owner to rent at any rate that appeared appropriate.

RENT CONTROLS AND CONDO-MINIUMS

The concept of owner-occupied condominium apartments offered the owners of existing apartments a means to be freed from the restraints of rent control. They turned rental units into condominiums and gave tenants the choice of either purchasing the units or vacating them.

The impact of this device on the less economically fortunate, disproportionately the elderly, was devastating. Purchase prices and costs of maintenance went far beyond their limited means. Once again there was pressure on government bodies to adopt regulations that would protect the tenants from either being gouged or being forced to occupy undesirable accommodations.

A true housing crisis was on. New laws were required for dealing with evictions. Families began to double up if at all possible, providing shelter for parents in the homes of children, when and if space was available and personal problems of the different age groups could be overcome.

The crisis was felt not only with apartment space. Many people had purchased mobile homes, locating them on rented small lot-sized spaces or in mobile home parks. But in the 1980s rents for mobile home spaces were, like those for their apartment counterparts, increased to the point where many occupants could not pay them. Most communities were reluctant to pass any kind of rent-control laws, and few if any did anything other than listen to the complaints of mobile-home occupants.

AFFORDABLE HOUSING

The population of the world is growing with each passing year. It could be assumed that the need for additional housing would be a matter of great concern internationally. As children grow up and greater numbers of families are formed, it might be assumed that the need for additional dwelling units would manifest itself in a building boom in most of the world. However, neither of these is absolutely the case. The gap between the growing need and the evolution of an effective demand constitutes a major gap in the housing market. Effective demand can be defined as the "desire for housing plus the ability to pay for it." With the cost of housing ever increasing in conjunction with economic dislocation of great numbers of families, the demand cannot become effective and the building of housing units falls short of need by a wide margin. Recent statistics indicate that only one-quarter of American households can afford new single-family housing. A decade ago, almost half the households could.

In the United States, the years leading into the 1980s saw all sorts of experiments. Most attempted to involve the private sector more than before, thus leading away from public housing and into the realm of subsidies to encourage private building for low- and middle-income groups.

HUD's position in the field of housing was weakened in the late 1970s. In the 1980s, for all practical purposes it was virtually eliminated through the efforts of the Reagan administration and the "New Federalism" programs that were espoused. These programs reduced the role that the federal government played in local community affairs by getting the federal government out of the housing and redevelopment business. While this panacea seemed attractive, it was hardly practical because of the limited financial capability of most communities, both large and small, to meet housing needs without federal assistance. This is particularly true in farm and industrial communities where poverty, unemployment, and homeless families are facts of life.

As with all new programs, new language came into the picture; in this case it was "affordable housing." The application of the term to the housing market was not uniform, since the definition of affordable was necessarily vague. It was intended to imply housing within the economic reach of the lower-middle income group. The cost for housing in this category runs from $50,000 to $75,000; even in the inflated economy of the 1970s–1980s this priced the units out of many would-be home purchasers' reach, especially with mortgage interest running between 13 and 20 percent. During the major recession of the early 1990s, when interest rates on housing loans fell to 12 percent or less, the housing market remained sluggish because of high unemployment, failures and scandals in the thrift industry, and insecurity among consumers about getting into debt. Even with population increases, the lack of effective demand for housing was apparent.

The housing industry has developed various devices to bring down costs. These include the lowering of standards of all types, including reduction in lot sizes, elimination of yards, decrease in the size of rooms, and lowering of ceilings. These and other practices ultimately may lead to overcrowding, congestion, conflicts, and the potential disruption of family life.

It begins to appear that new ideas for providing housing for the many thousands of families with modest incomes will emerge only from a greater degree of local participation, if and when local economic conditions permit. The so-called New Federalism did cut back on social programs, but it provided block grants that

Not-so-mobile homes near Oakland, 1992 (factory-built housing).

may be helpful in planning and building housing, especially in those communities where there is a reasonable concern for the welfare of the residents.

The Reagan administration proposed elimination of block grants as part of their 1985–86 budget. While still supporting and funding block grant programs, the federal government has made sure that, insofar as possible, funds are funneled to the cities through the states.

In the meantime, with federal assistance either limited or unavailable, the states and local communities have been authorized to issue tax-free municipal bonds as a means of securing housing for low- and middle-income families. Funds have also been provided for urban renewal through the issuance of Tax Increment bonds, the amortization coming from both income and property value appreciation. Refer to Chapter 38 for material on Tax Increment Financing.

Local Housing Financing

PART 5

THE PLANNING PROCESS

*If we could first know where we are,
and whither we are tending, we could better
judge what to do, and how to do it.*

—*Abraham Lincoln*

CHAPTER 18

RESEARCH FOR PLANNING

Planning is optimism, looking ahead, anticipating the potentials and limitations of urbanism and the quality of life that can be provided for humans and other animals.

Facts often quoted by opponents to planning are pessimistic . . . looking at past failure as reason for not trying to improve the living conditions.

The Greek philosopher Heraclitus once said that the difficulty confronting human society was to combine that degree of liberty without which law is tyranny with that degree of law without which liberty becomes license. The democracy of Athens, the Magna Carta in England, and the Constitution of the United States were wrought essentially from that same precept. Our society is organized on the basis of a group of laws established to guide the people in their conduct. The overriding purpose is to guarantee and protect liberty and justice for all.

Inspired by this freedom, the people of America created a vast domain of commercial and industrial enterprise. And they built great cities.

Today we see these cities scarred by congestion and decay, speculation and ugliness. We see the science and invention of our remarkable age snarled in the tangle of the urban network. At best our cities are mediocre. That mediocrity is a travesty of the productive genius and creative energy of America.

URBAN ANARCHY

It is not the desire of the people that their cities should be so built. Rather it is their ambition to create fine cities; otherwise the forward strides that have been taken would not even have been attempted. It is the essence of democracy that the people shall be masters of their destiny, that their behavior shall be guided by the precepts of law and order. Yet our cities suffer disorder and confusion as though born of anarchy. The most frantic antidotes of regulation appear inept and futile. The reasons for this state of urban affairs may be apparent upon examination.

Who are the city builders? They are the multitude of city people who invest in urban property and improvements. All the people participate. Some share by their investments of capital in physical improvements for conduct of profitable enterprise; others invest in municipal revenue bonds that pay for public improvements. All participate through their payment of taxes for the public services that make urban investment feasible.

Forty percent of the city area is public property: the streets, parks, schools, and variety of other publicly used elements. Within this area local government may shape the streets, traffic arteries, and open spaces according to the designs of official planners. But the bulk of city building, 60 percent of the total urban area, proceeds parcel by parcel as industry, business, and home-seekers find opportunity for investment.

Those who invest for profit are guided by the market for improvements. Investment in a city implies stability of values. By its nature the city is a permanent institution whose purpose is to shelter the continuing activities of people. An immediate market induces investment, and a continuing market makes of it a sound investment.

Stability in part depends upon the quality of the improvement itself. It also depends upon the quality of other improvements that have preceded and those that will follow. It depends upon the standards at which a community maintains itself, the level of maintenance of existing facilities, and the standards the community demands for future improvements. These determine the difference between environmental degeneration or stability, and upon them rests the difference between speculation and sound urban development.

Physical improvements on private land are not the only factors that affect the health of urban investment. The city functions through the circulation of goods and services. The warp, the infrastructure, of the community pattern is the network of streets, utilities, and transportation. The strength of the urban pattern is measured by the adequacy and convenience of the circulatory system and services; the stability of investment is measured by the level at which the community maintains itself.

Urban growth in some respects is analogous to processes in nature. The soil of fertile and prosperous citizenship is tilled, the seeds of investment are planted, and the garden is cultivated with urban management and maintenance, both public and private. All urban activities and functions are inseparable. The only area in which they may be isolated is that of speculation, and for that reason speculation is damaging.

Speculation—quick turnover for quick profit—contributes in large measure to building a city, but speculators assume no responsibility because they are not concerned with the use of the improvement. That responsibility and the obligation for maintaining it are shifted to others when the speculators transfer ownership. The motive of speculation consequently induces inferior quality; it is concerned only with the least possible initial cost and the greatest possible profit.

Speculative improvements are nonetheless an investment in the city. They are investments in which the public participates. Public services must be made available to all property, and the cost of these services is paid by taxes and public utility rates. These costs are determined to a large degree by the quality of the improvements to the elements that the city comprises. High quality resists spotty shifts in urban land use, the wasteful extension and duplication of public and private services and facilities, and holds stable values.

What determines the physical form of the city? It emerges from the initiative and enterprise of many people, acting individually and in groups. They are guided not by some preconceived model of the future city, however brilliant or inspired, but by a set of standards. The real plans for our cities are the standards prescribed by law: the codes and ordinances that regulate the development of urban property.

Laws form an integral part of the whole planning process, and all expression and action of those who design and invest in urban building are within the limits prescribed by law. City building is guided by the maximum quantity and minimum quality legally allowed.

That this process imposes a singular responsibility upon the citizen should be self-evident. It is the obligation of the people to determine the standards they deem appropriate for their community and to translate these standards into effective rules and regulations. It can be fairly stated that this responsibility has not been discharged with the intelligence and devotion demanded of citizenship in a democracy. Our cities hear violent testimony to that fact. If we are to bring improvement to the urban environment it devolves upon the people at large, upon leaders of business, industry, the arts, and in public office, to assume this responsibility with vision, integrity, and unflinching will to serve the public interest. In the final analysis, only the few reap profitable reward through violation of the general welfare.

Urban development implies a continuing responsibility, all forces associated in the process acting together and interdependently. The degree to which these forces are integrated reflects the aspirations, ambitions, and convictions of a community, and the initiative and responsibility of the citizenship as a whole and in each of its parts. When the forces that contribute to city building are unbalanced, inequities develop and the city declines. The energy is sapped, the city no longer provides a field for sound and continuing business investment, jobs disappear, and the environment degenerates.

Since the laws that apply to the physical development of the city set the standards for that development, it is important to examine the effect of these regulations and the prospects for improvement in them. It is important for those who invest their capital for profitable return and for those who pay the taxes that maintain the community. The cities themselves bear testimony to the ineffective nature of many of our laws and their administration. The legal framework that molds the urban pattern provides some advantages, but implementation appears to have drifted into a state approaching anarchy.

Until recently public contact with city planning has been limited; even today most people have little knowledge of planning practices or limitations, or its significance to their daily living. First contact usually comes when a building permit is sought and either granted or refused. If the permit is granted, the relationship of the individual and planning is a fleeting one and the ignorance continues. If, however, the permit is denied, the citizen may ask why. Informed that the law denies that right because what he or she wishes to do is inconsistent with the welfare of the community, the citizen may accept this interpretation of the law and leave the planning office. Or he or she may have the temerity to ask, What law? How does a community come by the right to restrain me from the free exercise of my will in developing property I own? Is this not the confiscation of private property without due process of law and without just compensation, both of which are violations of the Constitution of the United States?[1]

It is in the interest of the people that they be informed on these questions; they are the foundations of planning in democracy.

An Art or a Science?   The discussion of the planning process and the basis for determining decisions dealing with the development of communities has gone on endlessly, with much disparagement of its function in community affairs. Some have called it neither an art nor a science but rather guesswork at best and reaction to pressures at worst.

But forecasting the future is never precise. The best of economists fail to predict the directions that the market will take or what the national economy will do in the future. With the spread of the computer and all other electronic data-generating and gathering devices, the amount of existing knowledge can be collected and collated to provide a reasonable statement of where we have been and where we are. Alternative possible projections that can help in determining the path and directions that events in the future might take can be developed. It must not be forgotten, however, that even with these tools at our disposal, the unexpected events generated by external forces—changing of wind direction, a change in political climate—can, for good or evil, change need, timing, economics, or desire for any given planning program.

The debate therefore is academic. Both art and science, along with a lot of intuitive activity, are involved, together with that most precious ingredient imagination. Thus planning must be understood as an effort to bring orderly development into urban communities and reduce social and economic conflicts that would endanger life and property.

THE EARLIEST PLANNING

The time when land was first allocated to specific uses is, of course, shrouded in prehistoric mystery. The failure of land to respond to cultivation demonstrated that certain land was not adapted to agricultural use, but, since there were few ways of passing this information on to others, it was probably necessary for successive users to learn by trial and error that such areas were unfit.

Tribal experience indicated that certain land was suitable for raising crops, other land was better for grazing animals, and some was unproductive. When these

---

1. Federal Constitution, Fourteenth Amendment, 1869, Section 1: "No State shall make or enforce any law which shall abridge the privileges or immunities of citizens of the United States, nor shall any State deprive any person of life, liberty or property without due process of law, nor deny to any person within its jurisdiction the equal protection of the laws."

experiences were transmitted from generation to generation by word of mouth and custom, we had the first haphazard land use plan. Certainly enforcement was effective; struggle for survival in a not-too-friendly world left the line between life and death too thin for people to cultivate land a second time after it had refused to give them food the first time. Thus land was identified as either agricultural or nonagricultural; if the latter, it had little value. Since people were few in number and land was abundant, nomadic peoples found little need to limit themselves to any single place; they could keep moving on to fruitful areas. Where the land gave bountiful harvest from the plantings, it is believed these nomads settled down and formed the first permanent agrarian communities.

Customs of land use in humankind's earliest days defined the planting and harvesting seasons; then the first descriptions of crop rotation made their appearance, along with the idea of resting the land after a number of years of use. Priests of powerful religions wielded tremendous persuasive powers, and many codes of land use were incorporated in religious doctrines. Some of these are part of religious observations today in certain parts of the world.

The land gave humans many resources other than food. Minerals in the earth provided metals for useful implements of war or peace, the land's stone and wood provided materials for homes and fortifications. The earth itself became a prime building material, as structures were molded into shelters of mud, clay, brick, and so on.

As civilization developed and cities were built as population grew, land took on other values than those attached to agricultural use. The fixed site of the marketplace marked a land use of great value; the land given over to the public open space—the forum—and the commons became important as the centers of the town. Special places were designated for the residences of the aristocracy. It did not take rulers long to recognize that the relationship between and among land uses was of paramount importance, that the slaughterhouses had no proper place on the windward side of their palaces. In our present-day cities we have taken far less care in locating smoke- and dust-producing industries. It is true, of course, that protection of a few homes from obnoxious conditions was a far simpler task than controlling industrial development in relation to the mushrooming residential areas that crowd our urban landscape today. Nonetheless, some greater application of this principle might have given us a far less objectionable environment in our urban communities.

HISTORICAL BACKGROUND

Although the storage of powder in a convenient place was important to the people's defense, it was soon recognized as a menace when too near their homes. With such early concepts of danger and discomfiture began the first official designation of areas within which certain uses were segregated as a matter of protection of the people in a community.

In ancient cities people were themselves regulated as to where they might live. Workers were restricted to areas outside the fortress walls and were called within when required to protect the interests of rulers.

As cities grew in size and power, certain minority groups were restricted to specified areas. These ghettos were always the overcrowded slums and the center of poverty. When disease struck the city, the people in these areas suffered most. Limitation of living areas was extended to restrictions on the work the inhabitants might perform and the places they might travel. The regulations, enforced by the government and sanctioned by the public, often carried a penalty of death on violation. The groups thus segregated differed in various periods and in different parts of the world, but history repeatedly records their plight, their misery and deprivation.

To assume that such conditions are confined to past history or to remote places is unrealistic. There remains today considerable regulation over the rights of minority groups; the areas in which they live for social and economic reasons rather than legal ones are not officially called ghettos, but some retain the ghetto's historic characteristics: overcrowding, blighted or slum housing, poor health and sanitary conditions, poverty, racial or ethnic segregation.

CHAPTER 19

PUBLIC PLANNING

Public planning is accomplished through the activities of many agencies and authorities. The number of persons involved and the process may vary at different levels of government and with different enabling legislation, but in most parts of the United States the responsibilities are largely similar.

The regulation of private and public affairs essential to the general welfare has come under attack in recent years, and the drive to deregulate has had more than a little success. The best-known efforts are those associated with airlines, oil production, gas extraction, communications, and other activities that impact greatly on the nation's and the people's economic and other welfare. It has had an effect on planning and zoning, in that developers have demanded a freer hand to build without the constraints that often face them. However, even the most vocal opponents realize that many aspects of the very regulatory process they oppose have had material benefits for them and the security of their profitable operations.

Policy guidelines establish the structure and elements to be considered in planning. At a national level, The President's Urban Policy Report of August 1978 was submitted to the Congress as the first biennial report in accordance with the provisions of the Housing Act as amended in 1977. The report dealt with America's old perception and new realities, changing urban patterns, the need to assist urban residents in distressed areas; presented a new partnership for conserving urban America; and put forth a national urban policy.

ESTABLISHING GUIDELINES

199

In the chapter defining the policy, President Jimmy Carter stated:

> I think that we stand at the turning point in history. If, a hundred years from now, this nation's experiment in democracy has failed, I suspect that historians will trace that failure to our own era, when a process of decay began in our inner cities and was allowed to spread unchecked throughout our society.
>
> But I do not believe that must happen. I believe that by working together, we can turn the tide, stop the decay, and set into motion a process of growth that by the end of the century can give us cities worthy of the greatest nation on earth.

Needless to say, these policy guidelines had little or no impact in the years that followed. No such statement of direction has been forthcoming since 1977.

In October 1977 the American Institute of Planners (AIP), devoted to the study and advancement of the art and science of city, regional, state, and national planning,[1] published a series of guidelines. They were intended as a guide to practitioners as well as an educational effort directed toward legislators and the courts. The text was in two parts: (1) planning functions and their role in the decision-making process, and (2) planning goals—areas of major interest to practicing planners. The AIP stated, "The planning process may be, and often is, used within each of these areas (functional planning), as well as for coordination between them (comprehensive planning.)"[2]

The areas named were the following:

> Growth management
>
> Economic development
>
> Environmental quality
>
> Energy and other resource conservation and development
>
> Aesthetics and historic preservation
>
> Transportation
>
> Health, education, and welfare
>
> Public safety
>
> Leisure, recreation, and cultural opportunities

The AIP recommendations continued:

1. Planning should be widely practiced by the private sector and by all levels and branches of government.

2. Plans should be articulated cogently to private decision makers, the general public, and any others who may be involved.

3. The planning process should provide public and private decision makers and those seeking to influence decision makers with the best possible information, analysis of alternatives, and long range and short range impacts so that issues may be decided in the best interest of the public and conflicts and duplication among public policies may be avoided.

4. The planning process should coordinate functional and comprehensive planning among all levels of government and should integrate planning and programming with the budgetary and legislative processes.

---

1. The American Institute of Planners joined the American Society of Planning Officials in 1978 to become the American Planning Association.

2. *Planning Policies* (Washington, D.C.: American Institute of Planners, 1977).

5. The planning process should strive to involve significantly all responsible and affected parties.

6. Public agencies at all levels of government should provide the data needed to adequately support all stages of the planning process—from problem definition through implementation to subsequent program evaluation. The data should be as correct and current as would be cost effective.

The legislation of each state sets forth the objectives of the state government with regard to the contents and practice of planning programs. For instance, the California state law on planning states, "Each planning agency shall prepare and the legislative body of each county and city shall adopt a comprehensive general plan for the physical development of the county or city and of any land outside of its boundaries which in the planning agency's judgment bears relations to its planning."[3] Thereafter the elements that are to be included are identified. These may differ in name from those of the AIP, but they are similar in intent. It is in these policy statements of the legislative bodies that the mandate for public planning is established.

Private corporations need no enabling legislation for the internal operation of their programs. The boards of directors must accurately estimate the need for their product or activity and set goals. No large corporation would remain viable for very long without such forecasting.

Planning in the United States that deals with state, regional, and local affairs is left to the states and communities to promulgate and implement. Exceptions occur in those areas where the economic support of the national government is required to meet local needs. There has always been concern that "Big Brother" be kept out of local affairs. Thus city and regional planning and implementation often are not reviewed by the state or by national planning agencies.

In general, planning can be divided into two major categories: the private sector and government agencies. The right of the government to regulate the private sector is under constant challenge by those who feel that land ownership includes the right to do with it what one wishes provided the rights of others are not violated. As cities have grown in size and complexity and land has changed hands frequently, some sense of order has needed to be established and accepted, and public regulation is often required.

Public planning takes place at all levels of government. The federal government plans, and its plans effect the everyday lives of people in many ways. In certain areas, especially in land use planning, it has been determined that the federal government does not have the right to regulate except on federal land. The states in turn usually delegate this authority to local communities for all but state land, either through the state constitution or through the enactment of specific laws. Sometimes planning laws are flexible and permissive; sometimes they are rigid and mandatory.

Communities, cities, and counties enact laws and ordinances that define the areas of planning that they are by state law or local charter allowed to direct. If a community seeks financial assistance through one of the many federal programs, comprehensive plans must be prepared, detailing proposals for land use, circula-

PLANNING AT STATE AND LOCAL LEVELS

---
3. Section 65300, California Laws Related to Conservation and Planning.

tion, health, housing, energy, safety factors, educational and recreational facilities, means of conservation and other elements that relate to the social, economic,
and physical structure of the community.

In most cases legislative bodies create planning commissions and departments to
carry out the mandate of the laws that have been adopted. These bodies in turn
are responsible to the legislative body that created them.

ELEMENTS OF THE PROCEDURE

The planning process begins with an in-depth study of the physical, social, economic, and political structure of the community. The study includes material on
soil and topographic conditions, hydrology, seismic problems, if any, and air,
wind, and temperature conditions. Other factors are also discussed: population
growth rates and potentials, employment opportunities, health and welfare conditions, availability of utilities and public facilities, and a myriad other data. All
of this together identifies the nature and possible choices for future growth and
prosperity.

After the gathering of basic data the material is analyzed and computerized. In
the form of maps, charts, and text, the information is reviewed by the planning
agencies and becomes the basis for projections. After internal reviews, the basic
data and proposals are presented to the public at regularly scheduled study ses-
sions. These are followed by public hearings before the planning commission
and legislative body.

Almost every matter dealing with the use of land requires that the planning
commission and, more important, the legislative body hold one or more public
hearings before the rendering of a decision. In controversial matters, many hearings may be held before a vote is taken to determine the outcome of the issue.

Hearings can be many things. They are often fruitful and productive. But sometimes they are the scene of angry debates. The people may speak and the decision
makers listen but not hear, having already reached a predetermined conclusion.
Sometimes the proponents of a plan are dealt with gently and the opponents
challenged in a way that betrays the prejudice of the legislators. Corruption and
hidden economic involvement are not unknown.

When the inputs from the public and the official agencies are digested, and official
actions are taken in conformity with local law, the plans become effective and are
the basis for future decisions on many facets of planning for the future.

Decisions: A Comment

When decisions are not made by natural forces themselves, such as earthquakes,
floods, volcanoes, or similar external factors, they are made by humans. Human
forces—decisions—have aided and fashioned the form and substance of our
urban communities. Sometimes they have been helped by natural forces and
sometimes they have been eliminated. Urbanism in the Nile Valley was conditioned by the annual floods of the Nile River. Pompeii was destroyed by the
volcanic actions of Mt. Vesuvius. San Francisco was nearly destroyed by earthquake. Other examples abound in all parts of the world. The recognition of
which natural elements are favorable or unfavorable should be a serious determining factor in future courses of action. Urban areas should be built outside
flood plains, away from locations subject to seismic or other potentially catastrophic forces. Yet Pompeii was rebuilt in the same place, and San Francisco is
as prone to earthquakes as in the past. A day seldom passes without news of the

impact of improper or unwise land use decisions on the welfare of great numbers of people.

Human actions have been just as destructive of urban development as natural ones. The city of Jerusalem had been destroyed time and time again by Crusaders and other rampaging armies. Wars have made rubble of cities worldwide.

It is clear that human decisions related to current urban growth and development are (or should be) increasingly involved in dealing with the forces of nature and politics and are conditioned by logic, reason, sentiment, greed, and outright corruption. The mix of these forces determines the quality of government and its impact on the life-style and welfare of all the residents of that area.

Some Unstated Factors

The composition of the decision-making bodies has a great deal to do with the quality of the decisions made. Members of legislative bodies are elected by the residents and citizens of the local communities. In many instances they are interested in the welfare of the entire community, but in some they consider themselves to represent only the particular precinct, ward, or district that elected them. When special-interest groups influence their political behavior to the extent of special deals or projects, the larger community may well be the loser. This holds true as well for agreements with other legislators for projects that will benefit solely their constituency: "pork barrel" projects.

The comprehensive plan and policies associated with it are intended to provide the legislative body with a visible basis for decisions on land use. However, the comprehensive plan is viewed all too often only as a guide and as such is sometimes ignored as "too general and too idealistic." If the plan gets in the way of short-term interests, it is amended to make the desired activities possible. In the city of Torrance, California, for example, an application was made for an oil drilling permit in the city's central business district. Both the comprehensive plan and the zoning plan prohibited oil drilling and extraction in the area. Yet the city council approved the permit after stormy hearings, amending both plan and zoning to accommodate the powerful applicant.

In almost every community there is an individual or group of individuals that wields tremendous influence on public decisions, quite often behind the scenes. This group is identified as the local power structure, a basic element in decisions. Input into the process can occur at the country club or social affair, over the telephone, or in an editorial. This is not intended to indicate that all influence is evil in intent, but there is no doubt that it is a factor in normal community affairs.

Environmental impact studies and assessments are another device intended to provide legislative bodies with as many facts as possible. But casual observation would indicate that many of these assessments are merely "boiler plate" and are tossed aside with "negative declarations" or merely filed.

One wonders about the number of decision makers who read and understand the contents of some of these complicated and specialized reports.

PARTICIPANTS IN DECISIONS

Governmental

The Legislative Body. The role of the legislative body is that of decision maker; ultimately its members determine the character the city shall aspire to achieve. It activates the planning commission, provides finances for its staff, approves its membership, and supports its activities through regard for its recommendations. Except for the relatively narrow limits of administrative determination reserved to the planning commission, decisions on all planning policies rest with the elected representatives of the people. Acting upon recommendations of the commission, the legislative body translates the plan into action. It may also act as a board of appeals on commission decisions, but this function is usually assigned to an administrative committee specifically charged with the responsibility. Policies directing the shape of the city reflect the capacity of the planning commission and the stature of the legislative body.

The Planning Commission. The planning commission is the legal agency of the community through which most planning is performed. In many localities the official family is few in number and the planning commission may not have staff, as the engineer or clerk is largely responsible for the preparation of all plans. Large cities, however, usually have well-staffed organizations of qualified personnel.

The commission is a group of private citizens appointed and approved by the area's legislative bodies. The commissioners are community leaders in real estate, banking, the chamber of commerce, or attorneys, architects, doctors, labor representatives, social workers, and so on. It might be assumed that some commissioners, by the nature of their backgrounds and personal interests, would be devoted to the preservation of property values rather than the general community welfare. Although it cannot be denied that such has sometimes been the case, it is not infrequently found that people who have experience in the private business of community building are well qualified to serve the public interest and respond accordingly when given positions of genuine public responsibility.

New commissioners are seldom adequately informed about the planning process and its purposes or objectives, and they may require some time for training and for familiarizing themselves with the nature of their responsibility. Some communities appoint ex officio members to the planning commission to assist the new commissioners in their tasks. These members may be in the legislature or may be the heads of various departments of the local government: the engineer, the road commissioner, the county surveyor, the attorney, the public works officer, and so on. They advise the commission on matters of which they have special knowledge, but they seldom enjoy the privilege of voting upon the proceeding before the commission.

Exclusive of ex officio members, the commission varies between five and nine in number, depending on local charter regulations or state legislation. The frequency of meetings depends upon the extent of the planning program. In some large cities the program is sufficiently active to warrant the establishment of a separate commission to administer the zoning ordinances.

The planning commission usually serves in an advisory capacity to the legislative body, the council, or the board of supervisors. These bodies refer matters of planning to the commission for reports and recommendations, which the legislative body may then accept or reject. As a rule the preparation of the comprehensive and other plans for civic development is specified in the enabling legislation that created the commission. In such activities the commission requires no specific instructions from the legislative body. However, these functions require an appropriation of funds for an adequate staff. Unless the legislative body is sympathetic to the planning program, it can effectively delay and seriously hamper the commission's performance.

The planning commission recommends plans to the legislative body after it has held public hearings, which then may or may not adopt it. When a plan is adopted, it becomes law, governing the actions of all the people in the community as well as local governmental agencies. Because this is so, all public departments are required to refer any plans for specific improvements to the planning commission for review and approval. This coordination prevents the duplication of services and the functioning at cross-purposes that can easily occur in the wide range of urban activities. The coordinating functions are becoming increasingly important as the areas continue to grow.

Rather than use the planning commission in zoning controversies, some large cities have a separate zoning administrator and board of appeals. The board is responsible for interpreting the zoning law and creating such variances as unforeseen conditions may warrant. Normally the planning commission prepares the ordinance and the zoning administrator or local building and safety department enforces it.

Relief from the requirements of the planning policies established by law is provided all citizens if the law deprives them of property without just compensation or it is applied in a discriminatory manner. This relief may be obtained by appeal to the planning commission and the legislative body. In the event that the appeal fails to produce a satisfactory resolution of the case, it may be referred to the courts for decision. It is from such cases that the great fund of judicial opinions on the planning process has emerged.

Because the planning commission is only an advisory body with no legislative powers and with limited administrative authority, some persons have questioned the need for its existence. Rather than a commission, it has been suggested that a competent planning department should report directly to the administrative or executive office and the legislative body. The planning commission, however, plays a vital role as a catalyst for the variety of interests concerned with the objectives and consequences of planning. Providing a forum for deliberation of facts and opinions, the planning commission can serve to resolve issues and offer to the legislative body a well-defined and supported foundation for policy decisions. Some applicants ignore the planning commission's decisions when they are adverse and appeal to the legislative body, where political influence may negate planning logic.

The Planning Department. The planning commission depends for its effectiveness in large part upon the competence of the technical staff in the planning department. Whether the city charter provides for the planning director to report directly to the mayor or to the planning commission, the policies finally adopted by the legislative body depend upon the competence, skill, and enlightenment of the staff in the planning department. It is the staff that prepares the comprehensive plan—probably the most important single action affecting the future development of the city—and it is the staff that with legal guidance formulates the provisions of the zoning ordinance and subdivision regulations. Implementing the comprehensive plan, it coordinates with other departments of government with respect to streets and highways; health, education, and recreational facilities; utilities; police and fire protection; and all building and engineering activities. The department is, in many states, required by law to cooperate in the preparation of the city budget for both administrative and capital improvement programs. When the department's staff is endowed with that rare combination of vision, technical skill, and administrative talent, it becomes the heart of urban government.

Zoning Administrator. The amount and variety of improvements applied for in a large community may require an independent administrator for the zoning ordinance, who interprets the zoning ordinance for application in specific cases and may provide relief by variance permits when warranted. The administrator's decisions are final unless appealed, in sequence, to the planning commission, legislative body, appeals board, or court of competent jurisdiction.

The Appeals Board. As affairs of local government increase in complexity, usually proportionately with the size of communities, the interpretations of zoning ordinances and their variances have encouraged the creation of an appeals board. This agency derives its authority and is created in a way similar to that for the planning commission. It conducts hearings on appeals of planning commission or zoning administrator decisions and attempts to offer objective attention to appeals that may warrant reconsideration. On some occasions decisions by the appeal board are final, if so provided in local ordinances.

Outside Consultants

Outside consultants can give the planning commission the advantage of their particular in-depth experience, but their most vital contribution is their freedom from local pressures. They can help supply courage, conviction, and inspiration to the staff and commission. They may function in lieu of a full staff in small communities or serve as expert counsel on planning problems of particular complexity.

It is essential for the consultant to work intimately with the leaders of the community as well as with government agencies and their staffs. This involvement may include participation in public meetings and hearings on various proposals, including the adoption of the general plan, thereby giving greater assurance that the important policy statement would be received favorably by the community. It is equally important that the staff be adequately budgeted to maintain the planning process or employ outside consultants to serve in that capacity after adoption of the plan.

Consultants frequently represent both the private and the public sectors. However, when the consultant has at one time advised the community on a given matter, it would appear less than ethical for him or her to return at a later date to the same scene and represent a private client's opposition to the original recommendations. Unless, of course, there had been substantial changes in the physical, social, or economic environment.

The Public

Citizen participation is an essential function of the democratic political process. It may be characterized by courteous support or by confrontation and may be extensive or slight. The current emphasis is on the participation of as broad a segment of citizens as possible in the planning process.

To be effective, this participation must be based upon information acquired by study and clear presentation of facts. Recommendations from the public are generally tempered by politicians' understanding of the public's needs, as they try to make reasonable decisions. All too often citizen participation has involved passionate expressions of prejudices for or against a particular proposal, when behind-the-scenes lobbying may have already determined the decision makers' conclusions.

Most if not all of the federal programs that provide financial assistance to local communities call for citizen participation. The effort to determine the nature of the programs locally and thus gain support for them has seldom been successful in spite of some heroic attempts. People tend to become involved defensively; a controversial issue seems to be required to rouse the public. Even then, interest and participation tend to disappear as soon as the issue is resolved.

There is no doubt that the concept of public participation is an excellent one. Citizen involvement in public issues is the best way to obtain effective, responsible, and responsive government. What must be determined is the best way to achieve it.

The community at large tends not to participate at governmental hearings. The people do not have the information they need about the possible consequences of the proposed action. This lack of involvement prevents the community from manifesting its concern for matters that will directly affect it. Mainly special-interest groups are "the public" in the minds of the legislators.

On the other hand, the wishes of local residents can be made known, especially when they form themselves into a pressure group. They may not have the financial resources of the organized proponents of the plan, but their voting strength gives them power in the community. At times these groups unfortunately take positions of blind opposition to any development, planned or unplanned, good or poor.

The planning profession has made considerable progress in its advisory role, particularly as legislative directives have expanded the programs and broadened the administrative responsibilities of the staff. This position will become more influential, not less so, as the public is informed of the implications of the proposals under consideration. Planners must be open to suggestions made by community members even when these suggestions differ from their point of view. Their task should be to bring together diverse viewpoints for the benefit of the entire community.

The Advocacy Planner. In a sense every proposal presented to a planning commission or legislative body can be considered "advocacy planning" since the plans are intended to serve the special needs of the applicant.

More realistically, the advocacy planner is meant to ensure that those not able to attend public hearings have their interests represented, so that the influential and affluent do not dominate public policy. In recent years this has come to imply the representation of minority groups and the poor. In fact, this seldom occurs. Most cities do not employ anyone whose responsibilities include involvement with these "special-interest" groups. A plan's effect on the least mobile, least powerful elements of society is rarely taken into account.

intentions not actually implemented.

Design centers in some cities have assumed these responsibilities. These are locally established organizations supported by federal funds funneled through an area university. They are usually meant to serve the planning needs of the poorer elements of the community. The designs center in San Francisco is supported through the University of California in Berkeley, the one in Kansas city through the University of Kansas.

Lawyers and the Law. The city attorney or the district attorney's office serves as the legal adviser to public agencies. The staff reviews all proposed legislation, prepares codes and ordinances, and represents their agencies in litigations. Their role is generally defensive: their purpose is to protect communities from involvements in costly suits.

Although the decisions of legislative bodies are usually final, the courts become part of the planning process when there are charges of violation of the law, whether state or federal.

The Media. The role of the media is often overlooked. Most people are informed through newspapers, radio, or television. Local news items may deal with planning, especially if it becomes controversial. All too often a commentator or reporter presents a personal point of view, making it appear to be fact. The power of the media to influence final decisions cannot be underestimated. Their views are usually set forth convincingly, are not subject to an immediate counterpresentation, and carry the weight of authority because of who they are.

The Ombudsman. The ombudsman is a mediator, the person or persons who attempt to resolve conflicts before they reach the public arena. Misunderstandings or lack of knowledge are often the basis of conflicts that can frustrate or defeat even the most worthy of programs, and the ombudsman explains the program and finds out where the problems lie. Primarily listeners, they help individuals let off steam and frustration and frequently direct them to officials who can provide answers—probably their most important function. They are not always included in the staffing of both public and private planning offices, but it would seem they should be.

The Referendum and the Initiative. There are occasions when the general public becomes more deeply concerned than usual with the actions taken or about to be taken by their local legislative bodies. If the actions are sufficiently controversial or if disagreement is widespread, petitions with the public's point of view may then be made up and circulated. The number of registered voters required to sign is stipulated in state law pertaining to the action. The petitions are filed with the local governing body, and eventually an election is held and the legislative action is put to a vote. This is the *referendum.* If the action or law is voted down, it is no longer valid.

The *initiative* is simpler. A proposed law is promulgated by the legislative body or by interested citizens and voted upon by the public. If it is approved by the voters, it goes into effect.

THE PROFESSIONAL PLANNER

Planners are employed by most public or private organizations to carry out their official policies. There appears to be more than a suggestion that the planner in municipal government has a role to play in dealings with the community. However, that role invariably becomes entangled in several basic conflicts.

Are planners the representatives of the elected public official or officials and, as such, carrying out their policies? Or is their role to initiate programs and seek public understanding and support for them? Do planners have implicit powers that outrank those of elected public officials? Can or should they arouse public opinion on an issue that will undermine the authority of elected officials? Can they appear in court as friends of the court on issues that transcend the traditional, established, politically inspired policies and attitudes? Should planners merely prepare the plans? Or, in the best interest of the community, should they ''sell'' them to the public? Should they interpret the desires of one or another lobbying group? Or should they be merely advisers whose advice may be disregarded if it is not consistent with a given segment of community opinion?

No matter how these conflicts are resolved, whether the planners are involved in the public or private sector, certain professional responsibilities should be understood and adhered to as they make their recommendations to the decision makers, be they corporate executives or community legislators. They could be called the professional planner's creed.

Planners should be trained in and have knowledge of the various aspects of their specialty. They should be willing to listen and learn. They should be objective and as free as possible of prejudices toward people or proposals.

"The Planners Creed"

Planners should have an active imagination and be able to portray the future in graphic terms by projecting trends, practices, and policies.

Planners should have convictions. They must be believers in the planning process and the ultimate good that it can do for the orderly development of the community.

Planners must be ethical purists. There should never be a suspicion of favoritism, especially toward one's self, as the basis for a recommendation.

Planners must be communicators, able to provide decision makers with clear and concise material upon which to base their judgments. The ability to communicate with the public on all agenda items and proposals is mandatory.

Planners must have respect for those they work for and with as well as the public at large. Being civil and polite at all times marks the successful planner and administrator.

Planners should have courage. Difficult problems are the lot of the profession; without them there might be no need for the planner. Ability to make a controversial recommendation in a palatable manner is an art essential for a successful program.

Planners are team players. They must understand the policies and the limits within which they operate. When problems arise, they must be able to consult their peers effectively in the effort to better serve the public.

Planners should understand that in the preparation of a comprehensive plan there must be participation by specialists from allied fields such as engineering, real estate, hydrology, transportation, economics, social sciences, and political sciences. Their expertise can assist in both the preparation and the implementation of the plan proposals. Above all, planners should not become dilettantes in all fields and lead the community into ill-conceived and ill-considered decisions.

Planners should document all findings and recommendations, keeping full and complete records of all discussions and actions. Telephone messages should be logged along with meetings with applicants, commissioners, and legislators.

In sum, planners must be dedicated to the public's welfare regardless of the sector within which they may work.

The Planner and Social Issues

Developments in the fields of social welfare and the physical environment have intensified the essentially affirmative role that planners play as advocates protecting the public interest.

In recent years the American Planners Association (APA) has consistently expressed a growing concern for the fate of those individuals and groups who have not received an equitable share of the benefits of our affluent society. Since rearrangement of the physical environment inevitably affects the distribution of social and economic costs and benefits, virtually all public planning bears strong social welfare implications.

If these developments tend to project the planner into the role of advocate for social well-being, it is hardly a new role. A good city is the intended historical objective of the planner; it should be designed for social well-being. Planners seek to restore cities to a favorable environment for all inhabitants. But such a goal cannot be achieved by remaining in the passive role of "expert technicians." Planning commissioners have an obligation to assert the public interest on all measures embraced in the planning process. Our institutions of higher learning must generate the perception, talent, and capacity for creative contributions to the transformation of the urban structure and instill in their students the commitment to stand for them as advocates.

Among the social welfare issues that directly affect the quality of urban life, housing is a major priority. The professional planner may not be expected to present all the solutions to the housing problem, but he or she must maintain a healthy perspective.

Planners should recognize that juggling statistics of housing production does not produce adequate housing for the underprivileged. They should understand that ethnic discrimination will not disappear, nor will social comfort and compatibility appear, simply by the dispersal of "low-cost" housing in affluent suburbs. They should know that the major financial obstacle to building better housing is the high interest rate on home mortgages, not only the costs of labor or materials. Fundamentally, the planner must understand that as long as landowners may reap the benefit of values created by community prosperity, not only by their own investments, the public will be obliged to deal with unabated rises in land costs in its subsidy of low-cost housing.

The planner should realize that "ghettoization" is not a result of ethnic discrimination alone. People of all groups seek to maintain some vestige of social cohesiveness and economic, religious, and cultural identity: it happens in Scarsdale, Grosse Point, Palm Beach, and Beverly Hills, as well as in Harlem, Watts, and the barrios.

And the planner should recognize that the stain of slums and the blight of physical deterioration must be erased from the face of the city if the human dignity of any people is to be preserved. Toward this goal, the planner must encourage the general public to view problems of the less privileged as community responsibilities to be faced and resolved through the efforts of an informed society, both the general population and public officials. Housing, health, culture, and social amenities are interrelated and must be resolved by local agencies.

The Young Planner's Dilemma

In 1946, when the young men and women returned to the collegiate planning programs from the battlefields of Europe and Asia, they were filled with idealism

Education for planning. *Hands-on training with experienced planner as professor.*

and energy and with thoughts of how to take advantage of the "world that they helped save for democracy." Not unlike these young people, the graduates of the higher levels of academia go forth with fire in their eyes, the wholesome desire to make the world a better place in which to live, and thoughts of how planning should be done and what the process should accomplish.

Developing an ideal vision of what might be, however, is but the first step in the world of planning. The next step is the problem of reconciling that vision with the everyday realm of political and legal realities. That is where the true planning begins. Planners may find well intentioned laws that lead to unwieldy constraints on good planning. Taken at face value these laws seem to make sense, but they often tend to become handicaps to the pursuit of the high standards that young planners feel are required to bring about planning with farsighted goals. For example, the "concept" that the comprehensive plan is a sound basis for the development of long-range policies and goals is generally accepted. However, the requirement in the recent laws that zoning be consistent with the comprehensive plan has in many communities been interpreted to mean that the comprehensive plan be consistent with the zoning, making for an "as is plan" with nowhere to go as a guide to the future. The irony of this condition is that the bright young planners find themselves constrained by the political and legal arena within which they have to work. Sometimes the really bright persons become discouraged and depart into other fields, leaving the planning profession with the less capable to become the bureaucrats that find solace in preparing "no plan plans."

If our cities are to survive in the current political climate, the philosophy behind the comprehensive plan must be restored and assume its place in providing vision

attitude perseverance (handwritten margin note)

balanced with reality. The planning profession should be encouraged to "think ahead" to ways to bring about better living conditions for the people of the communities within which they provide their services. Young planners should not abandon their enthusiasm about the potentials of the profession or lose their idealism. Without either of these virtues the contributions to their chosen field will not have the spirit that will eventually breathe life into their ideas and concepts. It takes time for ideas that are new, no matter how good they may be, to germinate. Look about you and you will observe how ideas of 10 or 20 years ago have miraculously become realities today.

Education of Planners and Decision Makers

knowledgeable in order to make educated decisions (handwritten margin note)

Decisions are often made by planning commissions comprising persons who know little or nothing about planning or the matters that come before them. If the ideas sound good, they vote for them; if the person presenting them is in disfavor, they vote against them, regardless of the merits of the case. It seems to the author that, before accepting the responsibility for guiding the growth and development of a community, people who are selected should be required to attend seminars which define the role and duties of the position of commissioner.

The people who enter the field of professional planning should participate in seminars and courses leading to a degree from a recognized professional school where they learn the social and cultural background of planning as undergraduates. In addition they should take courses in economics and engineering since many of the duties of the professional planner demand an understanding of the active role of these fields in the planning process and an appreciation of their contribution to the practical aspects of programs. Graduate schools should provide exposure to all of the techniques and philosophy inherent in the profession, as well as the many facets of the occupation as practiced in public or private offices. Knowledge of the use of the computer and the many tasks that can be accomplished through this "magic" assistant should permit the planner to make decisions more rapidly and more accurately and precisely than was possible in the past.

In-service training, working in a planning office while attending school, should be a mandatory part of all graduate school programs.

After completing their formal education, students tend to advance rapidly in the professional world as advisers to decision makers; as members of the economic, health preservation, crime prevention, and physical planning segments of communities. They work with individuals in many other disciplines, using the methods of research, analysis, and creative projection to set goals and determine means and methods to achieve them. Very few are trained as designers or land planners unless they are also schooled in engineering, architecture, landscape architecture, or other design disciplines. The design-oriented planners should also be familiar with the science and techniques of land utilization (agriculture, business, residential, industrial, etc.). They should know the value of open space, the importance of "greening the community," and the relationship between all these elements and the circulation system, which includes walkways, streets, mass transit, parking, and roadways.

PATENT MEDICINE MEN

Planning, like all fields of endeavor, has its own fast-talking brand of supersalespeople who show clients "the new way" of performing old, badly conceived ideas that are espoused as the "only way to go to save the world from the bad guys." By using commonly recognized shortcomings in community development practices they foist questionable panaceas, in a flow of neatly packaged phrases, accompanied by a lantern show, on a public eager for improved living arrangements. Examining their ideas in the cold light of day, one finds that their cure of the urban ills may be no better or worse than the diseases they purport to remedy.

The American Institute of Certified Planners (AICP) requires its members to adhere to the ethical standards of the detailed Code of Ethics and Professional Conduct. The principles and requirements of the Code are under the following chief headings: [4]

The Planner's Responsibility to the Public
A planner's primary obligation is to serve the public interest. While the definition of the public interest is formulated through continuous debate, a planner owes allegiance to a conscientiously attained concept of the public interest.

The Planner's Responsibility to Clients and Employers
A planner owes diligent, creative, independent, and competent performance of work in pursuit of the client's or employer's interest. Such performance should be consistent with the planner's faithful service to the public interest.

The Planner's Responsibility to the Profession and to Colleagues
A planner should contribute to the development of the profession by improving knowledge and techniques, making work relevant to solutions of community problems, and increasing public understanding of planning activities. A planner should treat fairly the professional views of qualified colleagues and members of other professions.

The Planner's Self-Responsibility
A planner should strive for high standards of professional integrity, proficiency, and knowledge.

CODE OF ETHICS AND PROFESSIONAL CONDUCT

Kathryn Tobias, a member of the American Institute of Certified Planners and a land-use attorney with Downey, Brand, Seymour & Rohwer, Sacramento, California, offers the following encouragement:

> Today, the careful balancing of growth that a community deserves and expects is more possible than ever. Planning staffs have more professionally trained planners than ever. Compared to the early post–Proposition 13 years, there seem to be increasing financial resources for government to do the job properly.
>
> Planning commissioners are much more representative than they used to be. Many educational opportunities exist for training planning commissioners. Every year, more citizen groups spring up to educate and lobby elected officials to embrace their version of how our cities should look and function.
>
> For the balance between roles to be maintained, we need to build in trust: Trust that developers will try to respond to the mood, desires and needs of the community. Trust that planning staffs can understand the demands of both the public and property owners and can accurately evaluate and convey that information to commissioners and elected officials. Trust that elected officials will balance the needs of individual neighborhoods with the needs of the city or even the region as a whole.
>
> With trust re-established as an integral part of the permitting process, we can again expect accountability from our elected officials.

AN ENCOURAGING NOTE

---

4. Planners Code of Ethics, American Institute of Certified Planners, February 1991, Washington, D.C.

If the city does not look or function like we want it to, we shouldn't blame "rabid environmentalists" or "slimebag developers" or "burned-out staff" or even "hired-gun" land-use attorneys.

As statewide initiatives have allowed legislators to escape blame for not making tough decisions or for kowtowing to special interests, putting the blame on the wrong people (a form of role confusion) allows local officials to escape their responsibility for planning and creating both the vision and reality of cities for the next century.

We must not confuse the roles each of us plays in deciding land-use policy. Individual interest groups, neighborhoods, developers and bureaucrats must realize that at the top, our elected decision-makers are ultimately responsible for balancing interests in development.

THE FUTURE OF PUBLIC PLANNING

Although planning has become a more important part of the activities of the private sector, it seems to be subject to a questionable future as an implement of public policy. The full impact of federal actions in deleting or reducing support for planning at state and local levels was accentuated when Section 701 of the Housing Act was done away with. This financial support for local planning was the lodestone of assistance that made it possible for many communities to develop both long-range comprehensive plans and up-to-date zoning and subdivision regulations.

With the severe financial limitations placed upon local government, it is increasingly difficult to employ the staff or consultants to keep the planning programs current, let alone administer the regulations in an effective manner. The future does not necessarily seem bright.

However, practically all communities, large and small, have the essence of a planning staff, although many are untrained individuals who perform limited service in the protection of the environment.

CHAPTER 20

PRIVATE PLANNING

Land seems to have intrinsic characteristics that no other element on earth possesses.

The development of land as real estate in the United States has not been distinguished by its attention to the amenities of a living environment. Speculation was the moving spirit as the frontiers widened and were pushed forward. This was not a characteristic reserved to enterprising Americans alone. Rather, it reflects the desires that caused the people to seek this land and points to a difference between the opportunities open to the people of America as opposed to those of countries elsewhere. Freedom from oppression and tyranny implied certain rights, among them the right to a piece of land upon which to build a home. The abuse of the privilege was not a new characteristic of human beings.

During the colonial period the mother country granted land as a just reward due the leaders of colonization. Subdivision and sale of the land so acquired were common practices. When it was not lucrative enough, some of the large land estates were preserved through the English system of long-term leases rather than sale.

In the latter half of the nineteenth century whole towns were used as a speculative medium, and they sprang up almost at random along the railroads that stretched across the land. Some of these towns have become cities, many have vanished, and others remain as ghosts of the speculative orgy in gold and silver.

LAND AND REAL ESTATE

In real estate practice, land is considered a commodity to be bought at the lowest prices and sold at the highest. The sole purpose of the professional's services is to handle property that belongs to other persons for a fee. Land entering the market in large units may be divided into small elements called lots or building sites. Where the land is so subdivided, local laws govern and influence the manner in which the action is to take place; the final sale is to be approved by the state real estate commissioner to assure the buyer that no fraud is involved and that all local laws have been observed.

REALTOR AND DEVELOPER

Realtors—real estate agents or expeditors—are the intermediaries—"middlemen"—in real estate transactions. In most cases they have no economic interest in the properties they handle, other than in the commission obtained by bringing buyers and sellers together and consummating a transfer of ownership. Sometimes they may indicate what they believe is the fair market price, but in most cases they recommend using an appraiser. He or she then studies the property's condition and location and reviews the records for the sale of other property in the vicinity as well as the sales history of the property in question.

Developers play a different role. They acquire large parcels of land, prepare plans for the proposed use of the property, process the plans through the necessary public agencies, and install the utilities and facilities that are required. Only then, either through their own organization or through a separate real estate brokerage, do they place the development on the market, as a whole or in parts that can be absorbed within a reasonable time. Developers take large risks and in general invest a considerable amount of time and money in a venture before they secure a return for their efforts.

THE SUBURBAN COMMUNITY

Although the history of land speculation has not been the most savory, there were those who chose this medium as an instrument to improve land development. This choice was not motivated by the high purpose of the garden city movement in England, for instance, nor was it prompted by deep concern for the nature of the city or its social and economic welfare. It was rather the natural result of competitive necessity, no doubt prodded by the satisfaction that achievement invariably delivers.

With the dawn of the twentieth century high land costs squeezed the single-family dwelling farther and farther to the outskirts. As the city swelled, the outskirts moved to such distances that the community facilities originally able to serve the whole urban population ceased to be readily accessible. The consequent development of extensive facilities in the suburbs gave them the character of satellite communities. Decentralization was in progress.

Originally, only the land surveyor was involved in the layout of land subdivisions, but in recent times the planner became a more active participant in the development of independent residential communities. One of the earliest large-scale residential subdivisions was a 1,600-acre tract to be known as Riverside, near Chicago, designed by Frederick Law Olmsted and Calvert Vaux in 1869. Garden City, Long Island, was another such development; it has since become a substantial self-contained community.

The gridiron street system was typical of real estate development, offering the subdivider the most convenient pattern for surveying and recording deeds. But it offered little in return as a living environment. The exceptions are, therefore, the more noteworthy for the progress in planning they demonstrated.

Roland Park in Baltimore, begun in 1891, was distinguished for singularly high standards of physical development. It was designed for fine residences, but at that time few suburbs were not so intended. Forest Hills in New York's Long Island, started in 1913, was one of the earliest planned residential suburbs. The development company undertook the construction of many of the homes, apartments, and shopping facilities.

After World War I a number of well-planned communities were initiated. Mariemont, a satellite of Cincinnati designed by John Nolen in 1921, was devoted primarily to single-family homes with a density of six or seven units per acre. Apartment clusters were developed in connection with the principal shopping center, an arrangement subsequently true of much development planning.

About this time two other distinguished developments were begun in widely different sections of the country. River Oaks in Houston, Texas, occupying 1,000 acres, was planned with a full complement of community facilities including a golf course and market center. In 1923 the Palos Verdes Estates south of Los Angeles was planned for a dramatic site overlooking the Pacific ocean. About one-quarter of the total 3,000-acre area was allocated to schools, parks, houses of worship, libraries, shopping, and a golf course; residential lots of ½ acre to 30 acres occupied the remainder. A few small apartment areas were proposed adjacent to the small shopping centers. One-half of the land adjacent to the centers is in roads and landscaped parkways. The quality of all these developments has remained high as the project has been constructed in accordance with the plan.

Among other notable subdivisions in this country are Shaker Heights in Cleveland, the Country Club District in Kansas City, St. Francis Woods in San Francisco, Nassau Shores, Long Island, and Westwood Village in Los Angeles. Some of these developments mark a high level of planning. The subdividers had no serious intention to cope with housing for families of low income in these com-

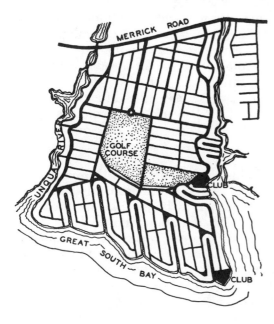

Nassau Shores, Long Island. *Nassau Shores, begun in about 1926 on approximately 500 acres, was designed to take advantage of the waterfront location. The area was subdivided in lots 20 by 100 feet, and it was customary to require two lots for each dwelling.*

munities. They intended them for the upper-income group and promoted them accordingly.

The contrast between these developments and the average subdivision is made the more apparent when we observe the rank and file of urban expansion. Most of it was not planned; it simply oozed over the edges of the growing metropolis. A minimum of improvements in streets, walks, sewers, water, electricity, and gas distribution was installed. The unaware purchaser was left to foot the bill individually at some later date or the burden was shifted to the urban taxpayer.

Local governments gradually awoke to the havoc being wrought in the suburbs, and legislation was enacted to require subdividers to make certain improvements as a condition of approval. These early regulations were feeble, but they were an acknowledgment that some measure of control was necessary to protect the city for the people who live in it.

THE MOBILE POPULATION

Suburban expansion was encouraged by urban growth, but it did not drain off the excess population from the center of cities. People responded to their natural desire to live near their work, and employment opportunities concentrated in the city center. Then, the nature of these opportunities changed from the prefactory system. Stable industrial employment became uncertain. With expanding commercial enterprise, the tendency to shift from job to job extended to movement from city to city. For practical reasons, mobility of the family offered advantages over fixed tenure.

The urban population thus became transient in character. Freedom to move was not desirable in itself but it was necessary. The rental apartment satisfied this need and became popular. The familiar central city tenement of the nineteenth century remained for the poor, but the new multifamily building was not confined to the low-income family. It achieved a new dignity as a form of urban living. Park Avenue, the Gold Coast, and Nob Hill were as popular among the well-to-do as, for example, New York's Lower East Side was necessary for the immigrant family.

Oddly enough, planning standards did not vary among the income groups who found the apartment popular. Lots forty and fifty feet wide were more common than the nineteenth-century twenty-five-foot lot and New York's dumbbell tenement had been outlawed, but the arrangement, size, and number of rooms in "high-class" apartments took up much of the additional lot area. In addition, narrow interior courts and side yards with little or no setbacks at front or rear prevailed as standard practice. Consequently, there was little difference in the amount of open space between the building of the "swank" trade and the "efficiency" apartment building of the middle-income white-collar clerk or the tenement of the low-income industrial worker.

The city was having growing pains. The industrial economy had thrown out of gear all previous concepts of what a city should be. The traditional dwelling for the average American family had been the single-family house. But the industrial metropolis had engulfed the village of homes. The family no longer dwelt in its home; it hired apartment space for temporary occupancy. The speculative opportunities for profit in this form of building enterprise were obvious and full advantage was taken of them, but the apartment as a form of investment for capital was not yet fully realized. Adjustment to the new kind of city was, and still is, slow. But there were signs of improvements.

CHAPTER 21

THE LEGAL FOUNDATION

IT'S THE LAW

Laws of all kinds have impact on the planning of cities and rural areas. Some laws are permissive; others are mandatory. No matter which way you turn, regulations and laws specify what you may build and where you may build it. These regulations include international compacts, the U.S. Constitution, federal laws, state constitutions and laws, local laws and ordinances. It is wise, therefore, that planners understand their responsibilities under the laws in the area where they practice and to try to strengthen them, in the public interest, when they feel that they are lax or inadequate to provide the improvements essential to protect the public welfare.

Legal Trappings

Legal action on zoning affairs went through two basic stages of development. Initially cases were brought to court that dealt with "nuisance uses." The courts treated these as separate and individual matters, deciding in each specific case whether a use was detrimental to the public health, safety, and welfare. In effect this was simple zoning, legally brought about. As time passed, the courts required more and broader evidence, such that would "indicate the character of a community," before it was willing to rule upon the validity of a use. This call for a larger and more comprehensive view of a community's purpose is now answered in the general plan of land use.

A California ordinance that prohibited a slaughterhouse, hog storage, and the curing of hides in certain areas of the city was upheld in the courts.[1] A Los

---

1. *Ex parte Shrader*, San Francisco (1867).

Angeles ordinance that prohibited the operation of a steam shoddying plant within one hundred feet of a church was upheld in 1895; in this latter case the court considered not only the nature of the specific use but the relationship between uses.[2]

The legality of the establishment of fire zones or districts has been upheld in most courts, the structural nature of buildings and their relation to space being admitted as an important factor in determining the uses permitted within a structure. In San Francisco, because of the great number of wooden buildings with party walls, certain districts were established by ordinance within which hand laundries were prohibited; wood fires were burned in the stoves upon which the laundry was boiled and several serious fires resulted. This ordinance was taken to the state supreme court and was held unconstitutional and invalid, not because of the regulation itself but because it was a breach of the Fourteenth Amendment of the Constitution. It was pointed out that the washing of clothes was not opposed to good public morals nor was it subversive of public decency, but the court cited the fact that all of but one of the non-Chinese applicants were issued permits in a similar business in like areas and were permitted to continue in business, whereas the petitioner and two hundred others of his race were denied permits. The court held that the ordinance was not unreasonable, but that its application was arbitrary class legislation discriminating against one group in favor of another. It thus violated the Fourteenth Amendment, and the ordinance was declared to be invalid.[3] The fair administration of a law is an integral part of the provisions of the law in the eyes of the courts.

One of the earliest court decisions in this country upholding an ordinance in the nature of a zoning regulation was made in 1920. In sustaining a town plan before it, the opinion said: "It betters the health and safety of the community; it betters the transportation facilities; and it adds to the appearance and the wholesomeness of the place, and as a consequence it reacts upon the moral and spiritual power of the people who live under such surroundings."[4]

The Use of the Police Power

The power to pass and enforce laws to protect the welfare of all the people, whether they be enacted at a local or a national level, is called the exercise of the police power.[5] In this country the power was retained by the sovereign states at the time of formation of the federal government. Only when the national welfare is involved and when the local government is unable to cope with a situation does the state deem it necessary to call for assistance from the federal government. Federal laws, however, do affect the relationships between the states: the Interstate Commerce Commission regulates rates on railroads dealing in interstate commerce, and the national labor laws regulate wages and hours of persons employed in industries that sell their products through interstate commerce. These instances constitute uses of the police power by the federal government.

Some states give the police power to cities and counties by specific legislative acts; others grant this right to communities in their state constitutions. The

---

2. *Ex parte Lacey*, 108 California 326.

3. *Yick Wo v. Hopkins*, 118 U.S. 356 (1895).

4. *Windsor v. Whitney*, 95 Connecticut 357, 363.

5. Police power was expressed in ancient law as follows: "Due regulation of domestic order of the kingdom where members of the state, like a family, are bound to conform their behavior in good propriety . . . to be good members and an orderly part of the community"; and later, "Police power . . . is the name given to the inherent sovereignty which is the right and duty to exercise when the public policy demands enforcement of such regulations for the general welfare as are necessary for the regulation of economic conditions to provide for adequate community life." *Parker v. Otis*, 130 California 322.

purpose of the police power is in general always the same, but the manner in which the power is granted differs in the various states. The power to make laws and regulations dealing with the activities of a community's citizens and the property they possess is a key to the planning process and particularly to that phase called *zoning*.

Today it is a widely accepted principle that the source of all power lies in the hands of the majority of the people. This implies that the people of a city or town, through the governing body, have the right to enact laws and regulations that support their ideas of what is best for their community. The distinction between this principle and the exercise of power in the past, whether by a minority or majority, is our recognition that regulations of law today apply to all the people, and no class or element is to be immune. The principal restraint upon law is that it shall not be in conflict with the Constitution of the United States or the constitution of the state in which it is enacted.

It is necessary that the police power be exercised for a worthy purpose and with definitely stated objectives. In cases where that power is used to regulate or deny the use of property without compensation, it must be clearly shown that the continued use of that property would be inimical to the best interests of the community. A house that is structurally unsound or badly infested with rats may be dangerous to the public in general as well as to the persons living in it, and it is thus subject to being closed under the police power without compensation to the owner. The equity for such actions rests upon the assumption that the people are obligated to maintain their property at standards that will not impose a nuisance on the community and that the necessity to exercise the police power to abate such a nuisance does not warrant compensation to the owners of the affected property.

Taking land for a public purpose when the owner does not want to sell is not to be confused with use of the police power; the former is known as the exercise of eminent domain. Condemnation of the property is instituted in the courts, which then establish a fair price based upon testimony from witnesses representing the owner, those speaking for the community, and impartial appraisers. The principal difference between the police power and the right of eminent domain lies in the matter of compensation to the owner; under the police power the state does not "take" the property from its owner: it regulates the right of use on behalf of the public welfare.

The police power of a community is limited to the area within its political boundaries. Thus state laws may be enforced within any part of the state unless otherwise provided in the laws, the county laws only within the county, and city or township laws only within their limits. Beyond this, cooperation among governmental agencies constitutes the only effective method for coordinated action or regulation. In the state of Texas, however, cities can regulate the subdivision of land in the unincorporated (county) areas within an established area of influence, a distance of 5 miles beyond their political boundaries. Nonetheless, zoning control in these extended areas is not granted to the cities.

A Sound Idea Corrupted

As with all laws and public regulations, there are those who seek and find ways of circumventing the provisions for their personal gain. Zoning was fair game for those who sought special privilege. Requests were made for special zoning classifications for a highly profitable land use in areas where the general provisions of the law did not provide it. Called *spot zoning*, this soon became so prevalent in some communities that residents or landowners in the vicinity protested the loss of protection that the zoning was supposed to provide.

When the spot zoning process was attacked in the courts, new devices were introduced to provide sanction for the granting of the same special privileges, among them the *variance*. Public officials were required to make a finding that special conditions existed and that the standard features of the ordinance did not apply, and therefore the community could attach those conditions necessary to adjust the specific use to its surroundings. Public agencies found it very convenient to invent all types of deceptive reasons for granting variances.

When variances became a recognized problem in local affairs, especially after broad community objection to the abuse of the function, a new device called a *conditional use permit* was invented, which permitted a specific use in a given location where it purportedly was essential to the welfare of the community. Like the variance and the spot zone, the conditional use permit became an instrument for illegal grants of special privilege. It appeared that any profitmaking use could be found to be in the interest of the community, if only from the standpoint of tax revenue.

Some communities, under the guise of protecting property values, require extensive and time-consuming reviews of plans that show such details as elevations of buildings as well as the use of the land, denying approval to projects that do not meet the architectural tastes of the reviewing agency. Long delays can become a device to make the applicants change their proposals to conform to the board's judgments of "good taste." Challenging the opinions of these boards in the courts can be a less than satisfying procedure.

Other communities use an unwritten regulatory system. Proposals of all kinds are reviewed and acted upon by the legislators on the basis of their personal prejudices or desire to grant favors. Plans are not comprehensive, nor defined for viewing. Zoning ordinances have no standards; all items before the commission and legislative bodies are decided at meetings that fall far short of being public hearings.

Of course, some people genuinely believe that the elimination or reduction of regulations would free planners, public and private, to do their work without constraint. Without hindrance, their approach to the future would be more open and creative. Local ordinances and regulations dealing with the general health, safety, and welfare would be reduced to the minimum, the sole constraint being that no harm be done to neighbors or community. Failing that, activity would be subject to the consequences of court action for damages (shades of Ayn Rand's *Fountainhead*!). It appears that this process would create a heyday for members of the legal profession as they dealt with people—those who could afford it—who believed they had suffered abuse by their neighbors.

EVASION OF THE LAW

To assume that the participants in the planning process, both public and private, are free from the temptations leading to corruption is to live in a dream world. The amount of money involved in construction is great and time of processing can be costly. It is not surprising that efforts are directed to secure favors of public officials and employees. Since lobbying is an accepted part of the political process, decisions favoring an applicant are subject to both political and financial pressures and sometimes poor planning recommendations and actions. The laws are there to be evaded through activities crafted to favor an individual or corporation guided by persons knowledgeable in the laws and the devices that are available to circumvent them.

It is not difficult to forecast that for every regulation there is a way to circumvent it. Some attorneys represent the interest of their clients by finding loopholes in the law or interpreting the provisions in a manner different from the intent of the legislators who framed the supposedly offending or restricting laws. Some of the techniques used to "get what you want" are as follows:

Circumvention

> Proposing amendment in or changing the planning ordinances to permit their friends' or financial supporters' proposals. This is not illegal, but it may undermine the plan.

> Supporting the election of persons to the decision-making body who would either change or disregard the provisions of the law. This too, is not illegal, but it does not reflect good planning or good administration.

> Spreading "favors" among the decision makers to induce them to be sympathetic to the needs of the petitioner. This, if disclosed, is, of course, corruption.

The more frequent and more easily concealed types of irresponsibility are the following:

> Some planners might try to blackmail an applicant to obtain money or favors (gratuities) for supporting an application with a favorable report even though the proposal is unworthy of support and is in conflict with the community comprehensive plan and policy.

> Politicians or planners might purchase property in their community and recommend changes in the community plans to favor their economic interests, thereafter directing potential purchasers to their property.

> Planners might prepare plans to comply with the language of the enabling legislation, but not with its specified intent. This is most likely to lead to the preparation of "as is" plans which are not plans at all, but a reflection of existing conditions of land use in the community, giving no guidance for the future.

> Planners might knowingly disregard known dangerous areas where the physical conditions may, if the land is developed, lead to loss of life and property by disguising problem areas to favor the landowners and their ability to sell land. Future users of the property rely on the government and laws to protect their welfare in marginal areas and should, at least, be warned of the potential dangers.

During the 1970–80 decade many efforts were initiated to protect the environment. Some of these involved including provisions in zoning ordinances to limit the extent and direction of the growth of cities to a certain number of dwelling units per year. Other provisions protected agricultural land from being depleted by urban expansion into prime areas. In most cases the growth management provisions were a separate part of the comprehensive plan and were supported by separate ordinances rather than by zoning.

A MEANS OF GROWTH MANAGEMENT

In legal actions brought against them, these provisions were described as placing limits on people's freedom of movement and therefore unconstitutional. However, in several important cases the highest courts upheld the right of communities to control their growth as long as the provisions related to the ability of the community to serve and protect the residents.

As a corollary to this, it was argued in 1987 and 1989 before the U.S. Supreme Court that communities that reserve land for public use or purpose and deny the landowners use of the property involved must pay compensation, since for all practical purpose the land was "taken" from the owner by the act of zoning. The "taking" issue is discussed later in this chapter.

CHANGING INTERPRE-TATIONS OF THE LAW

Some very significant changes have taken place in the courts' interpretation of laws regulating the use of property. The growth of communities into large cities has necessitated detailed and complicated legislation to govern more and more human behavior. What may be accepted in a small community as an unavoidable nuisance may be viewed as dangerous and contested actively in a metropolis. Thus the keeping of pigs, horses, and chickens would be considered a right in a farm town but would be looked upon with horror on Manhattan Island. The maintenance of open privies in backyards may be accepted practice in nonurban areas with no funds for sewage disposal, whereas the same condition in any large city would have the entire population declaring it a menace to the health and life of all the people.

The dangers of disease, crime, delinquency, fire, and traffic injury are rapidly multiplied as the housing, commerce, and industry of the large city absorb the open space that formerly helped to insulate people against these dangers. The courts have seen the necessity of recognizing these problems. Thus there came into being the concept that people have the right to protect themselves against these and other hazards by planning and zoning an environment that will meet the requirements of safe urban living. Where we have relied in the past upon the police power to prohibit acts that the courts determined to be a violation of a law, today we enact laws that tend to discourage in advance those acts that can be prevented.

Our philosophy of urban conduct is no longer confined to the public health, safety, and general welfare but has extended to the use of the police power for the maintenance of such matters as "public convenience and comfort." The Supreme Court has said: "The police power of a state embraces regulations designed to promote the public convenience or the general prosperity as well as regulations designed to promote the public health, the public morals, or the public safety."[6] Traffic laws that prohibit parking on certain streets are justified on the grounds that they make access to important areas a matter of greater convenience as well as ensure the safety of people. Laws that prohibit dangerous or obnoxious uses from residential areas are considered to protect values from depreciation and, in this manner, protect the general prosperity as well as health and safety.

Red Tape   In many areas of the country the planning and zoning processes have become so cumbersome that applicants are strongly dissuaded from participating in development. Some communities require approval by the planning commission, an architectural review board, the legislative body, and sometimes, after vigorous citizen protests, approval by the courts. In some states the referendum on a

6. *Chicago B. & R. Co. v. Drainage Commissioners,* 200 U.S. 561, 592.

proposal requires a vote by the electorate before a proposed development can become a reality. The time and money that is involved can become monumental —more than all but the very powerful and wealthy can afford.

It has been assumed by much of the public that the only direction for zoning change is to increase the law's permissiveness, to allow those changes that would permit landowners to anticipate greater potential profits from the use of their land. Few legislative bodies have had the temerity to tell owners that their land cannot be used as intensively as had been legislated in the past.

Up Zoning–Down Zoning

Recent court rulings, however, indicate that, like any other legislative act of government, zoning is subject to modification if required to protect the public health, safety, or welfare. Legislative bodies make judgments based upon data. With new facts before it, a legislative body has an obligation and responsibility to make such modifications and changes as would bring the zoning into a consistent position with the community's long-range comprehensive plan and recognized professional practices.

There is no doubt that persons paying for land on the basis of existing zoning for commercial uses would believe that rezoning for residential uses would be tantamount to taking property without just compensation. However, persons who own residential land make no such complaint, nor do they offer compensation to the community when the legislative body decides to rezone the land for commerce or industry. In each case, there must be careful analysis to be certain that the decision is based on sound planning and zoning principles and that no favoritism, prejudice, or discrimination influenced the decision.

In most instances where down zoning has occurred, the subject property was not developed for the permitted use. Meanwhile the land around it often developed a pattern indicating that the contested zoning would have been incompatible with its surroundings. If development has already taken place, the legislative body may enact a "nonconforming" provision that could include a reasonable amortization period, after which the existing use would have to conform to the surroundings.

Where property owners do not agree with the public action in down zoning their property, they challenge the procedure as being in effect the taking of the property by inverse condemnation, the taking of a substantial property right without just compensation. However, a California court held:

> A zoning action which merely decreases the market value of property does not violate state or federal constitutional provision forbidding uncompensated taking or damaging of property. Accordingly, an inverse condemnation action by property owners, in which it was alleged that plaintiffs purchased property zoned commercial and that thereafter the city rezoned the property to residential so that the property was worth only a fraction of its value under the commercial zoning, did not state a cause of action and the trial court correctly sustained the city's demur without leave to amend.[7]

The old debates about the applicability of the initiative and referendum provisions to zoning cases, especially in those states where the constitution provides for these remedies to actions taken by the legislative body, seem to have been resolved in a case in Colorado.

Administrative or Legislative Acts

---

7. Cal. Jur. 2d. Eminent Domain. no. 85: Am. Jur. 2d. Eminent Domain. no. 157 et seq.

In the case involving Margolis versus the District Court in and for the County of Arapahoe, the state supreme court found that the zoning decisions by the legislative body were subject to the initiative and referendum provisions of the state constitution. (This was also the finding of the California supreme court in a case involving the city of Claremont.) The opponents to the finding expressed the opinion that this decision would lead to delays in development and would ultimately result in unplanned growth. The court rejected this view, citing the fact that no real problems had occurred in other states where the initiative and referendum processes had been used.

THE PUBLIC WELFARE

The courts were called upon to rule on some mighty problems in the early days of zoning. What was the public welfare? When was public health or life endangered? What was an "obnoxious use"? At what point is the establishment of a district reasonable and at what point does it become only arbitrary? Was it proper for the court to substitute its judgment for that of the legislative body on matters of the "substance" of a zoning ordinance? When can a community permit a use in one area and deny it in another?

A series of court decisions over the years reveals much difference of opinion, but filtering through them all are sound precedents for the community's right to establish zoning districts and regulate the use of property. The 1913 Hadacheck case in Los Angeles provided one of the basic considerations in all zoning law. Although it preceded recognized zoning statutes, it dealt with the violation of a city ordinance prohibiting the maintenance of brickyards and kilns within a designated residential district of some three square miles. The court ruled that this use of property must cease and desist since the smoke, dust, and fumes emanating from the plant were damaging to the health of the people living nearby. In this case the brickyard was located and operating in the area before it was occupied by residences, but the court did not consider the property right claimed by the owner to be as important as the health and welfare of the people. The claim of discrimination was raised by the owner since brickyards and kilns were permitted in other areas near residential developments, but it was disallowed on the grounds that "it is no objection to the validity of the ordinance that in other districts similarly situated brick kilns are not prohibited. It is for the council to say whether the prohibition should be extended to such other districts."[8]

In 1915 the California city of South Pasadena attempted to restrict the operation of a rock crusher in a high-class residential district.[9] The district was then sparsely developed, whereas similar operations were permitted in other and more heavily populated residential districts. The ordinance was declared void on the grounds that it was unreasonable to prohibit such use in a lightly settled district when the same use was permitted in a densely populated district. The court made much of the fact that the poorer class of homes surrounding the industrial district is entitled to the same protection as the fine homes. In this case, and in others dealing with the mining of natural resources, the courts held that these minerals are only located in certain areas and can only be extracted where they are found. If this activity is denied there would be no material for construction.

A related issue was raised in a case involving rock quarries in the Los Angeles Roscoe area. As each pit's rock supply became exhausted a new site was opened,

---

8. *Ex Parte Hadacheck*, 165 California 416 (1913); *Hadacheck v. Sebastian*, 2390 Supreme Court 394; 60 Law Edition 348.

9. *Matter of Throop*, 169 California 92 (1915).

thus extending the mining area. Eventually it was brought cheek by jowl with the homes of those who had moved there for reasons of health in the excellent climate. The expansion of rock quarrying, it was contended, undermined the value of the climatic resource to the point that the lives of the people were jeopardized. The residents pointed out that the air was filled with dust particles, that the unfenced and abandoned pits were dangerous, and that children had been killed and injured. The community's planning commission upheld the residents' contention, but the city council reversed this stand. The lower courts upheld the legislative body, refusing to substitute its judgment for that of the council on matters of "substance."

The interpretation of the general welfare clause is fundamental to all zoning, and planning rests upon the thesis that regulation of property use will secure numerous benefits to the community. Among others it will lessen congestion on streets, secure greater safety from fire, panic, and similar dangers, promote health by requiring adequate light and air, prevent overcrowding of the land, avoid undue concentrations of population, facilitate the provision of adequate transportation, water supply, sewage disposal, and other basic necessities such as schools, parks, playgrounds, and civic and cultural amenities. Property values are preserved and stabilized, the city's income from taxation will be greater, and the tax rate to supply the required services will be lower. Blight, obsolescence, and slums are discouraged, the city retains a good character and appearance, and an overall improvement of the community reduces the need for and the cost of many social services.

Maintenance of the "general welfare and prosperity" as a reason for imposing race restrictions by means of zoning was termed an illegal use of the police power by the United States Supreme Court. A group of property owners sought to prove that the intrusion of "nonwhite" families into a "white" district caused a loss of property values and thus endangered the prosperity of the community. The court held that the agencies of government could not be used to enforce a law that specifically violated the Fourteenth Amendment of the Constitution. In many other cases the courts have ruled that financial gains or losses are not in themselves sufficient to decide the validity or constitutionality of a law.[10]

Tests of the community's right to prescribe the manner of development within its boundaries engulfed the courts during the 1920s. The newness of zoning law resulted in some phrasing that suggested discrimination to the courts, and decisions were more likely to support the individual against the community welfare, the courts being reluctant to take action which would infringe upon property rights.

As zoning received wider acceptance as a proper use of the police power, a variety of features were incorporated in the ordinances in attempts to dilute their restrictive purpose. There were efforts to use the law as a device to protect the property of the few while permitting the remainder of the city to continue unprotected. Occasionally, in concert with the land speculator, property was zoned for a use that would bring the highest price at the moment; whether the use was commercial, residential, or industrial was of little concern. A weird pattern of spot zoning covered the land like a crazy quilt. Purchasers were informed they could use the vacant land for any purpose they willed, and their neighbors were helpless to

---

10. *Smith v. Collison,* 119 California Appellate 180 (1931). Depreciation in value of property is not fatal to the validity of the ordinance.

protect their investments. Efforts of public officials to maintain conformance with the given character of a neighborhood were hotly contested. "Interim ordinances" were sometimes enacted to forbid encroachments upon "fine" residential districts. Some of these were sustained, but in general the courts found them invalid because of the arbitrary nature of their boundaries; the guarantee of a special area from detrimental uses was viewed as a discriminatory act since the same encroachments were permitted unchecked elsewhere.

Court decisions hammered at a thesis that has since become a cornerstone of zoning: to be valid the law must be both reasonable and fairly applied. The courts were actually leading the way toward the planning of cities; they were directly and indirectly appealing for a comprehensive plan that would provide a foundation for zoning acts and decisions of equity in the shaping and administration of these acts.

Community Character

Euclid 1926 case

One of the most important legal decisions in the history of zoning was the Euclid case in 1926. In his ruling, Associate Justice George Sutherland of the Supreme Court pointed out that each community had the right and the responsibility to determine its own character, and that as long as that determination did not disturb the orderly growth of the region or the nation, it was a valid use of the police power.

> Point is raised by the appellees that the Village of Euclid was a mere suburb of Cleveland, and that the industrial development of the latter had extended to the village, and that in the obvious course of things would soon absorb the entire area for industrial enterprise, and that the effect of the ordinance was to divert such natural development or expansion elsewhere, to the consequent loss of increased values to the owners of land within the village. But this village, though physically a suburb of Cleveland, is a separate municipality, with powers of its own and authority to govern itself as it sees fit within the organic laws of its creation and the state and Federal constitutions. The will of its people determines, not that the industrial development shall cease at its boundaries, but that such development shall proceed between fixed lines. If therefore it is proper exercise of the police power to regulate industrial establishments to localities separated from residential sections, it is not easy to find sufficient reason for denying the power because its effect would be to divert an industrial flow from a course which would result in injury to the residential public to another course where such injury would be obviated. This should not exclude the possibility of cases where the general interest so far outweighs the interest of the municipality, that the latter should not be allowed to stand in its way.[11]

The decision made it abundantly clear that a community may determine the nature of development within its boundaries; it may plan and regulate the use of land as the people of the community may consider it to be in the public interest.

Justice Sutherland enunciated another principle: a community is obliged to relate its plans to the area outside its boundaries. Again the courts anticipate the planning process. Cities are not surrounded by walls; they are each a part of their region, and each is obliged to plan the spaces within its boundaries as an integral part of the plan for spaces outside its boundaries. This suggests, for instance, that a highway plan prepared without consideration of the routes of major importance within the regional plan would constitute an improper use of the police power. A community has both the right to determine its character and the obligation to relate its plan to its regional environs.

---

11. *Village of Euclid, Ohio v. Amber Realty Company*, 272 U.S. 365 (1926).

The drab, uninspired appearance of our cities approaches offensive ugliness. The lack of a long tradition of the arts in society has dulled our response to the visual plunder in our surroundings. The grace and charm of a European village or New England town, the delight of Paris, Venice, and Vienna, arose by way of the manners and morals of the time quite as much as by craftsmanship. Our values have undoubtedly been contorted by materialism and the sheer preoccupation with the practical chores of everyday urban housekeeping. It should not be conceivable in a democratic society with balanced cultural values, but improvement of the aesthetic quality of our cities has actually been attempted through legislative action.

Aesthetic Concerns

In the past, legislative bodies have been reluctant to embody aesthetic considerations in legislation. Judge Swayze of New Jersey specifically expressed this sentiment:

> No case has been cited, nor are we aware of any case, which holds that a man may be deprived of his property because his tastes are not those of his neighbor. Esthetic considerations are a matter of luxury and indulgence rather than of necessity, and it is necessity alone which justifies the police power to take property without compensation.[12]

An early step toward aesthetic control was directed to regulations against the use of billboards along highways. As the advertising mania spread, the extravagant use of signs and billboards reached intolerable proportions. The police power was invoked when in 1905 the Metropolitan Park Commission of Massachusetts sought to prohibit signs near a parkway. This regulation was held invalid by the court, but restrictions against the wanton blight of the billboard rash gained momentum. In 1935 the same court in Massachusetts supported the use of the police power to regulate signs and billboards.

Although there is precedent for aesthetic control in areas of particular historic importance,[13] the device of architectural control is usually avoided; the prospect of imposing a hierarchy of taste upon a community is approached with caution. However, in a unanimous 1954 opinion of the Supreme Court, Justice William O. Douglas clearly affirmed that a community need not tolerate ugliness and may take legal steps to correct it.

> Public safety, public health, morality, peace and quiet, law and order—these are some of the more conspicuous examples of the traditional application of the police power to municipal affairs. Yet they merely illustrate the scope of the power and do not delimit it. Miserable and disreputable housing conditions may do more than spread disease and crime and immorality. They may also suffocate the spirit by reducing the people who live there to the status of cattle. They may indeed make living an almost insufferable burden. They may also be an ugly sore, a blight on the community which robs it of charm, which makes it a place from which men turn. The misery of housing may despoil a community as an open sewer may ruin a river.

> We do not sit to determine whether a particular housing project is or is not desirable. The concept of the public welfare is broad and inclusive. The values it represents are spiritual as well as physical, aesthetic as well as monetary. It is within the power of the legislature to determine that the community should be beautiful as well as healthy, spacious as well as clean, well-balanced as well as carefully patrolled. In the present case, the Congress and its authorized agencies have made

---

12. *Passaic v. Paterson Bill Posting Co.* 62A, 267 (1905) New Jersey Supreme Court.

13. 333 Mass. 773 and 783 (1955).

determinations that take into account a wide variety of values. It is not for us to reappraise them. If those who govern the District of Columbia decide that the nation's Capital should be beautiful as well as sanitary, there is nothing in the Fifth Amendment that stands in the way. . . . In the present case, Congress and its authorized agencies attack the problem of the blighted parts of the community on an area rather than on a structure-by-structure basis. That, too, is opposed by appellants. They maintain that since their building does not imperil health or safety nor contribute to the making of a slum or a blighted area, it cannot be swept into a redevelopment plan by the mere dictum of the Planning Commission or the Commissioners. The particular uses to be made of the land in the project were determined with regard to the needs of the particular community. The experts concluded that if the community were to be healthy, if it were not to revert again to a blighted or slum area, as though possessed of a congenital disease, the area must be planned as a whole. It was not enough, they believed, to remove existing buildings that were unsanitary or unsightly. It was important to redesign the whole area so as to eliminate the conditions that cause slums—the overcrowding of dwellings, the lack of parks, the lack of adequate streets and alleys, the absence of recreational areas, the lack of light and air, the presence of outmoded street patterns. It was believed that the piecemeal approach, the removal of individual structures that were offensive, would be only a palliative. The entire area needed redesigning so that a balanced, integrated plan could be developed for the region, including not only new homes but also schools, churches, parks, streets and shopping centers. In this way it was hoped that the cycle of decay of the area could be controlled and the birth of future slums prevented. Such diversification in future use is plainly relevant to the maintenance of the desired housing standards and therefore within congressional power. . . .[14]

The decision acknowledged that the appearance of the city stands with other features that involve the public interest. In this case it pertained to conditions that existed and found that the spiritual welfare of the people was imperiled by these conditions, but the point is no less valid. It provides a foundation for legislation that employs the police power to discontinue such conditions. We apparently have yet to establish means by which such conditions may not at the outset be created.

The public can assert its interests directly in two areas. One is in the public domain, since some 40 percent of the city consists of streets, walks, parks, and civic reserves. Herein is a broad and impressive arena for creative treatment of space arrangement, landscaping, street furniture, lighting, signs, and structures. The second area is in the realm of public regulation of three-dimensional volumes related to community design. This involves integrated use of land—open space and landscape—structures, the character of building design, advertising media, and ingress and egress for pedestrians and vehicles. Sensitive attention to the formulation of these regulations may accomplish some effective results without impinging on good taste. In the final analysis, the creation of beauty is the result of a desire that it be produced as well as the talent to produce it, and this demands the cultivation of cultural values.

The importance and validity of aesthetic considerations has been upheld in a case involving the county of Santa Barbara in California. The county zoning ordinance established an amortization period for outdoor advertising structures along its main highway. The outdoor advertisers sued the county, implying that zoning for aesthetic purposes was unconstitutional, that beauty is a matter of personal taste, that outdoor advertising was a legitimate commercial enterprise and there-

14. *Berman v. Parker*, 348 U.S. 26, 75 Sup. Ct. 98, 99 L. Ed. 27 (1954).

fore must be given the same rights as other commercial uses. The court held that the scenic quality of Santa Barbara county was one of its most important economic assets in attracting tourists and visitors, and as such must be protected for the general welfare. The billboards were therefore ordered to be removed. There was no appeal.

A case involving the Coachella Valley of California, however, turned out somewhat differently. An attempt to restrict the erection of billboards on land held in Indian ownership was rejected, on the grounds that since Indian land was subject only to regulation by the federal government, local laws did not apply.

The decade of the 1980s found the comprehensive plan the subject of attention in the courts with several important challenges. The importance of the comprehensive plan as a process was not criticized, but the quality and the contents of the plans which fell short of the essential legal requirements were subject to close scrutiny and legal rulings. The consistency of zoning with the comprehensive plan was measured, and in many cases neither the zoning nor the elements of the plan were consistent with the other or with the regional planning for the area. Three cases illustrate the legal positioning which strengthened the value of the comprehensive plan in the overall scheme of governmental efforts to obtain sound planning.

RECENT LEGAL CHALLENGES

In 1978, a series of subdivision maps was approved by Mendicino County.[15] Suits were filed against the county involving two different map approvals on the grounds that the county comprehensive plan was inadequate and that a tentative map could not be approved where such deficiencies existed. In the suit the court determined that the land use, housing, and noise elements were inadequate and ordered the county to adopt a better plan. In reviewing the plan the court identified specific deficiencies, including the failure to set forth population density standards, building intensity standards, and plans for the improvement of housing construction and sites. Nor did the plan provide a problem-solving strategy for the county's growth or a long-term projection of prospective need for market rate housing. In addition it failed to provide noise exposure information and did not monitor noise-sensitive areas. Finally it did not correlate the circulation element with the land use element.

MENDICINO COUNTY SUBDIVISION

The court ruled that injunctive relief against new developments was an appropriate remedy where the county failed to adopt an adequate comprehensive plan.

In April 1982, the Calaveras County Board of Supervisors adopted a new comprehensive plan for the county.[16] Subsequently a group of concerned citizens filed a writ of mandate alleging that the comprehensive plan was inadequate because (1) the land use element and circulation element were internally inconsistent and insufficiently correlated, (2) solid and liquid waste disposal facilities were not designated, (3) the plan omitted population density standards for three areas of the county.

INADEQUACY OF COMPREHENSIVE PLAN

---

15. *Camp v. Board of Supervisors,* Calif. Court of Appeals, 123 Ca. App 3d 331 (Sept. 1, 1981).

16. *Concerned Citizens of Calaveras County v. Board of Supervisors of Calaveras County,* Mar. 26, 1985, 166 Ca. App 3 90, Third District Court of Appeal.

The appellate court determined that the land use and circulation elements were not sufficiently correlated and thus violated the state law. The court emphasized, in advising cities and counties in the process of reviewing or preparing their comprehensive plans, to evaluate their circulation plans to determine whether they could accommodate the future traffic demands associated with the uses designated in the land use element.

ENVIRON- MENTAL IMPACT REPORT AND COMPRE- HENSIVE PLAN

The Twin Harte Homeowners Association, Inc., filed suit to compel the county to rescind certification of the environmental impact report (EIR), claiming that the wording changes in the EIR created potential environmental impacts that it did not address.[17] The association also stated that the land use, circulation, and housing elements of the comprehensive plan were inadequate.

The court of appeals held that the EIR was deficient in two respects resulting from the wording changes made to the draft plan after certification of the EIR. The changes deleted provisions restricting heavy industrial development in a certain area and amended a policy statement regarding seismic safety. The court held that these changes, without further analysis in the EIR, constituted an abuse of the county's authority. The court also ruled that the land use and circulation elements were inadequate. The land use element failed to include standards of population density and building intensity as required by state law.

GROWTH CONTROL AND THE COMPRE- HENSIVE PLAN

Two growth control initiatives in the city of Riverside were invalidated because the comprehensive plan was inadequate.[18] The people of the city of Riverside adopted two initiative measures related to the use of open space and agricultural land and called on the city to plan restricted development for the unincorporated areas within the city's area of influence.

The court determined that the city's comprehensive plan was invalid because it was internally inconsistent; it was also out of date and its organization and format were such that it was physically unavailable to the public, landowners, city staff, and decision makers. In addition the court held that various plan elements did not meet statutory requirements such as building intensity standards for nonresidential uses. In addition to the lack of correlation of land use and circulation, the noise element had not been updated to reflect the latest circulation and transportation elements.

THE "TAKING" ISSUE

Historically it has been the practice that when citizens appear before a public agency to secure permission to develop their property under provisions of subdivision or zoning laws and where such action is not permitted without public sanction, at that time the community can request or require an "exaction" from the applicant. This exaction may take the form of financial support for parks or schools or of dedication of accessways, easements, and so forth. Normally, if a community wants property for public use it must pay the owner a fair market price for the land to be taken. In many cases it is necessary to go through condemnation procedures where the court determines the price. Requiring exactions now appears to be a questionable practice.

---

17. *Twain Harte Homeowners Association Inc. v. the County of Tuolumne,* December 1982, 138 Ca. App 3d 664, California Court of Appeal.

18. *Garat v. City of Riverside,* Aug. 1, 1989, Riverside County Superior Court Case no. 191567.

The owner of a 2-acre parcel of land wished to split his land into two 1-acre lots, which would be similar in size to all the other parcels in the area. The request was submitted to the Los Angeles County Regional Planning Commission as a lot split. Since the request was consistent with the zoning for the area and the development already in place, the commission approved the request on the condition, related to a requirement of the Coastal Commission, that beach access be provided. The owner said that this was a taking of his property without just compensation. Furthermore, the owner felt that the value of both of his lots would be diminished by the pedestrian thoroughfare through it. In addition he cited the fact that the property frontage was on a narrow street and that parked cars of the persons using the accessway would create congestion and accident hazards. The county persisted, stating that there was a public need for access to the public beach. The owner withdrew his request, stating that the loss of privacy and the potential danger were far greater than the gain from the sale of the lot.

The Pennsylvania Bituminous Mine Subsidence and Land Conservation Act prohibits underground coal mining below existing public buildings, dwellings, and cemeteries.[19] To prevent subsidence (sinking of the land), the state's regulations implementing the act require coal mining companies not to mine 50 percent of the coal, in accordance with protected land uses. The act also authorizes the State Department of Environmental Resources (DER) to revoke a mining permit if the mining activities lead to subsidence under protected uses and if within 6 months the mining company has not repaired the property damage, paid for the damage, or made a security deposit with the DER equal to the cost of the repairs.

In 1982 four of the coal mining companies filed suit to enjoin the DER from enforcing the subsidence act and implementing regulations. They said that the acts subjected them to property damage liabilities despite generation-old agreements under which many surface property owners established their rights to damage claims.

The Supreme Court of the United States in its "taking" analysis found that a *taking* occurs when a regulation, (1) does not substantially advance legitimate state interests or (2) denies the owner economically viable use of his or her land. In conclusion the court held that the petitioners had not satisfied their burden of showing that the subsidence act constitutes a taking.

Further, the court held, "The public interest in preventing dangerous activities was similar to a public nuisance and a substantial one, which in many instances has not required compensation. The subsidence act . . . plainly seeks to further such an interest."

The First Lutheran Church of Glendale established a campground for handicapped children along Mill Creek in Los Angeles County. In 1977 a forest fire denuded the watershed above the camp, and in the following year runoff from heavy rain caused Mill Creek to flood, destroying the camp buildings.

In response to the flood, Los Angeles County enacted an interim ordinance in January 1979, prohibiting the construction or reconstruction or enlargement of any building or structure within an interim flood protection area that included

THE MALIBU CASE

PENNSYL-VANIA BITUMINOUS MINE SUBSIDENCE AND LAND CONSER-VATION ACT

FLOOD CONTROL TAKING

19. *Keystone Bituminous Coal Association v. DeBenedictis,* Mar. 9, 1987, 107 S Ct. 1232 United States Supreme Court.

Lutherglen. The church brought suit, declaring that they were denied use of their property and seeking damages for the taking.[20]

The United States Supreme Court held that landowners are entitled to just compensation for the loss of the use of their land while the property is subjected to overly restrictive land use regulation. Consequently just compensation is the proper remedy for a regulatory "taking" that is only temporary in effect.

As a basis for the holding the majority opinion of the court cited the just compensation clause of the Fifth Amendment of the U. S. Constitution, which says, "Private property shall not be taken for public use without just compensation." The court also noted its general rule that property may be regulated to some extent, but if the regulation "goes too far," it will be recognized as a taking.

The Supreme Court, in this case, did not rule as to whether a taking was involved and remanded the case to the appellate court for that decision on the basis of the phrase "goes too far." The court also left open the possibility that certain safety-based regulations were not takings.

The California Court of Appeals determined that the county ordinance was not an unconstitutional taking without compensation. This decision was based on *Nollan v. California Coastal Commission* (described later) that the building restriction clearly advanced the paramount interest of the state by preventing death and injury during the next flood. In addition, the court found that the ordinance did not apply to use of all of the church property and that the church could still use the land for camping and recreation as well as for agriculture. It placed an interim temporary limitation only on construction.

NOLLAN V. CALIFORNIA COASTAL COMMISSION

The Nollans own a beachfront house in Ventura County. In 1982 they wanted to replace a small, rundown house with a larger three-bedroom unit.[21] The application to the Coastal Commission was approved with the proviso that a public accessway be granted across a portion of their lot. The Superior Court struck the easement condition and reversed the appellate action on the grounds that it violated the taking provision of the Fifth Amendment to the Constitution. The court held that if the state wanted the easement, they would have to pay for it.

Another element had to be considered by the court, that of whether a demand for an easement as part of a permit procedure constituted a taking. The case findings indicate that when the court determines the validity of a development permit condition, it will look for the "nexus" (the connection between the condition imposed and the governmental purpose or interests affected by the development proposal) as the basis for their decisions.

INVERSE CONDEM-NATION

In April 1985, the California Coastal Commission approved the demolition and rebuilding of a house in Del Mar, California.[22] The approval was conditioned on the dedication of a public access easement along a strip of beach in front of the

---

20. *First English Evangelical Lutheran Church of Glendale v. County of Los Angeles*, June 9, 1987, 55 USLW 4781, U.S. Supreme Court.

21. *Nollan v. California Coastal Commission*, June 26, 1987, 55 USLW 5145 United States Supreme Court.

22. *California Coastal Commission v. Superior Court*, May 18, 1989, as modified June 9, 1989, 210 Cal App 3d 1488 Fourth District Court of Appeal.

new house. The applicant complied and the commission issued the required permits. In July 1988 the owner sued the state of California and the Coastal Commission for inverse condemnation, claiming that the easement requirement was an unconstitutional taking without compensation. The basis for the owner's claim was the U.S. Supreme Court's rulings in the *Nollan* and First English cases.

The state contended that the owner waived his opportunity to challenge the easement requirement by failing to seek a writ of administrative mandate within the 60-day statute of limitations after the granting of the permit. According to the court, an administrative mandate action filed within the 60-day statute of limitations alerts the commission that it may be liable for inverse condemnation damages.

Friends of the court tried to argue that an exception to *res judicata* occurs when an agency's action exceeds its jurisdiction and suggested that the unconstitutional permit exceeded the commission's jurisdiction. The appellate court concluded, however, that *jurisdiction* in this sense refers to jurisdiction of a most fundamental kind. If the owner believed that the commission was wrong, he could have remedied the decision by way of judicial review. Having failed to avail himself of this recourse, he had no basis for complaint.

The grant of police power by the states to the cities and counties vests these political subdivisions with the power to regulate their affairs and enforce the regulations. It is nevertheless found necessary on occasion for the state to enact legislation for the specific use of that power. Such legislation is in the form of what is generally termed "enabling acts." The purpose may be twofold. It may be for the purpose of affirming state policy in matters of vital interest to the people at any given time and thereby encouraging local communities to act; or the special legislation may be for the purpose of removing doubt that the police power was intended for the specific subject of the act. The preamble of all such legislation states the purposes in detail. Such enabling acts are drawn to establish clearly the relation between the use for which the police power is granted and the public health, safety, convenience, and general welfare.

ENABLING LEGISLATION

The state sometimes passes zoning enabling acts when cities and counties previously delegated the police power but are reluctant to exercise it until the state has specifically signified that it be so used. These special enabling acts are usually written in greater detail than the general grant of the police power. They define the scope of zoning, the procedure for adoption of the ordinance, the composition of the zoning board and its powers and functions, and the methods for modification or exceptions to the ordinance.

State planning acts are a form of special enabling legislation, although they generally establish a state agency to coordinate planning functions at the state level in addition to setting forth the specifications for local planning activities. Such acts describe the functions of a state planning board and prescribe the process for each city and county to accomplish a complete planning job for itself. These laws usually call for the preparation of a comprehensive plan, list the scope of the plan, and specify the methods for its adoption and enforcement. Power is sometimes given to the local planning commission to levy a special tax for funds to administer the law, but this power is seldom invoked; planning commissions prefer to work within the departmental family of the city government and draw their support from the general tax funds.

Another form of enabling legislation is that which creates new agencies in the state, cities, or counties to cope with problems of a particular nature. Housing and urban redevelopment acts are of this type, local agencies being created with powers conferred upon the city or county to engage in the program prescribed in the state statute.

Just as specific enabling legislation is created at the state level to cover certain fields of urban activity, so special ordinances are drawn at the local level to define in detail the manner in which city charter provisions are to be executed. In cities where there is no "freeholders' charter"[23] the state laws are in effect; in cities having charters that define the exercise of the police power in stricter terms than the state, the local law takes precedence.[24] Thus, if a state speed limit in a school zone is 20 miles per hour and the city law restricts the speed to 15 miles per hour, the city law is enforceable. If, on the other hand, the city has a limit of 25 miles per hour or no regulation at all for those specific areas, the state law is then enforceable. In terms almost identical to the state enabling legislation, city charters often define the functions of a planning commission; as long as all the duties included in the state law are included in terms not less restrictive, the city charter provisions apply.

Too frequently there is no penalty provision for failure to abide by the requirements of state legislation. An example would be the case in which states call for all counties to have planning commissions and many small counties ignore the requirement; there are few ways to compel the local government to conform. However, in some states the local governments are restricted from the benefits of funds appropriated by the state for public improvements until they conform with state laws. There are occasions when funds for the state highway system, for example, are withheld until the counties adopt general plans for highways that show the relationship between the state routes and local roads. But all too often great resources are dissipated without control.

TRANSITION

Since the inception of action against the use of property deemed a menace to health and life, zoning changed considerably. It has passed from regulation of land uses for the preservation of property values to the present position of responsibility not only for protection of the status quo but also for the creation of a better city, better state, and more prosperous nation. It is true that, as zoning becomes a more effective instrument for improvement of the good city, it becomes less like the traditional instrument called "zoning" and more like the act of planning the city, for many factors other than the ones usually identified with zoning enter the scene.

Recently zoning has become a means for both conservation and planning; the narrow concept is extended to the broadest interpretation of the use of the police power for the protection of the public welfare. In these instances zoning law anticipates the future and guides the development of areas through planned uses rather than waiting until the die is cast and merely fixing land uses that already exist. In the cutover areas of Michigan, Wisconsin, and Minnesota, where erosion threatened to rip the growing heart out of the soil and create dust-bowl conditions, legal steps were taken to label as submarginal the worst of the land. In this

---

23. An act of municipal incorporation, provided for in the constitutions of the individual states.

24. *Brougher v. Board of Public Works*, 205 California 426 (1928). A city charter need not follow the procedures of the state zoning enabling act.

way use of rural land was discouraged until such time as the topsoil could be replaced and refertilized. Further mining of trees in the areas not entirely destroyed was forbidden. A reforestation program, under the guidance and with the assistance of the federal government, now assures the people of a continuing supply of lumber for future generations. Thus the priceless possession of fertile land will not be wantonly wasted. The Hawaii State Planning Act of 1961 encompasses more than conservation. It provides for urban, agricultural, and conservation land-use classifications and requires that tax-assessing authorities be guided by these zoned land uses in establishing assessed values for real property.

J. H. Bradley, in his *Autobiography of Earth*, has stated: "the fabric of human life has been woven on earthen looms." We must use every device in our legal system to protect our land and devote it to its highest and best uses for we cannot escape to new frontiers after abusing and ruining what we have. Almost two centuries ago George Washington observed: "Our lands . . . were originally very good; but use and abuse have made them quite otherwise. . . . We ruin the lands that are already cleared, and either cut down more wood, if we have it, or emigrate into Western country." [25]

The use of police power—zoning—to ensure our future seems neither arbitrary nor in contradiction of any freedom assured to the people by the Constitution. [26]

25. U.S. Department of Agriculture, *To Hold This Soil,* Publication No. 321 (Washington, D.C.: U.S. Government Printing Office, 1938).

26. U.S. Department of Agriculture, *The Why and How of Rural Zoning* (Washington, D.C.: U.S. Government Printing Office, December 1958).

PART 6

PLANNING

FOR THE

FUTURE

*Zoning in its best sense looks not
only backward to protect districts already
established but forward to aid in the development
of new districts according to a comprehensive
plan having as its basis the welfare
of the city as a whole.*

—*California Supreme Court*

CHAPTER 22

THE COMPREHENSIVE PLAN

In recent years the courts have almost uniformly held that the comprehensive plan is the basis for planning. All zoning and other planning activities must be consistent with both the intent and the purpose of the comprehensive plan.

Patrick Geddes promoted the philosophy that called for the integration of natural and social planning and the integration of the natural and social worlds.

All too many persons believe that the comprehensive plan deals only with the use of land and that its most definitive forms are the zoning and subdivision regulations. To be meaningful, the plan must cover a much wider range than that; it must encompass the social, economic, and political elements that guide and implement the life of our communities and those who live within them.

The comprehensive plan must be farsighted, anticipating the needs and desires of the community. It must provide the guidance essential to the preparation of specific plans and the budgeting to accomplish them. In order to be comprehensive it must become the people's plan, supported by them when timely proposals are to be implemented by action agencies.

Neither the master plan nor the general plan is the same thing as the comprehensive plan. The term *master plan* has been applied to almost every scheme for property development, from an individual lot to a large estate, a shopping center,

COMPRE-HENSIVE PLAN DEFINED

or a city. The term *general plan* identifies long-range, comprehensive planning by or for a government agency as a foundation for overall land development policies within specific corporate limits. These terms were interchangeable, but *general plan* was adopted to distinguish it from the varied nongovernmental applications associated with *master plan*.

The term *comprehensive plan* was added to the planner's vocabulary in recent years to indicate that current community planning is more than "general." These planning programs now include many social and economic elements that were not included in the earlier days of professional practice. Students graduating from the universities where urban planning degrees are offered frequently are equipped to participate in a variety of programs, many of which have little or nothing to do with the physical planning that formed the basis for the early development of the profession. This should not demean the importance of physical planning; it merely adds a new dimension to it.

Nor should *comprehensive planning* and *a comprehensive plan* be confused. Comprehensive planning may range from the preparation of a series of highly specialized studies to an intensive study of a development plan for an entire area. The comprehensive plan, however, must include a review of the physical structure of a city or planning area; a measurement of development trends; a definition of goals and objectives for future growth and change; proposals to protect and promote health, education, and the general welfare; and specific recommendations, policies, and graphics that delineate the plan and establish standards in support of it.

HISTORICAL BACKGROUND

Every comprehensive plan for an area should begin with a study of the history of the community and the environmental and ecological characteristics that were present at the time that the community began. It should include the major events that have taken place during the years of its existence, featuring the important buildings, people, and cultural activities that have given the community its substance and character and have determined its growth and its place in the regional environment, or where it has grown or withered as a result of external or internal conditions or events.

The history should also describe the local sensitivities and pride as well as concerns for both the present and future.

WHY IT IS NEEDED

After the early adventures in zoning it became increasingly apparent that this use of the police power to safeguard the public welfare could not stand by itself. The courts had upheld the right of a community to exercise the police power in legislating regulations governing the use of land. They had granted that a community has the right to determine its own character. Conservatives such as Justice George Sutherland of the Supreme Court had supported this right, and there was a growing popular acceptance of zoning as a means to protect the interests of a community.

But the courts perceived that if a community was to determine the appropriate uses of its land properly and provide a firm basis for its control as prescribed in zoning ordinances, it needed to appraise the use of all land within its political jurisdiction and give consideration to conditions in areas contiguous to it as well. The courts found good reason for this view. They had observed numerous abuses of the police power. For example, many small districts would be established as a way to prevent the construction of some particular improvement or deny a use deemed undesirable in some existing structure; sometimes a zoning ordinance was intended to create or protect a monopoly.

To assure that districts were not arbitrarily or discriminatorily determined, the courts required evidence that the various zones were related to an overall evaluation of land use in the city. There was a growing insistence upon a "comprehensive plan" as a foundation for zoning ordinances; Justice George Sutherland's opinion in the Euclid case clearly expressed this need. Thus the process of the comprehensive plan evolved.

Seeking techniques with which to satisfy the requirement for a comprehensive plan, some communities willfully avoided the issue by employing specious devices. One of these was to zone all land to the least restrictive use with the exception of certain limited "refined" districts. The community could thus allege in court that it had enacted a comprehensive zoning ordinance since every parcel of land in the city was within a zoning district. Although that statement was true, it was not a plan. Another device was to zone all land not specifically zoned for other purposes as a residential district, with the provision for variances from the residential use. In the administration of the ordinance each variation was then interpreted as an act of making the original plan more "precise." Neither of these techniques stood the test for long since they were evasions of the basic principles of planning.

Too frequently zoning practices resolved themselves into a process of "freezing" existing land uses, including all the misuses that had previously established themselves. In some communities, an inventory and classification of all existing land uses were adopted as the "plan" of the city. Travesties of planning, these practices are gradually being replaced by a more enlightened awareness of the advantages of planning to civic growth and development. As a means to provide a pattern for future development of the city, the comprehensive plan has become a generally accepted instrument.

LEGAL STATUS OF THE COMPREHENSIVE PLAN

In recent cases the courts have challenged comprehensive (general) plans that were in themselves inconsistent with the plans for the region in which the subject community was located. For instance:

- How can a plan be truly comprehensive if it does not take into account the state highways and freeways plans, both those on the ground and those that are being planned?
- How can a plan be comprehensive if it does not consider the dangers of air pollution and the need to plan for air quality improvement?
- How can a plan be comprehensive if it does not understand and respect the decisions on land use in the neighboring communities? After all, planning should not stop at an artificially established community border. Uses must be planned to adjust to each other in order not to create conflicts that endanger life.
- How can a plan be comprehensive if the sewage, storm drain, and similar regional activities are not dealt with on a broader basis than one's own community?
- How can a plan be comprehensive if it does not deal with waste and traffic congestion management?

These and many other regional problems must be addressed and resolved before any plan can be called truly comprehensive.

The comprehensive plan has sometimes been regarded as only a reference guide for the planning commission and the legislative body, being subject neither to formal public hearings nor to official action by the governing body. This arrangement appears to prevent the cumbersome proceedings that accompany formal action to modify the plan, thus affording maximum flexibility at the discretion of the commission and staff, but also potential for abuse of the process.

CONTENTS AND FUNCTION

Many states mandate by law that comprehensive integrated plans be prepared and that they be used as the basis for later decisions involving public activity. The 1982 California law is not untypical. It summarizes in a rather brief statement what the contents of the plan shall be and the process that shall be employed in implementing it.

(a) Each demonstration county and city shall prepare an integrated comprehensive plan which contains the following:
  (1) Goals, policies, and programs for the physical, social, and economic development of the community;
  (2) Documentation of the data and analysis upon which these goals, policies, and programs are based;
  (3) Assessment of the fiscal capacity of the county or city to implement the plan; and
  (4) An implementation schedule that links the plan to the allocation of public resources, including capital expenditures, the annual budget, and federal and state funding for local programs.

(b) The planning process developed to prepare the integrated comprehensive plan should include provision for:
  (1) Integration, to the extent possible, of other required planning processes with the general plan process; including, in the case of counties, social services planning;
  (2) To the extent feasible, integration of plans with required regional or county plans, plans and programs of special districts, and with state-wide goals and policies;
  (3) Assessment of the potential physical, environmental, social, and economic impacts of alternative plan proposals; and
  (4) Specific mechanisms for involvement of citizens in the planning process.

(c) The demonstration counties or cities shall record and analyze the cost of development, maintenance, and implementation of the alternative plan.

PURPOSE

The modern city is a complex organism. It is a great human enterprise that should serve the material and spiritual needs of humanity. It is a segment of the land that people have selected as their place to live and to work, to learn and to trade, to play and to pray. It is a mosaic of homes and shops, factories and offices, schools and libraries, theaters and hospitals, parks and religious institutions, meeting places and government centers, fire stations and post offices. These are woven together by a network of streets and transportation routes, water, sanitation, and communication channels, and held together by social bonds and economic conditions.

To arrange all these essential facilities properly as the city develops is the purpose of the comprehensive plan. The city is a cumbersome affair, at once sensitive to the multitude of small shifts and yet capable of absorbing great shocks. A change in any part affects other parts of this structure. A new home means more places of employment, more traffic on the streets, extra mail in a letter carrier's bag, another customer in the supermarket, more children in the school, more water for the lawn, more picnics in the park. It also means more revenue in taxes. But growth does not always mean strength and prosperity for the community. This rests with the standards a community determines to maintain and the balanced use of its land and resources.

> The comprehensive plan is a guide to orderly city development to promote the health, safety, welfare, and convenience of the people of a community. It organizes and coordinates the complex relationships between urban land uses and many civic activities. It charts a course for growth and change. It expresses the aims and ambitions of a community, delineating the form and character it seeks to achieve. It reflects the policies by which these goals may be reached. It is responsive to appropriate change and for maintaining its essential vitality and is subject to continual review. It directs the physical development of the community and its environs in relation to its social and economic well-being for the fulfillment of the rightful common destiny, according to a "master plan" based on "careful and comprehensive surveys and studies of present conditions and the prospects of future growth of the municipality, and embodying scientific teachings and creative experience." In a word, this is an exercise of the State's inherent authority, antedating the Constitution itself, to have recourse to such measures as may serve the basic common moral and material needs. Planning to this end is as old as government itself—of the very essence of an ordered and civilized society.[1]

THE PLAN AS PROCESS

State legislation usually requires the preparation of a comprehensive plan and sets forth the scope. A passage from the California law reads, in part:

> Each commission or planning department shall prepare and the commission shall adopt a comprehensive, long-term general plan for the physical development of the city, county, area, or region, and of the land outside its boundaries which in the commission's judgment bears relation to its planning. The plan may be referred to as the master or general plan and shall be officially certified by the planning commission and the legislative body.[2]

After the comprehensive plan has been adopted by the legislative body,

> no road, street, highway, square, park, or other public way, ground or open space shall be acquired by dedication or otherwise, and no street, road, highway or public way shall be closed or abandoned, and no public building or structure shall be constructed or authorized in the area . . . until the location, character, and extent thereof shall be submitted to and shall have been reported on by the planning commission.[3]

Such statements of official policy establish the planning process in our cities, and it is such statements that have been upheld by the courts of our land because they recognize the necessity for a city plan.

Ladislas Segoe described the comprehensive plan in these terms:

> The comprehensive city plan or master plan, while it must be thoroughly practical and sound economically, must give expression also to other than the purely mater-

---

1. *Mansfield & Sweet, Inc. v. Town of West Orange.*

2. State of California, *Laws Relating to Conservation, Planning and Zoning*, 1959.

3. Ibid.

ialistic aspirations of the people of a community. Only then will the process possess —in addition to its influence toward a more convenient, efficient economical development—the inspirational force that will force civic interest, devotion and loyalty essential for building better cities.

The comprehensive city plan or master plan must therefore be—first, a balanced and otherwise attractive general design best suited to present and probable future needs; second, in scale with the population and economic prospects of the community; and third, in scale with its financial resources, present and prospective. The satisfying of the above criteria calls for the application of scientific as well as artistic effort, in order to produce a city plan of attractive form, pleasing balance and detail, attuned to the economic and social activities of the community. . . .[4]

It is probably more accurate to describe a comprehensive plan as a process rather than as a conclusive statement. It is a pattern for the physical development of the city, a pattern to guide the city builders in locating their investments and measuring the prospect for success. It is a design for the physical, social, economic, and political framework for the city; it welds the sociological, economic, and geographic properties of the city into a structure.

To suggest that the plan is a fluid process may imply that decisions are not represented in it. The plan for a city will be modified as conditions may alter the affairs of people from time to time, but a comprehensive plan represents certain decisions of vital importance to the welfare of the people and their city. It represents a decision as to the number of people the city may build to accommodate; it represents the standards by which the city will be developed. It represents decisions on the appropriate relation between the uses of land and the relation between the land to be developed for residential, commercial, and industrial enterprise. It calls for decisions on the lines of communication that link these areas—the circulation system and the infrastructure required to serve the residents. And it represents decisions on the plan: for public schools, parks, and reservation of open space throughout the city.

These are broad decisions, but they are essential to the formulation of a pattern for city building. It is upon these decisions that the health of urban development rests, for they express the aspirations of a community and set the goals toward which the city may advance.

CONSISTENCY

The comprehensive plan establishes these land use policies as the legal criteria for implementation through detailed zoning. This public document is of sufficient importance that it is subject to public response and discussion and thorough consideration by the legislative body, as well as to adoption as the official plan. It, and subsequent revisions to it, should be adopted by resolution of the legislative body. It serves as the basic frame of reference for all administrative and regulatory measures relating to urban renewal, the capital improvement expenditures. The financial solvency of a city hinges on a program of public facilities that maintains a balance between expenditure and revenue. The plan aids in weighing this balance. The seven basic elements of the comprehensive plan are:

1. Plan for land use

2. Plan for circulation

3. Plan for infrastructure

---

4. Ladislas Segoe, *Local Planning Administration* (Chicago: International City Managers' Association, 1942), first edition.

4. Capital improvement budgeting
5. Transportation element
6. Housing element
7. Many other elements, as described in this book

ECONOMIC, SOCIAL, AND HISTORICAL CONSIDERATIONS

If the data on the nature of the physical character of the city seem to be complicated, the social and economic facts are even more so. People are not inclined to conceal the manner in which they use the land unless an evasion of the law is involved, but they are reluctant to divulge their ages, incomes, or health; such information is naturally considered to be of a personal nature. To plan for the community welfare, however, it is important to know about the people for whom the plan is intended.

One of the principal source of economic and social data is the U.S. Census; the elements included have been described earlier. Based upon these data, the Bureau of the Census analyzes the spending habits of the various income groups, indicating the amount each spent for rent, clothes, food, amusement, and other living necessities. However, much of the latter information is given for the whole city and is difficult to relate to the census tracts, the units in which urban statistics are usually tabulated. The exception is housing data, which are listed by blocks in the census and provide a source of information for the land-use survey.

Although most public and private local agencies normally assemble only the information on the social and economic structure of the community in which they are directly interested, the planning agency may obtain and correlate this special information to form an overall picture. Since the various agencies may interpret similar data in different ways, these differences must be resolved by the planners on the basis of the best available known facts.

Care must be taken with the use of these facts: It is a well-known cliché that anything can be proved with statistics; the corollary is that statistics may not prove anything. Thus it is all the more important that they not be misleading. As an illustration, an increase in the number of families and the number of houses built may be nearly the same and therefore indicate no shortage of dwellings. But these "pure" numbers mean little as an evaluation of the housing supply in relation to housing supply and need. The number of families formerly doubled-up, the cost brackets of the new residences, the absence of a normal vacancy factor, and the occupancy of substandard housing facilities are among the statistics to be evaluated with those on the number of families and the housing supply in order for the evaluation of need to be accurate. Such caution and consideration of all related factors are essential for the proper and correct use of statistics.

Availability Of Data

The economic base of urban communities will differ from one geographical area to another, depending upon the nature of the local ecology and environment. Some areas will depend upon the preservation of natural resources, others will depend upon their extraction and exploitation. In general terms the types of activities considered as factors in the economic base include the following, much of which may be in computerized form:

Industry and agriculture	Retirement pensions	Transportation
Wholesaling and retailing	Property income	Insurance and finance
Services	Tourism	Government
Military		

General and Family Characteristics: 1980

The Area Neighborhoods	The Area 06-180	Neighborhood 001	Neighborhood 002	Neighborhood 003	Neighborhood 004	Neighborhood 005	Neighborhood 006	Neighborhood 007	Neighborhood 008	Neighborhood 009	Neighborhood 010
URBAN AND RURAL											
Total persons	32 584	2 506	1 016	1 529	1 015	1 747	2 329	1 067	1 697	993	1 152
Urban	32 480	2 506	1 016	1 529	1 015	1 747	2 329	1 067	1 697	993	1 152
Inside urbanized areas	32 480	2 506	1 016	1 529	1 015	1 747	2 329	1 067	1 697	993	1 152
Outside urbanized areas	—	—	—	—	—	—	—	—	—	—	—
Rural	104	—	—	—	—	—	—	—	—	—	—
RACE AND SPANISH ORIGIN											
White	28 963	2 325	938	1 499	58	1 487	1 987	1 017	1 513	944	1 097
Black	1 575	50	28	5	941	45	78	14	144	8	6
Percent of total persons	4.8	2.0	2.8	0.3	92.7	2.6	3.3	1.3	8.5	0.8	0.5
American Indian, Eskimo, and Aleut	184	6	2	6	1	16	12	2	12	7	24
Asian and Pacific islander[1]	786	72	15	15	6	26	79	9	17	17	8
Other	1 076	53	33	4	9	173	173	25	11	17	17
Spanish origin[2]	2 932	260	67	48	22	350	301	59	86	48	43
Percent of total persons	9.0	10.4	6.6	3.1	2.2	20.0	12.9	5.5	5.1	4.8	3.7
AGE											
Total persons	32 584	2 506	1 016	1 529	1 015	1 747	2 329	1 067	1 697	993	1 152
Under 5 years	1 265	94	38	22	82	104	209	8	39	11	55
5 to 9 years	1 316	138	32	39	93	75	193	12	31	41	49
10 to 14 years	1 577	189	29	69	128	99	136	18	43	46	64
15 to 19 years	1 914	190	49	68	110	137	166	34	47	57	76
20 to 24 years	2 264	150	97	64	85	217	222	34	47	33	64
25 to 29 years	2 205	204	87	44	65	155	276	46	49	27	65
30 to 34 years	1 986	222	47	55	54	122	239	49	28	41	79
35 to 44 years	3 234	291	117	138	108	225	283	68	77	124	138
45 to 54 years	3 795	307	96	241	112	180	226	110	145	128	145
55 to 59 years	2 388	132	58	146	36	110	130	71	150	97	118
60 to 64 years	2 505	165	64	163	40	78	85	102	232	84	81
65 to 74 years	5 122	251	146	337	76	143	120	283	581	165	143
75 to 84 years	2 477	126	106	125	24	80	37	200	198	115	64
85 years and over	536	47	50	18	2	22	7	32	30	24	11
Median	46.4	37.3	46.3	55.8	25.7	33.5	29.3	64.1	64.3	54.1	44.0
Female	17 287	1 274	592	815	548	877	1 148	571	952	512	606
Under 5 years	604	48	18	10	32	53	94	4	20	4	30
5 to 9 years	642	71	15	22	47	35	89	5	15	25	28
10 to 14 years	801	91	15	27	65	51	68	9	24	23	27
15 to 19 years	959	78	26	36	51	66	82	19	31	28	41
20 to 24 years	1 060	68	49	33	48	104	94	20	26	19	27
25 to 29 years	1 088	96	43	22	44	71	141	26	21	14	37
30 to 34 years	961	106	23	36	28	47	120	18	17	18	38
35 to 44 years	1 677	156	61	74	53	107	133	24	44	65	75
45 to 54 years	2 056	147	49	138	65	97	131	53	87	64	77
55 to 59 years	1 363	78	34	87	21	52	62	43	96	52	68
60 to 64 years	1 413	93	39	84	22	47	45	49	141	43	43
65 to 74 years	2 920	138	102	177	55	84	63	167	313	85	79
75 to 84 years	1 414	75	78	57	17	50	21	117	101	63	31
85 years and over	329	29	40	12	—	13	5	17	16	9	5
Median	49.1	40.1	54.4	55.5	28.5	36.1	30.2	65.9	63.6	54.4	45.0
HOUSEHOLD TYPE AND RELATIONSHIP											
Total persons	32 584	2 506	1 016	1 529	1 015	1 747	2 329	1 067	1 697	993	1 152
In households	32 305	2 428	921	1 529	1 014	1 747	2 329	1 067	1 697	993	1 152
Family householder	8 997	664	227	503	246	403	623	280	594	290	340
Nonfamily householder: Male	2 589	162	88	88	16	213	129	171	73	80	69
Female	3 682	140	168	154	49	192	91	221	214	79	91
Spouse	7 455	536	186	456	134	295	495	250	548	263	290
Other relatives	7 716	777	199	272	534	473	847	96	227	196	316
Nonrelatives	1 866	149	53	56	35	171	144	49	41	85	46
Persons per household	2.12	2.51	1.91	2.05	3.26	2.16	2.76	1.59	1.93	2.21	2.30
Persons per family	2.69	2.98	2.70	2.45	3.72	2.91	3.15	2.24	2.30	2.58	2.78
In group quarters	279	78	95	—	1						
Persons 65 years and over	8 135	424	302	480	102	245	164	515	809	304	218
In households	7 882	346	223	480	102	245	164	515	809	304	218
Family householder	2 908	132	59	198	46	84	66	166	354	121	86
Nonfamily householder: Male	515	22	16	28	1	17	7	52	27	22	21
Female	1 808	44	89	73	28	64	23	140	145	49	27
Spouse	2 078	87	44	148	17	51	36	140	258	86	64
Other relatives	417	40	13	28	10	18	29	11	13	14	17
Nonrelatives	156	21	2	5	—	11	3	6	12	12	3
In group quarters	253	78	79	—	—	—	—	—	—	—	—
PERSONS IN HOUSEHOLDS											
Households	15 268	966	483	745	311	808	843	672	881	449	500
1 person	5 200	226	221	204	59	310	153	356	259	118	130
2 persons	6 427	378	157	402	82	269	280	267	528	226	213
3 persons	1 740	148	62	73	49	114	185	34	41	48	77
4 persons	1 064	124	25	43	39	59	134	6	25	31	51
5 persons	470	51	13	12	44	31	46	6	18	9	16
6 or more persons	367	39	5	11	38	25	45	3	10	17	13
MARITAL STATUS											
Male, 15 years and over	13 186	1 021	373	643	308	731	894	476	691	435	463
Single	3 373	306	101	110	120	288	243	102	70	94	107
Now married, except separated	7 874	574	205	470	150	334	533	262	560	277	305
Separated	277	19	10	8	10	18	27	13	8	6	2
Widowed	437	31	19	26	5	12	12	25	22	17	11
Divorced	1 225	91	38	29	23	79	79	74	31	41	38
Female, 15 years and over	15 240	1 064	544	756	404	738	897	553	893	460	521
Single	2 445	176	110	90	113	178	160	85	72	54	86
Now married, except separated	7 756	570	208	465	147	310	520	258	557	272	297
Separated	407	22	20	16	27	29	28	12	11	13	10
Widowed	2 648	157	135	112	63	111	78	125	176	82	69
Divorced	1 984	139	71	73	54	110	111	73	77	39	59

[1] Excludes "Other Asian and Pacific islander" groups identified in sample tabulations.   [2] Persons of Spanish origin may be of any race.

Sample of 1980 Federal Census of the United States

These and many other forms of labor and goods exchange constitute the manner in which residents of a given area support themselves and maintain a reasonable level of community life.

Information on the economic development and prospects of the community is usually available through the chamber of commerce, and these data can be cross-referenced with reports by Dun and Bradstreet and the U.S. Department of Commerce, the U.S. Department of Labor, state employment offices, local agencies and industries, and so on. Trends in industrialization and increases in the working force have a decided effect on the planning process. Data on the earning capacity, the average years of employment, the social security structure, types and diversification of employment, and the income groups represented in the working population are necessary to calculate the purchasing power of the community and the ability to pay rents and taxes. Such information can be traced through the U.S. Department of Labor, the state employment services, and local industries. These statistics are important as a basis for the comprehensive plan.

Other social statistics are available from a wide variety of sources. Data on disease and health can be obtained from the health departments of cities, counties, and states, as well as associations concerned with specific diseases. Local police and probation department files record the location of criminal incidents and the residences of convicted offenders. Foundations, service clubs, veterans' organizations, universities, charitable groups, and other private agencies have valuable data. The birth and death rates, infant mortality rate, marriage and divorce rates, population immigration and emigration, educational level, occupations of the working force, the cultural inclinations—all this is among the data the planning commission must correlate objectively for the best and most workable plan.

The planner can fundamentally be said to be a social scientist. Too frequently the social scientist has been cast in the role of historian of economic facts, reporting past trends and current conditions. The economic aspects of planning have thus been limited to an inventory of data that presents the status quo. Statistical techniques are employed in the projection of population and related fields of importance to planning, but the general effect is a kind of resignation by all concerned to the prospects that these projections imply. If planning means anything, it is the endeavor to direct future growth and development, quite the opposite of drifting with the currents of unregulated trends. The tools of socio-economic analysis are therefore essential in the effort to find a balance among the basic urban activities. And this balance may require that accepted trends be altered, diverted, or redirected—but this is planning.

The Use of Data

The increase in population is a natural phenomenon, and the trend of population growth in cities is a consequence of broad economic and social pressures. But to be effective, urban planning cannot succumb to the weight of statistical evidence alone. Survival of the urban population is at stake and so is the prospect for building decent cities. Means may be developed to control the number of people who are born, as there have been means to lengthen the lifespan. With the reduction of disease and famine, particularly in the Western world, so-called natural ways of stabilizing the population short of war are meager. However, we have the means, through planning and legislation, to regulate the distribution of the urban population, the amounts of land required for the various functions of an urban community, and the standards for the development of the land. To determine the appropriate allocation of land in both amount and location, the economic demands must be measured. The physical structure must be arranged to accommodate the facilities required for economic survival, and accommodate them in a manner that will produce good places in which to live and work.

The social scientist carries a heavy responsibility for creative analysis of the relationships between people and their employment opportunities, the production resources, and the commerce and industry needed to support an urban population. The city must be built on a firm economic base or it cannot provide the amenities of a civilized community. The future of cities as desirable social environments will depend on our capacity to integrate physical and economic planning. In 1945 Walter Blucher, then executive director of the American Society of Planning Officials, stated:

> What is the responsibility of the planning agency for a determination of employment possibilities outside of public works? You may think the planning agency has no such responsibility. I don't see how we can do an effective planning job in any community, however, unless we know what the population of the community will be and what the economic possibilities for that population are.[5]

CHANGING COMMUNITY CHARACTER

With the assembly of the data—that part of the planning process identified as research—we learn the nature of the existing city. This is the knowledge needed for analysis of the city; from it we learn why the city was begun, how it grew, and why it prospered.

The sleepy village of the eighteenth century has apparently little in common with the metropolis of today. There may remain marks of its origin, but the functions may have altered completely. As the city grew in size, as the population increased, and as new enterprises developed, the city's character may have altered. Perhaps the quality of community living deteriorated in the growth from a small, intimate town to the unfriendly metropolitan machine it now seems to be. Much may have been lost in this process, enough to question whether the city can recover the human values by which the true living standards of people are measured.

There are reasons why each city is located where it is; they were important reasons in its history, and they bear upon its future. They may be important as a pattern for continuous development, or they may reveal what changes have overtaken the city and indicate the new directions for which the city must be planned. The reasons for the founding of a city may have multiplied or they may have vanished. There may be entirely new purposes for the city than those that motivated its original settlement.

The changes in urban character reflected in the growth and the deterioration of neighborhood life are illustrated in all our cities. It is apparent in a growing metropolis like Los Angeles. Hardly more than fifty years ago this community was renowned for its climate, its recreational opportunities, its beaches, and the grandeur of its mountains. The quality of its living environment and the pleasant mildness of its weather made Los Angeles a haven for travelers from all parts of the world.

The population of Los Angeles was 500,000 in 1920: in 1990 it was more than 3,485,398, and the city had spread over the entire 450 square miles of its area.

---

5. Walter H. Blucher, executive director, American Society of Planning Officials, in *Planning, 1945,* Part 1, Chicago, May 16–17, 1945.

From its beginning as the center of a predominantly agricultural area, it has developed an important industrial economy. Industrial plants have sprung up with little or no attention to their probable effect on the living conditions of the region and its inhabitants. Water was carried more than 250 miles to supply the growing population. Congestion overtook this city of "open space," blight and slums are taking their toll, and smoke and fumes taint the air.

This story differs only in degree and detail in all our cities; it is the tale of the metropolis. The native advantages of our urban communities have not been respected by the people who built them; in the name of a bigger and more prosperous city, they have been desecrated, and the people are retreating. The people are fleeing the city and it remains neglected, but the same indifference is guiding development on the outskirts. Rather than capitalizing on the native characteristics of a region, exploitation of the urban community is undermining its own investments.

The comprehensive plan of a city or region has two objectives: forestalling the drift into chaos in the yet undeveloped areas of the city, and gradually reconstructing the developed area of the city with particular attention to blighted sections and improved circulation. The present chaotic development of the city is a trend, but this trend can be corrected and redirected to benefit all the people through planning.

The changing nature of the city must be appraised and the natural character defined. Shifts in the emphasis of the urban economy and the services and functions it performs require adjustments in the living habits of the people, the land use, and the transportation, if they are to continue as favorable environments in which to live and work. The comprehensive plan will reflect these adjustments and thereby become a guide for the future growth and development of the community. This demands inquiry into every facet of urban existence. It calls for the coordination of a team of trained decision-makers (both public and private) and enlightened and enthusiastic citizens.

ELEMENTS OF THE PLAN

Knowledge of the physical structure of the city will reveal certain natural uses for the land and existing uses that deserve particular respect in the plan. There may be well-established industrial areas, commercial centers, residential development, a great park, waterways, railroads, and historical and natural features. This knowledge will also indicate some apparent maladjustments in current land use for which corrective measures are obviously necessary. It will also indicate an appropriate relation between industrial and residential areas. With these broad strokes the comprehensive plan is begun.

The city is linked with its neighbor cities and towns and its environs by the highways, railroads, and mass transportation facilities; these form the main arteries of circulation about the city, and they will form the boundaries of the neighborhood units. The freeways, parkways, rapid transit, and railroads will establish the relation between the sources of employment in commerce and industry and the residential neighborhoods.

Laid upon this comprehensive plan will be the reservation of open spaces, the areas adapted for natural parks, or the submarginal lands unsuited for active urban development. In this process the plan begins to take shape. It will reflect the local policies on desirable population density consistent with the character of the city in its residential areas, and it will indicate the standards for the relation of building bulk and open space in these areas and in the commercial and industrial districts. Within the broad land use plan and guided by these standards, the precise plans for the various areas of the city may be refined as the time for their development approaches. The schools and playgrounds may be located within the neighborhood units, and requirements for local shopping centers may be determined. Space may be reserved for the freeways and rapid transit rights-of-way. Detailed plans for the improvement of the "downtown" business center may be formulated, and the reconstruction of blighted areas in the central section of the city may be planned and executed. The comprehensive plan will set forth the appropriate use to which the land in the city should be devoted so that the enterprise of city building may have a tangible guide in its determinations for investment.

TEAMWORK

It takes teamwork to produce a comprehensive plan that contains the inspired will of a people bent upon building a decent and fine city. It takes boundless enthusiasm and enlightened civic interest, and it takes a competent staff of trained planners to perform the job of coordination and translation.

The preparation of the comprehensive plan, which represents the aims and ambitions of a community in shaping its environment, requires a shift in the usual roles of allied professionals on the planning team: the social scientist must set aside the role of social critic, the economist the role of statistician, the lawyer the role of legalistic obstructionist, the real estate professional the role of super salesman or saleswoman, the engineer the role of computer expert. These essential participants on the planning team then become creative urban analysts.

Commercial centers and industrial areas may be fairly defined and single-family suburbs readily delineated, but the process becomes complex within the twilight areas of the city which are, in planners' parlance, "transition zones." With public financial assistance, redevelopment in large cities may be planned as components of the city as a whole. Transition areas are older residential sections trapped between chaotic commercial and industrial development and new residential subdivisions. Although blighted areas may have begun, and they may have become the refuge of ethnic minorities, these areas often contain vintage homes and handsome trees that represent the only vestige of urban charm.

It is standard procedure for planners to sweep these transition areas with a broad brush into land use classifications of apartments, and a mixture of commercial zoning. With no modification of the original land subdivision, the intrusion of mediocre apartments on single-family lots erodes residential quality and reduces the prospect of neighborhood cohesiveness.

The city is in constant transition. The comprehensive plan delineates the concept of the city the people seek to achieve. Zoning is one of the instruments by which that concept is implemented, but as an instrument of transition it is suffering from atrophy. Conventional zoning regulations are obsolete. Sensitive teamwork to untangle the chaos of urban land uses and shape new instruments of regulation, while guarding the general social well-being, requires, as Jacob Crane observed, "intuition, imagination, and bold action."[6]

---

6. Jacob Crane, *Urban Planning—Illusion and Reality: A New Philosophy for Planned City Building* (New York: Vantage Press, 1973).

Planning is plagued with platitudes. Some familiar expressions have almost reached the stature of symbols, the mere mention of which presumably is sufficient to convey a significant message. It would be well to examine some of these phrases in order to recognize their meaning.

"Flexibility." We frequently refer to the necessity for "flexibility" in city planning. It is suggested that city plans must be adjustable to changing conditions, that cities grow like "living cells." These are convenient terms and contain much truth. Unfortunately they, too, generally become picturesque phrases. There are some very specific limitations upon their value and application.

A city is more than buildings, streets, utilities, steel, concrete, and glass. Nevertheless these are the materials of which the physical structure is made. They are inert. They have chemical properties, but they are not elastic. Once in place they cannot be shifted about to suit either fancy or "changing conditions." They are static. The width of a street does not pulsate with the intensity of traffic flow, nor can a building flex its beams and columns.

In these important particulars the analogy of city building to a "living organism" is literary confection. The pictorial similarity between a medieval town plan and the cross-section of a tree or the veins in the human arm becomes pure poetry. Lifted out of the rarefied atmosphere of romantic fantasy, "flexibility" means enough space to bring the products of industrial genius into useful service in the city structure.

Cities are inflexible because they are so crowded there is no room for the various elements to "work." They are frozen into congestion, and flexibility will be attained only through the establishment of adequate standards to guide those who participate in building the city.

There comes a moment when decisions must be made. When that moment arrives, there is a degree of finality implied by the act of decision. The structure of the city does not float; it cannot be tugged or pushed about. When a building or other civic improvement is erected, it is there to stay. Flexibility in the plan of a city will be accomplished by standards for city building that preserve enough space for all improvements without overcrowding.

"Trends." In nearly every kind of business enterprise there is reference to "trends." New conditions, scientific development, and social improvement require adjustment in the conduct of enterprise. They likewise require adjustments in the city. Shifts in the growth of cities prompted by such changes and accompanied by some degree of orderly direction serve as a measure of trends in healthy city development.

But these shifts are confused with quite another sort of change: the urge to escape from the contagious disease of obsolescence and unrestrained speculation. Healthy enterprise shuns association with derelict neighbors; unbridled physical deterioration repels improvement. Shifts in the urban pattern compelled by these desultory forces do not mark trends. They report a rout, a desperate and disorderly retreat. Diagnosing this disease as a trend is to spread the contagion further and ignore or misinterpret the only value that observation of trends can provide: a guide to the natural and appropriate use of land in the growing city.

"Economy." A familiar slogan. It is also a worthy aim. In practice, however, it has unfortunately been too frequently reduced to a fiction. Expenditures for civil

PLANNING PLATITUDES

improvements are generally decided upon by their budget appeal, not their adequacy. Patchwork improvements display such an appeal; they appear to be "economical." The question of whether they may actually solve any particular problem is usually overlooked or avoided. Economy may really be, and usually is, quite another matter. We have seen a street-widening prove inadequate almost on the day it was completed. We have seen the immediate need for another improvement added. We have seen the value of adjacent land enhanced with each such piecemeal improvement, and new buildings erected about it. We have then seen the public forced to pay the increment of land and building "value" each of these improvements has induced. This process is characteristic of urban "economy," but it is not economical.

Each new or improved utility service introduced to a city crowds some equally needed service. The utility system—sewers, water, gas, electricity—distributes the energy to operate a city of a million people. Yet these vital veins are, with some rare exceptions, buried beneath or suspended above the arteries that carry the stream of daily traffic. The conflict between these services is experienced day in and day out. A utility line breaks down and the repair job stops the circulation of automobiles and other vehicles. These conflicts choke an already congested city and are not economical.

"Prematurity." Many times comprehensive plan proposals have been deemed "premature." One must examine the use of this term as it applies to proposals for the future. What is premature in assessing the appropriate relationships between the several uses of the land before they happen? If one were to place a time factor for the development of specific uses, then one might say that is too far into the future, but where the time factor is not defined, and in many instances the variables in both economic and social conditions are too many to make accurate predictions, the exact development time is less important than satisfying the questions related to the appropriateness of the use in a compatible location when it will be needed to serve the residents of a community.

"Efficiency." Another ingrown term. Efficiency obviously has virtue; that virtue is the elimination of waste. In the name of "efficient" planning, however, are examples of the creation of waste. We have observed acres of subdivisions, planned with alleged efficiency, that are actually a waste of urban resources. We have seen the width of a street, the size of a house, or the lot it occupies squeezed to an efficient minimum so low it is reduced to nothing more than a cheap commodity.

In the light of the studies by Sir Raymond Unwin and Henry Wright, efficient planning is more than an obsession to save; it is also a method to improve. Standards are the measurements by which we must be guided rather than remain content with what Elizabeth Denby called "the intellectual pleasure which the architect got from a triumphant arrangement of inadequate space."[7]

"Neo-traditional." Neo-traditional is a newcomer. It seems to mean the same as good site planning with the appropriate provision for essential amenities such as schools, parks, and open spaces with appropriate land uses in a completely integrated harmonious plan.

---

7. Elizabeth Denby, *Europe Rehoused* (New York: W. W. Norton, 1938).

Village plans of this type have been developed in many parts of Europe and America for many years: witness the Radburn "idea" and the development at Lake Vista in New Orleans, Columbia in Maryland, and Reston in Virginia.

It must be clear that space in a city must first and foremost provide for adequacy: it must be ample.

The measure of adequacy will be the capacity of the space to receive the buildings of a city without itself being lost completely. It means enough space so that buildings may stand alone or together without violating the sensibilities of those who see and use them. It means that cities will provide space into which the buildings are built rather than a solid mass of buildings through which the fissures we call streets are carved.

The concept of space means relatively constant limitations on population density regardless of the heights that structures may reach. The prospect of squeezing more people into the same space creates instability, not only in land value but also in urban services. It imposes an extravagance on the installation of service facilities. Water, sewers, gas and electric distribution, telephones, streets, walks, transportation, fire, health, educational and recreational facilities cannot be estimated with any possible degree of efficiency. These services must be installed in sufficient size and quantity to meet unlimited future requirements or be repeatedly removed, altered, and replaced as the demand fluctuates. Either course is an extravagant venture as city budgets and utility bills attest.

Within a reasonable concept of space in the urban environment is room for the vehicles of transportation to circulate with ease and safety. This means enough

ADEQUATE SPACE

View of central Paris, France from the top of Hotel Concorde Lafayette.

room to separate the different types of vehicles and the direction of their travel; space enough to move about on the surface of the earth rather than burrow into the ground with subways. This means the city will no longer be a maze of streets and alleys slicing through a solid bulk of buildings.

This concept means that parking space for the free-moving vehicles of our contemporary age shall be a component of all floor space provided within or adjacent to buildings, and it means that this integration will move the relation between open space and building floor area into some degree of balance.

There will be enough room for all the essential utility conduits, a network of vital services arteries so aligned within their respective rights-of-way that interference is prevented at all times.

This concept of space means room enough for people to walk in safety and some degree of beauty; trees would not be unwelcome. Finally it means an environment in which the human spirit can rise above mediocrity; it means relief from the din and the danger that fray the human nerves and dull the human mind.

It may be suggested that the concept of space within the city described above is not a "practical" one. The planning of cities is rather cluttered with bromides, but hardly any is so overworked as "practical." Compromise is the inevitable road to satisfactory human relationships. The capacity to compromise is a requisite to accomplishment. It implies, however, that an objective is clearly defined. The objective of planning is the solution of a problem: in city planning the problem is that of an environment that is rapidly disintegrating under the spell of congestion and ugliness.

PRACTI-CALITY: DOES IT WORK?

Opinions may vary as to the way in which to arrive at the objective of decent cities, but no purpose is served until some area of agreement can be reached about the nature of the objective itself. Solutions call for ideas. They deal in ideas. Ideas are the tools with which we shape an objective, and they cannot be dismissed only because they may at first appear "impractical." We see about us the results of thus being practical; we see these results repeated time and again: more congestion, more traffic problems, more deterioration, more expense, and boundless confusion and bewilderment. If we peer behind this scene, we may well find the reason: the process of planning began with a compromise. The ideas that are the stuff of progress never reach the surface where they may be observed and tested for their validity.

Nor is this approach really practical. The first test of practicality is whether a thing works. Can it be claimed that our cities work? Is traffic congestion practical? Or the crowded business centers? Or the blighted areas and slums? Are the extravagant devices for parking automobiles—overhead and underground—practical? Are the mediocrity of the living and working environment and the obsolete transportation in our cities really practical? Is it practical to spend huge sums on surveys, consultations, and plans, then ignore them all? The urban malady of congestion is like an itch; scratching produces a sensation of relief. But common sense tells us the only practical treatment is a cure, not more irritation.

Must it be considered impractical to propose standards that have as their sole purpose a restoration of permanent values in the urban environment? Ample space for London was denigrated by F. J. Forty, chief planner for the rebuilding program, with the words "I want it [London] to be the leading place of commerce in the world and not—as some planners suggest—a park."[8] Must this be the interpretation of the need for adequate space within our cities? The original plan proposed for the City of London, a plan that offered little improvement over the city that was destroyed, was commented upon by Donald Tyerman in the *Observer* as "timid rebuilding proposals." He said, "The makers of this plan are not planners but pessimists."[9]

We might hark to the words of Lewis Mumford:

> As so often has happened during the last quarter century, the self-styled practical men turned out to be the weak, irresponsible dreamers, afraid to face unpleasant facts, while those of us who were called dreamers have, perhaps, some little right now to be accepted—at least belatedly—as practical men. By now history has caught up with our more dire prophecies. This is at once the justification of our thinking and the proof of its tragic failure to influence our contemporaries.[10]

FAILURES AND MISUSE

The record of successful use of comprehensive plans leaves a great deal to be desired. Research has indicated some of these reasons for this lack of success:

Lack of sound basis

Easy amendment

Political disregard

Lack of public support

Lack of comprehensiveness (warmed-over zoning)

Changing local political structure

Faulty interpretation

Changing economic and social conditions

Lack of coordination with other plans

Changing external forces (regional, state, national)

Lack of periodic review and overall comprehensive amendment

Faulty concept of "flexibility"

Lack of regional coordination

The importance of the comprehensive plan has been emphasized as much by the abuses to which it has been subjected as by the uses to which it has been put. Adoption of a plan has often been treated as a spurious political gesture; the less specific the plan, the more adaptable it is to political manipulation. Diagrams of existing land uses have been accepted as a plan; unrealistic agricultural or single-family zoning has been adopted for underdeveloped areas to avoid decisions on growth and development policies. Environmental impact statements for separate developments have become a convenient substitute for planning.

---

8. *Architectural Forum*, September 1944.

9. Ibid. The plan to which Mr. Tyerman referred was that proposed for the mile-square City of London by the Improvement and Town Planning Committee.

10. *Architectural Forum*, May 1945.

These irresponsible tactics have been politically expedient for incompetent civic leaders and have cast grave doubt on the social and economic usefulness of planning. The doubts are well founded; much of the planning has not been demonstrably effective in improving the urban environment. City and rural land has become an inviting medium for commercial exploitation and speculation. The extension of existing zoning, the legal regulation of land use, has also been misused as a substitute for the comprehensive plan in making decisions about changes in land uses.

Because of the reluctance of local communities to prepare and adopt significant long-range plans for community betterment, some states have found it necessary to require not only that these plans be prepared but also that they contain specific elements; they have further mandated that zoning conform to the plan. Besides the land use and circulation elements, these specific new elements include open space, conservation, noise control, seismic safety, and—for the well-being of all citizens—a housing element subject to state guidelines and review.

The long-range aspects of the plan were the least understood. Some legislators saw the plans as a "pie in the sky" dream of unrealistic academics who do not understand that government in general operated on short-term year-to-year programming. A 20-year plan (look into the future) was four times more unrealistic than the Russian "five-year plans." If proposals could not be financed under current budgetary allocations, then they were considered pure theory and to be deleted from the plan. This made planning a refinement of the current zoning map and eliminated all of the far-reaching implications of growth and the facilities and utilities that would be required as this growth takes place.

A San Francisco law professor, at the 1981 APA conference, stated that, in his opinion, the best defense a municipality can have is a comprehensive general plan. He also advised cities to develop an economic data base, which they can use to respond to landowners' charges that a planning commission action deprives them of a reasonable return on their land.

Alternatives

As more and more discussion took place in academic and professional forums, alternative approaches were sought to use the concepts included in the comprehensive plan but without the techniques that had become rote on the plans produced in the 1960–1980 era. New terms were tried on for size, such as short-range, middle-range, and long-range concept plans; and the direct use of the zoning plan as the land use plan, relating added utilities, facilities, and services on a haphazard demand basis. Other formulas intended to assist a community in keeping its house in order were invented, all more closely related to the pay as you go process. With the national drive toward massive elimination of regulations, the future of all efforts to guide community growth in economically reasonable directions appears in question.

The concept of looking ahead and preparing plans will continue, in some form represented by the comprehensive general plan, for it is through this process that order evolves in community development and services required for urban living. Even in instances where the physical structure of the community is entirely new and the impacts of history and tradition are not evident, human instincts and desires will lay a heavy hand on the disposition of the use of land and the manner in which the environment will be impacted upon as the people in the community react to natural forces and opportunities in a given locale.

In confronting the potential for improving already-built communities, from the smallest to the megametropolis, the questions that always arise are: Where do we begin, how shall we do it, how can we be sure that our concept will be accepted, how will our proposals fit in with the regional growth and change processes and programs, and, most of all, how will it be financed and who will pay for it?

Compared with the relatively simple processes involved in the planning of a new community on virgin soil, where the client is a single entity, person or corporation, and where the funds are available for the development of the new entity, be it a small village or larger new town, and the local laws governing development can be complied with or exceeded, the planning tasks can be completed rapidly and development can be achieved within reasonable time limits.

In existing communities the number of problems is infinite and in many instances complex beyond simple solutions. For instance, what are the conditions of the water and sewerage service facilities? Can the project be connected to them without overloading old and perhaps inadequate lines or treatment and storage and disposal facilities? Are storm drains adequate for the runoff from the new development? Are electrical and gas utility services available, or do new lines have to be extended to meet the needs, especially if the population density is to be increased? What about the need for off-site improvements? Are the limiting boundaries of the proposed improvement such that traffic loads will be funneled onto streets that are already inadequate as to width and condition of pavement and traffic capacity? These are but a few of the physical problems that face the already built community. However, they are minimal when compared with public relations and funding problems.

When confronted with the question of how to plan for the future of a city like New York, one consultant replied, "Start with a bulldozer." Spot improvements are possible, but changing the basic structure of the city piecemeal leaves much to be desired when the true impact of this type of developmental process is evaluated. The ethnic and racial problems alone that are involved when old areas are upset and friendship bonds are destroyed may be the icebergs upon which proposals will founder, no matter how well conceived or worthy they may be.

The use of well-planned rehabilitation of the older area may well be the logical answer for the treatment of the already-built communities. Sometimes the cost may be greater than the use of the wrecking ball, but the product may be better suited to the environment and, if created with sensitivity, less jarring to the neighbors or the neighborhood. Rehousing of the local people would be most likely to receive support if the total community participated in the financing through bond issues and the rents were kept affordable.

The effort to prepare plans for the changes that seem desirable for a large already fully developed community in many instances winds up with frustration or with half-baked proposals that are subject to instantaneous rejection by the public and local decision makers. A study by the Los Angeles City Planning staff suggested a means of facing the future together with the local citizenry. The city was divided into logical communities and each of these elements was studied to determine what changes were needed and what values were to be respected. Local bankers were invited to participate in the process to have their opinions and support that they might offer in causing the suggested changes and improvements. The product became the "Community Plan," part of the comprehensive plan for the city.

PLANNING THE ALREADY-BUILT COMMUNITY

CHAPTER 23

LAND USE ELEMENT

This we know. The earth does not belong to man; man belongs to the earth. This we know. All things are connected like the blood which unites one family. All things are connected.

Whatever befalls the earth befalls the sons of the earth. Man did not weave the web of life; he is merely a strand in it. Whatever he does to the web, he does to himself.

—*Great Chief of the Suguamish, Chief Seattle,* December 1854

Both economically and legally, past and present, all land has an owner, and title to that land provides for the more or less free use for homes, business, and other purposes. The Native Americans thought differently, as Chief Seattle's remarks make clear. The land was placed here by the Great Spirit, and we cannot sell it because we do not own it. But the belief in ownership is more common and deeply rooted. Even after earthquakes and fires that entirely destroy the structures on the land, titles and descriptions of specific parcels remain, and the title-holder rebuilds on the original site, setting old, often archaic patterns once again upon the land.

With the titles so firmly established on most land, the need for the planning of uses is of paramount importance. It should be self-evident that the use of each individual parcel is inextricably interwined with the use of all other parcels. And in fact the attempt to create a humanly satisfying environment was recognized by the courts as an important legitimate objective and resulted in support for the development of the first plans for land use.

It is the relationship between the variety of possible uses that becomes the problem of planning. Some are favorable to each other, whereas some are not only detrimental but also dangerous. The plan therefore begins with a definition of land uses and the appropriate location within the topographic, geologic, and geographic structure of the city. Upon these the city pattern should be developed.

Before any plan can be devised, the physical structure of the community—its rivers, its mountains, its plains and prairies, its hills, its climate, the direction of its winds—must be known and understood. Is the land suited to agriculture: is it good for grazing? Are there oil or mineral deposits, is it subject to floods, are there natural or historic features to be preserved? The geology, hydrography, meteorology, and geography must be rediscovered beneath the blanket of the built-up city.

The following statistics (based on Eisner and Associates studies, 1939–85) indicate the range of percentages found in most urban areas:

Residential	*35 to 39 percent*
Commercial	*4.8 to 5 percent*
Industrial	*10 to 11 percent*
Streets	*20 to 26 percent*
Open space, schools, parks, etc.	*10 to 18 percent*

In evaluating the space requirements for the various land uses in the comprehensive plan, the standards of development—population density and character of the physical environment appropriate to the region—introduce an additional factor: the building bulk and floor space that will occupy the land. This factor may be expressed as a ratio of building floor area to lot area and should be considered in formulating the basic concept of the comprehensive plan (chapter 22), the zoning plan (chapter 34), and commerce and industry (chapter 27).

The constant relationship of nature's three primary elements—land, water, and air—is necessary to the support of life. One can imagine controlled air conditions, and we know that water can be transported from distant mountain sources to semiarid regions, but the land is where you find it. Perhaps it can be built up, the marshes drained, fertility improved, and water increase its growing yield, but land itself must have the basic capacity for response to man's treatment. We classify it as good or bad according to its ability to provide life for humankind.

INVENTORY AND CLASSIFICATION

Regardless of the high aspirations a people may share for the future of their city or the distant range over which they prepare their plans for its development, the planning process must obviously begin with the city as it exists. It is consequently necessary to know how the land is used and maintain the inventory as a current record. From this inventory the physical characteristics of the city are discernible, those which warrant change or necessitate retention in the comprehensive plan may be determined, and some existing uses may become key controls over the pattern of future land use.

Actual Land Uses[1]

Use	CENTRAL CITIES	
	Per Cent of Total Developed Area	Acres per 100 Persons
Single-family dwellings	31.81	2.19
Two-family dwellings	4.79	0.33
Multifamily dwellings	3.01	0.21
Commercial areas	3.32	0.23
Light industry ⎫		
Heavy industry ⎬	11.30	0.78
Railroad property ⎭		
Parks and playgrounds	6.74	0.46
Public and semipublic property	10.93	0.75
Streets	28.10	1.94
Total	100.00	6.89

[1] Harland Bartholomew, *Land Uses in American Cities*, Harvard University Press, Cambridge, 1955.

Studies by Harland Bartholomew revealed the actual land uses in a number of survey cities. Three types of urban communities were included. The Central Cities are self-contained entities that perform the major social and economic functions of an urbanized area. They include fifty-three cities ranging in population from 1,740 to 821,960. The Satellite Cities are incorporated in and are economically dependent on an adjacent central city. They number thirty-three, ranging in population from 900 to 74,347. The Urban Areas are metropolitan areas that embrace a central city and an urbanized fringe. The eleven urban areas in the survey range in population from 7,150 to 119,825. The study does not include the largest metropolitan areas but presents a fair cross-section of urban land-use characteristics. (Each community is unique, and the land uses in each should reflect its special qualities.)

Land-use allocation varies from location to location, depending upon each community's attitude concerning the type of environment it hopes to create.

This prospect is particularly marked by the fact that the transition from an existing land use to another classification may span a great number of years. According to Anglo-Saxon law, if land has never been used for a particular purpose, it does not constitute a deprivation of property rights to deny the right to so use it in the future. On the other hand, it is assumed that zoning ordinances must not restrict property to uses considered less liberal than the existing use. The courts have held that zoning may not be retroactive, that existing land uses may not be "zoned out of existence." They must be permitted to continue as nonconforming uses if they are inconsistent with the use the zoning ordinance prescribes.

This may appear to permit the continuation of a nonconforming use that would prove to be a detriment to the surrounding development, like an obnoxious industry in a residential zone. The courts have pointed out that other means are available for relief from such intrusions; proof that a nonconforming use is a nuisance and a danger to the life and health of the inhabitants and the public welfare may be sufficient reason for the courts to deny a use to continue.

Nonconforming uses may not be renewed if destroyed by fire or act of God. The new structure must then conform to the provisions of the current zoning. In some ordinances a nonconforming structure may be repaired or slightly altered, but it may not be modified to the extent that the space or facilities are enlarged, nor may a different nonconforming use replace that which is removed.

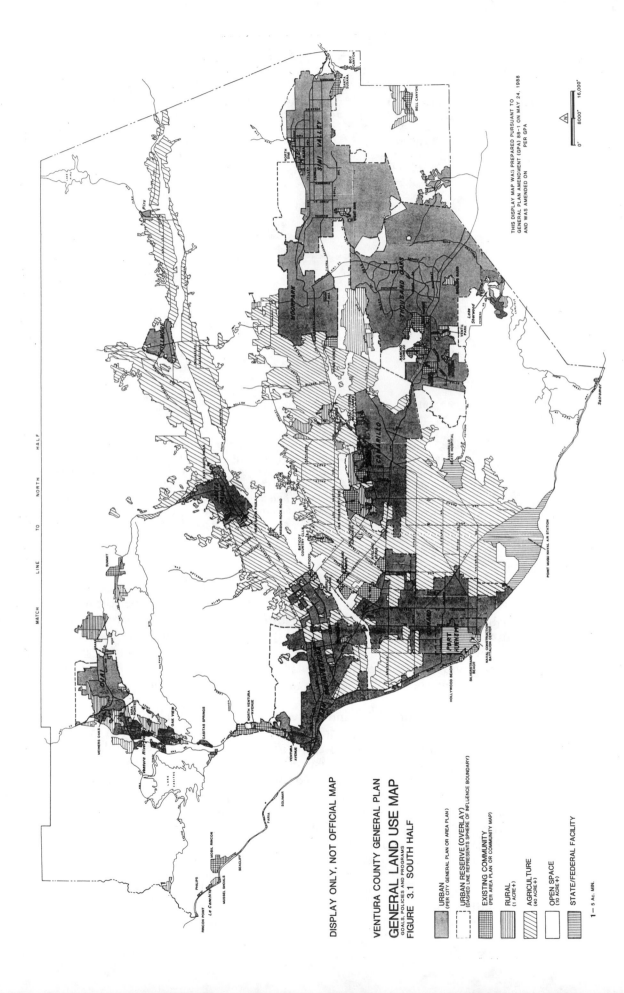

DISPLAY ONLY, NOT OFFICIAL MAP

VENTURA COUNTY GENERAL PLAN
GENERAL LAND USE MAP
GOALS, POLICIES AND PROGRAMS
FIGURE 3.1 SOUTH HALF

THIS DISPLAY MAP WAS PREPARED PURSUANT TO
GENERAL PLAN AMENDMENT (GPA) 88-1 ON MAY 24, 1988
AND WAS AMENDED ON ___ PER GPA

0'   8000'   16,000'

URBAN
(PER CITY GENERAL PLAN OR AREA PLAN)

URBAN RESERVE (OVERLAY)
(DASHED LINE REPRESENTS SPHERE OF INFLUENCE BOUNDARY)

EXISTING COMMUNITY
(PER AREA PLAN OR COMMUNITY MAP)

RURAL
(1 ACRE+)

AGRICULTURE
(40 ACRE+)

OPEN SPACE
(10 ACRE+)

STATE/FEDERAL FACILITY

1—5 Ac. MIN.

Comprehensive (general) plan.

SATELLITE CITIES		URBAN AREAS	
Per Cent of Total Developed Area	Acres per 100 Persons	Per Cent of Total Developed Area	Acres per 100 Persons
36.18	3.14	25.05	3.72
3.31	0.29	1.63	0.24
2.49	0.22	1.31	0.20
2.54	0.22	2.65	0.39
		1.87	0.28
12.51	1.09	3.77	0.56
		6.22	0.92
4.37	0.38	4.59	0.68
10.93	0.95	25.30	3.75
27.67	2.40	27.61	4.10
100.00	8.69	100.00	14.84

The following statistics (based on Eisner and Associates studies, 1939–85) indicate the range of percentages found in most urban areas:

Residential	*35 to 39 percent*
Commercial	*4.8 to 5 percent*
Industrial	*10 to 11 percent*
Streets	*20 to 26 percent*
Open space, schools, parks, etc.	*10 to 18 percent*

In evaluating the space requirements for the various land uses in the comprehensive plan, the standards of development—population density and character of the physical environment appropriate to the region—introduce an additional factor: the building bulk and floor space that will occupy the land. This factor may be expressed as a ratio of building floor area to lot area and should be considered in formulating the basic concept of the comprehensive plan (chapter 19), the zoning plan (chapter 28), and commerce and industry (chapter 22).

Some zoning ordinances specify a period during which a nonconforming use shall be retired. This time is equivalent to an amortization period with an established date for removal of the structure, the period being related to the years of use already experienced in the structure and the investment in it. In this way property values and human values may be reasonably balanced and intruding uses gradually removed to be replaced by conforming uses. The logic and equity of such a method would seem to impel cities to adopt it in the public interest.

Most cities classify their land in five major categories: (1) open space, (2) agricultural, (3) residential, (4) commercial, and (5) industrial. Each of these broad groups is subdivided into uses ranging from the most to the least obnoxious, from the most to the least restricted, from the most concentrated to the most open. This is generally identified as "step-down" classification as it is applied within each of the broad groups. Thus the general industrial classification contains heavy industry and light industry, expressing the difference between a boiler works and a tin shop, for example. A large department store would be classified in heavy commercial, whereas a neighborhood grocery store would be placed in the lightest commercial zone. Likewise a multistory apartment building would be in the least restricted residential zone, whereas a single-family detached house would be in the restricted area. Open space and agriculture are sometimes one classification.

The number of intermediate steps between the most intense use and the least intense use will vary in different communities as the complexity of the community warrants. In a very large city there may be as many as fifty classes of land use, whereas in a small town there may only be nine. This difference in the number of classifications does not suggest less accuracy in determining the classifications; it indicates that the manner in which the land is used in a small town is less complex than in a large city. The number of classifications should be as few as possible consistent with a complete coverage of the various uses of land and an accurate description of each.

A city should have a record of the way in which the land within its boundaries is used, as well as the quantity of space and structures which comprise it. A periodic inventory of these assets should be undertaken just as a well-organized and well-administered business maintains an inventory and the value of its stock. During the Depression of the thirties, land-use surveys in a number of cities were conducted under the auspices of the Works Progress Administration (WPA) of the federal government. These data were of immeasurable value to the planning commissions in the respective cities, yet there are few instances in which the records were subsequently maintained.

A continuous record may be maintained by reference to building permits and the tax assessor of the city. Other reference sources are aerial photography; the building and safety department of the city, which records levels of pest infestation, lack of sanitation facilities, and changes in building occupancy and alterations that indicate a change in the use of existing structures; and the local housing authority, from which information may generally be obtained on the physical condition of housing. Banking and lending institutions frequently maintain valid information on new building activity as well.

The record of urban land use is not only for the purpose of ascertaining the condition of the physical structure. It provides the information necessary to observe the rate at which the city is increasing or decreasing its physical plant in the various classifications of land use. It offers a basis for measuring the amount of land to be reserved in zoning for future developments of the city, the quantity of land, and the most appropriate location for the various uses.

The land use inventory is good urban business and should be maintained as a current record. It is not a plan; it is part of the vital data from which plans may be made. The inventory does not in itself reflect quality. A separate evaluation must be prepared dealing with this subject.

INVENTORY OF SPECIAL PLACES

In preparing the land use inventory special attention should be given to identification of those uses that are historical, culturally important, or intrinsically beautiful, making them outstanding features that define the community character. These uses when assembled and classified can become the basis for becoming a "place" to which people will be attracted and about which sound land use relationships and excellent planning can be organized and developed.

William H. Whyte in the *New Yorker* magazine (August, 1990) suggests that every community make an assessment of its landscape character, an inventory of the connectedness it has and of any broken connections that need mending. He points out that in aggregate, a host of small features and people's perception of them are what constitute true regional design.

LAND USE PLAN

The land use plan is intended as an important means of reaching physical, economic, and social community goals. The plan, through its effects on public and private decisions and investments, can be a powerful influence on the growth rate, character, quality, and pattern of the city's physical environment.

The plan sets forth policies intended to encourage the upgrading and preservation of the existing city and to provide for an orderly, efficient, and logical extension of urban development in the predominantly undeveloped area surrounding the city. A central issue in deciding the future pattern of development is the manner in which future growth is to be accommodated. Already developed areas can be used more intensively (higher average densities) or undeveloped land can be brought into use. A range of choices exists between these two extremes.

Until recently, many cities have emphasized expansion into new areas rather than the recycling and more intense use of existing areas. However, experience and analysis over the years have brought about a general acceptance of the fact that such an approach toward growth can raise the cost of city services and add to the severity of a number of environmental, social, and economic problems.

Many cities are now attempting to define a "balanced program of expansion and increased utilization." In large measure, each community's proper balance is unique. The balance is a function of the scale of priorities that a community attaches to its goals.

Another important factor affecting the community's choice is the existing pattern of development. The face of the city changes very slowly, and some choices may be feasible only in the long run. For example, an already intensely developed city may have little choice but to expand into new areas. Alternatively, a city "landlocked" by external development or jurisdiction (San Francisco, for example) can only accommodate growth internally.

Considerations

Land use considerations can be divided into five parts. The first identifies objectives and principles pertaining to residential, commercial, recreational, educational, and industrial uses and enumerates existing standards for such uses.

The second part focuses on the nature and pattern of development within the existing city boundaries. Descriptive data in this section provide the basis for answering in part questions as to what changes in the pattern of land use are needed and how much growth can be accommodated within the existing area of urban development.

The third part looks in detail at the area of land surrounding the community, the community's "area of influence." Existing uses of land are identified, and factors affecting the land's suitability for future development are discussed. Standards for new development and transportation are proposed.

When land is either in agricultural use or can be classified as prime agricultural land, great care must be taken to evaluate the environmental impact when providing for alternate uses that would deprive the public of the foods and fibers (such as flax and hemp) provided by the land. Agricultural land is a world asset that should be protected by careful planning.

The fourth part brings together the analysis and results of the preceding sections and proposes a coordinated, comprehensive land use plan for both the city and its area of influence, including all necessities, facilities, and amenities required to serve the people. This plan is an important element in efforts to manage growth and is based upon current expectations of future growth, the existing pattern of development, and community desires as to how growth can be physically and financially accommodated.

The fifth consideration explores and identifies tools that could be used to implement the proposed plan.

The land use plan establishes the location of neighborhood units with their several facilities, schools, parks, playgrounds, and shopping areas. It is the plan that sets the standards to guide the city builders in their various enterprises, and a complete plan will be more than a single map of the community. It will be a compilation of all the data from which the estimates of required areas were calculated and the standards determined. It will become a reference for all who are engaged in urban development.

This plan will chart the relation of the city to the region and indicate its integration with its satellite communities. It will be part of the regional transportation network and will define the areas and standards for subdivision of new land. This is the plan which forms the foundation for the precise plans for zoning, parks and recreation, schools and other public buildings, the civic center, cultural and sports centers. It is the plan that will guide the community and public utility corporations in the design of utilities: sewers, gas, water, electric distribution, street lighting, and police and fire protection. And this is the plan to which all can refer for guidance in determining their investments in the city.

THE BASIC URBAN UNIT

As the city grows in size, some areas within it assume homogeneous qualities that we have identified as neighborhoods. People who early emigrated to America frequently grouped together with those who spoke their language, shared their particular religious tenets, or had similar ethnic or racial backgrounds. When some became richer than the rest and enjoyed the greater mobility provided by a fine brace of horses and a carriage and differences in social and economic status became pronounced, they moved their residences to nearby hills and formed more exclusive neighborhoods. Different environmental standards were established, and people who desired and could afford them gathered there to secure these amenities.

Some neighborhoods developed, as in ancient times, more from compulsion than native choice; restrictions by prejudice, limitations of language, or economic pressures often forced the cultivation of neighborhoods identified by distinctions made other than by choice.

As open space in the growing city was built up, some neighborhoods were unable to retain their original identity, the economic level of the people living within them being inadequate to maintain the earlier standard of physical maintenance or community services. Decay set in and slums were on the way. Residents of formerly exclusive areas moved to new districts beyond the reach of this influence. The metropolis created by the Industrial Revolution completely dissipated whatever urban unity remained from the medieval town, and, except for exclusive residential districts that escaped from the sprawling industrial city, the distinctions between neighborhoods gradually merged into a common mediocrity. It was necessary to restore some semblance of human identity to the urban scene;

prodded by the social evils that enveloped the factory town, social workers began to function and developed the settlement house. Probably the settlement house movement, which began in London about 1885, marked the first conscious recognition of the neighborhood as a basic element in the urban structure; the house provided a nucleus for the restoration of human values that had dissolved within the indistinguishable mass of the industrial metropolis.

The dissolution of these values has created among urban dwellers a detachment from each other. Opinions among social scientists differ on the effectiveness of the neighborhood principle as a means to overcome this detachment. Some contend that it is imperative to reestablish a "face-to-face" relationship through neighborhood association; others expect that people will seek their friends no matter what distances may separate them even as they remain only chance acquaintances and even strangers with their next-door neighbors; and some oppose the neighborhood with the claim that it leads to a grouping of people that inevitably results in compulsory class distinctions.

These conflicting opinions notwithstanding, it has become a practical necessity to employ the neighborhood unit as a means to restore a recognizable form in the physical organization of the city. However large or small the city may be, there must be a workable unit of human scale with which to weave the urban pattern into a workable whole. Dissolution of human scale has allowed the industrial and commercial metropolis to become socially stagnant and physically flabby. As Benton McKaye said, "Mankind has cleared the jungle and replaced it with a labyrinth."[1]

Theoretical Neighborhood Unit Defined

The use of the term *Neighborhood Unit* is not intended to suggest a place where persons were to be forcefully segregated by race, religion, or income. It is defined as the physical environment wherein social, cultural, educational, and commercial facilities are within easy reach of the residents and where, in the past, it was found that people cooperated with one another in times of stress. It was also the "place" where one lived. It defines one's homesite in a large environment such as a city. It is a physical environment in which a mother knows that her child will have no busy streets to cross on the way to school, a school that is within easy walking distance from home. It is an environment in which the resident may have an easy walk to a shopping center where daily household goods may be bought and employed persons may find convenient transportation to and from work. It is an environment in which a well-equipped playground where the children may play in safety with their friends is located near the home; the parents may not care to maintain intimate friendships with their neighbors, but children are so inclined, and they need the facilities of recreation for the healthy development of the mind and spirit. Although the data cited in the following paragraphs are not current, the basic logic is the same today, and the standards will vary with the type of community and the family composition of a specific locale.

The unit measurement for space in urban society is the individual; the common denominator for the arrangement of that space is the family. To satisfy their relatively simple social wants, it is natural for families to seek the advantages that appropriately planned neighborhoods provide. The functions of a neighborhood have been described by C. J. Bushnell as maintenance, learning, control, and play.[2] One of the earliest authorities to attempt a definition of the neighborhood

---

1. Benton McKaye, *The New Exploration: A Philosophy of Regional Planning* (New York: Harcourt, Brace & Co., 1928).

2. "Community Center Movement as a Moral Force," *International Journal of Ethics*. Vol. 30, April 1920.

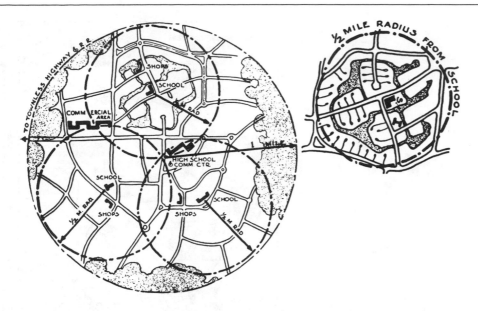

The neighborhood unit: Clarence Stein's conception. *These sketches show Clarence Stein's determinations of the proper design of the neighborhood unit.*
In the upper-right diagram the elementary school is at the center of the unit and within a one-half mile radius of all residents in the neighborhood. A small shopping center for daily needs is located near the school. Most residential streets are suggested as cul-de-sac or dead-end roads to eliminate through traffic, and park space flows through the neighborhood in a manner reminiscent of the Radburn plan. The upper-left diagram shows the grouping of three neighborhood units served by a high school and one or two major commercial centers; the radius for walking distance to these facilities is one mile.

in fairly specific terms was Clarence A. Perry. Although opinions differ to some degree, the definition he set forth in his 1929 *Regional Survey of New York and Its Environs* is still valid.

Perry described the neighborhood unit as the populated area that would require and support an elementary school. The neighborhood unit would occupy about 160 acres and have a shape that would render it unnecessary for any child to walk a distance of more than one-half mile to school. About 10 percent of the area would be allocated to recreation, and through-traffic arteries would be confined to the surrounding streets. Internal streets would be limited to service access for residents of the neighborhood. The unit would be served by shopping facilities, churches, a library, and a community center, the latter located in conjunction with the school.

The neighborhood unit or some equivalent is repeatedly referred to in proposals for urban reorganization. The suggested form varies widely, but the essential characteristics are fairly consistent: Perry was not far off. The suggested population appropriate for a unit has ranged between 3,000 and 12,000 people. In the plans for Chicago in 1942 the range was from 4,000 to 12,000; in Abercrombie and Forshaw's 1944 Greater London Plan, the size was 6,000 to 10,000. Some authorities have expressed a desire for smaller units than a school district, believing the nature of the neighborhood requires a relatively small size—generally 1,000 and not to exceed 1,500 families.

In its report in 1972 "A Strategy for Building a Better America," the American Institute of Architects adopted the neighborhood unit as the recommended

**Physical
Neighborhood**

AREA IN OPEN DEVELOPMENT PREFERABLY 160 ACRES •• IN ANY CASE IT SHOULD HOUSE ENOUGH PEOPLE TO REQUIRE ONE ELEMENTARY SCHOOL • EXACT SHAPE NOT ESSENTIAL BUT BEST WHEN ALL SIDES ARE FAIRLY EQUIDISTANT FROM CENTER

A SHOPPING DISTRICT MIGHT BE SUBSTITUTED FOR CHURCH SITE

SHOPPING DISTRICTS IN PERIPHERY AT TRAFFIC JUNCTIONS AND PREFERABLY BUNCHED IN FORM

ONLY NEIGHBORHOOD INSTITUTIONS AT COMMUNITY CENTER

TEN PERCENT OF AREA TO RECREATION AND PARK SPACE

INTERIOR STREETS NOT WIDER THAN REQUIRED FOR SPECIFIC USE AND GIVING EASY ACCESS TO SHOPS AND COMMUNITY CENTER

← TO BUSINESS CENTER   ARTERIAL   STREET

RADIUS   ¼ MILE

TRAFFIC JUNCTION

Clarence A. Perry's plan. *Perry was one of the first to give some consideration to the physical form of the neighborhood unit. It is substantially the same as in Stein's diagram but suggests that the maximum radius for walking be only one-quarter mile. Accepting the practice that was and still is prevalent, shopping areas are situated at intersecting traffic streets on the outside corners rather than at the center of the unit.*

Reproduced from New York Regional Survey

growth unit for future urban growth. The growth unit would range from 500 to 3,000 dwelling units (populations of between 1,700 and 10,000).[3]

Despite the variations the principle of the neighborhood unit runs through all considerations for social, physical, and political organization of the city; it represents a unit of the population with basic common needs for educational, recreational, and other service facilities, and it is the standards for these facilities from which the size and design of the neighborhood emerge.

N. L. Engelhardt, Jr., has presented a comprehensive pattern of the neighborhood as a component of the successively larger segments in a city structure. The unit includes the elementary school, a small shopping district, and a playground. These facilities are grouped near the center so that the walking distance between them and the home does not exceed one-half mile. An elementary school with an enrollment of between 600 and 800 pupils will represent a population of about 1,700 families in the neighborhood unit.[4]

Two such units (3,400 families) will support a junior high school with a recreation center in conjunction; the walking distance does not exceed one mile from the center to the most remote home. Four units (6,800 families) will require a senior high school and a larger commercial center. It will also be an appropriate size for a major park and recreation area. This grouping of four neighborhood units forms a community with a population of about 24,000 people. The components of this pattern are integrated, and such communities may be arranged in whatever combinations the sources of employment and communications to and from them may require.

---

3. *American Institute of Architects,* Washington, D.C.

4. N. L. Engelhardt, Jr., "The School-Neighborhood Nucleus," *Architectural Forum,* October 1943.

The latter part of the twentieth century has become an age of paranoid fear. We fear walking on our streets, and not only at night. We fear living in our homes as we place multiple locking devices on our doors and windows. We resort to living in securely protected buildings and communities. We construct communities within protective walls and employ security persons to guard us and our possessions. We isolate ourselves from our potential neighbors. We no longer live in a neighborhood other than one described by geography or a geographic symbol. Many of the joys that were derived from knowing and being with people have been lost.

There must be a way to restructure the environment in all of its elements to return to the sense of real security that can come only from a rebirth of communications with our neighbors and friends.

As a response to current conditions, however, a number of practical measures must be planned to increase the safety of the local neighborhoods. These include adequate night lighting of the streets, more than just at intersections; neighborhood watches where residents keep watch on their neighbors' properties and report suspicious activities; careful locking of entries to homes to dissuade the casual burglar from easy entry; assurance that police patrolling is adequate, especially during high crime hours. Burglar alarms and special patrols are expensive but may be necessary where a high-value property is at stake.

Protection from bodily injury requires greater concern for the welfare of the people in our neighborhoods. This must be more than a mere dedication to the creed that we are our brothers' keepers and that they deserve our interest in their well-being.

The school board in each community has its policy for extension and the design of the public school plant, but there are a few simple standards that are generally adopted as a key to the allocation of space. These standards link closely with recreational space, since the elementary school is the focal point within the neighborhood unit, and the junior and senior high schools the focal point within the group of neighborhoods we have identified as a community. The open space for recreation should become therefore an integral part of the school location and thereby provide the type of adult supervision and youth leadership necessary to guide the development of young people.

PUBLIC SCHOOLS

School service areas.

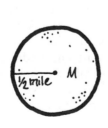

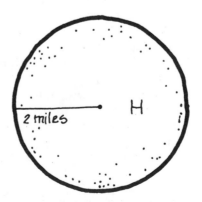

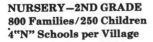

NURSERY–2ND GRADE
800 Families/250 Children
4"N" Schools per Village

MIDDLE SCHOOLS–3–8
1066 Families/600 Children
3 "M" Schools per Village

HIGH SCHOOLS–9–12
6400 Families/1500 Children
1 "H" School per 2 Villages

N. L. Engelhardt, Jr., has estimated one-half child of elementary school age (grades one through six) in the average family. The average for families among the low-income group is about 0.7 children, and 0.4 children per family in the high-income group.[5] Since most communities favor elementary schools with an enrollment between 600 and 800 pupils in the first six grades, a neighborhood designed about such a school would have a population of between 1,500 and 1,700 families, or between 5,000 and 6,000 people.

Two such neighborhoods would support a junior high school with enrollments between 1,000 and 1,200, and four neighborhoods would support a senior high school of about 1,500 enrollment. The walking distance for a junior high school (grades seven through nine) should not exceed one mile, and the senior high school (grades ten through twelve) should be a distance of not more than one and a half miles.

Although the public school system in most communities does not support nursery schools, it would be desirable to establish them by private means. The size recommended by Engelhardt is twenty-five children for each school within a radius not to exceed one-quarter mile from the most distant home served. The average is 0.1 child of nursery school age per family, and a nursery school would serve about 400 families.

It has been considered necessary too frequently in the past to select a school site after the population has arrived and the land has been absorbed for other uses than education or recreation. Consequently standards of adequate area for these facilities have been overshadowed by expedient decisions based upon the lowest price for land that might still be available. It is generally agreed, however, that a desirable standard for the three types of schools is: elementary, ten acres; junior high, fifteen acres; and senior high, fifty acres.

New Concepts

In the late 1960s educational authorities tried to solve the problem of school segregation resulting from racially segregated communities. It became clear that busing was not working and that a fresh approach was needed.

One such approach was the "educational park," a concept that emerged from a 1968 study done by the Bureau of Educational Research and Services for Litchfield Park, Arizona, entitled "Design for Lifetime Learning in a Dynamic Social Structure." The park was described as a complex of schools located in a large recreational area. The possibility of reduced educational costs and increased educational advantages made the idea attractive both to taxpayers and educators.

The system consisted of several related parts, serving different grade and age levels of young people within the community. For the youngest members of the community, a preschool program with facilities closely related to the neighborhood structure was suggested, the parent-child educational center is described in the following recommendations. For children in the elementary and junior high age range, facilities are planned at the village level with a cluster of schools on a large single site, bringing students with varying socioeconomic, ethnic, and reli-

---

5. Ibid. It should be noted that the school board and its staff have the authority to select public school sites and determine how the schools shall be designed and built, in conformity with state laws dealing with the design and construction of schools. However, it is required in California that the site must be reviewed by the planning commission and conform with the comprehensive plan; if it does not conform, the board shall not acquire the site for 30 days and then only after problems cited by the planning commission have been answered satisfactorily.

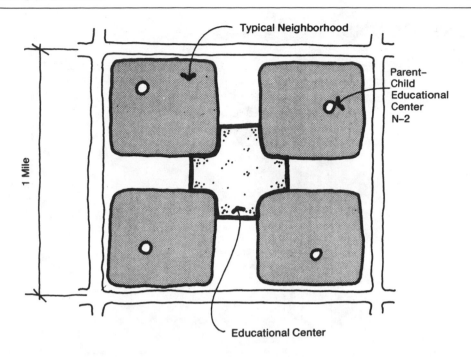

Typical Neighborhood

Parent–Child Educational Center N–2

Educational Center

gious backgrounds together. This new structure is the educational park. High-school educational facilities serve two or three villages.

Parent-Child Educational Center.

Each village is composed of three to four neighborhoods. Ideally, a Parent-Child Educational Center should be located in each neighborhood. The facility is intended as a social and recreational activity center for children from infancy through seven years (grades N-2) and their parents. These centers should be located within easy walking distance of the children's homes.

The Educational Park.

A village, roughly one square mile in area, containing approximately 8,500 people, could support an Educational Park. The park would provide a program of education for children of elementary and junior high/high school ages. The park would contain three or four middle schools, providing instruction for children in grades 3–8.

The goals of an Educational Park should be reflected in its shape and organization. An Educational Park's goals will be unique, reflecting the cultural, educational, and social values of a particular community.[6]

The object of the educational park is to create an environment in which learning becomes exciting and rewarding. The use of physical space to complement educational objectives is a principal objective.

During and after the seventies, in those areas of the country where busing was used to achieve racial balance, the public elementary school population fell off as an increasing number of parents who could afford the additional costs sent their children to private or parochial schools.

6. Study by the Bureau of Educational Research and Services for Litchfield Park, Arizona, 1968. Published in the General Development Plan for the Salt River Pima-Maricopa Indian Community, June 1970, Eisner & Associates, Consultants.

NEIGHBORHOOD PLAYGROUND

POPULATION

One site for 4,000 persons.

AGE GROUPS

5 to 14 years (active play).
Adults and tots (passive park).

AREA

5 acres minimum, including:
  3 acres active play area,
  2 acres passive park area, and
3 acres additional for school buildings when
  combined with elementary school.

TYPICAL FACILITIES

Softball	Basketball	Handball
Volleyball	Apparatus	Croquet
Table Games	Horseshoes	Tag
Tot-lot	Picnicking	Shuffleboard
Community	Off-street	Handicrafts
Building	Parking	

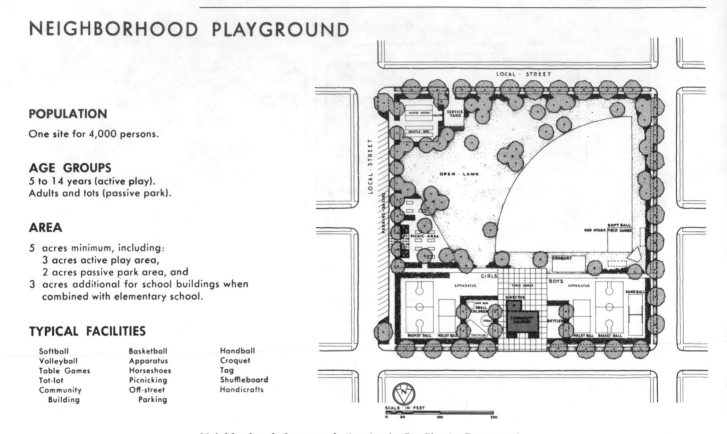

Neighborhood playground. *(Los Angeles City Planning Department.)*

EDUCATIONAL NEEDS

In addition to the improvements required in the quality of location and size and quality of the physical plants, the need for a better approach to education and improved training of teachers is apparent in all parts of the United States, especially for those areas where minorities reside. The best and most dedicated persons must be attracted to this critical task of bringing up intelligent, literate persons.

PUBLIC RECREATION

Open space in the city is usually considered as the area for recreation, and appropriately so. However, this space falls into a number of categories. There is space devoted primarily to active playgrounds for children, youth, and adults, and there is also space for adults' more passive relaxation. These spaces are those generally meant in a consideration of recreational facilities. Another classification should not be overlooked: the conservation of natural areas within as well as outside the city. This conservation may take the form of greenbelts to serve as buffers between different land uses—residential and industrial areas—or it may become a reservation of places of particular historic or geographic interest, or it may be space topographically unsuited for the satisfactory development of other urban improvements.

The standards for open space cannot adequately specify the required areas in a city for all these classifications; part of the distinction of cities derives from the way in which the natural site is shaped and planned. The spaces specified for defined recreational uses are not the full measure of adequacy of a recreational program under any circumstances; an abstract area of land in proportion to the population is but a part of the planning for recreation space in the city. It is the distribution of this space that measures the adequacy, not the amount alone.

To suggest that American communities are deficient in recreational facilities is only to repeat what has been often said by many authorities. The reasons for the deficiency are many; one of the most glaring is ill-planned land uses. Our present zoning practices provide extravagant areas for commercial and industrial uses, and the result is an urban pattern riddled with mixed land uses and an absence of stability in residential improvements. Consequently we face two predicaments; either land values render it too expensive to allot adequate open space for recreation or existing parks are swallowed by commercial and industrial areas, from which the people are trying desperately to escape to a better living environment.

A similar situation prevails with our schools. Because of unfortunate site selection, miscalculated population shifts, or lack of planning at the outset, schools are found languishing in the midst of business and factory areas, stranded between main traffic arteries, or situated in subdivisions too remote to serve the people. Recreation and education are linked with all other phases of urban development, whether they are planned or unplanned. Statistically, parks and playgrounds are deficient in number, but the maldistribution of available facilities is even more striking. This combination of circumstances makes it imperative to establish true neighborhood units in city planning.

As the machine has produced more and more with less and less manpower, and with the organization of labor, the work period was reduced from 60 hours to the 8-hour day and the 6-day week; then, during the 1930s, it was further reduced to 40 hours and in some trades to 35 hours. Not only has the change made more

Neighborhood playground in depressed area.

ADVANTAGES WHEN COMBINED WITH ELEMENTARY SCHOOL

- Playgrounds could be used by both educational and recreational agencies.

- Economy in maintenance and operation could be effected.

- Increased opportunities would be provided for public use of park and school facilities.

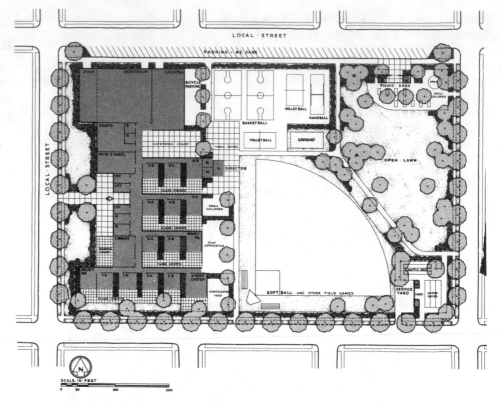

Neighborhood playground with elementary school. *(Los Angeles City Planning Department.)*

DISTRICT PLAYGROUND

POPULATION

One site for 30,000 persons.

AGE GROUPS

Youths 15 to 20 years (active play).
Adults (passive park).

AREA

15 acres minimum, including:
    10 acres active play area,
     5 acres passive park, and
10 acres additional for school buildings and
stadium when combined with high school.

TYPICAL FACILITIES

Hockey	Football	Soccer
Baseball	Softball	Tennis
Basketball	Volleyball	Handball
Table Games	Apparatus	Swimming
Horseshoes	Bathhouse	Pool
Bleachers	Community	Shuffleboard
	Building	

Off-street parking for at least 100 cars.

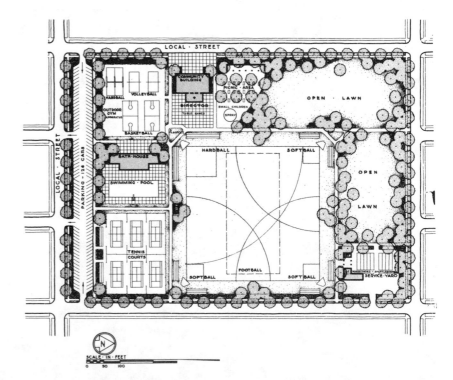

District playground. *(Los Angeles City Planning Department.)*

leisure time available, but the intensified nature of modern production has rendered the necessity for relaxation and recreation the more important.

Uncontrolled spread of blight hastened the flight to the suburbs, the process we usually identify as decentralization, and the absorption of open space within the central areas of our cities was a major factor in creating this blight. The combination of unplanned mixed land uses, physical deterioration, and lack of open space has created a situation that can hardly be cured by the injection of occasional playgrounds into these areas. They will improve the amenities within the hard and bare confines of blighted areas, but such devices will not remedy the condition; replanning and rebuilding will be needed in the great areas of our blighted and congested urban core. This process of rebuilding will necessarily be predicated upon the provisions of ample open space.

There are several excellent examples of the use of a regional stream or flood control channel as the basis for development of park and parkway systems. Several elements of circulation, flood control, and recreation are all planned as a unit and thus provide exceptional opportunities to conserve open space, protect human lives and property, and develop parks and green spaces that provide a community with a skeletal form about which to develop its other land uses. The parkway system in New York State is a fine example. In Arizona, the Indian Bend Wash in the city of Scottsdale is outstanding: linking neighborhood parks, golf courses, and flood control into one multimile strip of green space.

Integrated Recreation Systems

The City of Palm Springs, planning cooperatively with nearby cities and the Agua Caliente Indian landowners, has guided the development of the Tahquitz Creek flood control area into a scenic recreation area.

Bicycle and equestrian trails, municipal and private golf courses, scenic areas, and a water-related entertainment complex now occupy a spinal column of land normally reserved for flood control, providing open space intensively used by both residents and visitors.

There are three categories of recreation space for which the distribution as well as the amount of land is an important factor. They are identified by different terms in various localities. The National Recreation Association has classified them as (1) the playlot, (2) the neighborhood playground, and (3) the playfield. Each type fulfills a specific function in the design of neighborhoods and groups of neighborhoods.[7]

Neighborhood Recreation

The Playlot. The first category, the playlot, is for children of preschool age. In sparsely settled residential districts it is the equivalent of the back yard of homes, and in single-family districts the function is generally fulfilled by the usual open space about the homes. This is usually adequate when the street system is so designed that through traffic is discouraged or eliminated. In densely built apartment districts, however, the playlot assumes an important function.

There should be one playlot available for each group of families, the group ranging from 30 to 60 in number. The size of each lot should range in area from 1,500 to 2,500 square feet, and each should be located within a clear view of all the dwellings it serves. If a playground is more distant than several blocks or is separated from the residential district by a busy traffic street, the area of the

7. George Butler, *Recreation Areas* (National Recreation Association, 1958).

playlots should be increased to 2,000 to 4,000 square feet. Playlots should be equipped with such devices as low swings, slides, sandboxes, jungle gyms, and space for running and circle games; a portion of the lot should be paved.

All equipment should be designed and arranged for small children; authorities have pointed out the fascination of tots for objects such as low walls, logs, and common forms such as shallow trenches and small hills. Some form of enclosure, a hedge or fence, about the playlot is advisable, and a pergola and benches for parents should be included.

Neighborhood Playground. The second category is the neighborhood playground. Designed for children from six to fourteen, this playground is the neighborhood's center of recreation activities. Most authorities contend that a playground should be within one-quarter mile walking distance of the dwelling area it serves; this distance is particularly important in densely built districts, and it should not exceed one-half mile in the most sparsely settled residential areas. A study of five large cities surveyed a total of nearly 35,000 children; of this number two-thirds went to a playground within three blocks of their home and three-quarters lived within four blocks.

ADVANTAGES WHEN COMBINED WITH HIGH SCHOOL

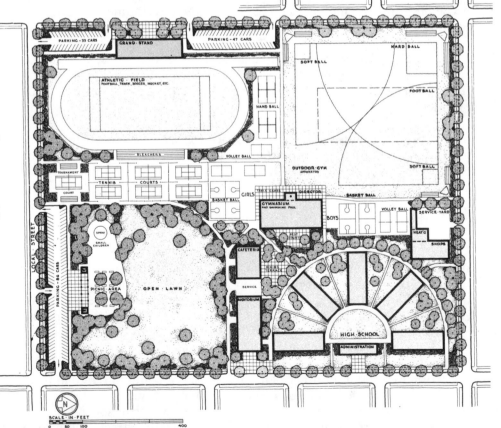

- Both school pupils and public could use athletic facilities on a suitable schedule.

- Park area would be available for public use at all times.

- Economy would be effected through joint maintenance and operation of playground and related facilities.

District playground with secondary school. *(Los Angeles City Planning Department.)*

Relation Between Net Residential Density and the Effective Service Distance of the Neighborhood Recreation Center*

	General Location in California	Average Family Size	Lot Size	Predominant Building Type	Effective Service Distance	Total Net Acres Excluding Streets and Public Uses	Population Within Effective Service Distance
⅜ Mile Radius 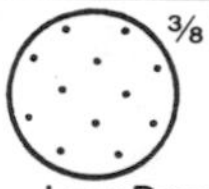 **Low Density 1** *15–20 persons per net acre* • = 200 people	coastal and valley nonmetropolitan mountain	3.5	7,000 to 10,000 sq. ft.	single-family detached house	¼ to ⅜ mile	206 ac.	2,500 to 3,000
¼ Mile Radius  **Low Density 2** *20–30 persons per net acre* • = 200 people	coastal and valley metropolitan desert	3.3	5,000 to 7,000 sq. ft.	single-family detached house	¼ mile	91 ac.	2,000 to 2,500
¼ Mile Radius  **Medium Density** *30–50 persons per net acre* • = 200 people	coastal and valley metropolitan	3.0	varies	duplex, row house, two- and three-story apartments	¼ mile	91 ac.	3,500 to 4,500
⅛ Mile Radius **High Density** *50–100 persons per net acre* • = 200 people	coastal and valley metropolitan	2.6	varies	multistory apartments	⅛ mile	23 ac.	2,000 to 4,000

* *Recreational Places*, Wayne Williams (New York, Reinhold Publishing Co., 1958).

The preferable location for a playground is adjacent to a community center or elementary school, where supervised recreation is possible. The following is a schedule of suggested space allowances.[8]

As a rule a playground for fewer than 200 children is economically impracticable to operate; use by more than 1,200 children requires two or more separate playgrounds. A minimum size of three acres for a playground is recommended.

The playground should provide an area for apparatus and an open space for informal play. There should be courts for various games such as soccer, softball, tennis, handball, and volleyball. Space is also needed for the quiet activities such as crafts, dramatics, and storytelling. A wading pool is desirable in warm climates, and a playlot with its facilities should be included in the playground. The lot should be near a shelter and rest area for adults. Lighting for evening use is desirable. Because economy in the operation and maintenance of recreation space in a community is highly important, it is impracticable to substitute a number of small play spaces throughout a residential development. The recommended sizes and design of spaces are more economical and avoid confusion between the various age groups who use the facilities.

The Playfield. The playfield is intended for young people and adults and provides a variety of recreational activities. A single playfield may serve four or five

8. Ibid.

Population	Number of Children	Size in Acres
2,000	450	3.25
3,000	600	4.0
4,000	800	5.0
5,000	1,000	6.0

neighborhoods; the walking distance should not exceed one mile, one-half-mile radius being preferred. One acre per 800 population is a desirable space standard, with a minimum size of 15 acres. Here again the standards vary, some cities holding to a minimum average area of one-half acre per 1,000 population. The space should be designed for the same facilities as a neighborhood playground, with the addition of space for such sports as football, baseball, hockey, and archery. It should contain a swimming pool, outdoor theater, bandshell, and recreation building. Night lighting should be provided.

Parks and Other Spaces

The three types of recreation spaces—playlot, neighborhood playground, and playfield—require the greatest attention with regard to their distribution in the community, the adequacy of space allotted to them, and their relation to the traffic arteries, community facilities, and accessibility from the homes. The total space for recreation is not confined to these categories, however. There are, in addition, the large city parks that supply the main facilities for citywide recreation, organized sports, public golf courses, open-air entertainment, and zoological and botanical gardens. These parks usually retain or reintroduce natural surroundings to the city and, where the sites are so adapted, they maintain the native wildlife as far as possible. They vary greatly in size, but they are usually of considerable area. Fairmount Park in Philadelphia and Griffith Park in Los Angeles each contain nearly 4,000 acres; Forest Park in St. Louis with its famous outdoor amphitheater has 1,380 acres, Balboa Park in San Diego has 1,100 acres, and Golden Gate Park in San Francisco contains about 1,000 acres. In addition to well-known Central Park, which contains only 840 acres, New York City has five other parks ranging from 1,000 to nearly 2,000 acres each.

Another type closely akin to the large park is the familiar "city" park, which serves as a breather in built-up urban areas. Their frequency depends a great deal upon the degree of population density: 5 miles apart is an average distance in congested areas and 10 miles is a standard in a highly decentralized city like Los Angeles. It is preferable that these parks be not smaller than about 30 acres, with a standard of about one acre per 2,000 people as a minimum area. This type of park is somewhat reminiscent of the Boston Commons (44 acres), but it is not intended to resemble a village green like the diminutive 6-acre public squares located in each quadrant of the original plan by Penn for Philadelphia. Such "squares" are little more than open space upon which some buildings may front. The city park should provide a natural atmosphere that may induce relaxation and some degree of repose.

The broadest reach of open space may be identified as the regional parks or park reserves. They comprise great areas of space, most of which is maintained in its natural state. Cook County Forest Preserve near Chicago is one of the greatest of these spaces devoted to conservation; it contains more than 30,000 acres. Others are the South Mountain Park of 15,000 acres near Phoenix, Arizona; the

Minimal Standards for Public Recreational Areas, City Planning Department, Los Angeles, California*

Nature of Recreation	Operational Agency	Ages Served	Minimum Acres	Service Radius	1 Acre Serves	1 Site Serves	Desirable Features Minimum Facilities
1 Playlot	Group Housing	Pre-school	⅛	1 block	—	136 tots	Housing projects only
2 Neighborhood Playground With Park Facilities	Elementary or junior high school or recreation dept.	5 to 14 and aged persons	Active area—3 Passive area—2	¼ to ⅜ miles Same	218 children 2000 tot. pop.	600–800 children 3000–10,000 tot. pop.	Space for juvenile tag and athletic games, crafts bldg., table games, rest area and boundary planting
3 District Playground and Park	Senior high school or recreation dept. and park dept.	15-20 and adults	Active area—10 Passive area—5	¾ to 1½ miles Same	290 youth 2,000 to 6,000 pop.	1,000–4,000 youth 10,000 to 50,000 pop.	Swimming pool, athletic field, all-purpose building, facilities for large group activities
4 Sports Center	Recreation dept.	Youth and adults	30	5-10 miles	Variable	500,000 pop.	Multiple facilities for field games, field house
5 Urban Park	Park dept.	All	30	5 miles	2,000 tot. pop.	50,000 to 100,000 pop.	Shade, lawn and water
6 Regional Park	Park dept.	All	No limit	No limit	Variable	Variable	Outstanding scenic or recr'l attractions
7 Beach	Recreation dept.	All	No limit	No limit	Variable	Variable	Multiple recreation facilities
8 Camp	Recreation dept. or school board	Various	20	No limit	Variable	Variable	Isolated location in primitive area
9 Specialized Park	Park dept.	Various	No limit	No limit	Variable	Variable	Golf course, or other special uses
10 Cultural Site	Semi-public or public	All	No limit	No limit	Variable	Variable	Historical, scientific, or educational interest
11 Miscellaneous Open Spaces	Any government agency	All	No limit	Local	Variable	Variable	Planted strips, squares, public bldg. grounds
12 Preserve or Reservation	Any government agency	All	No limit	Local	Variable	Variable	Protection of primitive or scenic areas

* April 1948.

10,000-acre reserve near Denver, Colorado; Tilden Regional Parks in Oakland, California; and the Westchester Park System in New York.

The great stretches of open space represented by these reserves or regional parks, and also some of the large city parks, stir the vision of the greenbelts many of these spaces might have become had they been formed as an integral part of the city plan. These parks frequently provide a transition between the urban development and the rural countryside, being situated beyond the center of population. They might have been formed as green buffers to separate the different land uses within the city and have been even more accessible to the people than their present locations allow.

There are many recreational spaces of a special nature: cultural centers including the museums and art galleries, beaches, amusement parks, sports centers including athletic fields, swimming pools, and stadiums. There are also the grand

Central Park, New York City.
A large urban park.

sweeps of broad parkways in which recreation areas are developed; the Outer Drive along the lakefront of Chicago is a magnificent illustration of this latter facility.

The overall minimum urban space devoted to the total of the foregoing recreational spaces ranges from about 3 acres per 1,000 population in the city to a desirable standard of 10 acres per thousand persons. It is further recommended that the urban area be planned for a reservation of about 10 percent of the gross area of the city to accommodate the space for an increase in population growth. In the vigorous replanning of London in preparation for the rebuilding program as a result of World War II's devastation, the standard of open space in the outlying areas of the county was 7 acres per 1,000 population, while the density of land use within the city boundaries where it is needed most forced a standard of no more than 4 acres per 1,000 persons.

The absence of open space within our cities may signal tomorrow's direction in planning. It will be a sad commentary, indeed, if 20 or 30 years hence our suburbs present the plight of the central city today.

Now is the time to prepare the open space within the growing subdivisions, for we cannot forget that the slums of today were the subdivisions of yesterday. This preparation was implemented by Title VII of the Housing Act of 1961. Identified as a provision for Open Space Land, it made financial assistance available for acquisition of open space in urban areas. Undeveloped or predominately undeveloped land in a comprehensive plan for parks and recreation, conservation of natural resources, and for historic or scenic purposes could be acquired by a city with the benefit of federal grants to meet the partial cost. This program was actively pursued through land acquisition, by dedications as part of the subdivision process, and by grants from state and federal agencies. The Bureau of Land Management reserved a great number of school and park sites adjacent to the city of Las Vegas, Nevada, as a result of cooperation based on the county comprehensive plan.

Strategically located in the city, the small urban park should provide for the variety of needs of ethnic and cultural groups that often may have special interests. These parks should vary in size, being able to respond to the local situations. The equipment should be carefully designed to withstand the pressures of usage and low maintenance costs. Special park areas should be designated for senior citizens and the physically impaired.

SMALL URBAN PARKS

In every state in the United States and in most other countries of the world there are park and camping areas, both in the wilderness and in special scenic wonderlands. These great landscape features tend to draw to them the people who thirst for and enjoy the freedom from the hustle and bustle of urban life. They include people who like to hunt and fish, hikers and mountain climbers, swimmers and horseback riders, all enriching their lives with the scent of fresh mountain air and sea breeze and greening of their eyes through the vision of great trees, wildflow-

OTHER OPPORTU-NITIES FOR OUTDOOR RECREATION

Grand Teton National Park, Wyoming. *Jackson Lake and Mount Moran in the background.*

Yosemite National Park. *Located in the Sierra Nevada Mountains in California, it can almost be considered an urban park in the summertime, serving both San Francisco and Los Angeles. Yosemite Valley, which is pictured, is a small part of the National Park.*

Type of Area	Acres per 1,000 Population	SIZE OF SITE (Acres)		Radius of Area Served (miles)
		Ideal	Minimum	
Playgrounds	1.5	4	2	0.5
Neighborhood parks	2.0	10	5	0.5
Playfields	1.5	15	10	1.5
Community parks	3.5	100	40	2.0
District parks	2.0	200	100	3.0
Regional parks and reservations	15.0	500–1,000	varies	10.0

School standards. *Intercounty Regional Planning Commission, Denver, Colorado.*

Urban Land, May 1961, by George Nez, Director, Inter-County Planning Commission, Denver, Colorado.

ers, and refreshing water. The experience is pure recreation, the rebirth of spirit often dulled by the routine of daily life.

SPRAWL: A LAND USE CANCER

Albert F. Appleton, a longtime conservationist, developed through study and observation a theoretical mathematical formula to describe and define the impact of scattered urban development on open agricultural land. His theory indicated that the first 5 percent of urbanization conditions the potential for continued agricultural use by about 50 percent on the adjoining land. The further urbanization increases the adverse effect on efficient agricultural practices by another 50 percent. Appleton indicated that regardless of the terrain and the individual condition, the same factors would apply.

William H. Whyte, a former editor of *Fortune* magazine suggested that planning and developing open vistas to bring view areas into the community; planting trees, especially along the borders and along rivers and creeks; removing signs and billboards, especially along the ridges, would tend to soften the impact of development on the environment. He recognized that some of these proposals might seem small but that the cumulative effect would be material.

CHAPTER 24

LONG HAUL TRANSPORTATION SYSTEMS ELEMENT

The important concept to study is not the amount and means of travel and transportation today but the roads that were traveled in arriving where we are. Only when we understand this can we estimate where we are going. The changes that have taken place in almost a hundred centuries seem astounding until we understand that this minute in the space of time revolutionized everything else we do.

In the technologically advanced portions of the world mobility is much like breathing: it comes with living. We travel about in our local communities, using every form of locomotion from the short walk to the flight into the wild blue yonder. Locally after walking and using a bicycle we turn to the automobile, the bus, the taxi, the subway, the commuter bus, and the train. When we travel long distances we use the airplane, and sometimes the train or bus. When we travel overseas we use the airplane or, on a leisurely cruise, the ship.

For shipping commodities we use the trucks on the highways and to some degree the railroads and airlines for longer hauls. For overseas, all large freight uses ships, many designed for hauling special cargo, such as the oil tankers and container ships that carry large amounts of boxed merchandise for specific destinations, many times to distant parts of the world.

Transportation, therefore, permeates every facet of our lives; it involves all types of people, from the sellers to the professionals who design the systems to the

TRANSPORTATION ELEMENT

Transportation: Who Uses It

professionals who build the system and those who use it. It involves traffic engineers, computer specialists, sociologists, city planners, economists, and, of course, the new breed, environmentalists.

The first transportation revolution occurred about 8,000 years ago, as dated by an archaeological find in the Ukraine. With the discovery of the remains of a horse that appeared to have been guided by a bit, the discoverers concluded that this was one of the first horses ridden by a human. With this invention humans were able to travel at greatly increased speed and to fight their wars more effectively and thus took the first steps into motion by other means than by use of their own physical energy.

The second transportation revolution occurred with the development of the wheel some 5,000 years ago. Having learned by experience that stones that were round were moved more easily than those that were flat or angular, humans concluded that their transportation needs might be met by using round objects as a sort of ball bearings; thus the steps toward a wheel were negotiated, slowly but significantly.

The third and perhaps most significant transportation revolution occurred when humans, subject to the dangers of lightning-caused forest and grass fires, saw the devastation caused by this form of energy and learned that safety involved hasty flight. This was also the reaction to another of nature's great displays of fire, the volcano. Learning to live with these forces and ultimately to harness them to human service was a tremendous step into the future. Can one think of any form of transportation that is not fueled by fire or the heat of radiation? From the simple railroad engine fired first by wood, then by coal, and later by oil we find that the basis of the energy was heat generated by combustion. This principle extends to the current forms of transportation, on the land, on the sea, and in the air.

CHANNELS OF MOVEMENT

Since people first charted the fleeting trace of a path across the landscape, routes of travel have been the vital threads in patterns of commerce, cultural exchange, and military conquest. For more than 3,000 years humans' mode of transportation was foot or horseback. Then came the Industrial Revolution and mechanization, steam for rail and water travel, the internal combustion engine for automobile and airplane, and the beginning of space travel—progressing from the path to the road, the river to the ocean, the rail to the sky.

LAND CARRIERS OF FREIGHT

Along with the railroads, trucks carry great volumes of cargo from farm to market and from production and storage areas to both near and distant points of final distribution. The service that streets, highways, and freeways provide for the distribution of freight is a major factor in the comprehensive transportation system. As a matter of fact, many state and national governments support the construction of higher standards for routes carrying high volumes of trucking, to permit these routes to withstand the heavier loads imposed on them by the trucks and trailers that use them daily for short and long hauling. The width of lanes, the grades in hilly and mountainous areas, are all designed to accommodate, along with the general traveling public, the trucks that travel on all major arteries. In addition, rest stops and parking areas suited to the needs of the truck drivers and their rigs must be planned and provided at reasonable intervals. Special demands are also manifested for parking facilities and loading areas at all terminal areas, especially at transfer points such as harbors, where loads or entire containers are transferred from the trailer unit to the container ships that carry the loads intact to their distant terminals.

THE TRAIL OF RAILS

Builders of railroads sought level terrain or followed the easy grades along watercourses. Cities sprang up along these routes, and industry developed on the lines of transportation. The passenger station was the entrance to the town, and the center of the city grew about it. Since this hub provided convenient commuting to and from the suburbs, the commercial district expanded about it.

With the passing of time and the neglect of orderly urban development, industry continued to creep along the railways and waterfronts. The city grew and new railroads entered to help build the metropolis. These lines of transportation were vital to the economic development of the urban area, and industries were accorded preferential sites along the rights-of-way as encouragement to locate in the city. Blocked by spur tracks and sidings, the street system was interrupted and traffic problems and other hazards were created.

Replacement of the various independent and scattered stations by the so-called union station improved the reception, dispatch, and interchange of passengers and freight, but cities like Chicago still suffered from the chaotic network of separate rail lines that stretched like tentacles in all directions. Consolidation of the various competing lines was slow because of complicated joint agreements, abandonment of rights-of-way, high cost of building new facilities for roads already equipped with terminals, signalization systems, and the necessity for coordination that tended to reduce possibilities for independent expansion—to say nothing of rivalries and ego. The reduction in the duplication of facilities that would have resulted from such consolidation, however, would have been of immeasurable profit to the city. Simplification of the street system, traffic routes, and by elimination of grade crossings alone would have vastly improved urban circulation and reduced the accident hazards and disorderly pattern that existed.

The current shipping of freight comprises a far larger part of railroad business than passenger traffic and presents more complicated planning problems. Except

Small British steam engine of yesteryear.

Early wood-burning steam engine.

for some terminal locations, a large part of the freight business is "through shipping," that is, freight destined for points beyond the city. As the city grew up and spread away from the railroad, the classification (vast spaces reserved for reordering the trains) yards remained a no-man's-land within the heart of the urban core. Occupying valuable land and disrupting the traffic system of the city, the current yards are generally too cramped for the efficient handing of the tremendous operations involved in the classification, sorting, and redistribution of freights, as well as storage, switching, and the makeup of trains.

Recently, planning studies have been conducted throughout America concerning the potential use of the waste land in the many abandoned classification yards that are so well located in numerous cities. The concepts for reuse range from new commercial centers, produce distribution complexes, and cultural or sports centers to retail and office applications, all to be supported by a partnership between the public and private sectors. Some cities in the eastern United States have been giving serious attention to such programs to gain the economic advantages that could be secured through this effort.

REBIRTH OF PASSENGER RAIL TRANSPORTATION

The adventures of the Japanese with their Bullet Train and the more recent addition of the modern French "TVG" high-speed system have given rise to the rehabilitation of railroads as a competitor to automobiles and airplanes as the means of traveling middle distances in many parts of the world. The efficiency of the Japanese system, its improved travel times and safety, along with its savings in energy and cost have now been recognized. Consideration is being given to similar experimental lines in the United States, for example, in the Los Angeles to San Diego corridor and in the Boston, New York, and Washington, D.C., corridor. As can be expected, opposition from cities along the proposed routes tends to delay some of these proposals.

Driver wheel on largest steam engine.

People's ability to free themselves from the surface of the earth created new problems. While the airplane was experimental, terminal facilities were located as far as possible from population centers. With millions of people now flying each year, location of the airport in urban centers and rapid delivery of passengers to their destinations are the joint concern of airline operators and the public. Connections from the airport to the destination in the city have become a greater problem than flight time between cities. During peak traffic hours the trip to or from Manhattan to La Guardia or Kennedy airports in New York and to or from O'Hare and Midway airports to the Chicago Loop can be interminable.

Airport planning is a component of the comprehensive plan for the city and region. It requires a complete analysis of the market comparable to what is done for other forms of transportation: it must consider the present and potential passenger, cargo, and mail business that may be expected in the community; meteorological data; the present and planned land use within and about the airport; the proposed extent of the operators' training program; the local traffic—intercity and interstate; transcontinental and international air routes; and prospects for development of private airfields.

Air transportation is in a state of flux. The equipment continues to change and policies of airline operators are constantly subject to modification with experience. The attitude of the urban population also varies: some desire complete immunity from proximity to flying fields and corridors; others are inclined to support the development of residential communities designed around the airplane as a vehicle for commuting.

The deregulation process, which has had an impact on many of the economic activities in the United States, has had an amazing effect on the airline industry. The number of airline companies has multiplied rapidly, and some communities with major airports have been in an uproar over the additional flights, the concern for air safety, and the additional noise and traffic that have been generated.

THE THIRD DIMENSION: FLIGHT

Several of the major airlines, new and old, have gone into bankruptcy while others have ceased to operate, as the current state plagues even the best of carriers. Deregulation may be synonymous with the "antiplanning" approach to the concept of a free market in which anyone can do as he or she wishes and cooperation and coordination of activities can be classified as a restraint of trade or conspiracy.

Planning for air transportation must be conceived on a regional scale. Airports should be located for convenient and rapid connections to the strategic parts of the city, by a variety of means that have not yet been settled. Downtown feeder airports through which small airplanes and helicopters carry passengers into the heart of the city are being considered. Helicopter flights from the major port to landing space in the city center for airmail and commuter service are already in operation. However, many heliports, other than those associated with medical emergency facilities, have been discontinued, for other than emergencies, because of local conflicts. Air transport is an integral part of the transportation system of the city, both passenger and cargo, and must be a component of the comprehensive plan.

Examples of the problems exist in all parts of the world. The crash of a plane in a populated area adjacent to New York's Kennedy Airport in 1975, the 1978 accident in the vicinity of San Diego, and the Chicago tragedy of 1982 are just a few well known examples that should make us give heed to the probability of future occurrences.

The danger of crashes may not be the major problem. Noise from the ever-increasing size and power of planes has constituted a major environmental difficulty. Overflights at low levels in the take-off and landing areas have generated petitions to close airports or to regulate their hours of operation or to use less noisy planes.

The future use of the "dead land" around airports after acquisition and clearance remains undecided. In the Los Angeles area, some of the land has been turned into parking lots. This use could be expanded and would be productive if the land were reasonably near the air terminal and were served by shuttle buses. In other areas the possibility of cemeteries or golf courses has been discussed. High-density housing or mobile home developments should be discouraged as a violation of the National Environmental Protection Act and common sense.

AIRPORT PLANNING

Several types of problems are related to the planning of airports, including new airports near existing metropolises, areas where existing airports are to be expanded, use of the land where airports are to be abandoned or where they are to be reduced in the types of service that they provide, or land uses around both regional and international types of airports.

Several cities are currently looking at the problems and evaluating the impact of the changes on air safety, for both the passengers and the residents of the areas immediately adjacent to the takeoff and landing zones.

Denver, Colorado, confronts an immediate problem as the current international facility at Stapleton Airport is to be closed as soon as the new airport near Boulder is completed. The service capabilities of this airport are not adequate to handle the role that is required at this major element of the national system. Moving the airport near the city of Boulder will make travel from the airport to the city of

Denver longer, and it must be assumed that, together with the new airport, an up-to-date transportation system will be planned to facilitate the transfer of persons and goods more rapidly than that which now depends only on the automobile or the buses for travel from Stapleton to the downtown area and surrounding communities.

To assume the role of regional facility, the new Denver airport must be based on a plan for the entire transportation system linking the airport with the surrounding communities by both freeways and mass transit services of the most modern kinds, to match the quality of service being planned for the new airport.

In the meantime there must be planning for the use of the land around the new airport to assure the City of Boulder that its present pristine environment will not be destroyed by noisy overflights nor danger from takeoff and landing. In a word, there must be a plan for the region that is sophisticated in all of the aspects of air transportation, as well as in the ground service and safety that the new facility should provide.

At the same time that the new facility is being constructed, the reuse of the existing site has to be considered. Currently studies and discussions are under way to determine which applications in this convenient area would do most to enhance the social and economic future of the Denver region. Should there be a small air-freight facility surrounded by clean industry? The types of uses permitted should take into account the inversion layer above Denver, which has created smog conditions in this mile-high community long known for its clean air. Once a prime health retreat for persons with lung illnesses, the city must do all that it can to recapture that reputation by planning its industrial and transportation systems to reduce the contaminants discharged into the air. No city with the potential of Denver could plan for less.

Many airports all over the world were originally built in open areas, since they required a large amount of space about them for safe landing and takeoff. In the meantime, with each passing year they have been engulfed and hemmed in by use of private land for urban development.

As a result property near airports has sometimes been condemned to prevent suits related to the health problems associated with noise and anxiety. In addition the traffic problems in the areas approaching the airports have multiplied to almost a stalemate. Parking at the airport proper, even though expanded both on the ground and in multiple decked structures, has been inadequate to handle the increasing demands for space.

HARBORS

In former times the harbors of the world were the centers of transportation activity, the locale for romance, the heart of developing civilization. It was to ports that ships of many nations carried their goods and passengers. They were the ties to the trade centers, the distribution points for all foreign exchange.

Today in the developed nations airplanes lead trains and ships in passenger travel. But ships still perform the important function of handling internationally bound bulk merchandise. The harbors of the world and the rail lines leading to and from them must be elements in any planning program. Harbors, unlike airports, cannot be moved from their natural locations. They may be deepened or extended or altered in function from industrial to recreational, but they are always at the water's edge.

Railroad flatbed designed to carry containers.

WATER FREIGHT TRANSPOR- TATION MIRACLE

Water transportation has been the main province of international freight shipments since the beginning of World War II. Ship passenger service for overseas destinations never did recover its role in the travel business except in the field of pleasure cruising. The main centers of activity for the pleasure cruise were the ports of Florida and to a lesser degree the Pacific coast. Although cruises seem to be a seasonal attraction, they take place year-round, especially in the tropics. All other personal travel went to the airlines, especially when jet planes, with a speed greater than 500 miles per hour, could reduce the travel time from New York to Europe to approximately 5 hours instead of the 4 to 5 days that some of the trips on the fastest ocean liners entailed.

In comparison, the handling of freight from coastal ports increased greatly, especially with the development of the cargo containers and the design of the great automated derricks at the ports that move the containers, like toys, and place them accurately aboard specially designed container ships, where they are piled high. The crafts are not beautiful to see, but they are efficient in doing what they were designed to do.

In the movement of crude petroleum, the tankers have grown to immense size and are able to carry millions of gallons of petroleum products from the shipping points to the refineries in designated ports. The very size of the ships has been a factor in the great oil spills when these vessels run into difficulty.

Recent major oil spills in Alaska, in the Gulf of Mexico, and off the coast of California, due to collisions or accidents where a tanker or barge ran onto a reef or its anchor, indicate that vessels carrying crude oil require greater care in construction and maintenance as well as better management.

COMPUTER REVOLUTION

The organization of travel, both in the field of pleasure and in the field of handling freight cargo, has made the computer its bedmate. Every movement, every time schedule, every quantity of passengers or freight is handled through computerization. The origin and destination of every cargo is determined by the

Mechanical equipment for loading containers aboard ships.

computer input and the automation of the entire process. The handling of tagging and ticketing of freight and passengers on interrelated modes of travel is a miracle with the number of persons and carriers involved. John H. Mahoney of Intermodal Freight Transportation, Westport, Connecticut, has the following comments about the growth of computerized systems.[1]

> The computer revolution probably will turn out to be as important, if not more important, to intermodality as the container revolution. Computerization touches every aspect of intermodal movements: rating, routing, control of containers, clearance, billing, reporting, and all other functions. The container revolution produced an improvement in physical aspects, but the computer revolution makes the entire concept simple and workable, regardless of whether or not the freight is containerized.

> The number and variety of computerized systems for transportation are expanding rapidly. They handle jobs ranging from operations control to traffic movement and facilitation. Railroads, trucklines, airlines, and shiplines have their systems, as do freight forwarders, other middlemen, and shippers. Large shippers such as Xerox and Ingersoll-Rand have systems that incorporate order processing, inventory control, and customer service requirements, as well as transportation and customs clearance information. Airports and seaports are testing and adopting computerized systems that will permit rapid handling of pre-clearance of goods. Compliance by shippers and middlemen with the rules of the systems is required for use of airports or seaports.

Planners no longer think of the computer as an abacus with a memory, for it has become an integral part of the working tools of the profession. It also means a great deal to the other creative professions, including the architects and engineers. As a matter of fact, the computer has made itself an integral part of the scientific communities and the military and everything in between. The following excerpt indicates, in the language of computers, the roles that the system plays in the planning professions. One can readily imagine that other professions have their own systems to serve their needs.

PLANNING AND THE COMPUTER

---

1. *Transportation Quarterly*, Eno Foundation for Transportation, 1985, pp. 76–77.

Three automation technologies are generally considered by planning agencies:

CAD. Computer-aided design uses interactive graphics to automate, organize, and draft maps and other materials. The basic system stores graphic data as sets of primitive graphic features—points, lines, curves, circles, or composites of these—and organizes them into layers. The layers may be edited, manipulated, and displayed.

AM/FM. Automated mapping/facilities management systems are commonly used by utility companies, among others, to organize geographically based information, such as pole locations. AM/FM systems were originally used mainly for facilities management because their high degree of cartographic precision allows facility managers to keep close track of the company's assets. On the other hand, AM/FM systems may not be able to do the spatial analysis often required for planning applications.

GIS. Geographic information systems were once oriented toward spatial analysis and not the geographic precision of AM/FM systems. The systems available today are almost interchangeable with AM/FM systems.

GIS is particularly useful for projects where large quantities of data must be processed and reprocessed over a long period of time. The newer systems are designed to interface with other technologies, including CAD and AM/FM. Until recently GISs have usually been based on either large and expensive mainframe computers or on smaller minicomputers, but GIS software is now available for engineering workstations and personal computers, bringing the price down considerably.[2]

APPLICATION OF TECHNOLOGY

In the 1980s the entire Coachella Valley of California was computerized, with every bit of available data recorded, including detail down to lots, from the size and shape of parcels to the assessed values and utility systems available. The data were mapped for the entire valley. Unfortunately, as a result of the rivalry between the county staff and the cities that participated, the data were not kept current and the value of the undertaking turned to ashes.

The incredible impact of the computer on every aspect of contemporary human existence is evident in a widespread reliance on that ingenious instrument for solutions to problems of the urban environment. It has value as a mechanical tool, but it is gifted with neither conscience nor ultimate wisdom: it cannot make decisions related to social and economic welfare or the physical form of the city unless the concepts are devised by humans and imparted to its memory system.

WHAT LIES AHEAD

Interest in automation and computer-guided rapid transit has been renewed. The first working system was built in Morgantown, West Virginia, more than 20 years ago, and new technology has improved the system since then. Major use of the automated transit and railroad system, similar to the strides taken in the Bullet Trains of Japan and in the Bay Area Rapid Transit (Bart) system in the San Francisco Bay area, could come on-line universally before the year 2000. There is no question about the need for government support since there never was a transportation system that developed without help.

A great number of experiments have taken place in an effort to propel trains and mass transit safely at high speeds, using all forms of levitation and propulsion and employing nonpolluting fuels and magnetic drives.

---

2. Laura Lang, "Making a GIS Dream Come True," *Planning*, July 1990, 14–20.

It will take a major effort to change from the archaic system using fossil fuels to one that uses propellants from sources other than petroleum or other hydrocarbons because of the involvement of economic giants with an eye to their own survival.

For some time, in both architecture and engineering the computer has been used with the assistance of digitizing, to bring about three dimensional perspectives of topography and sketch plans of proposed projects. In the recent, 1992 Olympic games the art of morphing was used in creating images of people performing card stunts with such realism that one could easily believe that they were witnessing the real activities. Coordinated with crowd noises and music, both the sight and sounds gave people the feeling that they were at the event. Of course the presentation was conceived and developed in the minds of the programmers and other creative persons who could use the computer to sell ice cream at the north pole.

MORPHING . . . CREATIVE VISUAL IMAGING

CHAPTER 25

TRAFFIC ELEMENT

MASS TRANSIT AND PARKING

Managing transportation in cities is almost as old as Western civilization. Julius Caesar, in the early municipal laws of Rome, had considerable regulations as to how wagons should go through the streets of Rome and when they should not, and how they should be restricted during business hours.

Edward P. Morgan,
"Atlantic Dateline" broadcast,
German Marshall Fund of the U.S., 1982

CHANNELS OF MOVEMENT

Since people first charted the fleeting trace of a path across the landscape, routes of travel have been the vital threads in patterns of commerce, cultural exchange, and military conquest. For more than 3,000 years the mode of transportation was by foot or horseback. Then came the Industrial Revolution and mechanization, steam for rail and water travel, the internal combustion engine for automobile and airplane, and the beginning of space travel. Progressing from the path to the road, the river to the ocean, the rail to the sky, the space for movement of humans and their vehicles now occupies more than a quarter of the land in the urban community.

Of all of the products of a remarkable age, none has made more striking progress than the vehicle of transportation. With the variety in modes of travel came increased speed, extended lines of communication, and, most important, unprecedented mobility of countless millions of people.

The impact on the structure of our civilization is appalling. The industrial economy is rooted in large part in the production and circulation of vehicles of transportation. Commercial enterprise in metals, plastics, fuels, rubber, even in insurance, hospitals, and funeral parlors, depends to a large extent upon our capacity to move people and goods. Within our cities we are confronted with a paradox. On the one hand is the struggle to design a circulation system to accommodate vast changes in the speed of transportation; on the other we search desperately for a place for these vehicles to come to a halt. The freedom of movement afforded by the revolution in transportation has reached such an advanced stage of development it is now a major problem to slow down and stop. The automobile is trapped in the network of an archaic street system, but when the circulation routes are improved there must be a place to park at the points of destination. This paradox of conversion speed to pedestrian tempo is dramatized in airplane travel: the time consumed to and from the airport may be greater than a flight of a thousand miles.

In 1847 the Messagèries Nationales coach line in France traveled at six miles an hour and fifty-six miles a day. With the introduction of asphalt in about 1860, the improved roadways brought a further increase in the speed of travel. The Malles-Poste coaches traveled nine to twelve miles an hour and seventy-five miles a day. The automobile has the capacity for speeds several times that of the nineteenth-century horse-drawn coach, but the time consumed by the fits and starts along traffic streets, the search for a place to park, and then the walk to the office reduce the average speed of the commuter to an actually lesser rate.

An even greater issue than the speed of modern transportation is its safety. If urban travel were confined solely to the irritation of a traffic jam, we might withdraw to a point of vantage and view the scene as a farce. But the automobile has indeed become a weapon of murder. Between 1960 and 1987, the yearly accident rate in the U.S. increased from 10,400,000 to 18,121,000. At the same time, deaths increased from 38,600 to 48,700 per year, a national tragedy of major proportions. In California, where the automobile is a way of life (though not necessarily of living), deaths increased from 5,114 in 1970 to 5,860 in 1980.

In addition, deaths involving pedestrians and motor vehicles amounted, within 30 days of an accident, to 9,900 in 1970; to 9,200 in 1972 and to 6,600 in 1989. This pedestrian slaughter amounted to 25 percent of the persons who died from intervehicle accidents or from other automobile related deaths including collisions with trees, telephone poles, and buildings.[1]

Many of these tragedies are due to carelessness, but the tensions generating from the tempo and confusion of the modern city might be relieved through well-ordered street and highway design.

The function of a city's circulation system is to provide for the movement of people and goods. It ranges from the movement of an individual on foot to the daily hordes of commuters entering and leaving the city from distant points. It includes automobiles, buses, trucks, and railroads—on the surface, underground, and overhead—ships, and airplanes. It is the series of routes traversed for a variety of purposes: work, entertainment, shopping, transport of raw materials and manufactured products, education, relaxation, affairs of state and law en-

---

1. *Statistical Abstracts of the United States* (Washington, D.C.: Department of Commerce, Bureau of Statistics, 1991).

forcement. The mixture of these demands for transport, and vehicles to serve them, compounds the equation for the system. It embraces walkways, service lanes, major streets, highways, freeways, the rights-of-way for rail lines, and airway routes. Each of the elements in the circulation system we know today has been inherited from the premachine era. Adjustment to the mechanical vehicle has been an arduous process of wrestling some semblance of order and utility from the archaic layout.

The early surveyors usually laid out towns in gridiron sections one mile square. The major highways followed these section lines in ribbons 100 feet wide. Secondary highways eighty feet in width were aligned along the quarter section lines, and within these squares the interior roads were laid in sixty-feet rights-of-way. The system was adaptable to a regular division of land into lots, and people settled at strategic locations. The pattern continued as the population increased, and later through this network of streets, vehicles of modern transportation poured into and through the growing cities.

How Shall We Move?

Satellites in outer space make instantaneous audiovisual communication possible on a global scale. Spaceships carry human beings to the moon, and television is projected into our living rooms from moonwalkers. Yet this same technology only complicates the movement of earthbound persons in cities.

The ever-increasing number of motor vehicles crowd the streets and are trapped in their own self-perpetuating traffic jams. Once associated with social status and the individual's freedom to move anytime, anywhere, at any speed, the illusion of the automobile has been fleeting.

Traffic congestion in all of the cities of the world has become a headache, in some cities a migraine. The results have been air pollution and dependency on a vanishing resource, petroleum-based fuel. The use of the private automobile as a massive transportation system has provided for maximum individual mobility but at great cost, not only for the user of the vehicles but also in the loss of valuable land devoted to the sprawling communities that dot the landscape of many Western nations.

The expressway or freeway systems were conceived to relieve congestion. But the proliferation of automobiles strains them beyond their capacities. Armed with formulas for measuring "cost-benefit ratios," the limited vision of traffic experts justifies widening streets and adding more expressway lanes and extensive new routes, only to compound the congestion, multiply accidents, and increase injuries and deaths each year. Once expected to delineate the boundaries of neighborhoods, the expressways destroyed them; they became channels of escape from the congested city to the sprawling suburbs.

Automobile manufacture, with related oil, steel, and service enterprises, comprises a major element of the national economy. There are over three times as many new automobiles produced than babies born each year in the United States.

THE ROLE OF THE AUTOMOBILE

"Freedom" in many parts of the Western world has symbolically been the right to own and operate a motor vehicle—be it motorized bicycle, scooter, moped, motorcycle, or automobile. The typical American family owns at least two automobiles and depends on them for the ability to move from home to places of employment, for recreation and other activities. The love for the auto leads one to the opinion that, if possible, the owners would take their vehicles to bed with them, for surely the accelerator has become an integral part of the foot.

Each motor vehicle requires about 4,000 square feet of space in the form of real estate and structures, and the land rent may be as high as $5,000 per year for each car. These costs are paid for in many ways by the consumers as they visit their doctors, the shopping center, the bowling alley, and are added to the mortgage payment, tax bills, and the many other public and private elements of daily living expenses.

The heavily subsidized automobile has become a toy, a weapon, and a means whereby people can express their "macho" image. With the demise of mass-transportation alternatives that are attractive, convenient, and efficient, it has become an essential part of the comprehensive plan to develop streets and highways ranging from the local access ways to our homes to the mechanical marvels exemplified by our freeways and parkways.

As traffic grows, atmospheric pollution spreads across entire urban regions. Streets, expressways, parking lots, and multilevel garages consume valuable land, as exhausts poison precious air. There is not, nor can there be, enough space to accommodate the moving and standing flood of automobiles. In the 1930s Sir Raymond Unwin calculated that all the automobiles that enter New York City would absorb all the space on Manhattan Island. Victor Gruen estimated in the 1960s that nine stories of garage space covering Manhattan would be necessary to store automobiles if everyone entering that island came by car.[2] The Urban Land Institute reported in 1970 that parking for the 150,000 cars entering Pittsburgh's Golden Triangle each day would require 214 garages with 700-car capacity, at a cost of $535,000,000 exclusive of land.[3] These projections may seem preposterous. Yet of the sixty stories in the twin towers of the Marina City apartment complex built in Chicago in the 1960s, nineteen stories are a garage. In the 1990s these factors increased the cost of parking to astronomical levels, leading to a drive to reduce standards in the face of increases in the number of automobiles.

With city planners spurred by the conviction that relief from traffic congestion would come by way of broader streets, there followed a rash of street-widening projects along the established rights-of-way, and major and secondary highways were designated. Congestion was not relieved, however. More traffic was invited onto these broader streets, slow-moving and short-haul traffic mixed with vehicles destined for more distant points, left turns occurred at all intersections, truck and passenger vehicles vied for parking and loading space along the curbs, vehicular and pedestrian traffic conflicted, unlimited ingress and egress flowed from abutting property into the traffic lanes, frequent intersections impeded movement, and the multitude of commercial distractions along the streets brought chaos to the city.

The profligate waste of resources in materials and land has turned the personal freedom promised by the internal combustion engine into a frantic search for survival at the periphery of cities. Continued decentralization persists without concern for the cost of transportation or the arrangement of land uses related to economic and functional channels of mass transportation.

Relief from Congestion

2. Victor Gruen, *The Heart of Our Cities* (New York: Simon and Schuster, 1964).

3. George Prytula, *Community Mobility Systems*, Urban Land Institute, Special Report, 1970.

Therein lies a crux of the urban planning process: a structure of land uses and distribution of population within a network of mass transportation that can move people and goods with convenience, comfort, and economy. In great cities that evolved before the automobile—London, Paris, Moscow, São Paulo, New York, Chicago, Boston, Philadelphia, San Francisco—the concentration of land uses and the inadequate surface space have forced tunneling underground for subways. Yet building bulk in these cities continues to accelerate, and the equation between the concentration of people and transportation is continuously unbalanced.

If a planned balance between building concentration and transportation service were achieved (and there is no evidence that this is about to happen), the subway would not be desirable. Man is not by nature a subterranean creature; he needs bountiful natural light and air. Since broad rights-of-way are being acquired for vast systems of expressways, comparable channels could be provided for a system of surface transportation within existing city centers, as well as outlying areas.

Such an approach to a desirable system of urban transportation will be expensive; any system of adequate transportation will require vast sums of public financing, as the massive cost of freeways and highways testifies. But it will require much more than public funds; it will require a rare commitment by public and private leaders to the transformation, the reshaping of the city structure.

Perceptive minds since Ebenezer Howard have recognized the need to restructure the industrial city—now the commercial city—in the image of man himself. Recovery of human scale is at the root of every enlightened concept of the city of our age. Sir Raymond Unwin applied Howard's theory of the self-contained garden city to his own diagrams for the decentralized metropolis. The British New Towns, the planned decentralization of Stockholm, and Tapiola, near Helsinki in Finland, have pursued this same objective.

The urban structure must be designed or redesigned as a series of physically functioning neighborhoods and communities integrated with a circulation system of mass transportation. Whatever the sociological variations, physical facilities for education, worship, trade, recreation, and work are determined by essential human needs. Special services may fit into the basic pattern of facilities that make up the areas of common interest, the neighborhoods and communities.

People are now dependent on automobiles to get to and from homes, schools, stores, and parks. Walking distances are excessive, traffic confrontations too hazardous, and the surroundings are often unpleasant or downright ugly. Poorly located schools and efforts to bring about a socioethnic mix have made the school bus a familiar feature in almost every city and town.

The family car is an anachronism in an industrial system that presumes to glorify "efficiency and economy." The family uses the car for an average of eight to ten trips each day. Most are short hauls to local facilities—shopping, school, house of worship, playground, or friends—they are seldom emergencies. Yet the car is 2,000 pounds of steel, powered with a 250-or-more-horsepower engine, transporting fewer than 1.5 persons per trip (1.1 in the West).

Stable neighborhoods and communities should have local systems of small low-speed minibuses running on frequent convenient schedules; one may recall the "elephant trains" at the 1933 Century of Progress exposition in Chicago, the electric trams in Disneyland parking lots, the free bus systems in modern retirement colonies, moving sidewalks in large airports. With the resulting reduction or elimination of traffic accidents, both pedestrians and bicyclists could discover the joys of a relaxed tempo, as well as economy, in traveling to and from their daily activities. Technology, having successfully created spaceships, with some measure of human ingenuity might even produce a nonpolluting minibus with "piggyback" shopping carts.

Traffic engineering is necessary because the planning of the city circulation system has been neglected.

Traffic Engineering —A Palliative

Because the street plan of cities is insufficient to cope with traffic, various methods have been devised to control the operation of vehicles. It might be more accurate to describe these as measures of control by default, but they are essential to maintain any movement of vehicles through the city streets. The calculation and administration of these are known as "traffic engineering."

Traffic engineers find themselves in the awkward position of attempting to compel the movement of the irresistible force of traffic through the impenetrable obstacle of congestion. Many traffic engineers are repair persons rather than builders, devisers rather than planners, first-aid traffic corpsmen rather than surgeons.

Traffic engineering embraces the host of devices with which the city-dweller is familiar: stop-and-go signs at street intersections, slow-down warnings and speed limits, parking limits and prohibitions, the police whistle, the so-called safety islands at boarding points for buses, the white and yellow lines painted on the pavements to channel moving vehicles and the mechanical divisions sometimes employed for this purpose, and the one-way street. The list of these "solutions" is long, but none has singly or in combination brought any genuine relief of the traffic problem. The devices are more appropriately described as stunts rather than solutions; they are expedient measures to cope with immediate traffic problems in the form of first-aid treatment and offer no real improvement in the capacity of the transportation system to move people.

The automobile travels at a reasonably rapid speed with relative ease, comfort, and convenience. Interruption of the flow of travel conflicts with the effectiveness of the machine as a means for the mass transportation of people, and this interruption also creates hazards to safety. The synchronization of stoplights has improved the continuity of movement, but the effect of these interruptions remains. The average cycle for change of the traffic signal is one minute; cars traveling in one direction are stopped for thirty seconds and move for thirty seconds. The effect is a reduction of 40 percent in the number of cars that could pass a given point if the flow were uninterrupted. In other words, a street intersection controlled by traffic lights can accommodate only two-fifths the number of cars a free flow of traffic will carry.

The conversion of streets from two-way to one-way travel is a familiar system traffic engineers are frequently forced to employ. It is a method for channeling traffic that avoids the conflict of left-hand turns across lanes moving from the opposite direction. But the traffic signal is still necessary to permit the passage of pedestrians, and traffic flow continues to suffer periodic interruptions.

There is a reluctance to design streets for peak loads because of the alleged wasted space during the periods of less intensive use. The alternative is the conversion of six-lane trunk streets to four lanes in the direction of heavy flow and two lanes for the opposite direction during the morning rush, and the reversal of this process for the evening peak. While the painted channel lines are usually the only means for marking these lanes, some cities have mechanical barriers that may be raised and lowered from continuous slots along the channel separations.

Traffic engineers maintain data on the movement of people and vehicles, they measure the service of commercial centers by traffic counts of registered automobiles that park there, they measure the capacity of sidewalks by counts of pedestrians who traverse them; the probable effectiveness of street widening, of new streets and freeways, is estimated by counts of local and through traffic. The need for and effectiveness of traffic signals, prohibitions on left turns and curb parking, and special lanes for traffic flow are calculated by the traffic engineers from the variety of traffic counts and data compiled, and they aid the public transit companies in the routing of mass transportation vehicles.

The traffic engineers maintain a gallant struggle to cope with the imponderable traffic tangles they confront. Until the urban street system is designed for vehicles that traverse it, their devices will remain essential ingredients of our city circulation. It is a choice between two traffic evils: no control and complete chaos, or negative control to avoid paralysis.

PARKING PROBLEMS AND SOLUTIONS

Off-Street

Man's struggle to achieve speed has been successful, and we are confronted with a paradox: inadequate space to slow down and stop. Automobiles, buses, and trucks must have a storage place at both the origin and the destination of their travel routes. And they must have a place to come to temporary rest for the conduct of business or pleasure en route. This is the parking problem.

In the United States as well as in many European countries almost 85 percent of all surface travel in urban areas, except in a few large cities, is by means of the private automobile. The road system on which these vehicles circulate must be a major element in the community's comprehensive plan and must provide for adequate terminal facilities. A component is the accommodation of these vehicles at their destination. The moment when a driver is transformed to a pedestrian plagues the planner. The plan must provide for this.

The horseless carriage inherited the narrow street as a traffic route with the hitching post as a parking place. When the automobile attained its own identity, the number of vehicles burgeoned. They filled the streets, the rate of movement declined, "slot machines" were put on the hitching posts, and curb parking absorbed two street lanes urgently needed for moving vehicles. Although the parking meter produces some revenue for the city, the movement in and out of curb parking seriously interrupts the free flow of traffic along the free lanes. Off-street parking is an urgent need, and methods for both voluntary and mandatory parking have been varied. Parking districts and merchants' associations have been created, but relief from the parking jam in commercial districts remains inadequate.

With the decentralization of commercial facilities, ample parking was a primary prerequisite of the shopping center. This obvious competition forced a recognition of the necessity for off-street parking in built-up central commercial districts.

Provisions for off-street parking have been accepted in many zoning ordinances for both residential and commercial areas during recent years. The requirements vary, but none have coped with the situation in central business districts.

The necessity of freeing the streets of standing vehicles is hardly more pressing in the business districts than in the high-density multiple-family apartment districts. Off-street parking is but one important feature for improvement of the total environment. It would aid in achieving a balance between bulk and the capacity of the street system to accommodate the traffic flow.

The requirements for parking space will vary according to the structure of the city and the habits of motor travel. These standards are generally related to the building floor space, and this underscores the issue of excessive commercial zoning and consequent congestion. The issue may be restated by a question of whether it is our intention that cities become gargantuan parking lots partially occupied by buildings. The prospect that mass transportation may offer the solution seems remote; the private automobile is a phenomenon of our age, satisfying a basic instinct for freedom of movement whatever the consequences. The form of cities must be adapted to man's nature and the vehicles he creates. To be effective, cars must have the room to move *and* to stop.

Motorists wish to park as near their destination as possible. Surveys have indicated that they will do this, in many instances at the cost of illegal curb parking. Surveys have also indicated that motorists entering the downtown district for business or shopping do not wish to walk from their parking place a distance of more than 1,000 feet. If we assume the city block to be 600 feet long, it is apparent that those who wish to park for a short time—one-half hour or less—wish to be within 500 to 600 feet of their destination; those who park for about one hour wish to be no farther than about 1,000 feet from their destination, and those who intend to remain for a longer time would wish to be no farther than about 1,200 feet from their destination.

It must be granted that surveys deserve qualification. Consider the environment through which the urbanite must travel; it is little wonder the shopper dislikes walking in the downtown district or in many other sections of the contemporary metropolis. Ugliness is abhorrent and it repels a human being; it can hardly be expected that people will wish to walk about a business district fraught with every disagreeable feature and lacking convenient shopping and business facilities. When the cities acquire the self-respect that comes with pride in the physical beauty of an environment, the willingness of motorists to walk through these surroundings will probably reveal quite a different set of statistics.

About 80 percent of the parkers in the central business district remain for one hour or less, the number ranging from 60 to 90 percent. When curb parking is permitted, the average time is about 30 minutes because of the preponderance of people who enter the business district for brief periods. Relating these several factors, the parking facilities for the downtown business district could be consolidated in areas ranging between 500 and 1,000 feet in radius from the center of a well-planned group of stores and office buildings. Convenience would be enhanced by the elimination of congestion, discomfort, and the hazards caused by the conflict between pedestrian and vehicular traffic. It is possible that this new element of convenience might encourage pedestrians to walk more and increase business further.

Requirements for parking vary considerably, but experience has divulged some factors that assist in estimating the requirements. The average space per occupant in commercial buildings—office space—is approximately 150 square feet in floor area. If all regular occupants in these business structures were to use private automobiles for their transportation, an area of 150 square feet per person would be required in parking, the equivalent of a square foot of parking for each square foot of building floor space.

This space does not provide for people who patronize the business enterprise; and it may be estimated that an equal number enter the commercial district for this purpose as those who occupy the commercial buildings. In the average city, however, about 50 percent of the people entering the downtown district use the available means for mass transportation: rail or bus. This results in a required space for parking equal to the building floor area, a figure generally confirmed by authorities. Retail shopping imposes a considerably heavier burden on parking space. It is therefore necessary to adjust the required area for parking in central business districts according to the estimated uses to which the land will be put. These estimates will likewise warrant adjustment as mass transportation is improved and becomes capable of adequately moving the largest possible number of people entering and leaving the business district.

More recently, several studies conducted during the 1980s indicated changes considered reasonable for parking standards. Most reduced the number of parking spaces for commercial areas below those incorporated into most existing zoning ordinances. Where there were nonconcurrent uses, adjustments were made to reduce the number of spaces by a proportional amount, depending on the nature of the uses and the time of their maximum utilization.

Economics   Some of the most valuable land in the central core of urban areas is used for the parking of automobiles. In Los Angeles, a study prepared by the planning department indicated that over two-thirds of the entire area is given over to streets and the parking of motor vehicles. If the streets occupy approximately 25 percent of the central area space, it can be observed that over 41 percent of the land is utilized for the storage of cars. This is in addition to the off-street parking provided within the structure of buildings, since most new development required on-site or nearby parking for both tenants and visitors. The Civic Center Mall, in Los Angeles is honeycombed with multistory underground parking, and the land about the center is still covered with thousands of vehicles.

One can imagine what the island of Manhattan or the Loop in Chicago would look like if all the employees and patrons were to bring their automobiles into them. There would be no space for buildings. The cost of parking in Manhattan, however, discourages this practice even though the rapid transit system, extensive as it is, leaves many with concerns about safety and security and rush-hour crushes, causing them to use their automobiles regardless of cost for personal transportation.

The changing size of the motor vehicles will have some impact on the space needed for them in parking areas. A recent study by the Urban Land Institute found that the American automobile owners are questioning the "Queen Marys" that they have been accustomed to as gasoline guzzlers and are turning in increasing numbers to the European answer provided by smaller cars. The study also suggests new requirements for the number of spaces for various types of uses, including shopping centers.

Free parking? *The Marina Towers, adjacent to the Chicago River in the city of Chicago, provide in each of the twin towers more than thirteen stories of parking for residents, patrons, and visitors. Located as it is within easy walking distance of the business establishments in the Loop or central business district, the need for an automobile for local transportation should be minimal for the residents of the apartments that tower above the fringes of the core area. One can anticipate, however, that the occupants of the megastructures use their automobiles for transportation to places of employment and to do the daily shopping.*

While it may be true that, with the recent affluence of the upper middle class in America, the "Queen Marys" are becoming more prevalent in the sales statistics, the increased sales do not offset the large-scale purchase of small foreign automobiles. In competition with foreign imports, which have taken over the market, some of the largest of the American manufacturers are placing newly designed small, efficient cars on the market.

The answer to the widespread use of the personal transportation system, with an average of approximately 1.5 persons per vehicle, has not been resolved in most Western nations. With pressures from the freeway and highway builders, it may be a long way into the future before people give up the tremendous, if illusory, freedom that the automobile represents.

One often hears of "free parking"; except for parking in the open wilderness there is no such thing. This freedom is especially scarce in urban areas. Studies will show that even the simplest forms of space required for the storing of a motor vehicle are exceedingly expensive. Parking at residences often requires approximately 400 square feet of space in an enclosed garage, and most communities require garages in residential areas. The cost of the land and structure will add as much as $20,000 to the costs of an apartment unit.

Likewise, free parking on the street is a myth. The cost of the extra land for the parking lanes and the cost of paving and maintenance will have to be borne by the property owner in terms of initial costs and in later taxes to keep the space maintained for use.

Free Parking

Free parking at shopping centers is also anything but free. The valuable commercial land and the paving and maintenance of this area cost a great deal of money, which is passed on to the consumer as part of the cost of everything that he purchases. When parking land is either too expensive or not available, commercial enterprises resort to multistory parking structures as an answer both to serving their patrons and local zoning requirements. Either below ground or above, the cost is roughly equivalent to the construction of additional stories in the building. If underground, the designs must include retaining walls, drainage structures, ventilation, and lighting.

Some merchants and professionals provide for client parking through a validation system in which the business picks up the cost of the space. This forms part of the cost of the service that is rendered and therefore is far from free.

The following article by Dr. Donald C. Shoup, professor of urban planning at the University of California at Los Angeles, examines the cost of free parking.

> If you could have either free gasoline for driving to and from work, or free parking at work, which would you choose?
>
> If you are the median U.S. commuter, you drive ten miles round trip to work, and if your car's gasoline consumption is the U.S. average of twenty miles per gallon, you use half a gallon of gas for each round trip to work.★ If you commute to work twenty-two days a month, you use eleven gallons of gas a month for work trips; at, say, $1.25 a gallon, gasoline for commuting costs you $13.75 a month. Therefore, if you work where the fair market price of parking is more than $13.75 a month, free parking is worth more to you than free gas.
>
> An astonishing number of cars park free at work even in central business districts where parking is most expensive. For example, in 1974, slightly over half the 100,000 cars commuting to downtown Los Angeles parked free, although the market price of parking averaged $35 a month; in 1976, almost half the 140,000 cars commuting to downtown Washington, D.C., parked free, although the market price of parking averaged $50 a month. Nationwide, 90 percent of the labor force commutes to work in private vehicles, and 75 percent of them park free in employer-paid, off-street parking spaces.★★
>
> The income tax exemption of free parking at work encourages employers to pay for commuter parking rather than to pay higher salaries. Free parking at work may seem harmless, or even beneficial, but it indirectly pollutes the air, congests traffic, and wastes energy by inviting commuters to drive to work alone.
>
> A tax exemption in lieu of free parking would encourage employers to subsidize people, not cars. If employers pay higher salaries rather than pay for parking, many commuters will do in their self-interest just what they have long been urged to do in the public interest—ride the bus, carpool, bicycle, or walk to work.[4]

THE CIRCULATION PLAN

The circulation plan involves major highways and streets, routes for mass transportation, railroads, airfields, and waterways. It defines the through-traffic arteries, freeways, parkways, and their intersections and interchanges. It charts the course of rail and bus routes about the city and its environs. It is in this plan that

---

★ U.S. Department of Transportation, *Home-to-Work Trips and Travel: Report 4, 1977.* Nationwide Personal Transportation Study (FHWA/PL/81/002), December 1980. Page 1 of this report provides media commuting distance; average fuel efficiency for the 1977 auto fleet was 10 mpg (report 2, p. 33). Because average fuel efficiency has been increasing since 1977, a figure of 20 mpg seems a conservative estimate for 1982.

★★ Donald C. Shoup and Don H. Pickrell, *Free Parking as a Transportation Problem* (Washington, D.C.: U.S. Department of Transportation, Office of University Research, 1980).

4. Donald C. Shoup, *Transportation Quarterly* 36:351–64.

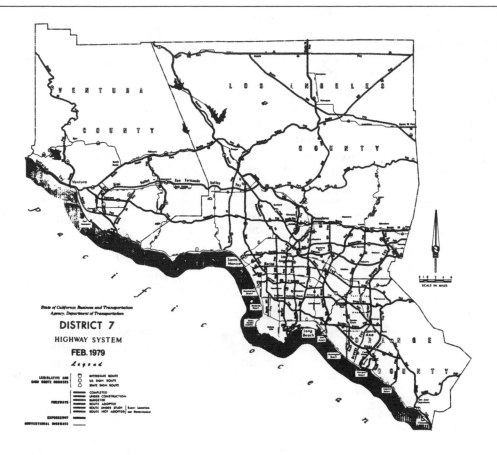

Map of freeway system, Los Angeles. *(State of California Business and Transportation Agency, Department of Transportation.)*

all lincs of vehicular communications are integrated for the circulation of the people and goods in and about the urban area.

The system of circulation should define the boundaries of neighborhood units. The street system within this broad framework need be determined only to the extent that it impinges on the through-traffic arteries and mass transportation routes. The internal design of the streets could remain unspecified until development is imminent and then be made precise.

As the city develops, the plan will become the reference for improvements and extensions of the circulation system. Precise plans may be made for railroad passenger and freight lines, yards, terminals and stations, air terminals and fields, and internal helicopter connections. Harbor and waterway development may be guided by this plan as improvements are proposed.

The plans for circulation and for land use require integration. They may require occasional modification, but there is no development within one category that can remain unrelated to the other.

Since approximately one-third of the land in some urban communities is devoted to the road system, it is pertinent to observe how this land came into public ownership. In early times travel over the safest and most easily traversed routes created "public" roadways through usage. Since the basic ownership of all land was the sovereign right of the state, it was normal for the ruler to designate "post" roads and highways to ensure that channels of communication between communities were protected. When ownership was granted to individuals, the

"Public" Ownership of Roads

head of state provided for a means of access to property, although some passage-ways remained toll roads until a very late date. In cities the subdivision of land into individual parcels was regulated by decree to maintain certain open spaces for travel and safety against fire.

This practice is reflected in modern subdivision design whereby the state, in granting the right to individuals to subdivide land, requires that the roadways that give access to property be dedicated to public use and be maintained by the city. Streets thus dedicated may either remain as public easements for such time as they are required as streets, or they may be deeded to the city in "fee simple." (*Fee simple* means that the possessor has full ownership of the land. When the right-of-way is no longer needed, the community can sell the land, just as it can any other property it owns.) When dedicated streets are vacated by the city, the land occupied by them is usually divided on the basis of the original dedication or deed, and title to it returned to the owners of abutting property.

STREET DESIGN

The gridiron street plan formed a pattern of rectangular blocks divided into rectangular lots that were usually very narrow to conserve on utility lines and very deep to conserve on streets. The curvilinear design was then devised to give some semblance of "character" to the subdivision, to subdue the deadly monotony of parallel streets stretching to infinity. The alternative soon developed into a curved grid, a series of parallel curved streets, with no more living amenities than the rectangular grid provided. The more exaggerated of the designs assumed the form of a violently swirling street system in which orientation was completely obscured.

It is customary to maintain the narrowest practicable width for local residential streets that serve only the abutting property. When parking is desired on each side of the street, the right-of-way is between 54 and 64 feet wide, with a pavement width of 36 feet. The paved surface may be as narrow as 30 feet, but this suggests parking on one side only since the traffic lanes should not be less than 10 feet wide. Although local streets of narrow width are more economical in their initial cost, the weaving of automobiles about parked cars is a safety hazard to children in the neighborhood.

Economy of street design has been more rationally approached through the effort to reduce the total length of streets rather than their width. Care in site planning brought about an abandoning of the artificial picturesqueness of the arbitrary street system and led to the use of the cul-de-sac and the loop street.

Cul-de-sac and the Loop Street

The cul-de-sac, or dead-end street, came into use to eliminate through traffic in a positive manner. Cul-de-sacs terminate in a circular or hammerhead turn-around. To retain their inherent advantages, they should be short—a maximum length of 450 feet is recommended. The advantages are dissipated in long cul-de-sacs, since they induce accelerated traffic speeds and render access for service and fire protection more complicated. Probably the most renowned example of the cul-de-sac street is in the community of Radburn, New Jersey. The system is fully exploited by the consolidation of open space and the reduction of street crossings, the separation between vehicular and pedestrian circulation being enhanced by the use of pedestrian underpasses beneath the major streets. Although this separation of traffic is desirable, the narrow tunnel shape of the usual pedestrian underpass tends to accumulate refuse and dirt and presents dangers that may be avoided by convenient pedestrian overpasses above slightly depressed streets.

Four-level intersection, Los Angeles.
(Courtesy Department of Public Works, Division of Highways, State of California.)

Simple Grade Separation between Two Highways

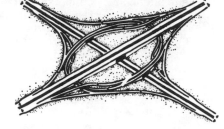

Universal Interchange

Braided or "T" Interchange

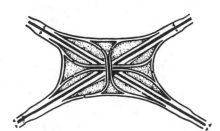

Four-Level Interchange

Simple Interchange of Freeway with Highway

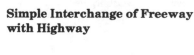

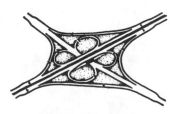

Cloverleaf Interchange

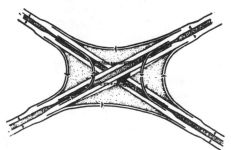

Bel Geddes Interchange

Highway interchanges.

Highway and Street Standards*

Type of Facility	Function and Design Features	Spacing	R.O.W. Width
Freeways	Provide regional and metropolitan continuity and unity. Limited access; no grade crossings; no traffic stops.	Variable; related to regional pattern of population and industrial centers	200–300 ft.
Expressways	Provide metropolitan and city continuity and unity. Limited access; some channelized grade crossings and signals at major intersections. Parking prohibited.	Variable; generally radial or circumferential	150–200 ft.
Major roads (major arterials)	Provide unity throughout contiguous urban area. Usually form boundaries for neighborhoods. Minor access control; channelized intersections; parking generally prohibited.	1 mile	120–150 ft.
Secondary roads (minor arterials)	Main feeder streets. Signals where needed; stop signs on side streets. Occasionally form boundaries for neighborhoods.	½ mile	80 ft.
Collector streets	Main interior streets. Stop signs on side streets.	¼–½ mile	60–70 ft.
Local streets	Local service streets. Non-conducive to through traffic.	at blocks	50–60 ft.
Cul-de-sac	Streets open at only one end, with provision for a turn-around at the other.	only wherever practical	50 ft. (90 ft. dia. turn-around)

* *Urban Land*, May 1961, by George Nez, Director, Inter-County Regional Planning Commission, Denver, Colorado. Standards revised 1979 by William A. Law, Linscott, Law, and Greenspan, Transportation Engineers, Los Angeles, Cal.

The loop street is a variation of the cul-de-sac and is employed in substantially the same manner. However, it eliminates the necessity for the turnaround and provides the continuous circulation that is required by some communities to assure no interference with the accessibility for public services. While it does not offer complete separation between vehicular and pedestrian traffic, it is as effective as the cul-de-sac in eliminating through traffic. The length of the loop street is not as important as that of the cul-de-sac, traffic is normally confined to residents' vehicles or vehicles for service and delivery within the block.

Pavement Width	Desirable Maximum Grades	Speed	Other Features
Varies; 15 ft. per lane; 10–14 ft. shoulders both sides of each roadway; 8–60 ft. median strip.	3%	65 mph 88.5 km/h	Depressed, at grade, or elevated. Preferably depressed through urban areas. Require intensive landscaping, service roads, or adequate rear lot building set-back lines (75 ft.) where service roads are not provided.
Varies; 12 ft. per lane; 8–10 ft. shoulders; 8–30 ft. median strip.	4%	45 mph 80.5 km/h	Generally at grade. Requires landscaping and service roads or adequate rear lot building set-back lines (75 ft.) where service roads are not provided.
84 ft. maximum for 4 lanes, parking, and median strip.	4%	35–40 mph 56–64 km/h	Require 5-ft.-wide detached sidewalks in urban areas, planting strips (5–10 ft. wide or more) and adequate building set-back lines (30 ft.) for buildings fronting on street; 60 ft. for buildings backing on street.
60 ft.	5%	35–40 mph 56–64 km/h	Require 5-ft.-wide detached sidewalks, planting strips between sidewalks and curb 5–10 ft. or more, and adequate building set-back lines (30 ft.)
44 ft. (2–12 ft. traffic lanes; 2–10 ft. parking lanes)	5%	30 mph 48 km/h	Require at least 4-ft.-wide detached sidewalks; vertical curbs; planting strips are desirable; building set-back lines 30 ft. from right of way.
36 ft. where street parking is permitted	6%	25 mph 40 km/h	Sidewalks at least 5 ft. in width for densities greater than 1 d.u./acre, and curbs and gutters.
30–36 ft. (75 ft. turn-around)	5%		Should not have a length greater than 500 ft.

There are some disadvantages in the cul-de-sac and the loop street, but careful planning can reduce these to a minimum. It is sometimes alleged that circulation about a community becomes confusing, although a simple plan can overcome much of this objection. House numbering and street naming require attention since they vary from the customary pattern for which the usual systems have been devised.

The collector street is, as the name suggests, the street into which the local residential streets feed. It may be designed to flow into the secondary or major traffic arteries, in which case the right-of-way is usually 60 feet wide with a pavement 36 feet wide. Frequently however, the collector streets are comparable in traffic load to a secondary highway and must be so designed.

Collector Streets and Other Traffic Arteries

The traffic load from the local residential streets and their collector roadways is carried by the secondary and major highways and, although a difference in function is suggested by this terminology, there is often little real distinction between the traffic they carry. The secondary highway is intended to serve areas intermediate between the major traffic street and thence connect to the major highway. However, major highways have grown so congested that much traffic escapes along the secondary and collector streets, thus rendering each the equivalent of a major traffic artery.

Secondary highways are usually 80 or 86 feet in width of right-of-way with a pavement width of 64 feet; they have four lanes for traffic and two for parking. The major highways are customarily 110 feet in width with a pavement width of about 76 feet, with six lanes for moving traffic and two for parking.

It is gradually becoming apparent that access from abutting property to major and secondary highways must be denied. The movement of traffic cannot be maintained when it is repeatedly interrupted by the ingress or egress of vehicles from frequent side streets or driveways. Frontages along these main traffic routes must obtain their service access either from alleys or minor service roads parallel to the highway. A service road is generally 28 feet in width, allowing parking on one side only, and the usual width of alley is 20 feet with parking prohibited. Service roads may be screened from the highways with a planting strip; the highway is thus enhanced while the abutting property is shielded from it, an asset to the development of residential neighborhoods contiguous to highways.

THE REGIONAL HIGHWAY SYSTEM

Following old native American trails, the winding, twisting, meandering routes between communities became the post roads, the plank roads, and the high roads. These were the trade routes between centers of population and between the rural areas where products were grown and the towns where they were marketed. Like the roads in the center of the early city, they followed the easy way irrespective of property boundaries. As property ownership was formalized, the roads served as dividing lines. They represented access to property and a way to and from markets. Most of the important regional links follow, to some extent, these original lines. With the expansion of communities, many of these primitive roadways have been lost in the maze of internal growth. They left their mark, however, as the basis for the orientation of other streets and highways parallel and perpendicular to these original spinal lines.

With the expansion and congestion of cities, the intercommunity roads collapsed under the impact of traffic loads. They carried less and less traffic. Accidents were a by-product of too many intersections, ill-designed roadbeds and curves, lack of sufficient sight distances, and vertical curves. Widening the roads only intensified the situation by drawing more of the ever-increasing number of vehicles to them. Then the "free-way" introduced the first change in highway design.

The freeway provided a new approach; it released the roadway from old alignments, from abutting property, from intersections at grades, from outmoded design standards, from old right-of-way limitations. The traffic problem remains unsolved, and it is true that at peak hours the freeway can become the longest parking lot in the world. The freeway nonetheless has embraced the salient characteristics of a travelway for free- and fast-moving vehicles. It has yet to find its appropriate relation to the future shape of the evolving modern city.

A freeway is essentially a pair of parallel roadways, each of which carries one-way traffic moving in opposite directions, with complete separation from each other and freedom from all cross-traffic. Ingress and egress in either direction flow via accelerating and decelerating lanes. Traffic moves unimpeded by any interruptions from light signals or stop signs. All cross-traffic is carried over or under the freeway, and access from abutting property is closed from the freeway right-of-way.

Freeways

The freeway appeared on the American scene during the early 1930s with the construction of the Downtown Expressway parallel to the Hudson River in New York City; the Pulaski Skyway from Newark, New Jersey, to New York; and the commencement of the great Chicago Outer Drive. Later developments soon followed in New Jersey, Pennsylvania, New York, Connecticut, Delaware, California, and the vicinity of Washington, D.C. Many of these early routes were limited in scope, but they were designed for the unimpeded movement of vehicles by the shortest feasible route between points.

The freeway may parallel existing streets or cut across their present pattern. It marks the beginning of a new form of artery that may aid in the solution of the traffic problem and create the huge cells that will ultimately frame groups of neighborhood units as the city grows and is rebuilt. With the freeway a new urban form emerges.

The right-of-way for a freeway is necessarily broad; it must provide adequate space to be depressed or raised without adversely affecting abutting property. Limitations on the width vary with circumstances. Land cost may be one obvious prospect for forcing economy in land area, but another may appear in state laws that restrict the acquisition of property for public improvements to that required for the principal function of the facility.

Such restrictions would limit the right-of-way to the area required only for the traffic lanes and adjacent parkways, the acquisition for contiguous buffer spaces being considered excessive. To cope with such a situation in New York City, the routes were acquired by the Parks Department as park strips and the trafficways were built within them; the term *parkway* is consequently applied to them. Some states have enacted statutes to permit the acquisition of ample space for the freeway right-of-way; in California a space 150 feet on each side of the centerline of the roadway may be acquired, thus providing for purchase of marginal property to avoid the creation of small remnants of land otherwise unusable for development. In the 1990s additional rights of way are being acquired for mass transit lanes.

The freeway is usually designed for three lanes of traffic in each direction, rarely more than four. These are intended for the free movement of vehicles, and the greater the number of lanes, the greater is the interference from vehicles weaving between them seeking a satisfactory channel of speed or access to the decelerating lane from which they leave the freeway. Entrance and exit lanes and those for emergency parking should be in addition to the number of channels of clear traffic movement.

Ingress and egress are at infrequent intervals, not less than 1/2 mile apart and preferably at 1-mile distance; this frequency will permit adequate stops for bus connections if they are allowed on the freeway system. Lanes should be 15 feet in width rather than the usual highway standard of 12 feet, and loading and unloading zones must be separated from the clear channels of movement, with transition lanes leading to the stopping places.

The dividing strip between the roads going in opposite directions will vary in width according to the nature of the right-of-way. Some separations are landscaped spaces, but the usual width is between 10 and 20 feet. Because the freeway, presently intended for personal automotive vehicles, may someday provide a channel for mass transportation vehicles, an ample dividing strip may one day demonstrate the economy of its original purchase; a minimum of 30 feet and a desirable width of 50 feet should be planned. Oversight, indifference, or lack of vision in planning freeways will cost the people much in money as well as time, confusion, and discouragement; that is demonstrated today in some cities where the freeway and mass transportation plans were not integrated.

Safety and efficient flow of traffic have been enhanced by improvements in lighting and directional signs. Lighting for night travel has made great progress; some highways have become ribbons of lighted pavement requiring no headlights for adequate vision and safety. Although not yet fully developed and employed, color may be advantageously used to identify certain lanes for speeds and points of departure from the roadway. The scale of letters and placement of signs that indicate directions, places, and distances are important factors in the design of trafficways for smooth and safe circulation.

TRAFFIC LANES

Traffic hazards arise from excessive speed, but they may also be due to deficiencies in the design of roadways. Separations between traffic traveling in opposite directions and the elimination of intersections are essential. The provision of off-street parking so curb parking may be prohibited is necessary; a single disabled car can reduce a three-lane roadway to a two-lane street and add the hazard of rapid accumulation of vehicles at this bottleneck. Given the free flow of traffic that these improvements offer, the effectiveness of the car depends upon the shape of the roadway over which it travels.

Traffic lanes vary from 8 to 15 feet; this variation is not a fault until it occurs within the same line of travel. The local street may have a width of 10 feet and the through-traffic artery may be 12 feet, but the width should be constant for each. Local streets serving residential areas are customarily designed for a lane of 10 feet, being 4 feet wider than the standard American automobile and none too great a separation between two moving vehicles passing at a rate of 35 miles per hour. On highways the width is generally 12 feet, increased to 13 or 14 feet on the curves.[5] When the freeway is designed for the operation of trucks and buses, a lane 15 feet wide should be provided.

The width of the land intended for parking vehicles is usually 8 feet; this assumes the wheels will be 1 foot from the curb and allow 3 feet between it and a vehicle passing along the centerline of the adjacent moving lane. If the parked vehicle is a truck, it will project into the adjacent lane, creating a sideswiping hazard. It seems more sensible to make no distinction between the width of a lane for parking and one for moving vehicles; in peak hours when curb parking is prohibited, this lane adds a trafficway to the otherwise overcrowded street.

---

5. Frank H. Malley, *Location and Function of Urban Freeways, Post-War Patterns of City Growth* (New York: American Transit Association).

Adjustments to the new character of modern vehicular travel have been slow, and the change in approach to the design of roadways has probably been most apparent at the points of intersection. Traffic circles were the first attempts to merge traffic flow and avoid the conflicts of left turns. While traffic was light, the circle was adequate, but the increase in number of vehicles re-created congestion at these points.

The cloverleaf was the next step toward a solution of traffic interchange, but it has a weakness. Drivers intending to turn left must cross beyond the intersecting street for which they are destined and then make a right turn into a curve that leads back to the cross-street they seek. It is confusing for drivers traveling at a fair rate of speed to find themselves beyond the intersection they want and then to turn right for a left-hand direction. Familiarity with a roadway offsets this sort of confusion, but it is not an assurance of the safest form of traffic artery.

Other types of interchange structures have been designed for the purpose of overcoming the weaknesses of the circle and cloverleaf, and most have incorporated the best features of each. However, all designs assume that slow vehicles remain on the right-hand side of the roadway and, because left-hand turns on level roads are a handicap to speed and safety, movement from the freeway is channeled to the right regardless of the destination of the vehicle. In the General Motors exhibit at the 1939 New York World's Fair, Norman Bel Geddes presented a freeway design in which a driver would turn left from a completely separate left-hand lane. This turn would have the same radius of curvature as the right-hand turn. He observed that the term *slow lane* is a contradiction of the freeway system and that the speed of vehicles would probably be similar in all lanes. Bel Geddes proposed that the number of through lanes continue undiminished regardless of the left and right turns, and he provided a lane for transition into the left-hand turn as was customary for the right-hand turn. Similarly the transition lanes for entrance to the freeway would be from both left and right sides of the roadway.

The adoption of this logic after 50 years has been rather slow, since it suggests some changes in the engineering that established the habits of drivers who have grown accustomed to the present formula for turning right out of a freeway no matter what direction may be the ultimate destination. It also necessitates some changes in the attitudes of the engineers who design the highway system. Meanwhile, the knotty problem of the smooth and safe intersection of traffic is met by some rather fantastic combinations of the circle, the universal, and the cloverleaf.

INTERSTATE HIGHWAYS

For many years names like "Santa Fe Trail" and "Lincoln Highway" have lent romance to the roads that cross our vast countryside. The Bureau of Public Roads has supervised the construction of highways and has received federal aid since 1916. Highway planning is currently being performed by the separate states in cooperation with the Bureau of Public Roads.

By 1989 the Interstate Highway System had been expanded to include 49,629 miles, much of which is freeway. In addition the Federal Aid System includes over 400,000 miles of secondary highways, most of which are in metropolitan areas. Rural areas are served by 3,131,669 miles of roadways. During the 1980s, because of economic recession, new routes and some maintenance was delayed.

However, in 1990 and 1991 the President and Congress approved billions of dollars to upgrade and expand the Interstate system.[6]

1991 Federal Legislative Action

Surface Transportation (S. 904/H.R. 2950)

Allows state and metro areas, for the first time, to choose highways, mass transit, bikeways, or pedestrian paths. Six-year, $151 billion program more than doubles existing planning funds.

Billboard Reform (S. 593/H.R. 1344)

Restores to state and local governments the right to regulate billboards. Prohibits new billboards along federally assisted roads.

Scenic Byways (S. 1490/H.R. 2957)

Establishes new program to designate and protect scenic areas along highways. Includes $80 million over six years for corridor management planning, scenic easement purchases, and billboard removal.

Great highways such as the Pennsylvania Turnpike have been designed for modern motor travel over long distances and at rapid and steady speeds. Uninterrupted by traffic crossings and modeled to the topography of the countryside, these sweeping freeways are unmarred by the stigma of commercial advertising. Roadside restaurants and service stations punctuate the route at convenient intervals. It is now possible to travel from New York City to Chicago and beyond on roadways with limited access rights and few, if any, crossings at grade.

MOVEMENT OF PEOPLE

In the movement of people about the city every form of mass transportation, except railways and subways, is routed on a street system originally laid out for the easy subdivision of land and at the time when the horse and buggy was the common mode of conveyance. The result is a paradox: the automobile, which has become the principal means of both local and regional travel, receives the most attention in plans for the improvement of urban traffic but is the least efficient form of urban transport. Furthermore, the bus has replaced the streetcar and the electric train, although they were essentially the most efficient forms of rapid transit for the mass movement of people. That the development of effective transit is the most economical as well as the most efficient means for the mass transportation of the urban population may be apparent by comparison of the characteristics of vehicles and the roadways they use. Many cities are recreating mass transit systems in streets and in special private rights of way.

A typical traffic street with the usual intersections will accommodate 700 to 800 private-passenger automobiles per lane per hour passing a given point. It will carry about 180 buses per lane per hour. Since it is the movement of people rather than the movement of vehicles with which we are concerned, the capacity of the street must be translated into the number of people these vehicles will transport. Studies have demonstrated that private autos carry an average of 1.5 persons per car. Modern "neoplan" buses will carry about 42 persons seated. Articulated buses will seat 60 persons, and double-decker buses will seat 82. The single lane of the typical trunk street will therefore accommodate about 1,200 passengers per hour in private autos, whereas the bus carries 7,200. The capacity of the bus may be further increased with standing passengers, raising the capacity of the bus to 9,000 per hour.[7]

---

6. Bureau of the Census, Statistical Abstracts of the United States, 1991.

7. *Moving People in the Modern City* (New York: American Transit Association, 1944).

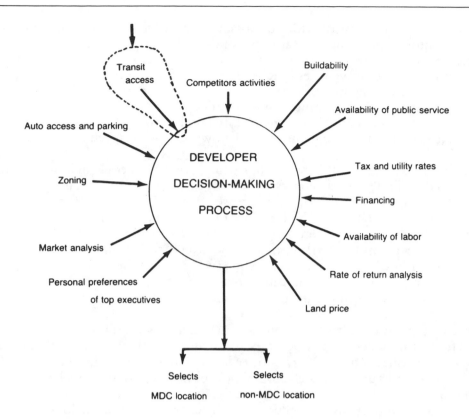

Transit access

Competitors activities

Buildability

Availability of public service

Auto access and parking

DEVELOPER
DECISION-MAKING
PROCESS

Tax and utility rates

Financing

Zoning

Availability of labor

Market analysis

Rate of return analysis

Personal preferences
of top executives

Land price

Selects
MDC location

Selects
non-MDC location

Developer decision-making process. *Developers operate in a complex environment, as exemplified by the diagrammatic description of the many factors that govern their participation in the urban scene. "Toward a Multinodal Urban Structure," Dr. Mary Jo Nuth,* Transportation Quarterly, Eno Foundation, *April 1983. Based on research by Jerry B. Schneider, University of Washington.*

These figures apply to the capacity of a single lane for each type of vehicle. A proportionate increase in the capacity would occur by the addition of lanes if they could be retained as clear channels. The effect of weaving measurably reduces the efficiency of the street. Surveys have shown that weaving reduces the capacity of the second lane of traffic to 75 percent of the single lane, the capacity of the third lane is 56 percent of the single lane, and that of a fourth lane is only 26 percent of the single lane.[8] Three lanes in one direction with unrestricted weaving have a capacity of only two and one-third lanes of clear channels with no weaving.

Studies by the American Transit Association demonstrate the increase in movement of people by the addition of mass transportation facilities on the city streets. A typical city arterial with a pavement width of 60 feet and no curb parking provides three lanes of traffic in each direction. This highway will accommodate about 2,100 private autos in three lanes, assuming reasonable restrictions on weaving, and carry 3,700 passengers per hour. If one lane of autos is replaced by a bus lane, the number of autos is decreased to 1,200 and their passenger load to 3,100, but the bus lane carries 7,200 seated passengers and 9,000 including standees, increasing the total capacity of the route to 9,300 seated and 11,100 including standing passengers.

This study shows that the substitution of a bus lane for a lane of cars on the ordinary arterial will carry two and one-half times the number of people carried by three lanes of cars alone. When standing passengers are included, the capacity of the street is increased to three times the number of people in cars.

8. Ibid.

A limited-access highway with no crossing materially increases the capacity of private automobiles, but this capacity is not increased proportionately with the speed that cars can reach with interrupted flow. Studies show that the theoretical maximum number of vehicles is accommodated at a speed of about 32 miles per hour and that the theoretical maximum number of cars is about 2,060 per hour per lane. The practical maximum number of cars that can be carried at this speed, however, is only about 75 percent of this number, or 1,500 cars per hour per lane, the capacity decreasing above and below this critical speed.

A freeway carrying 1,500 cars per hour will move 2,500 people in a single lane as compared with 1,200 passengers on the ordinary city street. The number of seated passengers carried by a bus increases from 7,200 to 10,000 per hour and 13,000 including standees. The free flow of uninterrupted rail lines (either in the form of a subway or an elevated line such as a monorail) further permits the effective use of multiple trains that carry 27,000 seated and 40,000 including standees per hour on a single track, while two tracks in the same direction, with one local and one express train, can increase the total capacity per hour to 70,000 seated and 100,000 or more including standing passengers.[9]

A six-lane freeway—three lanes in each direction—will reduce the capacity per lane for automobiles from 1,500 cars per hour for a single lane to about 2,700 cars for two lanes and 3,500 cars in three lanes. Three lanes will carry about 6,000 passengers per hour in private automobiles compared with one bus lane carrying 7,200 seated and 9,000 including standees.[10] Buses operating on a three-lane freeway would probably also be reduced in efficiency because of the inevitable conflict with automobiles. If the same decrease as applies to automobiles were applied to the bus, the latter would still carry 8,000 seated persons and more than 11,000 including standees.

Rapid transit lines or some form of overhead train system (the elevated train or monorail) incorporated in a freeway both require a fairly commodious right-of-way. Because there is a firm reluctance to remove any of the land surface from present or potential use for commercial development in existing urban centers, there is resistance to either of these forms of surface transportation into the heart of the city. Because of the overwhelming congestion on city streets and the inadequacy of rapid transit systems to move the people with convenience, comfort, or speed, the subway was constructed as the natural but costly alternative.

The subway marks the final evidence that the city has succumbed to strangulation by urban congestion. An uninterrupted flow of travel for multiple electric trains is accomplished, but at a cost that exceeds every other form of mass transportation. Only the private automobile exceeds the cost of subways; it is four or five times the cost per passenger mile.

MASS TRANSIT SYSTEMS

The future of mass transit lies in the development of an integrated system that will serve the people who need the service most. The fares must be geared to the income level of its primary users. The aged and lowest-income groups should ride free. The system must be built to take people to places of employment and centers of activity. Most of all the system should be a part of the reconstruction

9. Ibid.

10. Ibid.

of those portions of the city that have fallen into decay. In this way it would be built into the development itself and people would use it, especially if there were no garages for the storage of automobiles and no off-street or on-street parking permitted other than for brief periods or in cases of emergency.

Every large city in the world has some type of mass transit system. One can imagine what travel would be like in cities such as New York, Paris, and London if mass transit did not exist and automobiles carried no more than 1.5 passengers per unit. Congestion would be absolute: movement would not be possible.

The subway is a mass transit means that does not impinge on vehicular street movement. There are subway systems in London, Paris, São Paulo, Peking, Hong Kong, San Francisco, New York, Chicago, Montreal, Washington, D.C., and Moscow, as well as in other cities. One may be critical of a system that at times packs people together as if they were inanimate objects, but a better method for moving large numbers of people has yet to be found.

Recent mass transit systems such as the BART system in San Francisco have been criticized because their highly sophisticated mechanisms sometimes break down easily. Another criticism has been that these systems do not fulfill their intended purpose of reducing automobile traffic into the central city. Further, critics claim they do not serve poor people, the people who need them most, as service runs mainly through the affluent areas where personal transportation is more readily available.

How to finance mass rapid transit has been a controversial public issue. Studies all over the world indicate that nearly all systems need heavy subsidy, even if fares are substantially raised.

Statistics have indicated that, for most public transit agencies, 40 percent or less of the cost of operations is generated at the fare box. However, considerable additional revenue is generated from the increases in property taxes by the improvements located adjacent to the transit stations, mainly from increases in both the intensity of uses and the densities of the new housing developments built after or concurrent with the development of the mass transit routes. The funds derived from the tax revenues usually go into the general fund and only thereafter possibly appear as a subsidy for the transit operations.

Support, Cost, and Revenue

No great city's public transportation is supported by user fares except Hong Kong's. Public transportation nevertheless can stand as the hallmark of a great city. When transit systems are designed and constructed after the city has developed, as is usually the case, the costs tend to become exorbitant and the construction disrupts the fabric of the city physically, socially, and economically. Resistance to building becomes great as potential impacts on residential and commercial activities over an extended period of time are contemplated.

During the latter days of President Jimmy Carter's administration massive financial assistance was provided to cities interested in the development of experimental transit systems that would modernize the services in critical locations. The Urban Mass Transit Agency (UMTA) granted funds for development of "people movers" in many cities, discussed later in this chapter.

Subways

Tokyo has the most extensive subway system in the world, over 300 miles reaching from the heart of the city to the suburbs. The system carries more

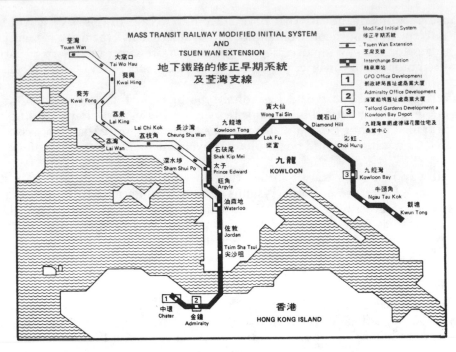

Hong Kong mass transit system.

passengers per day than any other except the Moscow system. It is integrated with the interurban and intercommunity system that leads to all parts of Japan. The trains are modern, color-coded to make use easy even for the uninitiated foreign traveler. The Hong Kong subway has been in operation since March 1980. Called the Modified Initial System, it is 25.8 miles long with 38 stations, twelve underground and three above ground.[11] Apart from a short overhead section at the Kwun Tong end, construction has mainly been accomplished by bored tunnel with an immersed tube under the harbor. The service provides transportation for 2.1 million passengers a day at fares varying from 30 cents to 1 U.S. dollar a trip.

In July 1977 approval was given to extend the Modified Initial System from Prince Edward Station in north Nathan Road to the Tsuen Wan new town in the New Territories. The extension commenced operation in late 1982 and is to be completed in 1992.

The new underground stations are being constructed by the "cut-and-cover" method. They have been designed around the central island platform concept in order to segregate passenger movements in urban areas. Stations are spaced at intervals of about 0.6 mile; across the harbor between Admiralty Station and Tsim Sha Tsui, the spacing is 1.5 miles.

"People Movers" All forms of transportation that carry persons from one location to another can be classified as people movers. However, during the 1970s and 1980s the term took on a different connotation. It meant the introduction of special forms of local transportation, some bordering on the fanciful. Moving sidewalks were used at airports to take people to boarding gates. Los Angeles proposed building a system in the central business district; the idea still persists, to the point of funds

11. Hong Kong Government Information Service Publication, June 1991.

Subway and station, Washington, D.C.

being allocated to plan the system. Denver has a people-mover system made up of low-slung buses that make boarding from the curb most convenient; the buses go from the capitol to the central business district. The Denver program entailed much more than a transportation system; concurrent with the people mover was the major redevelopment of its corridor, designed to the highest standards, resulting in an area of greatest beauty as well as providing for convenient travel. UMTA funded the entire program.

The city of San Bernardino, California, has been talking for many years about an overhead system that will connect its two major shopping areas and continue up into the San Bernardino Mountains to serve the resorts located there. Such a system would be especially convenient for skiers during winter months; current economic conditions, however, do not warrant this facility. Disneyland in Anaheim has used a monorail people mover to take people to the main hotel center. Seattle, Washington, built a monorail for the World's Fair held there in the 1960s. This type of people mover has been in use for many years in Germany.

Monorails have captured the imagination of the futurist. Examples, however, indicate that they are no more than a modernized elevated railway, with the same blighting effect on street architecture. The stations occupy large spaces at critical locations. The posts and columns rooted in the street and the heavy structure of the monorail track interrupt the streets and reduce their carrying capacities.

A variety of specially designed transit systems, coupled with the standard bus, streetcar, subway, and elevated railroad, constitute the major efforts by the Urban Mass Transit Agency of the federal government to make local transportation more convenient and, in some cases, safer.

The greatest failing of the mass transit system, if it can be called a system, is that it consists of an unintegrated grouping of individual operations, each functioning in its own little world without cross-transfers or transfer points.

The Multimodal System

The monorail, Seattle. *The impact of the overhead structure on the street and adjacent property is obvious in the photographs.*

Many transit systems need a comprehensive, coordinated plan and program of operation, in which the passengers could move rapidly and conveniently from points of origin to destinations with a maximum of comfort. The program could coordinate trains, subways, buses, helicopters, and ferries into a planned operational system where movement from one form to another could be accomplished at centralized locations.

Multimodal transfer systems are difficult to achieve. They take years to integrate and require political cooperation between cities for the benefit of the whole. The

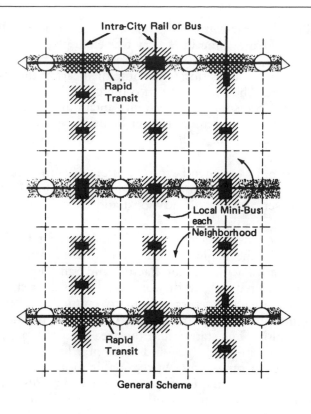

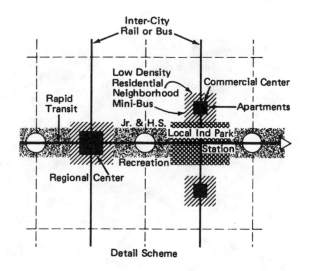

Multinodal mass transit. *The neighborhood unit is the common denominator in the urban structure. In this plan, a minibus system serves each neighborhood, circulating to and from the local commercial centers, parks, playgrounds, and schools. An intracity and intercity rail or bus system links the commercial centers with major rapid transit service to central business districts, cultural facilities, airports, railroad lines, and concentrated industrial or other employment centers. Although technically the system would be organized in a general grid, this does not imply a "gridiron" street layout or pattern of land uses. Alignment would be adjusted either to variations in natural terrain or in existing cities, to established and desirable permanent land uses. Weaning people from the automobile to mass transit will require both convenient and frequent local transit— the minibus—and parking restrictions in concentrated business and cultural centers. Until most of the urban community recognizes the extravagance of the automobile, and until a convenient mass transportation system is available, massive automobile parking space will be required at rapid transit stations. In the diagram, solid lines indicate the transit lines; solid spaces, the local and regional commercial centers; cross-hatched areas, the local industrial parks; circles, community, elementary, or high schools; dotted areas, recreation facilities. Dash lines outline neighborhood areas.*

Metro system of Washington, D.C., had eleven separate governmental entities to deal with in discussions of fares and transfers. The system in Paris, France, fared much better; there was a maximum degree of consideration and cooperation among all parties involved.

Transportation Centers. Most multimodal systems will need a central terminal where easy exchange of type of transportation will be possible. During the age of rail transportation, there developed in the world's large cities fine examples of terminal structures, well located to serve the heart of the cities in which they were located. With the near demise of passenger rail service in all but a few parts of the world, these old and sometimes very fine examples of classical architecture have been abandoned, many destroyed. However, those that through chance have remained are now in a position to become the heart of the future multimodal transportation system. They can bring into the critical areas of a community all the elements of the transportation system, including commuter helicopters, trains, buses, subways, and even commuter boats from offshore islands as in the Atlantic and Pacific oceans, the Gulf of Mexico, and the Great Lakes.

These reconstituted hubs can then become centers of commerce as well as transportation, reclaiming old areas and encouraging the rehabilitation of both the housing and public services that already exist and are in need of attention.

In the mid–1980s the Los Angeles Rapid Transit district began condemnation proceedings to obtain the neglected Union Railroad station, which is owned jointly by the Southern Pacific, Union Pacific, and Santa Fe railroads. This magnificent structure is located close to the central business district, the historical area adjacent to the plaza, the civic center, and many cultural facilities. It would serve as the multimodal center for the totally integrated transportation system serving the Los Angeles region. The station and the area around it are readily adaptable to serve as the locus of railroad, bus, and helicopter lines, as well as the subway lines that are under serious study. With imagination, this multimodal center could become one of the prime terminal and transfer points for all of the local, interurban, and long distance travel modes. Vast areas for automobile parking could be located within easy walking distance.

Multimodal transport system.
Rail, highway, and freeway, Santa Monica, California. (Courtesy of State of California Department of Public Works, Division of Highways.)

Multimodal transport system. *Gondolas, vaporettos, and seagoing ships, Venice, Italy.*

In the October 1990 issue of the *Transportation Quarterly* of the Eno Foundation for Transportation, Westport, Connecticut, Dr. William F. Stephens describes the following techniques for improving the effectiveness of ride-sharing programs.

Car Pools and Ride Sharing. People working in the same area or industry can share the ride to work with their neighbors. Thus one person's automobile would be used once a week while their neighbors ride free, thus saving energy, nerves, and considerable money in fuel and parking fees.

Park and Ride Areas. These locations along the travel route are set aside by the local community for persons arranging rides with someone they know or using a local shuttle bus to take them to their jobs. The arrangement of travel schedules would be through the employer's offices, since the cost to the employer would be minuscule compared with the cost of land and improvements for on-site parking.

Well-Planned Urban Transit Built to Serve the People. This could be a joint venture, with the local people and business community sharing the costs. The service should be convenient in terms of time and location of destinations, as well as cost-effective for the riders in comparison with driving their individual automobiles.

All over the United States and Canada light rail and subway systems have spread to reduce the tremendous space requirements of the automobile. Atlanta has the MARTA subway-surface system; Baltimore has a 14-mile Metro line; Buffalo has a light rail system; Calgary has a fine light rail system in the street and in private rights-of-way; Edmonton has a light rail system and a subway; Chicago has an extensive system, including the ancient elevated railway and many miles

Partial Solutions to Traffic Overload

Progress in Development of Light Rail and Subways

of transit in the median strip of its freeways, a total of 97 miles of mass transit lines; Miami, Montreal, New Orleans, Philadelphia, Sacramento, San Francisco, Los Angeles, San Diego (a private right-of-way to the Mexican border), Washington, D.C., and many other cities have engaged in construction of ways to relieve motor vehicle congestion.

Transit vehicles are being designed with spacious aisles and seats; most have accommodations for people who have disabilities and provide reduced fares for senior citizens. When rising gasoline prices and shortages and the high cost of parking in the central cores are combined with the bumper-to-bumper road conditions, number of accidents, and rising insurance premiums, there may in the near future be a greater demand for mass transit.

CONGESTION MANAGEMENT PROGRAM

In recent years one of the mandatory programs in the comprehensive plan deals with highway congestion management. This program involves both planners and traffic engineers. The planners' responsibilities relate to the appropriate designation of land uses in the land use element of the comprehensive plan, in the zoning plan, and in specific plans adopted to implement long-range programs.

The planners in cooperation with the traffic engineers must design the highway plan to eliminate congestion wherever it tends to occur. The use of by-passes and one-way streets, the elimination of left turns wherever intersection congestion is prone to happen, implementation of appropriate signal plans for critical intersections, prevention of traffic tie-ups due to crossing blockage, and use of other mechanical devices such as signal controls to assure continuous flow are but a few of the joint contributions to the solution of the problem.

Major highways which have had three traffic and a parking lane for each direction of travel, have converted the configuration to two wider lanes in each direction plus a central well defined deceleration lane for left turn movements wherever it is necessary to gain access to abutting property.

Bicycle transit—*a way of life in China.*

Other types of planning to prevent congestion include arrangement of working hours to reduce the volume of traffic in areas where concentrations of employees are engaged in economic activity. Cooperation between plant operators and traffic congestion elimination programmers is essential to this aspect of the solution to the problem. Both public and private pressures and incentives may have to be applied to assure the accomplishment of program goals.

THE BICYCLE

The bicycle, used as a health and pleasure vehicle for many years, has become an important link in the transportation chain. The energy shortage in 1976 caused their widespread purchase. Perhaps their use in urban areas in America has not yet become as important as it has been in many of the European cities, such as Amsterdam, Holland, but it is approaching this in certain localities. In Davis, California, college students attending the University of California campus use the bicycle as their primary means of movement within the city.

In the People's Republic of China the bicycle is the major means of transportation in cities. While buses serve along major routes, bicyclists are primary occupants of public highways.

The bicycle, like the pedestrian, poses many problems as it competes with the automobile for the use of the streets. The visibility of the bicycle rider going in the same direction as the automobile traffic creates a target. Reactions on the part of both motorist and cyclist are uncertain. Bicycles must move across intersecting streets. Bike lanes adjacent to the curbs often end at parked vehicles, and the bicycle must veer out into the traffic flow. This danger is apparently overcome by prohibiting parking, but there are still the problems of enforcement. Night riding, when the bicycle may not be as visible, may also lead to accidents.

The proper training of bike riders has become as essential as the proper training of automobile drivers. They should be licensed only after passing tests dealing with their safety and that of others.

Bicycle and pedestrian walk, Tapiola, Finland. *The routes are carefully marked to separate the pedestrian from the cyclist.*

Bicycle and pedestrian parkway in wide setback, Palm Springs, California.

Bicycle transportation means parking must be provided.

However, the only truly safe way to deal with the bicyclist is to construct separate roadways paralleling sidewalks. The separation of the pedestrian from the motor vehicle has been a part of the Radburn plan since the 1940s. It is only reasonable to extend this idea to the bicyclist.

THE PEDESTRIAN

People walked on all occasions during urbanization in prehistoric times. The horse, mule, and the like, permitted people to move a little more rapidly. After the wheel came to be used in conjunction with the horse, locomotion became still more rapid. During the mechanical age, steam, electrical energy, and petrochemicals gave the wheel added power. For all practical purposes, motorized vehicles took people off their feet. Briefly stated, industry had produced mechanized mobility for the masses.

Today one seldom goes to the marketplace on foot. In cities where mass transportation is inadequate, the individual automobile is practically indispensable, although in cities like New York it is generally impractical because of limited and expensive parking facilities.

Chicago Loop. *Adequate setback and space are provided, but the environment for walking is uninviting, discouraging pedestrian use.*

When the automobile is put to rest in a parking lot, people momentarily become pedestrians once again. They are on their feet as they travel the short distances from parking to place of employment, or to the shopping areas that have been designed to make pedestrians' activities convenient and comfortable.

At these shopping areas, unless the car is separated from pedestrian travel lanes, people become targets for the automobile. Statistics indicate that more than 300,000 pedestrian accidents occur across the United States each year, with more than 8,000 fatalities.[12] This latter statistic represents one-sixth of the total national highway death toll.

Improvements. As the accident rates and death tolls have increased, there have been efforts to provide for greater pedestrian safety through better street design, improved lighting of crosswalks, the use of traffic lights, and the slowing of traffic in areas where pedestrian movement is greatest.

---

12. David I. Davis and Lawrence A. Pavlinski, *Traffic Quarterly*, Eno Foundation for Transportation, July 1978.

Palm Springs. *Inadequate width and conflicting utility uses make this sidewalk both dangerous and impractical for pedestrian use.*

The shopping areas themselves have been improved. Almost all of the newly developed major shopping centers are enclosed groupings of stores with a pedestrian safety area in the center. This is not a new concept, but it is newly used in most planned commercial centers. However, in the places between where the automobile is parked and the pedestrian safety areas, it is still open season on pedestrians.

Pedestrian grade separations have been a part of the more sophisticated and costly arterial designs, but they are seldom placed in local areas where people are supposed to do most of their walking. These separations can go over or under the arterial. They were given their best treatment by Clarence Stein and Henry Wright. Here the separation caused the roadway to rise slightly and the underpass to depress about an equal amount. The dangers associated with the overpass, such as vandals throwing objects at moving automobiles, were eliminated, as were the dark, often dirty corridors of the underpass. The midway approach provided safety for the pedestrian as well as visibility in the corners: This type of underpass can be found in many of the new towns in Sweden.

The following recommendations for pedestrian safety were made in a July 1978 article in the Eno Foundation for Transportation *Traffic Quarterly:*

1. Pedestrian Midblock Crossing Barriers. At locations where significant numbers of pedestrian accidents result from midblock street crossings, physical barriers along the curbline or in the median of a divided roadway are effective in channelizing these crossings into intersections, where vehicular movements can be controlled by traffic signals or stop signs.
2. Midblock Crosswalks. Although midblock crossing of streets by pedestrians is generally more hazardous than the use of intersection crosswalks, under certain conditions a marked crosswalk at a midblock location between two widely spaced intersections will reduce pedestrian accidents.
   An example would be a midblock location that has a large parking facility on one side of the street and a major pedestrian trip generator on the other side— such as the entrance to a large shopping center, a university campus, or a sports stadium. Rather than erect barriers to force people to walk relatively long distances from the parking area to their destination, a marked crosswalk may be preferable particularly if traffic signals are installed to control vehicular movements.
3. Diagonal On-Street Parking. On main streets with business frontages, and with only one or two lanes for traffic in each direction, diagonal on-street parking has been found to be hazardous in terms of collisions between motor vehicles. But in terms of pedestrian accidents, such diagonal parking has been found to be safer than parallel parking at the curb. This is because it reduces "dart-out" accidents—the leading type of pedestrian accident—which occur when a person runs between parked cars onto the street.

Since many cities all over the world have been built to accommodate the automobile and it's 1.5-person average occupancy, it would appear to be less than reasonable to suggest walking as a means of transportation to and from places of employment or shopping. The workplace is often far from the home, which is in a low-density outlying subdivision. Planning for adequate systems of streets and arterials is therefore most likely to be with us for quite a while, at least until humans gain the wisdom to find adequate, desirable homes for themselves and their children in close proximity to the workplace and shopping centers. Experience has indicated that the two ingredients in that formula, finding a home close to work and finding work in one's field in an environment of highly individualistic, self-interested industrial location policy, seems unlikely.

So while diagonal on-street parking is not recommended on main streets unless they have ample width for vehicles to back out of parking spaces without disturbing the traffic flow, it can sometimes be applied with pedestrian safety benefits on wide residential streets.

How can these various and diverse characteristics of contemporary vehicles be merged into an effective transportation system?

INTEGRATION OR DISINTEGRATION

It is apparent that a change must be made in the present street system, and this change may affect other aspects of land use. The freeway has been hailed as an instrument with which to create a new framework for the community of tomorrow. The freeway can aid in relief of congestion in the central areas of the city, but the rebuilding of these areas to provide ample parking space and an environment as attractive as the outlying areas of the city must be created; otherwise, the freeways may become the arteries that carry the people past the outmoded central districts to the shopping districts that have their stakes in a well-planned, convenient, and pleasant environment of this day.

Adequate parking space, planned open space, and commercial development may be substituted for the futile strip zoning along traffic arteries which themselves will be replaced by the freeways. With replanning, the business district will be removed from traffic congestion and obtain ingress and egress for vehicles and pedestrians. Curb parking may become a thing of the past; with some exceptions the space along the curbs in central areas is less than one-fifth the amount of parking provided in lots and garages, and yet it is all hopelessly inadequate. Traffic flow is reduced about one-half by curb parking on the average street, making it a serious obstruction to traffic movement. The courts have held that streets are for the movement of traffic and not places for storage of vehicles. Since they are separate functions, terminal parking space for cars, the traffic arteries, and the space for circulation of pedestrians with their access to shopping and commercial enterprise, will be planned as separate but integrated elements.

There must be a plan for transportation, and this plan must become a guide for each improvement in the city. During the long and arduous period in which the plan is being formulated, first-aid remedies will be necessary. Traffic bandages and tourniquets, splints and casts, will be needed. It is necessary, however, that the distinction between the expedient nature of these measures and permanent solutions be continually recognized. The breakdown represented by traffic congestion must be treated in the most infectious spots to keep the urban traffic stream flowing, but these devices of traffic engineering must not be confused with basic improvements in the street pattern and mass transportation. Too frequently they are interpreted as one and the same, with the result that the prospect of a solution to the urban traffic and transportation dilemma is given up as hopeless. Students of the problem realize that disintegration will eat deeper into the cores of the urban environment and lead gradually to an eventual complete loss of values, unless basic changes are made.

The evidence is already present in cities. We see the decay at its worst in the movement or, to put it more accurately, the retreat of sound business from the blight that has consumed former "high-class" districts. We also see the creation of entirely new business centers, and we see them growing temporarily prosperous at the expense of the older established areas. Finally, we see the first-aid methods being repeatedly used in the vain attempt to revive the dying areas.

TRANSPOR-TATION PLANNING

We can see our problems on all sides, in the confusion and waste in time and energy as well as in the accidents and loss of life that are the response to an almost anarchic approach to the manner in which we conduct our affairs. It is not enough to say that we must plan better, for we must do that too, but there should be a charting of a direction by which we can resolve the ever-worsening conditions. There must be a will to doing and the direction of the fertile minds of our inventors and technicians to solving the problems we know and can see. There must be a plan for action allocation of our financial resources to see the jobs done. There must be a reorientation of our education to rescue our people away from the diseducating influences of the current radio and television concentration on violence and scenes of the good life of the rich and famous.

Boris Pushkarev and Jeffrey Zupan, in an article published in the *Transportation Quarterly* of the Eno Foundation for Transportation, set forth their opinions on measures that combine transport and community development to restore the use of mass transportation:

> Public policies favoring dispersal of urban settlement and the proliferation of the automobile have contributed to a decline of public transportation in the United States. Today, 95% of all motorized travel in urban areas is by automobile; only 4% is on public transportation, compared to some 14% twenty-five years ago. And 40% of the nation's transit travel is confined to the Tri-State New York Region—with less than one-tenth of the nation's population.

> Yet political pressure for more and better transit remains firm to:

> • Enlarge the mobility of those who for reasons of health, age, or income cannot drive.
> • Strengthen urban centers and reduce their need for highways.
> • Reduce pollution and conserve energy.[13]

This article demonstrates that only changes in the nation's urban development pattern will achieve all of these goals effectively. Improvements in transit service and fare cuts will increase transit ridership, but they will not cut nationwide auto use much. Restraints on auto use will shift some trips to public transportation.

> Of course, increasing the density of urban areas in American cities flies in the face of a long-term trend. The huge investment in spread-out development cannot be easily abandoned. Return to the older cities is further discouraged by poverty, crime, lack of amenities and high tax rates. Land development practices favor construction on vacant land over redevelopment. Nevertheless, with smaller households, for whom low density is necessarily an asset, with more white-collar and service occupations suited to city environments, with a rising concern for preservation of agricultural and open land, a potential for reinforcing higher density areas does exist. It could lead to less mechanical travel, greater choice, and a more urbane way of life.

> This potential will have to be realized if the nation confronts the need to reduce its consumption of energy and other physical resources. With dwindling reserves of liquid fuels and with the inevitably higher cost of foreseeable substitutes, the long-term viability of an auto-dominated urban pattern is uncertain. Moreover, higher densities save energy and materials not only in transportation but also in domestic and commercial consumption, and by preserving open land.

> There are also more immediate considerations of efficiency. Both labor and other resource costs of public transportation depend on the level of its use; to keep these costs within reason, there must be substantial passenger demand, which in turn depends on the density of settlement. High quality transit service in areas of low density and low demand can easily exceed the costs of the automobile not only in dollars, but also in energy and materials consumption.

Findings

The land-use policies that will do most for public transportation are those that will help cluster nonresidential floorspace in downtowns and other compact development.

> By contrast, increasing the size and compactness of downtowns and other clusters of employment and increasing residential densities, particularly near downtowns, will cut auto trips without reducing people's mobility as much as when the auto is restrained directly: more auto trips will shift to public transportation, and there will also be more opportunities for trips on foot.[14]

---

13. *Urban Transportation, Perspectives and Prospects,* ed. Herbert S. Levinson and Robert A. Weant (Westport, Conn.: Eno Foundation for Transportation, 1982).

14. Ibid.

CHAPTER 26

HOUSING ELEMENT

The continuing problem of housing lower-income groups has plagued society and has roused the conscience of the concerned citizens of the world. As a result of the efforts made, especially in Europe, during the early days of the twentieth century, the improvements were scattered and merely touched on the major problems of big city slums, which remained to fester as part of the disease of poverty.

In the United States, great debate took place between the representatives of the real estate profession and planning–housing improvement supporters. Hugh Pomeroy and Alfred Bettment, prominent planners, proposed massive slum clearance programs and public housing to help eradicate the blight on the landscape and the worst of living conditions for the residents of the slum areas. The real estate profession, led by Herbert U. Nelson, executive vice president of the National Association of Real Estate Boards and the Urban Land Institute, recognized the problem but recommended the "filtering-down process" as the means for solving it. Opponents to this point of view, led by Pomeroy, the executive director of the National Association of Housing Officials, pointed out that that process had only caused discarded obsolete housing to become part of the filtered housing in areas where these substandard conditions were already evident.

As a result of the debate the Housing Act of 1949 was passed by Congress and approved by President Truman. William L. C. Wheaton, former professor at

Harvard University, wrote, "The adoption of the Housing Act of 1949 is the most significant event in the development of city planning in the recent history of the United States . . . that congress had at last recognized the importance of cities to the national welfare and the necessity for comprehensive planning. . . ."[1]

In reading the legislation and the intent, it is obvious that this was a housing act and that the redevelopment program was supposed to bring the private sector into the process by providing the incentive of reduced land and improvement costs in the redevelopment area and that the residents of these areas would not be cast adrift to be replaced by persons who could pay the going price for housing. It became the role of public housing thereafter to be the recipient of those who lived in the redevelopment areas, many of whom were untrained in or not knowledgeable about the care and use of the new minimal facilities. These housing areas have therefore deteriorated over the years, especially since the public funds available for maintenance and upkeep were slashed by recent administrations.

Other major objectives of the housing act, which provided for limited commercial uses to satisfy the needs of the residents of the redeveloped area, were soon forgotten. The language of the act was modified to emphasize commercial renewal with a passing gesture at "low- and middle-income housing" located off in one corner of the projects, where it would not disturb the continuity of the commercial developments. Although the redevelopment program is making real changes in the structure of the cities, it has in the opinion of many concerned citizens turned out to be a people removal program and a violation of the intent of the original dedication to solving the housing problems of lower-income people.

Shelter is one of the most important ingredients in the urban pattern. The many programs developed over the years have seldom resulted in an overall plan for meeting all levels of community need. From the broad scope of the Housing Act of 1949 to the present drastic reductions of federal financial participation, there has been little evidence indicating that those with the greatest need for shelter protection have been provided for. In the past, federal government assistance made some inroads on the solution of the most pressing conditions. In recent years, however, that assistance has diminished greatly and the burdens have fallen on state, county, and city governments, only a few of which have the economic resources or social conscience that are essential.

The major reasons for the lack of adequate shelter for low- and middle-income groups are not only the cost of land but also the facilities that are required to satisfy local laws and ordinances, the inflated costs of construction, and the cost of money itself.

Perhaps the most difficult facet of the comprehensive plan to achieve is the housing element. It requires maximum participation by the private sector in order to accomplish the objectives and to deal with the economic problems associated with those features that involve low- and moderate-income groups; these require extensive subsidy by public agencies, many of which are hard pressed to meet even their everyday financial obligations.

---

1. "Housing Act of 1949," *Journal of the American Institute of Planners* 15, Fall 1949.

The essence of the housing element is described in the following extract from the California Planning Law. To a great degree it follows other state laws and is consistent with federal regulations.

Legislative Policy

(a) The availability of housing is of vital statewide importance, and the early attainment of decent housing and a suitable living environment for every family is a priority of the highest order.

(b) The early attainment of this goal requires the cooperative participation of government and the private sector in an effort to expand housing opportunities and accommodate the housing needs of all economic levels.

(c) The provision of housing affordable to low- and moderate-income households requires the cooperation of all levels of government.

(d) Local and state governments have a responsibility to use the powers vested in them to facilitate the improvement and development of housing to make adequate provision for the housing needs of all economic segments of the community.

(e) The Legislature recognizes that in carrying out this responsibility, each local government also has the responsibility to consider economic, environmental, and fiscal factors and community goals set forth in the general plan and to cooperate with other local governments and the state in addressing regional housing needs.

Intent

It is the intent of the Legislature in enacting this article:

(a) To assure that counties and cities recognize their responsibilities in contributing to the attainment of the state housing goal.

(b) To assure that counties and cities will prepare and implement housing elements which, along with federal and state programs, will move toward attainment of the state housing goal.

(c) To recognize that each locality is best capable of determining what efforts are required by it to contribute to the attainment of the state housing goal, provided such a determination is compatible with the state housing goal and regional housing needs. To ensure that each local government cooperates with other local governments in order to address regional housing needs.

Housing Element Content

The housing element shall consist of an identification and analysis of existing and projected housing needs and a statement of goals, policies, quantified objectives, and scheduled programs for the preservation, improvement, and development of housing. The housing element shall identify adequate sites for housing, including rental housing, factory-built housing, and mobile homes, and shall make adequate provision for the existing and projected needs of all economic segments of the community. The element shall contain all of the following:

(a) An assessment of housing needs and an inventory of resources and constraints relevant to the meeting of these needs. The assessment and inventory shall include the following:

    (1) Analysis of population and employment trends and documentation of projections and a qualification of the locality's existing and projected housing needs for all income levels. Such existing and projected needs shall include the locality's share of the regional housing need.

    (2) Analysis and documentation of household characteristics, including level of payment compared to ability to pay, housing characteristics, including overcrowding, and housing stock condition.

(3) An inventory of land suitable for residential development, including vacant sites and sites having potential for redevelopment, and an analysis of the relationship of zoning and public facilities and services to these sites.

(4) Analysis of potential and actual governmental constraints upon the maintenance, improvement, or development of housing for all income levels, including land use controls, building codes and their enforcement, site improvements, fees and other exactions required of developers, and local processing and permit procedures.

(5) Analysis of potential and actual nongovernmental constraints upon the maintenance, improvement, or development of housing for all income levels, including the availability of finding, the price of land, and the cost of construction.

(6) Analysis of any special housing needs, such as those of the handicapped, elderly, large families, farmworkers, and families with female head of household.

(7) Analysis of opportunities for energy conservation with respect to residential development.

A statement of the community's goals, quantified objectives, and policies relative to the maintenance, improvement, and development of housing.

Goals, Objectives, and Policies

It is recognized that the total housing needs identified pursuant to a subdivision may exceed available resources and the community's ability to satisfy this need within the context of the comprehensive plan requirements. Under these circumstances, the quantified objectives need not be identical to the identified existing housing needs, but should establish the maximum number of housing units that can be constructed, rehabilitated, and conserved over a five-year time frame.

Implementation Program

A program which sets forth a five-year schedule of actions the local government is undertaking or intends to undertake to implement the policies and achieve the goals and objectives of the housing element through the administration of land use and development controls, provision of regulatory concessions and incentives, and the utilization of appropriate federal and state financing and subsidy programs when available. In order to make adequate provision for the housing needs of all economic segments of the community, the program shall do all of the following:

(1) Identify adequate sites which will be made available through appropriate zoning and development standards and with public services and facilities needed to facilitate and encourage the development of a variety of types of housing for all income levels, including rental housing, factory-built housing and mobile homes, in order to meet the community's housing goals.

(2) Assist in the development of adequate housing to meet the needs of low- and moderate-income households.

(3) Address and, where appropriate and legally possible, remove governmental constraints to the maintenance, improvement, and development of housing.

(4) Conserve and improve the condition of the existing affordable housing stock.

(5) Promote housing opportunities for all persons regardless of race, religion, sex, marital status, ancestry, national origin, or color.

The program shall include an identification of the agencies and officials responsible for the implementation of the various actions and the means by which consistency will be achieved with other comprehensive plan elements and community goals. The local government shall make a diligent effort to achieve public participation of all economic segments of the community in the development of the housing element, and the program shall describe this effort.

Regional Housing Needs

While it is the intent that each community take care of its own housing needs for all elements of the housing spectrum, it is obvious that many cannot for a multitude of reasons, sometimes related to the lack of available land or the costs involved in the local scene. In these cases it is sometimes possible to participate with nearby communities where these conditions do not exist. It is also a fact that the community may be removed some distance from places of employment or without a reasonable transportation system, thus making the community unsuitable for that segment of the population that has the greatest need.

It is therefore essential that housing be viewed on a broad areawide basis, involving the preparation of a regional plan for the housing element, one that relates housing not only to the needs of people but also to their areas of employment and the availability of a reasonable transportation system.

The California Planning Law contains the following provisions for regional housing needs:

(a) A locality's share of the regional housing needs includes that share of the housing need of persons at all income levels within the area significantly affected by a jurisdiction's comprehensive plan. The distribution of regional housing needs shall, based upon available data, take into consideration market demand for housing, employment opportunities, the availability of suitable sites and public facilities, commuting patterns, type and tenure of housing need, and the housing needs of farmworkers. The distribution shall seek to avoid further impaction of localities with relatively high proportions of lower income households. Based upon data provided by the State Department of Housing and Community Development relative to the statewide need for housing, each council of governments shall determine the existing and projected housing need for its region. The State Department of Housing and Community Development shall ensure that this determination is consistent with the statewide housing need and may revise the determination of the council of governments if necessary to obtain this consistency. Each locality's share shall be determined by the appropriate council of governments consistent with the criteria above with the advice of the department subject to the established procedure.

(b) For areas with no council of governments, the State Department of Housing and Community Development shall determine housing market areas and define the regional housing need for localities within these areas. Where the department determines that a local government possesses the capability and resources and has agreed to accept the responsibility, with respect to its jurisdiction, for the identification and determination of housing market areas and regional housing needs, the department shall delegate this responsibility to the local governments within these areas.

PERPETU-ATION OF DISCRIM-INATION

The free association of families in "desirable neighborhoods" is not usually looked at as "ghettoization" since those living in the confined area are not forced by law to reside there. In fact, however, the prohibitively expensive rents or prices of homes in some areas have made these communities ghettos, effectively excluding from them those ethnic groups unable to afford the price of housing in the area.

A Supreme Court decision in 1964 held that racial or ethnic agreements based on law could not be enforced in the courts since they violated the Fourteenth Amendment of the Constitution. This decision, however, did not terminate the "gentlemen's agreements" that limited the availability of property to certain ethnic groups.

In order to overcome some of the educational problems derived from ethnic and economic segregation, the Supreme Court held that "separate and equal" educational programs were in fact unequal and thus violated the Fourteenth Amendment. It was obvious that the poorer economic districts, black or white, obtained the poorest of facilities and least qualified teachers.

In the mid-1970s the method developed to solve this problem was to introduce the busing of children from one area to schools in other areas in an effort to produce racial and ethnic balance. In some instances, the children are required to travel a considerable distance from their homes. Protests from both the majority and minority sectors became routine, not only in the South but also in all parts of the country. Obviously, the problem of segregation was not being solved by this effort. In fact greater alienation between whites and racial minorities often resulted.

A court decision in California decreed that taxes collected in a city or county shall be distributed to the schools on a student enrollment basis and not on the amount of taxes collected from any one district.

Stratified Communities

Regardless of court decisions, our communities are still highly stratified on the bases of age, color, national origin, and economic status. There are communities where only those people over fifty may reside. We have other locales where only millionaires call the area "home." Recently a project was proposed near Palm Springs, California, where eighteen homes would be located between the greens on a 160-acre golf course. Only 40 acres would be used for the homesites and intended swimming pools and tennis courts. At the other end of the spectrum, as mentioned elsewhere, people are being provided with small homes on parcels of land ever-decreasing in size.

HOUSING THE HOMELESS

No other housing need has spread across the world in the 1980–1990 period faster than that of the tremendous number of homeless men, women, and children. In every city, one finds people sleeping in the parks and in the doorways of buildings. The ages of these people range from the very old to the nursing young, and the physical condition of many indicates the ravages of poverty, illness, and unemployment. It is all too easy to sweep the problems under the rug by claiming that these are human derelicts or people who want to live under these intolerable conditions. "Kind and gentle people" want the federal government to develop a comprehensive program to give these needy people a decent habitat and a chance to rehabilitate themselves into the fabric of the country, in every country where this condition exists. Where the needs are apparent, local communities can do much to assist in the solution of the problems, but many, if not most, are without financial resources to do it alone or are unsympathetic to the needs.

CLUSTER HOUSING DEVELOPMENTS

Ruth Eckdish Knack describes the theories and principles of clustering housing in order to preserve open space.[2] It seems obvious that clustering does have value when it is done to prevent the destruction of valued open space such as agricultural and forest land. Unfortunately, in already urbanized areas where single-family detached dwellings are only one part of the zoning standard, it is achieved by reduced lot sizes. The so-called open spaces provided are inadequate and

---

2. *Planning*, September 1990.

represent only the creation of a minimal living environment with little to compensate for the crowding of homes on ever-smaller parcels of land. As in many other adventures into urban design, the end product, 20 years after, is the measure of what has been gained and what has been lost.

There can be no argument against clustering dwellings in multiple-family zones, where people want freedom from the yard maintenance associated with single-family dwellings. All multiple-family structures, however, should provide insulation against noise intrusion by their neighbors. Space between buildings is supposed to provide that in single-family residential areas. One buys or rents a multiple dwelling with the expectation of conditions that characterize that style of living. Here crowding is normal and the lack of close contact with neighbors guards against loss of privacy. In general, it might be observed that this concern for privacy makes for few "neighbors" in high-rise apartments or in other living areas where close proximity is the mode. There are very few high-density "neighborhoods"—just high-rise buildings and congestion.

CHAPTER 27

COMMERCE AND INDUSTRY ELEMENT

COMMERCE

The marketplace has always been the focal point of the city, a center for the exchange of goods. In the most ancient times it was the open space to which farmers and craftsmen brought their products for barter. The development of transportation and money systems implemented the transfer of goods, and the barter system shifted to a form of retail enterprise. Expansion of commerce created a merchant class dealing in the exchange of goods produced by others than themselves. The importance of cities increased as centers of wholesale and retail trade.

As it did with so many other human activities, the industrial system brought more changes in the nature of the marketplace. Not only did the transportation of goods quicken, but also the growing systems of communications accelerated the exchange of goods. The great cities became the trading centers in which world commerce was concentrated. With the growth of urban population the city continued its functions as the center of trade, but emphasis in the great business centers of the city shifted from the commodities being exchanged to the methods and processes for trading in them. Goods are replaced by pieces of paper —documents—that purport to represent them, and transactions for the transfer of commodities are consummated by an exchange of these documents. Negotiations for the sale and payment of goods transferred from a merchant in Montevideo to a merchant in Buenos Aires were transacted in a London banking house, or the exchange of grain and meat between the producer on the farm and the consumer in the city next door is arranged through the trading centers of New

York or Chicago. The industrial system has introduced to the city a variety of commercial functions never present in the simple marketplace of the ancient town.

Several recognizable types of commercial districts have emerged in the modern city. The most clearcut are the following.

The "downtown" of the large metropolitan city is familiar to every urban dweller. It is the financial and administrative center of its region and, in some cities, it has become the center of business for the nation. New York has its Wall Street, Chicago its LaSalle Street, Paris its Bourse, and London its Exchange district, but every city has its financial center, even though it may serve as a satellite of a greater center. "Downtown" includes the wholesale and retail centers for service to the satellite districts within the city proper or the region. These centers have not been planned; they have simply crept outward and upward within the network of obsolete and confining streets as the fortune of cities and nations fluctuated. The central business district serves a vital and useful purpose as the heart of the city, and its deterioration presents a challenge to business and civic enterprise. Affected by intolerable congestion, noise, fumes, exorbitant land values, and overcrowding, business enterprise shifts restlessly away from the blight eating into the urban core.

A second type of commercial area is the small business district of the satellite community. Dependent upon the metropolitan center for major administrative and wholesale functions, the small commercial center contains the chain retail stores, professional offices, service supply enterprises, motion picture theaters, branch banks, and stock exchanges. In the small, self-contained city, this district will also provide wholesale facilities and include the necessary administrative and transportation centers.

The third type is represented by outlying shopping areas of the city, the community or regional shopping centers. They may overlap with or be the counterpart of the commercial center of the satellite community, but they contain the large-scale service facilities that do not lend themselves to further subdivision and distribution. Among these facilities are large food markets, chain stores of various types, branch banks, telegraph, telephone, and postal district offices, motion picture theaters, branch libraries, and medical and dental offices.

The smallest commercial unit is the neighborhood center. The modern counterpart of the "corner grocery store," the neighborhood shopping center provides the day-by-day commodities for the direct convenience of a limited population. Here, the housewife may perform her regular shopping for the staple goods. It may have an independent grocery store and meat market, television and appliance shop, shoe repair shop, hardware store. a bakery, drug and stationery store, coin laundry, and barber and beauty shop.

Each of the different commercial types are discussed later in this chapter.

The shopping center is just one of many elements that comprise the commercial structure of a city. Legal services, banking, building construction, real estate, and accounting are just a few of the numerous economic activities a city requires. They are as important to the urban pattern as the shopping center, often occupying more total land within a city since they are not usually found in concentrated areas like shopping centers.

Malls are not just another type of shopping area. They are an architectural form wherein the pedestrian shopper is freed from vehicular traffic and where the environment is shaped to encourage shopping and entertain the potential customers.

General business offices are also a part of the commercial structure of a city. Large office complexes in the centers of all of the major cities of the world are occupied by a great variety of businesses and corporation headquarters. Government offices and courts of many types also occupy facilities in or immediately adjacent to business districts. Central city areas that have lost their retail sales attraction are often converted to office or light industrial uses such as garment manufacturing.

The medical center may be one of the exceptions to the scattering usually discerned in other services. The medical center is often located next to a major hospital. It may include rest homes, clinics, and convalescent homes, as well as doctors' offices. Such centers exist in Santa Barbara, California, and El Paso, Texas, and in many communities throughout the United States.

necessary proximity

When communities were small and served a vast outlying area, commercial uses were permitted along both sides of principal traffic routes. A highway passing through the center of a town became the axis for the central business district, and "strip" business developed at random along its route. As the population of the community expanded, additional traffic routes were provided and more business stretched along them. It was then presumed that the highway was the appropriate location for commercial enterprise and, with little further examination of the amount of business a community could support, all existing and proposed street frontage was zoned for commercial use. It is now impossible to classify almost any of these business areas as shopping "centers."

OVERZONING FOR COMMERCE

linear expansion

About one-quarter of the streets in our cities are used as main thoroughfares with the property fronting on them zoned for business use. Harland Bartholomew, internationally recognized planning consultant, estimated that some 25 percent of the total area of the average city is occupied by commercial zoning, whereas the area actually used by retail business is only about 3 percent of the total developed area of the city. This contrast gives some measure of the degree to which cities have been overzoned for business development along the traffic arteries.

The gross excess of commercial zoning weighs heavily on the city. Despite the relatively small proportion of commercial zoning actually developed for business, much of this enterprise operates on a marginal basis. The mortality rate is extremely high: between 15 and 25 percent of retail stores go out of business each

	Business Starts	Buiness Failures
1981	118,000	16,800
1985	249,770	57,253
1986	253,092	NA
1987	233,710	NA
1988	NA	57,096
1989	NA	50,389

year. About one-third of all retail stores have a lifespan of 1 year or less, one-half remain in business no longer than 2 years, and less than one-quarter remain as long as 10 years. Robert Dowling, a prominent real estate counselor in New York City, estimated that four or five times as many stores are in business as the need demands.

Inducement to engage in uneconomic ventures is apparently strong, and the impact spreads far beyond the failure of an individual entrepreneur. Unstable business enterprise breeds physical blight; the "shoe-string" investments in retail business are analogous to the strip character of zoning. In some cities fully half the property zoned for business is used for residences, and these unplanned mixtures of land uses not only create an undesirable environment but also reduce the prospect for consolidation of shopping facilities for convenient access.

Each community has local conditions and practices peculiar to it that will bear upon estimates of the amount of land required, but investigations in a number of cities have shed some light on the relation between population and the business area as a point of departure in developing appropriate standards for the allocation of space for commercial districts. The familiar rule of thumb for commercial development is 50 feet of street frontage for each 100 persons in the area to be served. That the overall amount of space to be devoted to business is an inadequate measure is evident from the observation of cities as well as statistics of land use. The distribution of the space is equally important, if not more vital, to the welfare and service of a city than the total area allocated. The Bartholomew survey disclosed that 44 percent of the total commercial area was in the central business district and 56 percent distributed in the residential neighborhoods. This proportion has shifted somewhat with the development of huge decentralized shopping malls and the conversion of central business districts to offices and light industry.

A survey by the Los Angeles Regional Planning Commission showed a further breakdown in the types of commercial districts.[1] Combined commercial uses amounted to 2.72 acres of land per 1,000 persons throughout the county of Los Angeles. Of this area 1.19 acres was in neighborhood shopping districts, while local or community business districts occupied 0.92 acre; the balance, 0.46 acre per 1,000 persons, was in the satellite commercial centers. An additional 0.15 acre per 1,000 persons was contained in the main "downtown" business center of the city of Los Angeles. These classifications of districts correspond to the four types described at the beginning of this chapter. The Los Angeles County survey included a great variety of communities, ranging from the great metropolitan area of the city of Los Angeles, through the small towns surrounding the city, to semirural areas served by village centers.

In 1990 a research was authorized by a consortium composed of Los Angeles, San Bernardino, Riverside, and Ventura Counties; as well as several public utility companies. The program was coordinated by the Southern California Council of Governments. The study contained material on housing and population, as well as commercial and other types of land use. The research utilized aerial photography and the findings were converted to a digital file for computer analysis. The research was completed in February, 1992.

---

1. Master Plan of Land Use (Inventory and Classification), Regional Planning Commission, County of Los Angeles, California, 1939, p. 38.

Statistical Chart—Commercial Land Use, Los Angeles County, 1990[2]

	Sq. Miles	Acres	Acres/1000
General Office Uses			
Low-medium rise major office uses	11.814	7,561	.853
High rise major office uses	1.535	982	.111
Skyscrapers	0.106	67	.007
Totals	13.455	8,611	.971
Retail sales and commercial services			
Regional shopping malls	3.424	2,119	.239
Retail centers (non strip with contiguous interconnected off-street parking)	11.373	7,278	.821
Modern strip commercial	34.674	22,190	2.504
Old strip development	21.835	13,974	1.577
Totals	71.306	45,561	5.141
Other commercial			
Commercial storage	1.590	1,018	.115
Commercial recreation	5.098	3,263	.368
Hotels and motels	1.981	1,268	.143
Attended pay public parking	0.700	448	.050
Totals	9.369	5,997	.676

Total acres per 1000 people 6.79 (1990 L.A. County Population—8,863,164)

The 60,170 acres of commercial land equates to 2.78 percent of the total land in Los Angeles County (3,952 square miles—or 2,524,280 acres).

Relating the statistics to the urban portions of the county it is necessary to deduct the following:

Open space	33,954 acres
Agriculture	72,769 acres
Vacant land	1,617,039 acres (desert, mountains, etc.)
Water	27,279 acres (rivers, flood control basins, harbors, reservoirs, etc.)
Total	1,751,032 acres
Remaining urban land	778,248 acres
Commercial land	60,170 acres
	Urban land in commercial use 7.75 percent

The 1986 data on commercial uses in the city of Los Angeles, provided by the City Planning Department, indicates that within the 464 square miles of area there were 3,103,000 people and 12,300 net acres of commercial land, a ratio of 4.0 acres per 1,000 people.

An unpublished study by John H. Riedercorn and F. R. Hearle, prepared for the Rand Corporation, Santa Monica, California, in 1968 indicated the land-use trends in forty-eight large American cities. This study indicated that less than 5 percent of the land was used for commercial purposes.[3] In 1987 a report by David B. Van Horn was published in *Viewpoint,* an Urban Land Institute publication. This study of 12 cities in all regions of the United States concluded that 7.7 acres per 1,000 people was the average allocation for cities ranging from 60,000 to 90,000 persons.

---

2. This material was furnished by the Los Angeles County Regional Planning Commission.

3. *Community Builders Handbook* (Washington, D.C.: Urban Land Institute, 1968).

Observation of the structure of cities as they grow and develop seems to indicate that the pattern of commerce and the use of highway frontages as the locale for retail sales has not changed in the minds of highway frontage property owners. Their logic is that highways are inappropriate locations for residential developments and therefore, per se, they are suitable only for business.

THE METROPOLIS AS A CENTER OF COMMERCE

The megacenter is, in its location and activities, the hub of both international and national commercial activity. Its location at great seaports or at the heart of rail and highway and communication networks makes it the pivot about which important decisions are made and trades and exchanges consummated. Few if any of the megacenters were planned, but by their location and initiative they attracted the gathering of groups because of the ease with which they could conduct their affairs. All are part of large concentrations of population, since their services require people to carry on the quantities of work that constituted their services to the nation and the world.

There are many cities of all sizes and shapes in the world, but few can be thought of as megacenters. Some of the most obvious are New York, Paris, London, Rio de Janeiro, São Paulo, Tokyo, Montreal, Berlin, Moscow, and Beijing.

In the United States we find New York City, Boston, and Philadelphia dominate the East Coast. In the South, New Orleans, Dallas–Fort Worth, and El Paso serve as the centers of vast geographic areas, as Chicago, Pittsburgh, and Denver do in the north central area. On the West Coast Los Angeles, San Francisco, and Seattle fit the description. These cities vary in their size and their role in the national economy, but they resemble each other in their function as focal points in the vast regions they serve.

THE FUTURE OF METROPOLITAN DOWNTOWN

There is a widely held view that continued growth in most metropolitan regions is inevitable, and many if not most local governments in these regions have made policy choices in their comprehensive plans and other land use regulations to accommodate, if not actively promote, growth. Typically public debates focus not on whether or how much the region or an individual city should grow but on where growth should occur and how to mitigate undesirable consequences such as traffic congestion and air pollution.

The Role of Downtown in the Region

Despite the existing dispersed development pattern and the individual growth plans of a region's local governments, there is a general consensus in most metropolitan regions that metropolitan downtown is, and should remain, the administrative, cultural, and urban heart of the region. The central role of downtown in the region is a fundamental concept in most metropolitan comprehensive plans.

Even elected officials and planners in satellite cities having very ambitious growth plans of their own would probably concede the primacy of the metropolitan downtown.

If downtown is to continue to serve as the administrative, cultural, and urban heart of the growing metropolitan area, it will, and it should, continue to intensify and expand to accommodate additional jobs, retail activity, and housing. As downtown expands and intensifies, the pattern will take three forms: it will grow up, it will infill, and it will be reused.

When measured against New York, Chicago, and Los Angeles, most California metropolitan downtown's still have relatively low skylines. This has begun to change in recent years as many buildings of twenty or more stories have been built in existing central city core areas and in other emerging high-intensity clusters elsewhere in the expanded metropolitan downtown.

Upward Growth of Downtown

There appears to be general agreement that infill and reuse within the existing urban areas could be better than urban sprawl, and that this will help solve a host of sprawl-related environmental problems. With the danger of additional congestion looming as a consequence of unrelated commerce and transportation systems, infill and reuse are practical means by which to achieve an expanded and intensified regional downtown.

Infill and Reuse of Urban Areas

PRACTICALITY

There is beginning to be a shift in urban development and demographic patterns throughout the United States. The pace of suburbanization is slowing and the pace of central city development is accelerating. This "reurbanization" is occurring in three forms.

First, existing developments are being expanded and intensified.

Second, underutilized parcels and areas are being recycled for commercial, office, and residential uses.

Third, vacant parcels which were skipped-over in the development process are being filled in.

While debate continues about the extent and cause of these changing patterns and whether they are positive or negative, there is support for the proposition that the reurbanization of central cities is both a positive trend and sound public policy. Compared to scattered development on the urban fringe or in isolated agricultural areas, infill and reuse can help to achieve the following urban objectives:

- More efficient use of existing infrastructure
- Increased economic feasibility of transit systems
- Reduced dependence on automobiles
- Reduced air pollution
- Reduced energy consumption
- Enhanced mobility for persons without automobiles, such as the low income persons and the elderly
- Minimized need to convert agricultural lands to urban and suburban uses [4]

One example of where changes are taking place is in the central core or "heart" of Los Angeles, California. Here, through the use of the tax increment laws, tremendous rebuilding of whole areas on the west and northerly side of the central city has occurred. Mostly high-rise commercial structures include some moderate-income housing to fulfill some of the demands of the redevelopment laws and public policy. While not changing the existing street capacities within the core areas, other than developing one-way systems, the freeways have had to handle motor traffic and buses into the area. At present a subway system is being constructed to connect the people who live to the west with the central area and,

4. J. Laurence Mintier, A.I.C.P., is a planning consultant in Sacramento, California.

ultimately, to the San Fernando Valley with its large concentration of residents. All these changes take time and many are late in coming and seldom arrive at their planned destination, like a kitten chasing its tail.

The Skyscraper— Symbol of Big Business

From earliest times people in urban communities placed the temples symbolizing their devotion at the central location of the communities' development. It was almost always either the tallest structure or built upon the highest promontory. In small cities it was the religious institution or the city hall, topped with steeple or dome to thus identify the center of local interest. The Parthenon in Athens is an example of how people felt about their most important institution.

In the age of business, the skyscraper represents the symbol of concentrated interest. It rises above its surroundings and gives the urban area an accent, a rallying point about which to cluster activities. These huge structures are the product of the genius of the American architects, engineers, and builders. When constructed in Europe or elsewhere they are called the "American architectural style."

Beginning with the Woolworth Building to the completion of the twin towers of the World Trade Center in New York City more than half a century later, skyscrapers became the identification for the center of large cities. Other examples include the Sears Tower in Chicago, the Bank of America Building in San Francisco, and the many others constructed in Houston, Texas, and elsewhere. In a sense these structures are the symbol of American devotion to "bigness." Architects and engineers vie with each other to devise techniques to build even higher and create intensity of use in the central core of those cities that have achieved the level of economic maturity to accommodate them.

The skyscrapers are a spectacular venture in city building, but like many other manmade spectacular objects they are subject to monumental problems in times of emergency, the simplest of which may be power failure, when elevators fail to operate.

The striving to meet the sky in the central portion of an already established city exaggerates a multitude of problems at the street level, where hordes of people are concentrated in a limited area about these magnificent structures. The ingenuity of the city planners has yet to devise a solution to the problems associated with a limited street system or to develop the services and amenities that should be planned and constructed hand-in-hand with edifices of this stature.

Floor Space

The amount of land area devoted to commercial uses is but a tentative guide for planning. It may, in fact, be deceptive. It omits the primary measure of floor space. Since the inventive genius of man produced the capability to build structures of unlimited heights, the area of land they occupy has been reduced to a relatively insignificant factor in calculating the capacity to accommodate people and their manifold activities. A defect in zoning practice has been the absence of this measurement in allocating space for the various uses in the urban plan. This was illustrated in the Regional Survey of New York and Its Environs of 1931. That study showed that within the eight-square-mile area between Fifty-ninth Street and the Battery in Manhattan, the average building height was only six stories covering 60 percent of the land, and the average in the Wall Street district was less than eleven stories covering less than 50 percent of the ground area. The lower Manhattan area bristled with the most dramatic display of skyscrapers the

Lakeshore Tower, Chicago. *Mies Vander Rohe, Architect.*

world had ever seen, and some of the tallest buildings ever built were held in the palm of midtown Manhattan. Within the relatively limited land area of the great city of New York, the zoning regulations permitted enough floor space to accommodate a business population of 344,000,000 people. Fifteen thousand people could work in the Empire State Building alone. Of course, these numbers pale when compared to current figures.

The significance of floor space to ground area is further illustrated in the floor area ratio provisions of the 1957 Chicago zoning ordinance which permitted floor space ranging from seven to sixteen times the lot area.

Each community has characteristics that form the basis for determining the appropriate relation between population and the space required for the commercial facilities to serve it. In large part it is the restoration of a balance between the open space for the movement of people and the enclosed space they occupy on which the health of city development depends. Although the differences among cities are recognized, Larry Smith and Company has estimated the relative range

**Metropolitan Per Capita Floor Area Requirements
for Selected Activities**

Activities	Floor Area per Capita (Square Feet)
Retail	20 to 55
Office	2 to 15
Parking (on the ground floor or in structures)	4 to 16
Public	1 to 3.5
Quasipublic	1 to 3.5
Wholesale	5 to 15
Industrial	2 to 15
Residential	200 to 400

of floor space for the principal uses in the urban community, as indicated in the accompanying table.[5]

Parking

Directly related to the amount of floor space occupied by commercial enterprise is the requirement for vehicular parking to serve it.[6] The future stability of commercial districts will depend in large measure on the adequacy and convenience of space for automobile parking available to customers, employees, and services. The effects of deficient parking may be measured by the shifts in commercial space to outlying areas of the city.

The automobile is a special breed of locomotion. By far the most uneconomical mode of transportation, it continues to gain in popularity year after year. The phenomenon may be explained in large part by the extended freedom of movement the automobile offers to the driver. Although excessive in physical bulk, this remarkable machine carries few passengers. That excessive bulk clogs the

Panorama of Manhattan Island, New York. *Looking north from the top of one of the Twin Towers—Congestion.*

5. Larry Smith, "Space for the CBD's Functions," *Journal of the American Institute of Planners,* February 1961.

6. See chapter 34, "The Zoning Plan."

city streets and requires extravagant space for parking. A standing automobile requires 175 square feet of space.

Space for automobile parking is a feature of the shopping center. The requirements vary: some specialty shops are reasonably well served with fewer than five car spaces for each 1,000 square feet of gross floor area, whereas supermarkets may require as many as ten spaces for each 1,000 square feet. An average may be struck at six spaces for each 1,000 square feet in neighborhood centers and eight spaces for each 1,000 square feet in community and regional centers.

An estimate of 5 square feet should be provided per person for sidewalk space. Assuming that there is an average of 100 square feet of building space per occupant and that one-third of the occupants use the sidewalks at one time, it has been estimated that if commercial space in New York City were built to what even the revised zoning ordinance permitted, pedestrians would have less than three and one-half square feet per person in the combined areas of sidewalks and streets.

The enigma compounds. The pedestrian has become a human jumping-jack in the struggle for a place on the sidewalk, and when streets are widened sidewalks are narrowed. Curb parking impedes the traffic lanes and renders the street obsolete as a channel for movement. Land prices exceed any economic value for surface parking, and multideck garages are built. Commercial enterprise is gradually forced to seek other locations in order to conduct business. Mass transportation shows little evidence of correcting the situation. The availability of economical off-street parking is a critical necessity. Chapter 25 contains additional material on parking and its economic impacts.

DOWNTOWN

There is a romance associated with the downtown of almost any city. It represents the tradition that springs from and clings to a place of the beginning. It has been the place where generation after generation has witnessed the vicissitudes of time. It has been the core from which the vitality of the city has found nourishment and energy. It has been the civic center, the place of the city hall, the "big" stores, the theaters. It has been the place people went to when they went to work, and the place they went to when they "went out." It has been the terminus, the hub for railroads, commuting trains, and buses. It has been the headquarters for firms and institutions. It has been the symbol of the life of the city. The central business district and downtown are often synonymous and are used interchangeably. Within this central area of most communities we find businesses, government offices, services, warehousing, and manufacturing. Each operation, in a well-planned city, is in its own segment of the core area, but they all seem to function well together.

A downtown area's strength[7] depends on its ability to remain the employment center of the metropolitan economic region. To help ensure or regain a position of economic dominance, urban centers often look to associations of businesses that are dependent on the center's health. Privately funded central business district associations have frequently been able to help through joint venture planning, by helping develop programs in their respective cities, and by influencing legislation critical to the urban center's well-being.

---

7. The following material is based on the Eno Foundation for Transportation Board of Directors and Board of Consultants, *Report on Joint Conference*, October 1981.

Urban revitalization does not mean returning to the downtown retail function of 20 or 30 years ago. It means becoming vital to the metropolitan area as a service center, a place to work, a place to visit, and even a place to live. It means involving all government levels in a more efficient and productive manner.

Downtown areas are typically major tax revenue generators, and while their land areas are relatively minute, the assessed valuation of downtown improvements are typically a major portion of those of the entire city. Downtown areas have the in-place infrastructure necessary to support economic growth. And oftentimes it is a city's urban centers which form the image of the community.

States are placing great emphasis on revitalizing urban centers. State-sponsored special programs for this purpose are increasing. Perhaps the most effective state action has been enabling legislation that encourages downtown reinvestment. Urban enterprise zones, industrial revenue bonds, grants and low-interest loan programs, tax abatements, and support for public-private venturing are among the legislative milestones passed by state governments. But urban center revitalization remains far from being assured. Inflation coupled with high interest rates are decimating what narrow chance distressed cities have of being competitive.

(The structure of the city is undergoing major changes while downtown is slow to respond.) Its future is uncertain, not because it is expected to disappear beneath the waves of change, but because of the resistance it poses to change itself, the reluctance of its response to the demands these changes are imposing upon it. Whole districts have deteriorated. Throngs of people mingle in the snarl and ugly tangle of traffic and buildings. It is suffocating under an economic oxygen tent, and breath is coming in shorter and shorter gasps. Choked by obsolescent circulation, people and vehicles have too little room to move. Worn haggard, and with shattered nerves, the urbanite bears testimony to these tensions.

The forces gnawing at downtown are manifold, and the lag in positive response to the competition is hurting. Decentralization of retail shopping to major regional centers has been a natural evolution of urban expansion, and the relative position of the downtown business district is headed for modification. Until the Depression of the thirties, over 90 percent of general merchandise trade was concentrated in the downtown area. In recent years the amount of this trade in shopping centers surpassed that in downtown in all cities with more than a million people. While the rate of this increase spirals ever upward, the dollar volume of trade in the downtown areas has been more than halved.[8]

This trend will not subside automatically nor from natural causes. Aggressive and imaginative attention to and understanding of the function of the downtown area as the heart of the city is necessary.

The central city was once the transportation hub. Except in a few large cities the private automobile is the primary carrier today. The central district is jammed with traffic, but one-half or more of the vehicles that crowd the streets are passing through downtown for destinations beyond. Yet the district, bulging with vehicles, resembles an endless parking lot. A striking image of the central city is Los Angeles, where two-thirds of the downtown area is devoted to streets, alleys,

8. Homer Hoyt, *Urban Land,* September 1961.

and parking lots. It is not that this allocation of space is disproportionate when compared with modern shopping centers, but the inferior quality of the space, created by the disorderly scattering of buildings among automobile repositories and traffic-ridden streets, is spoiling the district.

Dispersion of the residential population from the environs of the downtown area has altered the economic base. Those who could afford to have escaped to the outskirts, and a ring of slums chokes the central city. The flight of the suburbs has drawn with it a decentralization of consumer retail business. Perhaps more insidious in its effect, however, is the shifting of other traditional downtown activities caught in this centrifugal movement. Restaurants, department stores, theaters, civic and cultural facilities—museums, art galleries, libraries, auditoriums and sports centers, government offices—and a variety of business firms are moving to new locations along the fingers of commerce stretching outward from the core. These shifts are sporadic, but they seem to be persistent. Consumer shopping naturally seeks proximity to its direct market, but most of the movement is not necessarily induced by improved geographic location nor compatible relationships; it is flight from the congestion of downtown.

A virtue of the central district is its compact form. The hard core of the center is of relatively limited size, rarely exceeding 160 acres. It thus becomes a natural area for ready access by pedestrian communications. The spearheads of commercial expansion spreading outward overextend these lines of communication and drain the internal energy rather than buttress the economy of the core. Property owners seek to sustain their values, but the incentive to risk capital for improvement by absentee owners lags so long as property yields an acceptable return on the investment. Concerted action is thus slow in forming. Oblique maneuvers, slogans, cleanup campaigns, sidewalk twig planting, reflect a basic pessimism. Enthusiasm will be expressed by a frontal attack, a bold and imaginative plan by business leaders to revitalize the district.

It is possible that major retail commerce may not be equated with the future central business district as the functions of downtown evolve. The central area of a great city usually forms into specialized districts: the financial district, theater and hotel district, business and professional offices, the large department stores and shops, and offices of government. These several functions may mingle in a single district of a small city, where they form a fairly compact unit, having their own identification and supporting services.

The future of downtown demands more than piecemeal rehabilitation. The occasional bright new building, replacing some old and wornout structure, is attractive. But the impact of increasing intensity of land use, without change in the street system and parking accommodations, only aggravates an already overburdened circulation system. Business enterprise thus exercises its option to use land more productively, but the public responsibility has not been exercised to update the circulation system and terminal facilities. The "golden noose" draws tighter.

Vehicular and pedestrian circulation are not rehabilitation measures, nor is parking. Rebuilding the broad fringe of slums and blight encircling the city center could attract a multitude of those who have fled to the outskirts. Integrated replanning from within the central district outward, and across the wide twilight zone surrounding it, may restore an enriched quality to this critical area of the city.

The Nature of the Central Core

SIZE AND CONTENTS OF THE CENTRAL BUSINESS DISTRICT

The size and contents of the central business district will be different in each community. Since each urban area of any size has one, the range of the differences will relate to the services that each one performs in the total urban pattern. In a well-planned central business district the types of uses will be in nodes; where the retailing area will be compact and attractive, the financial cluster and general office should be integrated in a "wall street." Banking will be scattered in close relation to the retailing. The wholesaling sector will be distinct and on the periphery as will any manufacturing operations, not interspersed and interfering with the continuity of the retailing. The types and locations of the internal circulation will favor the pedestrian in the heart of the area. Vehicular traffic will be held to the perimeter of the retailing area, and parking facilities integrated with the circulation, not necessarily penetrating into the heart of the retailing area.

Where mass transit serves the central business district it should be closely associated with the heart of the area, making walking distance between terminals and stores short and convenient. When subways are involved they could have station exits into stores, as in Boston and downtown Montreal and midtown Manhattan as well as other cities.

If a major governmental center is also located in the central business district, it should also be in a tightly knit entity on the edge of the district but close enough to the office center to make use of the courts and legal offices an easy relationship.

Cultural facilities such as a major theater district are often an important part of the central business district. It should be closely related to the retail sector and restaurants so that people who use the theaters will find themselves in a lively location where there is a feeling of excitement both before and after a performance. When these facilities are located near a civic center, as in Los Angeles, there are few related social activities near the area and it is dead at night.

Shopping area in front of the opera house, Stockholm, Sweden.

In the past 20 years there has been an enormous investment in the central core of many cities, large and small. As the rebuilding of the core area has taken place, many residents who inhabited the area during the years the poorly maintained properties provided shelter were displaced. Although there were some efforts to make the transition easy, great numbers of the low- and middle-income families became victims of the changes taking place. In San Francisco the mayor initiated a program whereby 20 percent of a project in the core areas was required to provide housing for low- and middle-income families. Other cities are following the same pattern of social responsibility toward their residents.

SHOPPING CENTERS

Population changes between 1960 and 1990 clearly indicate the shift of the urban population away from the central city to the peripheral areas, either just outside of the central city or to the rural countryside. The natural consequence of this change in the location of peoples was the development of commercial uses close to where the people now lived. The nature of the retail commercial establishments changed to meet the shopping habits of the people. While small convenience types of retail commerce continued to develop along highway frontages, some of this type of retail use began to cluster in "minimalls" with their offstreet parking. In addition major retail uses clustered in large and small shopping centers with their variety of outlets and provision of ample offstreet parking, both in the open and in major indoor areas.[9]

Retail enterprise to serve the sprawling residential suburbs gathered in scattered clusters. The corner grocery store was transformed into the neighborhood shopping center. This "new look" suggested a strong contrast with the shabby and congested commercial streets of conventional business districts. Convenient parking without charge was a novel and refreshing experience. Nourished by the volume of new population, the shopping center became popular. The distinguishing feature of the new center is the positive separation between the automobile and pedestrian. Smarting under this new form of competition, the downtown business districts of the large cities and small towns made belated efforts to improve shopping conditions.

Shopping center statistics of the 1960s are still valid in the 1990s. They can be divided into three general categories:[10]

1. The *neighborhood center* is the local source for staples and daily services for a population of between 7,500 and 20,000 people. The average size is about 40,000 square feet of gross floor area, but it may range between 30,000 and 75,000 square feet. The site should be four to ten acres in area. It is usually designed about a supermarket as the principal retail service.

2. The *community center* may serve a population of between 20,000 and 100,000, and extends the services of the neighborhood center by providing a variety store or small department store as the major tenant. The average size is 150,000 square feet of gross floor area with a range of between 100,000 and 300,000 square feet, requiring a site between ten to thirty acres in size.

3. The *regional center* is usually built about one or more major department stores and includes a full complement and range of retail facilities usually found in a balanced small city. It can serve a population from 100,000 to 250,000 people.

---

9. *Statistical Abstracts of the United States,* U.S. Bureau of the Census, Department of Commerce, 1990.

10. *Community Builders Handbook,* Executive Edition (Washington, D.C.: Urban Land Institute, 1960).

Fort Worth, Texas—*Victor Gruen and Associates, architects. This well-known plan for reshaping the central business district of Forth Worth combines the features of the regional shopping center, which are lacking in the downtown of most cities. A circumferential highway system about the district feeds six four-story parking garages. Each garage projects into the central core, and convenient walking distance from the garages to the center encourages the closing of internal streets to serve as pedestrian shopping malls. Service to business establishments is through underground tunnels.*

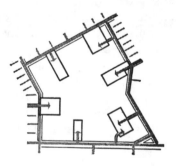

An average size is about 400,000 square feet of gross floor area, although it may range as high as 1,000,000 square feet. A minimum site of forty acres is required; the largest centers require as many as 100 acres.

Examination of the economic base for retail trade is the initial stage in planning the shopping center, and the techniques of market analysis have come into full play by authorities in their development. The steps in such an analysis follow a logical sequence:

1. The trading area involves an investigation of the population, income levels, places and direction of its growth, the existing and potential location and volume of trade in competitive establishments. This information will indicate the volume of trade in relation to the site of the new center.

2. The gross potential sales for the center is derived from estimated expenditures in the trading area. Family income data will disclose the portion devoted to

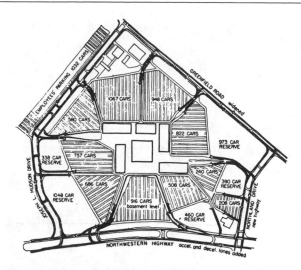

Northland Center, Detroit—*Victor Gruen and Associates, architects. A major regional center of 1,100,000 square feet in retail space, this development includes a theater, auditorium, and community center. Parking space is available for 10,000 cars, and the center is patronized by as many as 70,000 people per day.*

various goods and services—food, furniture, clothing, appliances, drugs, automotive equipment, restaurants, entertainment, miscellaneous merchandise.

3. The potential net sales volume for a new center is related to the sales volume in existing and potential competitive enterprise in the trading area. This requires informed judgment of the proportion of existing trade that may be attracted to the new location. The sales volume per square foot of retail floor space for the various goods will aid in estimating the gross sales in existing establishments offering comparable goods.

4. The physical space that can be supported by the net sales from the trading area may be estimated from the average annual sales per square foot of floor space in the several retail facilities.

5. Anticipated income from the center may be determined by application of the probable rental rates per square foot of retail space, less operating and management costs, taxes, insurance, interest and amortization on the loan for the capital cost for the complete development. The balance represents the net return that may be expected by the developer on his equity investment.

Regional Shopping Centers Revisited

Enthusiasm for regional shopping centers has waned. Originally intended to bolster the city, shopping centers have become magnets for decentralization, hastening the decline of the downtown area as a retail center.

One of the major proponents of large-scale shopping centers and the architect of many throughout the United States, Victor Gruen, recently indicated that they are far from what he had envisaged them to be. He had thought that shopping centers could combine retailing with recreational and cultural activities, thereby promoting the revitalization of central city areas. While not accomplishing all the goals initially expected of them, regional shopping centers have nevertheless been built in central core areas in an effort to reestablish their retail function. Urban renewal has often been the vehicle to free land for such centers.

THE MALL

An animated, colorful scene is the attraction of city streets. The gaudy array of signs by day and night conveys a carnival spirit. The kaleidoscopic spectacle is a

Lincoln Road Mall, Miami Beach—*Morris Lapidus Associates, architects.*

tasteless, even vulgar, display, but it is the asset of the street. People warm to the crowds and the excitement of variety. Shouting out to the passerby by means of vivid display is a commercial necessity. City streets have become traffic arteries. Capturing and holding the attention of a passing motorist intensifies the pressure on advertising. Business notices must project themselves into the street with a galaxy of illuminated devices. (Signs grow in size and novelty in direct ratio to the congestion of traffic.) It is a grim, bizarre reality. Design reform could sterilize the city street scene. Neither the shopper-driver nor the shopkeeper can forsake the nervous disorder. The anachronism is obvious. The automobile is not a natural means of locomotion for shopping; the patron of business is essentially a pedestrian, not a motorist.

It is quite possible that much of the distasteful quality of the commercial street would disappear under its own weight if the patron were readily converted from a driver to a pedestrian. The necessity for the raucous display could be replaced by attention to the goods for sale. Again the shopping center makes the case; the automobile is removed from the street, the shopper returns to the natural status of pedestrian, and the animation of the scene is enhanced. As though it were "proof positive," more dollar volume of business results.

The mall has acquired a magic ring. Contrary to some impressions, it is not accomplished by the simple gesture of closing a street to vehicular traffic. It becomes a complex arrangement of traffic rerouting, parking, service for merchandise delivery and refuse collection, adjustments in utilities, illumination, fire and police protection, and maintenance. Nor is the mall a panacea for the ills that beset downtown. It may become an important element in replanning the central business district, but it is effective only to the extent that the traffic, parking, and general spatial rearrangement are integrated. Not the least element in the program for a revitalized downtown is the spirit with which the property owners and tenants participate. Full cooperation may produce a metamorphosis in downtown and restore it as the heart of the city.

The tragedy of physical and economic neglect that has disfigured so many areas of cities is apparent in the futile and desperate efforts to breathe life into already dead city centers by conversion of traffic streets to pedestrian ways—malls that traverse a desert of vacant stores, empty lots, and outworn advertising signs. The penalty for no planning or bad planning is underscored by this dilemma. In new shopping centers space is reserved for pedestrians separate from automobile parking, and a handsome environment is created free from ugly advertising. The unattractive strip commercial traffic street cannot compete with those advantages. With the deterioration of city centers and in the absence of planning foresight, retail enterprise has been allowed to disperse carelessly to the new shopping centers. The retail function of the city centers further declines until remedies for their recovery are too little and too late.

Some 150 pedestrian malls—including transit malls—have been built in the United States in the last two decades. Most haven't failed outright, but few have lived up to their billing as the salvation of downtown retailing. Just about as many department stores and first-run movie theaters have closed in towns with malls as without, and just as many wig stores, fast-food places, and video-game arcades have opened up.

What's different about the malls is the trees and grass and children's playgrounds—and the ubiquitous Muzak. Now some analysts are questioning whether the park-like atmosphere is conducive to retailing, and some places are going to the other extreme and ripping up their malls. Most, though, are sticking with the mall, while searching for ways to bring it up to date.[11]

The Answer?

Model for proposals for Upland town center. *Using the existing commercial facilities and streets, this mall plan for the small city of Upland eliminated the proposed bypass road system and turned the proposed central pedestrian way into a diagonal parking lot for shoppers' automobiles. The community abandoned the plan for the pedestrian mall as a result of shop owners' fears that the inconvenience of walking a few yards from a parking lot to their stores would deter customers.*

11. Ruth Eckdish Knack, "Pedestrian Malls—20 Years Later," *APA Planning,* December 1982.

Basic to the problems facing street malls is the fact that they are a last-ditch effort to save bankrupt merchants who have done little with their merchandising and less with their investments toward upkeep and modernization. Many street malls in these already deteriorated areas become like "flowers at a funeral" and the streets are reopened to vehicular traffic and diagonal parking.

SOME SUCCESSFUL STREET MALLS AND SOME FAILURES

The street mall in Boulder, Colorado, appears to be a striking success in that it is a "people place," with shops well maintained and the mall forming the core of the working central business district for the city. The mall in Denver can be considered a success, not as a shopping center, but as a people place. At noontime the workers in local office buildings find it a place of rest and relaxation. The buses that ply the center of the mall provide free transportation to the capitol and the cluster of private and public uses nearby. The Capitol Mall in Washington, D.C., and the State Capitol Mall in Sacramento, California, are both monumental parklike approaches for major public buildings.

On the other hand, the "Golden Mall" in Burbank, California, has been bulldozed back to a vehicular traffic street with some diagonal parking while the Santa Monica Mall remains a sad reminder that the businesses facing the pedestrian area must have the potential for attracting shoppers and sustaining their interest. The mall in Fresno, California, does not seem to have lived up to its initial publicity and may suffer as it tries to compete with new air-conditioned shopping centers, especially during the hot summer months.

It would appear that the really successful malls are the totally integrated enclosed developments surrounded by ample free parking and containing a full complement of shops while providing a pleasant atmosphere for the shoppers. Even some of these centers have failed, but the really good ones which are located appropriately to serve a supporting population are doing very well.

BASIC INDUSTRY

The industrial segment of economic activity brings dollars to a region from other areas. Traditional examples are manufacturing, mining, and agriculture. The products of all of these activities are exported (sold) to other regions. The money thus drawn into the local economy is used to purchase locally provided goods and services as well as items that must be imported from other regions. Other, less traditional examples of basic industry are tourism, higher education, and retirement activities, all of which also attract money to a region.

NONBASIC INDUSTRY

The economic activity of nonbasic industry is supported by the circulation of dollars within a region. Examples are the wholesale, retail, and service functions that supply goods and services to local sources of demand, such as businesses, public agencies, and households.

LOCATIONAL CRITERIA

Heavy industry usually has been located where raw materials are available or on sites that are served with adequate transportation of these materials to the manufacturing or processing facilities. There should be adequate transportation to the marketplaces for the products. In addition, many industries require great amounts of power, supplied by generating plants or other sources of energy, such as petroleum or alternate types of fuel. Adequate supply of workers, suitably skilled, is another essential to the success of an industry. Large amounts of capital

Light industrial area in Northern California.

are essential to the construction and maintenance of the plants and the operation of the industrial activity.

Light industry means industrial pursuits that border on commercial, in the sense that they can be accommodated in or near residential areas without conflict with their neighbors. These uses include microcomputer centers such as Silicon Valley located in and around San José and Palo Alto, California. These uses rely heavily on the educational institutions that furnish the scientific personnel on whom they depend and are, therefore, located in or near large universities or groups of universities.

Some cities are substantially developed industrially. These afford their residents opportunities for employment in manufacturing. This does not indicate that a majority of the land area of cities, even those like Gary, Indiana, and south San Francisco, are occupied totally by manufacturing. Even Santa Fe Springs, California, which has 85 percent of its land either used or zoned for industry, has a substantial residential population. Generally, however, industrial cities use only about 10 to 15 percent of their land for manufacturing. Some form of industrial activity is always an essential part of a community's economic structure. However, the term *industry* has many facets. Places of employment, research and development centers, electronic assembly plants, heavy industry, factories, and the testing of atomic bombs all come under the heading of "industry." The kind of industry that a community permits within its confines will determine its quality of life.

Industry involves a wide range of activities, varying from the assembly of small premanufactured items into larger elements to the huge steel mills and chemical plants that are the heart of the economic life of many communities. The past behavior of these industries left scars on the areas where they were located. The buildings were most often ugly and dilapidated. The operations were both noisy and contributed to pollution. Their impact was not only on the physical appearance of the area but often adversely affected the health of nearby residents as well.

With the beginnings of planning—as far back as in prerevolutionary Boston, where wind conditions were taken into account in the location of slaughtering plants—communities began to be concerned about location. Not until recently

Land use pattern; housing, school, and industry.

have communities become involved in regulation of the appearance of establishments and in the control of both sound and odors and other impacts on the health of people in surrounding areas. Atomic energy plants have been a subject of great concern in the present decade.

In cities such as Santa Barbara, Miami Beach, Palm Springs, and Las Vegas, major industry takes the form of tourism. There are also alternate sources of employment for the residents of these communities in commerce, real estate, and general services, but they are usually in some way related to tourism and recreation.

In some communities, educational institutions are the major "industry." They bring financial support to the area through the employment of faculty and service personnel. These people in turn support the shopkeepers and the other institutions that provide housing, food, and other services. One of the purest forms of the educational community is in Davis, California. Once an agricultural college, the University of California at Davis was in 1992 a full-fledged university with approximately 18,000 students. Its influence on the surrounding community is enormous.

Industrial Parks   The development of industrial parks has been due to the efforts of specialized industries to become more completely integrated with the home areas of their employees. The development of excellent architecture within a landscaped environment, the maintaining of noiseless, pollution-free operations, and service roads designed not to conflict with the residential area of the community have made the industrial park welcome in many communities, even the most restricted ones.

Typical standards include the establishment of an architectural board of review, minimum setbacks of twenty-five feet with complete landscape treatment of the open areas, provision of adequate enclosed parking and loading spaces, exclusion of any operation that emits smoke or fumes, and the limiting of noise levels. Performance standards for landscaped areas and plant operations are established to ensure that high standards are maintained.

New Orleans is looking to its improved industrial future with the development of the Almonaster-Michoud industrial corridor, which constitutes one of the few remaining large tracts of undeveloped property in the city. This proposed development will be the largest of its kind in the United States, involving approximately 12,000 acres. Many years of planning led to the adoption of an overall master plan for the projected development.

After a difficult start due to the lack of proper drainage and sewerage systems and a roadway network, Anthony De Vaney, director of the Industrial Corridor District indicated that through fine cooperation with the city of New Orleans many of the handicaps were removed and new large industries like the Pic-n-Save distribution center have joined with corporations like Folgers Coffee, Georgia Pacific, Siemans-Allis Electronics, and Litton Industries to occupy large sites. With the adoption of Mayor Morial's economic development program the city took responsibility for the infrastructure and for the development of the corridor which will include the 7,000 acres established under state law as the Almonaster-Michoud Industrial District. The legislation paved the way for a permanent funding source and a real property tax of 20 mills.

In 1982 a controversy raged over Detroit's "Poletown" neighborhood when General Motors threatened Detroit with the relocation of its Cadillac assembly plant and forced the city to destroy a longstanding ethnic working-class community for a new plant. In an attempt to retain a few thousand industrial jobs, Detroit gave GM 12 years of tax abatements, spent $200 million in public funds for land, and razed more than one thousand houses. This is almost an exaggerated example of reindustrialization, born of Detroit's hard-fought decision to choose economic revival over community preservation.

Business plays a major role in the urbanization process. The commerce and industry that make up business not only produce and distribute products important to life, but also provide employment for the millions who reside in urban places. The health of the national economy of all nations depends on the success of the business ventures that are part of their environment.

In addition to its own values, the business community has a responsibility in many aspects of community affairs. These include, beside the payment of fair wages and provision of safe working conditions, keeping the environment free of congestion and the air free of smog, acid rain, and other forms of pollution.

Large cities are losing their hold on important job producing industries. The reasons, cited in the *New York Post* editorial on April 30, 1987, are a composite of problems, both physical and economic. The article lists city and state taxes, federal tax reforms that reduced the value of deductions allowed to industries, lack of affordable housing, poor public education, and serious crime as discouraging to upper-level corporate executives trying to keep their homes and raise their children in a deteriorating atmosphere.

RESPONSI-BILITIES OF COMMERCE AND INDUSTRY

CORPORATE EXODUS FROM LARGE CITIES

CHAPTER 28

PUBLIC SERVICES, INSTITUTIONS, AND FACILITIES ELEMENT

CIVIC CENTERS

Every nation, state, city, and town has a center where public services are grouped. Some are pretentious like Washington, D.C., which is the service center for the United States and, like the capitol of any other nation, is big because of the number of functions that are involved, local, state, national, and foreign. States, too, have large civic centers where the operations of state government take place and where the counties and cities have their representatives. Counties often group their governmental activities in the same civic center as the cities, especially the larger cities that act as the nucleus of all local functions. In all of these centers laws, ordinances, and regulations are enacted and enforced. Taxes are promulgated and collected at federal, state, and city levels, sometimes for the same things.

Some civic centers are large and ornate, with public buildings that attempt to look like the Parthenon in Athens or St. Peter's in Rome. In other instances they are modest, occupying a store in the business district. In some cases they are in a park or city square, where the landscaping provides a setting of dignity to the seat of government. In most cases they are part of the business center even though they may be at the edge, for in fact they are the center of business, public business, and many of the services rendered are to the private business sector. The courts, for instance, and the offices housing attorneys find it convenient to be in close proximity to the jails and bail bond brokers and law libraries.

For the most part, even the smallest communities have built their town centers with special architectural features to display the pride that they have in their community. This is the one evidence of what they own jointly, and it establishes their identity.

It should be mentioned that the civic centers, large and small, are the locations of offices for all of the special interests (lobbyists) that participate in influencing, for personal or corporate purposes, the members of the legislature and the public officials.

PUBLIC SAFETY

Police, firefighting, paramedical, emergency, and other public safety functions are essential parts of the community services that must be provided with adequate resources, equipment, and housing. Headquarters and substations should be strategically located to provide required services rapidly when emergencies require rapid deployment. Traffic routes should be designated from stations to areas of greatest potential need. The number of substations should be determined by the nature of the community. The location of dangerous industrial activities and other areas where problems are known to exist, including those subject to seismic activity, wildfire potential, and landslides, should be identified to permit rapid response in emergencies.

THE JUSTICE SYSTEM

Handling matters ranging from family disputes to violent crimes, the courts and detention or correctional systems occupy important roles in society and require facilities for their operations. The judicial system extends from justices of the peace to municipal courts, superior courts, and appellate courts to supreme courts, both state and national.

Part of this system of justice are jails, prisons, and correctional institutions, all of which require locations and facilities related to their functions. Location of new or expanded centers is, as mentioned elsewhere, highly controversial, as sug-

North Dakota state capitol, Bismarck.

California state capitol, Sacramento *(left). The dome is reminiscent of St. Peter's Cathedral in Rome, but on a smaller scale.* **City hall in Pasadena, California** *(right). Still like St. Peter's, but even smaller.*

gested by the acronym NIMBY: not in my Back Yard. The logic of easy access to the courts falls flat on the sensitivities of the potential neighbors and their fears of diminished safety and property values.

PUBLIC WORKS

All cities have a major department concerned with public works, including engineering, street maintenance and improvements, tree trimming, garbage collection, and many other services that keep the city functioning. Storm drains and local flood control can be major operations in many communities. Street lighting also falls within the responsibility of the public works department.

Only the offices concerned with public works, such as the engineering department, are located in the civic center; all other functions are usually located in the "yards" where large equipment and supplies are stored. Street maintenance, sewerage disposal, and many similar functions of government are also usually grouped under the "public works umbrella."

BUILDING AND SAFETY

The building and safety department checks all requests for building permits and reviews working drawings for buildings proposed for construction in the city. It also has a staff of field inspectors who check on the construction at all stages of the work and sign certificates of completion when each phase is completed satisfactorily. No building may be occupied before the final inspection, which determines that the structure is safe for occupancy.

PLANNING AND ZONING

The planning and zoning departments are located in the civic center because of the widespread contacts that are necessary to advise the public of the laws and ordinances that affect the use of their property. In large cities local offices are dispersed into the community centers to allow the public to conduct their business locally rather than traveling into the downtown areas where the civic centers are usually located.

Utility services are provided by different agencies in different cities. Some large cities provide all of the services through separate agencies; for instance, Los Angeles has its own water, power, and light departments. Other cities have private water, power, and light companies servicing their residents.

PUBLIC UTILITIES: WATER, POWER, LIGHT, AND GAS

Public Utility Companies

In addition to special districts, privately owned companies under the jurisdiction of the Public Utilities Commission, including gas, electric, water, sewer, and transit companies and railroads, make services available and carry out public works directly bearing on the comprehensive plan. The law specifically requires cities and counties to provide opportunities for the involvement of public utility companies in preparing and implementing the plan.

Some of the public institutions of higher education are supported by the state or local communities that they serve. Private universities and colleges are sponsored and supported by either religious organizations or wealthy donors. Most are nonprofit institutions, and many in both categories offer excellent opportunities for higher education.

PUBLIC EDUCATION, UNIVERSITIES, AND COLLEGES

The campus requirements of a university can involve as much as a full square mile to accommodate and house the many students, faculty members, and activ-

Scale model of the central area of the city of Los Angeles. *The Civic Center site, prepared by the WPA in 1940.*

Civic center plan for Los Angeles.
This plan was approved by city, county, state, and federal government early in 1941. In the intervening years, the construction programs of all the agencies exceeded all of the most venturesome elements of the plan. Many private organizations have added to the enclave, spreading it far beyond the original boundaries. In addition, the entire central mall is honeycombed with multilevel underground parking.

ities multiple-degree programs involve. Smaller colleges, many located in the center of cities, require less space and are considered "downtown" functions. As time passes and the educational opportunity demands increase, even these colleges tend to expand their campuses, often through eminent domain, when residential or commercial areas are cleared for the expansion.

University and college activities are often the most important events of a community, and the interest of the public makes additional demands on the spatial requirements for stadiums, accessibility, and offstreet parking.

The economic advantages of having a large and important institution of higher education in the community are many, since they offer programs that attract students and faculty from all over the nation and the world. They also are major cultural centers, offering many programs that involve the general public, including libraries, theaters, and museums. Private housing demands are increased and other commercial services are required as the number of persons involved increases. Smaller colleges tend to have less impact on the area economically, as most of the students are local residents and live at home. In all cases, however, the demand for offstreet parking is directly related to the number of students and faculty involved.

PUBLIC LIBRARIES

From the earliest times in recorded history the library has been a major factor in the educational process as the works of the great philosophers and writers have been housed and made available to the public. All research, it seems, must begin by leaning on the contents of libraries, both public and private. From the tremendous repository in the Library of Congress to the smallest in the tiny community funded by Andrew Carnegie, we find treasure houses of information and hours of pleasure in reading the works of fine authors. Large cities like New York have magnificent public structures housing the writings of the literary world. Every university, college, and high school has a library for the use of students and the public.

As part of the cultural life of every city, town, and village, the public library is a magnet to seekers of knowledge.

MUSEUMS

Most larger cities have one or more museums, some devoted to art, others to natural history, and many others to the cultural interests of the people. Like the libraries, these institutions contain physical reminders of the world of the past as well as the work of current artists and craftspeople. Many private museums add to the sum of knowledge and pleasure contained in the public institutions. The Huntington Library in Pasadena, California, is an example of a private institution that is library, museum, and art gallery, housing works considered some of the finest in the world. In Washington D.C., the Smithsonian Institute contains in its several buildings along the Mall, a superb collection of art.

PARKS AND RECREATION

The parks and recreation organization has multiple service responsibilities. It functions as the operation and maintenance organization for the parks and landscaped areas of the city and as the leader in the organization of recreational activities from dancing to football and baseball tournaments.

MAJOR HEALTH FACILITIES

No community that can call itself a city can be without a major hospital to care for sick persons, both those capable of paying and those who are indigent. In the past cities have operated these hospitals, but increasingly the assignment has been taken over by the county, state, and federal governments. In addition to public hospitals, which are limited in capacity, many private hospitals, sponsored and supported by religious and fraternal organizations, are available to provide the major portion of medical and surgical care. Small neighborhood hospitals handle minor problems and emergencies that can be managed by a limited staff; such facilities are almost totally privately owned organizations.

The Los Angeles Civic Center. *Viewed from the City Hall Tower, 1991. This depicts the conformity (in general) with the original plan.*

WASTE MANAGEMENT

Collection and disposal of waste are in many cities public functions. In some communities, however, these functions are performed through contracts with private firms. Many disposal areas are on public property. Some major violators of the health and safety codes are the private ones, which are subject to public regulation. In recent years both the federal and local governments have been involved in requiring the cleanup of some of the worst offenders.

ANIMAL CONTROL

The animal control department is responsible for managing unruly animals and disposing of dead animals that have either been poisoned or run over by motor vehicles. They also pick up stray animals and confine them until the owners claim them.

In addition to those listed, many other essential facilities add to the services provided to urban areas as well as to many rural homes and industries.

SITES FOR ESSENTIAL OR CONTRO-VERSIAL USES

Locational planning for institutional uses can become a crucial political problem in the decision-making process. Although "hot issues" such as determination of a site for a neighborhood shopping center can raise havoc at public hearings, they are like Sunday school picnics compared with hearings that deal with prisons, asylums, hospitals, sewage treatment plants, solid and chemical waste disposal areas, power stations, power transmission lines, and other essentials to protect the health and safety of all urban areas. Even religious institutions become the focus of heated discussion and opposition from potential neighbors. Likewise, elementary schools and parks, which serve the children of a neighborhood, find opposition from adjacent property owners. The cry is always the same: put the facility in someone else's backyard. The important factor in all of the problems centers on the attempt to insert these essential functions after the character of a community has been established, by which time the proposed uses are obviously not in conformity with the surrounds.

It is essential, therefore, that these uses be assigned predetermined locations where potential residents will be aware that they are a part of the community. In addition, the buffering of the uses and the provision of adequate access routes, parking, and traffic controls are essential prerequisites to the construction that will take place.

CHAPTER 29

SEISMIC SAFETY ELEMENT

Just what is an earthquake? It is the shaking that occurs when a slowly accumulated strain in the Earth's crust is suddenly released, typically along preexisting fracture lines called faults.

Stress most often builds up in places where parts of the Earth's crust are moving past each other along faults. Scientists believe the crust is actually a number of gigantic plates that are driven by the movement of the underlying convecting mantle. In some places, as along California's San Andreas fault, one plate is slipping horizontally along the edge of another. In others, as along the coast of Peru, one plate is diving beneath another.

Improved zoning is the first and most fundamental step in reducing earthquake damage. The better we get at delineating areas of seismic risk, the better we can decide where to build—not only homes, but schools, hospitals, dams, bridges, high-rise buildings, and power plants. Some older buildings can be made more earthquake resistant: houses can be improved, for example, by anchoring the sill to the foundation, adding bracing to supports for floor joists and the load-bearing walls of garages, and strapping the chimney to the house. New buildings can incorporate the latest technology, including shear walls that bend into parallelograms rather than crack when subjected to horizontal force. Gas-, electricity-, and water-distribution systems can be made less susceptible to disruption.

Even knowing that an area will be quake-free for a considerable length of time because it is early in its seismic-gap time period can be an incentive for investment in buildings that need only that much longevity to realize a profit. It may make

WHEN THE EARTH IS STRAINED TOO FAR

economic sense to build at a place that has just had an earthquake since the Earth's stresses have been relieved.[1]

SEISMIC RISKS

A look at a world seismicity map reveals the truly global incidence of earthquakes. Except for Northern Europe, most of the other regions of very low seismicity are largely uninhabited: Greenland, Siberia, Northern Canada, most of Australia, the Amazon basin, the Sahara, and Antarctica.

Most of the great historic architectural styles have occurred in seismic regions, but it does not seem that the architecture that evolved in these areas consciously expresses seismic design principles. The seismic factor has not induced the evolution of indigenous construction forms as sophisticated and effective as the large variety of climatically-determined responses with which we are now familiar.

Much of the explanation for this lies in the fact that the physical characteristics of earthquakes have not been well understood until this century. Prior to this time earthquakes tended to be regarded as acts of God, and proper mitigation measures consisted of prayer rather than architecture and engineering. By the time of the 1906 San Francisco earthquake, the idea that the design of buildings would affect their seismic performance was beginning to be established, and by the 1923 Tokyo earthquake seismic design principles, based primarily on empirical methods, were firmly established. Following the Tokyo disaster the study of earthquake engineering occupied some of the best engineering and geological minds in the world and analytical methods became highly developed.

In the United States research into seismic design was concentrated in California, spurred on by periodic events—Santa Barbara 1925, Long Beach 1933, Kern County 1952, and the San Francisco area again in 1989—that reminded the public and responsible officials of the seriousness of the problem without, fortunately, providing the impetus of a major disaster.[2]

Two of the most severe earthquakes in the United States did not happen on the West Coast but in the East and Midwest. One was in Charleston, South Carolina, in 1886 and the other was a series of three shocks in New Madrid, Missouri, a small town in the Mississippi River Valley, in 1811 and 1812. The "felt area" was 2 million square miles.

Approximately 180 years later, on September 26, 1990, the New Madrid area was shaken again, this time with a 4.6 quake. The tremor was felt not only in the Missouri Valley but in the neighboring states of Illinois, Kentucky, Arkansas, and Tennessee. It seems apparent to the casual observer that the Mississippi River, just below the point where the Ohio River joins it, may be a rift in the tectonic plates and that earthquakes are evidence of the movement in the ever-changing face of the earth.

PREDICTION OF SEISMIC OCCURRENCES

As of now there is little evidence that seismic events can be predicted accurately. As with volcanic activity, time lapses of hundreds of years are not unusual. The Filipino experience of June 1991 illustrates the point, for Mt. Pinatubo had not erupted for more than 600 years. Although seismic disturbances were frequent before the eruption, they were considered part of the normal life of the area.

1. Richard L. Williams, *Smithsonian,* April 1983 and July 1983.

2. Christopher Arnold and Robert Reitherman, *Building Configuration and Seismic Design* (San Mateo, Calif.: Building Systems Development, 1981).

Earthquakes are a national problem. Over 70 million people in the United States live in areas threatened with severe earthquake activity. Another 115 million are exposed to moderate risks. Ground shaking and faulting are not the only hazards connected with earthquakes. Landslides, flooding, and fires that can follow a quake often cause more damage than the quake itself.

Two other activities can take place after an earthquake. First, in locations with a high water table, subsidence resulting from liquefaction, the conversion of earth to a fluid state, can occur. In such areas special foundation structures should be developed to prevent residences from unequal settlement and the fractures that occur. Second, less frequently and only in certain coastal areas, earthquakes can generate a tsunami or the violent wave action often called a tidal wave. In the massive earthquake that struck Japan in 1983, the major damage was the result of the tsunami. Very little can be done to prevent danger to life and property from this type of activity, other than to disallow construction in low-lying areas adjacent to ocean frontal zones.

While new engineering techniques have been developed, especially in Japan, the structures have not as yet been empirically tested with seismic forces of the intensity of those that leveled San Francisco or Tokyo in the early part of this century. Many high-rise buildings, especially in the zones where seismic faults are known to exist, were built without the benefit of the new techniques and safeguards and thus are open to dangers to both life and property. It seems that disregard for the environment allowed public officials to change the regulations related to building heights for the greater profit of a few and risk to the welfare of the many.

The April 1983 earthquakes in Coalinga, California, once again confirmed the danger in codes that permitted structures in critical areas to be built of brick held together with lime mortar and no reinforcement or ties of any type. The miraculous lack of deaths in the midst of structural destruction should serve as a warning of the dangers that could become tragedies of immense proportions, should the same type of seismic action take place in an area of intensive land use and tall buildings or great glass exterior walls—the current fashion in many large cities.

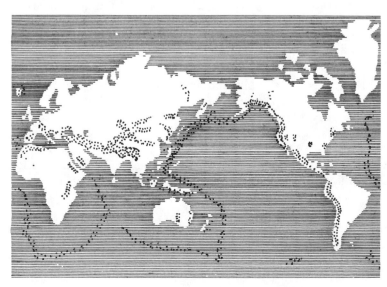

World seismicity map showing distribution of mid-twentieth-century seismic events. *Christopher Arnold and Robert Reitherman*

Structural engineers advance the theory that most recent high buildings are adequately designed to withstand a force of eight on the Richter scale. However, they believe that falling glass and masonry would endanger lives outside of the buildings and that most of the interiors would be damaged severely.

The Value of Parks

The people of Tokyo learned the value of parks and open spaces at the time of the great earthquake in 1923. They were useful in checking the fires that followed the quakes and also provided space for shelter during the aftermath of the great disaster. After that great earthquake an additional fifty-two small neighborhood parks were planned, laid out in a modern fashion, and opened to the public in a short time.

EARTHQUAKE IMPACTS: THE PLANNER'S NIGHTMARE

Earthquake—in California the word has special meaning. As the most seismically active of the forty-eight contiguous states, California (like Japan) is a place where earthquakes are a fundamental fact of life. Fully 90 percent of its population centers are earthquake-prone.

It should follow, therefore, that 90 percent of the population centers are also earthquake-prepared. But that is unfortunately not the case.

For planners, preparedness is a critical issue. Comprehensive earthquake preparedness can save lives, minimize damage, and cushion long-term economic impact. These are goals which can realistically be achieved because the special considerations and specific planning measures which California's unique environment should mandate are certainly familiar to planners.

The real challenge lies in obtaining essential public support. Faced with a barrage of issues, choices, dilemmas, and controversies, many citizens feel overwhelmed. With so many critical questions before them, the public finds it increasingly difficult to select priorities effectively.

Special events do stimulate interest. Virtually every major event is followed by a focus on one particular area of concern. Most recently, the Loma Prieta (San Francisco) earthquake of 1989 certainly energized a focus on transportation issues. The image of a collapsed section of the Cypress elevated freeway and the Bay Bridge was the strongest possible message. It generated tremendous concern about the safety of highway structures, the existence of alternative route planning, and the capacity of public transportation systems.

The transportation question offered an easily understood, straightforward issue for planners, city managers, and elected officials. Politically, it is easier to develop needed legislation and pass effective ordinances successfully when and allocate adequate funds public concern is so focused. Historically, this is the pattern.

In 1983 a major earthquake in Coalinga caused shocking levels of building damage. In the aftermath, public concern and response zeroed in on a construction issue: unreinforced masonry.

After the Los Angeles earthquake of 1971, fears of hospital damage and concern that the Van Norman Dam might fail spurred the enactment of the Hospital Act and a strengthening of the Dam Safety Act. Both of these measures, direct responses to imminent threat, were intended to protect the public against powerful natural events.

Other earthquakes have also inspired legislative reaction. After a 1933 earthquake in Long Beach the Field Act, addressing the question of school safety, was enacted. At the same time the Garrison Act, which strengthened building codes, passed through the legislature.

In response to the 1989 San Francisco earthquake, a new statewide insurance measure was enacted. And although this legislation does provide some important protections, it also begs the true question. Strictly responsive in nature, it ignores the geological hazards which caused this earthquake, will cause others, and must become a permanent factor in planning within California.

In effect, the insurance bill will speed recovery. But other recovery measures have been based on funding which can only be described as fragile. These include Disaster Federal Relief funds and special tax increases which cannot depend on indefinite or unlimited public support.

The pattern of official city reaction to earthquakes is as familiar as the pattern of the earthquakes themselves. High levels of attention and energy immediately after the event are also relatively quick to fade. Legislation that may seem critically important in the immediate aftermath, especially that related to sensitive issues such as improved building codes, is viewed as less essential a few months later. Yesterday's all-important need becomes today's uncomfortable issue—at least until the next event.

no long term commitment

Yet there is no doubt that meaningful legislation is the most potentially effective means of limiting the devastation which earthquakes, and other disasters, can impose. It is the role of planners, engineers, and architects to make city officials aware of how that goal can be achieved.

In making comprehensive proposals, the planning team should consider a specific group of criteria.

First, land-use planning: How do preventive measures fit in with the overall vision of community development of local officials over the long range? Next, public utilities and communication: What will stand, and what will fall? What special factors must be taken into consideration so that essential services and communications continue after a disastrous event?

Transportation planning is also critical. Will roads, bridges, elevated freeways, and other transportation structures remain intact in the face of disaster? What structural engineering measures must be implemented so that public transportation will continue to function? And what alternative routes must be designated to minimize potential disruption?

Evacuation planning ties in closely. Routes and travel modes must be available on a large scale. Destination facilities must be identified. Communications systems must be readied to provide evacuation information under the most difficult circumstances. Would it seem unreasonable to condemn all dangerous buildings before their occupants were condemned to injury and death during a severe earthquake?

Planning for recovery is also fundamental. Each city and township should have such a plan as a security measure, so that citizens can be confident that community services will endure and community resources will remain available.

If that confidence is to be found, other questions must be considered: Would it not be wise to limit development in hazardous areas? And should we not, at the very least, require far higher standards in hazardous areas?

These issues seem even more critical given the limited current recovery planning. In Santa Cruz, little has been done since the 1989 disaster. The city in 1992 appears to a large degree as if the event occurred weeks, rather than more than 2 years, ago.

Those communities which do address the problem often do so as a result of direct experience. The Coalinga earthquake hit that city especially hard, because it occurred in conjunction with another economic problem, an oil depression which had awakened city management to the fact that its income base, resource extraction, was vulnerable.

The disaster impacted not just the city's physical structure but its economic structure. "As businesses go out, they can't kick in the sales tax," says Assistant City Manager Blair King. "City revenues went flat because you're providing a high level of services in a short period of time." Economic recovery, in terms of reestablishing or attracting retail enterprises, takes years and is especially difficult in a town with limited economic potential.

With that lesson firmly in mind, Coalinga moved in two directions: first, the establishment of a postdisaster recovery strategy and, second, a strong move toward economic diversification.

One safety problem, unreinforced masonry construction, was literally eliminated in a single day in 1933. The city's subsequent strict rebuilding and safety standards have created at atmosphere of confidence. "There's always personal loss in an earthquake," says King, "but I can honestly say that I would much rather be in Coalinga during an earthquake than any other city."

Effective preparedness plans are legislatively based, at two essential levels. First is the one which we have already examined, recovery from the event. Legislation works to aid rebuilding, assist the population most severely affected, and perhaps address local issues of preparedness. In the energized atmosphere that follows an event, city council members and other officials are able to act quickly and effectively.

But it is in the calm between storms when the most significant legislation is considered and too rarely enacted. Preventive legislation is the key to preparedness. But gaining approval of such measures is difficult.

Preventive legislation impacts areas which are, quite literally, too close to home. Building codes, the seismic portion of the Safety Elements, and other requirements seem excessively stringent and costly in a calm environment. Comprehensive proposals meant to help communities achieve preparedness on a large scale may well be seen as overly alarming measures, if not perceived as outright scare tactics.

Effective planning must therefore address two areas with equal vigor. First is the preventive measures themselves; although they may be far more politically palatable, the limited measures which are sometimes taken are terribly inadequate.

To achieve even the most basic levels of preparedness, the issue of awareness must also be incorporated into the overall planning process. Without comprehensive public awareness and public knowledge, there will be no public support.

Creating a solid base of support within such a confused group as the inconstant public is a daunting prospect. But the essential preventive measures which must actually be a part of any program are considerably more straightforward.

Proper building codes are an important first step. Currently, building codes are designed to ensure human safety but not continued function. Regulation of the size and type of structure allowed within specific earthquake zones is a fundamental element of earthquake-effective building codes. That regulation does not presently exist.

The second most significant consideration is the seismic portion of the Safety Element. The current requirement is that seismic considerations be built into the element. But even once that evaluation is available, there is no follow-up requirement that any specific action be taken.

We know, for example, that specific areas within fault zones are hazardous for any building. In the Los Angeles earthquake of 1971 two facilities collapsed, causing many deaths. The Sylmar Veterans' Hospital and the Olive View Hospital had both been constructed near a fault line, with tragic results.

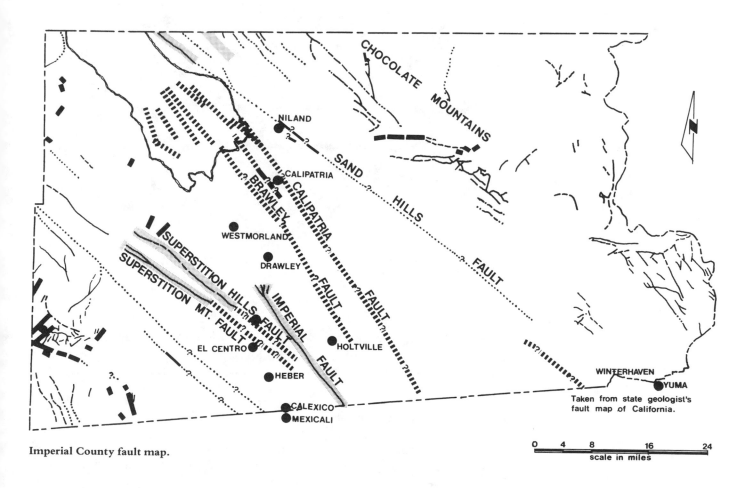

Taken from state geologist's fault map of California.

Imperial County fault map.

scale in miles

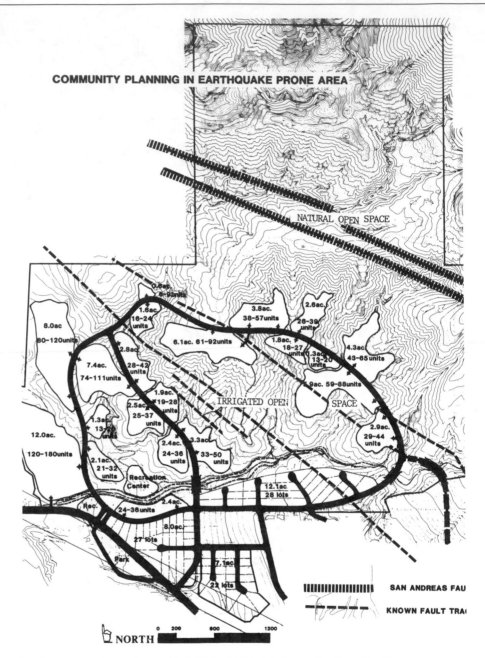

Planning in an area where seismic risk is high. *Highland Hills area, San Bernardino County.*

Other, equally dangerous building practices continue despite the hazards. We know, for instance, that more stringent building height requirements are basic in certain earthquake-prone areas, yet they have rarely been imposed.

In San Francisco, the district south of Market Street is built on an underlying plain of alluvium, a material which liquifies when shaken, causing subsidence.

And although earthquakes may most often be the galvanizing event, preventive planning is important for other reasons as well. Throughout California, homes and businesses are located on unstable slopes, subject to slippage, or along canyons which may be devastated by rivers of mud during winter storms.

At this moment, planning is under way for the construction of an entire new community in Sacramento's North Natomas, an area which is in a clearly identified flood plain.

In many ways, it seems that our civilized sophistication has led us to disregard nature's most fundamental messages. Native Americans, in selecting areas to establish villages, took careful heed of all the signs. One sign is the presence of many round stones. Recognizing that that signifies the presence of water flows and flooding, the population moves elsewhere.

Modern people are less inclined to heed these obvious indicators. Rather, we seem to believe that we can develop anywhere at all. We remain more than reluctant to address the difficult questions which arise in an atmosphere of growth.

Just as it is a fact that earthquakes and other disasters are an element of California life, so is it a fact that we have the technical ability to prepare for them, and for their effects. Preparedness is rarely easy, never convenient, and far from inexpensive. It is, however, the only form of planning which makes sense.

The purpose of seismic safety planning is to protect the health, safety, and general welfare of persons living in areas subject to seismic occurrences. As in all comprehensive planning, it calls for the highest degree of cooperation between the public agencies that would be involved if catastrophic events were to occur and the general public whose safety and welfare would be directly affected. Con-

SEISMIC SAFETY PLANNING

Earthquake destruction in Pasadena, California, 1987. *The epicenter of the quake was about 20 miles to the south, causing major damage in the city of Whittier. (Courtesy of BAREPP, Bay Area Regional Earthquake Preparedness Planning, Oakland, California.)*

Environmental Issues

Objectives	Policies
A. *Seismic Faults* • Minimize risk of seismic damage.	• Prohibit development on the main faults. • Avoid development on faults where possible. • If development straddles a fault, ensure no buildings are near the fault. • Provide numerous escape routes from the site. • Specify standards for foundation design.
B. *Liquefaction* • Eliminate the risk of liquefaction.	• Fill over areas prone to liquefaction. • Pump water for irrigation to lower level of water table. • Provide special building foundation design.
C. *Fire Safety* • Minimize fire hazards. • Comply with all city regulations.	• Provide numerous access points to site. • Provide choice of routes to exits (loop street systems). • Create landscaped, irrigated greenbelts. • Design streets at 10 percent grade or less. • Minimize 12 percent grades. • Plan short cul-de-sacs/loop streets where possible.
D. *Flooding* • Eliminate exposure of residential areas to flooding. • Design for containment of 10- and 100-year storms.	• Retain major drainage courses. • Construct debris basin(s) along canyons. • Bridge over major drainage courses to prevent road closures. • Design curbs, gutters, and culverts to carry 10-year storms in street rights-of-way.
E. *Topography* • Minimize grading. • Respect existing topography and maintain major features. • Balance cut and fill.	• Use the cluster concept of development using hilltops and valleys. • Preserve hillsides and natural drainage courses where possible. • Blend cut-and-fill slopes with existing topography using contour grading.

Public Facilities Issues

Objectives	Policies
F. *Open Space Amenity* • Create a coherent open space system. • Retain natural amenities on the site such as mature trees.	• Retain major drainage courses and existing vegetation. • Use cluster concept to allow direct visual access to open space for almost all housing units. • Provide community park. • Provide bicycle paths and jogging trails. • Provide recreation amenities in housing area.
G. *Circulation, Access, Traffic Safety* • Provide a coherent circulation system capable of carrying all traffic loads.	• Use a street system with a simple pattern based on loops and functionally divided into collectors and local streets.

Seismic damage in Mexico City in 1985. *The epicenter was determined to have been in the Pacific Ocean about 50 miles to the west. (Courtesy of BAREPP)*

Building collapse in Mexico City. *Illustrates the violence to major structures, and gives a clear picture of the human suffering that was involved. (Courtesy of BAR-EPP.)*

cerned scientists question the knowledge that planners and civic leaders have about their own communities, and what steps would have to be taken to cut down on injuries, death, and destruction of public and private property.

The following guidelines were developed as part of the Highland Hills Specific Plan for the city of San Bernardino, California, and are based on county standards:[3]

Coordination of Public Response

The preceding outline indicates the actions that should be considered and implemented before a seismic occurrence. The programs essential to dealing with people and property after a major earthquake are still in the study stage. The Seismic Safety Commission of the State of California is deeply involved in the effort to establish the level of coordination essential to care for the needs of residents of an area that has experienced temblors. Funds are being provided by both the federal government and the state to examine the aftermath of earthquakes in the continental United States, Japan, and Mexico City.

---

3. Prepared by Eisner, Smith and Associates, Planning Consultants, Palm Springs, California, June 1982.

CHAPTER 30

NOISE ELEMENT

Sound is all around us. Some sounds are constant, others intermittent. Some are pleasant, others annoying. Sounds become "noise" when they disturb us, sometimes even causing danger to health and the general welfare. Sounds can be controlled through use of amplifiers or suppressors, natural or electronic.

In the planning of a community it is essential to be aware of the relationship between sound-producing sources and the habitat of people subject to them. This can be accomplished by locating the habitat in an environment free of high intensity sounds, or by providing for acoustical treatment that will reduce the intensity of the sound to a tolerable level.

Some of the principal noise sources in urban development are related to railways running through the heart of a town or city. Freeways have replaced the railroad in the present day. Airplanes, as they approach and take off from airports in major urban centers, cause the greatest threat to health in areas immediately adjacent to the approaches. Heavy industries, for example foundries, are poor residential neighbors.

All of the worst causes of noise, especially those that result from human decisions, can be tempered. Remedial measures to reduce the impact of existing sources are essential parts of the planning responsibility; good planning for the coming development is crucial.

Highway-related noise can become a violent part of the urban environment. The Chinese city of Shanghai is one of the noisiest in the world. The sound of horns on a variety of motor vehicles, mingling with the sound of bells on the bicycles that compete with pedestrians for the use of limited roadways, results in chaos. Other cities, both in China and in other parts of the world, have regulations prohibiting the use of automobile horns other than in emergencies.

GUIDELINES

The Noise Element of the comprehensive plan provides a basis for local programs to control and abate environmental noise and to protect citizens from excessive exposure.[1] The fundamental goals of the Noise Element are the following:

To provide sufficient information concerning the community noise environment so that noise may be effectively considered in the land use planning process. In so doing, the necessary groundwork will have been developed so that a community noise ordinance may be utilized to resolve noise complaints.

To develop strategies for abating excessive noise exposure through cost-effective mitigating measures in combination with zoning, as appropriate, to avoid incompatible land uses.

To protect those existing regions of the planning area whose noise environments are deemed acceptable and also those locations throughout the community deemed "noise sensitive."

To utilize the definition of the community noise environment, in the form of CNEL [community noise equivalent level] or Ldn [day-night average level] noise contours as provided in the Noise Element for local compliance with the State Noise Insulation Standards. These standards require specified levels of outdoor to indoor noise reduction for new multi-family residential constructions in areas where the outdoor noise exposure exceeds CNEL (or Ldn) 60 dB.

Noise Element Requirements

A Noise Element shall identify and appraise noise problems in the community. It shall recognize the guidelines established by the Office of Noise Control in the State Department of Health Services and shall analyze and quantify, to the extent practicable, as determined by the legislative body, current and projected noise levels for all of the following sources:

(1) Highways and freeways.
(2) Primary arterials and major local streets.
(3) Passenger and freight on-line railroad operations and ground rapid transit systems.
(4) Commercial, general aviation, heliport, helistop, and military airport operations, aircraft overflights, jet engine test stands, and all other ground facilities and maintenance functions related to airport operation.
(5) Local industrial plants, including, but not limited to, railroad classification yards.
(6) Other ground stationary sources identified by local agencies as contributing to the community noise environment. Noise contours shall be shown for all of these sources and stated in terms of community noise equivalent level (CNEL) or day-night average level (Ldn). The noise contours shall be prepared on the basis of noise monitoring or following generally accepted noise modeling techniques for the various sources identified in paragraphs (1) to (6), inclusive.

The noise contours shall be used as a guide for establishing a pattern of land uses in the land use element that minimizes the exposure of community residents to excessive noise.

---

1. The excerpts are from the *Noise Element Guidelines* published in *The Planning Commissioner's Handbook* by the League of California Cities 1984.

The noise element shall include implementation measures and possible solutions that address existing and foreseeable noise problems, if any. The adopted noise element shall serve as a guideline for compliance with the state's noise insulation standards.

Noise Mitigation Measures

Based upon the relative importance of noise sources in order of community impact and local attitudes toward these sources, the noise element should include implementation measures and possible solutions that address existing and foreseeable noise problems, if any.

Selection of these noise mitigating measures should be coordinated through all local agencies in order to be most effective. Minimization of noise emissions from all local government-controlled or sanctioned activities should be a priority item. This includes low noise specifications for new city or county owned and operated vehicles (and noise reduction retrofitting where economically possible) and noise emission limits on public works projects. Local government should ensure that public buildings (especially schools) are sufficiently insulated to allow their intended function to be uninterrupted by exterior noise. Local agencies can work with State and Federal bodies to minimize transportation noise, primarily through transit way design, location or configuration modifications.

Additional measures might include such policies as limitation of siren usage by police, fire, and ambulance units within populated areas. Animal control units may be encouraged to minimize barking dog complaints through use of an improved public relations campaign termed "Animal Philosophy." This involves working with pet owners to determine why the dog barks and attempting solutions rather than just issuing citations. Local zoning and subdivision ordinances may require the use of noise reducing building materials or the installation of sound insulating walls along major roads in new construction and subdivisions.

In general, local noise reduction programs need to address the problems specific to each community, with the ultimate goals being the reduction of complaint frequency and the provision of a healthful noise environment for all residents of the community.

NOISE AND THE COMPREHENSIVE PLAN

The noise element is related to the land use, housing, circulation, and open space elements. Recognition of the interrelationship of noise and these four mandated elements is necessary to prepare an integrated general plan. The relationship between noise and these four elements is briefly discussed.

Land Use

A key objective of the noise element is to provide noise exposure information for use in the land use element. When integrated with the noise element, the land use element will show acceptable land uses in relation to existing and projected noise contours.

The noise contours should be used as a guide for establishing a pattern of land in the land use element that minimizes the exposure of community residents to excessive noise.

Housing

The housing element considers the provision of adequate sites for new housing and standards for housing stock. Since residential land use is among the most noise sensitive, the noise exposure information provided in the noise element must be considered when planning the location of new housing. Also, state laws

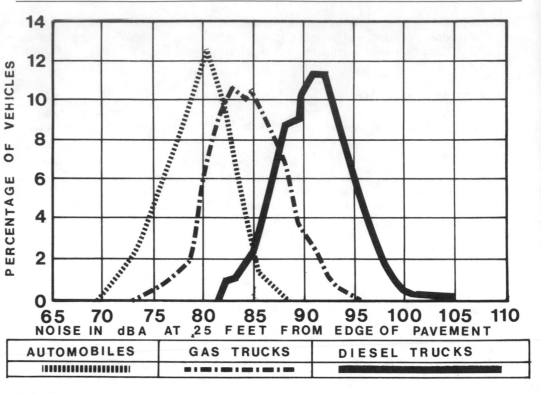

Noise distribution curves of highway vehicles.

should requires special noise insulation of new multi-family dwellings constructed within the 60 dB (CNEL or Ldn) noise exposure contour. This requirement may influence the location and cost of this housing type. In some cases, the noise environment may be a constraint on housing opportunities.

Circulation

The circulation system must be correlated with the land use element and is one of the major sources of noise. Noise exposure will thus be a decisive factor in the location and design of new transportation facilities and the possible mitigation of noise from existing facilities in relation to existing and planned land use. The local planning agency may wish to review the circulation and land use elements simultaneously to assess their compatibility with the noise element.

CRITERIA FOR NOISE COMPATIBLE LAND USE

Excessive noise can adversely affect the enjoyment of recreational pursuits in designated open space. Thus, noise exposure levels should be considered when planning for this kind of open space use. Conversely, open space can be used to buffer sensitive land uses from noise sources through the use of setback and landscaping. Open space designation can also effectively exclude other land uses from excessively noisy areas.

The suggested use of the CNEL/Ldn metrics for evaluating land use noise compatibility has been summarized in the figure that follows. Such criteria require a rather broad interpretation, as illustrated by the ranges of acceptability for a given land use within a defined range of noise exposures.

Freeway Noise Abatement

Where freeways are planned or where they exist in urban areas, high masonry walls are being constructed to reduce the sounds created by large numbers of motor vehicles, especially when the freeways carry trucks and other diesel prime movers.

As in the case of the freeways, many new industrial plants are being designed in a manner that prevents the noises associated with their operations from passing into the outside atmosphere. Some plants, like those in Palo Alto, California, are not only noise-free but set back and landscaped, making them good neighbors in any residential area.

CHAPTER 31

CONSERVATION ELEMENT

WHERE WE'VE BEEN

The basic questions regarding environmental management have not changed. Just as past generations have had to define the optimum value and use of environmental resources for themselves and posterity, so do people today. Just as past generations have had to determine the different functions of the public sector and private enterprise in developing natural resources, so do people today. And, just as population levels, economic development, and technological capability have helped to shape the environmental attitudes of past generations, so too will these factors influence value judgments today.

For the early colonists, environmental values were dominated by the need for survival, both physical and economic. Because in those precarious times when human labor was more scarce than natural resources, it is understandable that they valued these resources less than we do today. The early colonists made little effort to ensure continued yields from virgin forests or to protect wildlife. Nor did they practice methods of farming which preserved or replenished surface soils. Instead, they responded in a resourceful way to both the problems and possibilities posed by a seemingly limitless wilderness.

During the century after 1776 the federal government bought, or was ceded, vast areas of land which were added to the territory of the United States. The midwestern land claims of the original states expanded the new nation's boundaries, and successive events—the Louisiana Purchase (1803), the Oregon Compromise (1846), the Treaty of Guadalupe Hidalgo (1848), the Gadsden Purchase (1853), and the Alaska Purchase (1867)—added 1.8 billion acres to this young country. The federal government continued the common colonial practice of assigning property rights to new lands by distributing rights through sales, homesteading, and land grants to military veterans, states, local governments, and railroads.

The abundance of land contributed to the uniqueness of America. Instead of the republic of classical antiquity—territorially small, ethnically homogenous, socially conservative, and economically stable—the American republic became big, diverse, exuberant, innovative, and expansive. Slow, planned growth favored by many eastern politicians was replaced by the sprawling, brawling, impatient expansion that characterized the American frontier. America became a republic of hope, opportunity, experimentation, mobility, and personal independence.[1]

We have become inured to early obsolescence. Goods are plastic-packaged for early discarding. Fashions are outdated as soon as acquired; the trim on automobiles is still shiny when they are replaced by newer models. Commercial prosperity has been geared to the principle of early obsolescence; quantity production substitutes for quality.

Wasteful consumption by an affluent society has become a malady: the passion to consume has been satisfied by the remarkable productivity of an aggressively expanding industrial system. Our appetites have become so gluttonous that the Environmental Protection Agency had to report even in 1970: "The United States, with about 6 percent of the world's population, consumes 40 percent of the total nonreplaceable materials and 40 percent of the world's energy." The oil shortage that surfaced in 1973, dubbed the "energy crisis," exposed only one aspect of the overconsumption that plagues the industrial nations of the world.

The urban environment directly reflects the excesses to which society has become habituated. Commercial enterprise has created gigantic symbols of economic power in urban centers. For more than three decades the 1,250-foot tower of the Empire State Building was the tallest emblem of commercial aggrandizement. But in the sixties, the two 110-story towers of the World Trade Center rose 1,350 feet into the air, while in Chicago the 100-story John Hancock Tower, looming 1,127 feet high, was soon topped by the 1,136-foot Standard Oil Tower, and in 1972, the Chicago Sears Tower triumphed over all competitors with a height of 1,450 feet. The famous architect Eliel Saarinen had pleaded, "Surely the city's form and coherence must not be left at the mercy of commercial speculation,"[2] yet the architect of the World Trade Center, Minoru Yamasaki, claimed that venture was the "living representation of Man's belief in humanity."[3]

Lower Manhattan seen from the Statue of Liberty, the view of mammoth towers through the trees of Central Park, the silhouette of San Francisco from the Bay, the lakefront skyline of Chicago, are among the dramatic spectacles of urban America. But these are not the views seen by most urban dwellers. Most of the people some of the time and some of the people all of the time experience streets denuded of trees, paved with oil-stained asphalt and concrete, overburdened with buildings and vehicles, strung with wires and glaring advertising signs. Their intimate environment is a jungle of noise, tainted odors, incessant movement, and visual chaos. The refuse of the industrial system, spewed with abandon into rivers, lakes, and the atmosphere, pollutes the water and air nature has bountifully supplied. An economy of planned obsolescence scars the urbanscape.

WHERE WE ARE

---

1. Council on Environmental Quality, *Environmental Quality—1981: The 12th Annual Report of the Council on Environmental Quality* (Washington. D.C.: U.S. Government Printing Office, 1982), p. 3.

2. Eliel Saarinen, *The City—Its Growth, Its Decay, Its Future* (New York: Reinhold Publishers, 1943).

3. Paul Heyer, *Architects on Architecture* (New York: Walker, 1966), p. 195.

Psychological and physiological damage is wrought upon the human mind and body. Those who can afford it find refuge in suburbia. Precious open space is devoured, hills are unmercifully bulldozed, and valleys filled to accommodate the burgeoning population. When God created men and women, he admonished them to "replenish the earth and subdue it," but they neglected to distinguish between *subdue* and *destroy*. We have impaired the balance of nature and contaminated our environment.

This, then, is the challenge we confront as we prepare for the twenty-first century. A beginning has been made with our growing awareness of our impact on the environment; these lessons have slowly grown clear as the twentieth century progresses.

Previously unfamiliar words have entered the popular vocabulary. *Environmentalists* protect against the destructive exploitation of natural resources. A new awareness of *ecology* reveals the scope and intricacy of the interlocking relationships between land uses and services required in a manmade environment. Disposal of the waste created by overconsumption and planned obsolescence is a difficult, complex task, and unforeseen scarcities give the term *recycling* a new significance.

Securing food in the city usually means going to the supermarket or the restaurant. Our concept of the creation of clothing is going through racks in a department store. Our understanding of energy resources until recently was limited to the pump at the gas station. We are dependent on the unknown producers of these items, and we would have a difficult time surviving if the real sources ceased to exist. Nevertheless, we encroach on the best agricultural land and foul the air, giving little thought to the end products of our actions.

The Essential Element

Conservation is not new. In ancient lands flood control was necessary for human survival. Blessed with apparently unlimited land and resources, the United States has been tardy and erratic in conserving its resources. When one resource is depleted, it has been taken for granted that some new technology will certainly replace it. That optimism cannot be applied to land. The amount of land on this earth is fixed, and when the supply, for whatever purpose it may be used, is exhausted, there is no substitute. Land is not yet recognized as the precious natural resource it is, and the civilized concept of limiting speculative gains from land exploitation has not penetrated the American consciousness.

The nineteenth century was rife with disposition of public lands for the ostensible purpose of encouraging economic development. In the early twentieth century the public interest was asserted by the creation of the National Parks and Forest Services. A third (765 million acres) of the land area of the fifty states is still owned by the federal government. Of this federal reserve, 312 million acres have been allocated to specific jurisdictions: the National Parks Service, the Forest Service, the Department of Defense, the Bureau of Indian Affairs, the Bureau of Fisheries and Wildlife, the Bureau of Reclamation, the Department of State, the Atomic Energy Commission, the Tennessee Valley Authority, and the National Aeronautics and Space Administration. To administer the remaining 435 million acres, the Bureau of Land Management was created in 1946. Occupying nearly one-half of the western states, this precious resource is, in the words of Charles S. Watson, Jr., "the land nobody knows."[4]

---

4. *Sierra Club Bulletin*, September 1973.

Conservation, therefore, implies both the protection of the open lands and resources as well as the preservation of urban areas. Our propensity toward a discard economy and planned obsolescence must be changed. Many states require conservation guidelines in their comprehensive plans. The purpose of these guidelines is to promote the prudent use of our natural resources. Understanding the interconnection of these resources through the activities of man is important to achieving effective conservation.

Implementing land conservation policies through zoning, subdivision ordinances, and growth management will help forestall premature or unwarranted expansion of urbanism into the agricultural areas. The city zoning ordinance can provide for an agricultural district requiring large minimum lot sizes to protect the integrity of agricultural activity within and surrounding the cities in its area of influence.

THE ROUTE TO SURVIVAL

Many farsighted individuals and groups have fostered the protection of our natural resources. Proponents succeeded in obtaining presidential support for a National Parks System and the conservation of some of the historical areas of America. For many years European nations have worked to preserve natural landmarks. In recent years, the importance of preserving our soil and forests has received much public attention.

Frequently, however, we think of conservation as applicable only to wilderness areas. While this is crucial, the protection of our urban environments is equally important. Cities and their hinterlands are an intertwined entity. If we are careless with either, both will fall. We seldom realize the role that rural agricultural land plays in the lives of city dwellers. Without farms and forests the basic necessities of life (food, clothing, and shelter) could not (except for synthetics) be produced.

PRESERVATION OF THE BIOSPHERE

The course of shifting social values is made evident in the observations of the prominent public health engineer Frank Stead.[5] When he began his career in 1931, public health occupied a privileged position: "When we said something was hazardous to health . . . that ended it. Everything else yielded—economics, property rights, everything." Administration of more recent water and air regulations, however, is intended to "balance environmental quality against economic production." The exposure to poor environmental conditions is an unacceptable concept of "trade-offs" with public health. Stead states the imperative of protecting the

> total biospheric support system . . . that relatively thin zone at the surface of the earth that contains the land surface only a few hundred feet below the surface and ground waters, and the atmospheric envelope only a few thousand feet above the surface of the earth. Together with solar energy, these are the total resources on which all living things depend.

"The real fact is," he emphasizes, "that we must give first place to the preservation of the biosphere, and within that mandate develop the ability to support an economically productive system to keep our civilization viable." To achieve that,

---

5. *Health News,* August 1974. A graduate in public health engineering from Harvard University, Frank Stead, instituted the first industrial hygiene program by the Los Angeles County Health Department and for 20 years was chief of the Division of Environmental Sanitation, California Department of Public Health. In the early sixties he asserted that by 1980 "the gasoline powered engine must be phased out."

he says, "we will have to make changes far more fundamental than getting rid of the internal combustion engine."

IMPORTANCE OF THE COMPREHENSIVE PLAN

With increased pressures of commercialism and urbanization, conservation has become a necessary element of the comprehensive plan. To preserve the theory of local autonomy, most legislative authority is delegated by state governments to local communities. With public authority thus divided among various local governments, essential conservation measures are beyond the authority of competing local jurisdictions. Although some internal flood control, preservation of watersheds, protection of historic sites, and extraction of minerals may be effectively administered at the local level, the broad conservation measures related to public health and welfare, domestic water supply, fish, plants and game, land and water reclamation, disposal of refuse and sewage, air quality, timber supply, and agriculture extend beyond city boundaries to regional, state, or interstate dimensions. Conservation at the local level has consequently been equated with provisions in the comprehensive plan and zoning ordinances for preservation of parks and recreation areas.

Each city determines the space and distribution of its playgrounds and parks. Rampant land subdivision practices have often failed to provide space for recreation. Planned developments have improved this situation, but cities must require all residential development to allocate land for recreation and schools in accordance with local space standards. In the event that scattered subdivisions are too small to provide a park, prorated payment should be substituted, and the money should be maintained in a revolving fund for acquisition for parks, playgrounds, and school sites as the demand evolves.

The county tax assessor, more than the planning commission and city council, influences the disposition of open space. The office of property tax assessment is required by state law to assess taxes on the basis of "fair market value," and those appraisers determine the values. Regardless of the zoning designation, land that is in the path of development usually acquires a value consistent with that potential development. Land thus taxed cannot be long held off the market for development, nor can the pressure for zoning changes to accommodate "higher economic" use be long resisted by local authorities. Urban sprawl eats into agricultural zones, speculators are rewarded, plans are ignored, and open space disappears.

One tentative remedy is the contract between the state and the landowner to maintain an agricultural use for a specified period (ten years) in return for tax assessments based upon agricultural value.[6] This tax shelter only postpones the inevitable change to urban development, unless the comprehensive plan and zoning ordinance become the recognized reference for land value and tax assessment or, as recommended by the American Institute of Architects,[7] unless public policy provides for the public to recover that increase in land value that is created not through the productive enterprise of the owner but as the result of public investment and community prosperity.

This policy deserves thorough exploration by civic leaders and authorities on urban law and economics of development. Comprehensive planning of the urban

---

6. Hawaii State Zoning; Williamson Act in California; Land Conservation and Development Act, 1973, in Oregon.

7. *A Strategy for Building a Better America*, 1972.

environment is seriously impeded by ineffective land use controls. Their ineffectiveness, according to Robert H. Freilich,

> stems from a supposed constitutional inability to adequately govern the decisions of the private land owner. It is stated to be a constitutional problem limiting the extent of regulatory powers over land use regardless of the political unit which is exercising decision-making authority. The United States has a deep-seated tradition which believes in "absolute" ownership of land. The view that land ownership is "absolute" is, of course, erroneous under American law. All property is held subject to police power, regulations of the State being necessary to preserve the public health, safety, and welfare of the community, a power which is the least limitable and most expansive of all governmental power.[8]

It should be within the power of government to recover that increment of land value that is created by community action through zoning decisions and investment of public funds for capital improvements. Value created by the action of a city council or other governing body in changing a permissible land use from residential to commercial, for example, or the installation of public facilities that enhance the use of property, is unearned by a landowner; it is an increment of value created by public action and should be recovered by the public. Conversely, changes in land use necessary to achieve an improvement of the environment, such as rollback zoning from high to low density of land use, and that result in a reduction of the vested land value, should be accompanied by a compensation to the owner by the public for that increment of lower value. Donald Hagman has referred to the policy as "trading windfalls for wipeouts."[9]

This policy is comparable to the British program of compensation and betterment and, benefiting from the experience in England, both the success and the equity of the policy will depend in large measure on the simplicity of the administrative procedures designed for its implementation. It should be instituted neither as a punitive measure nor as a means to produce revenue. To prevent a possible disruption of the land market, it should be implemented in stages.

Open space in accordance with local standards for parks, playgrounds, and other amenities for built-up districts must be acquired with public funds or special assessment districts. Efforts to preserve open space to enhance the general amenity and enrich the aesthetic quality of a city confront the eternal conflict between the public good and private property rights.

POSSIBLE APPROACHES

Buffer Areas

Open space, however, implies more than a street or a neighborhood park or playground. It includes the broad areas of land that separate urban developments from the rural areas. Open space can include regional parks, agricultural land, forested areas, rivers, oceans, lakes, or land masses with dimension adequate to supply breathing requirements in contrast to the congestion of urban development of even the lowest density. Reports indicate that the city of Sochi in the Commonwealth of Independent Republics (Georgia) has devoted approximately 70 percent of its land to the protection of open space in the form of forests, parks, recreational areas, and similar uses. The government of Sweden acquired and is holding greenbelts around its major cities to conserve both the quality of urban life and the welfare of the rural hinterland. These greenbelts give form to the

---

8. Robert H. Freilich and John W. Ragsdale, Jr., *Development Framework Data Report,* Metropolitan Council of Twin City Area, January 1974. See also the *Minnesota Law Review* (58 Minn. L. Rev. 1,009) (1974).

9. "A New Deal: Trading Windfalls for Wipeouts," *Planning,* Association of Planning Officials, September 1974.

urban communities, preserve the air's freshness, and provide areas nearby for the production of foodstuffs.

Cities blessed with hilly terrain within or around them can turn this natural asset into a beautiful urban form, or they can allow it to be chewed up for the homes of status-seekers. We seem to have great difficulty in accepting the fact that the modern city is not the natural habitat of hill dwellers. The site for a medieval castle was not selected for its view, although views of a beautiful countryside were magnificent. The noble's real concern was the observation of approaching enemies, and the compact hill towns that huddled about the castles were built for protection of the inhabitants. Modern city builders generally seek plains and broad valleys for industry, business, transportation, and housing. Lovely hills should be looked at, not cut to ribbons for flatland lots. The undulating ridges and slopes should be preserved. Development should not climb above a 20 percent slope.

Philanthropy rarely extends to gifts of land to enhance the amenities of a city, and political action to restrict development of land for either utility or beauty meets with the claim of "inverse condemnation." But if we intend to halt further destruction of the natural character of our environment, the public and the government must act.

Cherishing the beautiful site of their city along the foothills of the Rocky Mountains, the people of Boulder, Colorado, took action to protect their birthright. Adding to an original 1899 federal grant of 3,000 acres of foothills, donations by enlightened citizens increased their Mountain Parks System. The people of Boulder took the initiative in financing the preservation of open space when potential development threatened the city, as it does other cities. A greenbelt program was approved by referendum in 1967: the people assessed themselves an additional 1 percent sales and use tax for land acquisition and the lease or retirement of bonds. A cooperative city-county comprehensive plan encompassed a greenbelt system of parks, recreation, wildlife sanctuaries, and scenic trails. By means of density transfer[10] (compensatory density), open space in planned developments became integral links with the greenbelt. The citizens of Boulder thus have demonstrated that when the people are determined to maintain their environmental assets, they can. Aspen, Colorado, followed suit; so should other cities.

The resolute determination of the people of St. George, Vermont, to maintain the quality of their environment is also instructive. After their population more than tripled in a decade, from 108 in 1960 to 477 in 1970, the people of St. George acted. Recognizing that they must deal with the right to develop land rather than the right to own land, St. George required the transfer of development rights for the open space of its lovely environment to the community, to be used for the new village center it planned for the future.[11]

Fearful that "development" would destroy the foothills of the city, Palo Alto, California, undertook a comparative study of open space versus urbanization. The study revealed that the cost of public services for residential development would exceed acquisition cost for preservation as open space.[12] Failing to support

10. The basic density for residential development is four dwelling units per acre. It may increase to six dwelling units per acre with open space thus consolidated to link with the greenbelt.

11. Leonard U. Wilson, "Precedent-Setting Swap in Vermont," *Journal of American Institute of Architects,* March 1974.

12. The professional study was conducted by Livingston and Blayney, Planners, San Francisco, California.

a $4 million bond issue for land purchase, the city rezoned the land to minimum lot sizes of ten acres.

The California Office of the Bureau of Land Management has, in cooperation with the city of Palm Springs, prepared plans to preserve the habitat of a band of desert big horn sheep. By this action, a large open space in mountainous terrain has become a permanent open area to provide a refuge for the endangered species and breathing space for people. Another of the bureau's projects is preservation of the great California desert, which was abused by uncontrolled off-road vehicles ranging from motorcycles to dune buggies. Areas are provided for these recreational vehicles, while the more fragile sections are off limits to all but persons on foot or on horseback.

Margins

The most critical areas of our world are the margins, the edges where related conditions require careful planning and decisions to determine the use of land on both sides of a border. In the broadest sense, the relationship between the earth and the space within which it moves requires that we carefully plan our activities not to destroy the protective environment that permits life to continue with a reasonable degree of safety. In more finite situations we have many margins that require special attention and planning if the advantages and disadvantages provided by nature are to be respected.

Perhaps one of the most interesting and challenging margins is where water (oceans, lakes, and streams) meets land. Here, in the past, there has been an almost total disregard of the need for careful planning and nondestructive use. We have placed some of the most obnoxious of industries along the waterfront. We have thrust our sewage and refuse into the waters and polluted them with a

Urban waterfront development. The Harbor, Portofino, Italy. *Serving as seaport on the Mediterranean as well as the town center for a recreational complex, the harbor at Portofino is an attractive, dynamic place for the residents and tourists who gather here at all times of the year.*

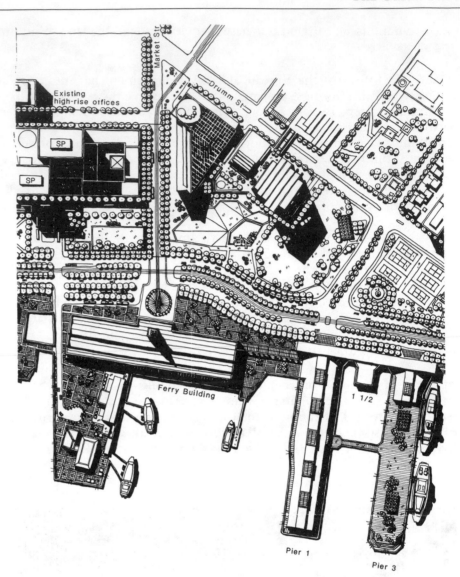

San Francisco's waterfront. *One of the treasures of the world. The relationship of waterfront areas to the hearts of the cities they serve requires the special concern and planning now being given to the San Francisco area.*

reckless abandon. The delightful developments that might have been created at many of these critical and limited areas have been destroyed, as we have literally fouled our nest. In recent years there have been major and costly efforts to restore these margins for recreational uses to the benefit of the residents, not only those close by but also from other regions and the nation as a whole. Los Angeles County began in 1940 to plan for the recovery of its precious ocean frontage. Now, after more than 50 years, through local and state funding, a great deal has been acquired for beaches to be enjoyed by the general public.

Another critical margin is that which separates urban areas from the agricultural areas that form the rural environment. In nations where legislative determination through open space zoning for agriculture has been the rule, it is believed to be but a slow-burning fuse to a time bomb that will explode as soon as pressures are placed upon local legislative bodies to change the zoning for more profitable uses for the landowners. Vast areas of productive agricultural land have been converted to urban uses, sometimes—as in the San Jose area of California—by hopscotching and leaving parcels of uneconomically sized agricultural land to wither as they are surrounded by urban development.

Paul Revere's House
*(top). Located in Central
Boston, Massachusetts.*

Urban Conservation
*(left). Historical buildings
showing late 19th century
architecture in Oakland,
California.*

The General Grant Se-
quoia, Sequoia National
Park, California *(right)*.
Wanton destruction of
giant sequoias *(bottom)*.

Even more dangerous, perhaps, is the unplanned development at the margins of land exposed to great dangers. Some of these dangers are manmade, such as at the edges of or on landfills where dangerous wastes have been disposed of over the years. Developments along the fringes of earthquake faults also constitute an unwarranted ignoring of conditions that could endanger both life and property. Likewise, the edges of areas subject to period flooding should be respected.

Many other critical margins provide opportunities for development where conditions could, at one time or another, have significant impact upon humans. These must be defined, understood, and respected in the planning of our urban communities.

Harbors by their nature have been the locale for industrial and warehousing developments. Unfortunately, these areas of potential open space and scenic attractiveness have become shabby with the neglect often associated with the industrial workplace. The visual recreation that should be associated with the activities of the large and small ships and the business of loading and unloading of cargos from far-off places has been overlooked. In some cases, the waterfront has become an unkempt neglected asset. The planned conservation of these limited resources is an essential task for the people of our time.

The seashores and riverfronts are priceless recreational areas wherever they are found in the world. They constitute a limited resource since they are often scattered and in some places inaccessible. The reclaiming of land along these frontages has been a major accomplishment of many European nations as well as America. These special lands have been opened to public use rather than allowing them to remain the private reserve of the few. Millions of people now enjoy

Harbors and Seashores

Scale of Sequoia gigantea. *Measured by a human being. Some are more than 300 feet tall.*

The Four Guardsmen.

swimming, fishing, and boating in the oceans and rivers as a result of state and federal as well as local programs.

Valued Architecture

Many cities have made efforts to preserve buildings that have historical value architecturally. These are the gems of eras past, some showing the flamboyance of their period, others fine detailing and sensitive design. In the East, the home of Paul Revere in Boston is but one example of history preserved for future generations to enjoy. In the West, where the structures are relatively young, many of the residences of the 1880s and 1890s are being gathered into centers to form a living museum of the classics of their time.

The architect Philip Johnson once stated that whereas Europe has its great cathedrals, America has the Grand Central Station. The Supreme Court decision in 1983 that saved the Grand Central Station in New York City from demolition set the stage for the preservation of other fine old structures in many American cities. Even the Pan Am Building that looms above it on Forty-second Street as one looks uptown on Park Avenue has not destroyed the impact that the station has as one views the architecture of the grand facade.

Beautiful natural areas with fine stands of trees, such as the sequoias in California, are also a part of the natural architecture of our environment; they should be looked upon almost with reverence. Although these areas are protected by federal and state laws, encroachment is a constant threat to their survival. A famous man once stated, "When you have seen one of these trees you have seen them all," implying that there was nothing wrong with harvesting some of them for building material or fence posts.

During the period from 1970 to 1990, there has been a renaissance of the effort to preserve and restore historical buildings in all parts of the world. The efforts of conservationists have not been limited to natural settings but include as well the classification of buildings worthy of preservation—those that have historical significance even though they may not represent what some purists would call

Washington, D.C.: view of the capitol building.

Washington, D.C.: view of street leading to the capitol.

"fine architecture." This is a reflection of the concept that, whereas our historical era is relatively short, it is getting longer each year and, without these evidences of earlier days, we will never have an American past to study and understand.

There must be concerted and continuous effort to preserve our natural and man-made environment if we and our children are to have the pleasure of observing how the world in which we live has developed. We must not turn our backs on our history. We must learn to respect our heritage, for it tells us much about who we are and how we survived to the present.

GRAND CENTRAL TERMINAL

The Grand Central Terminal— Reed & Sterm and Warren & Wetmore, Architects, William Wilgus, Engineer— *The Pioneer and Landmark Jury of the American Institute of Certified Planners (AICP) in November, 1992 designated The Grand Central Terminal in New York City as a National Landmark, citing it for both its architectural beauty and skillful transportation planning and engineering (Photograph by Frank English, Metro-North Commuter Railroad.)*

Not just a pretty building, Grand Central Terminal is indeed a planning landmark. As a significant symbol of transportation infrastructure and great public space as any of our great housing or community projects, it has been hailed as one of the greatest railway terminals in the world. The comprehensive terminal plan was largely "inspired by a great engineering vice-president of the railroad, William Wilgus," whose 1903 scheme contained most of the essential features ultimately carried out by the architectural firms of Reed & Sterm and Warren & Wetmore. Construction lasted ten years.

CHAPTER 32

WASTE MANAGEMENT ELEMENT

America recycles only 10 percent of its garbage, incinerates 10 percent, and deposits a whopping 80 percent in landfills. As a result, we are having to cope with a monumental solid waste problem.

Americans throw away about 160 million tons of garbage a year. According to a recent study, plastics make up about 18 percent of the volume of solid waste in our landfills, paper and paperboard account for about 38 percent; metals, 14 percent; glass, 2 percent; and other wastes, 28 percent, all by volume.

As a result, in the past 10 years our country's landfills have decreased by about 1,850 to 6,000. In five years, 2,000 more will probably close.

The seriousness of the problem, in the face of the population increase predicted, requires a plan which will cover the multiplicity of elements that the problem comprises. These should include at least the following:

Produce goods that have a longer use life and repair and rehabilitate items wherever possible rather than disposing of them at some half life time;

Learn to respect food as an essential to life (i.e., don't waste food);

Develop garbage recycling plants, turning food and rubbish into fertilizer;

Recycle all glass, metals, and paper, again and again, saving the great trees of our forests and the metals that are in short supply or costly to produce.

VANISHING LAND FILL SITES

PLANNING THE FUTURE TREATMENT OF WASTE

Scow carrying waste out of the New York Harbor to points unknown.

The following excerpt is from a report by the Council on Environmental Quality, published in 1981:

> Future concerns related to solid wastes are likely to be focused on two issues. First, new waste treatment and disposal sites will have to be established which adequately protect surrounding property. Second, market mechanisms will have to be encouraged which either reduce waste generation through more efficient manufacturing techniques or which allow for the exchange or sale of wastes for reuse.
>
> To solve the waste disposal problem by eliminating waste does not imply that smaller volumes of chemicals will be manufactured. Rather, the internalization of waste disposal costs will encourage waste-generating industries to make their chemical processes more efficient and to investigate methods of turning wastes into saleable commodities.[1]

In presenting the 1990 *Annual Report of the Council on Environmental Quality,* President George Bush optimistically stated:

> We have not solved all our environmental problems. Some we have only begun to understand. But over the past two decades we have proven to ourselves, and to the rest of the world, that we are willing to act on our beliefs. If the best prophet of the future is the past, as Lord Byron once wrote, then our children and grandchildren can look forward to the same good health, clean environment, and abundant natural resources that so many Americans have been so fortunate to share.[2]

HAZARDOUS WASTES

Although wastes which are considered hazardous represent less than 1 percent of the total waste produced in this country, they have become the subject of increasing environmental concern. Major efforts were made in 1981 by industry and government both at the federal and state levels to translate this concern into effective management and environmentally sound disposal of these wastes.

---

1. *Annual Report of the Council on Environmental Quality,* 1981.

2. *Annual Report of the Council on Environmental Quality,* 1990.

Identification

There are two major methods for identifying a hazardous waste: listing a waste as hazardous (the most common method for defining a hazardous waste in European countries) and testing a waste to determine if it exhibits one of four characteristics adopted by the Environmental Protection Agency (EPA). EPA lists as hazardous any waste that contains any of 90 chemicals that have a reported toxic, carcinogenic, mutagenic, or teratogenic effect on humans or other life forms. The current hazardous waste list contains 13 categories of waste from nonspecific sources, such as halogenated solvents used in degreasing operations; 76 wastes from specific sources, such as wastewater treatment sludge from the production of chlordane; and more than 300 commercial chemical products that are deemed hazardous if discarded. Since promulgation of the hazardous waste regulations in May 1980, a number of additional wastes has been added to the hazardous waste list.

The four criteria for identifying a hazardous waste are based upon measurable characteristics—ignitability, corrosivity, reactivity, toxicity—for which standardized tests are available. Of these four characteristics, the first three produce acute effects capable of causing immediate damage; the fourth creates chronic effects more likely to appear over a longer period. The core characteristics are defined as follows:

- Ignitability—waste that poses a fire hazard during routine management;
- Corrosivity—wastes requiring special containers because of their ability to corrode standard materials or requiring segregation from other wastes because of their ability to dissolve and thus mobilize other toxic contaminants;
- Reactivity—wastes that, during routine management, tend to react spontaneously, to react vigorously with air or water, to be unstable to shock or heat, to generate toxic gases, or to explode;
- Toxicity—wastes that when improperly managed, may release toxicants in sufficient quantities to pose substantial hazard to human health or environment.

Probably one of the greatest hidden dangers from waste is that which is generated at land fills that become "toxic leakers." In these cases, the effluent from the dump penetrates the underground water supply and literally contaminates the water in active wells, thus entering into the homes being served. An instance, recently in communities on the perimeter of Los Angeles had to shut down certain wells that had become contaminated, the sources not indicated.[3]

The section dealing with hazardous waste reflects the attitude of the president. Concerned persons should continue to be concerned.

Control and remediation technologies for hazardous waste have been improved substantially over the past 20 years. In 1970 solid and semisolid wastes that now would be classified as hazardous wastes were usually placed in unlined landfills, while liquid wastes were placed in impoundments, and neither landfills nor impoundments were sited to minimize environmental effects. Those facilities did not collect leachate, and they did not monitor the groundwater to detect leakage. After the useful life of the facility, owners often walked away without a proper closing.

Today's land disposal facilities are much improved. Wastes are not just dumped in the ground; they are placed into facilities with synthetic liners that hold wastes inside the facility and leachate collection systems that keep hydraulic pressure from building and rupturing the liners. Such facilities also monitor groundwater to detect leaks. Finally, because of Environmental Protection Agency regulations,

HAZARDOUS WASTE CONTROL AND REMEDIATION

---

3. California Environmental Quality Guidelines, Sacramento, California, 1981.

many wastes now are treated prior to their emplacement in land disposal facilities to limit the mobility of the waste and reduce its toxicity.

Not only is land disposal safer, but treatment alternatives have been developed that change the character of waste to render it less hazardous or nonhazardous, or that reduce the volume of the waste. Incineration is one such form of treatment. It is a thermal process primarily used to burn organic liquids and solids. Modern incinerators can remove or destroy over 99.99 percent of the principal hazardous organic constituents of a waste stream. Other treatment technologies, like neutralization to adjust the pH of a waste, precipitation to remove heavy metals, and stabilization to prevent hazardous constituents from leaching out, also are used widely.

Although modern waste management technologies are comparatively nonpolluting, past practices left a legacy of contamination to be remediated. Fortunately, progress in development of remediation technologies has been considerable. In 1970, because few people understood that groundwater could be contaminated, little attempt was made to clean it. Today well established methods are used to delineate the extent of contaminated groundwater plumes, determine the optimal number and configuration of withdrawal wells, and treat the contaminated groundwater to remove pollutants.

Methods for controlling the source of the groundwater contamination also have improved. In the early days of Superfund, pollution control at a Superfund site usually was limited to capping the soil—covering it with a clay cover to limit infiltration of rainwater and thus reduce leaching from the soil into the groundwater. Unfortunately, capping was not a permanent remedy; it did little to reduce the toxicity or the mobility of the waste stream.

Remediation managers can now select from technologies like solvent extraction, solvent washing, biological degradation, in situ vitrification, soil washing, liquid/solid contact digestion, in situ stabilization, and ultraviolet/oxidation treatment for liquids.[4]

Exploit the use of waste as a potential alternate for producing energy, thus reducing the demands for atomic plants and the tremendous use of petroleum and coal. This would include water power (and old friend), sun power (an even older friend), wind power, the ocean, where both motions and temperature differentials can produce energy. For instance, the Israelis have developed an energy production operation in the Dead Sea where the differences in the salinity of water of the Mediterranean and the Dead Sea are used to develop electrical energy. Most of all, the inventive genius that can place man on the Moon can certainly solve the problem of waste before it engulfs the world.

TOXIC LEGACY IN FOREIGN LANDS

Concern has been voiced in the press about the toxic legacy revolving about the far-flung military bases operating in secrecy far outside the jurisdiction of American environmental regulations. The quagmire of chemical contamination could cost billions of dollars to clean up and without responsible action damage U.S. foreign policy for years to come.

---

4. Ibid.

The one form of hazardous waste that at this time cannot be safely disposed of or converted for other useful purposes is nuclear waste. That waste comprises plutonium and other nuclear wastes resulting from the production of energy either for human services, such as power and light, or from the obsolete atomic weaponry that is part of the worldwide killing inventory. Lacking the potential for conversion or recycling that characterizes other forms of waste, atomic waste must be put, like the genie, back into a "bottle" for endless storage and be disposed of deep in the earth or concrete bunkers in far-away places, which are getting closer and closer to human settlements every day. A related matter is the safe shipping of these encapsulated genies to wherever their final resting place may be.

With the rate of proliferation of the atomic energy plants all over the world, even in remote countries, the problems grow to frightening proportions. With France's using atomic energy almost exclusively and Japan's developing 25 percent of its energy from this source, one can see the direction of the programs. As Israel, Pakistan, India, the Commonwealth of Independent Republics and others all participate, the menace of hazardous waste production and disposal has become a management problem, one which demands an international approach and convention that is committed to saving the world from itself.

NUCLEAR ENERGY WASTE

PART 7

IMPLEMENTATION

PUTTING PLANS TO WORK: TURNING IDEAS INTO REALITY

CHAPTER 33

THE IMPLEMENTATION PROCESS

Implementation is carrying a plan through to action. Thus the implementation of a proposed plan presumes that the initial political action that made its preparation possible will also make its utilization equally possible. Therefore the first step is the enabling legislation that spells out the responsibilities of the action agencies and the scope of the work to be accomplished. Following this, there must be funding of the activities or construction to permit local personnel to carry out the given goals and objectives.

DEFINITION

Sometimes goals and objectives are viewed as similar, but in the implementation process they should be differentiated. The goals are set in the long-range comprehensive plan. The objectives are the short-range action programs to be accomplished when a time limit is placed on one or more elements of the long-range plan, and which involve the preparation of budgets for the physical improvement of the community. These are capital improvements, and they involve those structures or equipment that have a relatively long life, such as public buildings, fire and police vehicles, park equipment, and similar facilities that are costly, must be anticipated in advance, and must be in accordance with the long-term guidelines of the comprehensive plan.

GOALS AND OBJECTIVES

Implementation involves participation in several types of political action on administrative, legislative, and citizen-action levels. Laws must be prepared by legal advisors and are subject to public hearings before planning commissions and

POLITICAL ACTION

legislative bodies. Once approved, they enable the development of either social programs or programs of construction for physical improvements. The actions that implement such developments may be described as:

Permissive. The preparation and adoption of laws or ordinances that will permit or encourage the development of plans or programs.

Directive. The actions by the legislative authority that permit the first stages of a program to be initiated and define the scope of the work to be accomplished.

Supportive. The arrangement of the financial programs through the budgeting process to permit the projects or programs to become a reality.

Active. The launching of a social or economic program; the construction of a building; the acquisition of goods and services; the acquisition of land for open space or other essential purposes.

All of the several activities involved in implementation require extensive planning based upon research and analysis of the community's needs and potentials.

THE COMPRE-HENSIVE PLAN

The most important aspect of the implementation process is that it is based on the comprehensive plan. It fits into the overall structural framework of that document and the carefully analyzed financial capabilities of the community as well.

As the overview of the future of the community, the comprehensive plan must contain a wide range of projects, to be added or subtracted from as time and circumstances warrant. Its very nature implies that it cannot be implemented in total in a short period of time. The plan contemplates changes and additions to accommodate growth, and this implies in turn that the plan should contain a carefully defined program for implementation of those timely parts capable of being financed in the first phase of the growth period.

In the past there has been the implicit common understanding that the state or federal government would offer assistance to meet emergencies when the local communities did not have the resources to accomplish what was essential. Today the changes in the decade of the 1980s make this assumption subject to reexamination.

When local communities did not have the funds necessary to perform the essentials associated with the mandated portions of the comprehensive plan and/or local attitudes mitigated against federal assistance, all too often they would find a way to comply with the letter of the law but hardly its intent. An "as is" plan would be prepared that merely rounded off the corners of the zoning map and showed existing facilities such as schools and parks and existing streets and highways. By then placing the title "Comprehensive Plan" on the map, the community appeared to abide by the law. Few of these communities ever prepared a report or followed up with the programming of essential improvements.

IMPLEMEN-TATION PROBLEMS

The implementation of a land-use plan requires that government and the private sector have a reasonably similar view of the future. This presupposes that the comprehensive plan has been prepared on a rational basis and decisions have been made without collusion with special-interest groups. If the comprehensive plan is followed up with sound growth management (the timely meeting of people

Examples of Tools for Implementing the Comprehensive Plan [1]

Corporate Powers (Acquisition and Development)	Police Powers (Regulatory)
• Construction of streets, roads, and water and sewage treatment facilities	• Specific plans
• Acquisition and development of parks	• Zoning: Open-space zoning Environmental hazard zoning Inclusionary zoning Planned unit development zoning
• Acquisition of sites for low- and moderate-income housing	• Subdivision regulation
• Purchase of development rights and scenic easements	• Park dedication requirements
• Establishment of policies governing the timing of improvements to public services	• School dedication requirements
• Creation of development corporations	• Review and regulation of public works
Others	• Housing and building regulation
• Redevelopment	• Code enforcement
• Intergovernmental coordination	• Environmental review procedures
• Public information	• Design review
• Data management	• Program for maintenance of public facilities (streets, water and sewer lines, drainage, buildings, vehicles, etc.)
• Monitoring	
• Cooperative arrangements with the private sector	

[1] California State Guidelines for Implementing the Comprehensive Plan.

and the facilities that they require), then development can be readily implemented.

However, in many areas of the country long-range planning is still considered only a guide for future growth, to be respected if the politicians see fit and to be disregarded if short-range personal gain is considered paramount. In the latter case development will be uncontrolled, and the decisions on the land use will be made on the basis of momentary advantages to the landowner with little concern for long-term cost of services and inconvenience to residents at large.

Perhaps the most important obstacle to appropriate plan implementation exists in the political process that permits the plan to be amended without sound reason or ignores the plan as though it did not have a definitive role in producing compatible development. A major problem with many plans is that there is no schedule for their development. The past lack of growth management techniques has created plans that are not chronologically and sequentially phased. There was no sound basis for the extension and installation of the infrastructure, and thus there was no indication of where, how, or when the community could implement the plan.

Objections by citizens' groups often will delay or halt the implementation of portions of a plan. For example, changes in a zone to permit a shopping facility can bring out residents to oppose the facility because it will be incompatible with their concept of their area. Residents of Montecito, California, objected strongly to including such facilities in their hillside areas. They did not mind traveling on

Public Opposition

narrow streets to obtain convenience items, preferring the travel problems to the danger, as they saw it, of the intrusion of commercial uses and the possibility that these uses might spread to depreciate their rather pristine properties further.

In Arcadia, California, tremendous local opposition was registered to the development of a regional shopping center. Local opposition was overcome when a citywide referendum on the matter indicated that the residents in areas away from the site supported the proposal. The matter was decided on political grounds even though the site was admirably suited for the project insofar as strategic location was concerned. However, the shopping center did present the problem of heavy traffic so special traffic and aesthetic design features were initiated to protect the area.

CHAPTER 34

THE ZONING PLAN

Since zoning ordinances are, in effect, law and since they apply to almost every person in a community where zoning is applicable, it is imperative that they be clear in all of the regulations that apply to a given zone in the specific community. There should be adequate definitions to clarify technical and legal language. The standards should be brief and clear and not require the public to search from one section to another to finally determine the regulations that apply to a particular property or the use thereof. The uses permitted, those subject to limitations, and those specifically prohibited should be in the same section of the ordinance. The language should be simply stated and positive.

Ordinances should include all of the zones necessary to have the regulations carry out the intent of the comprehensive plan and reflect the goals and objectives which determine the community character. If the ordinance fails to meet the changed environment of the community, it should not become a patchwork of changes. A new ordinance should be drafted and deal affirmatively with the changing needs.

Communities, both urban and rural, have a great deal of latitude in making decisions on the number of districts they create and the way those districts are delineated on the zoning map, as long as both processes are consistent with the comprehensive plan and the policies established therein. Thus some zoning boundaries may be determined by topography, some by relationships to other districts and the uses that are permitted, and others by provision of adequate circulation and transportation facilities. The character of a community and the quality of life within its boundaries may be determined by the sensitivity of the decision makers and the influence of the property owners.

PRECISE PLANS: PUBLIC DECISIONS

The comprehensive plan sets the basic policies for development of the city, the general relations of the various land uses: residential, commercial, and industrial. In brief, it forms the framework of the urban structure. From time to time this general framework is translated into precise plans that specify the zoning for land use, streets and highways, mass transit, recreation and conservation, subdivision expansion, utilities, railways and airports, civic centers, schools, and urban redevelopment. These precise plans interpret the basic policies reflected in the comprehensive plan and serve to adjust it to new situations and conditions as they arise.

The plans serve a dual function. On the one hand, they define the standards for development of the city, the standards of population density, the design of the circulation system, and the amount and location of open space and physical facilities for business and residence. On the other hand, they provide a program for development, establish a basis of timing proposed improvements in the city, the location, design, and installation of utilities, schools, parks, the extension of subdivision development, and the redevelopment of blighted areas. In this way the need for public improvements may be linked with the ability to finance such improvements and maintain a coordinated pace with expansion of private development.

These functions presume continuous attention to the process of urban planning. A comprehensive plan that collects dust in the archives of the city hall is a monument on the grave of lost opportunities in urban improvement. Planning involves an entire process that anticipates the needs of a community, proposes ways and means for the satisfaction of these needs, and relates these proposals to the orderly development of the city through the realization of the comprehensive plan. The precise plans are the action-oriented instruments with which these functions are performed.

ZONING DEFINED

Zoning is the legal regulation of the use of land. It is an application of the police power for the protection of the public health, welfare, and safety. The regulations include provisions for the use of property and limitations on the shape and bulk of buildings that occupy the land. The law comprises two parts: the ordinance in which the regulations are defined, and the zoning map that delineates the districts within which the provisions of the ordinance apply.

For all too many years zoning has been considered planning. The zoning map was seen as the "grand plan" for the community when in fact it was a generalization of existing conditions, freezing them into a format that reflected only the past and frequently thoughtless individual desires of influential property owners supported by their political friends.

The zoning plan is neither a substitute nor an alternative for the comprehensive plan. The latter expresses the basic policies that shape the community character and the general land use; the former establishes the specific limitations that apply to land use as one of the instruments for achieving the goals set forth in the comprehensive plan. A guide for urban development, the comprehensive plan is usually adopted as a resolution by the legislative body. The zoning plan is adopted as a legal ordinance with penalties associated with violations.

Many people believe that zoning or any public regulation of the use of land is not only unnecessary but unconstitutional. In their opinion zoning has a detrimental effect on the development process. They would substitute the free market process, in which economic forces at any time determine what is the best use for a given parcel of land.

Often cited as an example of a city without zoning is Houston, Texas. Not mentioned, however, are the many land use regulations that affect the free use of land in that city, such as the 10,000 deed restrictions and regulations enforced by residents' associations that cover two-thirds of the city. The deed restrictions are applied in a fragmented manner, and there is the potential for unfortunate changes after the effective period has expired. Nonetheless, the major difference between them and zoning seems to be only that the regulations are applied by a private local body to a local area instead of by official governmental institutions on a city-wide basis.

The question remains improperly posed and unanswered. Although there may be a limited number of legal problems at this time in Houston, there may still be tests of the reasonableness of the deed restrictions when they are at a point near termination and the participating property owners start expressing opinions that may not have legal precedent and thus be supportable in a court of law.

Over the years zoning has been an accepted means of regulating the use of land, not only in the United States but also in almost every nation of the world. In some countries the democratic processes involved in the United States are not observed, the government making land use decisions and applying them as it sees fit. Planning in these countries is in many cases arbitrary, expressing only the will of a few in the administration.

Criteria

The validity of the zoning ordinance has been subjected to several court tests; the decisions have generally supported the following criteria:

- The plan (ordinance and map) shall be comprehensive.
- The same regulations shall apply to all districts having similar zone classifications.
- The plan shall demonstrate protection of health, welfare, and safety.
- There shall be neither discrimination nor capricious intent in the plan.
- Administration of the ordinance shall be reasonable and free from arbitrary decisions.

ELEMENTS OF A TYPICAL ZONING ORDINANCE

A. *Text*

    Intent and purpose
    Definitions
    Delineation of zones
    Schedules for decisions
        Planning commission
        Board of appeals
        Legislative body
        Amendments
        Court of competent jurisdiction

B. *Preparation and adoption of the zoning map*
     Consistency of map with the comprehensive plan
     Costs of various procedures
        Changes
        Applications
        Appeals

PROCEDURES FOR ALTERATIONS

Complications inevitably arise in the administration of zoning, and procedures must be provided to cope with them. These situations may involve natural or synthetic conditions of the land, unusual demands not evident when the ordinance was adopted, or developments in which the exacting limitations of zoning do not accommodate reasonable latitude for the adoption of new ideas. Some examples follow.

Density Transfer

In cases where there are reasonably large landholdings that contain areas where flooding or other potential dangers exist, some zoning ordinances provide for the overall transfer of the permitted densities from the endangered land to safe locations. This process becomes a useful planning device when the endangered land can become a valuable open space or a recreational area during periods of low danger. It is often recommended that the land be either deeded to the community for permanent open space, in which case the owners enjoy a tax benefit, or that it be dedicated as permanent open space, in which case the land remains in private ownership subject to the requirement that it remain open in perpetuity or at least until such time as the dangerous conditions are mitigated to public satisfaction. In the development of the Indian Bend Wash in Scottsdale, Arizona, this technique was used to provide open space without cost either to the community or the property owners. The owner is permitted the same number of dwelling units or commercial intensities on the remaining land that he would have been permitted if the transaction had not taken place.

The Zone Change or Amendment

The most frequent alterations occur when property owners require a change for the classification of their properties from one zoning district to another, usually for the purpose of enjoying greater economic values. Changes to the zoning map should be made only when such changes conform to the comprehensive plan. Otherwise they may, while being beneficial to an individual, be detrimental and costly to the community in terms of their effects on utilities and public facilities.

Amendments to the text of the ordinance are also made quite often. These amendments include changes in terminology; inclusion or deletion of certain uses; changes in standards, either raising or lowering them; and changes in procedures.

Regardless of whether the map or the text is modified, the procedure requires public hearings and discussions prior to any changes becoming effective. The procedure is generally identical with that required for the adoption of the original ordinance.

The Zoning Variance

A variance is a permission granted as relief from some specific and unusual hardship imposed by the strict interpretation of the ordinance. It is a means to adjust the property development standards of the ordinance that, by reason of location, topography, shape, or size, are impossible to comply with. The variance permits a property owner to use his land at the same intensity allowed to others in the same zone; however, it should not allow uses not permitted in the zone. Being readily subject to discriminatory administration and unsound planning, the variance is perhaps the most abused of all zoning procedures. It is not intended to be an alternative to spot zoning or a device to circumvent the intent of the ordinance by a grant of special privilege, nor is it proposed as a means to solve personal problems. The following advice by a high state court in its review of a case involving rezoning brings the issue into clear focus:

> We feel impelled to express briefly our view of the proper theory of zoning as relates to the making of changes in an original comprehensive ordinance. We think the theory is that after the enactment of the original ordinance there should be a continuous or periodic study of the development of property uses, the nature of population trends, and the commercial and industrial growth, both actual and prospective. On the basis of each study changes may be made intelligently, systematically, and according to a coordinated plan designed to promote zoning objectives. An examination of the multitude of zoning cases that have reached this court leads us to the conclusion that the common practice of zoning agencies, after the adoption of the original ordinance, is simply to wait until some property owner finds an opportunity to acquire a financial advantage by devoting his property to a use other than that for which it is zoned, and then struggle with the question of whether some excuse can be found for complying with his request for a rezoning. The result has been that in most of the rezoning cases reaching the courts there has actually been spot zoning, and the courts have upheld or invalidated the change according to how flagrant the violation of the true zoning principles has been. It is to be hoped that in the future zoning authorities will give recognition to the fact that an essential feature of zoning is *planning*.[1]

Conditional Use Permit

There are occasions when a special use is necessary for the welfare of a community but not permitted within the applicable zone. Permission for such uses may be granted by the conditional use permit. Unlike the variance, evidence of unusual hardship in the development of a property is not required. The permit is for the purpose of meeting a special need of the community based on evidence that the proposed location will serve this special purpose. Protection from adverse effects on abutting property must be assured, and measures for this must be included in the permit. As with the variance, the conditional use permit (C.U.P.) is not a substitute for rezoning. It is designed to meet a special situation in the general public interest; it is not a device by which a new use may be indiscriminately introduced within an established zoning district. The zoning ordinance usually provides for a variety of sharply defined uses within a district, and the C.U.P. offers a degree of flexibility in adjusting to new demands within the framework of the ordinance.

There remains a difference of opinion on the manner in which a conditional use permit should be granted. Some authorities hold it to be essentially an administrative decision at the discretion of the planning commission. Others contend that it should be subject to approval by the legislative body. It is generally agreed that the ordinance should clearly stipulate the circumstances and indicate the areas under which conditional use permits may be granted as a protection to the community and to investors in property.

Administrative Committees

Zoning ordinances contain a variety of provisions, compliance with which may require some form of review and approval. Among these may be the location and size of signs or engineering and architectural design and arrangement. The ordinance may therefore provide for administrative committees vested with the

---

1. *Fritts v. City of Ashland,* Court of Appeals of Kentucky, 348 S.W. 2d 712 (June 16, 1961); quoted in *Zoning Digest,* American Society of Planning Officials, October 1961.

responsibility and authority to pass upon plans subject to these provisions. Such committees are particularly effective when both public officials and lay persons compose their membership.

ZONING DISTRICTS

In the zoning plan the community is divided into districts in which the land is restricted to certain classified uses. The size, shape, and location of these districts reflect the major uses indicated by the comprehensive plan and should be formed to invite the natural development of neighborhoods. The comprehensive plan may indicate an area to be appropriate for single-family dwellings, whereas the zoning plan may permit a commercial use within specified limits to be developed as a shopping center and contribute to the neighborhood quality of the area. A site for a school and a park may also be provided within such an area. Such developments of the precise plans are refinements of the comprehensive plan, their purpose being the creation of balanced community design.

Most zoning ordinances provide for different densities of population in different districts. One residential district may permit only single-family houses with a density of five families per acre, whereas another district may permit "unlimited multiple residential" use in which the density can reach hundreds of people per acre. These variations must be reflected in other precise plans for the city since they affect the provisions of all community facilities and services. The size and location of schools, commercial land use and transportation, police and fire protection, and the size of utility services vary considerably with the number of people to be served.

The land use categories that follow are among the major districts that may appear in the zoning ordinance. Their classification will differ in various communities. Local customs and requirements will determine the definition of each classification.

Open Land

This classification of open land districts, though not included in most urban ordinances, applies to areas in which the public interest requires the prohibition or restriction of urbanization to protect or enhance the reasonable growth and development of the community. Open land districts may include areas of particular scenic or historic importance, areas too steep to be built upon, areas subject to flooding, and areas where water and sanitary facilities or police and fire protection cannot be provided without excessive cost, both physical and financial, to the community.

Agricultural

Areas designated as agricultural districts permit the use of land consistent with economically feasible agricultural enterprise, the subdivision of land being governed by the type of agriculture normal to the area. Those about some urban areas may establish minimum lot areas of 40, 20, 10, 5, and 2 acres; others include 1-acre lots. Uses considered generally permissible include farming, poultry raising, dairying, and cattle and horse grazing. Restricted residential uses may also be permitted, provided the agricultural uses are not adversely affected. Hog raising may be prohibited in some agricultural zones because it is generally interpreted as an obnoxious use. There are usually provisions in the zoning ordinance for exceptions by special permit if an investigation of the particular situation demonstrates no prospect of endangering the general welfare.

Estate

Estate districts are sometimes created with a variety of lot sizes and thus provide property owners the opportunity to establish the character of a residential development of large-sized lots. Such a district can be used to establish a rural quality in some suburban developments. Some agricultural uses are frequently permitted, such as poultry raising for domestic consumption or keeping of saddle horses. This is generally the most restricted residential zone, the minimum lot sizes ranging from 20,000 to 40,000 square feet or more in area. The districts are usually established at the behest of property owners or developers desiring to attract clientele who want reasonably large tracts protected from the infiltration of small-lot subdivision. Other factors sometimes warrant the establishment of estate zones: it may be advisable to limit the population in an area when facilities for sewage disposal are absent or limited, where police and fire protection are not readily available, or community facilities such as schools or commercial districts are remotely situated. Entire cities zoned for only large lots were declared "exclusionary" and an "unconstitutional exercise of police powers." See Chapter 21 [Mt. Laural].

Single Family

In single-family districts land use is restricted to a single dwelling unit per lot. The ordinance establishes a minimum lot area permitted in these zones and frequently specifies the minimum lot measurements. The standards vary considerably; some cities still permit lot widths of twenty-five feet street frontage, but a width of sixty feet or more is accepted in most communities as the minimum, with a minimum lot area of 6,000 square feet. Such restrictions are not retroactive, and property owners are not obliged to comply with area and lot size regulations enacted subsequent to the recording of subdivisions with lesser restrictions.

The sanctity of the original concept of the single-family home as the residence of a nuclear family is not sustainable. Based on numerous court decisions, it is apparent that a community can regulate what may be placed on a lot and what the population density may be, but not who shall constitute that density of population. In other words, the definition of "family" no longer seems to mean only those people related by blood or marriage.

Two Family

The two-family district classification has been rather generously used in the past to permit the "duplex" type of dwelling, i.e., two dwelling units within a single structure. With the increasing use of density control rather than classification of building type, a provision specifying the density, such as a minimum lot area per dwelling unit, is more equitable than a limitation of two dwellings per lot. Application of a uniform density provision offers a desirable flexibility for lots of varying size, rather than freezing the limitation regardless of the lot area.

Multiple Family

Any residential district in which more than a single one-family dwelling is permitted to occupy a single lot is a multiple-family district. A gradation of dwelling unit densities is usually provided within this classification.

Medium Density

The "medium" permitted in medium-density districts is quite different in a great city from that in a small town. In large cities medium density ranges from twenty to forty dwellings per net acre. It may be prescribed as four times the density of the single-family district. If the minimum single-family lot area is 6,000 square feet, the medium density then requires 1,500 square feet of lot per dwelling. Some communities permit a lot area as low as 1,000 square feet per dwelling in this district.

High Density

High densities ranging from 50 to 150 families per net acre (lot area exclusive of streets and alleys) in some districts are not uncommon in large cities, and some laws permit as many as 200 to 300 families per acre. With the increasing congestion of traffic and the growing intensity of the parking problem, zoning ordinances permitting these high densities are due for a critical review. The classification may be defined as a multiple of a minimum single-family lot size. Assuming a density standard of some fifty dwellings per acre and a minimum lot size for the single-family district of 6,000 square feet, the high-density district would permit about eight times the single-family density, or about 750 square feet of lot area per dwelling unit. Some ordinances further grade these requirements according to the size of the dwelling apartment. Thus 300 square feet of lot area may be permitted for "bachelor" units, 400 square feet for one-bedroom units, 600 square feet for two-bedroom units, and 800 square feet for three-bedroom units.

Densities may be limited to levels far below what may be permitted in a district when, for instance, the offstreet parking requirements cannot be observed; the height limits restrict the number of units that can be built on a parcel; the street capacity does not accommodate the traffic that will be generated; or the utility systems, mainly water lines and sewers, do not have the capacity to accept the number of families that will occupy the dwellings under the density proposed.

Mobile Home   The mobility of the population in the United States is demonstrated by the expanding use of the so-called mobile home as a relatively permanent dwelling. It possesses unique characteristics and plays an important role in the housing supply in moderate climates. The essential amenities for this mode of living should be regulated in zoning ordinances. Well-designed mobile-home parks accommodate between six and eight factory-built units per acre, or approximately 4,000 square feet of ground space for each unit. The Federal Housing Administration standards and the recommendations of the Mobile Homes Association support the lesser density as the desirable space requirement.

Hotel   The density and lot area requirements for hotel districts are the least restrictive of the residential zones, except in areas where the particular character of the environment warrants special attention to density. Hotels may also be included in the provisions for commercial districts. With the exception of limitations on setbacks for side, rear, and front yards, there has been little control of density, but reconsideration of hotel densities is as urgent as it is with high-density apartment and commercial zones. Recent off-street parking requirements actually determine the number of hotel rooms allowed upon a particular site.

Commercial   The complex structure of the modern urban community has introduced changes affecting the arrangement of commercial facilities, as it has in other land uses. The "mom and pop" grocery store has blossomed into the neighborhood convenience center; the expanding suburbs have forced the decentralization of retail enterprise and the development of the regional shopping center. The density of "downtown" hangs in the balance. Special service facilities, from professional offices to light manufacturing establishments where commodities are also sold across the counter, must be accommodated within the fabric of commercial zoning regulations. Consideration of the relation between these several commercial functions and other land uses must be reflected in the comprehensive plan as a foundation for the zoning plan. Excessive land area and permissible floor space, typical of present zoning, is related to traffic congestion and the parking problem. Transition from the burden of strip zoning for business uses along the major streets to the consolidation of commercial centers will be an arduous task and require a long period of time. The shopping center has confirmed the necessity and provided the impetus for this conversion in the pattern of commercial land use.

Initiated by the federal government, the enterprise zones take on different forms in various parts of the United States. The intent of the zoning is to free the sickly central business areas from generally applicable zoning and to offer tax incentives and subsidies to encourage investments in the revitalization process.

Enterprise Zones

Two questions are most often asked about this subsidized laissez-faire proposal: (1) Who will benefit? Will underfinanced small businesses gain a betterment of their economic plight? (2) Will the redevelopment of the depressed area result in greater employment opportunities for the disadvantaged residents?

Perhaps the most serious unanswered question relates to the propriety of providing a wide range of subsidies for business at a time when public assistance to needy residential families of the unemployed is reduced and children's free lunch programs are curtailed.

The classification of an industrial district ranges from the most restricted uses for light industry, in which only electric power may be employed or in which smoke, odors, and sound are rigidly controlled, to the unrestricted heavy industry district, in which any type of manufacturing enterprise or process is permitted. Certain industrial uses which may endanger the public are frequently restricted to specific areas, and still others may require special permits by legislative action in order to conduct business. The manufacture of fireworks or fertilizer or the dumping of refuse and garbage, when allowed, may be confined to areas at least 500 feet from other unrestricted uses, if permitted at all.

Industrial Districts

The phrase "industrial district" has acquired an unsavory association with rundown hovels in the shadow of the factory. The successful development of the planned industrial district, or industrial park, has therefore been a singular advance. The intensity of land use identified with the crowded workshops of the past is relieved in such a park. A density of some thirty to fifty workers per acre is not uncommon in industrial areas, but in industrial parks it ranges between fifteen and twenty per acre, with areas of heavy industry having fewer than ten workers per acre. Regulations prescribe restrictions on building height, space between buildings, setbacks from property lines, signs, off-street parking and loading, and landscaping.

The reservation of industrial parks for the exclusive use of industry encourages the planned integration of residential communities, with mutually beneficial results: efficiency in industrial operation and convenience to employment in a desirable residential environment.

In recent ordinances, the manner in which operations are conducted, rather than the type of the industry, is the basis for the classification of an industrial district. The adoption of performance standards may obviate the need for arbitrary distinctions between light and heavy industry and provide a more rational use of industrial land. It could also become a means to integrate places of employment and places of residence more closely.

In some regions and states the emission of contaminants from the various types of industries has necessitated the creation of an independent air pollution control agency, but normally performance standards prescribe regulations for control of smoke, odor, glare, vibration, dust, sound, radiation, water or sewer pollution, and moisture. They are enforced through the measurement of the effects of plant operation at prescribed points and at frequent intervals.

INDUSTRIAL PERFORMANCE STANDARDS

The industry performance standards established in the zoning ordinances of such cities as New York, Chicago, and Denver have been analyzed by the Urban Land Institute and the American Society of Planning Officials. The following standards are derived from those analyses.

Fire and Explosion Hazards

All activities involving inflammable and explosive materials and/or their storage shall be provided with adequate safety devices against the hazard of fire and explosion and adequate fire-fighting and fire-suppression equipment and devices standard in industry. All incineration is prohibited.

Radioactivity or Electrical Disturbance

Devices that radiate radio-frequency energy shall be so operated as not to cause interference with any activity carried on beyond the boundary line of the property upon which the device is located. Radio-frequency energy is electromagnetic energy at any frequency in the radio spectrum between 10 kilocycles and 3 million megacycles.

Noise

The maximum sound pressure level radiated by any use or facility when measured at the boundary line of the property on which sound is generated shall not exceed the values shown in the following table:

Octave-Band Range in Cycles per Second	Sound Pressure Level in Decibels, 0.0002 cyne/cm²
Below 75	72
75–150	67
151–300	59
301–600	52
601–1200	46
1201–2400	40
2401–4800	34
Above 4800	32

If the noise is not smooth and continuous or is present between the hours of 10 P.M. and 7 A.M., one or more of the following corrections shall be applied to the above octave-band levels:

	Correction in Decibels
Daytime operation only	+5
Noise source operates less than 20 percent of any one-hour period	+5
Noise source operates less than 5 percent of any one-hour period	+10
Noise of impulsive character, such as hammering	−5
Noise of periodic character, such as humming or screeching	−5

The sound pressure level shall be measured with a sound level meter and associate octave band analyzer conforming to standards prescribed by the American Standards Association as set forth in a pamphlet published by the association entitled "American Standard Sound Level Meters for Measurement of Noise and Other Sounds No. Z24.3," published in 1944, and in another pamphlet published by the same association entitled "American Standard Specification for an Octave-Band Filter Set for the Analysis of Noise and Other Sounds No. Z24.10," published in 1953.

Vibration

Every use shall be so operated that the ground vibration inherently and recurrently generated is not perceptible, without instruments, at any point on any boundary line of the lot on which the use is located.

Smoke

No emission shall be permitted at any point, from any chimney or otherwise, of visible gray smoke of a shade equal to or darker than No. 1 on the Power's Micro-Ringlemann Chart, published by McGraw-Hill Publishing Company, Inc., and copyright 1954 (being a direct facsimile reproduction of the standard Ringlemann Chart as issued by the United States Bureau of Mines), except that visible gray smoke of a shade equal to No. 1 on said chart may be emitted for four minutes in any thirty minutes. These provisions applicable to visible gray smoke shall also apply to visible smoke of a different color but with an apparently equivalent capacity.

Emission of Dust, Heat, and Glare

Every use shall be so operated that it does not emit dust, heat, or glare in such quantities or degree as to be readily detectable on any boundary line of the lot on which the use is located.

Emission of Odors

No emission shall be permitted of odorous gases or other odorous matter in quantities which exceed those proportions shown in Table III, "Odor Thresholds," in chapter 5 of the *Air Pollution Abatement Manual,* copyright 1951 by Manufacturing Chemists' Association, Inc., Washington, D.C.

Outdoor Storage and Waste Disposal

All outdoor storage facilities for fuel, raw materials, and products shall be enclosed by a fence or wall adequate to conceal such facilities from adjacent property. No materials or wastes shall be deposited on a subject lot in such form or manner that they may be transferred off the lot by natural causes or forces. All materials or wastes that might cause pollution due to radiation fumes or dust or that constitute a fire hazard or that may be edible by or otherwise attractive to rodents or insects shall be stored outdoors only in approved closed containers and in specific disposal areas.

Special Uses

In some communities land may be subject to special uses, such as drilling for oil and mining for rock or minerals. It is customary to control uses of such a special nature by requiring individual action by the planning commission and the issuance of permits by official action of the city council. The establishment of cemeteries may also come within this category and be subject to similar control.

The development of nuclear energy has introduced a new element of regional concern. The location of nuclear power plants, as well as performance standards, becomes a matter of state concern. Citizens, as well as wildlife and coastal waters, must be protected from the pollution that can result from the disposal of the plants' waste, and must also be protected from possible ill effects of radioactive material.

HEIGHT AND BULK

One of the most critical problems of zoning is the relationship between buildings and the space around them. The question of space was once predicated on the necessity of preserving adequate light and air for the interior. Sufficient light, air, sound control, and privacy continue to be criteria in measuring adequate space between buildings, but their relative importance has been modified by advances in artificial illumination, sound insulation, and air conditioning. It is possible that the necessity for space in the future will derive far more from the exterior requirements than from the interior demands. The amount of building floor space in relation to exterior circulation—streets, sidewalks, and parks—may become the critical factor. The space for vehicular and pedestrian traffic circulation now presents an almost insurmountable problem, and it is compounding annually. The dissipation of exterior space in which the environment may be enriched with landscaping and in which the human scale may be restored is a mounting challenge. This challenge, however, will be best answered in new areas where open land is to be developed or in renewal areas where land is assembled into large plots. The current concern for space to protect light, air, and so on, will still be an important consideration in dealing with old areas divided into small, narrow, individual lots. More than a gesture should be made toward the quantity and shape of the open space.

Over the years there has been a constant effort to increase the distances between buildings and property lines and to devise methods by which setbacks might compensate for increasing building heights. The ground space reserved by these provisions has never been sufficient for its purpose; the setback distances and lot coverage restrictions have rather been token grants of space sacrificed after the land had acquired great value. The initial method of front, side, and rear yard requirements was later augmented by "envelope" provisions to cope with excessive building heights. The modest side yard of five to six feet in residential zones has increased to ten feet for multiple-family districts in some ordinances, with provisions for setbacks above the first or second floors. The space between buildings reserved by these provisions is not adequate for reasonable privacy, but opposition to increasing the space has been adamant. Awareness of the deficiency, however, has induced the subdivision of land into larger lot sizes and the consolidation of small properties. This trend has increased the efficiency of land use and site planning, but successful large-scale developments demonstrate that the conventional regulations have no actual bearing on good planning.

There is an inflexibility in current methods for preserving open space; the minimum standards permitted by law become the maximum standards in practice. The primary issue in the future seems to be the need for regulations directed to a balance between building bulk and exterior space required for circulation, vehicular storage, and the evolution of an urbanscape that satisfies more of the basic material needs of humanity.

The principle of the "floor area ratio" offers some encouragement in this direction. It involves the ratio between the area of building floor space and the area of the lot it occupies. A floor area ratio of two, for example, would permit 100 percent of the lot to be covered by a two-story building or 50 percent of the lot to be covered by a four-story building. Recent applications of the floor area ratio introduce the features of "bonus" or premium space. Chicago adopted such inducements in its revised ordinance of 1957, and they have been proposed in Philadelphia. The first major overhaul of the New York City ordinance since the history-making zoning law of 1916 occurred in 1960. The conventional setback requirements that produced the familiar shapes variously referred to as "cake-mold" or "ziggurat" were modified by adoption of the "sky exposure plane" for commercial zones and the "open space ratio" for multifamily residential districts. The effect of these provisions, in combination with the inducements of increased permissible floor space in proportion to the open space reserved at the ground level, is comparable to the floor area ratio method of regulation.

This approach affords a flexibility in the shape of buildings to serve their particular functions and removes the arbitrary limitations on building heights unless such limitations may be desirable for particular purposes. As with other regulations to control the bulk of buildings on the land, the floor area ratio will be effective to the extent that it produces the required balance between enclosed floor space occupied by people and adequate ground space for vehicles and living things, be they human, animal, or plant.

Historical preservation starts with the protection of sites of ancient civilizations, whether in the deserts or the mountainous areas of the world. Buried in the fields adjacent to Rome are evidences of a great road system, and adjacent to the roads can be found walls and foundations of other types of structures. In North Africa, the remains of an ancient civilization can be observed at Moulay Idriss in Morocco and locations in the many other nations that lie along the Mediterranean rim. Native American Indian artifacts are to be found in many parts of Arizona, and developments are required to devise means for the preservation of vast areas where ancient villages were once located. The ruins at Mesa Verde, Colorado, now a part of a national park, are splendidly preserved remains of a vanished civilization.

HISTORICAL PRESERVATION

Brussels, Belgium. *Town Hall and Guild Houses.*

The Vieux Carré, New Orleans, Louisiana.

These sites require protection from destruction, not to mention modern-day "grave robbers." The need has diverted many developments because extensive investigations and removal of the artifacts discovered caused great delay. Interested citizens have formed associations dedicated to the protection and preservation of these critical areas. Ordinances have been adopted in many communities' zoning areas containing historic remains or where historical buildings constitute a link with the past.

Historical preservation also takes into account the need to protect and preserve rare and endangered species of all forms of wildlife, ranging from whales to fringe-toed lizards.

In urban areas historical preservation deals primarily with two conditions. The first is the historical site or building. Immediately coming to mind are the classical city hall, the fine old colonial mansion, the architecturally exquisite cathedral. These are in many instances isolated structures. The second is the historical area, which may contain a collection of fine structures, be a generously landscaped area with historical significance, a locale where historical events took place such as at Lexington or Concord, or a collection of governmental buildings such as those in Washington, D.C. It may also be a fine example of architectural style in a commercial composition, such as in the Vieux Carré in New Orleans or Tivoli Gardens in Copenhagen.

It would not be appropriate to create a one-building zoning district to preserve the historical site. More appropriate would be the acquisition of the building by either a private institution or by a governmental body, thus establishing not only a permanent future for the structure but also providing funds for essential maintenance.

The historical district can be a zoned area with many regulations to protect the existing buildings, provide for the architectural consistency of new structures, and deal with new building heights and setbacks, signs, and other elements. The buildings may be in separate ownerships, and the owners may take pride in the opportunity they have to participate in a national program as well as possibly enjoy a profit. The regulations can be in the form of restrictive covenants if they are more restrictive than the community zoning, or they can simply be a community action taken by the legislative body.

A national carelessness about our rich natural and cultural heritage has been another byproduct of building for commercial enterprise. The unique grandeur of many natural wonders has been protected through the National Parks Service, but efforts to preserve structures and sites of historical or artistic importance have been severely hampered by economic unfeasibility and social indifference. In some regions significant historic buildings are protected by special government action, and a few have been saved by private philanthropy. The continued maintenance of existing structures, however, is a serious problem. Historically important buildings are often not economically practical, especially since zoning regulations usually permit structures of greater height in bulk in these areas. Professor John J. Castonis of the University of Illinois has proposed that owners of such landmark buildings be allowed to sell the development rights to additional stories (or the bulk that the zoning would permit) to developers of another building on another acceptable site. This would allow the protection of famous and historic buildings without the sacrifice of the property rights that usually preclude preservation.[2]

Several cities followed the lead of New Orleans, which adopted a zoning provision for the protection of the Vieux Carré (French Quarter). The principle involved here is the protection of an area's unity, intended to preserve not only a historical structure, a natural feature, or a site, but also the entire surroundings.

The city of Redlands, California, has acquired some thirty acres of orange groves in order to preserve a portion of its agricultural history in the face of intensive urban pressure. The groves produce crops each year, and the fruit is marketed to provide revenue to compensate for the cost of the grove and its maintenance.

The historical area must have a distinct and desirable character worthy of preservation. The standards for its preservation should assure a continuity of scale and design even if demolition, alteration, renovation, removal, or relocation takes place. A certificate of appropriateness is often required for any change in occupancy, construction, demolition, removal, or relocation, or any modification of the site that would alter its original form or structure.

Historical preservation commissions are created by the legislative body. The members of the commission must be residents of the special zone. All members must demonstrate knowledge of and interest in the preservation of the area. Santa Barbara, California, always deeply concerned about its early history, has adopted

2. The first application of this proposal is the Heurich House, a Victorian mansion in Washington, D.C., owned and occupied by the Columbia Historical Society. A building ninety feet high could legally occupy the site. The city zoning commission permitted a developer of a high-rise structure on a nearby site to erect a building forty feet higher than the zoning code usually allowed, from which the additional income is to be used for the maintenance of the old building. A similar application is being considered for the Chicago Loop, where many significant buildings of the nineteenth-century Chicago School remain. Report in the *AIA Journal*, American Institute of Architects, March 1974.

Interior courtyard in the Vieux Carré.

a historical preservation zone to protect the old presidio area where the remains of the city's early days are found. San Diego has also adopted such an ordinance to protect an area containing remnants of its historical heritage.

In 1952 Mr. and Mrs. Henry N. Flynt founded the historic Deerfield district to carry on the tradition of historic preservation of this picturesque western Massachusetts village. It was the last outpost on New England's frontier when it was settled in 1669. Devastated twice, by the Bloody Brook Massacre of 1675 and the Deerfield Massacre of 1704, its resettlement brought agricultural prosperity and a determination never to forget its past. The district maintains twelve house museums, a research library, and an active education program, all devoted to the study of the history of Deerfield, the culture of the Connecticut Valley, and the arts in early American life.

Outside America

Other countries seem on the whole to be more aware of the need to maintain visible contact with the past through the preservation of structures and areas of historical or cultural importance. This may be so because these countries are so much older than the United States. Some examples of this attempt at preservation follow.

Warsaw, Poland. The Nazis leveled Warsaw in World War II. Damaged areas considered of great historical importance were not replaced with new structures, rather the existing buildings were reconstructed in a manner consistent with the past. The cost of doing this is often far greater than that of clearance and rebuilding with "modern" structures. However, the value of retaining a taste of the past sometimes seems more important than the cost involved. There can be no doubt of the need to preserve architecturally and historically important buildings, especially if they can be made functionally suitable.

Prague, Czechoslovakia. The government of Czechoslovakia has spent more than $200 million a year on restoration in Prague. The Committee to Preserve Old

Jackson Square in the French Quarter of New Orleans, Louisiana.

Prague would not let planners tear down the graceful but outmoded main railway station, so a new one was built underneath. In general, Prague's one million inhabitants amble down cobbled lanes under spires and buttresses. They pass Hradcany Castle, rising fairytale-like on one of the city's seven hills.

People's Republic of China. In Beijing great concern has been expressed over the past disregard for the preservation of many of the historical and interesting struc-

Hutongs: *the narrow streets that serve both residential and commercial areas that lie between the main highways serving the large urban areas.*

tures in order to make way for new hotels, modern residential structures, and subway routes and stations. An element of major interest is the preservation of the *hutongs,* residential areas built about courtyards on interior streets. A major protest occurred when a street with many fine old buildings was demolished. People, both locally and internationally, requested that the structures be rebuilt to the original style, rather than replaced with modern ones. This protest succeeded. Local Chinese city planners are dedicated to the premise that the city must become a blend of the new and the old in order to retain the worldwide interest it creates because of its character and the quality of its many ancient temples, pagodas, shrines, and hutongs.

Government Assistance: The Tax Reform Act of 1976

Since passage of the Tax Reform Act of 1976, federal tax incentives have been responsible for stimulating more than $1.2 billion in private investment in more than 2,500 preservation projects nationwide. Historic buildings listed in the National Register of Historic Places and within registered historic districts in all fifty states have been rehabilitated, including hotels, office buildings, factories, and apartment buildings. The benefits have meant more than financial gain for owners and investors. Whole neighborhoods and business districts have been favorably affected by well-timed and well-placed investment in historical buildings.

The Economic Recovery Tax Act, signed into law on August 13, 1981, makes dramatic and sweeping changes that directly benefit investment in real estate. The tax incentives in the new law make rehabilitation of historic buildings a more attractive investment than before. A new 25 percent investment tax credit will replace the existing incentives, together with new depreciation schedules and recapture rules. Along with the National Historic Preservation Act Amendments of 1980, the new law should provide further impetus to encourage capital investment in historic buildings and to spur revitalization of historic business districts and neighborhoods.[3]

SOME COMMON ZONING DEFICIENCIES

Zoning regulations are predicated upon good principles of land control, but many fail to establish standards of urban development that produce good cities. Harland Bartholomew has said:

> Zoning has come about partly through the desire of certain better residential districts to obtain a protection which is difficult, if not impossible, to secure by private initiative, and partly through municipal authorities seeking to curtail the enormous losses brought about by uncontrolled growth. Zoning as now practiced, however, has scarcely succeeded in attaining either of these objectives. Owing to inaccurate and, more particularly, insufficient information, our zoning ordinances have been quite out of scale with actual needs. The same forces of speculation that have warped city growth in the past continue to do so through distortion of zoning ordinances.[4]

Because zoning is a vital instrument, these deficiencies deserve attention. The design of commercial zoning persists in retaining "horse and buggy" features. It is an established community attitude in most areas that all land on highways should be zoned for business. In the early days of the village the road led to the door of the shop. The horse was tied to the hitching post in front and "parked at an angle." This form of curb parking has lingered on while the automobile replaced the horse and buggy, while the number of motor vehicles leaped from

3. Educational Service/Tax Conference. National Trust for Historic Preservation, Washington, D.C.

4. Harland Bartholomew, *Urban Land Uses,* Harvard City Planning Series (Cambridge, Mass.: Harvard University Press, 1932).

8,000 at the turn of the century to more than 120,000,000 in 1970, and to 183,468,000 in 1988, and while the electric streetcar and motorbus made the horsecar extinct.

The shopping promenade of yesterday has become the traffic artery of today, but the design of business zoning remains unchanged. Mile after mile of highways are stripped with excessive zoning for commercial use. Strip zoning with its curb parking has become a curse. Through traffic does not mix well with the ready ingress and egress needed for parking and service on shopping streets. Submarginal business enterprises, blighted houses, and acres of weed patches on unimproved lots stretch along streets zoned for business, creating a state of built-in blight. The result is a plan impractical for traffic and undesirable for shopping.

The property protection expected of zoning has been largely confined to single-family dwellings. It is a peculiarity of current zoning that each lesser economic classification is permitted in zones of greater economic intensity. Single-family dwellings are permitted in multiple-dwelling districts, and both uses are permitted in commercial districts. Some ordinances still permit all uses in industrial zones. As a result, the only zone restricted to the use for which it is designed is the single-family zone; in this zone only single-family dwellings are permitted. The industrial park is a step forward because it is restricted to industry, but this feature has thus far been infrequently incorporated into zoning ordinances. Unplanned mixture of land uses are not economically sound. Land occupied by dwellings in an industrial zone reduces the efficiency of service facilities for industrial operations, and the safety and convenience of a residential community are denied to the residents scattered through an industrial district. Zoning and planning will achieve compatibility only when the zoning ordinance restricts uses in each zone to those for which the zone is designated.

The areas of land zoned for their respective uses are usually far in excess of the requirements of the city. The amount of land zoned for commercial use has been estimated at three to ten times the area that will ever be needed in the locations zoned. This not only compels the mixture of incompatible uses but induces the spread of uneconomic commercial enterprise. Submarginal business degenerates into blight and, in turn, creates an unhealthy environment for its more prosperous neighbors. Were land uses restricted to the classifications for which they are zoned, the temptation to retain or seek zoning for uses that cannot be sustained economically would undoubtedly fade. High taxes on commercially zoned land, used or not, could cause a realistic attitude toward zoning of property with little or no potential for use.

The tremendous burden of building bulk occupying urban land has contributed to the congestion of people and traffic, the disappearance of space, and ugliness. Zoning regulates the type of use permitted on the land; it also regulates the amount of permissible floor space. The regulations are expressed in terms of setbacks from property lines—front, side, and rear yards—volume envelope, sloping planes from street lines, maximum heights, lot coverage. The building volume resulting from these regulations is the measure of the floor space and population density set by the zoning ordinance. The maximum density permitted by prevailing ordinances is so excessive that open space has disappeared, the streets cannot handle the traffic generated, and there is no room to store vehicles.

A final consequence, more difficult to measure but nonetheless vital to the economic health of the community, is the imbalance between the demand for space and the amount of excess space permitted by zoning laws. In most communities neither the total amount of land nor the total amount of permissible floor space can be absorbed for the designated land use. As land development reaches a saturation point, new improvements that exploit the permissible zoning volume drain away the opportunities of less fortunate neighbors to sustain economical business operations. Physical deterioration follows economic blight, and the adverse effects injure both the overbuilt and the underbuilt properties. The potential intensity permitted by the ordinance defeats its purpose as a regulatory measure. Land values are subject to extremes of speculative irresponsibility, and decent standards of open space and site planning occur, if at all, despite the law. Zoning must allow adequate space for dynamic growth, but it must also avoid the excesses that nourish economic and physical blight.

An indiscriminate, unplanned mixture of different land uses can be detrimental to the quality of the physical environment. This is observed in the careless practice of spot zoning—the intrusion of service stations in residential neighborhoods, for example. The convenience of a modest shopping center, however, may enhance a residential neighborhood if it does not lead to undesirable noise, excessive night lighting, and an increase of traffic on residential streets, and if adequate on-site parking and landscaping are components of the plan. With appropriate density control, apartments may not only harmonize with single-family districts but also enrich the appearance of a neighborhood with a variety of form and open space. *Compatibility, rather than similarity of uses, is the key to a harmonious relation between land uses.*

The dull uniformity of mass-produced houses in suburban "cookie-cutter" subdivisions has prompted the effort to achieve visual interest and some degree of individual identification; a variety of setbacks and decorative exterior designs are used to camouflage the similarity in floor plans. These superficial efforts are unpleasant reminders that few custom-built homes have been erected in recent decades. Most homes are produced by a new profession of speculative, large-scale homebuilders. The home, once every man's castle, has been reduced to a piece of merchandise, a commodity for trade.

FLEXIBLE ZONING

It appears that zoning is already adequately flexible. Hardly a day goes by when there is no application for a change in the ordinance regulations or a change in the map to permit uses currently disallowed. The requests for exceptions, variances, conditional use permits, and a variety of other escapes from the rigid enforcement of the law are major items on every planning commission and council agenda. Many of the requests are reasonable and appropriate to the variety of conditions associated with the nature of the land and environment and must be approved, but the vast majority are the result of efforts to gain special privileges and economic advantages beyond the intent and purpose of the law.

But the fact is flexible zoning is necessary. Exploration of methods by which flexibility may be incorporated has produced the technique of density control. The monotony of subdivision design that has resulted from the single-family land use classification combined with lot-size regulations is relieved by this method. The zoning classification and prescribed lot size that prevail for a given tract establish the overall density and maximum number of lots permissible in the subdivision. The density control provision permits the developer to reduce the minimum lot size, providing the maximum number of lots is not exceeded and the balance of the land is developed for recreation or park space.

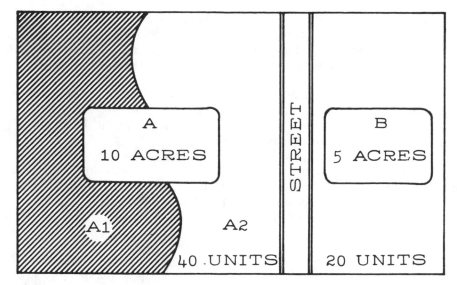

Incentive concept:

A & B   *Parcels zoned for four units per net acre.*
A1   *Dedicated 5 acres for flood control and recreation.*
A2   *Forty units permitted on the remaining parcel (5 acres) provided the number of units on the residual land is not greater than two times the units allowed on similar acreage of adjacent land.*

The technique identified as "planned development" or "community unit" is another advance in the achievement of zoning flexibility. This permits the planned integration of land uses and, although its application is directed primarily to large developments of raw land in suburban areas, it may be applied to built-up sections of the city. It offers the opportunity to plan for the full range of uses required by a well-balanced community—shopping, parks, schools, and a variety of housing types—uses not generally provided for within the framework of conventional zoning.

Mixed-Use Land Concept

Most of the classical zoning ordinances have consistently advocated the protection of single-family residential areas from intrusion by higher-density residential uses, even more so from commercial and industrial uses. Only in planned unit developments where the homes could be adequately protected from the nonconforming developments and activities associated with them have these been permitted.

The main objection to "unplanned" mixtures of uses remains a valid consideration in the planning of communities, especially in those already built, where there is concern about the conflicts that can and often do arise as a consequence of increased traffic, inadequate streets, lack of parking, noise, and other activities that violate the health, safety, and quiet desired by residents.

On the other hand, where uses are planned in a reasonable relationship to each other, and the problems associated with spot zoning and variances that offer special privilege are dealt with in advance, there can be excellent urban planning opportunities for the careful mixing of uses to provide for the needs of the residents without violating their privacy and safety.

Development Agreements

Over the years the theory that zoning cannot be subject to conditions other than those set forth in the ordinance has been the basis for many court cases, with findings in support of the concept. As mentioned elsewhere, new devices are always entering the process to make zoning more flexible. In a sense the newly devised development agreements are, following approval by the community, a more rigid contract between both the community and the developer.

First, the development agreement does not take the place of any existing law or regulation or any of the approval requirements. It is more like the regulations for a planned unit development used for a complex proposal, in which the regulations set forth the basic outlines for the development.

Second, and most important to the developer, the community agrees not to change its planning and zoning laws applicable to the development for a specific period of time. This assures the developer that he can safely engage in large expenditures for detailed planning and construction during the valid period of the agreement.

Third, in return for the above guarantee, the community may require, and the developer may agree to, the construction of specific improvements, public facilities, and services and develop the land according to a specific schedule. The community may also require other commitments that it otherwise has no right to compel a developer to perform.

Fourth, statutory requirements indicate that a development agreement must specify the time during which the city agrees not to change its regulations dealing with the permitted use of the property, the density or intensity of uses, the size of buildings, and the requirement for dedication or reservation of land for public purposes. The agreement may also include other terms and agreements, including a time schedule for additional public services and facilities to be provided by the developer.

Fifth, once an agreement has been entered into, the local agency must periodically review the progress made by the developer to comply with the terms of the agreement at least once every twelve months.

Some projects are more subject than others are to development agreements. They can provide security to developers of large-scale multiphased projects, where substantial investments for planning, engineering, and the installation of public facilities are involved.

In addition, the agreements can become a valuable tool in dealing with smaller parcels. This is particularly so where there are many public service problems or where the community seeks to induce the property owners to dedicate land or participate in the construction of new public facilities even though the owner is not ready to develop the property.

The community could also hold out the development agreement as an incentive to encourage a developer to provide low-income housing, extra open space, or other provisions that the community might desire.

PITFALLS

Zoning decisions may often be challenged on the basis of both legislative enactments and constitutional issues. These would include:

Conspiracy, the actions either open or covert, to grant a privilege to a person or organization, either for friendship or financial reward. Contributions to future political campaigns fall into this suspect area.

Antitrust, the denial of equal protection under the law by granting a zoning or other development favor to one party and denying it to another whose property is in a similar situation.

Freedom of speech, the regulation of signs, billboards, certain religious organizations, or certain games and activities that may offend a segment of the populace. Careful treatment in the design of regulations must prevent the appearance of outright prohibition.

Excessive demands for improvement, in the form of fees, licenses, and exactions, especially in those states where other means of securing improvements are not available.

Failure to follow due process, not holding adequate public hearings, providing for appeals, posting public notices in local media, failure to disqualify decision-makers with personal interests in a case, failure to keep adequate records, and illegal conduct of meetings (actions without quorums, for example).

Exclusionary zoning, where a community seeks through zoning to establish such high standards for development that the excessive costs involved in land and improvements will per se exclude all but the most affluent segment of the population from the jurisdiction. The New Jersey Supreme Court, in *Mount Laurel I* and *Mount Laurel 2,* has ruled that communities shall provide opportunities for the development of a fair share of its housing to be available for low- and moderate-income families.[5] This housing must be provided for in each community and not just in the region.

As the zoning process is reviewed it is possible to conclude that, like much else in the field of public law, it is full of potential for proper use as well as misuse. As indicated, however, it is still one of the better ways in which to implement the comprehensive plan. The flaws become fewer when there is good government and when the ordinance is administered in a reasonable manner.

In some communities, where attention to details is lax, the legislative body may permit applicants to provide sketchy plans and depend on the goodwill of the developer to carry out the proposed program with little if any further approvals. This type of casual approval results in losing control of the actions to be taken at a later date and is considered the contracting away of public power.

---

5. *Southern Burlington County NAACP v. Township of Mount Laurel,* 336 A 2d. 713 (N.J. 1975).

CHAPTER 35

THE SPECIFIC PLAN

It is a well-known principle that zoning requirements cannot be waived except in minor matters prescribed in the ordinance itself, under conditional uses allowed by special permit or variance after a minor deviation from the code is carefully inspected, found consistent with the intent and purpose of the law, and determined to pose no problems for others in the same zone.

Over the years the planning department receives proposals that cannot, without violating the law, be approved; such requests for special privileges are rejected.

With this as background the state adopted a means to allow the planning commission and legislative body to approve projects under circumstances that would accommodate the applicant's request. Specified conditions with special fees and exactions would give the public a quid pro quo: financial and physical advantages to the community and reasonable protection for the surrounding residents and their property rights. A community of regulations applicable to a single zone or property would be the product of this procedure.

In the early days of zoning this type of favoritism would be called "spot zoning." If the zone was large enough and was consistent with the comprehensive plan, a legal change of zone classification based on enabling laws was made. There is no question that when this option was used poorly, the process would be viewed as corrupt.

Specific plans have rejuvenated central business districts, preserved open space, built residential and mixed-use developments, and widened streets. Such plans are versatile, applicable to both small and large areas. The city of Mountain View used one for a 4-acre mixed-use project that combined commercial and residential development along a major city street. At the other end of the scale, the 18,000-acre Chino Hills Specific Plan in San Bernardino County allowed more than 200 landowners to participate.

Processing time for tentative maps, zone changes, and environmental review can be cut with the use of a specific plan. Because this plan must analyze the targeted area in detail and set development standards, there is no need for other design reviews once the tentative map is approved. Simi Valley in Ventura County, California, expects to reduce subdivision processing time by up to 75 percent under its Wood Ranch Specific Plan.

A developer's uncertainty about whether the total area of a large multistage project will be approved is also lessened, since a local legislative body must set its priorities for appropriate land uses when the specific plan is designed. Because the location and size of capital facilities and public improvements have already been decided, a developer knows from the outset how to design a project to take the greatest advantage of the area. And the local government can keep its expenses to a minimum. In the 1,700-acre Northeast Specific Plan of Visalia in Tulare County, California, the city lowered the cost of road construction by $1.5 million by designing streets 32 feet wide instead of the standard 60 feet of conventional subdivisions. The city and private utilities also saved money by eliminating the need to install larger storm drains and sewer systems and more telephone lines than necessary. The specific plan had spelled it all out.

The use of specific plans is increasing even though a number of jurisdictions are still reluctant to employ them. Some local planning departments feel that their requirements make their use too limited and the process too complex. Others believe that land use controls, such as area plans, planned unit developments, neighborhood plans, and community plans, offer greater flexibility. Some are confused as to whether specific plans are regulatory measures similar to zoning laws or alternate means of implementing comprehensive plans.

DEFINITION OF A SPECIFIC PLAN

Specific plans have developed as a bridge between the local comprehensive plan and individual development proposals. Whether written by the developer or by the local government, they contain both planning policies and regulations. They often combine zoning regulations, capital improvement programs, detailed development standards, and other regulatory schemes in one document which can be tailored to meet the needs of the specific area.

Specific plans are often confused with area plans and planned unit developments. *Area plans* are adopted as part of the comprehensive plan in the same manner as elements and do not ordinarily contain regulatory mechanisms. *Planned unit developments* differ from specific plans in that they are a form of zoning that generally allows for mixing housing types and implementing other uses. Specific plans, however, may be prepared for uses other than residential and may include zoning regulations.

Local planning agencies may designate areas within their jurisdiction as ones for which a specific plan is necessary or convenient. Some communities use their comprehensive plans or municipal codes to identify these areas, which are often undeveloped or transitional areas where greater detail will eventually be necessary to implement the comprehensive plan. Norwalk, California, in Los Angeles County has amended its comprehensive plan to create a specific plan land use designation to apply to underdeveloped areas of the city with unique characteristics. Simi Valley (Ventura County, California) has identified seven areas of the community with unique characteristics or problems. It plans to require a specific plan for each. Still other communities may require that all undeveloped areas above a certain acreage have a specific plan.

**CONTENTS OF
A SPECIFIC
PLAN**

A specific plan should include all detailed regulations, conditions, programs, and proposed legislation which will be necessary for the systematic implementation of each element of the general plan.

The following excerpts regarding mandatory contents, flexibility, California Environmental Quality Act (CEQA) exemption, and consistency are taken from the California General Guidelines of June 1987:

> A specific plan is a tool for the "systematic implementation" of the comprehensive plan. It may be applied to all or a portion of the area covered by a comprehensive plan. Any interested party may request the adoption, amendment or repeal of a specific plan. While a plan may be prepared by either the public or private sectors, plan adoption, amendment and repeal are the responsibility of the local legislature. As a legislative act, however, a specific plan is subject to the referendum and initiative processes.

> ### Mandatory Contents
> At a minimum, a specific plan must include a statement of its relationship to the comprehensive plan and a text and diagram(s) that specify all of the following in detail:
>
> The distribution, location, and extent of the uses of land, including open space, within the area covered by the plan.
>
> The proposed distribution, location, and extent and intensity of major components of public and private transportation, sewage, water, drainage, solid waste disposal, energy, and other essential facilities proposed to be located within the area covered by the plan and needed to support the land uses described in the plan.
>
> Standards and criteria by which development will proceed, and standards for the conservation, development, and utilization of natural resources, where applicable.
>
> A program of implementation measures including regulations, programs, public works projects and financing measures necessary to carry out the provisions of the preceding three paragraphs.
>
> These requirements are general and enable a local government to select from a wide range of land use criteria and implementation programs. Specific plans may also address any other subject which is in the judgment of the planning agency necessary or desirable for comprehensive plan implementation.

> ### Flexibility
> Such flexibility allows a community to assemble, in one package, a set of land use specifications and implementation programs tailored to the unique characteristics of a particular site. Therefore, specific plans are particularly useful for sites with major environmental and fiscal constraints.
>
> A fundamental question regarding specific plans is whether they are regulatory or policy documents or both. A review of the specific plan statutes does not provide a

clear answer. However, specific plans adopted by ordinance are more regulatory than those adopted by resolution.

A regulatory specific plan with its characteristic flexibility would have certain advantages over zoning, which is inherently rigid in its application. A community's control of development phasing provides a good example. The regulatory effects of zoning are immediate while the provisions of a comprehensive plan are long-term. If a comprehensive plan's implementation is limited to zoning, it may be difficult for a city to phase a long-term development so that it meets the comprehensive plan's development objectives. A series of zone changes, including the use of holding zones, may be required; whereas, the one-time adoption of a specific plan can easily resolve the problem. Along with specifying land uses, a regulatory specific plan could stipulate development timing by means of a phasing program.

CEQA Exemption

The advantages of a specific plan are not limited to those inherent in its flexibility. Residential development projects are exempt from the California Environmental Quality Act if they implement and are consistent with a specific plan for which an environmental impact report (EIR) or supplemental EIR has been prepared. Hence, application processing times should be reduced for residential projects, including subdivisions and rezonings.

In addition to saving time, a specific plan reduces development costs. For example, a specific plan's land use specifications in combination with its capital improvements program eliminates uncertainties as to future utility capacities. Developers can avoid costly oversizing.

Consistency

In light of these benefits, it is important to note that specific plans may not be imposed arbitrarily. They must be consistent with their jurisdiction's comprehensive plan. In turn, zoning ordinances, subdivisions (including tentative tract and parcel maps), public works projects, development agreements and land projects must be consistent with specific plans. A local agency may not approve a final subdivision map for a land project unless the agency has first adopted a specific plan covering the project area. Furthermore, a special district, school district or agency created by a joint powers agreement may not carry out its capital improvement program if the program (or a part of it) is found to be inconsistent with a comprehensive or specific plan of an affected city or county.

CHAPTER 36

SUBDIVISION OF LAND

The earth is our primary resource. It took hundreds of thousands of years to create the few inches of soil that support humanity. People's greed and neglect have often destroyed what nature took eons to develop. The story of humankind's improvidence with the land is suggested by Walter Havighurst:

> In 1823 a little Norwegian wanderer, named Cleng Peerson, walked overland from New York to the western territories. At Chicago he turned north. For six days he printed his steps in the blank sands of Lake Michigan. At evening he boiled his kettle at lake's edge. He slept under the soothing drones of water. At the site of Milwaukee (three log huts, one of them empty) he found a tall man, naked to the waist, beside a cabin hung with traps and snowshoes.

> "What will I find if I continue north from here?" Cleng Peerson asked.

> Solomon Juneau was a fur trader. He knew the great twilight of the forests.

> "Woods to the world's end," he replied.

> It was literally true. Woods for 600 miles. In that day six-sevenths of Wisconsin was forest. Two-thirds of Minnesota was forest. The upper peninsula of Michigan was all forest. And the forest began beyond Lake Superior, stretching away toward Hudson Bay. A country as big as France and every mile of it mysterious with forest twilight and haunted with the sound of running water. . . . Cedar, hemlock, tamarack and pine. A forest rich and vast enough for the needs of a nation forever.

> Try to find that forest now. . . .

> The timber cruisers came, walked through the country. . . . Behind them came the lumber kings and the great corporations. They logged off the forest in a furious

442

assault. "Come and get it" was the cry of the lumber camp. . . . "Come and get it" was the slogan of the corporations. . . .

How did the big corporations get hold of all the timber? There was the Stone and Timber Act of Congress, designed to safeguard national resources. But the corporations found the loopholes, and they got the timber. . . .

Following the mining of timber came the fires that swept not only the fallen timber but the seeds as well . . . so there was no second growth. Conservation of this forest came fifty years too late.[1]

We have done the same with all of our resources. In our desire to provide a maximum of opportunity and a minimum of regulation, we are prone to pass on a heritage of poverty in natural resources. So often our willingness to protect our resources emerges only after irreparable damage has been done. The control of land subdivision has been similar to that of soil conservation. It is accepted only after most of the urban land has already been butchered into pieces that render our city the unhappy affair we now experience. Carol Aronovicci said: "Wisdom

The primitive forest that reached to the end of the world. Like most of the orange groves in Southern California they have faded away like the "snows of yesteryear" to be replaced with housing and other urban uses.

1. Walter Havighurst, "The Land and the People," *Land Policy Review*, June 1941.

is knowing what to do. Virtue is the doing it." In the subdivision of land, as in many other affairs, our virtue precedes our wisdom and, it might be observed, the "doing" of many subdivisions is without much virtue.

PRIVATE OWNERSHIP: A HISTORY

The history of land ownership commenced when people formed tribes. Living on wild food and game, prehistoric tribes appropriated the territory they occupied. Like the American Indian or the pastoral people of the Asiatic steppes, the primitives guarded their territory from intrusion by other tribes, but equality of use was open to all the members of their own community.

communal property

The land belonged to the tribe and not to the individual; in this we detect a precedent for the sovereign states as the true owner of all land. As the tribes grew in size and acquired territory by conquest or peaceful consolidation, they subdivided into villages. A degree of local autonomy was tolerated, but the land remained as community holding.

This ancient tradition of the land vested primarily in the community, with individuals granted rights to its use, has persisted despite the forms it has assumed at different times. Later, it was reflected in the feudal system when land was vested in the king as the head of the state.

The king granted land to his lords for their pledge of military support. They in turn allocated rights of land use to their serfs and *villeins,* these rights becoming an integral part of the social and political caste system. As the feudal system dissolved, the privileges of the lords were transformed into a form of ownership, and the landlord was born. In England the system of leasing land estates to tenants reached a stage in which the tenants were assured rights even more firm than those of the landlord-owner; the tenants' intimate association with the land and its use warranted secure protection against unfair eviction and the assurance of full compensation for any improvements they might effect.

The history and nature of land tenure is complicated, varying in different countries at different periods. While the landlord-tenant system prevails in some countries, peasant proprietorship is predominant in others. The concept of land ownership has gradually moved from that of possession—the land as a place to live and to cultivate or capture food for survival—to that of land as property; when it is the latter the land becomes a commodity and is associated with private land ownership.

Because of this identification with ownership it is necessary to recognize the relation between private ownership and community interest. In strict legal terms there is no absolute private right to land in our system. The state alone is vested with that right, which it cedes to the individual possessor only as a strictly defined subordinate right, subject to conditions enacted by the community from time to time. The article on land tenure in *The Encyclopaedia Britannica* is no less accurate in its mention of the British parliament:

> Land tenure, throughout the world, shows that it has pursued one unvarying course: commencing in the community as a tribal possession, land has everywhere by degrees been appropriated to the village, to the families, and to the individuals. But in every stage the condition of its enjoyment and use have been absolutely regulated by the community in reference to the general welfare. . . . Those who refuse to admit the right of the state to impose such conditions on private property as it deems for the general benefit, may be dismissed with brevity. Not only do

they show entire ignorance of the history of land tenure at all times, but they belie the daily action of the British legislature. Parliament seldom lets a session pass without making some laws which assert the right of the state to take possession of property for private or public benefit, to tax it, and to restrain or regulate the rights of its owners over it. Nor is there any theory of the basis of property which does not tacitly admit that it is subject to the authority of the community.[2]

Land in the United States was originally vested in the crown of the country that colonized the area. The English king made grants of land to the trading companies, and they in turn transferred the grants to individuals or groups of settlers. In New England these settlers customarily established compact villages with each family receiving twenty acres. Outside the area of these individual holdings, the land remained in custody of the community for use by all members of the group. In the South, large tracts were granted for agricultural development.

The King of Spain held absolute title to the land in the Spanish colonies. His subjects were dispatched to those areas the crown desired to be populated, and the land was leased for cultivation. The crops were specified, and if for any reason settlers neglected to cultivate the land, they were deported from the colony. Provisional grants of huge estates were made to crown favorites in the western country that later became California, the first in 1784. *Ranchos* like those of José Verdugo in the San Fernando Valley and Manuel Nietos between the Santa Ana and San Gabriel rivers occupied areas of 390,000 acres stretching from the mountains to the sea. These great holdings were roughly measured; the *vara,* the Spanish measurement of distance, was calculated by the distance covered on horseback in a given period of time, and the later problems of untangling disputed claims may well have originated with the relative spryness of some caballero's horse.

Like the Roman *praesidium,* the German *Marktplatz,* and the New England common, the plaza occupied the center of the Spanish colonial pueblos. House lots were grouped about the plaza, with planting fields and public pastureland lying beyond them. This layout historically was intended as protection from attack, but its social advantages were eventually realized and all pueblos and cities founded by the Spanish in North and South America are laid out in this way.

The town of Los Angeles illustrates the typical village plan. The eleven families who were the original settlers were joined by the garrison and the Indians in a gay fiesta to mark its establishment in 1781. (This was probably the first of the supercolossal premieres for which Hollywood later was to become famous.) Each of the settlers was permitted to cultivate fourteen acres of land outside the residential area, and an allowance of stock and equipment was given equally to each family. All had free range for their stock on lands outside the area designated for cultivation.

> The first subdivision of the City of Los Angeles was quite simple. It covered an area of four square leagues or about thirty-six square miles centered about the plaza which measured 275 by 180 feet. In accordance with De Neve's instructions, the old plaza lay with its corners to the cardinal points of the compass, the streets extending at right angles so that "no street would be swept by the wind." Upon three sides of the plaza were the house lots, fifty-five feet in width. One-half of the remaining side was reserved for public buildings, the other half was for open space.[3]

---

2. Chicago: Werner Company, 1893, vol. 14, p. 259 (American Revision).

3. *El Pueblo,* Security Trust and Savings Bank, Equitable Branch, Los Angeles, California, 1948.

After the American Revolution, land formerly held by the crown of England went to the respective states. To resolve the conflicting interests of the states, much of it was declared in the public domain by the federal government. The United States thereby became proprietor of the frontier areas. Because the government of the new nation needed revenue for its operation and the expansion of the vast country, settlement was encouraged by the sale of land at nominal prices, and grants were offered in return for development. The Homestead Act, entitling the citizen to 160 acres of land on the condition that he bring it under cultivation within 5 years, was one such instrument. Huge grants were made to the railroads as inducement to extend their rails across the western territories; about 10 percent of the public domain was turned over to them in 1867.

These policies overlooked the possible dissipation of the natural forest and mineral resources that later took place, and it has been subsequently necessary to devote much legislation to the restoration and protection of these domains. In urban communities the abuse of land through speculative excesses has paralleled the dissipation of the natural resources in rural areas.

STANDARDS SET BY ZONING

Standards for lot sizes, dimensions, and area are to be found in the zoning ordinance. These standards are different in each zone. They often differ for cities and counties; for example, large-lot zoning has been criticized in many urban areas, but is desired in rural regions where piecemeal urbanization could destroy the potential for economically sound agriculture.

Historically, lots in urban areas tended to be small, as illustrated in many of the early cities of the United States and Europe. San Francisco, with its twenty-five-foot-wide lots, exemplifies the conditions of overcrowding created by this pattern of development. Structures are built next to each other with no open space except the street in front and a small yard at the rear. It was only after earthquakes and fires that community planners realized that little if anything was to be gained by this overcrowding. The standards were thereafter increased to at least double those that had previously existed. The current drive to return to old standards is based on the exorbitant price of land in most communities coupled with the desire for greater profits for those participating in the real estate marketplace.

Single-Family Lots

The size of individual homesites varies from the lot 25 feet wide covering an area of 2,500 square feet, to the estate lots where the width may be 250 feet or more and the area extend into acreage. In between these are the so-called standard lots, where the width ranges from 40 feet to 60 feet and the areas from 5,000 to 7,200 square feet. Many suburban communities have minimum standards of 7,500 to 8,000 square feet in order to provide for the openness associated with the village life desired by many middle-class residents.

Zero Lot Line Developments

Zero lot line housing is a potential solution of dwindling land and resources, increasing housing costs, and the continuing need to conserve energy. By placing residential units on one lot line, the amount of usable open space is expanded. The wall on the lot line provides privacy and can be aesthetically pleasing to the residents of the directly adjacent lots. Such projects fulfill the owner's desire for single-family detached housing while maintaining an attractive appearance and conserving resources.

The zero lot line design concept potentially permits greater flexibility in provision for useable outdoor living, because it doubles the width of the side yard on one side of the dwelling. This would provide the flexibility in orienting the structure to take advantage of sun and shade. However, care must be taken in the design to protect the adjacent lot's privacy, and covenants must permit the portion of the structure on the zero side to be maintained. All roof drainage must be onto the resident's property.

However, developers seeking to utilize zero lot line procedures are less interested in providing greater amenities than they are in reducing the lot sizes and crowding the land. For instance, in Dade County, Florida, single-family lot areas were reduced from the standard 7,500 square foot requirement to 4,500 square feet. The maximum coverage was increased from 35 to 50 percent of the total lot area. Certain privacy safeguards were introduced by requiring solid walls on critical sides of a structure. To make maximum use of the limited outdoor space, a minimum of 15 percent of the building's walls had to open onto a patio or garden.

SPECULATION

As our nation grew in size and urban centers became large metropolitan areas, there was increased competition for land for all purposes. Great estates were broken up and sold in parcels of varying size. For the most part, land was still considered a base for some economic or social use. Not until recent years did it become a speculative commodity to be bought and sold for a profit like stocks and bonds and, not infrequently, for a loss.

Some of the wildest exploits in land sales occurred in Florida and California during the early 1920s. Florida land was sold at fantastic prices to people in such places as New York and New England, and much of the land was underwater. When the boom broke, thousands of people found themselves with worthless property and their life savings lost.

Real estate speculation in California involving *los Americanos* and the Spanish *rancheros* was no less fantastic. For example, at one time all land in an area was to be registered in the land office by a specified time or be declared free for claim by anyone desiring it. Various tricks were employed to deceive the Spanish rancheros: some notices were never published or they were "lost": some were phrased in language not understood by the Spanish landowners; or, as a last resort, owners were terrorized to keep them away from the registry office until the deadline passed.

In later days of speculation, land was subdivided and sold in flood areas and on precipitous hillsides; in one example the gridiron plotting of streets rendered the lots useless so that 90 percent of the land has since reverted to the state for failure to pay taxes. A multitude of 25-by-100-foot lots were laid out and sold for "a dollar down and a dollar a week." There were no sewers and no paved streets, and heavy rains washed out roads and water pipes. These subdivisions were not only poor investments for the purchasers; they were also wanton wastes of urban land resources.

As lots in these scattered "wildcat" subdivisions were sold off, the new owners demanded urban services and facilities and transportation, which could not be supported. When the boom died in California, as in Florida, thousands of lots, some improved and some devoid of pavements or utilities, remained as evidence of premature and irresponsible subdivision. Assessment districts, which had been formed to pay for the improvements promised by the subdivider, defaulted on their bonds. The scene was one of economic desperation.

The depths to which abuse of urban land subdivision sank is best illustrated by the contrast with the fine residential suburbs begun during the same period. Such developments as the Palos Verdes Estates near Los Angeles, St. Francis Woods in San Francisco, Roland Park in Baltimore, Forest Hills in New York, River Oaks in Houston, and the Country Club District in Kansas City are among a number in which the best techniques in land division and development were employed.

Escape!   The wanton neglect of the congested centers of our cities has been equaled only by the wastefulness of its sprawling expansion. People are fleeing from the city in search of relief from the ugly evils of congestion in their living and working environment. This does not raise the question of decentralization versus rebuilding. Cities are being continuously rebuilt, after a fashion, and decentralization is not only coming, it is here. The central problem is to turn the current exodus from a rout into an orderly expansion by way of planning and effective legislation to implement the execution of the plans.

Thus far, expansion has amounted to a scattering of homes over the available outlying countryside. This has provided a means to escape from the outmoded living environment within cities rather than as a means to accommodate the growing urban population gracefully. It has not been guided by the foresight of planners, enlightened civic leadership in business and government, nor wisdom in urban economics and finance. Credit for failure to meet the demand for better living must be given to the large-scale tract developers who produced the Levittowns and the thousands of similar but smaller "almost mass produced" clusters of homes. The only variations in the homes were the changes in orientation, the color of exterior finish of the homes, and the prices. The process of location was chaotic, unplanned in many instances, without reference to either places of employment or existing means of transportation.

Henry Ford said some years ago, "Plainly, so it seems to some of us, [that] the ultimate solution will be the abolition of the City, its abandonment as a blunder. . . . We shall solve the City problem by leaving the City."[4] This reflects the underlying discontent with cities, but can it be a milepost on the way to reaching a decent environment?

People have congregated in cities for their mutual welfare. They are now retreating from the congestion. Commercial and industrial expansion is moving to the outskirts to dodge the incredible land prices in the older areas. Decentralization is on the march, but this is an industrial age and the urban framework forms the basic pattern of our economic and social system. It is in the cities where people find their work. The surge of population to the cities has occurred at a remarkably accelerated rate, but this is not a phenomenon of recent origin.

Although exact figures are not available, the changes in industrial activities from 1947 to 1990 are indicated by the following statistics:

- The number of industrial establishments with more than twenty employees grew from 241,000 in 1947 to 809,000 in 1987.
- In 1981 there were approximately 112 million persons in the labor force. This was an increase from 71.5 million in 1960.
- The number of persons in manufacturing decreased from 18.5 million in 1972 to 12.5 million in 1988. This was a loss of 119.1 percent.

---

4. From "Mr. Ford's Page" in the *Dearborn Independent,* Dearborn, Michigan, 1922.

During the thirties three-quarters of all industrial jobs were within the major industrial centers, and these centers were confined to only 7 percent of all the counties in the United States. More than one-third of all jobs were in large cities and one-fifth in the peripheral areas and satellite communities contiguous to them.[5]

Industrial Employees in Manufacturing 1980 to 1989[1]

	ALL MANUFACTURING		
	1980	*1985*	*1989*
Manufacturing	20,285,000	19,260,000	19,426,000
Durable goods	12,158,000	11,463,000	11,422,000
	PRODUCTION WORKERS		
Manufacturing	14,214,000	13,082,000	13,257,000
Durable goods	8,472,000	7,673,000	7,615,000

[1] Statistical Abstracts of the United States National Data Book, U.S. Department of Commerce Economic and Statistical Division, Bureau of the Census Page 409, chart 669, 1991.
These statistics do not include the industrial and commercial unemployment that occurred in 1990 and 1991 due to the recession.

The urban population of the country was only 3 percent of the total in 1790, and it is almost 70 percent of the total in 1990, having increased nearly 30 percent during the 1950–60 decade. But the great central cities are losing population. This trend has also been evident since the thirties when the suburban districts of metropolitan areas under one million population gained twice as fast as the central cities themselves, with a similar trend in areas over one million. The suburban and satellite areas of Detroit and San Francisco-Oakland increased twice as fast as the central urban districts; the suburban and satellite communities around Chicago, New York, and Pittsburgh gained three times as fast as the central cities; around Philadelphia they gained six times as fast; around St. Louis more than ten times; and around Cleveland nearly eleven times.[6] The trend has advanced to the point where the population in ten of the twelve largest cities, with populations in excess of 700,000 and including the above-named cities, decreased during the 1950–1960 decade; only Los Angeles and Houston showed gains. The people are moving to the suburbs and satellite communities about them, but they seek to retain the advantages of the urban environment. More than three-quarters of the urban population live in the 212 metropolitan areas, and 40 percent of this urban population occupies the sixteen metropolitan areas of more than one million people.

The Statistical Abstracts of the U.S., 1984, indicate that between 1970 and 1980 the population of the U.S. increased 11.4 percent. Metropolitan areas gained 10.2 percent, the central cities 0.2 percent, the areas outside the central cities 18.2 percent, and the nonmetropolitan areas 15.1 percent.

Spreading at random about the metropolitan countryside, the subdivisions exact a heavy toll on the city. Extension of public services—utilities, streets, schools, transportation, police and fire protection—over sparsely occupied sections has

5. Daniel B. Creamer, *Is Industry Decentralizing?* (Philadelphia, Pa.: University of Pennsylvania Press, 1935).

6. Ladislas Segoe, *Population and Industrial Trends,* American Society of Planning Officials, 1935.

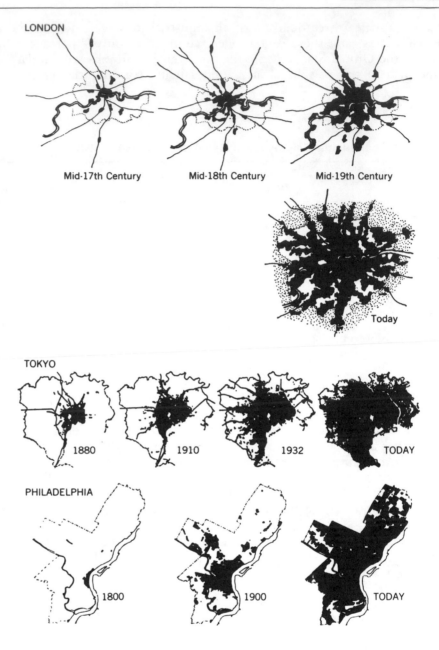

LONDON

Mid-17th Century   Mid-18th Century   Mid-19th Century

Today

TOKYO

1880   1910   1932   TODAY

PHILADELPHIA

1800   1900   TODAY

heaped a burden upon the city treasury. Financing the urban community has become a lingering illness. Debt hovers over property and improvements until a day when it is either paid in full or foreclosed. It hangs over the city hall and drains the taxpayer. Investments are unplanned; lending institutions compete for loans in the expanding suburbs, mushrooming over the countryside and sapping the strength of the central districts. "Lenders thus find themselves in the unpleasant situation of financing their own funeral."[7] The city invites chaos and awaits the day when the federal government must be summoned to bolster the crumbling local economy. Encouraged by the prospects for cheaper development, uninspired builders surge to the outskirts, create the blight of tomorrow, and retreat to other equally fruitful fields.

7. Miles Colean in a speech before the Mortgage Bankers Association, New York City, 1943.

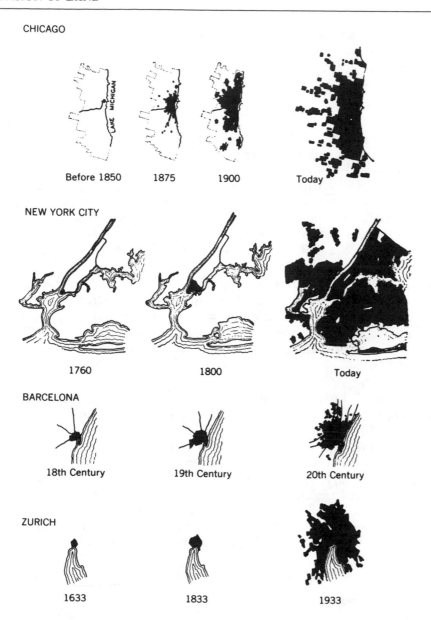

CHICAGO

Before 1850   1875   1900   Today

NEW YORK CITY

1760   1800   Today

BARCELONA

18th Century   19th Century   20th Century

ZURICH

1633   1833   1933

Subdivision records. *Cities everywhere are growing with disorder along the same pattern, each becoming a metropolis sprawling unplanned over the countryside. These diagrams illustrate the urban explosion since the Industrial Revolution. Rare among such cities, London built a greenbelt to restrict its expansion. This has resulted in the building of numerous New Towns outside of the boundaries of the London city area.*

Within every city is much land that is either vacant or inefficiently used. The speculative prospect for a future increase in the selling price is a strong inducement to withhold this land from development. The penalty of high real property taxation on improvements is a further deterrent to development. Henry George in 1879 evolved his theory of the single tax on land as a remedy for the situation,[8] and the graded real property tax in Pittsburgh assesses land at twice the value of improvements. Various methods have been proposed to emphasize taxation on land as a means to remove the speculative advantage of withholding land from development and conserve the public facilities and services of a community. Applied to all land, this principle could also discourage speculation in unproductive vacant land in the suburbs.

8. Henry George, *Progress and Poverty*, 1879.

The role of cities is vital. They provide the range and diversification of employment essential to free existence. Our task is not to destroy the city, but to build a better one.

REGULATIONS

Our conception of land has changed from one of soil cultivated for food and earth mined for minerals and other materials. The change has come about almost imperceptibly but nonetheless surely. Land is still used for the same primary purposes. However, it is not only used for the goods it produces: it is itself treated as goods to be bartered for trade. As such a commodity, urban land is frequently traded independently of its productive usefulness in the traditional sense. Ostensibly the value of land is linked with the manner in which it may be used, but possession is quite generally acquired for the purpose of exchanging it as a commodity rather than for its natural productive use.

As a result of this gradual shift in emphasis on land, we have grown unaware of the vital impact that the process of transforming raw acreage into improved urban lots exerts upon the community welfare. It is to assure the protection of the general welfare that subdivision regulations have been devised, with the knowledge that in the final analysis it is the general welfare that protects sound investment.

The questionable practices of the 1920s placed the subdivider of land in an extremely poor light, and the able practitioner was unavoidably identified with the unscrupulous. Reforms were overdue, and the necessity for regulations over the subdivision of urban land was urgent. These controls are based on the principle that the use and development of land constitute a right bestowed by the community upon the individual, and this right may be withdrawn or withheld when and if the individual violates the conditions upon which it is vested in him. The power of eminent domain, the police power, the power to tax real estate, and the power to regulate the use of land are expressions of this principle, and it provides the structure upon which the development of urban land is built.

The California State Subdivision Map Act defines a subdivision as follows:

> Any land, or portion thereof, shown on the last preceding tax rolls as a unit or as contiguous units, which is divided for the purposes of sale, either immediate or future, by any subdivider, into five or more parcels within any one year shall be considered to be a subdivision and requires the filing of a map for the approval of the planning commission and legislative body.

Such a definition or a similar one is usually contained in state laws that vest the right of police power in cities and counties for the regulation of land subdivision or in planning acts that outline the procedure for preparation of the comprehensive plan.

A definition of a subdivision such as the foregoing does not preclude the sale of a portion of an individual lot; this right is retained by the individual property owner. A parcel of land may be sold as a whole or in part at the discretion of the owner without the necessity to follow the subdivision procedures, provided no illegal lots are thereby created.

However, if more than one parcel is created it is necessary, before attempting to obtain a building permit, to secure the approval of the Planning Commission and to file the approved map with the County Recorder. It is usually required, even for a "lot split" where one lot is divided into two more lots (fewer than five), that all of the required improvements be installed before the lots are offered for sale. All developments on the parcels created are subject to all applicable laws and ordinances; substandard lots should not be approved.

There are many interests involved in the subdivision of land, including those of the original owner, the developer, the prospective buyer, and the city as a whole. Ladislas Segoe stated:

> To the land developer the subdividing of land is primarily a matter of profit. He is chiefly interested in realizing as much money as he can from the sale of his land in the shortest possible time. To the community the subdivision of land is a matter of serious public concern. The activities of the developers shape the future of the community and condition in a considerable measure the quality of the living and working conditions of its inhabitants. Where such activities are uncontrolled or inadequately controlled, they also may place an undue burden on the public treasury by reason of excessive cost of public improvements and maintenance, unnecessarily high operating costs of public services, and through the participation of the community in the financing of improvements in premature subdivisions.[9]

One of the first steps taken in some states for the control of subdivisions was the licensing of the subdivider. To obtain a license some education in the principles and practices of land sales was necessary, as well as knowledge of state and local laws pertaining to subdivision. It was generally required by law that the owner employ a licensed engineer to prepare the subdivision map for recording. This was an effort to ensure the accuracy of the subdivision maps and to avoid alteration in the development after it was recorded. In more recent years it has frequently been mandatory to record on the maps any unusual or hazardous conditions, such as the danger of floods in low areas. Such land has not necessarily been precluded from sale, but the purchasers were warned of what they were purchasing. If life was endangered, however, the public body could deny the right to subdivide and sell the land.

Subdivision is the method of transforming a city plan into a reality. The city plan is either realized or it is lost in the subdivision of land. Many of its overall elements are realized at the time the land is developed. Highways are dedicated, streets and alleys are paved, sewer and water lines and electric power are installed, new schools are constructed, transportation lines are extended, and police and fire protection are expanded. The control a community retains over land subdivision is one of the principal means by which elements of the comprehensive plan are enforced.

Having sovereign rights over the land within their boundaries, states pass laws governing the ownership, transfer, and use of private property, and they vest in cities and counties the right of police power to regulate the subdivision of land. Some states establish the procedures for subdividing land and have real estate commissions that ensure compliance with these procedures. The real estate commission operates in a manner similar to that of a corporation commission that regulates the sale of stocks and bonds. They check the legitimacy of sales organizations, the quality of the lots offered for sale, and ascertain that the required improvements are either installed or assured by a bond posted by the subdivider before approval of the subdivision and sale of land.

---

9. *Local Planning Administration* (Chicago: International City Managers' Association, 1941), p. 495.

The design of subdivisions is the responsibility of the local government of the community in which the land is situated. Under the provisions of the comprehensive plan, the local planning agency is generally charged with the responsibility for the administration of the standards for "community design" of subdivisions, the shape and size of lots, the size and length of streets, and the spaces to be reserved for community facilities, schools, and recreation.

In effect, the community reserves an equity in the land and vests in the individual the right to own and use land subject to the requirements for the general welfare of the community. Thus the city may require the subdivider to dedicate certain streets for access to property and it may demand that sewer lines be installed. If this facility is not available, the city may require larger lots to avoid the possibility of water and soil contamination by effluents from cesspools or septic tanks. The city may require service roads where land abuts a principal trafficway to control the ingress and egress to property, and it may require the installation of specific utilities and roads, walks and curbs, street lighting, electric distribution; alternatively, the city may require the subdivider to post a bond to cover the cost of such improvements before the final map of the subdivision is approved. The subdivider may be required to conform with a major highway plan for the community by establishing highway widths the proposed grades and alignment of city streets.

The local agency aids the subdivider in planning his land, suggests improved methods of site planning, and recommends to the legislative body exceptions of regulations that may be warranted by peculiar characteristics of the various sites. Material assistance has been rendered by the Federal Housing Administration in the improvement of subdivision design; this federal agency has performed a service in raising the quality of subdivision design in those communities where local laws are ineffectual or no trained planning officials are active.

One of the principal deficiencies in subdivision practice is the difference in standards for improvements that prevail in adjoining communities. These differences are apparent in the strange street alignments, blocked roadways, alternately wide and narrow streets, and differences in type of pavements frequently observable from one community to another. Perhaps less discernible, but more disastrous to the general community welfare and regional development, are the differences in standards for the design and construction of subdivisions. Some communities willfully lower their standards below those of neighboring areas to invite the subdivision and development of land within their boundaries, only to suffer the pain of a degenerated community at some later date. Many cities have made agreements to cooperate in matters of subdivision where the developments are within a certain distance of their respective boundaries. Where regional planning agencies are active, they have coordinated the subdivisions of the various cities within their jurisdiction. Here is a field ripe for significant service and progress.

A way to exercise quantitative control over land subdivision is yet unresolved, but it is urgently needed to restrain excessive and premature expansion of subdivisions. The repetition of the economically disastrous practices of the 1920s, many of which are recurring today, needs to be forestalled, but the method of legally accomplishing this purpose has not been developed. There were suggestions for issuing "certificates of necessity" during the 1920 decade when the effects of wildcat operations became painfully obvious. These certificates were to allow subdivision of land only when the developer could demonstrate the need for developing his property and produce some evidence of bona fide purchasers for it. The certificates never appeared.

The most effective means thus far of coping with excessive subdivision has been the requirement that a subdivider install all utilities and improvements, including streets and walks, in conformance with the standards established by the community at his or her expense and before sale. This transforms the subdivider from the usual position of a land speculator to that of a land developer. Required to meet the full capital costs of a complete improvement, it is likely that the developer will more thoroughly consider the financial soundness of a development before venturing willfully on a highly speculative enterprise.

PROCEDURE

Although procedures vary in different localities, the following steps may serve as a general description of the general sequence from an unimproved site to the development of parcels available for sale:

1. The land is surveyed to ascertain the precise description of its boundaries, the abutting streets, local drainage conditions, contours of the land, and the special features or structures that may occupy the site.

2. Official records are consulted to define the location of special easements or rights-of-way that must be retained in developing the land. There may be a proposed highway passing across the site of easements for sewers or power lines to serve the site or adjoining land. All restrictions on the use of the property must be determined: deed restrictions and zoning, the location of existing sewers or other requirements for sanitation, the height of the water table, the type of soil. The data on orientation and wind directions may affect the layout of streets and building sites. The surrounding land uses, both existing and permitted, require investigation. Adjoining streets are identified, and street names suggested.

3. Schools, parks, playgrounds, and other cultural and social facilities are located, and the availability of transportation and shopping facilities is evaluated in reference to the services they may provide to the residents in the proposed development.

4. The subdivision ordinances are consulted for restrictions that may apply to the size and shape of lots, the width and grade of streets, the setback lines to be observed, and the methods for presentation of the maps required by the local government agency: the planning department, real estate commission, or city engineer.

5. The developer should employ a planner or engineer to prepare the tentative or preliminary plan for the development of the property. This map should show, with reasonable accuracy, the manner in which the land is to be subdivided: the approximate size, shape, and the number of lots, the location of streets, their radii of curvature and grades, the method for providing drainage in all areas, and the utilities to be installed. The zoning and proposed land uses—open space to be reserved or developed for recreation, shopping, or other community facilities—should also be indicated.

6. An estimate is then prepared to show the probable total cost for development of the site and indicate the minimum selling price for the lots to defray the cost of the land, the improvements, and the overhead for subdivision commissions and profits.

7. Before filing the tentative map with the local agency, planning department, or city engineer, it is generally considered good practice to consult the Federal Housing Administration (FHA) land planning officials and lending agencies. This is particularly important if approval for mortgage insurance by FHA is expected to be ultimately sought by purchasers of the lots.

8. The tentative map is then filed with the local agency, planning commission, or engineer, and this agency submits it to the various city departments for advice on engineering, health, schools, fire and police protection, and recreation. The suggestions and requirements of each department are coordinated by the planning commission, the specific conditions being based upon the public health, safety, or the general welfare of the community. On many occasions the planning staff will prepare a revised plan to suggest improvements in the site design or indicate the manner in which the plan may better conform to local conditions and the comprehensive plan for the city.

9. After approval, the developer proceeds with the preparation of the final or precise engineering map for the land. The street improvements and utilities are shown, the lots are staked on the ground, and any minor changes that may be dictated by peculiarities in the site, such as hilly areas, are recorded. The final map is then filed with the city authorities, who check it for conformity with the approved tentative map. If compliance is apparent, the final map is submitted to the local legislative body and the mayor for final approval. It is then officially recorded.

10. Approval of the final map follows the installation of all required improvements or the posting of surety bonds to cover the cost of said improvements plus a factor of safety to offset inflation.

11. Before sale of the land may be undertaken the final recorded map must usually be filed with the state real estate commission and approval of sale obtained from that government agency.

CURRENT TRENDS

The subdivision of land is responding to the techniques of large-scale planning, and the magic words *mass production* are having their effect. Pressure to retreat from decent standards is strong, and resistance is difficult in periods when a housing shortage and high costs create social as well as economic problems for city dwellers. The necessity for and desirability of reasonable standards are generally recognized. It is in the broader implications of urban expansion that regulations of land subdivision need serious attention.

Conservation of the land is vital, not only to prevent reckless waste of this precious resource but also for the economic and social stability of the community. The sprawl of suburbia is a symptom of the revolt against congestion and exploitation in the central city. The crying need for reexamination of the nature of urbanism in our society is urgent, but the extension of urban facilities ad infinitum to serve the symptom postpones treatment of the malady. A common perhaps national fervor comparable to that which brought the London Plan and New Towns to England after World War II may be necessary to force the search for a pattern of urbanism appropriate to our time. Meanwhile, and without relaxing this search, the uneconomic expansion of suburbia will require some measure of curtailment. The unpleasant reality of deterioration throughout great areas of the central city demands attention, but prudent conservation of land is a companion to economy in the cost of government.

SUBDIVISION MAP CHART

Parcel Map
Filing Procedures

Tentative Map
Filing Procedures 1

Final Map
Filing Procedures

Map prepared by or under direction of a registered civil engineer or licensed land surveyor. Procedure for filing and obtaining approvals as provided by city ordinance.

↓

Transmitted after approval to county recorder through clerk of board of supervisors.

↓

County recorder must examine map and accept or reject it for filing within 10 days.

Map prepared by or under direction of a registered civil engineer or licensed land surveyor.

↓

Filed with Planning Director

↓

Public Works Director
City Engineer
Building Superintendent

↓

Planning Director

Map prepared by or under direction of a registered civil engineer or licensed land surveyor following approval or conditional approval of tentative map.

↓

Necessary certificates and acknowledgements obtained.

↓

Map filed with City Clerk (must be filed prior to expiration of tentative map)

↓

Planning Director and City Engineer

↓

If improvements not completed, improvement agreement entered into with local agency as a condition of approval.

↓

Map approved by City Council within 10 days or at its next regular meeting, if in substantial compliance with previously approved tentative map and conditions, if any, imposed on the tentative map have been met. (Deemed approved if no action taken within 10 day period.)

↓

Map transmitted after approval to county records through clerk of board of supervisors.

↓

County recorder must examine map and accept or reject for filing within 10 days.

Planning Commission

Approves, conditionally approves, or disapproves within 50 days after filing with clerk. (Deemed approved if no action taken within 50 days, but only insofar as map complies with act and city ordinances.)

↓

If dissatisfied, subdivider may appeal within 15 days to the City Council

↓

City Council

↓

At next regular meeting sets date (within 30 days thereafter) to consider map.

↓

Approves, conditionally approves, or dissapproves within the 30 day period. (Deemed approved if no action taken within the 30 day period, but only insofar as map complies with act and local ordinances.)

↓

Decision of City Council within 10 days. (Deemed approved if no action taken within time limits, but only insofar as map complies with act and city ordinances.)

The requirement that the land developer assume the cost of street and utility improvements in new subdivisions is accepted practice. Expansion creates the demand for a variety of facilities and services including schools, parks, playgrounds, health, fire and police protection, and highway and utility extensions. It is a public responsibility to assure the provision of these facilities. When the services are required to accommodate an increase in population, the added tax revenue to the community may maintain an economic balance with the cost of the facilities. Imbalance occurs, however, when the municipal facilities are necessarily duplicated to serve the population escaping from the central city, or where expansion is into an area that has no economic support.

The power to withhold permission to subdivide land is one control with which balance may be maintained. Denial of the right to subdivide land, however, is strong medicine, and other means may serve with greater equity and equal effectiveness. Independent of the land's market value, the public improvements and services necessary to development enhance the basic land value. Since this increment of increased value is created by public expenditure, it seems reasonable to assess a pro rata share of the cost against the subdivision.

A policy adopted in a growing number of cities is the requirement that the developer shall provide the new subdivision with a neighborhood park and playground. The policy is based on the premise that recreation space to serve a residential subdivision is in a category similar to public rights-of-way and improvements for streets, sidewalks, service roads, and parkways. Since the size of subdivisions varies, some being too small to require a local recreation area, the subdivider is assessed a charge that is deposited with the city to assure the development of this facility when the demand arises.

PLANNED DEVELOPMENT

The growing acceptance of the principles of community planning is one of the encouraging signs of an improvement in standards. Land in the heart of cities is already subdivided. Improvement in city planning within these huge areas must necessarily emerge with techniques of urban renewal and redevelopment. The major activity has consequently been taking place on the outskirts of the cities and will undoubtedly continue until renewal becomes an effective instrument for rebuilding the central areas.

Attention to the amenities of good community planning is apparent in the standards espoused by such organizations as the Urban Land Institute. The members include some of the pioneers in the development of subdivisions and the planning and building of residential communities. That good planning may also be good business is attested to by the appeal for an improvement in subdivision development by such men and organizations. The mediocre (and worse) product of speculative ventures has succeeded in the past and will continue to succeed as long as it remains a profitable enterprise. As the initiative of creative enterprise in community building produces better standards in the living environment, the speculative ventures will be reduced to a diminishing investment level; by this form of competition and the maintenance of decent standards of land subdivision —land planning—our cities may gradually improve as an environment for the people.

The Community Unit

In the comprehensive plan, the locations of future neighborhood centers—shopping centers, parks, and schools—are only approximately defined within the undeveloped areas of the city. The land use is usually shown by density classifications for residential purposes. The principles of community planning applied to large-scale subdivisions imply a balanced range of dwelling accommodations as well as a full range of community facilities. A provision for planned development, or the "community unit," has been incorporated in zoning ordinances to encourage and facilitate this integration of land uses.

Under this "community unit" provision an owner or group of owners may produce a complete development plan that, upon approval by the planning commission, may be adopted by the legislative body as the zoning plan for the entire area in lieu of prevailing zoning. This feature affords a flexibility not heretofore available. It implements planning for a diversification of dwelling types, characteristically lacking in conventional zoning, and ensures harmonious density within the plan for the entire area.

The neighborhood association is a familiar instrument for property owners to secure and maintain common amenities. Membership is usually stipulated in property deeds. The planned unit development embraces this legal instrument as a new level of self-government through cooperative or condominium ownership. The owner of a dwelling—apartment or house—in a *cooperative* owns shares of stock in the entire development with the right of occupancy in a specific dwelling. The owner of a *condominium* has title to the dwelling itself and a proportionate interest in the land and exterior facilities. The governing organization in both cases is an association of all owners with responsibility and authority for levying assessments for management and exterior maintenance. The condominium is generally preferred, since owners are financially responsible only for their own dwellings and for a portion of the related common areas and are not liable for obligations incurred by other owners.

The prospects for an improved environment warrant encouragement of this enlightened approach. The cumbersome procedures involved in the modification of conventional zoning fortify entrenched resistance to the flexibility community planning demands. Planned development may be a means to overcome current complications and achieve a variety in urban expansion not previously feasible. It could release the future subdivision of land from the straitjacket in which the built-up city and current subdivision practices are bound; it would provide the amenities and character of an urban environment associated with the central city without its concomitant faults. It may lead to a broader concept of planned decentralization for the metropolitan regions, where the great majority of the population is destined to find itself in the future industrial and scientific age.

Density Control

Conventional residential zoning classifies land uses according to building types: single family or multiple family. This method has its roots in the historical beginning of zoning when "fine" residential sections were protected from the intrusion of undesirable uses. The precedent has lingered while the protection has become a myth. Vast changes in the social and economic structure have completely altered the physical character of the city. The multifamily dwelling is no longer restricted to the "tenement house" class, nor is the single-family dwelling district the sole domain of the privileged class. The apartment and the detached house are not now distinguished by the difference in type of dwelling but rather by the quality of each, the geographic location, and particularly by the preferences of the residents and the composition of the family. Incompatibility revolves about the differences in the density of each type: the relative adequacy of interior and exterior space for comfort, convenience, and safety.

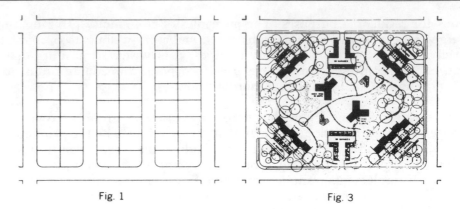

Fig. 1   Fig. 3

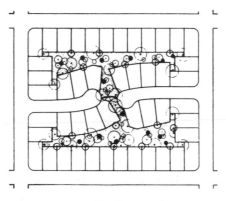

Fig. 2

Density control. *In this illustration Figure 1 represents a typical subdivision of forty-eight lots controlled by the minimum lot size. In Figure 2 relaxation of the minimum lot size as the basic control results in the same number of lots but reduces the area of internal streets, eliminates through traffic, and provides a common open space for all dwellings. It introduces a diversification in streets and an increase of recreation space.*

Planned development implements a desirable mix of dwelling accommodations to serve the needs of a balanced range of family sizes and preferences. The quality of the improvements placed upon the land and the level at which they are maintained contribute to the character of a community, but density is the key factor in planning. It establishes the texture of the physical form. It reflects the distinction, for instance, between a community of single-family homes and one of multistory apartments. It is a unit of measure for establishing a balance among all community facilities and circulation.

The term *density* is commonly employed as a measure of the number of dwellings that occupy or may occupy an area of land. *Net density* is identified with the number of dwellings in relation to the land area exclusive of public rights-of-way —the streets and sidewalks, parks and playgrounds, schools and commercial areas—whereas *gross density* usually pertains to the number of dwellings in relation to an area of land including all public rights-of-way and other related land uses. A distinction between these definitions may serve a useful purpose for certain technical measurements and comparisons, but the significant measure for the general texture of the physical form is expressed by gross density.

The pressure of urbanization has intensified the demand for land to accommodate the expanding urban population. Efforts to maintain the traditional single-family dwelling on its individual lot has forced the subdivision of land into increments of inadequate size; the typical "cookie-cutter" subdivision pattern has been inevitable. This, in combination with the pressure to reduce building and site development costs, has resulted in vast areas of mediocre residential tracts about our cities.

Every city will have its districts of single-family detached homes; this traditional form of family dwelling has virtues of particular value. In the very large metropolis these districts may be removed to the distant outskirts, but they should be planned with standards that actually produce the amenities of the detached house on its separate piece of land. In fact, however, in the attempt to preserve the single-family detached dwelling the minimum lot size has been reduced to dimensions that actually nullify the real advantages of this form. The narrow width of sideyards that separate dwellings denies privacy and renders the space wasteful; the conventional street setbacks have lost almost all semblance of usefulness since the automobile converted the street from a promenade to a service roadway. Insistence upon a distinction in zoning between subdivisions of high-density single-family lots and low-density apartment districts has consequently contributed in large measure to the extension of urban sprawl.

The genuine unit for the measurement of adequate planning standards is the individual human being. Family composition and characteristics vary, as do personal desires. Families need space in proportion to their sizes; children need space for active recreation, adults for sports, and older people for relaxation. Variations in these requirements may be more than absorbed in the "psychological elbow room" people need and now find wanting in their living environment. A diversification of dwelling types is necessary to satisfy the wide range of desires and family needs in a city. Insistence on the distinction between single-family classification of land use and the apartment district has tended to obscure the wide gap that exists between the amount of land per family in these two zoning categories. If the amount of space on the earth were related to the common denominator of the human being, the importance of density rather than the type of dwelling

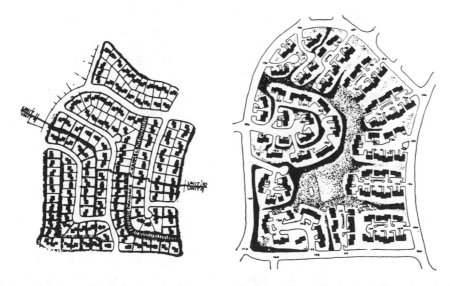

With the minimum prevailing lot as the unit of measurement for the overall gross density in the illustration, the site would accommodate as many as 200 dwellings. Adjusting the internal street system to the topography in a typical subdivision plan, with the usual odd lot sizes that result, would produce only 137 individual lots in conformance with the standard regulation (Fig. 1). With the principle of density control applied so that 200 dwellings are permitted, arranging clusters of row (alias "town," "group," "garden," or "patio") houses about cul-de-sac roads results in the allocation of about one-fifth of the site for park development (Fig. 2).
This is the primary community interest served by density control. Other advantages may accrue in the planning of individual dwellings, cul-de-sac roads, attractive plantings along the main circulation roads, and economy in site improvement costs. These costs may be reduced to as much as one-half of those of the conventional subdivision because of economy in grading, paving, drainage, and utilities. The degree to which the consumer of housing shares in these economies will extend the broad social advantages that may also accrue.
(Plans courtesy of Richard Leitch, Architect.)

Scarring of the hillsides with homes perched in precarious locations where narrow winding streets, exposure to wildfires, earth slippage, and other dangers are a constant threat.

Density Controls and Typical Urban Zoning Regulations

COMPREHENSIVE PLAN	GROSS AREA DENSITIES
Density Classification	*Not to Exceed (Gross Acres)*
Low	6 Dwelling units per acre
Medium	20 Dwelling units per acre
Medium high	60 Dwelling units per acre
High rise	200 Units per acre
ZONING CLASSIFICATION (FOR INDIVIDUAL LOT SALES—(NET AREA)	
Low D-1	6 Lots per acre
Medium D-2	12 Dwelling units per acre
	20 Dwelling units per acre
High (D-4 and D-5)	30–50 + Dwelling units per acre

Where land is to be developed as a complete planned unit, the plans shall be submitted for approval to the planning agency to be checked for compliance with regulations dealing with access, space between buildings, height limitations, parking design and location, building codes, water and sewage services, and access for fire and other safety vehicles.

Where land is to be subdivided into lots for individual sales all the requirements of the zoning ordinance shall apply to lot size and dimensions, building set backs and yards, building heights, etc. All provisions of the subdivision ordinance shall be complied with.

structure or the size of a lot could be employed as the desirable control for residential planning.

It is within the space of this wide gap that conventional subdivision practice and apartment zoning require overhauling. Were a relatively common standard of population density to be adopted as the measure of control for residential development, varied patterns could be woven within the overall texture of the physical form of the city. The apartment and the single house, the tall building and the low building, would then approach equal acceptability as neighbors and as places in which to live.

Poor subdivision regulations permit inappropriate types of trees in a limited parkway area, causing damage to sidewalk, curb, and gutter and dangerous conditions for pedestrians (left). Damage to sidewalks caused by tree roots (bottom).

The interpretation of density control may be extended to mean that the conventional minimum lot size represents an acceptable unit of measurement for the gross density in a community. The number of dwellings that may be placed on an area of land is thereby controlled by this density rather than the minimum lot size per dwelling. This method of control offers flexibility in planning the internal street system and the arrangement of the dwelling units. Efficient planning may also produce economy in development cost. As compensation for these advantages a predetermined proportion of the property would be reserved as open space for community recreation.

Oakland, California Fire Storm. *It has the appearance of a bombed-out city, October, 1991. (Bay Area Regional Earthquake Preparedness Program—BAREPP)*

THE OAKLAND FIRESTORM

Oakland–Berkeley firestorm. On a blistering hot Saturday afternoon, while sitting in the stadium in Berkeley one could observe smoke from a grass fire to the southeast, in Oakland. This event appeared to be under control. However, in the early evening a violent furnace like windstorm blew through the Oakland community. Early on the morning of October 20, 1991, a firestorm erupted casting a cloud of smoke over the bay area. Within a few hours some 3,000 homes and 400 apartments were completely destroyed. Twenty-five persons were incinerated in the catastrophe. Final calculations of the property lost will take some time. Personal articles such as art and family memorabilia have values that can never be determined.

Some of the factors contributing to the firestorm and the inability of the firefighters to stem its spread, included the following:

> the abnormal weather conditions which coupled with intense heat and blasting winds; the absence of an enforced weed abatement program that permitted more than six years of tinder dry growth to collect in the hill areas; the antiquity of the utility system, most of it installed under regulations and standards that could not respond to the demands of an emergency (For instance, the water main at the lower end of the lines tested to adequate pressure but the upper end was without a supply required to control the blaze); the rapidity of the spread of the flames (In the first hour one house was destroyed every 4 seconds and one house every 11 seconds for the duration of the fire); and many of the lives that were lost were a result of the elderly persons ignoring the warnings by the police to evacuate as they tried to save their treasured belongings.

The importance of this event is that it points to the dangers that face residents residing in hill areas where new development is added onto obsolete roads and utilities and where brush removal is not adequately enforced.

CHAPTER 37

GROWTH MANAGEMENT

The development of laws and ordinances to manage how and where growth may take place in a community did not "rise like Phoenix from some far off place in the sky." It is the result of the intensity of development that is taking place in many of the real estate "hot spots" in the world. Development that comes into being without the services (or the community ability to provide them) that are essential to meet the needs of the additions to the local population should not be allowed. In addition, valuable agricultural land, if not totally used for urban development, was made difficult for agriculture due to the proximity of the urban growth. Not only the health of the new residents but that of the existing community was at stake as the water and sewerage problems mounted while the community faced the threat of new taxes to install the needed facilities, a condition that few of the old or new residents favored.

Most of the worst conditions occurred in the unincorporated areas where the public officials representing the rural attitudes and interests failed to establish measures to support new urbanism in their midst. Many of the scattered developments soon became slums and a burden that the rural residents did not foresee. Some counties that included both rural areas and urban centers adopted regulations that permitted urban growth only in or adjacent to the existing development and then only if the developers provided the funds to develop essential infrastructure or to build new facilities to handle the problems that they were causing.

In Florida, for instance, as in other states, the growth management plans depended on the existence of a truly comprehensive plan and policies and financial resources to implement the critical parts of that plan in a timely procedure. Reginald R. Walters, planning director of Dade County, Florida, stated in the October 1990 issue of *Planning,* "Growth Management is not the mandate to plan, it is the mandate to implement your plan."

Another element in the Florida Growth Management Plan deals with a new term, concurrency. The term is new, but the demands that it makes as part of the management program are not new in that many communities over the years have required that essential improvements be made before a development was offered for sale to the public. Some communities provide that either the infrastructure (roads, utilities, sewerage treatment plants, school capacity, and parks) be in place or bonds be posted to assure the installation of the improvements within a fixed period. Unfortunately, in some cases the projects were occupied and the bond revenues were inadequate to install the facilities because of inflation or unexpected construction costs. Such costs are often due to unforeseen problems that would not have arisen if installation had been completed before the sale price of the homes was established. Communities sometimes require that 150 percent of the estimated cost be bonded to assure proper and timely installation. However, occupancy permits should never be issued before the roads; water, solid waste disposal, and drainage lines; and schools and recreational facilities are in place. This is "concurrency."

HOW SHALL WE GROW?

It has traditionally been assumed that continuous growth is essential to economic prosperity. But an unpleasant fact of life now becomes apparent: as urban population swells, public welfare and protection absorb increasing segments of city budgets. In the absence of a national or state policy to direct population distribution, individual cities are obliged to make their own decisions about growth and development.

Within the comprehensive plan land uses are designated and population densities distributed; thus the carrying capacity of the land in a city is measured. It is useful to know the rate of estimated population increase, through immigration and birth-death figures, in anticipating programs to improve and maintain city services. But it is the comprehensive plan that establishes how many people a city may accommodate and the quality of the environment to be provided for those people. The zoning ordinance translates the land use provisions of the comprehensive plan into specific terms. These instruments of planning policy represent the ultimate "growth policy" of a city. Where they are not so designed and not so implemented, the entire planning process is invalid.

These processes for guiding urban development are invalidated to a large extent by the common assumption that a city must find ways and means to accommodate all the people who may choose to live and work within it, and that regulations of land use that limit density are infringements on the "property rights" of landowners. Such allegations nullify the planning process and reflect a serious cultural and economic malady: the conflict between the recognition of land as the precious and rare natural resource it is and the concept of land as a commodity to be traded as merchandise. The "vested rights" of an owner to use his or her land as he or she chooses must be limited to uses that do not undermine the public interest; these are determined by the comprehensive plan and the zoning ordinances derived from it.

The small city of Petaluma in northern California, with a population of some 43,000, illustrates the dilemma. Confronted with inadequate public services, sewers, water supply, and schools to accommodate an unprecedented population growth, the city undertook the unusual measure of restricting further development to 500 dwellings a year. The well-financed Construction Industry Association protested the city ordinance and, in 1974, a federal court judge ruled: "No city can control its population growth numerically."[1]

The issue was drawn between the right of a city to determine its own character and the obligation to accept all the people who may choose to reside there. Petaluma's comprehensive plan of 1962 (when the population was 17,000) provided for growth to an estimated 77,000 by 1985. It also provided a guide for capital improvements of facilities and services in conjunction with expected city revenues.

The Supreme Court, however, reversed the lower court decision, holding that the city had developed a careful timetable for the expansion of city services. It ruled moreover that the city's carefully worked-out plan was predicated on expected tax revenues and so could not be altered.

The legal strife in Petaluma represents the struggle of cities across the land to control their own destiny. A 1972 zoning ordinance in Ramapo, New York, through which the timing and sequence of development could be made consistent with necessary capital improvements for public services, was upheld by the Supreme Court.[2] The issue of exclusionary zoning, however, is not fully resolved, and the equitable distribution of housing for all income levels is a complex issue. An ordinance in Fairfax County, Virginia, required that 15 percent of all units in multifamily housing be available to low-income families. It was declared unacceptable by the courts, which alleged the provision an illegal "taking" of private property for public purposes.

The impact of growth affects every city, town, and village. Boca Raton, Florida, grew at an alarming rate—from 7,000 in 1960 to 49,505 in 1980—and placed a ceiling on its ultimate growth with a limit of 40,000 dwelling units or about 120,000 people total. Sanbornton, New Hampshire, population 1,000, rezoned to a minimum of 6-acre sites to forestall compact development.

The issue of property rights versus public interest is subject to a variety of legal interpretations. Development of Great Salt Meadow in Stratford, Connecticut, was denied by the Environmental Protection Commission. The land was already zoned for industrial use, and the Rykbar Industrial Corporation contended that the action constituted a "taking," claiming $77,700,000 in damages. On the same grounds, disapproval of development of a 17-acre site at Fleur de Lac at Lake Tahoe, California, by the Tahoe Regional Planning Agency resulted in a claim for $4,500,000 compensation.

The dilemma is not confined to development of open land. The great concourse of Grand Central Station in New York City, owned by the Penn Central Rail-

---

1. Decision by Judge Lloyd H. Burke, Federal District Court, San Francisco, January 14, 1974.

2. In *Golden v. Planning Board of the Town of Ramapo* (1972), the Court stated: "There is then something inherently suspect in a scheme which apart from its professional purposes, effects a restriction upon the free mobility of a people until sometime in the future when projected facilities are available to meet increased demands. . . . What we will not countenance, then, under any guise, is community efforts at immunization or exclusion. But, far from being exclusionary, the present amendments merely seek, by the implementation of sequential development and timed growth, to provide a balanced cohesive community dedicated to the efficient utilization of land."

road, was declared a landmark by the New York City Landmarks Protection Commission in 1967. UGP Properties, Inc., had leased the air rights above this historical monument; denied the right to build a fifty-nine-story office building above it, the lessee claimed a "taking" and asked $8 million a year in damages. In 1972, after high-rise apartments near the bay front in San Francisco had obliterated dramatic views for inland dwellers, the city created a 40-foot height limit. It did not apply to the downtown area, where the increasing height of skyscraper office buildings was destroying the scale of the picturesque urban silhouette. Also threatened by high-rise apartments, San Diego set height limitations along its waterfront. The people of Santa Barbara by referendum established a stated limitation on the height of buildings in their charter, simply because they did not want high-rise structures.

How we shall grow to accommodate the new urban population and achieve the civilized quality of the environment toward which we aspire remains a crucial issue confronting cities as we approach the twenty-first century. Violation of the "constitutional right to freedom of movement," alleged in the Petaluma case against the city's restrictive ordinance, is a transparently superficial argument on behalf of those whose interest is the exploitation of land. It reinforces the necessity for distribution of population, but it should not abrogate the city's obligation, as well as its "right," to determine the number of people it shall accommodate and the environment it intends to provide for them.

Premature, scattered, or noncontiguous subdivision of land has perennially plagued city administrations. Agricultural zoning is a common protection, but it is usually a device for postponement rather than planning. It has become common practice for cities to finance extensions of public services—water, sewers, roads, and so on—to encourage urban expansion. These costs are then recovered by the city in whole or in part through taxes on development over ensuing years.

A multitude of other services, however, must immediately be assured to the new residents, schools and fire and police protection among them. Uncontrolled exploitation of land for development about the periphery of large and small cities exceeds the capacity to provide services and maintain desirable open space. People's desire to escape from the oppressive environment of congestion in cities accelerates the trend toward suburban growth. The goal of local administrations must be a balanced use of land and services within the economic capacity of a city to achieve and maintain the quality of the environment.

LINKAGE

As communities grow, both in the flat lands and in the hill areas they are sometimes confronted with the problems of linking up to ancient, narrow streets with substandard water and sewer lines, incapable of handling the additional services. In hilly areas, in particular, narrow streets become bottle necks and dangerous where the grades are steep and the right of way does not provide for passing vehicles, let alone essential parking even for emergency conditions. Grafting a new development onto an old one where the standards were low or absent, makes for health and safety problems as well as financial ones if there is an effort to remedy conditions.

Widening the streets and improving inadequate services lying in them could be a costly adventure. Many times street improvements eliminate front yards and often a portion, or all of the adjacent building. The costs could result in increased taxes and in other community hardships as families would be displaced. There are no simple remedies short of requiring all new construction to conform with current standards.

Requiring the new development to pay for the offsite improvements, even though they would be beneficial, would be so costly that it might either delay or stop the new development and wind up in legal actions.

An enlightened attitude toward the "right" to develop property may emerge as civilized values mature. Meanwhile, this right must be coupled with responsibility to assume the burden of cost it imposes on the public. This would require that landowners and developers accept the obligation for all the costs that may be entailed, including extension of facilities and services. Such a policy does not deny the right to use the property in accordance with the local land use regulations. It is simply a "carry your own weight" policy. Such regulations would act as one means of growth control and take the decision-making power away from the local bureaucracy, which is often arbitrary in its decisions or subject to political pressure.

There is flexibility in the planning process to amend plans and zoning ordinances, but that flexibility cannot be subverted by incompetent, capricious, or corrupt public administrators. Among the most damaging changing conditions to which a city is subject is the subordination of public interest to commercial exploitation, the easy zoning changes, casual conditional permits, and a variety of special concessions for private advantage.

A city plan that is a vague diagram or is hardly more than a record of existing land uses transcribed onto a map offers nothing but more of the same; for that there is no need for a plan. In contrast, a plan that embraces innovative and imaginative measures to correct social problems[3] and misuses of land can be a public commitment to progressive change.

The following guidelines for managing growth have been proposed by Katherine E. Stone of Feilich, Stone, Leitner, and Carlisle, Los Angeles:

Twelve Major Objectives of Growth Management
1. Preserve the character of the community and promote community identity.
2. Conserve agricultural land and preserve open space.
3. Encourage full utilization of existing facilities.
4. Control development of new areas to ensure coordination with existing and proposed facilities.
5. Maintain or improve the level of community services.
6. Improve housing opportunities, increase diversity, and promote better housing developments.
7. Avoid environmental problems.
8. Prevent sprawl.
9. Promote aesthetics and preserve historic or cultural features.

---

3. The Sketch Plan prepared by *California Tomorrow,* published in 1971, lists greater political participation, reduction in unemployment, improved educational opportunities, improved access to health service, combating of hunger, and the reduction of crime as social measures that strongly affect the poor of all ethnic groups.

10. Reduce traffic congestion and improve the road system.

11. Promote public safety.

12. Provide for flexibility to meet future needs.

Eighteen Growth Management Methods

1. Public acquisitions.

2. Public improvements.

3. Environmental controls.

4. Development rights transfer.

5. Restrictive covenants and other agreements running with the land.

6. Zoning techniques.

7. Conventional subdivision regulations.

8. Zoning subdivision controls relating to adequacy of off-site facilities.

9. Exactions and other requirements.

10. Tax and fee systems.

11. Annexation including timed and conditional boundary adjustments and servicing.

12. Official mapping (roads, streets, parks, and drainage systems).

13. The capital programming process.

14. The comprehensive plan and its elements.

15. Geographical restraints.

16. Numerical restraints or quota systems

17. Annexation and development agreements.

18. Other planning and management techniques (interim development controls, environmental impact assessment, cost/benefit analysis, information, education, monitoring, and technical assistance).

Thirteen Tips For Managing Growth

1. Maximize meaningful public input from diverse interest groups.

2. Identify principle goals and objectives.

3. Conduct studies and gather data concerning capacities of land, past and projected rate and location of growth, capacity of public facilities and services and a fiscal impact analysis.

4. Identify development constraints (e.g., infrastructure and service deficiencies, sensitive lands, areas of deteriorated air and water quality).

5. Identify those areas and resources to be protected (e.g., neighborhoods, hillsides, historic buildings) and those areas for development.

6. Develop policies to achieve the objectives that have broad, general applicability to deal with large scale, communitywide problems.

7. Prepare a comprehensive plan with some guidelines as to the amount and cost of new public facilities and utilities to support growth.

8. Prioritized development based on the city's general plan objectives and timely growth rather than cap the population.

9. Do not zone land any higher than necessary to achieve comprehensive plan objectives, to ensure adequate infrastructure capacity, ensure resource protection, and preserve quality of life. (You can upzone as facility needs are met.)

10. Limit non-priority development until infrastructure and/or resource impacts are remedied.

11. Tie fees, taxes, and other financing devices to your growth management plan.

12. Be careful to avoid infringing on vested rights and leave all landowners with a reasonable, beneficial, and/or economically viable use of his/her land within a reasonable period of time.

13. And finally: Be fair and reasonable, as always.[4]

Willdan Associates, Engineers & Planners, San Diego, have proposed the following outlines of the components of a program to manage growth.

Elements of a Growth Management Program
Ten steps of a growth management program, including affected departments in parenthesis:

1. Update city's comprehensive plan. *(Planning)*
2. Prepare a growth management element to the comprehensive plan. *(Planning)*
3. Identify the city standards for public facilities. *(All Departments)*
4. Develop a master plan for each public facility to be included such as:
   - A. Major Streets and Freeways *(Transportation Engineering Bridges and Structures)*
   - B. Water Distribution System and Storage Capacity *(Water Resource Engineering)*
   - C. Sewer Collection System and Treatment Capacity *(Sanitary Engineering)*
   - D. Drainage Facilities *(Drainage/Flood Control Engineering)*
   - E. Public Works Facilities *(Public Works Engineering)*
   - F. Police and Fire Stations *(Facility Planning)*
   - G. Libraries *(Facility Planning)*
   - H. Schools *(Facility Planning)*
   - I. Child Care Facilities *(Facility Planning)*
   - J. Civic Center Facilities *(Facility Planning)*
   - K. Parks *(Parks/Landscape Architecture)*
   - L. Open Space and Trails *(Planning/Parks)*

5. Develop an inventory and analysis of existing facilities. *(All Departments)*
6. Based on the projected buildout of comprehensive plan, identify the facilities needed to serve the fully developed city. *(All Departments)*
7. Develop a "point of need" threshold for each facility based upon the phasing of development. *(Planning/Engineering)*
8. Prepare a public facilities phasing plan through a long-term Capital Improvement Program Budget. *(Planning/Engineering/Finance)*
9. Review available financing methods and programs. Identify financing strategy or strategies for each facility. *(Finance)*
10. Prepare a computerized tracking and monitoring system. *(Computer Services/ Planning/Engineering)*[5]

---

4. Material presented at the American Planning Association Conference, Newport Beach, California, September 1990. Published in *Western City*, League of California Cities, May 1990.

5. Willdan Associates, 12900 Crossroads Parkway, Industry, California.

SETTING LIMITS TO GROWTH

Experience has indicated that setting numerical limits can result in serious difficulties as the community allocations are resolved by either beauty contests or the "First come, first served" approach. Even if the annual allocations are high, the scramble for a part of the pie becomes a contest among developers, who often seek favoritism in the final allocations. A better method for the allocation process is the rating of proposals and the selection of those that meet the highest criteria of quality and conformity with the provisions of the comprehensive and management plans.

COSTS

A central concern in plans for accommodating future population growth is determining where new residential development should take place, given the necessity of providing essential public services. Although the costs of additional roads, sewer collector lines, and water lines will be borne eventually by new homebuyers, there are other continuing services that must be provided by local governmental units.

For example, current expenditures for such services as police and fire protection, water and wastewater systems operation and maintenance, street maintenance, and solid waste collection amount to a substantial portion of general fund expenditures. The costs of police protection, waste collection, and street maintenance alone amount to about 37 percent of general fund expenditures in El Centro, California. The per capita costs of these services are particularly sensitive to the density of the residential developments, so that a widely dispersed pattern of developments can have a substantial impact on municipal finances and local tax rates.

GROWTH MANAGEMENT AND THE COMPREHENSIVE PLAN

The management of community growth and development is not a new technique. Every step taken since the adoption of the first zoning ordinances has been an effort to direct the structural pattern of a city in a way that would bring about the best, most efficient and desirable living environment for its people. Zoning, however, has not always taken into account the timing and sequence of development and thus has not been effective in indicating where or when services can be provided at levels essential to sound community living.

With the requirement that each community prepare a comprehensive plan for its future growth and development, there was still the lack of an instrument to provide for the phasing and direction of growth other than in a general way. Expansions into new areas are often piecemeal, without the essential studies to determine what the costs of scattered development might be.

Often the zoning of the land reflects decisions made before there was a comprehensive plan and, in most instances, before the decision by the state legislature that zoning must be consistent with the comprehensive plan. In the past, community leaders felt that the plan was a simple guide and therefore had no real meaning in law. In California, this has changed with the adoption of new state laws. The plan is now considered critical in all land use decisions, because it is the only real indication of how a community wants to grow and how it will attain its goals. Until the law was changed there had been a gap in the process; no ties between the comprehensive plan and timing of development existed. Now, however, growth management is to be the vehicle for implementing plan proposals by creating timing and directional guidelines based on the ability of the community to absorb growth.

The growth management program is therefore an outgrowth of efforts by community leaders not so much to stop growth and change as to direct and limit it to prescribed boundaries based on community capabilities.

The growth management plan is the bridge between planning and development. It is the evaluation system used to determine if the proposals submitted to the community can be accommodated within the fiscal abilities of the community without causing existing residents and commercial and industrial occupants to assume an unreasonable tax burden.

The growth management plan is the best means designed to date to bring about logical implementation of the long-range proposals of the comprehensive plan. Zoning thereafter becomes the legal vehicle that permits development to proceed in those areas where growth management finds it appropriate and timely.

There must be a well-designed comprehensive plan that establishes the densities and intensities of land uses and gives an indication of the facilities required to meet the needs of the residents. Where facilities and services exist, they would be evaluated in terms of the potential for expanded demands.

If there is a service shortfall there should be a determination of the ability of the individual services to expand to meet new demands, and when this expansion will be possible both physically and financially. Only after the determination of the "when and how" should zoning of the land be approved, which will allow for the development to take place at the densities and purposes set forth in the comprehensive plan.

A number of approaches and techniques have been developed to ensure that future growth occurs in a manner consistent with the community's ability to accommodate new growth. Some are described next.

FACTORS AND TECHNIQUES

Zoning

The place and distribution of growth can be affected by the following types of rezoning:

Downzoning is intended to reduce the ultimate holding capacity of an area, either in terms of the number of residences or the land available for business expansion. The objective is to reduce the pace of population or economic growth to a level consistent with the community's ability to absorb new people and businesses.

Upzoning is intended to increase the ultimate holding capacity of an area and can serve to attract development that might have occurred elsewhere. For example, the upzoning of central areas can help reduce growth pressures on undeveloped lands.

Moratoriums are intended to prevent further development for a relatively brief time in order to allow for the completion of studies and plans, and the implementation of controls directed toward managing and accommodating growth.

Building Quotas. These limit the number of housing units that can be built during a given period of time. They are intended to reduce population growth and to ease the burden of such growth on public facilities and services.

Total Population Densities. Techniques such as downzoning, moratoriums, and so on are used to ensure that a city's total population does not exceed some stipulated maximum. That maximum is set on the basis of the city's ability to provide services affecting the safety and general welfare of its residents.

Land Banking

Land is actually bought by local government and then made available for private development under carefully specified conditions (such as consistency with the comprehensive plan and the provision for some low-income housing), according to a timed-sequenced capital improvements program. This ensures that future growth occurs at a pace compatible with the city's financial resources.

Development Rights Transfer

All landowners receive development rights in proportion to the amount of undeveloped land owned within an area, with no single landowner initially owning enough rights to develop all of the land. Unexecuted rights are bought and sold on the free market (independent of land ownership) and tend to be transferred from rural areas to growth areas.

To develop a specific piece of property to the intensity of use designated on the comprehensive plan, a developer must accumulate sufficient rights.

Timing and Sequencing Controls

These controls are intended to affect the distribution of growth, as well as its pace. A well-known application of such controls occurred in Ramapo, New York. The controls, in conjunction with a master plan and a capital improvements plan, were used to constrain growth around existing developed areas, to prevent hopscotch development into agricultural areas, and to forestall development until necessary public services could be made available at reasonable costs.

Development Agreements

A city or county participating in a development agreement promises, for a specified time period, not to change certain rules, regulations and policies applicable to a development. The idea is to give developers, who have yet to attain a vested right to develop, a degree of assurance that their investment in project preparations will not be nullified by some future local policy or regulation change (e.g., the rezoning of a commercial project site to residential). In exchange for the privilege of a regulation "freeze," the developer may be willing to agree to certain concessions.

Procedure Cities or counties have the option of entering into development agreements with persons having legal or equitable interest in real property within their jurisdictions. A city may also enter into a development agreement with any person having legal or equitable interest in real property in unincorporated territory within that city's sphere of influence. In the latter case, however, the agreement will not be operative unless proceedings annexing the property to the city are completed within the period of time specified by the agreement.

Limitations Developers are not "home free" just because they sign an agreement. After specifying the types of existing rules, regulations, and official policies that a development agreement covers:

> A development agreement shall not prevent a city, county, or city and county, in subsequent actions applicable to the property, from applying new rules, regulations, and policies which do not conflict with those rules, regulations, and policies appli-

cable to the property as set forth herein, nor shall a development agreement prevent a city, county, or city and county from denying or conditionally approving any subsequent development project application on the basis of such existing or new rules, regulations, and policies.

For the sake of clarity, therefore, it is important that local governments stipulate which existing rules, regulations, and policies will be "frozen" by an agreement. In the absence of such specification, all development rules, regulations, and official policies noted in the Government Code that are in force upon the execution of an agreement will be "frozen." This could result in unanticipated consequences for both a developer and a new city or county.

It is also important that local officials know exactly how property under an agreement is going to be developed so they can avoid agreeing to an inadvertent forfeiture of their powers to control a development's impacts.

> A detailed specific plan prepared and adopted prior to an agreement could specify the development details for a site, including the regulations and policies that would apply under the agreement.

Duration In addition to carefully examining development details, local governments should exercise caution in specifying the duration of agreements. An agreement for less than a year probably would not afford a developer enough protection.

> An excessive agreement duration could impair a local government's response to community concerns and needs that change over time. Many cities have entered into agreements ranging in length from fifteen to twenty years.[6]

Each of these approaches must be evaluated on the basis of a number of legal, economic, and social criteria. The issue of the legality of a particular approach is complicated but tends to revolve around a number of basic questions: Is a regulation related to a "protectable goal" (such as health, safety, or general welfare)? Are equally situated landowners treated equally? Is the regulation "reasonable" in application as well as intent, and not discriminatory in its application? Is the regulation exclusionary or does it restrict free movement? Answers to each of these questions are currently being evaluated through the judicial process.

Economic criteria include the costs of application and administration. For example, land banking involves substantial public money. Also to be considered are the indirect effects of controls. Quotas, downzoning, and population ceilings can increase the costs of housing and may accelerate the rate of growth as developers rush to beat impending deadlines (often at higher cost). Social criteria include issues of equity and exclusion and the political impact of governmental intervention.

Small Cities

The cities of El Centro and Holtville lie within 10 miles of each other in a highly productive agricultural area in southeastern California. The problem of growth confronts each of these communities, but in different ways. Both are confronted with the potentials of growth, especially as it may be affected by the development of geothermal resources located in nearby areas. But each has special problems associated with the anticipated growth, and each has its own philosophic approach to dealing with it. El Centro wants to encourage growth. Holtville would discourage it in order to maintain its present rural, low-pressure way of living.

---

6. Excerpts from *The Planning Commission Handbook*, League of California Cities, Sacramento, California, June 1984.

In both cities, most of the land within the city limits has been occupied, and growth must come either by intensifying the uses within the current city or expanding into the agricultural hinterland. El Centro sees no problem in the expansion and annexation program, since the city's major support comes from government and services (the city is the county seat). Holtville, on the other hand, is governed largely by persons sympathetic to the preservation of its agricultural resources. The city sees any invasion into the agricultural area as a reduction of its economic base.

Both communities have utility problems. El Centro's sewage disposal system is operating at capacity. The plant could handle the products of growth if the sewer lines were replaced to prevent seepage into groundwaters. Holtville, however, is not troubled by line capacity, but the treatment plant is underdesigned and there needs to be a complete moratorium on building until plant capacity has been improved to prevent further pollution of local streams and the Salton Sea, a nearby recreational resource.

Water is a problem for Holtville but does not pose any difficulty for El Centro. Other utilities are private or in special districts that can meet even explosive rates of growth that may come into the valley. The potential of the geothermal resources may actually mitigate the energy problem for many years to come.

Thus in the management of growth the entire planning process depended on the abilities of the cities to meet the requirements of health and safety for both the current residents and for those who constitute the element of growth.

Two other cities in California base their growth management plans on entirely different criteria. Both San Juan Capistrano and Rancho Mirage, like many other communities in the world, are deeply concerned about the maintenance of the quality of their environment. They both fear that too-rapid growth may allow some development to slip by without adequate review. Local pressures against increasing the staff that deals with review projects suggest there will be a reduction in the number of applications acceptable at any one time.

As reasonable and logical as the growth management process is, its acceptance by many communities has been limited by the negative stance of potential developers and those landowners whose property might be affected. One of the critical factors in acceptance of the management process is determining the number of residential units that can be absorbed and serviced at any one time. Projects that are already in the "pipeline" pose additional problems. In fairness to the developers who have expended considerable amounts of money to prepare such plans, these individuals are seldom kept from completing their projects, even if they exceed the management allowances.

Since the premise on which most management programs are based is the ability of the community to provide facilities and services for the residents-to-be, the developer should provide funds for additional improvements where needed to accommodate his contribution to the growth of the community. One of the questions this raises is, How can one developer provide for a portion of a school or part of a sewage treatment plant or water supply system? All of these facilities and services must be in place if they are to meet the needs of the proposed addition to the community.

Growth management techniques can be applied to the older area of a community where change is both necessary and likely with aid of the city's housing programs for rehabilitation and conservation. Raising or lowering the densities in a new zoning classification would establish ways and means of determining the rehabilitation area. Through this process, the work of rehabilitation could go on in some units while the others remained occupied until the first units were reconditioned and available for occupancy. In this process the residents, most of them of advanced years, will be close to their normal area of interest, their friends and associates, and existing mass transit lines that take them to other parts of the city.

GROWTH MANAGEMENT IN OLDER AREAS

CHAPTER 38

THE FINANCIAL PLANS

Someone must pay for it.

METHODS OF FINANCING DEVELOPMENT

Financial limitations are perhaps the most frequently cited reason for failure to implement essential public portions of the planning program. The larger the project, regardless of the need, the more difficult it becomes to obtain financial support through the normal municipal budgeting process. In most cases, only state or federal intervention can provide the economic support to see projects completed.

ONE STATE'S ANSWER TO THE TAX FREEZE

When the freeze of assessments on the stock of housing built in the years before Proposition 13 was adopted and applied to commercial and industrial developments it appeared that services would have to be curtailed and cities would face bankruptcy. Property owners in all developments faced a new situation as their water bills now listed fees for sewerage and rubbish collection services—which were free before Proposition 13—and had the choice of paying water and light bills or having the service stopped. In addition other charges were tacked on, such as city and state taxes on both water and power. Proposition 13 also limited the tax rate.

There were also new fees for development and for processing of many of the services that were either nominal in cost or free before Proposition 13. In this case the developers and builders could pass on the added cost through the sale of their products. It is only the consumer, at the end of the chain, who has to assume the burden of the increases in cost.

THE BUDGET

The most important ingredient in the financing of community programs is the preparation of the budget. How much money will be needed? What are the sources for the funds? Will they be derived from local taxes, private sources, or state or federal grants or loans?

After the cost of services and potential sources of income are estimated, a phasing scenario in which the projects are arranged in order of importance within the financial schedule is prepared.

Capital Improvement Programs

Public funds are invested in the construction of community improvements through capital improvement programs. Each community anticipates its income over a period of years and prepares a budget for the accomplishment of certain essentials to the growth and prosperity of the area over which it has jurisdiction. Improvements include expansion of a sewage treatment plant, extension of trunk sewer or water lines, development of new parks and recreational areas, and many other projects of this type.

The new growth management plans are making it easier to project future needs, since they are under the control of the agencies responsible for implementing the capital improvements.

The location and nature of public improvements such as streets and public buildings are major factors in determining environmental quality. Expenditures for these public improvements should be allocated in accordance with a planned program that balances needs and priorities against available resources and in accordance with the provisions of the comprehensive plan.

Capital improvement planning should not be limited only to those items that require funds from the city budget. Significant programs carried out by other levels of government can have a great effect on the timing, financing, and location of city projects.

Capital Improvement Budgeting

Both public and private institutions budget for capital improvements. Cities prepare a 5-year capital expenditure program for street improvements, for new buildings and structures, for new motor vehicles, for acquisition and development of parks and other public facilities, and for those other items that have a multiyear use in the service of their community and its people. The capital improvement program must be reviewed and approved by the planning commission and conform with the comprehensive plan before it is submitted to the legislative body for action. The annual budget is then drawn; it is based on a priority system in which the most important items are ranked at the top of the expenditure list. The annual budget is drawn up by the city manager or a county counterpart and is provided to the governing body, the council or, in the case of the county, the board of supervisors. The governing body, acting as the politicians that they are, divide up the pie to make sure that each has taken care of his or her district or patrons.

Federal Assistance

Since all parts of a nation constitute a federation, whether in the United States or elsewhere in the world, it is understandable that economic and other assistance

The financial plan. (Photo of Wall Street)

can be advanced by the central power to its several integral entities when local conditions warrant. The vast differences that exist physically, socially, and psychologically in the several regions make some national concern for the less fortunate elements in the federation essential. Historically, governments have come to the aid of communities in times of emergency or disaster. Sometimes, through foreign aid, this assistance has been advanced to far-off parts of the world. It is thus not surprising that hopes for the abatement of the crisis in housing and community development should include extension of the hand of the federal government, making changes and improvements that strengthen the fiber of the entire federal structure possible.

Although many of the visible portions of the federal assistance programs are in the field of housing and highway construction, it is important to recognize that other aspects of the community physical improvements are also aided. Through incentives and direct financial subsidies to both local communities and private corporations, federal aid makes the development of sewage treatment plants, water supply systems, and programs involving nuclear, wind, solar, and geothermal energy possible.

In addition to financial assistance for physical improvements, the federal government grants aid to states—and through the states to the communities—in support of social programs that include education, welfare, and other activities that require funding beyond the resources of the local entities. Some federal grants of aid are made directly to local communities.

The government's power to tax on a broad national basis provides the economic base for the assistance where great need exists. Legislators in the Congress are always interested in providing programs for their home districts as one means of representing their constituency and, in the long run, of being reelected.

Change in national economic policies sponsored by Reaganomics and the so-called voodoo economic system was followed by deregulation, which left public and private business and industry as freebooters, who gobbled up more than they could chew in many cases. This resulted in savings and loans, bank, and business failures and the need for public "bailouts." Little money was left for the care and maintenance of the public services provided by local government. The drain on the taxpaying public was too great, and they therefore rejected bond issues which would have funded essential improvements.

Many of the federal financial assistance programs that helped local communities to improve their physical conditions have, since 1991, had their budgets either eliminated or reduced materially. Not only did the programs for modernization of water storage, distribution lines, and sewage treatment plants fall by the wayside, but support for other programs dealing with redevelopment and public health and education were substantially reduced. These were, in most cases, essential and worthwhile as sound expenditures of the revenues collected by the federal government from the very people that the programs served.

Recent Conditions

When certain economic conditions became critical in the 1980s, the newly elected administration cut many features dealing with urban renewal out of the budget. The government indicated to local communities that if they desired to continue the rebuilding process, to all intents and purposes they would have to devise means to do it on their own. Various devices were utilized to overcome the financial shortfall resulting from local taxation limitations. Fees, exactions, and charges for services and licenses were all increased to permit the essential services to be provided. Tax increment financing was conceived as a device that would provide an effective means of meeting the challenge of reduced federal activity in the redevelopment programs.

In 1980 Lyle Alton Stewart, a planning consultant in Medford, Oregon, submitted the following program describing the techniques involved, which was based on his experiences on the West Coast of the United States and in Canada and Mexico. The material was prepared to illustrate to the communities he advised how the program would work and what the benefits would be. Regardless of the local political attitudes toward redevelopment, this program is being widely used in small communities as well as in large cities, and is a useful tool wherever implemented.

**FINANCING
URBAN
RENEWAL**

New Legislation

In recent years tax increment financing has become the darling of the urban renewal programs. Since it is based upon the theory that all cities have some blight and since blight was rated broad in definition, some cities have designated large areas, some included vacant land, as blighted and any development therein added funds to write off the bonds issued to cover the program. Added to this, in California, the tax limitations of Proposition 13 did not apply since it was written to exclude development constructed after the effective date of the legislation. Needless to say, the Redevelopment Agencies have become, in many communities, both wealthy and powerful, since they have both bonding capacities and the rights of Eminent Domain.

Numerous states currently provide some form of tax increment financing as an integral part of their redevelopment enabling laws. Historically, tax increment financing has been limited for use only in retiring the public indebtedness incurred in implementing redevelopment plans. However, in more recent times, and as a result of local governments' interest in expanding their economic development capability, tax increment financing is being considered as a potential method of financing the needed infrastructure required to attract job-producing businesses and industries. In most states, however, to broaden the use of tax increment financing would require voter approval of state constitutional amendments as well as appropriate action by their legislatures. With a definite public interest in tax-limiting measures beginning with Proposition 13 in California, the broadening of the use of tax increment financing is by no means an automatic procedure.

Although there are variables in the several state tax increment provisions, the concept as originally conceived by the California legislature is basic to all of them.

When a redevelopment or urban renewal plan—the terms have identical meaning —is officially adopted, the tax assessor for the jurisdiction is required to certify the taxable assessed value, based on the tax roll last equalized, for the property encompassed by the redevelopment plan. This value is usually referred to as the "base year assessed value" or the "frozen assessed value."

All taxing agencies that receive ad valorem tax proceeds from this base year assessed value will continue to receive income based on the following equation:

$$\text{Tax Rate} \times \text{Base Assessed Value} = \text{Tax Proceeds}$$

During the period in which the division of ad valorem taxes (tax increment) is operative, the annual tax rate may increase or decrease in any subsequent year but the base assessed value will remain "frozen" throughout the life of the tax increment process.

In the years beyond the base year there usually is an increase in the assessed value of the redevelopment area resulting from a variety of renewal activities implemented. This increase in assessed value (above that of the base year) is referred to as *incremental assessed value*. The ad valorem taxes (tax increment) realized from this increased assessed value is calculated as follows:

$$\text{Tax Rate} \times \text{Incremental Assessed Value} = \text{Tax Increment Proceeds}$$

These tax increment proceeds are transferred to the agency charged with implementing the redevelopment plan to be used to retire debts incurred in the implementation process. Most state laws limit the agencies' right to receive these annual tax increment proceeds only when there is a legal debt to be serviced or retired. It follows then that an agency, with no indebtedness, cannot collect the proceeds, place them in an interest-bearing account, and use the accumulated fund at some future date. Indebtedness incurred by the agency may be in any legal form including loans, advances, notes, tax allocation bonds, contracts for services, construction contracts, etc.

Most states (including California and Oregon) have included provisions in their enabling laws that require the redevelopment plan or reports on the plan to state a maximum sum of tax increment proceeds to be collected, to estimate the time which the tax increment process will run, and to estimate the impact on the tax rates, taxing bodies, and the taxpayer.

In California, Proposition 13 fixed the tax rate at 1 percent of the assessed value. As such, the tax increment process has no effect on the tax rate. Before Proposition 13, tax increment proceeds that were diverted to the redevelopment agencies were subtracted from the various taxing agency's annual tax income. In Oregon, to generate the tax increment, the tax rate is increased by an amount necessary to produce the tax increment proceeds. Other states have subtle differences, but the Oregon and California procedures are in wide use in the many states that allow tax increment financing.

To illustrate how the tax increment process functions, the following example illustrates the one in Oregon, where the tax increment process was in place for 13 years (1962–1975). During the 13-year period the assessed value increased from a frozen base assessed value of $11.0 million in 1962 to $140 million in 1975: an increase of $129 million. The figure illustrates the continued growth in the project area to fiscal 1984–85, where the assessed value is estimated to reach $275 million. The tax rate in 1962–63 was approximately $23.00 per $1,000 of assessed value. The taxes produced that year and distributed to all applicable taxing agencies was $253,000 ($23 × $11,000). In 1975–76, the last tax increment year, the tax rate was $24.50 per $1,000 of assessed value. The following calculations illustrate how the tax proceeds are distributed. Taxes distributed to all taxing agencies based on the frozen base assessed value of $11.0 million was:

$$\$24.50 \times \$11,000 = \$269,500$$

Tax increment proceeds dedicated to the urban renewal agency were based on an incremental assessed value of $129.0 million ($140.0 million − $11.0 million).

$$\$24.50 \times \$129,000 = \$3,160,500$$

The $3,160,500 in tax increment proceeds for fiscal year 1975–76 was used by the urban renewal agency to retire all outstanding indebtedness in conjunction with implementing the urban renewal plan.

Following is a table based on a variety of developer and redeveloper commitments if the blighted conditions were corrected that illustrates the expected annual increase in assessed value as the resulting tax increment flow calculated at 1 percent per year of the incremental assessed value:

Fiscal Year	Annual Assessed Value Increase	Annual Tax Increment Proceeds
1980–81	0	Base year
1981–82	$ 11,000,000	$ 110,000
1982–83	22,700,800	227,000
1983–84	35,102,500	351,020
1984–85	48,242,500	482,420
1989–90	229,597,000	2,295,970
1994–95	425,970,000	4,259,700
2000–01	555,350,000	5,553,550
Totals (20 years)		$55,844,060

In this project, the redevelopment plan contains a provision that the maximum tax increment proceeds that will be collected will not exceed $55,200,000. The difference between the plan stated maximum and the total collected amount of $55,844,060 is $644,060. The tax increment process is estimated to be terminated in fiscal year 2000–01 and the surplus $644,060 over the maximum authorized amount of tax increment would be prorated back to the several affected taxing agencies.

It will be observed that in 20 years the redevelopment process is estimated to have stimulated an increase in the assessed value of $555,350,000. The total assessed value of $687,247,510 ($131,897,510 + $555,350,000) then will be available to all of the taxing agencies.

Redevelopment and Housing for the Homeless
Planners have long been aware of the problems of homeless people, but until recently have not had the tools or funds with which to propose solutions.

An innovative approach adopted by several California cities circumvents this lack of funding by using redevelopment funds set aside for housing. Through the cooperation of the local redevelopment agency, a number of programs such as construction of special shelters, are funded for the homeless.

Redevelopment agencies, under state law, are authorized to undertake a wide range of projects—not only housing related, but also commercial, industrial and civic improvement—that increase the value of taxable property in a project area.

Tax Increment. State law requires that the "tax increment" realized from a redevelopment project (the amount of new taxes collected in the project over and above the preredevelopment amount) be allocated to the agency to cover expenses incurred to finance the project.

Affordable housing advocates are taking advantage of the legally required use of these agency tax increment funds. The law requires agencies to set aside 20 percent

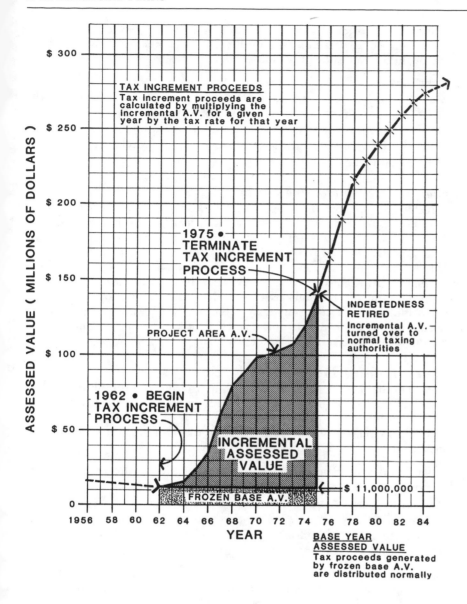

Lyle Alton Stewart, Planning Consultant, AICP

Tax increment proceeds chart.

of the tax increment "for the purposes of increasing and improving the community's supply of low and moderate income housing to persons of moderate, low and very low income."

The tax increment set-aside mechanism potentially makes available an enormous amount of money. In a recent survey by the Bay Area Council, it was found that 27 Northern California redevelopment agencies had set aside funds collectively amounting to over $33 million annually. Their affordable housing expenditures since 1985 reached close to $150 million.

Furthermore, few if any restrictions on the use of set asides are imposed (except for the mandate to expand affordable housing). This gives the agencies the ability to use funds in some very innovative ways.

Innovative Methods. A number of agencies have channeled their funds directly in homeless assistance programs, sometimes using set-aside funds in conjunction with other redevelopment income. For example, the city of San Mateo lends money to homeless persons to cover first and last month's rent, while the city of Santa Rosa's redevelopment agency funds the operation of a homeless shelter.

In 1987 alone, the Los Angeles Community Redevelopment Agency made construction loans and provided operating funds for eight emergency shelters; established "Homeless Shelter Trust Fund" funding 420 emergency shelter beds; assisted community organizations operating transitional housing facilities; acquired, rehabilitated, and managed single-room occupancy hotels; and financed a family moving assistance program.[1]

Trust Funds for Meeting Housing Needs

Housing Trust Funds are spreading rapidly at the state and local levels across the country in response to the diminished role of the federal government in housing. While there were only 7 such funds in 1985, more than 50 now exist and many others are in various stages of development. In California, San Francisco, Sacramento, Palo Alto, Menlo Park and Santa Monica have already established Trust Funds, and they are being considered in Los Angeles, Irvine and Oceanside. Sources of revenue for Housing Trust Funds are mostly derived from development and/or real estate fees and taxes. Those revenues are dedicated by legislation to the production of housing for lower income families, and are therefore largely immune from the uncertainties of the government budget process.

The San Diego Housing Trust Fund

In March of 1990 the San Diego City Council approved a $13.9 million housing trust fund, one of the largest in the country for a locality. The San Diego Housing Trust Fund is significant also because it dedicates at least 70% of the revenue to very low-income households and because it ensures that Housing Trust Fund housing remains affordable for at least 55 years.

A Housing Trust Fund was especially needed in San Diego, the city with the least affordable housing market in the nation, a city where more and more people are forced to live in the streets, in shelters, or in substandard and overcrowded housing, or are forced to pay up to 70% of their income on rent. It is perhaps because of the great need that the Housing Trust Fund idea sparked an extraordinary level of community involvement in San Diego.

An alliance of more than 50 community groups and organizations came together to form the Housing Trust Fund Coalition to promote the idea of a permanent Trust Fund that is broad based, equitable and committed to meeting the long term housing needs of the city. Revenue for the Housing Trust Fund will be derived from two sources: 1) 50% of the increment in Transient Occupancy Tax above the amount collected in FY89, for $1.9 million; and 2) A "linkage fee" for commercial development for $12 million ($2.00/sq. ft. for office, $1.50/sq. ft. for research and development, $1.20/sq. ft. for manufacturing, $0.50/sq. ft. for warehousing, $1.20/sq. ft. for retail and hotel).

Linkage fees are already being used successfully in Boston, San Francisco, and other cities. They are of special interest to planners because they are based on the legally established principle that a nexus exists between growth in commercial development and growth in the need for lower income housing. Many of the people who will work in new office towers, shopping centers, hotels, and factories will not be able to afford housing in the San Diego housing market without some form of assistance.

---

1. Christopher Ho, in the June 1989 issue of *Planning* the publication of California Chapter of the American Planners Association. Mr. Ho is associated with Homebase Public Advocates, an organization that is a joint project of the Association of San Francisco Bay Area Governments and Public Advocates, Inc.

Planners should realize that one of the costs of growths in the commercial sector is the additional need that it creates for lower income housing, and that developers should help pay for that cost, at levels that would not adversely affect the feasibility of projects or the favorable business climate in their locality. It has been calculated that the linkage fee adopted in San Diego amounts to one tenth of what could be legally justifiable on the basis of the nexus calculation.[2]

Funding Sewage Disposal

The federal government has funded a large-scale construction grants program for municipal sewage treatment facilities. Unfortunately, the type of facility generally funded under the program, while appropriate for high-density urban areas, may not suit the needs of sparsely populated rural areas. In fact, the existence of such a large-scale federal program may inhibit consideration of alternative sewage disposal systems more appropriate to local circumstances.

The history of national concern over the quality and quantity of natural resources demonstrates that the nation's understanding of environment problems will evolve over time, as will its response to those problems. Just as the industry of one generation has caused unforeseen problems for the next, so have the environmental problems of one generation been confronted, and sometimes resolved, by the next. But if the nation is to continue to respond effectively to changing environmental circumstances, the laws of one generation cannot prescribe environmental legislation and regulations in such detail as to impede future, perhaps more informed efforts to protect environmental quality.[3]

Special Assessments

Special assessments are among the oldest techniques for funding construction of such physical improvements as sidewalks, sewers, streets, storm drains, lighting, and flood control that benefit identifiable areas. They have also been used to finance maintenance of some facilities. As discussed earlier, the courts have held that special assessments are not "special taxes" under Proposition 13 and, therefore, are not subject to the two-thirds vote requirement. Assessments are also exempt from the Proposition 4 expenditure limit. In 1981 the Legislature authorized the use of special assessments for financing fire protection, although this use is still legally untested.

Bonds

Special assessment bonds are a traditional tool for financing sewer, water, street, sidewalk, street lighting, and similar improvements which benefit property owners within a given area. Assessment bonds issued under the California Improvement Act of 1911 are secured solely by the properties that benefit from and are assessed for the improvements. Assessment bonds issued under the Improvement Bond Act of 1915 are secured by the assessed property plus a special reserve fund to cover delinquencies.

Revenue bonds, which are backed by a reliable flow of future revenues from the facility or enterprise they fund, were not affected by Proposition 13. Thus, the Revenue Bond Law of 1941 will continue to be an important source of funds for

---

2. These innovative means of addressing local housing needs were described by Nico Calavita in the June 1990 *Planner*. Nico Calavita is associate professor and coordinator of the graduate program in City Planning at San Diego State University. He is a member of the San Diego Housing Trust Fund Coalition and was nominated by the San Diego City Council to the Housing Trust Fund Board of Trustees.

3. Nineteenth Annual Report of Council on Environmental Quality, (Washington, D.C., U.S. Government Printing Office, 1981).

the construction of hospitals, water facilities, sewer plants, parking facilities, bridges, auditoriums, and other such public facilities. Because revenue bonds are secured by the proceeds from the enterprise they fund, they carry higher interest rates than general obligation bonds.

Instead of being issued by the city or county, lease revenue bonds are issued by the nonprofit corporation or special authority which constructs a facility and leases it to the city or county. Lease payments provide the revenue to pay off the bond and when the bond is retired the facility is turned over to the city or county. Some local agencies have used this method to finance administrative centers and schools.

Lease-Purchase
The use of lease-purchase agreements and sale-leaseback arrangements with private entities such as banks and leasing companies is growing rapidly. The advantage of these agreements is that they can be transacted without voter approval and hence avoid some of the administrative delay and costs associated with bond issues. To increase the marketability of lease-purchase agreements, banks typically break up the obligations into units known as Certificates of Participation and sell them to individual investors. Sale-leaseback agreements, including "safe harbor" agreements, involve the transfer of important federal tax benefits from the lessee to the lessor, but their use is currently limited by several legal considerations, particularly in general law cities.

Privatization
Recent years have seen a growth in the popularity of *privatization* (the use of private contractors or private ownership) to provide local services such as garbage collection, fire protection, and street maintenance. Although it is not strictly a financing measure, it is a strategy used to stretch limited public funds. Privatization has certain advantages: government need not purchase and maintain special machinery, personnel for specialized or seasonal tasks need not be maintained on salary, and the costs to the local government of providing service may be reduced. It also has disadvantages: special skills are needed to establish and manage the contract with the private service provider, quality control is beyond the direct control of the local government, and if it is necessary to replace the contractor local government may face a period of interrupted service.

State Funding
In addition to general state support of local government, the Legislature may create a broad range of categorical programs of grants and loans which local governments use to finance the implementation of their comprehensive plans.

Financing Transportation Improvements
A great number of organizations are involved in the development of new arterials. They range from the federal government in its contribution to the development and maintenance of freeways and primary and secondary highways, to the states that support the development and maintenance of state routes, to the cities which are responsible for the care of all streets and highways that lie in their jurisdiction. The development of new local streets and highways and lesser roads is the responsibility, first of the land developers who seek to obtain subdivision approvals. The maintenance, later, is the responsibility of the community within which the improvements are located.

Public mass transit facilities are usually financed and operated by special Transit Districts. These districts are a separate entity operating under state law and financed by issuing tax exempt bonds, backed by the state. Airports likewise are operated by a special district authorized, under state law, to issue tax exempt bonds which in many instances are backed by revenues collected by the authority from tax on tickets and the merchants and airline operators who use the facilities.

Private Utilities

Private utility companies often issue stocks and bonds to fund the installation or improvement of the services that they render. Many private water companies and some of the largest power and light companies are in private ownership. Small companies usually issue water stock with the sale of lots, so the property owner also becomes a stockholder in the company serving them. The larger companies, such as Pacific Gas and Electric or Commonwealth Edison all issue common stock, preferred stock, bonds, and debentures. All of these issues are intended for the purpose of benefitting the company's economic position and improving the service facilities while presumably making a profit for the stock or bondholders.

Impact Fee

A fee, also called a development fee, levied on the developer of a project by a city, county, or other public agency as compensation for otherwise-unmitigated impacts the project will produce. California's Government Code specifies that development fees shall not exceed the estimated reasonable cost of providing the service for which the fee is charged. To lawfully impose a development fee, the public agency must verify its method of calculation and document proper restrictions on use of the fund.

In 1989 the voters of California, in the face of stringent budgeting for schools and public welfare, voted to improve the road and rail systems. William Fulton gives the following description of the action:

> ### West Coast Voters Say Yes to Taxes for Roads, Rail
> By a vote of 52 percent to 48 percent, voters in June elections in California approved Proposition 111, a transportation spending program that includes the state's first major tax increase in more than a decade. The yes vote will double the state's gas tax, raising $18.5 billion over a 10-year period for transportation.
>
> Voters also approved both Proposition 108, a $1 billion rail transit construction program that was linked to Proposition 111, and Proposition 116, a separate $2 billion rail transit program that California environmentalists placed on the ballet via the initiative process.
>
> Most of Proposition 111's funds will go toward road and highway improvements. The measure's most controversial provisions require local governments to take part in traffic reduction programs in order to qualify for funds. In this way, it is similar to a recent sales tax increase for transportation in Contra Costa County, near San Francisco, which requires local governments to adopt growth management programs before they may qualify for a share of tax revenues.[4]

CALIFORNIA VOTERS SUPPORT IMPROVEMENT IN TRANSPORTATION

---

4. William Fulton, *Planning,* the publication of the American Planners Association, July 1990, Washington, D.C.

NEOCLASSICAL METHOD OF FINFRA-STRUCTURE IMPROVE-MENTS

The need for some means to finance the tremendous job of updating obsolete water and sewerage facilities is increasing with each passing year. The suggestions James Krohe, Jr., describes for the development of a land bank may be new, but the idea of such an institution has been around for a long time. The opposition of the politicians to something different is, however, not new. Following are excerpts from Krohe's article:

> Paving The Way For Infrastructure Banks. Turning federal grants into loans—a new twist on the old revolving fund—seems like such a promising idea that it's hard to figure out why it hasn't caught on.
>
> Republican governors more often ride in Buicks than astride white chargers. But New Jersey's Thomas Kean looked a lot like a knight in 1982, when he rode to the rescue of state and local officials trying to fund ever-swelling infrastructure needs out of ever-shrinking budgets. His weapon: a state infrastructure bank that would convert federal grants into loans.
>
> For a while, Kean's bank looked like an idea whose time had come. As is true in much of the rest of the country, the state's transportation, water supply, and sewer systems are overused, underfinanced, or unbuilt, and the cost of rescue has been put in the billions. Even the growing number of observers who believe that the "infrastructure crisis" has been exaggerated have no doubt that better methods of allocating funds and of managing facilities are needed.
>
> At the same time, of course, federal grants for infrastructure projects have all but dried up. "New Jersey must look to its own resources," Kean told state lawmakers late in 1982, "its own initiatives, and its own innovative abilities to solve its infrastructure problems."
>
> The innovation was Kean's version of an infrastructure bank. Such a bank would lend money to local governments from a number of revolving loan accounts, one each for sewers, roads, and so on. The accounts would be filled initially by a pool of capital drawn from such traditional sources as bond sales as well as from federal grants. Loans would be made to local government units at below-market rates, payable over periods ranging up to 20 years. Repaid loans would be recycled to fund subsequent generations of improvements.
>
> Kean's bank idea quickly attracted national attention. Lawmakers in California, Minnesota, and Massachusetts began considering financing mechanisms loosely based on the New Jersey model. But, as is often true in government, the bank was less a new idea than a fertile blending of some old ones. Pooling capital is old hat in the dozen or so, mainly rural, states with state bond banks. Similarly, the revolving loan fund for capital improvements dates back to the 1940s. Such funds (with initial capital supplied by the sale of state-backed bonds) typically are used to finance water and sewage treatment projects whose revenues can be conveniently dedicated to paying off loans from the fund.[5]

Kean's proposal elaborated on these methods, extending the revolving fund concept to projects other than water and sewer improvements. The real innovation was his proposed conversion of federal grants into loans. Its practical appeal was not as a source of new money—many towns would find themselves having to pay for things they were used to getting almost free—but as a new way to spend it. The plan recommended itself to many planners, as will be noted, although politicians were less impressed.

---

5. *Planning*, August 1986.

PART 8

REBUILDING OUR CITIES

*Slowly, but surely humanity
acheives what its wise men
have dreamed.*

—*Samuel Johnson*

CHAPTER 39

WEEDS IN THE GARDEN AND URBAN RENEWAL

Physical decay has eaten deeply into the urban community. Unchecked obsolescence stretches its withering fingers over the environment and brings degeneration to the city. Irresponsible civic management invites it, and negligent urban housekeeping permits it to spread. It menaces health, breeds crime and delinquency, and brings traffic death and injury. It undermines civic pride, threatens municipal bankruptcy, and gnaws at the human mind and nerves.

Blight casts its sinister shadow across the face of the city. It decays the core of the business and industrial districts, and it disintegrates the outskirts. It is not confined to the slums, but it is most apparent there; it is there that we have failed to maintain the much-vaunted "American standard of living." Harold Buttenheim once said: "We not only need to defend our standard of living, we need to achieve it." [1]

The housing problem remains unsolved, but certain policies have taken shape during the past few decades. The necessity for government to render assistance in some form has been recognized. It has become apparent that private enterprise, unaided, is not able to provide an adequate supply of satisfactory housing to meet the wide variations in the income levels of all the people. This was made evident by the success of the mortgage insurance program of the Federal Housing Ad-

THE PENALTY FOR NEGLECT

---

1. "The American City," *Architectural Forum*, January 1945.

ministration. Initiated as a "pump-priming" measure during the Depression of the thirties, it continued to be popular through periods of high economic prosperity. Acceptance of public assistance through public housing for low-wage earners persists as an issue, but the history of housing in Europe and the situation in the United States indicate that the issue revolves around the extent to which public housing shall become an integral part of our economic and social machinery, not whether such a program should be instituted.

Practically every city is vested with the police power to require maintenance of adequate housing standards. Not only has the enforcement of these powers been ineffective but also the nature of the problem has moved beyond the scope of this device. Lack of planning, poor subdivision practices, excessive land values, ineffectual zoning, archaic streets, and inadequate transportation have created a condition of congestion, unplanned and incompatible mixed land uses, and economic distortions that render whole sections of the city in a process of built-in physical decay and social disintegration. The problem has transcended piecemeal treatment for improvement and has reached a stage where large-scale rehabilitation is the only feasible procedure. Such procedure implies the understanding of social and economic problems of the poor as well as the coordination and participation of all forces at the command of the urban population.

Sound business thrives on production and distribution; they create investment opportunities. Speculation travels in its wake, clinging like a leech and eating away its solvency. The effect is evident in the urban pattern. Industrial and commercial growth was expected to continue horizontally and outward from the center. But as speculation set in, land prices boomed, and industrial enterprise eluded the trap by hurdling to the outskirts. Commercial enterprise expanded vertically via the skyscraper or skipped to the expanding market in the suburbs.

What havoc has been wrought by this economic warfare! In its wake lies a mass of industrial, commercial, and residential derelicts, hemmed in by a network of obsolete streets and alleys. It has left land values so inflated they defy self-improvement through normal channels of enterprise. It has heaped a relentless burden of taxation upon the people, and it encourages the persistent exodus of the population to the periphery of cities and beyond.

City government is in partnership with this process. As the city deteriorates the cost of upkeep increases. Lip service is given to local responsibility, but it has been customary for city and state governments to avoid the issue of subsidy by transferring that responsibility to the federal government. The cost of maintaining obsolete cities has exacted heavy demands upon the taxpayer.

The Tax Burden   In the last few decades, many studies have indicated that slum areas do not generate nearly enough tax revenues to support the many services essential to the maintenance of decent communities. In recent times, with the federal government exacting a greater share of the tax dollar for its programs, and with less and less being funneled back into the local communities, the plight of all segments of urban areas has become increasingly difficult. Services are reduced, local taxes are increased, and cities are forced to allow their physical and social structures to decline, especially in those areas that are already blighted.

In the post-"Reaganomics" era, local government can no longer look to the federal government for meaningful financial assistance. As a reaction to the tax burden on property owners, legislation such as Proposition 13 in California and

Proposition $2\frac{1}{2}$ in Massachusetts has limited the taxing powers of all levels of local government to the point where many cities are faced with demands for services and are without the funds to provide them.

Tax-limit laws like these extend and increase the problems. They freeze the taxes on older structures at past assessed values and thus reduce available income required to update and rehabilitate obsolescent areas. To circumvent the drastic reductions of city income, special charges are now assessed for such essentials as sewage collection and processing, rubbish collection, and many other services heretofore covered by property taxes. Additional city revenue is obtained by increased development and processing fees that in the past had been nominal.

One essential item not covered in all the discussion of the need for tax limits is the repayment of debts and interest owed for bonds and for the installations of facilities and utilities before enactment of the legislation. This can be a considerable burden upon the capacity of the city to finance, and it could also undermine the capacity to make future improvements that might be subject to bonded indebtedness.

Although concern over the deterioration of cities was confined for a time to social reformers and a few utopians, leadership in all phases of urban enterprise was awakened to the hazards to the people and institutions whose roots are in the city, to its life and its economy. Some persons were stimulated to action by an aversion to public housing serving a single role—as an instrument for rebuilding. They were genuinely disturbed by the downward trend in the physical environment and became convinced that broad steps were necessary to stem the tide. Emotions and reason were mixed among those who, comprehending the social and economic evils rooted in our cities, recoiled at the prospect of saving the financial souls of those allegedly responsible for and profiting from the slums, and those who, confessing the evils, were reluctant to admit the inability of conventional enterprise to cope with them. As these forces moved toward the center, the issues gradually came into clearer focus. In the absence of concerted willingness or ability among those who own urban property to check disintegration, it fell to the lot of the public through the instrument of government. "The legitimate object of government," said Abraham Lincoln, "is to do for a community of people whatever they need to have done but cannot do at all or cannot do so well for themselves in their separate and individual capacities."

The central problem of urban rebuilding is the cost of land and financing. Measured by any standard of appropriate use the land will cost too much; it will be out of all proportion to the economic value for acceptable redevelopment, and any other terms will make the venture worthless. If we are to restore decency to the urban scene, the excess cost of land must be liquidated—written off as a loss by the owners, or when acquired by the government by purchase, or by eminent domain. No magic will make it vanish. The cost of rebuilding our cities is the price that must be paid to restore a decent standard of city building. It is the penalty for permitting such congestion that rebuilding is not an economic possibility. Responsibility for this error rests with every community in which it has occurred.

If the processes of rebuilding cities to the standards considered appropriate to the times in which we live are to begin, it will be essential for the people of the communities to understand their vested interest in the structure of their urban environment and what it can mean to them and the future of their families. This

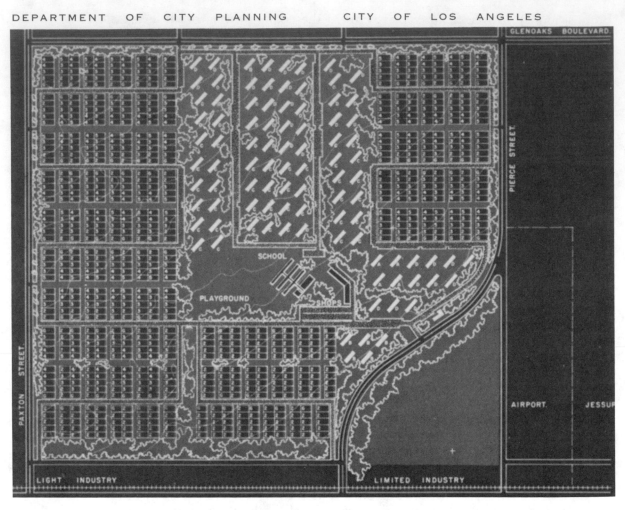

The Pacoima Plan, San Fernando Valley—Los Angeles, 1950.

interest, based on knowledge and understanding, must be translated to participatory democracy through activities that will be reflected in political action by elected officials.

OBSOLES-CENCE AND URBAN RENEWAL

The accelerated rate of physical deterioration in our cities was among the deficiencies in our national well-being recognized in the year after the Depression of the thirties. It was then estimated that urban housing was becoming obsolete five times as fast as it was being replaced. As a consequence, the Housing Act of 1954 extended the role of the federal government to include rehabilitation and conservation, and the program was expanded from redevelopment to urban renewal. As part of the new program aggressive enforcement of the building codes to maintain housing standards must be pursued, but the limitations of such piecemeal renewal should be recognized. The physical improvement of old buildings is but one aspect of effective renewal, and it may result in the postponement of the planning corrections necessary to improve traffic conditions and alleviate the undesirable mixture of incompatible uses that also contributes to community blight.

Blight: Weeds in the Garden

Blight is the critical stage of urban obsolescence. Defining an area as blighted serves as the basis for redevelopment. Its elimination and prevention are justifications for using eminent domain to acquire and assemble sites for private devel-

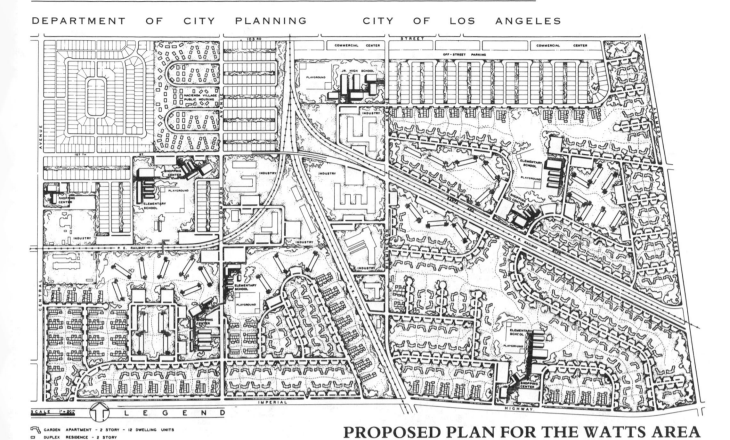

DEPARTMENT OF CITY PLANNING   CITY OF LOS ANGELES

PROPOSED PLAN FOR THE WATTS AREA

LEGEND

GARDEN APARTMENT - 2 STORY - 12 DWELLING UNITS
DUPLEX RESIDENCE - 2 STORY
ROW TYPE DWELLING - 2 STORY - 5 DWELLING UNITS
APARTMENT - 3 STORY - 54 DWELLING UNITS
GROSS AREA OF PROJECT - 982 ACRES

opment, for the expenditure of public funds including tax increment moneys, and for the imposition of controls in the project area.

The definitions that follow are part of California's health and safety code, but they can be usefully applied to any city.[2]

Structural blight refers to buildings and structures used for living, commercial, industrial, or other purposes, that are unfit or unsafe to occupy and may cause ill health, transmission of disease, infant mortality, juvenile delinquency, and crime, because of any one or a combination of the following factors:

Defective design and character of physical construction;

Faulty interior arrangement and exterior spacing;

High density of population and overcrowding;

Inadequate provision for ventilation, light, sanitation, open spaces, and recreational facilities; and/or

Age, obsolescence, deterioration, dilapidation, mixed character, or shifting of uses.

Los Angeles urban renewal planning in the 1950s. *Large-scale projects were the norm in the early days of the urban renewal programs. Vast areas considered blighted—usually the neighborhoods inhabited by poor minority groups—were to be swept clean, and a new "fabric" of development placed on the land. The costs in money and inconvenience to the residents were pushed into the background in an effort to renew the structure of the city. The scope of these concepts was so extensive that in most areas local and federal governmental agencies viewed the plans as artists' conceptions without the substance to achieve reality. Above is the Watts Area Plan, and page 496 displays the Pacoima Plan, San Fernando Valley; and page 498 shows the Jefferson Area Plan.*

---

2. "Introduction to Redevelopment," compiled by the Community Redevelopment Agencies Association. The definitions are based on California Health and Safety Code Sections 33030-2, 33320-1, and 33367.

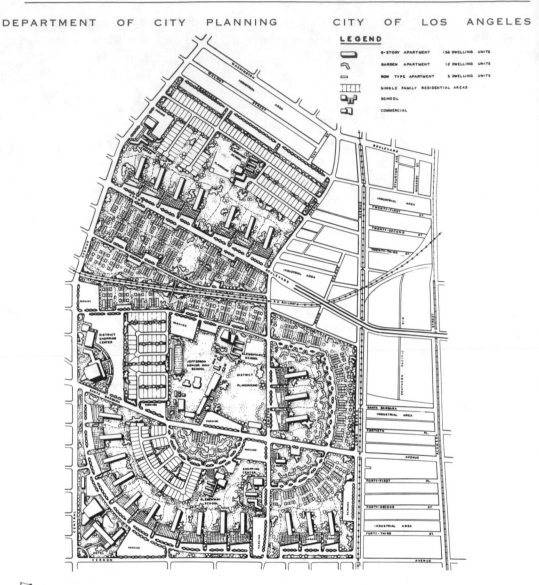

The Jefferson Area Plan—Los Angeles, 1950.

Economic blight refers to properties that suffer economic dislocation, deterioration, or disuse because of one or more of the following factors:

Any economic dislocation, deterioration, or disuse resulting from faulty planning;

The subdividing and sale of lots of irregular form and shape and inadequate size for proper usefulness and development;

The laying out of lots in disregard of the contours and other topographic or physical characteristics of the ground and surrounding conditions;

The existence of inadequate public improvements, public facilities, open spaces, and utilities that cannot be remedied by private or governmental action without redevelopment;

A prevalence of depreciated values, impaired investments, and social and economic maladjustment; and/or

The existence of lots or other areas that are subject to being submerged by water; provided that any ecologically valuable existing features in such areas shall, to the maximum extent feasible, be preserved.

Such conditions must cause a reduction of, or lack of, proper utilization of the area to such an extent that it constitutes a serious physical, social, or economic burden on the community, one that cannot reasonably be expected to be reversed or alleviated by private enterprise acting alone.

The conditions of blight should predominate and injuriously affect the entire project area. Nonblighted properties may be included if their inclusion is necessary for effective redevelopment; they shall not be included for purposes of tax increments without other substantial justification for their inclusion.

Noncontiguous areas should either be blighted or, if not blighted, necessary for effective redevelopment. An unblighted, noncontiguous area is not deemed necessary for effective redevelopment if included only for purposes of tax increments.

The legislative body must make findings of blight and must justify inclusion of nonblighted properties in the ordinance adopting a redevelopment plan. The findings must be supported by substantial evidence in the record. A preponderance of the evidence is not necessary. Evidence need only be substantial enough for the legislative body to make a good-faith finding. If there is no legal challenge to the finding within 60 days after adoption of the ordinance, the existence of blight in the project area is conclusively presumed.

The wasteful neglect of the resources within the broad belt of blight about our city centers has been underscored by the shift in emphasis from redevelopment to renewal. The 1960 Housing Act provided for pilot rehabilitation projects. Local agencies could purchase individual dwelling units, remodel and sell them to private owners. Each such project was limited to fifty units or not more than 2 percent of the total units in any renewal project.

Bunker Hill, Los Angeles. *Originally planned as a residential community as this plan (a student project) shows, it was intended to replace existing homes close to the center of the city. The plan conformed to the intent of the Housing Act of 1949 that established the purposes of redevelopment for residential uses and supportive services.*

Urban and rural slums: residential blight in barrios in South America. *All too many people are compelled by economic conditions to live in areas such as these in all parts of the world.*

The 1949 Housing Act requirement that a project be "predominantly housing" reflected the general assumption that the low-cost housing program was being transferred, along with "slum clearance," from the public to the private sector. Public housing had grown in disfavor, and political resistance to its continuation accounts for some of the reluctance to adopt the redevelopment provisions of the act at an earlier date. It was consequently assumed that the redevelopment program would shift the emphasis from public housing as the means by which slums and blight could be overcome. The fact that the physical deterioration is not confined to housing areas alone was overlooked. Such deterioration is the result of the general neglect of the basic standards that guide the building and the

Piecemeal urban redevelopment: New York City. *Making way for a new development on individual parcels of land.*

maintenance of the whole physical environment. The restriction therefore interfered with a comprehensive approach to redevelopment until 1954, when the Housing Act was amended to permit 10 percent of the federal grants for nonresidential sections of a redevelopment project.

Congress has been slow to acknowledge the responsibility of the government in the total problem of urban blight, persistently inclining to the position that housing is the primary concern. Nevertheless, relaxation from this firm position has been demonstrated. In 1959 the restriction was again modified to permit 20 percent nonresidential uses in redevelopment projects, and it has since been increased to 30 percent. Concern about the displacement of families from renewal areas and the destruction of socially viable communities led to a new emphasis on rehabilitation rather than wholesale clearance. To expand the effectiveness of the program, use of funds for nonresidential purposes was again increased to 35 percent. Rehabilitation demands unusually sensitive planning or it may become a deterrent to genuine improvement; the physical condition of individual buildings is but one of the elements in the creation of a living environment.

However, positive steps taken toward a comprehensive attack on the physical decay of the urban community have since been altered. Redevelopment programs were almost completely modified to favor the development of commercial structures. Only a minor effort was directed toward the construction of housing, which was the original intent of the redevelopment legislation passed in 1949. Bunker Hill in Los Angeles is a prime example. The original plan proposed mainly residential structures. But the projects constructed since 1980 and those now being constructed are largely for office buildings, hotels, and other cultural and commercial uses. The major proportion of the redevelopment area, once almost totally residential, now has only a small portion of the land devoted to that use.

THE WORKABLE PROGRAM

An innovation in the 1954 Housing Act made local agencies responsible for the development of an action plan for renewal: an overall community program for the removal of slums and blight. Known as the Workable Program, this important requirement deserved a more imaginative title.

"There is no justification for federal assistance except to cities which will face up to the whole process of urban decay and undertake long-range programs." That statement is from the 1953 report of the President's Advisory Committee on Government Housing Policies and Programs. It sums up the challenge to cities laid down by the Workable Program.

A POSSIBLE SOLUTION

Congestion created high land values and congestion now threatens to destroy them. To ward off this imminent disaster, the protection of land values is a compelling motive for improvement of the environment. Land is a natural resource; it is not a product of human toil. Value attached to it is essentially a byproduct, a value not of the land itself but of the way in which it may be used. Stable values can be maintained only through social controls cast in the form of laws that prescribe the limits of its use. This has not occurred. Stimulated by the almost anarchic nature of laws governing urban development, speculation has enjoyed a violent career. Inflation bubbles blow up, they burst; land prices quiver but rise again to unprecedented heights. More than 60 years ago, Harland Bartholomew said, "Too often is the American city considered an unlimited speculation in real estate."[3]

Negligence and abuse have sapped some of the vitality of our traditional practices. The public power of eminent domain is summoned to force adjustment, and public funds are drawn upon to aid in purging the economic congestion. Condemnation and public credit now receive general acceptance as necessary instruments for urban rebuilding. These are not measures to be taken as tempo-

---

3. Introduction to *Urban Land Uses,* Harvard City Planning Series (Cambridge, Mass.: Harvard University Press, 1932).

rary sedatives. The high cost should produce a cure; it is reasonable to expect them to prevent a recurrence of the same ills.

State laws for urban redevelopment provide that land acquired by condemnation may be resold. It is generally provided that the new use to which the land is put shall comply with standards of use which conform to a comprehensive plan for redevelopment.

Public financial assistance for urban rehabilitation serves a dual purpose. It implements rebuilding at standards of land use that will restore a decent environment, and it provides unlimited opportunities for sound and profitable investment by private enterprise. The investment of public funds as subsidies is warranted on the condition that the resulting improvement is permanent, and there must be assurance that the same investment to cure the same ills will not be repeated every generation. It is of vital importance, therefore, to ascertain that the new standards of land use are of a reasonable lengthy duration.

To determine this, it is necessary to refer to the laws that apply to urban building. A comprehensive plan is not a permanent document, nor are the "administrative decisions" that emanate from a planning agency preparing that document. A comprehensive plan is only part of a series of legislative acts controlling the development of cities. An immediate improvement may conform to the new standards administratively determined within the scope of a comprehensive plan, but subsequent use of land will depend entirely upon later revisions and modifications that may emerge. To rely upon administrative policy, no matter how inspired, is to invite inevitable chaos and abuse.

Adequate protection is afforded only by the laws that set the standards, and there is little evidence that reasonable legal standards are yet remotely intended. This raises a question as to the advisability of delivering land, acquired by the public power of condemnation, back to the same abuses that have made it necessary to exercise that power. The question may be elaborated by inquiring whether justice is served by taking land from some private owners and selling it to other private interests at a reduced price. The purpose of public funds is to bring land costs down to an economic value for redevelopment at standards of decent land use. To that extent the public interest is served and to that extent it must be protected. To sell land at a subsidized price is to make a gift of public funds as an inducement to engage in urban rebuilding for profit. Such a policy is somewhat of a distortion of the high purpose for which it is designed.

Thus we come to the central question: Rather than buy land only to sell it at reduced cost, other considerations aside, thereby creating potential dangers for the future, why should not publicly owned land be leased for redevelopment use?

The suggestion is not new. In 1942 an English Royal Commission reported its recommendations for a reconstruction program. That report said in part, "We recommend . . . that once any interest in land has passed into public ownership it should be disposed of by way of lease only and not by way of sale, and that the authority should have the power to impose such covenants in the lease as planning requirements make desirable, breach of such covenants to be enforceable by re-entry."[4]

---

4. Report of the Expert Committee on Compensation and Betterment presented to Parliament by Minister of Works and Planning, September 1942.

Building on leased land is by no means rare. It is common practice in commercial enterprise and offers no deterrent to sound investment. It need offer no obstruction to the sale of improvements on the land. Nor would tax revenue be affected, since a lease value would return revenue to the city, and the usual taxes could be assessed against the improvement. The objections of the local bureaucracy could be avoided by obtaining the services of competent and established firms in property management.

We are confronted with a situation in which public powers must be called into action to restore the productive enterprise of our cities and the initiative of private enterprise in our urban economy, and, in so doing, create an urban environment consistent with our contemporary capacities and skills. The fact that land values obstruct the path to this goal becomes a matter of concern to the people—a public responsibility—and the gains made at the expense of the people should be retained by them.

CONTROL OF OBSOLESCENCE: TAXATION

An effective method of controlling the spread of obsolescence is not yet available. The police power to restrain the "nuisance" of blight has limitations. Obsolescence is an obstruction to full production of housing. Normal competitive enterprise does not and cannot cope with it, as the accumulation of huge areas of blighted districts testifies.

When blight sets in, the land is deemed ripe for more intensive land use. As single-family districts, some being the "fine old sections," begin to run down, their only salvation seems to be a change to apartment development. Intensity of land use moves relentlessly from the city center, and the "old" areas are drawn into this ever-widening vortex. The greater density permitted in apartment zoning then swiftly moves to reinforce a claim to higher land values. Thenceforth only multiple-dwelling development can be afforded. Old residences are converted to apartments, and the district declines further. Strip zoning for business use is soon permitted, and unplanned stores are spotted in the neighborhood. After that, "light" industrial uses seep in. The "salvation" of revised zoning is dissipated among unplanned mixed land uses, and the community environment decays.

Pressure is ever present to "save" obsolescent areas by permitting a greater intensity of land use. Indeed, there are a few instances where this usually insidious process has restored to blighted areas a decent standard of residential or commercial development. More normally, the careless mixture of land uses leaves a series of derelicts in its wake. Land values increase rather than decrease as blight eats its way from the central core of the city, and they defy recovery of neighborhood values. Good development retreats from these damaging blows and seeks protection of new and more economical land at a safe distance. Disorderly expansion continues. Self-maintenance is the urgent need: a form of preventive treatment that will build resistance to decay and render major operations less necessary.

Federal, state, county, and city taxes in general are intended to provide for sound governance and essential public services to protect the health, safety, and public welfare. Certain portions of the funds collected by the federal and state governments have been returned to communities to assist in the financing of many local services, mainly education, transportation, and, in the recent past, public housing and urban renewal. Taxes associated with property, sometimes called *ad valorem taxes,* affect urban development directly. In the mid-1980s and since then much discussion in the federal administration was directed to the reduction in assistance to local government, especially in revenue sharing, support of education, health and transportation. Curtailing of this sharing of federal taxes places additional burdens upon the already limited assets of state and local governments. Federal interest in the urban renewal programs has been all but eliminated, with the threat of curtailing the functions of HUD in the process.

The use of public funds to assist—that is, to subsidize—urban development is not a new function of government. However, the extent and direction of both legislative and financial assistance increased immeasurably after the first and second world wars, when much of Europe was so devastated that it required public assistance to become socially and economically viable once again. In addition, the recessions and Depression that followed the wars highlighted the conditions of the poor, and programs were initiated to construct and reconstruct those areas hardest hit.

One factor has remained consistent over the years. Changes are made in all programs to aid urban areas as different political groups come into power. Some once abandoned as unworkable are revived under a different name, thereby proving that people remember and learn little from experience. The previously mentioned shift in emphasis, from rehousing the poor in areas to be redeveloped to support for supercommercial development, is an example of the pendulum swing in recent years; it is a far cry from the initial intent of the programs.

Buildings are built to provide space in which to live or conduct business. Taxes are collected to support the public services that make these building ventures possible and profitable. Today taxes are measured by the assessed value of land and buildings. The value of land may increase. The value of physical improvements, on the other hand, depreciates with age and use. At the same time the cost of public services increases as physical deterioration continues. Yet the present assessment of taxation actually works in reverse of this: tax revenue goes down as the cost of urban maintenance goes up.

Taxation in Reverse

There is little inducement for an owner to remove obsolete buildings as long as it is possible to derive a profit from them. The present order of real property taxation penalizes new construction and encourages the retention of old buildings until they have reached the last stages of decay. It retards sound real estate development and management, makes unhealthy communities, and adds to the burden of the taxpayer. This trend must be checked and reversed.

Taxation is our traditional instrument for maintaining economic and social equilibrium. Our system of enterprise is intended to give the individual full freedom of choice and initiative; devices employed by government to serve the public welfare should remain consistent with this pattern. It is up to the individual to measure his opportunity for investment; he must determine the extent to which he, in his own interest, will take part in the building of a community. But his interest cannot be served when a system of taxation imposes the penalty of high taxes on new building while it encourages competition from old buildings. Yet that is our current method of ad valorem taxation, and it is inimical to the full use of our productive resources.

It would be productive to look at a common technique used to reduce taxes in business enterprises: the cost of improvements to carry on the business may be deducted from gross income. Applying this principle to real property taxation would establish a logical order: as buildings deteriorate with age, thus contributing to the spread of blight and retarding new building, taxes would increase rather than decrease. Taxation would serve as an effective instrument to encourage expanding production and protect against blight, as well as no doubt adding revenue to the community for public services. This technique would be the more effective because real property taxes are levied primarily by local government and are thereby readily subject to such periodic adjustment as changing local conditions may warrant.

The Economic Life of Buildings

The control of obsolescence has a twofold purpose: the maintenance of a stable economy through continuing full production, and the maintenance of adequate standards through continuous improvement. The FHA program introduced the repayment of loans for urban construction in regular installments over a predetermined period: amortization. This helped to stabilize financing, but more than that it recognizes the vital role of time in our economic machinery. It acknowledges that buildings have an "economic life," a period during which they are economically useful. The wheels of the system are kept turning by the circulation of money, and the time required to pay for buildings marks the frequency of the circulation of money. Unless the demand for building continues to exceed the existing supply, circulation of building money diminishes or ceases. The building industry then slows down or stops.

In *Building Height, Bulk and Form,*[5] George B. Ford pointed out that the average life of skyscrapers was calculated at 25 to 30 years. The period of residential financing ranges between 15 and 25 years. Except for commercial dwelling structures that have become a sordid blight, few acceptable buildings remain in use for more than 35 years without such major alterations that they become the equivalent of new buildings. The obsolete buildings need to be weeded out of the urban environment.

If the physical life of buildings were linked to their economic life, money would continue to flow into the production of new structures. Improved methods would find normal reception and application. But as long as old and obsolete buildings remain on the market, they suffocate new production. Rundown and wornout buildings sustain themselves too long on no maintenance and low rents. It is that type of competition that must be weeded out. Control of obsolescence would maintain the economic flow of goods and services and therefore a higher level of decency in the urban environment. Taxation could be effectively used to establish this control if the rate were related to the economic life of buildings.

It would be possible to establish a low tax base for new buildings and thereafter increase the tax rate from year to year. During the early life of a building—about 10 years—the increase would be moderate. Thereafter it would gradually accelerate for the succeeding 15 to 20 years. After that the increase would move rapidly upward at such a rate that a major improvement to sustain a profitable income on the building or a complete removal to make way for a new structure more suitable to the market and the community would be induced by the time the structure had reached 35 years. A major improvement would cause a building to revert to a proportionately lower tax bracket rather than be penalized by an increased assessment, as occurs with current policy. Standards of construction

5. Harvard City Planning Series, Vol. II.

Changes occur, even in cities where property values are exceedingly high and where redevelopment occurs on a lot-by-lot basis—as in New York.

would be improved because they would benefit from lower taxes rather than be discouraged by the present ad valorem system.[6]

Such a method rejects the traditional supposition that a building may remain as long as it produces revenue satisfactory to its owner. It may seem to be bitter medicine, but the accelerating degeneration of our cities has amply demonstrated that neither the public welfare nor sound private enterprise is served by current methods. The proposal does not presume to solve the broad problem of taxation, but it would put our current tax system in a logical order. Without such a change, the regulations of today offer no prospect for correcting the insidious evil of obsolescence.

No surgeon ever performed an operation without destroying some live tissue. The physician's aim is to save the patient, knowing that time will heal the wounds and restore the living cells. Our economy as well as our social well-being depend upon our capacity to carve out the parasite of decay with the destruction of as little useful tissue as is practically possible. But we cannot continue to rely upon vagaries of chance. In an organized society it must become a matter of law.

It may be alleged that this order of taxation would impose undue hardship on low-income homeowners who depend upon their dwelling solely as a place to live. The most articulate protests of this nature will undoubtedly come from those who profit most from blighted property, but the criticism has some validity. Nonetheless, every community will have to face, sooner or later, this ques-

6. This approach to building improvements could be coordinated with some form of taxation on land.

tion: How long can the accumulation of obsolete buildings and "improvements" that deface the environment and eat away at the civic solvency be tolerated? Each community is obliged to address itself to that question and deliberate the problems—all the problems—it poses. Only then will cities begin the long road out of the sordid morass that the anarchy of urban development has wrought.

All things grow obsolete with time and change. That is inevitable. But obsolescence must be brought under control, as weeds are kept out of a prosperous garden. Degeneration of the urban environment is an epidemic feeding upon lack of attention. The absence of public control and effective treatment is like the underwriting of obsolescence by law. It has become a public liability. It is consequently a public responsibility to devise machinery to put its house in order, and to keep it in order by the progressive regulation of obsolescence.

RENEWAL IS FOR PEOPLE

There is little doubt that slum conditions must be eradicated and the families living in them must have decent housing. Blight must be removed and further spread prevented. Rundown business sections need rehabilitation, and industrial areas must be cleaned up. The decay must be carved out. But there are some related issues from which a program of renewal and rehabilitation cannot be dissociated. Bright new projects replace the slums. Buildings rise high and open space appears where there was none before. The apartments all have a view. Efficiency and convenience replace the drudgery of a house and yard; services are well maintained by management. The great new buildings are quite urbane, the parking garages and traffic circulation ingenious. But as the program progresses there is evidence that money, buildings, and bulldozers are receiving somewhat more attention than people. For what people are these giant developments intended? Certainly not those displaced during the clearance.

Further, are these projects an expression of the environment we really seek? Is the agglomeration of cells in huge building blocks the design for future family life? Have we become incapable of distinguishing between "habitable" and "livable"?

The frequency with which these questions have been asked is reason enough to ponder them. It is the human spirit of the city, rather than land prices, which renewal is presumed to sustain. As the prospects for orderly rebuilding of our cities loom brighter, we cannot be unmindful of its underlying purpose: recreation of an urban environment in which the functions of the contemporary city can be performed with order. Other advantages will accrue, but we may be guided by Aristotle's advice: "A city should be built to give its inhabitants security and happiness."

Urban renewal is not supposed to be solely for the purpose of restoring stability to real estate values, although this will result. It is not for the purpose of bailing out the investments of landed gentry, since much of the decaying city pays dividends to its absentee owners. It is not intended to recover speculative losses, since the curse of blight has fallen upon the property of those who cannot afford to join the flight to better places. It is not for the purpose of reinforcing government bureaucracy, although the public that these bureaus represent has a heavy stake in the problem. It is not for the purpose of providing employment, although it will create unlimited opportunities for labor in field and factory. Urban renewal is for none of these specifically, but each is a part serving the main objective: building a decent city for people.

Cities are for people. Cities are not objects to be coddled by zealots nor commodities to satisfy speculative greed. The philosophy of escape from the city is a retreat from reality; within this philosophy are the seeds of our own destruction. To deny the place of the city in our industrial age is to invite economic slavery and social suicide. Our proper course is not the destruction of urban life; it is the building of a better one.

John Osman, then vice president of the Ford Foundation for Adult Education, once stated:

> Building a city is a sacramental act on the part of the whole people. For a city is the physical manifestation of an invisible reality: the soul of its people. Ancient cities were worshipped by their citizens. Americans appear to hate their cities. We do all we can to demean and disgrace them.
>
> But there is an intangible spirit at the heart of a contemporary commercial city that must find its expression in and give purpose to the city building of its people. We should endeavor to make an art out of our town building.
>
> The citizens of a city must discover the character of the city if they are to build an image of its soul. They must understand its nature and its function before they can design it. For the design of a city is not to be found on the drawing board of the city planner. The forms of the city live in its people. They emerge out of the mind and spirit of its citizens. They reside in the very history of "the place." . . .[7]

It is well to think about that counsel as we consider the confused maze of housing "programs" intended to improve the lot of the poor while rebuilding rundown areas in our cities. Civic and political leaders, disenchanted with the public housing programs after World War II, decided private enterprise should clear slums and build decent housing for low-income families. Urban renewal programs failed to take into account the plight of families who, for economic, ethnic, or social reasons, were not eligible for or could not afford the new high-rise apartments that replaced the blight. Where the new buildings were intended for underprivileged families, it was discovered that high-rise cell blocks were incompatible with the living mores of their intended occupants.

The bizarre example of the Pruitt–Igoe public housing development in St. Louis should alert our attention to the human element in the housing equation. Because the development had such an oppressive atmosphere to the low-income occupants for whom it had been planned, less than a quarter of the dwellings were ever occupied. Eventually, in 1972, the government ordered two of the eleven-story towers destroyed by dynamite; the remaining towers were reduced to less than half their original height.

Despite such an incredible experience, housing is seldom designed for compatible living patterns. The drama of high-rise buildings appeals not only to architects and engineers who design them; it also satisfies the land-economists and government officials who consider land prices more than the basic needs of people for a compatible living environment. Urban renewal moves toward apartments designed for upper-income groups who want to return to city life and the amenities it offers, or else accommodations for commercial institutions are promoted to replace the blight.

With the drifting course of government assistance to housing, the fact that many low-income families in the nation cannot afford the cost of decent housing—the

---

7. *Architectural Forum*, August 1957.

property taxes, insurance, and maintenance—has been obscured in the enthusiasm to subsidize the private sector in real estate and development. It is quite possible that when the ambition for large projects attractive to planners, architects, and government officials has abated, public housing may be integrated within neighborhoods where the less economically privileged may find a compatible environment.

It would be well to heed the observations of Paul Gaff, urban affairs editor of the *Chicago Tribune*. Despite new Neanderthal monsters in the heart of the city, such as the Prudential Building, the Marina City Towers, the John Hancock Building, the Standard Oil Building, and the Sears Tower, Chicago "is losing its battle with the suburbs." Confronted with the lethargy of the City Planning Department, privately financed plans by the architectural firm of Skidmore, Owings, and Merrill in 1966 envisioned a restructuring of the look of Chicago and the lakefront, a leviathan "new town in town" on 600 acres along the river for a population of 120,000. But Graff suggests:

> Perhaps it is already too late. . . . The nature of the growth points to a day when the last middle-class white family has fled the city—when only the wealthy remain within their fortified apartment towers along the lake and the rest of Chicago is populated by the poor. This is no doomsday fantasy. . . . Chicago, which keeps telling itself to "make no little plans," continues to move toward the time when it will have little left to plan for.[8]

The changes that have taken place in the central area of Chicago, and in the core areas of many other large cities, indicate a reversal to the earlier trend of white, middle-class flight to the suburbs. Although the "new town in town" program has generally been considered a commercial experiment, there has been a residential revival. Old structures have been rehabilitated and are now occupied by affluent individuals and families seeking the social advantages associated with the business institutions and cultural establishments, as well as places of employment, located nearby.

URBAN REHABILITATION (REGENERATION IN ENGLAND)

In all cities, large or small, there are areas that have grown old along with the people who reside in dilapidated, antiquated buildings which are served by public utilities that are long due for replacement. The normal approach is to label these areas as "blighted" and prepare plans for razing the structures and replacing them with new shiny buildings for persons other than the local residents, who cannot afford the cost of the replacement housing.

These areas are generally in the heart of the city near many services, health, welfare, and shopping that are geared to serve the need of the elderly. The redevelopment of these areas creates in many ways a new group of homeless people without income to secure even the so-called affordable housing.

It would seem mere logic, since the project areas and their housing are available at relatively low cost, if they are not already publicly owned and are available for the development of rehabilitation projects designed to serve the residents of the areas, to rehabilitate them. It is true that the costs of rehabilitation run high, almost as high as those of new construction, but with the write-off on the land and a recognition of the needs of the resident population, it would seem more than just being a "do gooder" to preserve these areas, many of which contain

---

8. *Architectural Forum*, January-February 1974.

buildings that are interesting historically as they demonstrate the style of a particular architectural period.

In preparing plans for the growth and development of a city, it seems reasonable to designate such areas in a protective category while the community budgets for the revitalization are designated.

All cities have older areas where people are drawn together for many cultural reasons. These can be neighborhoods of artists, artisans, musicians, or producers of special services that must be located in close proximity to each other and to their public to perform their services to society most effectively. These include medical centers with all of the related occupations which are interdependent. There are educational neighborhoods, generally centering about a university, within which the reasons for living close to the institution are important both to faculty and students. Many more examples could be cited to suggest that all clusters of persons with common interests tend to group into neighborhoods. The rehabilitation of these areas would do much to preserve the housing stock, and both the individual people served and the community as a whole would benefit.

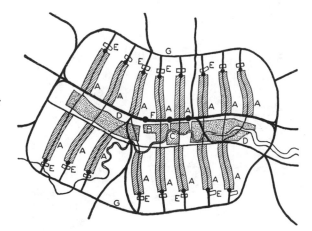

PLAN FOR LONDON

by the M.A.R.S. Group

A   Residential Units
B   Main Shopping Center
C   Administrative and Cultural Center
D   Heavy Industry
E   Local Industry
F   Main Railway and Passenger Stations
G   Belt Rail Line

Plans for renewal of London.

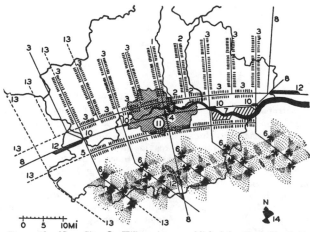

DIAGRAMMATIC SKETCH FOR LONDON, by Hilberseimer, 1941

1   Political Administration
2   Financial Administration
3   Commercial Administration
4   Central Station
5   Smokeless Industry
6   Smoke-producing Industry
7   Port of London
8   Long-distance Railroad
10 Main Railroad Station
11 Airport
12 Railroad Yards
13 Possible Extensions
14 Wind Diagram

Areas 1, 2, 3, 5, and 6 include Residential Districts

From *The New City*, L. Hilberseimer, published by Paul Theobald

Urban reorganization, La Cité Industriel.

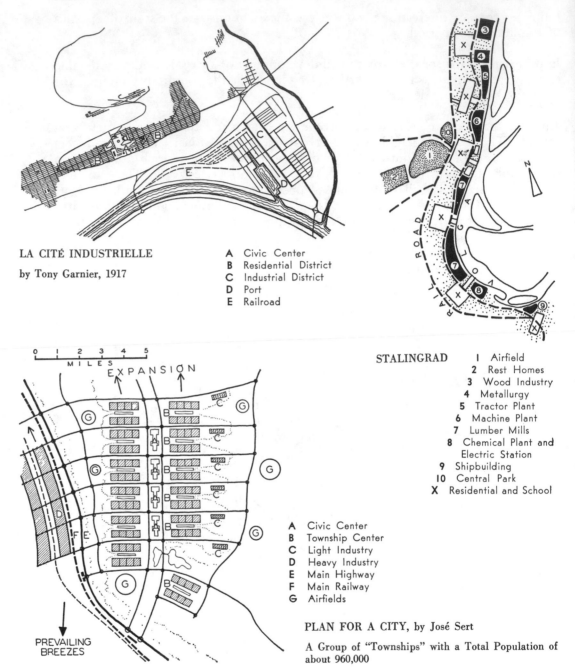

LA CITÉ INDUSTRIELLE

by Tony Garnier, 1917

A   Civic Center
B   Residential District
C   Industrial District
D   Port
E   Railroad

STALINGRAD
1   Airfield
2   Rest Homes
3   Wood Industry
4   Metallurgy
5   Tractor Plant
6   Machine Plant
7   Lumber Mills
8   Chemical Plant and
    Electric Station
9   Shipbuilding
10 Central Park
X   Residential and School

A   Civic Center
B   Township Center
C   Light Industry
D   Heavy Industry
E   Main Highway
F   Main Railway
G   Airfields

PLAN FOR A CITY, by José Sert

A Group of "Townships" with a Total Population of about 960,000

URBAN REORGANIZATION

Searching for an urban form appropriate to the metropolis of the industrial age, the New Utopians have produced some principles which may guide a reorganization of the city of tomorrow. These principles merge the common characteristics of the "linear" and the "concentric" city forms; they accept the physical properties of the neighborhood unit in favor of the basic needs of the family and regain the prospect for identity of the individual parts of the great city now lost within the dreary grayness of the present metropolis. Because the city form must change if it is to survive and because it must survive as an integral element of the industrial age, the proposals of the New Utopians are essential ingredients of urban thought and action.

As Garnier's "La Cité Industrielle" used the greenbelt for separation between the factory and the home not present in Howard's "garden city," and the plan for Stalingrad suggests a cellular organization of residential and industrial units not present in the linear city of Soria y Mata, so the Ascoral plans by Le Corbusier synthesize the essential characteristics of a new urban form.

The variety of this synthesis is further expressed in the diagrammatic presentation of other proposals.

CHAPTER 40

DEVELOPMENT PROCESSES

PROCEDURE

Before any public or private development can take place the developers must take a number of steps. Among them, they must observe the comprehensive plan as it affects the land, the zoning ordinance and its many regulations, and the subdivision laws of both the local community and the state; they must abide by the findings of the environmental review agency, which will determine if the project impacts unfavorably on environment, energy use, or endangered species; they must follow the building code and all of its many components, and, if the site is near the coast, must pass the muster of the critical eye of local and state coastal commissions. Finally, they may have to convince citizens' committees, environmental protection associations, and other groups that are opposed to development on personal or philosophic grounds.

Having cleared all of these steps, the developer is then faced with the costs related to the required procedures and improvements. It is important to recognize that many of the costs now part of the development process are due to past excesses mismanagement or the problems directly related to earlier lack of adequate regulation.

Fees

Some of the types of fees assessed the subdivider or developer are given in the chart that follows. These are determined at the local level and relate to the costs of both materials and manpower at a given time. The data serve only to illustrate the impact of those local government requirements, which are meant to assure the ultimate users of the land that they are not walking into an untenable situation

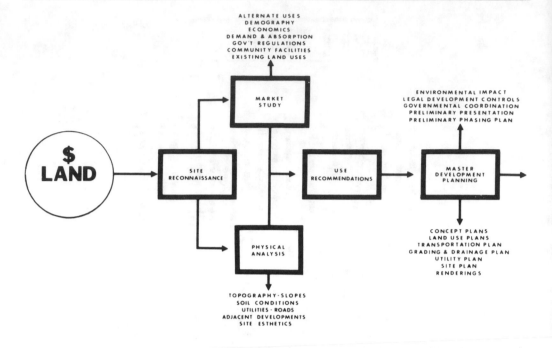

of great expense in the future. Later installation often involves lengthy individual negotiations with a multitude of occupants and a variety of economic situations. In many instances the "after-occupancy" efforts to bring a development up to acceptable levels result in failure and frustration. It is far better to have the improvements included in the original costs so that installations can be done on a mass basis at much less expense.

THE INFRA-STRUCTURE

Infrastructure includes all essential facilities, such as water, sewers, streets and highways, public utilities, schools, libraries, parks, and police and fire services, and many other facilities related to the protection of the health, safety, and general welfare. Before any property can be offered for sale, there must be a major investment in the infrastructure. The installation of the various elements involves both the public and private sectors identified with a proposed development.

The infrastructure must be in conformity with the comprehensive plan and all other regulations dealing with services to people. All must be related to the density of population proposed or the intensity of the commercial or industrial uses intended for the land.

Many of the elements of the infrastructure are installed prior to the occupancy of the sites. Others can follow when the need arises. Schools must be in place at the time the people and children are on the land. Water, sewers, and other utilities must be available at the time the land is to be occupied. The utilities must be in the streets before paving is done. The timing and sequence of the installation of improvements must be carefully planned. They must be tied into existing lines that have the capacity to accept the additional loading as foreseen in the comprehensive plan. Offsite connections may become a critical financial problem for the developer.

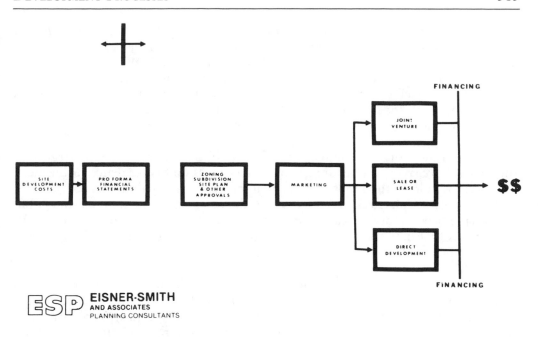

FINANCING

| SITE DEVELOPMENT COSTS | → | PRO FORMA FINANCIAL STATEMENTS | → | ZONING SUBDIVISION SITE PLAN & OTHER APPROVALS | → | MARKETING | → | JOINT VENTURE / SALE OR LEASE / DIRECT DEVELOPMENT | → | $$ |

FINANCING

ESP EISNER-SMITH AND ASSOCIATES PLANNING CONSULTANTS

Although the developer is required to install and pay for most improvements, like all other costs they are passed on to the consumer. If the proposed development is detached from the already urbanized area, the offsite costs are also borne by the developer, but as the in-between spaces are filled the funds collected are returned to the initial activator. In many ways these funds are clear profit since the total cost of the development has already been passed on to the occupants, be they residential, industrial, or commercial.

Beyond the baseline items, there are several other costs. Schools and parks are often assessed against the developer in the form of either demands for land or in-lieu fees. This cost is, of course, related only to those facilities that serve the people who directly benefit from them. In California, early efforts to secure neighborhood parks were declared illegal on the grounds that the state subdivision law did not list them as improvements; the state law was thereafter amended to include parks. A formula was devised to require the subdivider to allocate either land or in-lieu fees. In addition, in 1977 the state recognized the overcrowded conditions in local schools and adopted legislation to require the allocation of land or in-lieu fees to assist communities in securing temporary buildings and sites for school purposes.

Installation of many of the elements of the infrastructure has generally been established as the responsibility of the persons who develop land. However, the responsibility for the maintenance and replacement of aging elements in the underground and surface systems is almost universally the responsibility of the public agencies called "government." These are elements that in general are related to the supply of water and gas and the disposal of sewage and solid wastes, among other things.

Maintenance

Very little thought has ever been given to the useful life of these elements of the urban structure, almost with the thought that once in place they live to eternity.

Since most urban areas are aged and many facilities outlive their useful life, the economic problems facing communities are often beyond their capability to cope. The condition grows worse and more dangerous to health and safety with each passing year. Aside from the broken pavement and chuckholes on the surface, most of these facilities cannot be seen by the general public and consequently there is no outcry for improvement. There seems to have been no long-term plan for dealing with the infrastructure that is so essential to urban life.

Obtaining funds for the maintenance of the public domain has rested largely on the general taxpayer and his obligation to pay taxes on his residence or business. Taxpayer revolts in the 1980s reduced many communities' ability to continue the protection of the physical environment. In the past, efforts to maintain the public ways have been funded by capital grants from the federal and state governments, from taxes that they have collected. But recent programs based on these sources have also been reduced or cut out altogether.

Few people consider the congestion that occurs in the unseen workings of our urban communities. As in the human body time and use fill the concealed arteries with rust, metal accumulations caused by electrolysis, and just plain garbage to the point where the service plants can no longer function efficiently. When bridges fail or roads become unusable, we respond more readily than we do when water or sewer lines fail. It has been said that conditions in the city of New York are so bad that it would cost over $40 billion to rebuild the infrastructure, and it would take more than 10 years to accomplish the most essential portions of this task. Every large city faces the same problems. Although the extent and the costs may not be as great, the ability to perform the tasks is even more limited financially.

Dr. Pat Choate, author of *American in Ruins,* noted in his comments at a 1983 meeting of the California Infrastructure Task Force that "between $2 and $3 trillion is due to be spent on infrastructure between now and the year 2000." It is far cheaper, he said, to institute timely maintenance procedures on existing structures than to implement new projects.

CHAPTER 41

NEW TOWNS, SATELLITES, AND VILLAGES

An appropriate form for the future city has not yet emerged. Nonetheless, serious attention has been directed to the nature of the modern city in two major areas: the redevelopment of the internal urban structure, and planned decentralization —the new towns. The results are not yet conclusive in either, but our present consideration of the new towns may serve as important experience in shaping our vision of the city of tomorrow.

Every large city has a planning department, often a very large one. The results of their planning may be primarily confined to patchwork efforts dealing with zoning, to beautification of the streets, and, where they exist, the building setback areas.

NEED

Big cities do not respond to large-scale comprehensive planning since the changes that take place deal for the most part with individual projects involving one or more contiguous properties. One may observe New York City rebuilding itself with the tearing down of a large structure and the replacing of it with a larger one. Nothing can be done about the circulation system as the traffic becomes more congested with each intensification of use. Parking is required for the new uses, but the amounts are never adequate and the costs for the spaces are prohibitive. Chicago and San Francisco suffer the same situations. Planning for the future of the Chicago Loop was an excellent exercise when sponsored by Carson Pierie and Scott. The changes since the completion do not reflect the ambitious plans that were submitted.

The same problems face the cities of the Orient, only in exaggerated form. Shanghai represents the essence of the problems: too many people housed in inadequate shelter. Both the housing and circulation systems, handed down from the past, are based on the political rivalries and antagonisms that were associated with nineteenth-century imperialism. Here we have, today, a city that was three separate entities. Street systems were not coordinated. Separate utility systems served the areas. Transportation was largely by foot. Replanning from a base such as this will take generations, since the rehousing of even a few families means the destruction of existing shelters, as mean as they may be.

The answer to all these problems may well be the almost universal development of new towns on open land where people can be provided with new shelter and opportunities for employment in new locations as the older areas are cleared for renewed uses. It is important to understand the difference between "new towns" and "new cities." Since World War II, there has been a tremendous growth of new cities in the United States. In Los Angeles County, for example, 88 new cities have appeared since 1940. The county population, which includes both the cities and the unincorporated areas, has increased from 2,785,642 in 1940 to 8,863,164 in 1990. These new cities are *not* in the classical sense new towns, however. Rather, they are existing clusters of population, in either rural or urban areas, that want to have greater control over their local affairs than was being provided by the county government.

New towns, of which there are very few in the United States, are completely designed and constructed urban complexes. Some are self-sufficient entities while others are satellites to nearby major communities. The distinguishing feature of the new town is that it is designed in advance and is not merely a political "divorce" from an existing urbanized, developed community.

The United States

Creating facilities to accommodate 40 million more urban inhabitants in the United States by the turn of the century cannot be left to chance. Cities will require massive rehabilitation, regrouping of densities, allocation of open space, and effective mass transportation. Left to speculation and exploitation by free enterprise, suburbanization outside corporate city limits seriously impairs the economic viability of the cities. In Europe, decentralization has been planned by government authorities to distribute the population, industry, and commerce in satellite towns, notably around London and Stockholm. As socially responsible attitudes develop in the United States, large American cities will collaborate with county or regional enterprises for the same kind of orderly decentralization of population.

Big cities are swollen and decaying. Some states can only accept more population to their own detriment economically, socially, physically. Florida is already suffering. Oregon chooses not to grow in population. In its plan and land use regulations, each state has to consider its particular attributes. Responsibility devolves upon the federal government to harmonize state policies with the national imperative. There is much land, and, though it is perhaps underdeveloped, it is precious.

A "new cities" program, comparable to the British New Towns or Swedish satellites, may be implemented in the United States though no such program has yet been initiated. Any equivalent of British public development corporations will conflict with the ingrained American assumption that the public role shall be subordinate to the role of free enterprise, which is necessarily contingent on the degree to which financial profit is assured. Free enterprise has thus far been primarily engaged in existing cities and urban expansion where a full range of public facilities and services is available.

In his review of the New Communities Act of 1968, the veteran British New Town proponent Sir Frederic J. Osborn anticipated the administrative problems

> of a Federal department without town-funding experience confronting developers necessarily concerned for profitability but themselves not having staffs adapted to building complete towns, and local municipalities accustomed only to providing public services for adventurous growth rather than cooperating in town design. Some think that good new-town creation is only possible if a public body comparable with our development corporation is entrusted with the land ownership and groundwork, leaving the provision of building mainly to commercial developers. They are probably right.[1]

The record of large land-development companies across the nation does not bode well for their effectiveness in town building. From Cape Coral and Palm Coast in Florida to Adirondack Park in Pennsylvania; Treasure Lake in Georgia to Colonias de Santa Fe in New Mexico; Lake Winnebago near Kansas City to Lake Tahoe in California: the consuming objective has been the rapid sale of land, not the building of cities. "Decisions about where millions of Americans should be encouraged to migrate are left to land speculators while the National, State and Local Governments give up by default the right of the public to say what land use or growth policy should be."[2]

Time is growing short. As the population grows, vigorous redevelopment of existing cities can upgrade the environment and accommodate more people. Based on the assumption that "most of America's expected growth from now until the end of the century will occur within existing metropolitan areas,"[3] the National Task Force of the American Institute of Architects recommended that future urban growth should proceed in neighborhood increments identified as "growth units."[4] The estimated increase in national urban population during that period, however, can hardly be absorbed in existing metropolitan areas without a massive multiplicity of such growth units.

Numerous and extensive land subdivision has occurred on the periphery of the cities of America. Many of these developments have incorporated parks, schools, and shopping centers, but usually they have been random residential tracts without benefit of a plan for decentralization of the cities to which they are attached. The planning and development of complete self-contained towns in North America are rare. Kitimat in British Columbia, planned by Clarence Stein, and Don Mills near Toronto, discussed later in this chapter, are exceptions.

Exploitation of desirable open space proceeds in the guise of "new towns," although most serve as expansion of suburbs for discontented refugees who can afford to escape from the city or own a second home. The growth of suburbia is

1. "Planning Commentary—U.S.A. on the Way to New Town," *Town and Country Planning,* October-November 1968.

2. Robert Cahn, "Land in Jeopardy," *The Christian Science Monitor,* January 17–January 24, 1973. Reprinted by permission of The Christian Science Monitor, © 1972. The Christian Science Publishing Society. All rights reserved.

3. American Institute of Architects, *A Plan for Urban Growth: Report of the National Policy Task Force,* January 1982, page 3, Item G.

4. American Institute of Architects, National Task Force, *Strategy for Building a Better America,* December 1971; Report of Constraints Conference, May 1972; *Structure for a National Policy,* October 1973.

not confined to ticky-tacky subdivisions for the middle class. Wealthier citizens are in the market for fine, well-planned, and expensive communities with a full complement of commercial and recreational enterprises.[5] These are not independent new towns, however, and the economic and social stratification increases pressures upon low-income families, ethnic minorities, and the elderly.

The Urban Land Institute defines a *new town* as a

> land development project having acreage sufficiently large to encompass land use elements of residence, business, and industry which, when built, provide opportunities for (a) living and working within the community; (b) a full spectrum of housing types and price ranges; (c) permanent open space in passive and active recreation areas with sufficient land on the periphery to protect the identity; (d) strong esthetic controls.[6]

History   Planning new towns is certainly not a novel activity for Americans. Williamsburg was a new town in 1633, Savannah in 1733, Washington in 1791, and Chicago as late as 1833. The "company town" of the nineteenth century was notorious, such as the town of Pullman near Chicago, built for the workers of the Pullman Car Company. Many large and fine residential communities were developed near large cities in the twentieth century, and independent new towns were promoted to serve major industrial enterprises—Gary, Indiana (1906); Kingsport, Tennessee (1910); Kohler, Wisconsin (1913); Tyrone, New Mexico (1915); and Longview, Washington (1923), among them. Radburn, New Jersey, begun in 1928 as the Town of the Motor Age, will be remembered for the greenbelt circulation through the community. In the thirties, the Resettlement Administration communities of Greenbelt, Maryland; Greendale, Wisconsin; and Greenhills, Ohio, were planned after the Radburn prototype.

An ambitious program for a new "city" of Irvine was incorporated in 1972 on a huge singly owned ranch in southern California. Although elaborately planned for a population of nearly 500,000, the community depends on neighboring cities for most urban facilities and services. With an expanding campus for the University of California, an airport, and a large industrial park, the new city emerges as a series of planned real estate developments in a street system for automobiles. Later developments based on changes in the corporation policies seemed to turn the excellent planning of the early stages into a look-alike scheme of the usual large-scale speculative subdivisions, without the originally provided amenities or the careful preservation of open spaces that gave special character to the community.

Reston, Virginia, and Columbia, Maryland, are both new towns begun in the early sixties. In 1989 Reston, with a population of 44,000, is near Washington, D.C.; Columbia, with a population of 70,900, lies between Baltimore and Washington. Each is a well-planned, privately financed community. Although some industrial-research development is anticipated in both, the principal economic base is the nearby federal government.

In Europe new towns are public ventures of a high order. A city is a political entity of citizens; it is not a private domain, a corporate "company town."

---

5. Florida is "blessed" with such high-class developments, such as North Palm Beach, and California has its share; Rancho San Bernardo and Laguna California in San Diego County, Laguna Niguel in Orange County, Conejo Village in Ventura County, and Valencia and Westlake Village in Los Angeles County are examples.

6. *The Community Builders Handbook,* (Washington, D.C.: Urban Land Institute, 1968).

Lake Anne village center. *Aerial view of Reston's first village center, Lake Anne, designed by the architects Conklin and Rossant, showing the fifteen-story Heron House apartments; the J-shaped Washington Plaza shopping area; the 30-acre Lake Anne, with the townhouse clusters, single-family detached and patio homes, and rental and condominium garden apartments that surround the lake.*

Although the city in the United States is, for many, a "fat calf" to be exploited for private gain, accommodation of the growing population will require aggressive public initiative, implemented by the equivalent of the British development corporation to administer public funds for initial investment in land and public facilities. New York set a precedent with the creation of the State Urban Development Corporation in 1968. With some tax support from the state, the corporation was empowered to issue tax-exempt bonds as its major source of funds. Its function was to initiate needed public facilities with emphasis on housing for low-income families. With the power of eminent domain and to deviate from local codes and zoning ordinances where necessary, the corporation used private capital in its developments. Roosevelt Island was a major project, financed with federal assistance under the Communities Development Act.

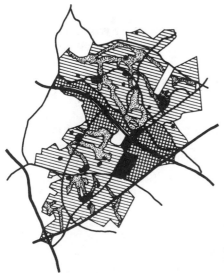

Reston, Virginia: master plan. *Lines indicate residential areas, which include low-, medium-, and high-density mixtures; cross-hatching includes industrial and "advanced educational" uses; solid areas denote commercial centers; round dots are high schools; the dotted areas, internal recreational space, lakes, and ponds. No permanent surrounding open space was planned.*

Alert to the need for new urban communities, competent and experienced developers recognize the necessity for public participation in new town building to achieve the full range of housing and urban facilities. "There is absolutely no means whatsoever by which the home-building industry, as it is now constituted in America, can develop the sensibly organized new communities that America needs to accommodate its future growth," said James Rouse, developer of Columbia. "The country needs to enlarge the application of the process by which Columbia was built. It cannot afford to rely on the capacity or the whim of the private developer alone."[7] Philip Klutznick observed the need for public assistance to meet the need for housing and basic facilities of all income groups, and Emmanuel Cartsonis, director of planning and design of Litchfield Park near Phoenix, Arizona, developed for the Goodyear Tire and Rubber Company, asserted the need for federal assistance in site acquisition and low-interest financing for this well-planned and partially developed new community.[8]

New towns, as depicted in the developments that have taken place since the end of World War II, are different from the clusters that developed previously. These new entities incorporated all of the best features designed by the architects, engineers, scientists, and planners during the later part of the nineteenth century and added to that formula consideration for human safety by the separation of pedestrians from the then-recent invention the automobile. In addition, streets were designed to a width adequate not only to accommodate the moving cars but in some cases to provide space for their parking. These new towns, most important of all, provided ample open space, parks, and schools in locations where they would serve the children safely and conveniently. In most European examples the homes were designed as part of the completely planned multifamily arrangements and of detached single-family units. Near the commercial center, some high-rise apartment structures were planned. All areas were well landscaped to produce an atmosphere of living in a park.

VILLAGES, SATELLITE TOWNS, AND NEW TOWNS

New towns fall into three distinct classifications; the first is the small cluster of residences which form a *village*. Here the facilities are limited and many of the essentials are located in the larger town. The elementary school and convenient shopping facilities are provided; the village depends on the large towns for all other essential goods and services. Employment also is a function of the nearby cities.

The second classification is the major residential complex, which has many of the essential facilities but depends on a nearby city for almost all of its economic support. These are the satellite towns, which, like all current satellites, are separated from the "earth" but tied to it by gravity—the railroad and freeways and other means of communications.

The third type of new town is the complete urban complex. Larger than the other types, it contains many sources of employment, in commerce, in light industry, and in services. It also provides a full range of educational opportunities, many of which are designed to serve the satellites that tend to cluster about

---

7. James Rouse, *Taming Metropolis: How to Manage an Urbanized World* (New York: Doubleday & Company, Inc., Anchor Books, 1967).

8. Shirley Weiss, *New Town Development in the U.S.,* New Towns Research, Center for Urban and Regional Studies (Chapel Hill: University of North Carolina Press, March 1973).

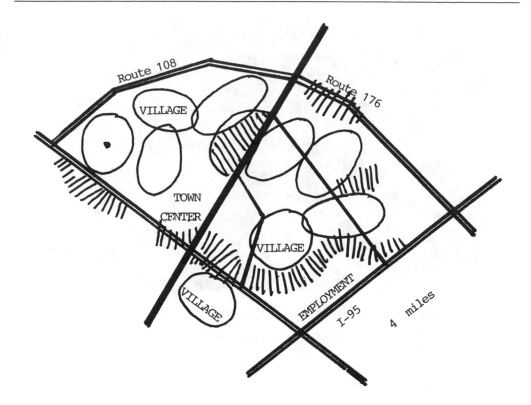

Diagramatic Sketch of Columbia, Maryland, by Robert Tennenbaum, A.P.A. Planning—May, 1990.

its periphery, such as shopping centers, special schools, colleges, and universities. Also, major health facilities are developed here because, like many other services, they cannot be decentralized efficiently. The main feature of all of these new complexes is their separation from the older cities by open space. In many of the nations where they are located, they are in the greenbelts that have been secured by the state or city to provide the setting that is essential to give them identity.

Dr. Harvey S. Perloff, former dean of the School of Architecture and Urban Planning at the University of California at Los Angeles, presented his vision of the New Town Intown in an article published in the *AIP Journal,* May 1966. The following excerpt indicates the premises on which his ideas are based:

NEW TOWNS INTOWN

> The heart of the new town idea is the creation of an urban community conceived as an integrated and harmonious whole. Starting from scratch in an open area, the new town can provide the most modern of facilities, whether schools, shopping or parking. The ability to develop through an overall plan makes possible community amenities and aesthetic qualities normally not realized. Because people today have both rising income and expanding leisure time, recreation receives an important role in the new town plan. (Reston, Virginia, for example, has made a golf course, an artificial lake, riding stables and bridle paths, and other recreational facilities the very backbone of the community.) The more advanced new town makes an effort to provide a balance between workplaces and homes. It has a distinctive center with important functional and visual purposes. High-rise apartments as well as low-lying buildings and individual homes help to provide variety as well as a superior design for living.
>
> With adequate imagination and purpose, the essence of all this can be applied to the older parts of the metropolis. Since replanning is much more difficult than starting from scratch, it will require particularly good planning—aimed at the same goals of harmony and balance. It will normally require some strategic rebuilding as well

New Town Intown, Roosevelt Island, New York City, New York State Urban Development Corporation. *A 150-acre site developed for 25 percent housing, 16 percent commercial/industrial, 44 percent open space and public use, 15 percent circulation. Of 5,000 dwelling units, 30 percent are for low income, 25 percent for moderate income, and 45 percent unsubsidized.*

as rehabilitation for continuous improvement according to a plan. An essential element would be a working partnership in planned urban development between the people of the area, a variety of public agencies, and private enterprise. The aim should not be to create communities that are all alike; each should have its own special character, its own focal points, its own attractions.

The New Town Intown concept can greatly help in transforming the physical environment of the city in keeping with social objectives and human resources needs. It cannot solve the human problems of the city, nor even all the physical problems. It can provide a valuable lever for both. If we hope to achieve the objectives of the antipoverty and other social programs, it will be necessary, among other things, to transform the total environment of poverty—the physical aspects as well as the social, economic, and political. It is important to create an environment in which the community as well as the individual family are important.

The New Town Intown concept involves the large-scale rehabilitation, modernization, and redevelopment of the core of the city. It is proposed that the functions of the area be changed to make for a viable living environment that will be attractive and safe for persons of all ages who like to be in the heart of a city where interesting and exciting activities are available. The concept involves recognition that the central city areas are too important to discard. To reconstitute the central core as a total living environment is a challenging idea. To make it an economically sound as well as socially desirable part of the total city is imperative. The changes called for will take time and monumental efforts on the part of both government and the private sector to complete. The old format for the area must be abandoned. Vehicular traffic must be reduced or confined to special locations, the concentration of pollutants must be eliminated, the streets must be well-lighted and protected against vandalism and crime.

Many buildings have been rehabilitated. These buildings, like the warehouses in the SoHo artist district of New York City, have been converted to special uses both commercial and residential, and bring people with like interests together.

The effect of this rehabilitation is to bring economic stability into areas on the verge of collapse.

As a means of coping with the tremendous urban dilemma, the Urban Growth and Community Development Act of 1970 provided federal financial aid until the early 1980s for the New Towns Intown program. Intended to recover a human scale through comprehensive redevelopment of large cities, it provides more flexibility than was embodied in previous redevelopment "projects." The Housing and Urban Development Agency does not make its usual requirement that a site be a minimum of 100 acres, and wholesale condemnation is not necessary. A full range of urban facilities and social amenities may be incorporated to achieve an effective community. Cedar-Riverside in Minneapolis was the first development to be undertaken; Roosevelt Island in New York was the second.

Plans for sweeping redevelopment should open avenues to the essential restructuring of the urban form, to phase out strip commercial zoning and substitute genuine commercial centers, and to readjust land uses to a system of mass transportation without which large cities will continue to strangle themselves in an endless network of streets, highways, and parking facilities. It will take time, in some cities a desperately long time, to achieve the transformation. But it has taken a long and dreary time for cities to reach the current stalemate, and it should be worth the time to recover. It is the public's responsibility to replan cities for the integration of renewal through redevelopment programs, and a combined public and private responsibility to ensure that each new development will serve that purpose.

BRITISH PLANNING POLICY

Throughout the nineteenth century the British were stirred by the woeful impact of the Industrial Revolution on the living environment. Improvement in housing conditions was the focus of concern and action. In 1909 there began a series of legislative steps up the ladder of urban planning. It was a cogent, complete experience in the search for a physical structure to accommodate the people and the functions of urbanization. The Housing and Town Planning Act of 1909 granted powers to local authorities to prepare plans for their respective jurisdictions. To encourage building after World War I the Housing and Town Planning Acts of 1919 for both England and Scotland introduced the policy of joint planning action among several local authorities, and in 1923 the act empowered the local authorities to plan for built-up as well as undeveloped areas. In 1925 planning functions were separated from the field of housing alone for the first time. The Town and Country Planning Acts of 1932 for England, Wales, and Scotland extended the responsibility of local authorities to urban and rural land and included the preservation of historic buildings and the natural landscape. The powers under these acts were only permissive (i.e., not mandated), and they were conferred on all local authorities. As a consequence, the local authorities were subject to excessive compensation for any claims that might result from the exercise of their powers. These acts, however, with the addition of the Ribbon Development Act of 1935 that regulated the space along the highways, provided the basic framework in Great Britain for the following 15 years.

In 1937 a royal commission was established under the chairmanship of Sir Montague Barlow to inquire into the distribution of industrial population and the social, economic, and strategic disadvantages arising from the concentration of industry and working people in large, built-up communities. The commission report, published in 1940, contained recommendations for redevelopment of congested areas, the dispersal of population from such areas, the creation of balanced industrial employment throughout Great Britain, and the establishment of a national authority to deal with these matters.

In 1941 two new committees were created to study the recommendations of the Barlow report: the Scott Committee on Land Utilization in Rural Areas and the Uthwatt Committee on Compensation and Betterment. From these committees came recommendations for the creation of a central planning authority, measures to ensure state control of development, increased powers of local planning authorities for compulsory purchase (eminent domain), and major revisions in the laws on compensation and betterment.

The Scott and Uthwatt reports led to the adoption of a new series of town planning acts. The first, in 1943, created a new office of minister of town and country planning for England, Wales, and Scotland and strengthened the powers of local authorities to control development. The Town and Country Planning Act of 1944 for England and the 1945 act for Scotland gave local authorities power to enforce comprehensive redevelopment of obsolete and war-damaged areas and implemented the acquisition of land for both open space and a balanced arrangement of land uses. These acts culminated in the Town and Country Planning Act of 1947 for England and Wales and a counterpart for Scotland. The principal features were (a) to establish a framework of land use throughout the country based on development plans by local authorities, approved by the minister of town and country planning (now the minister of housing and local government) or the secretary of state for Scotland; (b) to control all development by making it subject to permission from the local planning authorities; (c) to extend to local authorities all necessary powers to acquire land for planning or development and provide for grants from the central government for these purposes; and (d) to ensure the preservation of buildings of historic interest and the natural character of the landscape. In contrast to prior legislation, this act conferred these powers upon only 188 local authorities in large cities and county boroughs, and rendered their exercise mandatory rather than permissive.[9]

Compensation and Betterment

During the past hundred years the policy of "compensation and betterment" became an accepted procedure in the regulation of land use in Great Britain. The principle that the use of private property is subject to regulation for the community welfare was complemented by a dual provision: just compensation is due to private owners for any restrictions public authorities create that impair the value of land; and, the enhancement of property values that accrue through public planning decisions may be assessed by the local authorities. It was assumed that the public funds expended for compensation to property owners would be balanced by the assessments for the betterments that resulted from land use regulations. The administration of this policy, however, became unduly complicated. Assessments for betterments for improved values were awkward to determine and almost impossible to collect. As a consequence, local authorities had inadequate resources upon which to draw to fulfill their obligations for payment of compensation.

A major task of the Uthwatt Committee was to investigate this entire policy and to make recommendations for improvement. Based on the report of the com-

9. Beverley J. Pooley, *The Evolution of British Planning Legislation* (Ann Arbor, Mich.: University of Michigan Law School, 1960).

mittee, the 1947 act introduced a comprehensive modification in land policy with the provision that the state shall reserve all rights to the *development* of land; the government was empowered to expropriate all development rights. This sweeping revision, while following the principle of compensation and betterment, was intended to remove the involved processes in the collection of betterments and the determination of appropriate compensation. Owners of property approved for development at the time the legislation was enacted were entitled to compensation for the loss of these rights at land values prevailing in 1947. A central land board was appointed to administer these negotiations, and a fund of £300 million was set aside by the national government for this purpose. As permission was subsequently granted by local planning authorities to develop property, the landowners were required to pay a development charge to the government. This charge was in the amount of the difference between the value of the land for the existing use and the value of the new development approved by the planning authority. Since, under the act, owners who had suffered loss through expropriation of development rights were to have been compensated for this loss, all landowners were subsequently liable for the development charge. A permitted use that resulted in a lesser land value entitled the owner to compensation for the difference, whereas one that would support a land value greater than the existing use entitled the government to charge the owner for this difference.

This remarkable and very timely land policy was developed under a coalition government, similar to that under Winston Churchill when he was prime minister. The committee that recommended it included conservative members with a sound knowledge both of British tradition and the problems of land development. The chairman, the Honorable Augustus Uthwatt, was a lord judge of appeal, a high rank in the public affairs of England. But opposition to the entire procedure formed soon after passage of the act and its administration became increasingly cumbersome. In 1951 a Conservative government came into power and, in an act of 1953, abolished this feature. Permission to develop land was still required, but landowners were thereafter free to realize the values on the open market. Sadly, the long tradition embraced in the principle of compensation and betterment as a basic policy for the equitable regulation of land in the implementation of the planning process was ended.

The administration of planning in England has been vested in the public authorities of large localities, the county, and borough councils. Contrary to the practice in the United States, zoning as a means to regulate land use has not prevailed. Local planning authorities are required to prepare a 20-year development plan, approval of which is required by the government. This plan is reviewed every 5 years and has the statutory effect of establishing the land use policy by which the authorities are guided in granting permission for development. The power to grant permission is the vehicle for the control of development within the policy set forth in the plan, and this procedure has been retained for the purpose of maintaining flexibility to meet changing conditions.

Although the enlightened landownership policy embraced in the act of 1947 is absent and the experience in Great Britain demonstrated its difficulties, the tradition of responsibility by public authorities may yet offer the prospect for favorable land development in that country. There are planning authorities who believe these difficulties might have been materially altered if the landowners had shared in the increment of increased property value by a development charge fixed at a lower level, such as 75 percent of the difference in value.

This issue will undoubtedly remain alive. It revolves about the relation between the necessary public control of land use and the element of monopoly that such control vests in land values. Any form of public control over land use, whether it may be permission for development from planning authorities as in England, or by zoning regulations as in the United States, conveys to some owners and withholds from others privileges that accrue because of the relative location of land. The maintenance of a balance between the open channels of competition and the effect of monopoly values that sound planning may confer is an unresolved issue in the United States as in Britain. An equitable distribution of all the benefits of planning was the basic purpose of compensation and betterment; the operation of this principle may yet restore an appropriate measure of equity in the conduct of urban affairs.

London Region

England suffered heavy damage to its cities during World War II. One-third of its 13 million dwellings were damaged, and there was practically no new building. With devastation all about them, the people found it necessary to consider plans for reconstruction. The 1944 Town and Country Planning Act had extended financial aid to local authorities for the purchase of land when rebuilding became possible.

A large proportion of the English live in urban communities, but there are only seven large industrial centers. These are agglomerations of urban areas ranging from two to eight million people, and congestion in these cities is acute. Nonetheless it remains the British ideal to live in "cottages." A density of twelve families per acre was suggested by Ebenezer Howard and became the standard density for the garden cities; Sir Raymond Unwin dwelt upon it at length as a desirable standard. It remains today the standard toward which enlightened planners strive.

The destruction of large urban areas impressed many thoughtful people with the possibility of recapturing some open space within their congested urban centers in the large-scale rebuilding that was necessary. The British realized that they should try to cope with the problem of congestion in their cities. Launching the postwar planning program, they began where they were with what they had and sought the way to a new concept of the urban structure.

The elements of the garden city held strong appeal for the British; the characteristics of the village, in contrast with the metropolis, attracted them. Proximity to the beautiful countryside was a natural desire. They prefer the bicycle to the subway. They probably enjoy walking more than motoring. The two successful garden cities, Letchworth and Welwyn, were before them for comparison with the huge and congested cities. The English people have seen the advantages of the small community as a better way of life. They have been justly proud of their delightful rural country, and preservation of the countryside has occupied the aggressive attention of the most influential peers of England.

To the people of Britain, London is their great and noble city, the capital of the Commonwealth, and as colorful as any city in history. It is also synonymous with overcrowding. The County of London covers an area of 117 square miles.

In 1944 it had a population of over 4 million. At the core of this area is the City of London, one mile square, with 5,000 people. This is the financial and political heart of the British Commonwealth. Fanning out from this center, Greater London in 1990 had a population of over 9 million in an area of 700 square miles.

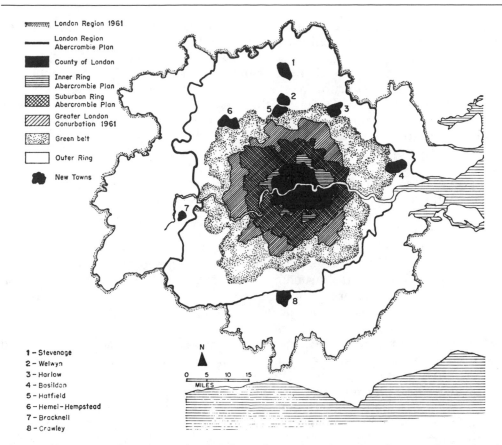

Legend:

- London Region 1961
- London Region Abercrombie Plan
- County of London
- Inner Ring Abercrombie Plan
- Suburban Ring Abercrombie Plan
- Greater London Conurbation 1961
- Green belt
- Outer Ring
- New Towns

1 – Stevenage
2 – Welwyn
3 – Harlow
4 – Basildon
5 – Hatfield
6 – Hemel-Hempstead
7 – Bracknell
8 – Crawley

N

0   5   10   15
MILES

The London region. *The Greater London plan of 1944, by Patrick J. Abercrombie and F. J. Forshaw, embraced a region of 2,600 square miles. A series of four rings surrounded the County of London. The population within the heavily urbanized areas of the county and the inner ring was to be reduced by some 1 million people by dispersal within the suburban and outer rings. The urban conurbation (concentration) of the region has extended the boundaries of the suburban ring beyond the limits of the plan and has forced attention to the preservation and expansion of the greenbelt. The regional sphere is also extended to some 4,600 square miles since the plan was conceived, and the total population has grown from 8 million to 10 million.*
The development of the New Towns may not have resulted in the hoped-for population reduction in the city of London. However, no one can deny that these well-planned communities have provided residents a healthful environment in new facilities.

The planning program of 1944, under the direction of Patrick Abercrombie and F. J. Forshaw, was directed toward a dual objective: rebuilding the wartorn city and relieving the intolerable overcrowding and congestion.

The essential elements of the Abercrombie plan for Greater London were the reduction of the population within the congested center, the creation of a greenbelt to contain Greater London, and the movement of industry to an outer ring. This was consistent with the enlightened planning tradition in England, but it demanded courageous conviction and bold decision. A major issue at the outset was the standard of population density to be sought within the overcrowded center. Although some authorities held to a density of about 70 to 75 persons (20 dwellings) per acre as a desirable maximum, the London planners proposed a density of 100 to 150 persons; the inner districts of the county are being redeveloped in this latter range. The density within the inner ring ranges from 70 to 100 persons per acre, and in the suburban ring it is maintained at about 50 persons. About this complex a broad greenbelt ring ranging from 5 to 15 miles wide has been reserved. Within this greenbelt the existing towns are permitted to increase within the plotted areas of their jurisdictions, but the balance is reserved for recreation. Beyond the greenbelt and within the Greater London region are the outer ring of villages and small towns separated by open countryside.

The plan encompassed a total area of some 2,600 square miles. The population densities involved a reduction of about 40 percent, or more than 6,000, in the county, and more than 400,000 in the inner urban ring. Some increase was proposed for the suburban ring, but the population of Greater London was reduced by a total of over one million people. This program for the decentralization of vast population resulted in the New Towns Act of 1946.

As in the United States, the structure of urban government in Great Britain was designed for an era when the administration was relatively simple. With the growth of the metropolis and its accretions of urban entities, the governmental organization bears no relation to the real character of a metropolitan area. Legislation was implemented to establish a single authority, the Greater London Council, for the 800 square miles and over 9 million people of metropolitan London. Within this council structure there are boroughs, each with a population of about 200,000, that are responsible for all local administration except the functions of metropolitan scope, including planning.

The adoption of the policy that more than a million people had to be removed from the central districts of London was of major consequence. It represented a conviction that the overcrowding within the city must be relieved, that the expansion of the city must be controlled, and that the amenities of urban life could be achieved only by decentralization of employment and residential communities. The New Towns were conceived in the tradition of the garden cities, as self-contained communities with all facilities that make an independent environment. They were not intended to be satellite dormitories connected to the central city. Some were related to the larger orbit of London, however, to make available to the people of the New Towns the special facilities of the central city and, being thus attractively near, to encourage movement from London to release the city for a program of redevelopment.

The New Towns Act provided for the creation of development corporations to plan, build, and manage the New Towns. The corporation obtained 60-year loans from the Ministry of Housing and Local Government (now the Department of the Environment) to finance the acquisition of land, prepare the plans, and improve the land with all utilities and road systems. The corporation could construct buildings to rent to business and industry, or could lease sites for private development. Lease arrangements were generally for a period of 99 years. Housing could also be built by the corporation and, to ensure adequate housing for industry employees, the corporation did build most of it. Increasing participation by private enterprise has been encouraged. The Minister of Housing and Local Government has general jurisdiction over the program and all plans for development are subject to approval by the ministry. The New Towns Act of 1959 determined to dissolve each corporation when the town was completed and transfer management to a commission for New Towns, made up of members appointed by the Minister of Housing and by local government.

The earliest towns, beginning with Stevenage in 1946, were located in the London region. Eight were so designated, including Welwyn, which was begun in 1920 but taken under the jurisdiction of the New Towns Act. These towns, from 18 to 30 miles from London, were intended to accommodate the overspill of people and industry to implement the London Plan.

Town and Country Planning Association

Some of the New Towns in Great Britain and Northern Ireland. *Locations of the first thirty-two New Towns are shown on the map of England, Wales, and Scotland. The towns are experiments in the design of an environment in which the human scale predominates. They are self-contained communities seeking a balance between sources of employment, business enterprise, shopping, education, and recreation for those who live in them. They are, however, significant for another important reason: they are essentially an organic element in a broad program of decentralization of the congested urban centers, the London region having received the principal attention.*

Two of the towns related to the London region are shown in diagrammatic plans. Stevenage, begun in 1949, was the first of these towns. The site comprises 6,100 acres, and the original population of 60,000 for which the town was planned has expanded to 80,000.

Overspill from large cities has not been the principal reason for building more New Towns. The purpose has shifted to economic support and development on a regional scale. As reported by the Town and Country Planning Association: "The regional aim of new towns is both to assist the restructuring and growth of our major urban regions and to bring the advantages of strong growth points to relatively depressed regions." [10]

Thirty-three towns had been authorized by the end of 1973. Of these, in 1982, twenty-eight had been built. Today each of these towns houses between 60,000 and 250,000 persons. Thus about 2 million people reside in these planned communities, in both urban and rural settings. By the end of the century, if the program is continued to the authorized number, it is predicted that the figure will grow to 3.5 million.

> The 32 new towns designed since 1946—21 in England, two in Wales, five in Scotland and four in Northern Ireland—have now largely achieved their aims of dispersal of industry and population from congested cities and the stimulation of regional economies. They have a total population of over 2 million; several have become regional centres for shopping and office accommodation. The new town development corporations' priorities now are to maximise private investment in

---

10. Report by the Association to the House of Commons Sub-Committee of the Expenditure Committee, November 1973.

housing and employment, and to achieve balanced communities able to generate their own growth.

> With the completion of the new towns programme, the development corporations which administered the new towns are being dissolved. The remaining two corporations in England will be wound up in 1992 and dissolution of the five Scottish development corporations will begin in 1991. In Wales responsibility for Newtown rests with the Development Board for Rural Wales, while the corporation responsible for Cwmbran was dissolved in 1988.[11]

This planning at a national level in support of regional development is an important first step toward the regeneration of congested urban centers and the general improvement of the living and working environment, as well as a rational approach to accommodating a growing national population.[12]

Planned as clusters of neighborhoods around a business and civic center, the New Towns are predominantly made up of row cottages, ranging in density from twelve to fifteen per acre. The neighborhoods have populations of 4,000 to 8,000, each with its own schools, recreation facilities, churches, and a small shopping center. There is convenient and efficiently arranged access to industrial areas.

In an effort to overcome the monotony of the standard two-story cottage, some high-rise apartment buildings have been introduced. Commenting on this trend, Dame Evelyn Sharp, permanent secretary of the Ministry of Housing and Local Government, said: "The architect likes the occasional high block; whether the new town tenant really does is one of the great debates."[13] The apartment is considered objectionable for the large numbers of families with children; 5 to 15 percent of the apartment buildings are planned for single people and childless couples.

Industrial enterprise, though initially slow to move to the New Towns, became attracted by the efficient operating conditions, the availability of good sites, and the stable employment conditions. The expanding range of industries settling in the New Towns offers a desirable diversification of employment, although skilled and professional workers predominate.

Retail services are arranged in the conventional manner of shopping centers in the United States, with a variety of facilities arranged around a pedestrian mall or plaza. Automobile ownership increased in the New Towns beyond that anticipated in the early plans, and it has been necessary in some towns to build garages to augment shopping center parking. Ownership in the original eight towns within the London ring ranged between 50 percent and 60 percent and has reached 70 percent in Stevenage, as compared with 42 percent in Greater London and 46 percent in Wales and England.[14]

An experimental "superbus" system in Stevenage doubled bus travel but the New Towns in Great Britain were not planned for internal mass transit. The London-region towns are connected by rail to London. Only in Runcorn is there

11. Planning, Urban Regeneration and Housing in Britain, Foreign and Commonwealth Office, London, England, page 3, August/September, 1990.

12. See Chapter 18 for a discussion of national and state planning in the United States.

13. *Town and Country Planning,* January 1961.

14. Report of the United Nations Seminar, London, June 1973, the Office of International Affairs, U.S. Department of Housing and Urban Development, Washington, D.C.

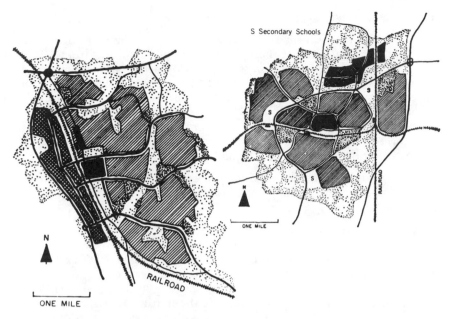

Stevenage (left), designed by Clifford Holliday; Crawley (right), designed by Anthony Minoprio.
The town of Crawley, originally planned for a population of 50,000 on a site of 6,000 acres, will have a population of 70,000. Two existing villages—Three Bridges and Crawley—have been absorbed, and the town center occupies the latter. An industrial area of 264 acres is planned for 8,500 workers. Nine neighborhoods have populations of 4,000 to 7,000, and the density is about twenty-nine persons per acre.
Each neighborhood in the New Towns has a small subcenter for shopping, a primary school, playfields, and social facilities. The secondary schools serve several neighborhoods; in Crawley they are combined in three separate campuses (S).
The residential neighborhoods are indicated by cross-hatched areas, industrial areas by heavy cross-hatching, and the town center by black. Open space and farmland, forming a greenbelt about the towns, are indicated by dotted areas. A desirable attribute of the New Towns is their relatively small size, designed to encourage pedestrian circulation and maintain close proximity to surrounding open space. The plans indicate an abundance of space flowing throughout the community as separations between the neighborhoods. The preservation of natural wooded areas or unusual topographical characteristics within this space is advantageous, but the proportionate quantity of land reserved for permanent open space may be excessive in view of the surrounding greenbelt, low density, and internal recreation fields. This abundant open space may overextend walking distances, exaggerate the separation between neighborhood cells, and thus tend to nullify the advantages of the modest size of the towns.

provision for an exclusive bus lane along the road system, but Cumbernauld New Town, near Glasgow, was designed for complete separation of pedestrians and motor traffic. Cumbernauld is also unusual in the design of its commercial center.

The New Towns, in the words of Dame Evelyn Sharp, "have been a great experiment and are on their way to being a great success. Mistakes have been made and there are many problems still to resolve. But for thousands of families they are providing living conditions among the best in Britain; and for industry they are providing the conditions for efficiency. They will prove a first-class investment, in money as well as health and productivity."[15]

After 31 years of growth and maturity, the New Towns have been highly successful in providing decent housing and a healthful environment for the residents. The number of nations that have adopted the concept provides the best evidence that the New Towns are both self-sustaining and supportive of the regional centers (as a result of effective transportation ties).

15. *Town and Country Planning*, January 1961.

An American assessment stated:

> The crowning achievement of British planning is not the new towns themselves, but rather the protection of the bulk of beautiful landscape around London and other major cities. Along with control of development in new towns and expanded areas designated for growth, all are coordinated with a sensible rapid transit system. The British have found the formula for coordinated regional and national planning and curbing of urban sprawl, which may be ten years away in the United States. There is no *direct* cost for this 610,000-acre greenbelt. It would have been impossible to purchase in full fee at market prices, which is the only permanently successful way to protect the landscape on a significant scale.

> The success with the greenbelt is not immediately transferable to the United States. It is based upon several factors which makes it successful, but which are difficult to transfer.

> A concept of government ownership of the incremental value of property derived from public improvements and zoning, where property owners need not be compensated for permanent freezing of land use in open space of existing uses. This would be impossible under current court rulings under the Fourteenth Amendment in the U.S., where freezing of large areas, not subject to natural hazards, in nondevelopment could be challenged as taking without just compensation.[16]

IMPACT

Since, to some degree, the New Town policies of the British government were intended to reduce the overcrowding of the central cities, especially after the end of World War II, many have wondered about the degree of the success of this program and what its impact might be on the central city and its industrial base. Peter Gripaios responds to this in part in the following excerpts.

Locational Influences

The very concentration of population and economic activity in the London area indicates that at one time it must have been, relatively, a very profitable location. Have there then been changes in this relative profitability such that London firms have been forced to go into liquidation or to move elsewhere? If London can be compared with other cities it does seem likely that this has been the case. There have been net firm losses in many large cities throughout the world and locational factors have been shown to be an important influence. Studies of New York (Hoover and Vernon, 1959; Lichtenberg, 1960; Leone, 1971), Chicago (Moses and Williamson, 1967), Sydney (Logan, 1966), and Glasgow (Firn and Hughes, 1973) indicate that this is particularly true with regard to the decentralization of manufacturing industry.

These studies reveal that firms have been driven out of central areas by lack of room for expansion, difficulties of access, competition from other uses and high factor costs. They have been pulled to peripheral locations as a result of improvements in transportation, technology and communications and by the existence of plentiful supplies of factors of production. Certainly, there can be no doubt that the development of motor transportation has radically altered the pattern of location. Modern road systems and vehicles mean that distance within urban areas is now unimportant and that it does not much matter where factories are located. In addition, the flexibility of road transport has enabled manufacturing firms to capitalize on improvements in production technology. They have been able to utilize space in peripheral locations to build large single-storey plants operating with assembly-line techniques. Finally, improvements in communications have enabled such firms to

---

16. A report by the Office of International Affairs of the Department of Housing and Urban Development on the United Nations Seminar of New Towns in London, June 1973. The report, written by Jack A. Underhill of the Office of New Communities Development, HUD, clearly stipulates that "the material presented does not necessarily represent the views of the Department."

differentiate their production activities from those requiring face-to-face contacts. As a result, production establishments can be moved to low-cost "greenfield" sites and only small head offices maintained in the metropolitan core. Such factors may well have contributed significantly to employment decline in London. Certainly, various questionnaire studies of relocating firms have revealed that shortages of space and skilled labour and access difficulties figure prominently in the relocation decision (Keeble, 1968; South East Joint Planning Team, 1971). Moreover, in the case of London it seems possible that such factors have been reinforced by the spatial policy measures of national and local governments (below) with regard to their effect on the relative profitability of an inner London location.

Does then, the South East London evidence support the contention that the profitability of an inner London location has changed? It is difficult to be certain one way or the other given the simultaneous interaction of various possible influences but it does appear that the evidence is at least consistent with this contention.

(1) One would expect such problems as access difficulties, shortages of space for expansion, high costs and unsuitable buildings to be more serious in the older and more densely populated inner parts of the city. This would in turn suggest that the percentage loss of firms and employment would be higher the more central the location.

(2) Since the studies of other cities have emphasized that the improvements in production, transportation and communications have particularly affected the viability of an inner city location for manufacturing industry, one would expect, ceteris paribus, the loss of jobs and firms to be concentrated in this sector. This was especially true of the loss of jobs in South East London, 90 percent of the jobs lost 1961–71 being in manufacturing industry. The survey of closures indicated that though manufacturing establishments declined more than their service counterparts, service industry nevertheless declined significantly.

(3) Assuming that the cost of land, labour and the cost of obtaining suitable premises in general increases with the centrality of the location, one would expect the direction of firm movements to be outward. It might further be expected that manufacturing firms with (in general) less need to be close to the market and an assumed higher average land/output ratio than service firms would be moving farther afield than the latter. The data on firm movements confirms both expectations. It can be seen that, regarding the total number of firms, most tended to move from South East London to other areas of the capital, outside of the central area, in that such moves accounted for over 40 percent of all moves.

There is no breakdown of movement within Greater London but the fact that there were very few moves (4) to the central area and a large number of moves to beyond the Greater London area indicates, in general, that the movement was certainly outwards. The data, surprisingly, do not show widespread local movement (probably as a result of the bias of the sample between large firms). In general, the movement of internal relocaters was also outwards—the fourteen internal moves consisting of ten outward, one orbital and three inward moves. The destination of moves differed greatly between manufacturing and service firms. Internal relocations were the most significant in the case of service industry whereas, in manufacturing, moves to elsewhere in Greater London and to the area beyond were most significant, accounting for 42 percent and 37 percent of all moves respectively.

Urban and Regional Policy

There have been two aspects of spatial policy which have affected the London labour market. Regional policy has been aimed to induce firms to move from prosperous to depressed areas and urban planning policy has attempted to move population and jobs from congested areas to new towns. Local government redevelopment schemes have been an additional influence. There can be no doubt that both aspects of policy have to some extent been responsible for part of the job loss. Regional policy tried to stop firms growing in London and encouraged them to move to Development Areas.[17]

"NEW TOWNS" OUTSIDE ENGLAND

The British New Towns were an expression of the national disposition in the aftermath of World War II. Whereas most of the people live in the great industrial centers, the English village and the open countryside represent the cherished qualities of an ideal environment. This ideal was given tangible expression by Ebenezer Howard and established as a traditional British objective in the garden city. Urban desires have not followed this firm direction in other places, however. The strong affirmative approach to decentralization represented by the English New Town program has exerted positive influence elsewhere, but the traditional bond with the older cities in most countries is strong. The self-sufficient community as a module for decentralization does not present the same attraction in other countries as it has in Great Britain. As a consequence, the movement of planned decentralization is marked by variations of the British theme.

Gideon Golany, professor of urban and regional planning at Pennsylvania State College, presented an excellent overview of new towns in both Europe and the Orient in *Cities*.[18] His comments deal with conditions and policies in the many nations that have been experimenting with the development of this effort to improve the housing and environmental conditions of their people. The following material includes excerpts from his intensive studies.

Canada

The community of Don Mills was begun in 1953 by the Don Mills Development Corporation, a private land and investment company. Being part of North York, one of the thirteen municipalities in the Toronto metropolitan area, it is not politically independent but represents an approach similar to the New Towns of England. Occupying a site of 2,058 acres, it was planned as a new industrial community for a population of 25,000. However, in 1988 the estimated population in the two wards that are identified as DON MILLS PARKWAY/RAILSIDE ROAD INDUSTRIAL AREA contained 84,351 persons. In 1991 there were 200 business establishments, employing 4,250 workers. The majority of the employment is in manufacturing and warehousing, accounting for 47 percent.[19] Located one-half mile from a limited-access highway and 25 minutes from the Toronto airport, it is served also by two railways that traverse the site. The sponsoring development company has encouraged a wide diversification of industrial enterprise, and the entire town has been developed by private companies. It is distinguished for the high level of architectural quality that prevails.

Perhaps the most significant aspect of this new town is the policy of the development company to seek an economic balance between residential and industrial or commercial development. It is the objective to maintain a ratio of 60 percent in the assessed values of residential development and 40 percent in industrial and commercial development. This policy of a balanced economy in the administration of urban affairs suggests an approach to the regulation of urban growth and development everywhere, not merely in new town developments.

---

17. Peter Gripaios, Division of Economics, Plymouth Polytechnic, Devon, England.

18. Nancy Akre, ed. *Cities* (New York: Cooper Hewitt Museum, 1982).

19. Statistics provided by the Department of Property and Development, City of North York, Janaury 1992, through the good offices of the Ontario Tourist office, Government of Ontario, Ministry of Industry, Trade and Technology, Los Angeles.

Fundamentally, however:

> Canada has also suffered from a fragmented policy towards new-town planning. The Canadians have had a long history of pioneering settlements and exploration of new areas, but it was not until 1973 that a New Communities Act provided capital and planning and management assistance for new towns. The Act also provided 100 million dollars per year until 1978 for land acquisitions. While the Act aims at many of the same things planners implemented elsewhere—stabilization of population movement and stimulation of economic growth—the Canadian policy has suffered from use as a complement to urban growth strategies rather than as a part of a regional, more comprehensive plan.[20]

Around the middle of the twentieth century Copacabana, near Rio de Janeiro, was a seaside paradise. A quarter of a century later, 250,000 people occupy tall buildings in 3 square miles by the sea. A new city is now planned 10 miles away. Barra de Tijuca, occupying 75 square miles of open space and mountains stretching along 14 miles of beach, was planned in 1969 by Lucio Costa, the planner of Brasília. Planned as a series of urban communities of 12,000 separated by greenbelts and two large centers for 80,000 to 100,000 people each, the new city is expected to accommodate a population of 2 million. The population in 1985 was estimated at 1,576,657. Designed with the flair of the architect Oscar Niemeyer, the first center is dominated by seventy thirty-four-story apartment towers, six office buildings, and elaborate associated amenities. The grandiose concept of Barra de Tijuca is in the Latin American tradition of dramatic scale.

Brazil

Aratu was also planned by Lucio Costa. An extension of Salvador in the province of Bahia, it was planned for a population of 1,500,000. Aratu is a neighboring city rather than a satellite community; Salvador itself has a population of less than 1 million. The land for Aratu, the first completely planned industrial city in Brazil, was purchased by the state and sold at low cost to developers of industry and housing. Tax incentives were also granted for development. The National Housing Bank (NHB), founded in 1964, is the primary source of financing for urban development; several thousand low-income dwellings have been built in Aratu with NHB loans.

NHB funds are obtained by a tax on payrolls of all private enterprise in the country. The NHB borrows from this special fund (Fundo de Garantía do Tempo de Servico) to finance its urban housing programs, which are directed primarily to housing for families in the slum areas or *favellas*. These families pay from 1 to 10 percent interest on the loans, according to their income.

The unique program has elicited the interest of other countries, but it is not without problems. New outlying housing communities are far from sources of employment. The degree of authoritarian direction concerning the movement of families from the *favellas* to the new and unfamiliar living conditions, some of which include the proverbial high-rise apartments, has aroused resentment. The bank has also been confronted with the not uncommon predicament of many low-income families unable to meet the continuing financial obligations of home ownership.

The places of greatest historic interest in Paris, most of the important commercial, financial, educational, and political activity, and the entertainment center are

France

20. Nancy Ahre, ed. *Cities* (New York: Cooper Hewitt Museum, 1982).

confined to an area of less than 10 square miles in the heart of the city.[21] The city, however, covers an area of 40 square miles with a population of 8,709,000 in 1990. The density was 29,213 persons per square mile. The projected population for 2,000 is over 14 million. More than 4 million people have settled in surrounding districts. This region of between 7 million and 8 million people occupies 300 square miles. Since an urban population increase of 20 million is anticipated by the turn of the century, a multiplication of housing "colonies" is inadequate. Implementation of an urban policy of planned decentralization in the country has been slow. But the pressure of population and industrial growth has required positive action, and with the passage of the Boscher law in 1970 financial assistance for new towns became available. Five new towns with populations between 330,000 and 500,000 were built within a 10- to 12-mile radius of Paris. Existing villages have been integrated within new town developments here and elsewhere.

> A group of four new towns have been planned about the periphery of Paris . . . some thirty-five or more miles away from the center of the city. These towns are either tied into the central city or are to be by mass transit facilities to make possible a wide range of choice to the residents for places of employment.

> Many have thought that these new towns would become the locale for the poor of Paris as the central portion of that city was taken over by the wealthy. In the planning, however, it was the policy of the local and state planning groups, that government-assisted housing and the affluent would find facilities to meet their needs . . . sometimes just across the street from each other.

> One of the new towns is Evry. It has a centrum called, in the reflection of the Greek civilization, the Agora. In and about this commercial center are found all of the amenities that are desirable to meet the need of the local residents. Beautifully planned and developed, the Agora not only serves but it enriches the residents with cultural facilities. The Agora is an air-conditioned mall arranged for pedestrians.

> The residential sections are in the form of microneighborhoods containing clusters of approximately 100 dwellings. In the course of the development, the technicians worked closely with the existing and potential residents, especially in the middle class areas of Paris. These new towns are formed by a mix of existing residential communities with new, sometimes high-rise, structures. The French program is state-planned; private enterprise was enlisted in development. Other satellites are also under construction around Lille [for 150,000], Lyons [for 300,000], Marseilles [for 750,000], and Rouen [for 140,000]. The French new-town satellites are coming into their own as economic entities, and their population will exceed 100,000.[22]

Spain   In Spain, where the same concentration of population in large urban centers exists, a 1970 legislative decree created Urban Urgent Action (ACTUR), a plan for eight new satellite towns ranging in population from 60,000 to 120,000. Three of these are near Barcelona, the principal city of Spain, and the others serve Madrid, Seville, Valencia, and Cádiz.[23]

Sweden   Sweden was the first country in Europe to enact legislation for planning, with the Urban Building Act of 1874. However, the social and economic circumstances there have not compelled attention to planning on a regional scale. The first Town Planning Act of 1907 and the 1931 act were similar to the 1909 and 1932 planning acts in England, but emphasis was placed on site planning and street and building arrangements rather than on regional relationships.

---

21. The following data are from *New Communities in Selected European Countries*, U.S. Department of Housing and Urban Development (Washington, D.C.: U.S. Government Printing Office, April 1974).

22. Golany, *Cities*.

23. *New Communities*.

Courtesy Hugo Priivits

FARSTA—Town center

Courtesy Hugo Priivits

Courtesy Hugo Priivits

VALLINGBY—Town center

Courtesy Hugo Priivits

VALLINGBY—Town center
and apartments

Vallingby and Farsta. *Neither Vallingby nor Farsta are, nor were they intended to be, self-contained "new towns."
They are integral developments of the general plan for the decentralization of the city of Stockholm. They were planned,
however, to support a complete marketplace and business center, to provide industrial employment to complement the
employment opportunities in the central city, and to accommodate a diversification of dwelling types to meet the wide range
in family composition in a balanced community. When completed, Vallingby will have nearly 500,000 square feet of shops
and more than 1 million square feet in office space, social and welfare facilities, and entertainment. Some 40 percent of the
employment has been within the nearby new industrial district.*
*Visitors to the new towns in recent years have marveled at the way in which the homes, grounds, and overall living
environment have been maintained. Employment opportunities have increased as new firms are lured away from the more
intensively developed, older cities. The plight of London is an indication of the decentralization of industry to the open sites
in the new towns.*

The consumer cooperative movement reflected the direct and pragmatic approach to the solution of economic and social conditions for which the Swedish
people have demonstrated capability. The self-help small cottage or Magic-
House program initiated in 1927 is another example. One-tenth-acre plots on
city-owned land were made available for 60-year lease and a ground rent of 5
percent of the land value. Prefabricated houses were also made available for
erection by the owner, his or her labor amounting to 10 percent of the cost. The
balance of 90 percent was to be repaid to the city in thirty annual installments.
This program presented a practical means for families of low income to acquire
decent homes as a substitute for substandard tenements in the congested city.

The plan for the decentralization of Stockholm has resulted in two noteworthy
developments in urban planning, Vallingby and Farsta. Some 50,000 people with
sources of employment in the central city have had to seek dwellings within the
suburban districts. This is equivalent to about one-third of the housing in the
new suburban developments. These two new communities are therefore related
to the general plan of the city. They are served by a subway to the center. It was
intended that the usual development of small suburban increments, proved unable to support an adequate community center, be avoided. The Vallingby group
was therefore planned for a population of 60,000 that, including the immediate
existing suburbs about it, could support a complete shopping and commercial

center. The Farsta district, with a surrounding population of 35,000, was planned for the existing number. Industrial sites were reserved within the vicinity of both communities as part of the decentralization program.

These towns are built on publicly owned land. They attest to the wisdom of the policy adopted by the city many years ago to acquire large tracts of land about the periphery of the city. Planning for the greater city of Stockholm was thus implemented and the complete development of these new communities was made possible. The city built some of the housing, and land was leased to cooperatives and other private organizations for additional housing and commercial and industrial development. Open space for recreation was reserved between the towns and Stockholm, but the relatively convenient proximity (Vallingby 7 miles and Farsta 6 miles) to the central city offers a diversification of employment and the advantages of cultural facilities in the city.

Since these successful towns were founded, Skarholmen-Varherg and Soderby-Salen have also been built around Stockholm, and a dozen relatively small communities are distributed through the southern part of the country.

Denmark A series of urban concentrations in a linear alignment, known as the Finger Plan, was adopted in 1949, part of the plan for the development of an integrated decentralization of the entire metropolitan region of Copenhagen. It was estimated that the urban population of this region would increase 70 percent, about 1 million people, by 1980. The Finger Plan was expanded in 1958 with the recommendation for two large urban centers southwest of Copenhagen. Each of these new centers would accommodate 250,000 people, a population considered by the planners to be an optimal size to support all necessary major urban services, provide a desirable diversification of industrial employment, and yet facilitate the convenient circulation of motor vehicles without the congestion that afflicts the larger cities. Although the new communities were intended to have self-sufficient economic bases and their size and facilities would exclude them from the category of satellite towns, a key purpose of the Finger Plan is convenience of communication between the new centers as well as to the central city of Copenhagen. The aim is integration with, rather than isolation from, the metropolitan complex, and this linear structure is therefore dependent upon a rapid and efficient system of rail transportation.[24]

Finland The policy of planned decentralization is also illustrated in the new town of Tapiola in Finland. Situated on a superb wooded site 6 miles from Helsinki, the new satellite town is exemplary. Although it is relatively modest in size—a population of 17,000 on 670 acres—Arne Ervi's town plan, chosen by a competition in 1952, reflects the sensitivity and skill of the several architects who participated in its destiny, among them Jorma Jarvi, Keija and Heiki Siren, Viljo Rewell, and Aluis Blomstedt. Residential groups are situated among the forest areas in three neighborhoods of about 6,000 people. Each is provided with convenient shopping centers with indoor and outdoor recreational facilities. Bicycle and pedestrian ways are carefully separated from motor roads. Housing ranges from one- and two-story dwellings and three- and four-story walk-up apartments to eleven-story apartment towers. Dwellings are purchased with the aid of loans at low interest from the State Housing Board.

24. Eric Reade, *Journal of the Land Planning Institute,* London, December 1961–January 1962.

An area of light industry provides employment for about half the residents, and a short bus trip to Helsinki extends employment and cultural opportunities. Completed in 1965, Tapiola was administered by the Housing Foundation, an association of consumer, civil servant, and trade union organizations created in 1951. The town site was purchased by the Family Welfare League before the establishment of the Housing Foundation. With aggressive private initiative, this new town achieved an environment of unique distinction under the direction of Heiki von Hertze, chief of the Planning Department for the Foundation.

Poland

The changes that have taken place during the early part of the 1990s in Eastern Europe, with the defection of Poland from the Soviet camp, and the complete disintegration of the Soviet Union itself into a fragmented, balkanized federation of independent states is difficult to comprehend or evaluate.

Planning that was centrally performed while the nation was a whole has now shifted and is in the hands of persons with different skills, philosophies, and the usual lack of financial support.

The following material is helpful for an understanding of what existed and what were some of the ideas behind the programs.

> In Poland, the creation of new towns became an emergency issue after the destruction of Warsaw and other cities during World War II. After 1950, the Polish government built three free-standing new towns, six satellite towns, and forty-four new towns within Warsaw limits. Except for the satellites, the new towns were usually expansions of existing small towns. In their early stages, the new towns were characterized by geometric uniformity and "monumentalization," but the government later shaped new towns as entities of their own and developed the neighborhood as the unit of social focus. Some new towns lacked adequate old centers (such as Tychy) or convenient access (such as Konin), creating difficulties for planners. The government is responsible for assemblage, planning implementation, and operation of the new towns.

> In 1972, there were half a million people in the Polish new towns, but population will eventually reach 800,000. A large portion of the Polish new-town population is young married couples with small children who have come from all over the country. In the years just after the war, shortages in urban labor brought many workers from small towns who regarded the new towns as an improvement, although the standard of living was not and is not high.[25]

Soviet Union (Now the Commonwealth of Independent States) (C.I.S.)

The theory of the new towns was adopted by the Soviet Union. Industries were discouraged from settling in cities that have reached a population of 500,000 or more, but new communities were to become satellites of large cities, to assure proximity to cultural activities. Three population sizes are favored for new towns: 30,000–50,000; 80,000–100,000; and 100,000–300,000. In 1974 plans were made for five new towns of 100,000 for the region around Odessa. Eighteen such towns have been proposed for the region around Moscow, the first of which is Kryukov. The future size of this great urban complex will be limited to 5 million people.

> The Russians have employed a number of new-town designs. Some are dormitory towns for commuters, some are self-sustaining with local employment, some are built to sustain rural industry, and some are built to disperse the population for strategic military purposes.

---

25. Golany, *Cities.*

According to Russian sources more than 1,200 new towns have been built in Russia since 1926, housing more than 40 million people, or a quarter of the national population. Between 200 and 250 more new towns are to be built by 1985. A longer-range plan targets twenty-five cities and regional centers for intensive construction of small and medium cities by 1991, each with a population of up to 100,000.

Russian new towns have brought progress and technology to backward regions, have increased industrial production, have succeeded to some extent in population distribution, have supported natural resources exploitation, and have distributed industry.

But because of the immense cost of building new towns, coupled with harsh climatic conditions and the remoteness of many regions, the Soviet approach has had only limited success. Bringing population to the east and especially to Siberia has been a major problem, as has the complaint that many of the new towns are created and managed in "company-town" style, the result of planning a new town to serve a single industry.[26]

Israel   Israel faced several unique problems in planning new towns. First, the nation started entirely from scratch, in order to create a homeland for widely dispersed Jewish populations. Second, the geographical area involved is quite small and population must be spread away from the cities to avoid overconcentration on the Sharon (Mediterranean) coast. And third, the nation feels acute defense and geo-political needs, and towns are placed accordingly.

Most of the Israeli development towns are self-supporting communities built from the ground up. All of them were built through government support and planning, and all are considered in the public domain. More than 20 percent of the total population now resides and works within the twenty-eight development towns. There are no specific towns for specific jobs—all are planned for mixed land use and all provide basic social and daily services. Because many current residents came to Israel without any wealth, housing for the development towns is publicly subsidized.[27]

Israel has built many new towns in addition to the reconstruction and expansion of Jerusalem, Haifa, and Tel Aviv. New communities were developed, some as defense outposts, others as permanent homesites, for immigrants arriving from many parts of the world. Along the coast of the Mediterranean two important centers were constructed in the late 1960s and early 1970s, Ashdot and Askelon. The new town of Eilath was constructed at the northern end of the Gulf of Aqaba.

The government used British town planning standards and techniques. Most structures are two or three stories in height and built of masonry materials. The site planning is, for the most part, very good, with adequate open spaces for recreation and outdoor living in the temperate climate.

The decision to establish the new town of Arad was taken by the Israeli government in 1960. During the course of the following 2 years a team of planners was engaged in developing the physical, demographic, and economic basis of the town; and by the end of 1962 the first settlers arrived.

Arad is situated in the northern Negev east of Beersheba and borders the Judean Desert. It is located on a plateau 1,968 feet above the Mediterranean and 3,280

26. Ibid.

27. Ibid.

feet above the Dead Sea, overlooking them from the west. It is located 45 kilometers (27.9 miles) from Beersheba and 100 kilometers (62 miles) from Jerusalem. To the Dead Sea and its curative springs one has only to travel 25 kilometers (15.5 miles—a half hour). There are two highways leading to Massada—one by way of Sodom, the other, originating from within Arad itself, leading to the ancient Roman ramparts only 45 kilometers (27.9 miles) to the west.

Ancient Arad, as it is called in the Bible, is located 10 kilometers west of the new town. Archaeological excavations exposed an Israelite fortress dating back to the period of the kings of Judaea (seventh century B.C.) and an ancient Canaanite city no less than 5,000 years old.

The 1990 population of Arad was 15,400. Arad was planned during the sixties without the population pressures caused by the fifties' waves of mass immigration. Thus the types of planning errors that characterized and plagued development towns preceding Arad were prevented. The streets are wide, the apartments spacious, and the town itself is planned for a projected population of 70,000 inhabitants. Clearly established development priorities favor industrial expansion, high- and low-density housing, commercial growth, and the tourist hotel industry.

The local climate is uniquely suitable for sufferers from asthma and various allergies. From its inception, the town has actively prevented air pollution; the municipality of Arad directs special attention to the preservation of clean, dry, and refreshing air. Even the flora is controlled in order to preserve the air's unique properties.

Egypt

The late president of Egypt Anwar el-Sadat stated that until his administration, "not a single new city has been erected in Egypt since the opening of the Suez Canal." In the short course of his presidency a cluster of new towns was designed and construction started. Most of the efforts were directed to the developments in the delta land of the Nile adjacent to Cairo. Tenth of Ramadan new town lies 50 kilometers (31 miles) from the center of Cairo on the Cairo-Ismailia highway. It has a target population of 500,000, which may be reached before the year 2000. Tenth of Ramadan is to be an industrial city with medium industries. Some major facilities were already constructed and the school, shopping, and cultural facilities for the first unit were completed in 1980. Other communities include Sadat Industrial New Town is located about 104 miles from Cairo adjacent to the Cairo-Alexandria Desert Road. It, like Tenth of Ramadan, is planned for a population of approximately 500,000 by the year 2000 and an ultimate population of 1 million. El Obour is being planned for a population of over half a million, El Amria for approximately 1 million. Other new towns are in the planning stages.

The location of the new towns—between Cairo, Alexandria, and the Suez Canal—is intended to relieve the tremendous population concentration in Cairo, Alexandria, and Ismailia.

The housing types, as for example in Tenth of Ramadan, vary from one-story modest accommodations to two-story buildings of a rather handsome character. All are constructed of masonry.

People's Republic of China

While rapid changes have taken place in the other communist countries, the system appears to be holding in China. Cries for democracy that resulted in the massacre of students in Tien An Men Square as well as the terrific earthquake

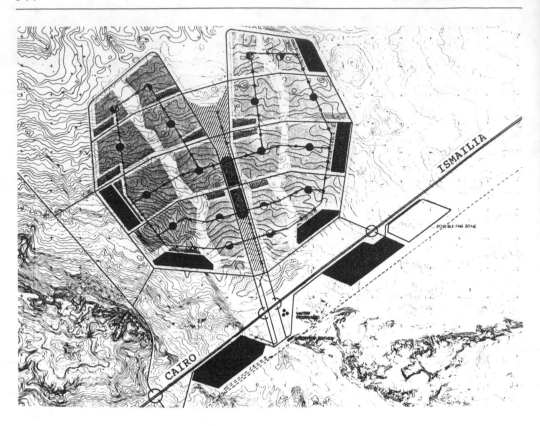

New town near Cairo, Egypt.
Plans for this new town are well on their way to completion. In 1980, having built an industrial plant and educational, religious, and cultural facilities, the town has also provided multiple family housing for its present and future residents.

that devastated Tangshan in July 1976 have not altered the current government's ways of planning. The following is a reflection of past progress.

Since 1949 more than ten industrial towns have been created in the suburbs around Shanghai. These towns are 18 to 42 miles away from the central city. They have been developed in conformity with sound city planning principles and provide for industrial, residential, and commercial areas as well as for greenbelts, railway stations, schools, parks, medical facilities, and other amenities. Some of these communities were built as an extension of existing small enclaves, where the population ranged from 3,000 to 5,000 persons. They have now grown into small industrial complexes with more than 70,000 residents. Ties with the existing central city have been constructed to ensure regional services such as energy and transportation. The open space between the old cities and the new towns is being utilized for intensive agriculture to provide food for the residents, thus narrowing the difference in attitude between city and country residents and workers.

One of the most exciting of the new town policies can be seen in action along the Chinese coastline. Four cities there have been developing new towns in what are called Special Economic Zones: Zuhai, near Portuguese Macau; Shenshen, near British Hong Kong; Shantou (Swatow), and Xiamen (Amoy). These will be an industrial base centered in manufacturing and export centers to attract foreign trade. It is the hope of the Chinese that these centers, while exporting goods, will become the educational institutions for teaching the Chinese people the ways of the Western world. They are or will soon be the leaders in the developing open door policy toward economic dealings with the other nations of the world.

To encourage foreign investments the Chinese government makes the land available free of cost for residential and commercial developments. Much of the capital being invested in the new areas comes from Hong Kong, as many of the people of that community seek better living and working accommodations than those available in that overcrowded Crown Colony.

Hong Kong

With virtually all of the urban land in Hong Kong and Kowloon in use, most new construction must be in the New Territories that border the People's Republic of China. Six new towns have been built in this area and a seventh is planned. The biggest is Tsuen Wan, which is well on its way to full occupancy, with a population of about 1 million people. Next biggest will be Sha Tin and Tuen Mun, each planned to have a population of about 500,000. The other new towns at Tai Po, Yuen Long, Fanling, Sheung Shui, and Sai Kung (under planning in 1985), will not be as large, but each will become the commercial and administrative hub of its district.

Japan

Japan's major cities are phenomena of congestion.

> In an attempt to deal with what is perhaps the world's most pronounced example of urban congestion, Japan's new-town program calls for satellite towns beyond the greenbelt surrounding large cities. Tsukuba, an academic new town under construction northeast of Tokyo in 1980, plans to accommodate forty-three educational institutions between 100 and 200 thousand people. More than half of the population is slated to live in high-rise buildings at the town's center. Senri, which was constructed to draw off Osaka's swelling population, now has a population of 150,000. In all, there are twenty-seven new towns in Japan, most of them started after 1960. The biggest problem now facing Japanese planners is locating the new towns so that not too much of the sorely needed agricultural land is displaced.[28]

Tama New Town, constructed just outside of Tokyo, is another excellent example of recent development in Japan. This site contains more than 7,500 acres of land on a hilly site. Housing is all in high-rise buildings. Access to central Tokyo is provided by two electric railway lines, both privately operated. Over 14,700 dwelling units were completed by January 1981. The town will ultimately provide housing for 370,000 people at a gross density of approximately fifty persons per acre. This density, when compared with the crowded conditions in the Tokyo metropolitan area, is very low.

Suma New Town, just outside the city of Kobe, was completed and occupied in 1985. This new town contains 31,420 dwelling units located on 2,237 acres of land and houses a population of 115,000 people. The goal of this town was to provide good-quality living conditions at a reasonable cost. In addition the planners aimed to provide for a "human-oriented" environment, safe and comfortable to live in. The town provides medical and cultural facilities as well as sports centers and other recreational facilities. The town comprises six housing complexes, formed as distinct but integrated neighborhoods. Municipal express trains link the central area and the industrial districts of Kobe.

A plan for the new town of Suzuran-Ko was prepared at the request of the Japanese Ministry of Transport. The proposed site was an area of approximately 2,918 acres located about nine kilometers northwest of downtown Kobe. The site analysis was conducted by means of a computerized system that offered appropriate synthesis for development areas compatible with environmental

28. Ibid.

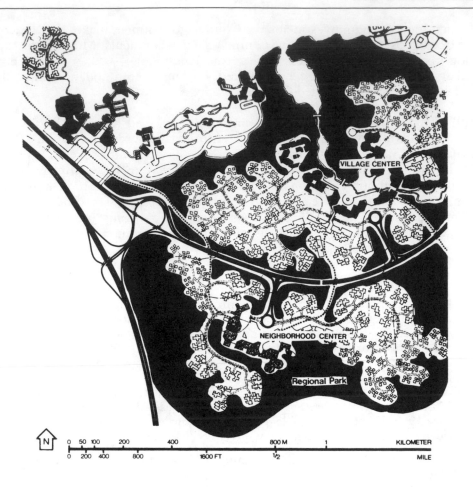

Suzuran-Ko New Town. *The creation of this town involved the movement of 350,000,000 cubic meters of earth to Kobe Bay to achieve the landfill for the creation of the new International Airport, together with the development of the site for Suzuran New Town. The new town will accommodate almost 26,000 dwelling units and all essential services.*

facts, thus reducing the overall impact of urban structures on the natural environment.

Suzuran-Ko (which means "Lily of the Valley") was intended to provide a variety of residential types totaling 25,945 dwelling units, together with 4,000 dwelling units for a special environmentally and urban-oriented university. The expected total population after 10 years of development was to be approximately 100,000 persons, with residential densities ranging from thirty-five families per gross acre (which includes streets) to forty-four families per net acre (which is the land that can be used for business and facilities).

Aside from featuring a cluster of nine villages gathered around a 325-acre lake formed by earth removal, Suzuran-Ko was to incorporate a special intercommunity transit system that would support town community centers, a regional park, and marina facilities. This transit system was designed to enable residents to be within 5 minutes' walking time to all sections of the town. Open space was to represent almost half of the total site area; much of it was to be developed for regional recreational use. The estimated cost for Suzuran-Ko was to be about 570 million yen.

Although this hypothetical new town was not built, Suma New Town may well have become a reality as a result of the intensive study devoted to Suzuran-Ko.

New town planning in Japan.
Courtesy Embassy of Japan Information Section, and Cooper Hewitt Museum, Cities, 1982.

Developing Countries

Developing countries face larger, more comprehensive problems in new-town planning, so perhaps intelligent planning now will yield more effective cities than those of the developed world. Venezuela, for example, has pooled large resources to build new towns, including Ciudad Guyana, a new center for 300,000 near the center of oil and iron production; Alta Gracía, built around the petrochemical industry and planning a population of 330,000; and Ciudad Losada, a satellite of Caracas. Mexico, which is looked to with increasing frequency as a proving ground for city planning, showed foresight when in 1959 planners named a Mexico City suburb Satellite City. Critics who chided planners for placing a satellite so far from the city were silenced, however, when the burgeoning city expanded past its own satellite a few years ago.[29]

NEW NATIONAL CAPITALS

The occasion to undertake the building of new cities to serve as government capitals is rare, and those in progress in Brazil and India are unusual both in this respect and in the boldness of their expression of urban form. Such planning is outside the context of towns as they relate to the mammoth problems of metropolitan urban expansion, but these two recent examples warrant attention: Chandigarh in India and Brasília in Brazil.

29. Ibid.

Brasília   The constitution of the Republic of Brazil in 1889 included a provision for a new capital for that country. The location was not determined until 1955, when a site at the confluence of two rivers some 600 miles from Rio de Janeiro was selected. A development corporation, appointed by the president, assumed charge of the building of the new city, and a competition for the plan was held in 1957. It was won by the Brazilian architect Lucio Costa. The creative talents of Oscar Niemeyer are among those employed for the dramatic architectural forms throughout the city.

The concept is bold: two huge axes in the sign of the cross. The principal multi-level traffic arteries traverse these axes. Separate centers for government, commerce, and entertainment are located along one axis, and the residential districts are distributed about the other. Building of the city has progressed as rapidly as funds are available. Great blocks of tall apartment buildings dominate the residential sections, and the entire theme of the city is a monumental expression of concrete and glass.

The positive conviction, uncompromising courage, and daring forms represented in the new city are inspiring. Perhaps a faint question can be heard through the powerful thrusts of this dynamic place: It is really for people? In 1978 the city seemed out of touch with its surrounding open space—somewhat sterile and with a building scale that made it difficult to comprehend it as a "city." Later, when visitors came to Brasília in the 1980s they commented on the condition of the buildings, noting that many were in disrepair. The bright, attractive new city

Brasília: general plan.

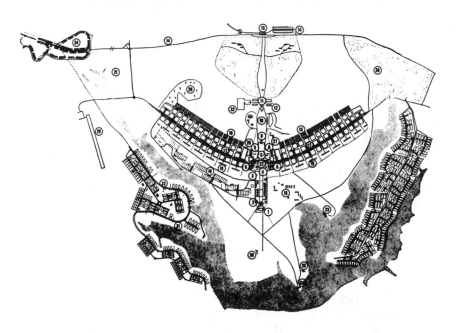

1. Plaza of the Three Powers
2. Esplanade of the Ministries
3. Cathedral
4. Cultural Area
5. Amusement Section
6. Books and Offices
7. Commercial Area   8. Hotels
9. Radio and Television Towers
10. Sports Area
11. Municipal Plaza
12. Sentry Outpost
13. Railroad Station
14. Warehouses, Small Industries
15. The University
16. Embassies and Legations
17. Residential Zone
18. Twin Houses
19. Twin Super-Blocks
20. Botanical Gardens
21. The Zoo
22. Highway Terminal
23. Yacht Club
24. Residential Palace
25. Tourists' Hotel
26. Exhibition Grounds
27. Horse Club
28. The Cemetery
29. Airport
30. Golf Club
31. Individual Residences (So.)
32. Printing Facilities
33. Individual Residences (No.)
34. Suburban Residences (Pky.)

had lost much of its glamor. The hopes that *favellas* would not develop on the outskirts are long gone. Workers and the poor flocked to the new city when it was under construction and have remained as evidence of the sad economic plight of many of the people of that lovely country.

The ancient capital city of the state of Punjab in India was Lahore. When India and Pakistan were partitioned, Lahore was contained within Pakistan. The site of Chandigarh, on the rolling plains near the foothills of the Himalayas, was selected for the new capital of the Punjab. Prime Minister Nehru appointed Le Corbusier to serve as adviser to the government for the plan of the new city. In collaboration with Maxwell Fry and Jane Drew of England and P. L. Varma, chief engineer for the state, a master plan was developed in 1951.

Chandigarh

A future population of 500,000 was anticipated, but the initial stage of the plan provided for a population of 150,000 on a 9,000-acre site. In 1989 the population grew to 218,743. The plan is a huge gridiron of major roads intersecting at distances of one-half mile in one direction and three-quarters of a mile in the other. These roads define neighborhood sectors, each 240 acres in size and housing about 15,000 people. The commercial and civic center occupies the heart of this great square.

The capital complex is set apart along one boundary of the city on a site of 220 acres. Comprising the palace of ministers or secretariat, the palace of the assembly, the palace of the high court, and the palace of the governor, this complex and the buildings within it were designed by Le Corbusier, who added a symbolic sculptural feature to the group—the Open Hand (representing Buddha's upraised palm).

The plan is no more bold than might be expected from the creative mind of Le Corbusier. Situated on a vast plain in a hot and arid region, it nevertheless evokes positive response from those who view it. The highly disciplined order and the sweeping scale of the entire concept are at once impressive. In this respect it shares an affinity with the tradition of the Mogul Empire which, during the period of Islamic domination in India, executed unsurpassed strokes of bold planning and city building. Yet there is a basic difference between the monumental group of this new capital and the earlier Mogul tradition. Even in a dead Mogul city like Fatepur-sikri, a human scale seems to pervade the paved courts and the varied structures within and about them. This city lived for only fifty years but, stark and empty though it now is, the relation between buildings and space, the light and shade of arcades and sheltered areas, convey a vivid impression that the place was meant for people. Somehow this quality is not present at Chandigarh.

At Chandigarh, the palace of ministers, a tremendous concrete structure 800 feet long and nine stories high, is one-quarter of a mile distant from the high court palace. Perhaps trees may one day provide a welcome canopy of shade within this vast space, but a rich landscape to cover the dimensions of the open space in this complex is hardly indigenous to the region nor reminiscent of the delightful gardens that once graced this country. The great structures are powerful expressions of abstract form and pattern, and the space between them is of mighty proportions. Yet they seem to withhold an invitation for people to share in the experience, and tender no protection from the burning sun. Thus one may ponder the art of planning and await the emergence of Chandigarh as a complete reality to evaluate the grand concept it represents.

Brasília central core, view toward administrative center.

Islamabad

When the new nation of Pakistan was formed, changing the status of the former Indian province to a separate state, it became necessary to select a capital. The provincial capital in the ancient city of Lahore was moved to Rawalpindi, located along the foothills of the Himalayas in West Pakistan. The facilities in Rawalpindi proved unsatisfactory to meet the needs of the new nation, and in 1959 a capital development authority was appointed to develop a new capital, Islamabad, nearby. The rigid geometrical plan, by the Greek architectural firm of Doxiadis Associates, is divided into residential sectors or neighborhood units of some 800 acres. Each sector is served by civic facilities, schools, health services, recreation facilities, and mosques. The administration center at the crossing of two main avenues contains the president's house, the secretariat, the assembly, the supreme court, and cultural buildings, with a large enclave for foreign missions. With a great national park and extravagantly monumental public buildings in Muslim tradition, the city of Islamabad should reflect the ambitions of the new nation.

OBSER-VATIONS

New towns the world over vary greatly. At Farsta in Sweden, built upon hilly terrain, the buildings rise excitingly from natural rock formations, providing for a happy marriage with the site upon which they have been built. British New Towns have, for the most part, been constructed on relatively flat or rolling land, where the topography does not add interesting variations. Tapiola in Finland contains a wide variety of building types, including both high- and low-rise structures, all within heavily forested land and with water as another sort of architectural relief.

As one meditates upon the qualities that charge a city with the human spirit, the images of many places loom in contrast to the remarkable new towns in Brazil and India. Probably none is more heartwarming than that of Paris. The charm of

Brazil legislative and administrative center, view of the Houses of Congress.

its monumental spaces, the saucy animation of its avenues, the delight in its varied perspectives, seem less to have been planned than to have blossomed.

Perhaps, more than an efficient arrangement of its streets or the abstract shape of its buildings, it takes "the music of men's lives" to give a city character.

Gideon Golany, who said it so well, observes:

> The experience of careful planning and allocation of resources has shown that new towns can be a successful alternative to increasingly cramped cities. In places where nations have been willing to adopt the recommendations of planners and create new towns, such as Great Britain and France, the towns that resulted were not only pleasant places in which to live, but also economic pluses for the area. As world and especially city population expands, the new-town concept will continue to be a sound and feasible option.[30]

There are geographic entities that have been incorporated as towns and have individual names but no reason for existence as separate political entities other than frustration or hatred for the treatment that their residents received from their former governing body. These areas, in many cases, are the sprawling suburbs that have grown about the periphery of all large cities that border on open or agricultural land.

Known by several names, including "bedroom communities," "escape estates," or just "the 'burbs" (suburbs), these "no-town towns" have no economic base,

NO-TOWN TOWNS

---

30. Ibid.

The new national capital: Islamabad.
(Courtesy of the Pakistan Embassy.)

offer no employment, and provide no strong social or cultural context. In many cases, incorporation as towns or small cities has followed fear of impact by county decision makers. These fears, usually associated with zoning practices, have led to the creation of jurisdictions with no tax base; no ability to provide services other than at minimum levels through contract with the county, special districts, and consultants; no sense of goal or policy direction. These are the towns with no reason to exist.

But exist they do. The urban history of Southern California is full of examples of cities that came into existence to escape from something—real or imagined. Actual bankruptcy or disincorporation has not yet happened. Eventually, rapid growth of major cities washed over these no-town towns and brought with it the minimalls, fast food outlets, and video rental stores that supplied enough tax base to allow local government to hang on. The result, however, is not a triumph of the virtues of local government. Rather it is a proliferation of poorly run, poorly financed, poorly organized governmental entities, each protecting its turf and avoiding dealing with other entities and regional problems.

CHAPTER 42

PLANNING WITH MINORITIES

The subject of the participation of members of minority groups in urban planning can and should become the basis for in-depth research and proposals since the problems are many, varied, and difficult to describe. In the case studies presented here only isolated efforts and conditions are presented to illustrate the complexity of the issues facing cooperative planning projects that involve people of different origins, cultures, needs, and desires.

The definition of a *minority* is similar to that of the environment: it is of an ever-changing human role depending on time and circumstances. The study requires the application of wisdom and understanding of the conditions that impact on humans in the struggle for a place in the sun, the right to a decent life in a competitive society where numbers are sometimes the only means of defining the extent and severity of problems. One has but to study the recent history of the city of Miami, Florida, to learn the full meaning of what can happen to the terms *majority* and *minority* insofar as numbers are concerned.

In a short 30 years the entire ethnicity of the city as well as that of Dade County changed as the Anglo population fled into the outlying areas and the core of the city population of 380,000 persons became 65 percent Hispanic and only 10 to 15 percent Anglo. In one year, 1980, 400,000 Haitians and 140,000 Cubans had to be accommodated.

SALT RIVER COMMUNITY PLANNING PROGRAM 1970–1978

Planning which involved the people of the Salt River Pima-Maricopa Indian Community in Arizona was assisted financially by Section 701 of the Housing Act as an important case study. Lying immediately to the east of the city of Scottsdale, the 100-square-mile area that comprised the original reservation is at present largely open land. The western half of the community is held in 5, 10, and 15-acre allotments. These allotments were given to member families of the community through the Bureau of Indian Affairs, division of the Department of the Interior of the U.S. government. These allotments, at least the smaller ones that lie in the southwestern portion of the community, have since been divided many times into fractions, as members of the families married either members of their own tribe or individuals from other reservations. This alone made enlisting the participation of the "landowners" both difficult and in some cases impossible since locating them was difficult.

Members of the tribes have their homes on smaller holdings. That is the land where water is available and agriculture can be engaged in profitably. Thus, since the tribe members have little business experience, these holdings have been leased to large California agribusiness organizations. In the late 1970s, when the planning began, the tribal members received $50 an acre annually for the use of their land. Perhaps this was, at that time, a reasonable compensation, but it did not in any way provide a satisfactory income for the people, who continued to depend on the Bureau of Indian Affairs to provide subsistence supplements.

There was some additional supplemental income as certain of the young people worked in the nearby communities, the women as maids in the hotels and motels in Scottsdale, Phoenix, Tempe, and Mesa; the men elsewhere in the labor force at whatever level their education and training would provide.

In the meantime many of the residents on the allotments, living in the poorest types of shelter, were being exposed to the spraying of the crops with fertilizers and pesticides. This condition exposed them to long-term health risks.

Just a few words about the government of the community: with the departure of the (Superintendent), an employee of the Bureau of Indian Affairs, the Pima-Maricopas were self-governing. They have a community council, a land board (planning commission), a police department, and a justice court. The community council had jurisdiction over tribal affairs. In addition there was a preschool facility for the children too young to be bussed to the public school system in Mesa, located across the Salt River, which, during winter flooding, constituted an almost impassible barrier. Older children attended the public schools in Mesa. Health care was administered in a small clinic in the community center and serious problems were treated in the Indian Hospital in central Phoenix. There was no ambulance on call for the needy in the community; medical service from agencies in the surrounding area was slow in arriving in emergencies, posing additional risk to life.

With this information as background, the planners looked to the people to try to determine their needs. It was clear that many of the substantial problems related to the economic plight of all of the members of the community. In instances where an individual tried to start a business, the limited resources and very small local population to support the venture usually caused the venture to fail after a short time. The main hope for economic development appeared to be on the boundary with Scottsdale or along the southern boundary near Mesa, where some small Anglo-owned industries had been started on leased land.

With this background the first cut at a plan was worked out with the apparent support of the members of the land board. The plan visualized what was termed a "duplex" system of land use, where the members of the community would continue to live on their allotments, something they demanded, and the eastern 50 square miles of the community, which was under tribal ownership, would be developed with a full complement of uses, similar to that in a standard urban community but with well-developed plans for preservation of open space. The land would be leased to developers at rates equivalent to those for first-class property in the nearby Scottsdale area; since the quality of the development would be high, it would seem to have a ready market in the rapidly growing Scottsdale-Phoenix region. The revenue income to the tribe would then permit the community to obtain better living accommodations, improved health facilities, and better schools and faculty to educate their children, and free them all from dependence on the Bureau of Indian Affairs.

After discussions among the tribal leaders, the land board, and the community council, the plan was adopted and reports were prepared for submission to the Bureau of Indian Affairs and the Department of the Interior.

No development resulted from the plan, and after several years the tribe determined that the plan needed revision, better to reflect the spirit of the people in the community. During the discussion that preceded the preparation of the revised plan, it was disclosed that the people felt that the plan did not conform with the philosophy of the tribe, in that it would invite great numbers of people who were not tribal members to live on the reservation. Some expressed the fear that the Native Americans would lose "jurisdiction" over their own affairs and that their customs would be jeopardized. Many questions raised at this time concerned the functioning of the community police and the courts when those outside the tribe were involved in accidents or criminal activities. The concern extended into the educational programs, which would be dominated by the

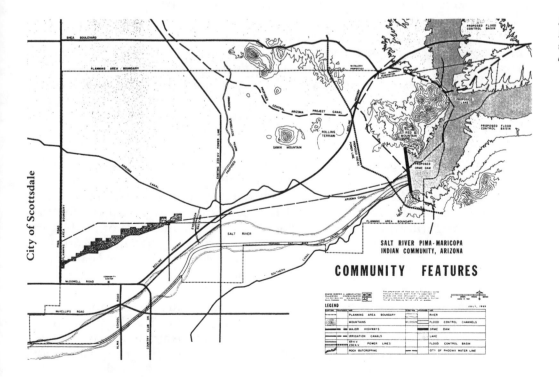

Site of the Salt River Pima Maricopa Indian Community (formerly Reservation), located immediately east of the city of Scottsdale, Arizona.

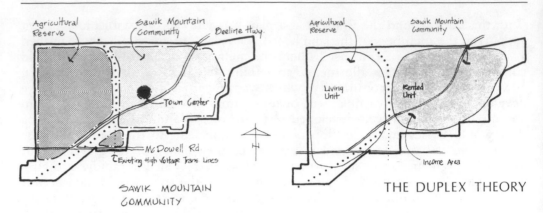

Outline plan for the Salt River Pima Maricopa Indian Community *(left).* **Duplex theory applied to the Salt River Community.** *The plan contemplated that the western half of the land would be retained for use and occupancy by the members of the tribes and their individual families. The eastern half of the land would be leased to the public for applications in conformity with the comprehensive plan. The income from these leases would go to the tribal council for uses beneficial to the members and their families (right).*

majority of the residents. The word *jurisdiction* meant the potential tribal loss, not only in political matters but in the more important issues related to eventual loss of their land and identity as a people with a history and culture important to each person in the community and, in fact, to the entire region.

With these facts in hand the planners turned their attention to the formation of a plan better suited to the values of the people and, in the end, to the protection of the environment, even though it did not satisfy the immediate economic needs addressed in the original plan.

The revised plan respected the residential desires of the allottees by showing that part of the reservation would remain agricultural, permitting the people to continue customary residential uses in special designated areas. The community-owned land was shown as permanent open space. Nodes of commerce were indicated along the western border adjacent to the city of Scottsdale, and industrial areas were set aside in the southern portion of the community adjacent to the one existing major arterial, a state highway, and backed up to the Salt River floodway.

It might be of interest to the readers to know that these proposals have brought a degree of prosperity to some of the landowners, where allotments bordered Pima Road, the western boundary of the community. In these areas, where groups of contiguous allotments were grouped for development purposes, the owners were successful in offering leases and attracting commercial interest and development.

In addition, the concept of having a community college on the reservation materialized and the campus was built on the northwestern corner of the land. The lease of the land to the school board set forth a condition that members of the tribe would in perpetuity be provided free education. The land used for the college was originally allotted for grazing uses in the plan because of the lack of community water facilities. However, since the college was adjacent to Scottsdale and the facilities would serve students from that city, water, fire, and police services were funded by a cooperative arrangement.

The years spent working closely with the tribal council and the members of the land board (planning commission in fact, if not in name) led the planners to realize that the preservation of the people's culture and aspirations was of paramount importance in the development of the revised plan. The plan would not

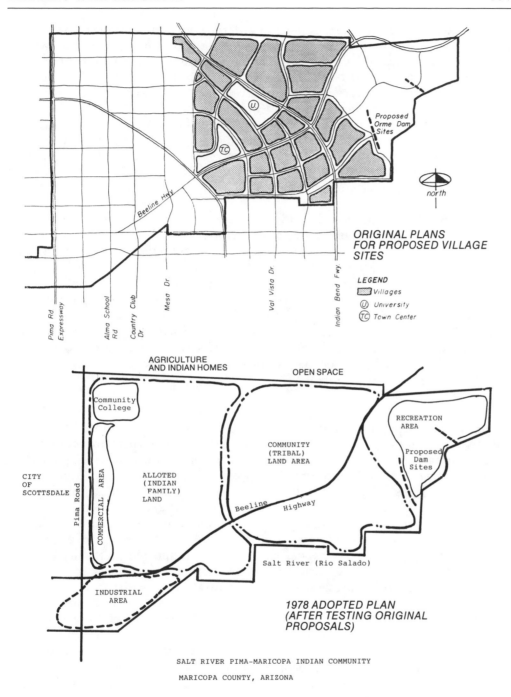

ORIGINAL PLANS
FOR PROPOSED VILLAGE
SITES

LEGEND

▨ Villages
Ⓤ University
Ⓣ Town Center

1978 ADOPTED PLAN
(AFTER TESTING ORIGINAL
PROPOSALS)

SALT RIVER PIMA-MARICOPA INDIAN COMMUNITY

MARICOPA COUNTY, ARIZONA

The proposed village for the community (top). The revised plan, adopted after 5 years of study (1978) by the members of the community, the land board, and the tribal council. No land would be leased for other than commercial or industrial uses, and then in accord with the comprehensive plan. Fear of loss of control of their land and jurisdiction over the uses was the policy basis for their decisions (bottom).

produce a copy of a typical non-Indian community but one that would preserve the people's values, cultural heritage, and dignity. The plan would keep the land under Indian control, rather than producing a suburban extension of the city of Scottsdale covered with housing and shopping centers and the traffic congestion associated with intensive urban development.

Lessons are sometimes learned the hard way, through experience. In this case, through work with a patient people who understood the threat to their existence inherent in following customs and practices that applied to different cultural and economic conditions, the plans ultimately developed better served the needs and aspirations of the majority of the members of the community.

SOME OTHER NATIVE AMERICAN COMMUNITIES

Other Native Americans were subject to different physical and social conditions. The Indians in Oklahoma, for instance, came into substantial economic wealth as the reservation was the location of great oil resources. Those living in the Palm Springs area of California owned scattered sections of land as part of a checkerboard pattern which interspersed Native American land with land given by the federal government to the railroads to induce them to open lines to the west. During the latter half of the twentieth century the growth of Palm Springs involved the leasing and development of land owned by the Agua Caliente tribe in the heart of the resort community. Strangely, most of the tribal members live off the reservation land, in and around the city of Los Angeles, where many are part of the impoverished minorities.

On the other hand, the Navajo and Hopi live on adjacent reservations, where they occupy a large part of the states of Arizona, New Mexico, Colorado, and Utah. The Navajo reservation alone occupies over 9,000,500 acres of land. The Hopi reservation, once a part of the Navajo reservation, lies to the northwest and abuts the Navajo land. One factor that ranks high in the mores of all tribes is love and respect for the land; all recognize the role that it plays in their lives and the continuation of their culture and history as a distinct people. Seldom do they relinquish title to the reservation land. Where it is used by people who are not tribal members, it is always through short-term leases. Unfortunately, many of the leases do not yield an adequate return because of poor economic contracts with non–Native American firms.

PLANNING WITH MINORITIES IN URBAN COMMUNITIES

Planning for a separate nation, such as a Native American community, where there is for the most part a defined land area within which there are more or less common goals, is in some ways simpler than planning for a diverse urban area. Minority racial, cultural, and ethnic groups in cities often occupy almost self-contained areas, like those settled by Chinese, Korean, and Japanese immigrants, whose cultural associations gathered them in concentrated areas with other immigrants who shared their language, food, religion, and social customs. These groupings may seem like ghettos, and they probably were in the beginning, when segregation of minorities was practiced and supported politically by laws and later by zoning. Now such restrictions cannot be enforced by law, but cultural affinities tend to preserve ethnic concentrations in some areas.

As members of a minority group become more affluent, they often seek a better environment for their families and the improved educational facilities found in more exclusive areas. In many instances, even today, there are methods that are employed to keep these well-off people out of the "pristine" areas. One device is the use of "gentlemen's agreements," whereby the real estate agent informs the interested persons, quietly, that there are no vacancies.

MINORITY ACTIVITIES IN THE PLANNING PROFESSION

Seldom are women thought of as a minority of our national population even though many are treated that way. Although women have made significant progress in the planning profession in the past 40 years, the percentage involved remains relatively low at the present time. Of those who are active, many are leaders, heading staffs and directing important projects. A study of the membership of the American Institute of Certified Planners (AICP), the professional society of the field, indicates that women constitute approximately 20 percent of the membership. The membership in the American Planning Association (APA) indicates that 22 percent of the membership in the California Chapter are women;

this figure was based on a 15 percent random sample of the 1989 roster of more than 4,000 members. The APA includes persons in other related fields, many of whom are also members of AICP. Many of the women in the field are extremely competent professionals, working as designers, economists, and policymakers as well as directors of their community staff.

The future looks more promising. A brief survey of universities in the Los Angeles area reveals impressive statistics. In UCLA's graduate program in the School of Architecture and Urban Planning approximately 51 percent of the students enrolled in the 1990–91 planning program are women and all are doing well. At USC, where the planning program provides education at both the undergraduate and graduate levels, the percentage of women in the programs also amounts to more than 50 percent of the student body. If the same condition exists at the other universities and colleges listed in the 1990–91 roster as offering accredited planning degrees, the planning profession will be enhanced by the addition of a great number of both men and women trained in the skills of the profession and capable of becoming the next generation of leaders. Sixty-two institutions are on the AICP accredited list and offer programs leading to undergraduate and graduate degrees.

Other minorities, including African Americans, Asian Americans, and Latin Americans, unfortunately still constitute a low percentage of the numbers of the profession. Even fewer play a leading role. At the recent conference of the California Chapter of the American Planning Association, which includes among its members many involved in related activities, such as law, banking, and real estate, the absence of minorities from the large assembly was noticeable. A number of women presented excellent papers, but they were greatly outnumbered by the male presenters.

As the profession matures and addresses the crucial programs concerned with the welfare of all of the people, it is imperative that greater efforts be made to attract participants from all segments of the population, especially those among whom the greatest need exists for improvements in their environment and increased opportunities to advance into the mainstream of society. To plan for a better nation we must not lose the opportunity to enrich our lives by providing greater exposure to the offerings of the varied cultures represented by our minority confrères.

CHAPTER 43

URBAN DESIGN

The attempt to give form, in terms of both beauty and function, to selected urban areas or to whole cities. Urban design is concerned with the location, mass, and design of various urban components and combines elements of urban planning, architecture, and landscape architecture.

—Naphthali Knox AICP, California Planning Roundtable, 1990

CITIZEN PARTIC- IPATION

There is an increasing demand for "a voice" in the design and planning of communities. Community cooperation and involvement through participation in meetings, hearings, workshops, and charettes are the most commonly used methods. Publicity is a major part of this process. A "small blurb" in the legal section of your local paper will not produce a large crowd. Contacting local groups, schools, and agencies and encouraging media publicity will ensure participation of a good cross section of your community. This should lessen the number of "NIMBY" at the development stage. Collaboration among public agencies, consultants, and citizens will result in a more harmonious community process.

Many large shopping centers have received community approval only when site planning of the highest quality was the basis for their development. Years of community conflict in Arcadia, California, resulted in excellent shopping center designs by Victor Gruen after the neighbors felt that their interest had been protected and the city approved the construction.

Critics of the concept of urban design say that in fact it does not exist. "Towns are not designed," said one. "They are pasted together, piece by piece." If that is true, it is the result of too many person's being involved in the developmental process and insufficient cooperation among them—time is a major factor.

In recent years several interesting concepts have been put forward to bind individual efforts into a compatible whole. The comprehensive plan with its emphasis on a coordinated, unified system of land use and circulation is at the heart of this effort. The creation of new techniques and acceptance of greater responsibility by the land developer in subdividing property is another important gain. The emphasis on building development in a subdivision has tended to reduce the speculation in vacant land; thus the city may become a place for living rather than a hopscotched checkerboard of partly used real estate. The costly ignoring of concern for the environment—especially in the areas of fire prevention and land erosion—has also made the notion of urban design more acceptable to many people.

IMPACT

Urban design has most impact when all of the theories of serving the residents with open space and amenities are reflected in a subsection of the comprehensive plan. Sound judgment must be applied to the relationships between the permitted number of dwellings and the spaces between them. The provision for access and parking and the responsibility for the maintenance of the open areas are issues that must be resolved before construction can start.

That democracy imposes great responsibility on the individual is self-evident: with the privilege of freedom comes responsibility. Harmony in the city of democracy calls for the exercise of individual responsibility and mutual respect. Since it was by autocratic means that a monarch was able to produce a vast venture like Versailles, so it is contrary to democratic principles that individuals should ignore the work of others to memorialize their own vanity or expand the contents of their purses. Rivalry for "bigger and better" cities can do no more to open the way to creative design than can the stamp of classic planning.

NEW DIMENSIONS

With the abundant labor of slaves ancient cities were built of blocks of stone and wood, their heavy forms refined by sculpturing the structural members. Laying stone upon stone, medieval builders formed soaring arches, flying buttresses, and intricate tracery. During these centuries all construction was wallbearing; all structural stresses were in compression.

The Industrial Revolution produced a violent change. The massive construction of ancient cities was transformed to the lightness of steel in tension. Processed in the crucibles of smelting plants and testing laboratories, materials were refined, their basic qualities extracted and synthesized. A wide range of synthetic materials was mechanically assembled on light structural frames. The dynamism of forces in tension replaced the static forms of compression, and the machine released a new freedom in the organization of space.

With the positive thrusts of railway, highway, and airway, new dimensions penetrated the twentieth-century city. Vehicles of transportation no longer mingled informally in the fashion of the Middle Ages. Seeking channels of uninterrupted directness, moving with uncompromising direction, straight ribbons stretch across level spaces and merge with irregular terrain in graceful sweeping curves. The highway is shaped to the contours of the land. Continuity is uninterrupted by natural obstacles; with almost defiant sureness bridges span chasms and tunnels pierce mountains. Unimpeded continuity is essential and insistent. Almost unnoticed, this new dimension has forced a new scale in city building.

The new scale appears in the Mount Vernon highway, the Westchester County parkways, the New York City highways and parkways, the Outer Drive in Chicago, and the freeways of Los Angeles. More rural than urban, the parkway in combination with clear-channel rapid transit for mass transportation is the salvation of the traffic dilemma in the heart of the city.

Matching the expanse of the parkway is the horizontal span of enclosed floor space. The city of today is a series of horizontal planes, one above the other, and the relatively constant floor heights retain the impression of human scale. Utility and economy are inconsistent with the inflated scale of the poorly conceived imitations of the past; excesses in scale that characterized the baroque city are restrained. Scale is not absent in the volume of floor space enclosed in tall buildings; it has been lost in the congestion of these buildings on the land—the absence of open space as a foil for their size. The skyscraper readily expresses the multiplicity of its floors, but the sense of scale has been destroyed by the oppressive bulk of buildings in proportion to the open space about them. It is toward the restoration of adequate space that the new dimensions of the city are forcing urban development.

The Penetration of Space

A rectilinear street arrangement has generally been interpreted as evidence of conscious planning. That assumption must be qualified by an appraisal of the purpose and functions for which the form was devised. The Roman city was patterned after the military camp and agricultural and urban land have been subdivided into rectilinear plots; but it does not necessarily follow that the organization of a military camp or a convenient form for legal description and the recording of deeds are keys to the conscious design of cities for the residence and commerce of people. On the other hand, Hippodamus adopted the checkerboard street arrangement for the purpose of allocating lots that would provide proper orientation of all the dwelling units erected upon them. Vehicular traffic was light, towns were small, and direct communication within them was of no particular import.

The Freeway

Today, the freeway or parkway brooks no interference; freedom of movement is continuous. The futility of the usual network of streets is exposed. Like an irresistible force meeting an immovable object, the freeway meets the gridiron: the city is the battleground. The static form of the right angle meets the dynamic thrust of free form; the tight gridiron of the surveyor versus the swirling twists of our "planned" suburbia. The battle is being waged in a vacuum; chaos prevails in both, the monotony of one, the variety of disorder in the other. The process is one of dividing the land rather than forming spaces, laying out roads and lots rather than planning appropriate and related uses, and allocating parcels as merchandise tagged with a price rather than arranging space for living or business.

Planning circulation about the city implies a twofold purpose: the direct and natural connection between two or more points, and clear direction for those traversing the roadways. The gridiron provides the latter, but it is essentially a devious zigzag route between two points. Complete loss of orientation is the curse of curving roadways, and no amount of picturesqueness can compensate for the confusion it creates.

A test of planning is the order it produces, and the freeway is a new instrument for orderly space arrangement. Its horizontal expanse clearly defines it as an artery with positive direction in contrast to minor roadways. Reliance on signs of nature or the rigid orientation of the gridiron in the old city is supplanted by the positive identification and direct action of the sweeping freeway. A dominant feature of the modern city, it brings time and space into harmony. The parkway is destined to force an orderly development not yet apparent in the cluttered urban environment, or it will sweep the city clean.

Just as the freeway has rendered obsolete the corridor and gridiron street, a new relation between buildings and open space was introduced in the great housing developments during the 1920–1930 decade. Parklike open space was incorporated in the eighteenth-century terrace dwellings of the Royal Crescent and Lansdowne Crescent in Bath and Regent's Park in London; the squares of Bloomsbury introduced the garden to residential streets. However, these developments were generally confined to the aristocracy, and the amenities were absent from the living environment of the majority of the urban population. During the early twentieth century Hendrik Pieter Berlage in Holland and Otto Wagner in Vienna strove to treat the dwellings of the people as integral parts of civic design, but they retained the corridor street and uniform facades reminiscent of baroque planning.

Open Space

When the international housing crisis after World War I forced a wide-spread program of dwelling construction, the new dimensions pierced the archaic armor of the city. Large-scale planning freed from the restrictions of single lots completely altered the relation between dwelling and open space. The corridor street was abandoned, space between building facades was no longer devoted exclusively to vehicular circulation, and building units were arranged in orderly groups within free open space.

Space was designed for use, traffic arteries bypassed residential groups, and internal circulation was by way of service roadways and pedestrian walks. Recreation space was accessible from all dwellings, and buildings were planned so that each dwelling unit enjoyed the same orientation as every other dwelling. For the first time since the building of Hellenic cities a common standard of amenities was applied uniformly to all dwellings in the community plan. There was an affinity between the continuity of breadth of space along the parkway, and the flow of space through the developments of large-scale housing.

The infiltration of space in the center of the city is insistent, although it expresses the anachronism of urban growth. While automobile parking lots expand and slums are cleared, adjacent lots are improved with a greater density than before, and congestion persists round about; one ugly improvement is substituted for another. Nevertheless, space is forcing its way into the heart of the city.

Much land still lies vacant within the city, and more lies fallow on the periphery. No pattern, no plan, and little thought have been directed to the future destiny of this land save for outmoded zoning and ineffective building laws. Should we not profit by experience? The tragic results of chaotic expansion lie all about us, the heavy hand of public debt gropes frantically to support the crumbling environment, and all because we waited too long!

Laws to prevent the abusive use of land are one step. Common sense suggests another: the reservation of space for public use—plan today our program for

The Future

tomorrow. We will not save by waiting: now is the time for decision. Now is the time, not later, to decide upon the orderly expansion of the urban pattern, or abandon it to the termites of civic decay. If we intend to restore decency to the environment, now is the time to prepare.

The failure of inaction is written in the spectacle of present cities. The success of action is demonstrated in those rare instances when vision triumphed. What would Manhattan do without Central Park, Chicago without Lincoln Park, San Francisco without Golden Gate Park? In contrast, what a price the people have paid to "make" the land for Chicago's lakefront and the Robert Moses Parkways in New York! If ample space for public facilities is not reserved now, speculation will grip only more firmly: sink its roots more deeply into the nourishment of urban expansion. To delay the day of reckoning will cost the future much too much.

Reservation of open space—greenbelts for recreation, broad thoroughfares, public services—is the least our urban program should include. It would make sense to plan regional park systems as permanent lungs and circulation to protect future expansion. It would make more sense for cities to acquire sections of outlying land as an antidote to the insidious effect of future speculative inflation.

There is a need for civic enterprise to provide leadership for urban growth and development rather than remain forever a step behind. Our society requires such leadership, which represents the dominant will of the people. Civic enterprise is the joint participation of private and public initiative; it is neither one nor the other alone. The ultimate goal in our democracy—the general welfare—is approached when both act in unison. And it is then that profit becomes a healthy motive in our economic, social, and political system. This purpose can be well served by preventing urban ills from infecting new development while the cancer is being carved from the old city. Prevention will come by reservation of ample space before the cost renders adequate room too expensive.

THE HABIT OF CONGESTION

Congestion has a strong grip on the megalopolitan city. Excess upon excess of people and building are heaped upon the land. Size is an accretion of ever-increasing population; people are piled in a pyramid expanding at the base in proportion to the accumulation at the center. The heavy burden of building bulk has created a Frankenstein monster of land values, and the result is a paradox.

The value of land is a product of its use. Presumably the use is designed as a service to people, and the value of the land is measured by the income derived from performing that service. When by increasing the intensity of land use the income from it can be increased, the value of the land is likewise increased.

Following this logic with enthusiasm, city building proceeded according to the "highest and best use" to which urban land could be put. Absorbed in the pursuit of this theory, attention to the basic concept of land value as derived from service to people shifted to the concept of land as a speculative commodity, and this is the status of urban land "economics" today.

It is not a new situation. Exploitation of land has been common throughout history. The degree of its effect on the development of cities has been dependent on the extent to which urban growth in any period has been dominated by speculative excess, or implemented by tempered investment.

The novel character of this process today is the self-consuming nature of land economics. The upward spiral of value has created congestion and, seeking to maintain an economic balance, more congestion is the usual antidote. As a result, value is not measured in terms of service to people; on the contrary, the people are now obliged to adjust themselves to congestion in order to maintain land values.

This paradox is at the root of the urban problem, but it is being resolved. Decentralization is gnawing at the values in congested areas, even though the unplanned and disorderly process has the effect of shifting the disease about the urban anatomy rather than curing the malady.

Congestion is a habit hard to break. We see it illustrated in some of the most courageous efforts to release the city from its shackles. The remarkable program of highways directed by Robert Moses in New York City may be fairly compared with achievements of the Roman Empire or Baron Haussmann in Paris. Yet the administrative prowess and engineering skill it represents are unconsciously tangled in the web of congestion.

Struggling to escape from congestion, the smooth freeways loosen themselves from one complicated intersection only to find themselves caught in another. High land cost is a challenge to engineering ingenuity, and the results are triumphs of technical skill, but the capacity to build these structures is sometimes a delusion. The ready escape from congestion offered by the freeways is part of the formula for dissipation of excessive land values, but the highway design is threatened with early obsolescence when it is warped into complicated and extravagant intersections to avoid high land cost. Avoidance of high land cost is inadequate compensation if the civic improvement is crippled and yields no permanent asset to the community. A full statement of the problem cannot omit the necessity for the most direct system of circulation integrated with redevelopment of congested areas.

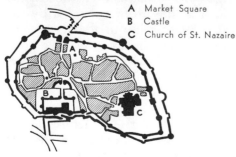

A Market Square
B Castle
C Church of St. Nazaire

Carcasonne, France: a walled city still functions. *A great tourist attraction (left).* **Genoa, Italy: a city built in accordance with a plan.** *The central feature is the beautifully landscaped park that terminated in a floral depiction of the Niña, Pinta, and Santa Maria, the ships that carried Columbus and his crew to the New World in 1492 (right).*

Palais Longchamps and the great central park, Marseilles, France.

High-Rise Buildings

Many architects as well as city planners believe that in order for there to be a real urban center there must be a change in the vertical scale of the buildings. The uplifting experience of the cathedral in the medieval town must be restored, a punctuation point that says, Here I am: the city centrum. Few, if any, large cities in the world fail to adhere to this as a principle of urban design. Economic reasons support the desires of the city builders.

Many factors lead to the decision to develop high-rise structures in the urban centers. Most frequently mentioned is the high price of land, even though the cost of construction sometimes consumes much of the profit provided by the intensified use of the land. In addition, the close relationship to activity or employment centers places the high-rise structure in an excellent competitive position in relation to the horizontal alternative, where land transportation becomes a major factor in the cost. Scarcity of space in already congested areas is also a factor.

Commercial building seems to be able to survive as high-rise structures in the central city and in some of the specially designed outlying centers, since the cost of the space can be written off both in the cost of products or services and in tax

Mont St. Michel: mountain in the sea. *An architectural gem on the Normandy coast of France, this small island is crowded with Gothic buildings. The first monastery was built on the summit in 708; the remaining structures were built in the thirteenth and fourteenth centuries (left).* **Red Square in Moscow, Russia.** *This tremendous open space where great public occasions are celebrated is remembered as providing one with a sense of place. The interesting architecture and the contrasting open space are retained when much else fades from one's memories (below).*

savings. On the other hand, high-rise housing structures generally call for rents that can be afforded by relatively few families; in many cases the units are acquired by corporations for their directors or top personnel.

There is no question that good urban design is essential to the development of pleasant urban communities. The real problems associated with the process are that there is either too little coordination of efforts or too little concern with the impact of one design upon others. Too many persons believe that the best urban design is that which has great variety based upon the freedom of the individual. The designation of good design is considered a matter of personal taste, or as being in the eye of the beholder.

In preparing an urban design plan for a city or for a specific area, effort should be directed to giving the observer a pleasing impression that will be retained in memory. Some examples of the "know that you are there when you are there" are the great Piazza of St. Mark's in Venice, Red Square in Moscow, and Tien An Men Square in Beijing, all of which are open spaces defined by dramatic groups of buildings. Outdoor areas that define "place" bring to mind the drama

DEVELOPING A SENSE OF PLACE

Tien An Men Square is part of a huge architectural composition which, as an open space, lies as the central plaza for the huge governmental building complex. The Forbidden City with its historical Chinese architectural style forms an interesting core within a great city.

of the Grand Canyon of the Colorado as that monumental colorful structure holds the thin wisp of the Colorado River in its hand. The scenic beauty that is Yosemite National Park is also a "place" one never forgets.

We cannot create a Grand Canyon or a Yosemite in our intimate communities, but it is possible to design a community center or feature a dramatic view that will always recall the quality of our special "place," of "our town."

GATEWAYS TO THE CITY

From ancient times the approach to the heart of the city was through one or more gateways. It was at this critical point that visitors were able to determine the character of the community and the quality of its features.

Among the main portals to a community are its airports and railroad stations and the principal highways that approach the heart: the community center. All of these features require handsome parkway treatment, stands of trees and other plants, some statuary, and carefully designed and controlled lighting and directional signs and identification of the routes to important places and events. Billboards and other garish signs should be prohibited.

Examples of airport approaches can be like that from Midway Airport into the central area of Chicago which traverses the crowded lower-income housing and commercial areas of Cicero. In contrast, the drive from Dulles Airport into Washington, D.C., established the magnificent visual character of the nation's capitol.

Visitors landing at the airport in Palm Springs, California, are treated to a view of the city through a palm-lined street, with flowers covering the median strip in the highway which leads to the city center. There are no power lines or other obstructions to limit the sight of the magnificent, often snow covered mountain backdrop for this desert recreational community.

The comprehensive plan for the city of Burbank, California, determined that the main entrance to the business district and civic center limited outdoor advertising; all billboards were prohibited in an effort to adhere to the city's plan for developing the visual quality of the approach to the business district.

The portal to the city of Palm Springs. When visitors arrive at the airport, they are greeted by a view of the fountain, the palm trees, the flowers, and above all the backdrop of snow-covered Mount San Jacinto, rising 10,000 feet above the desert floor, all extending a welcome.

The County of Santa Barbara in California determined legislatively that a portion of Highway 101, a major north/south highway, should be free of billboards, which would detract from the natural beauty of the coastal landscape. Similarly

Banff, Alberta, Canada, is a community that is sited like a jewel in a great wilderness of mountainous open space, especially when seen from the top of Mt. Norquay.

the city of Monterey, which lies along historic Highway 1, also acted to protect not only its coastline but also the tree-lined ridges that form the eastern backdrop to the community.

BASIC COMPONENTS OF URBAN DESIGN

Urban design encompasses all things perceived in the community. Perception refers to many components, including people, movement and circulation, time, mood, sound, light, color, touch, taste, and smell. Most of these are experienced whether driving, walking, or riding through a community, down a street, in a shopping area, or in your own yard. To achieve a cohesive satisfying environment all of the components of perception and sensitivity to the needs and goals of the community should be considered.

Movement, Circulation, and Time

Well-placed patterns of vehicular traffic meet the needs of destination and through traffic. Pedestrian movement and circulation should be major considerations of vehicular traffic patterns, for the speed of traffic determines the level of safety for pedestrians. Generally you will not find many pedestrians when the traffic is moving faster than 25 miles per hour. Well-designed vehicular circulation encourages pedestrian movement, saving energy. Commute time is always an important factor whether one is traveling to the store or to work.

Sound

A clean, well-maintained community can become unpleasant when noise levels are excessive. Siren, factory, traffic, and industrial sounds individually are tolerable; in excess they become unpleasant, at times frightening. Buffering these uses from each other and the surrounding areas can help minimize the noises produced by each.

Unity

When scale and character of nearby areas, structures, streets, landscaping, and open space are respected, the integrity of the design will promote a sense of unity.

Light

A light, bright area or community will appear safer for pedestrians and vehicles. In some areas natural landscaped screening is required for comfort and protection from the heat of the sun. Light and air circulation standards are strictly enforced in many cities where skyscrapers are prevalent.

Color

Harmony and contrast can be formed through color. A subtle, soothing atmosphere can be achieved or busy activity promoted with color. At times when scale and character of structures has been disregarded, harmony can be felt through color when there is no structural harmony. Contrast in color helps to break up monotony; however, random meaningless contrast has a disrupting effect on the overall design.

Color preference is extremely individual; thus it represents the identity of each and every individual city, town, and community.

Taste and Smell

Taste and smell are closely related. In a community where a bakery is making bread, the smell permeates the atmosphere and one can almost taste the bread. On the other hand, a pulp mill in a community can make one eager to leave. Pleasant odors can be overwhelmingly masked by vehicle exhaust and industry and factory odors, adversely affecting air quality—in some cases to such an extent that one never notices the aroma of the ocean, pine trees, or other pleasant natural features.

Some communities are associated with taste. Gilroy, California, is one of these because of its annual garlic festival. Other cities, towns, and communities are recognized for specific kinds of ethnic foods available in abundance.

The textures of the ground, structures, street furniture, landscaping, and roads all help to break the monotony of surroundings. Nature provides a wide array of textures to choose from when selecting construction and landscape materials. Wise decisions give an attractive, pleasing, comfortable feel and touch to any area or community.

Touch

Each building, street, highway, freeway, and open space is a part of the urban pattern. When any one basic component is overlooked, the continuity of the integral urban design is diminished.[1]

Guidelines for Urban Design

The following are suggested guidelines provided by Mark Brodeur from an article in the California Planner. These guidelines are needed to assist design professionals, developers, and builders to produce quality land planning and excellent architectural contributions for the communities in which they work. These guidelines, however, may have to be adjusted to conform with political and environmental limitations. Brodeur also recommended that the guidelines be made available to the design professionals and that they are clear and positive so the users will not find themselves in conflict with their public due to vague or unusual language.

1. Purpose and basis for guidelines
2. Urban design goals and objectives
3. Design components
    a. Site Planning: Setbacks, orientation, open space, circulation, grading, buffers, vistas, street scene, efficiency.
    b. Architecture: Height, bulk, and area of buildings, style, if any, with thorough description, color palette, roof type and pitch ratios, scale, wall articulation, solid to void ratios.
    c. Landscape Architecture: Overall concept, plant materials palette, hardscape palette, locations, size of landscape material, minimum coverage, lighting site furniture, solar orientation, color.
    d. Parking Design: Locations, circulation, access, efficiency, entry character, landscape, lighting, screening.
    e. Signage/Advertising: Character, location, type, materials, size, illumination, color, orientation.
    f. Special Items: Streetscape, commercial rehabilitation, historic building, guidelines, waterscape, entry monumentation, incentive and bonus programs.

Formal design review is a tool fashioned to meet certain community goals, but it requires considerable skill if it is to be put to proper use. The hazards of design review are considerable, and not all guidelines manage to avoid them.

The design review process has proved to be workable and effective, proving that good design and economic feasibility aren't mutually exclusive elements. They provide unique opportunities for both the developer/designer and the jurisdiction. For the developer/designer, the guidelines can provide a marketable image and design theme, ensuring development continuity. The guidelines can maintain and usually enhance property values because they ensure that neighborhood developments will be consistently evaluated and, ideally, well designed.[2]

---

1. Shelley Eisner, unpublished paper, 1991.

2. Excerpts from Mark J. Brodeur, *California Planner*, June 1987.

EARLY STUDIES IN COMMUNITY DESIGN

The art of community planning and urban design is set forth in the following material, which talks of the development of a livable setting for good quality of life, with all of the essential facilities and amenities provided. Current planners and community builders (and highway and street designers) might look askance at the street design and zoning, but one must realize that this was the "state of the art" at the time and made the approach acceptable and inevitable. As with all long-range planning the proposals were modified, but they provided a useful guide to the planning of the major arterials which actually structured future development.

Regional Planning Commission Approach to Urban Design

The earlier planning can be undertaken, the more powerful it becomes as an instrument for the prevention of waste and the production of an ideal community.

An essential and outstanding feature of the design is the careful proportioning of the various types of uses so as to make zoning easy and natural. Space is provided for industries, business, homes, parks, and public buildings in such a way that each has enough space, and, moreover, space is so selected as to be the most desirable for that particular use.

Another feature of importance is the sense of unity which is given by the use of a definite focal point for the community business center, the provision of gracefully curved streets bringing all parts of the area into easy communication, and the continuity of the parks and parkways.

NEED OF A PLAN FOR THE RANCHO LOS CERRITOS

The Montana Ranch, located northeast of the City of Long Beach, embraces the larger portion of the original Rancho Los Cerritos, which is a part of the grant from Spain to Manuel Nietos. In 1931, still largely undeveloped, this great ranch represented a rare opportunity for the ideal application of city planning principles and methods.

Directly adjoining the ranch, to the south are three large land holdings owned by Susanna Bixby Bryant, Fred Bixby, and The Bixby Land Company. Any development of any one of these holdings should be based upon a comprehensive plan that includes them all. With such a plan established, each independent development will contribute materially to the enhancement in value and attractiveness of the adjoining holding, as well as of the surrounding communities in general.

The total land of the planning area included four ownerships lying within Los Angeles County is approximately 10,000 acres. Taken as a unit this property presents an opportunity to develop a new community complete in every respect.

CERTAINTY OF DEVELOPMENT

The Rancho Los Cerritos and a large portion of the Rancho Los Alamitos have been held inviolate from the hands of land speculators since the time of the original Spanish grants, through the Mexican era, and under the regime of the United States to the present day.

A DISTINCTIVE PLAN

The Regional Planning Commission has carried out a careful study of a detailed development plan for the remaining 10,000 acres of these two great ranchos conducive to the best interests of the owners and future occupants.

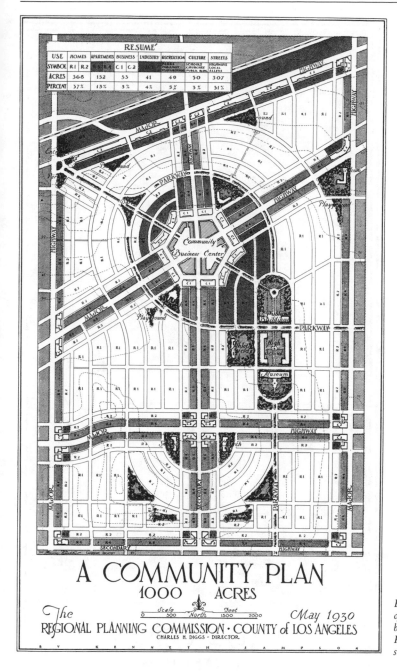

RESUME'						
USE	HOMES	APARTMENTS	BUSINESS	INDUSTRY	RECREATION	CULTURE	STREETS
SYMBOL	R1	R2	R3	R4	C1	C2		PARKS PARKWAY PLAYGROUND	SCHOOLS CHURCHES PUBLIC BLDG.	HIGHWAYS LOCAL ALLEYS
ACRES	368	152	55	41	49	30	307
PERCENT	37%	15%	5%	4%	5%	3%	31%

A COMMUNITY PLAN
1000 ACRES

The
REGIONAL PLANNING COMMISSION · COUNTY of LOS ANGELES
CHARLES H. DIGGS · DIRECTOR.

Scale   North   Feet
0   500   1500   2000

May 1930

BY KENNETH SAMPSON

Early example of the planning of a new community, prepared by the Los Angeles County Regional Planning Commission in 1930.

The main highways are direct and frequent, and yet they are so arranged that there is no congestion of many highways at a single point. The small number of crossings on these main highways results not only in safety and convenience for travelers upon them but also protects the interior streets from annoyance and danger of traffic. This arrangement of streets, by its very pattern, tends to regulate the uses to which the property is best suited.

Adequate neighborhood playground and recreation facilities are easily and economically located in each segment. Elementary school sites can be so placed that no small children have to cross busy highways. It is proposed that the land holder retain these areas at acreage prices, in order that they may be made available to the proper authorities when needed.

EACH SEGMENT OF THE PLAN—A NEIGHBOR-HOOD UNIT

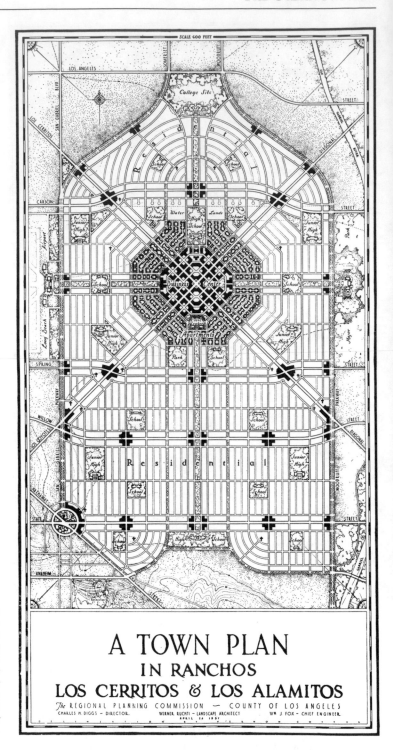

This community plan and the zonal proposals were also prepared by the Los Angeles County Regional Planning Commission to provide leadership for the many cities in the county and to coordinate the planning of the basic highway system, the impact of which can be observed in the current development of the study area.

In addition, six junior high schools, two senior high schools, and a college are provided for. The distribution of these has been very carefully worked out in relation to the population and to one another: 20 acres are allowed for each elementary school; 30 acres for each junior high school; 50 acres for each senior high school; and 130 acres for the college site.

Ample provision is made for apartment houses just outside the central business district, the gradation of uses being such as to protect property values. The civic center is conveniently located and carefully planned.[3]

To study an area subject to urban design we must study not only the graphics of site planning but also the laws governing development that are politically applicable, the offsite facilities such as adequate road ties and the extension of regional arterials, the ability of sewage treatment plants to handle effluent from the intensity of development that would be generated under peak conditions, the adequacy of water supply and the pressure essential to bring the water to its service area and adequate to provide the pressure and quantity to suppress fires when needed. The latter would include the appropriate design and location of hydrants and alarm boxes. Design really is the coordination of essential functions in a pleasing form that improves the quality of life in an urban area.

What Is Design Review?

Many publications and documents on design review speak of its purpose, but fail to provide a definition of design review. This omission leaves the planning profession without a conceptual framework within which to work. One goal will be to establish a working definition for foreign review.

Design review may be defined as the evaluation and interpretation of the placement of mass, form, and spatial elements using a set of predefined objectives. Typically, the design review process focuses on site planning, architectural consideration, and landscape requirements in order to determine compliance with stated objectives.

Why Have a Design Review Board?

It is difficult to translate every nuance of a stated objective into a set of regulations. A successful balance of community demands, project economics, and creativity is more likely to result in a good project and design. However, this balancing act is, in part, an inherently subjective process.

A design review board is one method to harness the subjective process into coherent standards and guidelines. Furthermore, design review boards are also the result of citizens' demands for a greater "say" in how a project should fit into the neighborhood.[4]

URBAN DESIGN: WHAT IS IT REALLY?

DESIGN REVIEW BOARDS

---

3. Los Angeles County Regional Planning Commission, *Regional Plan of Highway-Section 4 Report,* 1931.

4. R. Nicolas Brown, AICP, Palmdale, California, Dispatch News Letter of Los Angeles Chapter APA, August 8, 1990.

CHAPTER 44

ART IN THE CITY

Ideally a good building in itself should really be a work of art architecturally. It should not need another object to make it good. But if you have a first-rate sculpture next to an excellent building—and some rapport or tension between them—this can well lead to an enhancement of the urban surrounding. Good sculpture should be used on city sites with the same discrimination with which sensitive people put paintings and sculpture in their homes.

Henry Seldis, Henry Moore in America

COMMUNITY APPEARANCE

Not since the City Beautiful movement at the turn of the century has the planning of cities been accepted as an art. Planning shifted from the province of the landscape architect to engineers and techniques of zoning; planners' attention was diverted to zoning administration and urban management.

Industrial genius created the productive capacity of the world, but it was commercial genius that produced the wealth. The city became a vast commercial enterprise; everything was for sale. The billboard syndrome defaces strip commercial streets in every city, freeway rights-of-way, and most rural highways. Power poles and wires, competing traffic signals, a convulsive mass of distracting color, form, and motion, obscure the identity of individual signs. Every street looks like every other street; in the words of Gertrude Stein, "When one gets there, there is no there there."

Symbol of Peace. Rock Garden in Japanese Temple, Kyoto, Japan.

It has now become customary to include community appearance as part of a city's comprehensive plan. The refinement of urban form and space, respect for natural topographic features, scenic approaches, views of sea and sky, open space, relationships and identity of structures, have been skillfully advocated by competent designers.[1] It is perhaps the most nebulous element in the planning process.

But, caught up in the technicalities of urban housekeeping and confronted with apathy among the urban populace, administrative planners, public officials, and citizens alike have become inured to the ugliness around them and seem incompetent to make judgments on urban aesthetics.

Public authority has absolute jurisdiction over some 40 percent of the city area: streets, parks, and public facilities. Yet a street will be widened to accommodate more automobiles, even though doing so destroys trees and ruins the visual quality of adjacent property; a school or other public building will be crowded onto an inadequate lot, and acquisition of enough space is alleged to be "uneconomic" because it would cost more. An old city hall will be abandoned and a modern facility built elsewhere without concern for the historical value of the old building or the disruption of the city's sense of identity.

Despite official insensitivity to urban aesthetics, the city may improve or preserve attractive features within the area of its authority—if an alert citizenry and a competent planning staff are vigilant. But the balance, 60 percent of the city area, is within the province of private enterprise, and regulation of aesthetic quality by legislative processes is largely ineffectual. Strategic locations may be controlled

---

1. Kevin Lynch, *The Image of the City* (Cambridge, Mass.: Technology Press and Harvard University Press, 1960).

Street scene, Kowloon, Hong Kong, 1984: community art or anarchy?

Picasso's Woman, *Civic Center, Chicago, 1967.*

by regulations of height and bulk, and billboards may be eliminated in time by imposition of amortization zoning. The 1954 Supreme Court decision offers some encouragement, but the courts are generally reluctant to impose judgment on aesthetic issues alone. Subdivision ordinances can require underground power utilities, building setbacks, and open space. The planned unit development introduces the advantages of large-scale planning. But a city can exercise its major influence on aesthetic quality by the degree to which an orderly structure of land uses is planned: the relationship of streets to abutting property and their effectiveness for traffic movement, the elimination of strip commercial zoning (also by amortization zoning), the consolidation of commercial facilities in shopping centers, the maintenance of street trees, the preservation of open space and historic landmarks, the location and intensity of street lighting, and the design of street furniture such as benches, sculpture, as well as directional and identification signs.

LOCATIONAL PLANNING FOR THE ARTS

The arts, like other aspects of urban life, are affected by public regulations dealing with land use and structures. In certain cases, changes in such regulations can have a favorable impact on the expansion of the arts. It is obvious that there must be some changes in the current zoning laws in many cities if the artist is to be accommodated in the parts of the city where the mixing of studios and living accommodations is now prohibited.

Two areas of public regulation deal with the use of land and structures. These involve zoning and the approach to mixing land uses in an unplanned manner. Such regulations were basic to the establishment of zoning as a means of protecting the "sanctity of the home" as they barred all nonresidential uses from residential areas in particular. Other regulations, less frequently observed, restricted the intrusion of residential uses into commercial and industrial areas. The fear of mixing residential and nonresidential uses in an unplanned manner caused numerous communities to adopt prohibitions against the extension of the mixed uses and ordinances establishing "exclusive" zones. Changes in the concept of the desirable structure of commercial areas have caused some recent reversals of this policy, especially where nonconforming uses had existed on a large scale and where new techniques of urban design overcame prior objectionable conditions.

The Establishment of Artists' Colonies

In the postindustrial age which we are now entering, when service employment can be expected to be the mainstay of most cities' economies and when large older cities have to struggle to maintain their economic and financial viability, the creation of artists' enclaves seems particularly appropriate. Arts and cultural activities will inevitably have to be counted on as a significant part of city economy. The artists' enclave may well become an important symbol of the postindustrial city, suggesting the importance of art in its many forms to the economic and residential life of the city.

Some General Principles

Artists have special locational needs; they require large areas of work and storage space for their work and yet their income is frequently limited. Their hours of work do not necessarily correspond to the normal work patterns of others, often requiring either close proximity of residence and studio or their fusion. Art buyers must be able to visit the studios to acquire the work of the artists. The area should, therefore, be visually attractive and safe to lure potential middle-class art clients.

Opera House, Stockholm.

What seems ideally suited to these special needs is an individual large, substantial building in a preferred location or in an area that is being revitalized. Use of vacant loft buildings where they exist is best because it causes no displacement of persons occupying the space. The building must be substantial and be capable of being located in or adjacent to an attractive commercial area.

The main problem is economic. The cost of a building in a central location and of renovations to make it suitable for residential purposes as well as for studio activities is great and must be passed on to the occupant. Unless subsidies are available for artists, the district would be of value to a limited number of artists. Such rehabilitated structures become increasingly attractive to others, causing impressive increases in property values.[2] Many artists soon find themselves un-

2. The experience of SoHo (an abbreviation for South of Houston) in New York, where an art colony was encouraged, is instructive. When the rehabilitated space was offered for rent or lease, the immediate attraction of the project for renters caused rents to skyrocket. Rents originally ranging from $0.60 to $1.60 per square foot escalated up to $3.00 or more a square foot. In addition, people desiring apartments have paid several thousands of dollars as "key money" in order to secure a lease. The people now occupying the facilities are only those who can afford to pay rents at the inflated prices or were able to buy accommodations before this area became glamorous. Ms. Adriana R. Kleiman, AIP, principal planner on the staff of the Planning Department of New York City, has provided useful information on this topic.

Central Plaza, Madrid.

able to live in the enclave because of the increased costs. However, in a situation in which a central city is concerned about losing taxpaying residents—and many larger central cities are experiencing serious declines—it makes good sense for the city to sponsor such enclaves as a means of revitalizing itself. At the same time through federal assistance it is appropriate to subsidize at least some portion of the rents of artists.[3]

Under such circumstances it would be necessary to define rather carefully who is eligible to receive such assistance. New York City has already begun the task of definition, defining the "artist" as one "who is regularly engaged in the fine arts, such as painting and sculpture or in the performing or creative arts, including choreography and film making, or in the composition of music on a professional basis, and is so certified by the city department of cultural affairs and/or state council on the arts."[4]

3. Since people in the arts experience large-scale unemployment and relatively low annual income, it would seem reasonable for HUD "rent subsidy" provisions to be applied in potential programs.

4. Assembly Bill 7552-B, signed into law August 8, 1977 (State of New York) Article 7-B, Section 275.

THE SITUATION IN LOS ANGELES

The problem of locating artists' centers has some special features in Los Angeles.[5] As in other parts of the country, the city some years ago set up exclusive residential, commercial, and industrial districts. As a result of this action, it was necessary to develop a new zone for mixed occupancies to accommodate artists. The new zone permits residences in commercial or industrial structures.

Certain areas within the city of Los Angeles have already attracted many artists. These include Mt. Washington and the several canyons leading from Westwood and Beverly Hills to the San Fernando Valley. There is already a cultural appeal associated with these locations, and artists compete with affluent individuals for homes in these places. In residential zones, application of the ordinance requires the agreement of the residents of the area.

Insofar as commercial and industrial areas are concerned, there seems to be a better-than-average potential for artist use of specific buildings rather than zones for combined occupancy, especially in the Hollywood area, where, although there are no loft buildings as in New York, there are industrial structures that could lend themselves to the development of centers of artistic endeavor.

Downtown Los Angeles has vacancies in buildings where garment industry and banking offices were once located. One or more of these structures might become a center for the arts if upper floors were renovated. Because the cost of making the buildings habitable as residences might price the accommodations out of the range of artists, rent subsidies might be required. Although at present there is limited attraction in being located in the downtown business district of Los Angeles, the restoration and revitalization proposals outlined elsewhere in this book could fundamentally alter this situation. Downtown Los Angeles could become a significant center for artists to live and work.

A ZONING PROPOSAL

What follows is a comprehensive proposal for zoning that draws on features of existing ordinances in New York and Los Angeles. It is designed both to enable artists to practice their professions in a variety of urban settings and to anticipate problems this might generate.

Residential Districts

Single-family districts would permit the practice of the arts on the following basis: In detached housing, the practice by individuals of crafts (as defined in a "home occupation") would continue without constraint other than that related to a public nuisance or creating conditions dangerous to the general welfare. In detached housing, groups could form an "ensemble" subject to the obtaining of a commercial-low density residential (C-A) type of zone overlay and further subject to the following conditions: (1) that the performance of the art involving the group would not exceed a certain number at any one time, to prevent traffic and parking problems on residential streets; (2) that the hours of group work would be limited to daytime between 10:00 A.M. and 5:00 P.M.; (3) that all fire laws and the laws related to sound, vibration, and emission of noxious odors would be respected.

In multiple-family districts practice of the arts would be strictly limited to activities that are quiet and do not in any way tend to endanger adjoining residents.

---

5. Information has been provided by Calvin Hamilton, director of planning for the city of Los Angeles, and by members of his staff.

In all residential districts the sale of works of art or crafts would be limited to those produced on the premises. The hours of sales would be restricted to the daytime, when the use of the streets and parking areas would be minimal.

In commercial districts the practice of the arts is already permitted, subject to the types of art that are consistent with the nature of the district. For example:

In planning shopping centers the display and sale of all forms of the arts could be exercised either within the mall areas or in streets closed off with permission from traffic authorities, or there could be creative activities in the upper levels of multiple-story buildings. Where residential facilities are associated with artists' studios, they should be above the ground floor so as not to interrupt the continuity of the retail sales functions.

In strip commercial areas where vacant stores abound, the storefront could be used for a studio and the display and sale of artworks or, in some cases, performances. Where residential facilities are permitted (as they should be under the following conditions), they would be separate and to the rear of the work and sales area. The residential facilities would have to be in a safe and sanitary condition with all essential services available and usable.

In central business districts the buildings should limit studio residences to the floors above the ground floor and require that residential accommodations be safe, sanitary, and appropriate for residential purposes. The uses could be any that fire laws permit and space users should be required to have parking facilities related to residential occupancies and additional spaces for potential clients.

Provision of educational and recreational facilities for the families of artists living in the heart of a commercial district would have to be carefully considered or "no children accepted" regulations would have to be applied, thus creating adults-only communities.

Industrial Districts

Although it is necessary to limit zoning to exclusive industrial use in many areas, others might allow a planned, compact enclave where artists could work, provided their activities were not incompatible with industry and would not cause industrial practices to be limited by their presence. So many conditions within industrial districts create an undesirable environment for living that it would appear best that the current practice of excluding residential facilities be continued. There is no reason to exclude the studio itself, only the residential occupancy.

There may be isolated industrial buildings in small industrial zones which were created to provide space for uses that no longer exist. These structures may be located in places where their transformation into studios would be appropriate and where their use would be preferable to vacancy. Studios in Hollywood, Culver City, and part of Los Angeles might fit this description. Conditional-use permits might then be granted for the conversion of these structures to centers of the arts and related residential facilities.

In zones that permit the mixture of professional offices and residences, as long as artists conduct themselves as other professionals do there is no reason for limiting their professional activities. The residential area is a separate and distinct unit from the professional facility.

The types of zoning that might accommodate the various individuals who practice the arts might be viewed as follows:

Individual Practice. Where individuals practice the arts, it is possible to accommodate them in residential areas of most cities provided: (1) that their activities are not obnoxious to their neighbors, and (2) that as a home occupation they may merchandise their art or craft products on the premises. In the latter case, the business portion of the activity would be disclosed if the artist required a business telephone and therefore a business license. The level of sound would need to be controlled by some performing artists during hours of practice. The introduction of unusual amounts of traffic in a "school" situation and the consequent parking of excess vehicles could invite neighborhood antagonism and protest.

Group Practice. Whenever there is a large-scale operation, implying more than one artist or pupil, the areas open are generally in the commercial districts, although certain of the districts are reserved at present for highly specialized types of retail services (the neighborhood, district and regional shopping centers where areas are designed and specifically limited to retail sales operations). This does not mean that there could not be precincts in these centers for the practice of the arts, especially on second- or third-floor levels, which are usually not desirable for retail outlets (other than in large department stores).

The potential economic benefits of a genuinely flexible approach to zoning and locational planning for the arts are significant. It would enable artists to live and work in many areas of a city. If zoning changes were linked to the restoration and revitalization of the downtown, artists might choose it as a location for their work. This in turn would greatly enhance the center of the city and contribute to it the excitement and energy of creativity so sorely needed.

THE IMPACT OF CIVIC ART

People respond to improvement in their community; they are affected and their pride is lifted by evidence of cultural energy in their city. They may not appraise these deeds with accuracy or identify them with discrimination, but they are moved by the existence of urban enterprise that transcends mediocrity. This is illustrated by the popular response to Radio City in New York City. In reality the "court" is a relatively diminutive space, but, in contrast with the absence of space within the environs, the appearance of size is exaggerated and the people are impressed. It is space for which the urbanite yearns and seeks and it is the design of space that presents the challenge to city building in the future. It is also the attractive use of the space that make it important.

Attention to the proportion of open spaces and building masses was an integral part of city building in the great cultural periods of the past. Studies by Camillo Sitte indicated that certain relationships between space and buildings were recognized in the medieval town. From these observations he estimated that the minimum dimension of a plaza should be equal to the height of the principal building facing upon it and the maximum distance should not exceed twice the height of the building. He considered that the length of a plaza should not exceed three times the width.

Designers of the Renaissance were also apparently guided by rules of proportion between open spaces and building masses as well as the classic proportions of the buildings themselves. To obtain the effects they sought, the guides were more

Piazza D'Italia Fountain in New Orleans, Louisiana, designed by Charles Moore with the Urban Innovations Group, UCLA, and Perez and Associates, Architects, New Orleans, Louisiana (left). The unseen art. A rooftop view of almost any old city (right).

elaborate than those that appear in the medieval town. Studies by H. Maertens indicate that, to encompass the architectural detail within the height of a building, the spaccs were arranged so that the distance from the observer to the building would be equal to three times its height. These general proportions seem to have been considered in creating the great plazas of the Renaissance and Baroque periods and, as the scale of open spaces increased, the designers introduced sculptural forms—fountains, statues, and monuments—at appropriate intermediate points within the spaces.

WALL ART

In the latter part of the twentieth century development of an old artform (paintings on the walls of caves in France and elsewhere) into new dimensions took place. Starting, perhaps, with the crude efforts of graffiti that were scribbled over building walls and subway trains, the talented artists of many communities began a tremendous adventure that resulted in an outpouring of fine art on building walls, walls of flood control channels, and safety panels surrounding construction sites. Walls along the perimeter of freeways and underpasses were turned over to the artists for examples of their work, thus adding interest and in some cases real beauty to the otherwise barren concrete.

The history of the residents of the areas and the depiction of their cultural backgrounds and attitudes tell the story of the lives and struggles of many minorities as well as the richness of their festivals, their religious practices, their joys and sorrows. The political messages flow throughout the works describing the victories and losses.

A wall on a building near Canter's Restaurant on Fairfax Avenue in Los Angeles tells the story of the Jewish community in the city. The artwork, in black and white, is pictorial to a degree that makes it appear to be a photograph montage.

THE BIRTH OF ROCK & ROLL

Fine art on concrete walls of a flood control channel in the San Fernando Valley, Los Angeles (left). Artistic painting on wall enclosing housing project in the Barrio, Los Angeles (right).

The use of the land adjacent to the wall on the private commercial building is offstreet parking; thus the view of the artwork is open to the public. The city should plan to acquire the parking lot to assure the view of the artwork is not obstructed.

In recent years the Los Angeles Cultural Affairs Department sponsored a program titled "Neighborhood Pride—Great Walls Unlimited." In addition, the local Social and Public Art Resource Center sponsored a group of local artists, commissioning them to create a series of murals through the city of Los Angeles. To bring the neighborhood youth into the activity, they authorized the artists to employ teams of local youngsters to aid in the production of the murals and thus help them to develop their artistic and technical skill as well as imbuing them with a sense of pride and accomplishment.

Many gold country towns in Northern California have commissioned local artists to paint murals of the history of their communities on structures and walls. These graphic delights depict the struggles and triumphs of the people and many different techniques and tools used in mining the gold in that particular area. These murals are familiar sights in Auburn, Placerville, Grass Valley, and Nevada City.

COMMUNITY PROJECT OF A LOCAL GENIUS

The Watts Towers, conceived and constructed by Simon Rodia in the southeastern part of the city of Los Angeles, has been designated as a national treasure. Rodia, a retired worker, constructed the entire group of towers after the fashion of Antonio Gaudi's La Sagrada Familia in Barcelona, Spain. He used the same type of decorative material, bottles, broken dishes, and other colorful discarded junk, fashioning it all into monuments beautiful to behold. The Royal Palaces and temples in Bangkok, Thailand, use this means of decoration on exterior walls.

NEW UTOPIANS

In the wake of Le Corbusier's polemics, some recent new utopians have become increasingly esoteric. Abstract terminology is drawn upon to support imaginative concepts of urban form. Words acquire their own subtle and occult significance: a "continuum of constant change," "ever-fluid movement," "transiency of life-cycles," "mobility," a "new objectivity." The rhetoric is eloquent; words in the lexicon are employed with enviable conviction. Yet when the terms are con-

Paintings describing people and events in a cultural area (top, left). Paintings on the wall in an ethnic shopping area. The property adjacent is now used as a parking lot and should be acquired by the community to protect the view of this fine artistry (top, right). Painting on a temporary wall in front of a revitalization project in the city of Pasadena, California. This was developed as part of the city beautification program related to the New Year's Day Tournament of Roses (bottom).

verted to delineations of tangible form, they reveal a strong basic similarity to the conventional city. Any alternatives seem even less appealing than existing cities. At one time, a platform is proposed to cover Paris; at another, an urban bridge leaps across the English Channel.[6] Buckminster Fuller proposed a series of "floating neighborhoods" moored in New York City's East River.[7]

In their 1958 plan for the Haupstadt in Berlin, Peter and Alison Smithson were intent upon the theme of "mobility." Pedestrian and vehicular traffic were separated by a network of decks and bridges elevated above the road system. Sinuous "walls of office slabs" to contain the inner city would become as rigidly fixed as any conventional urban structure. In that proposal, as in their 1963 plan for Mehring Platz,[8] the Smithsons feature the motorway rather than a dynamic concept for mass transit that might have been expected to shape the modern city. Bearing strong resemblance to freeways in American cities, the new planning vision appears remarkably conventional and in fact rather old. There is little evidence that the new aesthetic of urban form would be any more adaptable to fluid change than existing cities.

Kenzo Tange and the Metabolists of Japan envision dramatic vertical and horizontal forms linked by automobile highways projecting into Tokyo Bay. The

6. Illustrated in Udo Kuterman, *New Architecture in the World* (New York: Universe Books, 1965). Paris Platform, Yona Friedman; Channel Bridge, Schulze-Fiedlitz and Friedman.

7. The "floating city" was developed under a grant by the Triton Foundation, Cambridge, Massachusetts, 1968.

8. Haupstadt Plan (1958), Peter and Alison Smithson and Sigmonde Wonke. Mehring Platz Plan (1963), Peter and Alison Smithson and Gunter Nitschke. See David Lewis (ed.), *Pedestrian in the City* (New York: D. Van Nostrand, 1966).

forms are exhilarating, but the fundamental difference between their proposal and the cities we have, and know to be outmoded, is not readily discernible.[9]

The Realities Where among the broad roadways in these theatrical visions is the mass of motor vehicles to be lodged? Where in the incessant movement of traffic can the automobiles stop? That function was featured in the visions of Louis Kahn for Philadelphia in 1956. He glorified the multilevel garage: among images of tall shafts, pyramids, and "tinker-toy" cages, a collection of great cylindrical garages, or "ports," dominated the scene.

The popular acceptance of the idea of the mechanistic beehives designed for a million or more people by the desert mystic Paolo Soleri[10] as recently as the 1970s and George Favre's "cellular agglomerates, clip-on or plug-in cities, grid structures, containers, submarine cities, cities in outer space, megastructures and all the gidgety-gadgety et ceteras":[11] both of these visions reflect the desperate malaise of a technologically oriented society.

The City Is More Than a Statistic Encompassing the full range of human activity, the city is the living image of the culture that spawns it. It reflects the social values, aspirations, and aesthetic sensibilities of the people who create and occupy it. These characteristics will be

9. Illustrated and described in Lewis, *Pedestrian in the City*.

10. Paolo Soleri, *Arcology: Cities in the Image of Man* (Cambridge, Mass.: MIT Press, 1969).

11. George Favre, "Cities Are for People . . . or Are They?" *Christian Science Monitor,* June 14, 1972.

Portrait of Simon Rodia, the creator and builder of the Watts Tower, in Los Angeles. Types of decoration used are reminders of the work of architect Gaudi on the towers of Segrada Familia in Barcelona, Spain and by Thailand's architects on the temples in Bangkok (page 588, left).

Watts Tower, located in the southeastern part of the city of Los Angeles, where Rodia lived and worked (page 588, right).

More details of Watts Tower (page 589).

represented in the comprehensive plan and zoning ordinances, the allocation of land uses, and regulations that accommodate individual and collective participation in city building. A city that functions adequately may not be aesthetically satisfying: but conversely it will not become an art form unless the functional parts work effectively.

In the final analysis, the aesthetic quality of the city is the measure of the cultural values of a community, values identified with the elevation of mind, morals, and taste of a society. Beautiful cities in the world are not only charming because of a colorful history or the patina of age. Cathedrals of Europe were beautiful when the stone was white. Paris and Venice were built to be beautiful, and they show that beautiful cities can grow old gracefully.

The city needs space for the free flow of transportation and movement of people, space in which to create a desirable environment for living and for work, space in which the functions of the city and the aesthetics of our time may be welded into an inseparable unity. Space in the city will encourage the inventive genius of humankind to fulfill the wants of people and free them from the wanton congestion that renders the city a detestable place in which to live and work.

The urban environment shrieks with the production of science and industry and the commodities of commercial enterprise. The city is like a cave in which a multitude of weird and raucous echoes create a psychological din. Self-discipline in organizing the advantages of our industrial age is lagging, and the citydweller is suffering distraction.

More details of Watts Tower.

Reams of statistics reveal the habits of the urbanite. They show, for example, the short distance people will walk from their parking place to their shopping destination. This reluctance to walk is interpreted as a significant characteristic of the present-day shopper, but the fact that these statistics also measure the repellent character of the urban environment is overlooked. There is ample evidence of the response of the people to studied civic design and their hunger for open space. The plaza in Rockefeller Center evokes spontaneous response, and the success of planned residential communities and neighborhood shopping centers attests to the good business of adequate space. Statistics may show the characteristics of the urban population, but they may also reveal the deficiencies of the environment that induces those traits; they may tell the story of how rank congestion violates human sensibilities and how abhorrent slums are to the human spirit.

THE CULTURAL VACUUM

City building is neglectful of human feeling; it is a cold, harsh enterprise devoid of the amenities for living. It explains the desire for escape that eclecticism provided, a refuge from reality in which the people could draw the walls of romanticism about themselves. The people did not live a real existence, but the romanticism showed that they could still dream, and it is dreams that will lead civilization out of the darkness—dreams of the future rather than the past.

The significance of freedom is not yet fully grasped; society is not yet adjusted to the democracy of our industrial age. Political rights have been won, and mechanical tools of phenomenal number and variety are at our disposal, but the significance of human achievement is blurred in its whirling presence. It was entertaining and amusing fiction that Jules Verne wrote in the nineteenth century. Today reality so far surpasses his visionary anecdotes that society is bewildered. There is a strangeness about the powers science has thrust into the hands of human beings; their capacity to manipulate these powers and the responsibility they bestow cast a spell upon society. When we contemplate their effect upon our social and economic life, the stupendous possibilities are appalling. Imagination pulsates with the vibrating tempo of the modern world.

Evidence of technical progress is all about us. The material benefits of our age are delivered ready-made; gadgets are a part of our daily existence and we take for granted the marvelous developments of science. But the assimilation of these accomplishments into our cultural environment is coming hard. Forging a culture from the technology of our time is a complicated process. Ultimately the adjustment of civilization to the reality of our age will generate the cultural climate in which the creative work of artists flourishes.

Meanwhile we are moving in a cultural vacuum, into which has been drawn the technological progress we misinterpret for culture itself. Mediocrity is the maximum standard bred of materialism. Inured to this standard, we are hardly conscious of its reality and unaware of the cultural potentials present but undeveloped. Their development offers a whole new frontier in our world of progress: the cultural expression of democratic freedom in which the vitality of contemporary art will shape our physical environment. There is resistance to a new aesthetic, but it is more passive than active. The pursuit of material welfare distracts attention from cultural achievement as we bow low before the great god Mammon, but the result is indifference more than willful denial. Economic distortions exert more convincing pressures for improvement of the urban environment than does the creative urge for a fine city. Land values lost to congestion and the economic burden of blight and social maladjustments are more impressive than the aesthetic and spiritual baseness to which the city has degenerated.

UNITY OF PURPOSE

The search for form in the urban environment would stagnate without the imagination of fertile minds. It is the more regrettable that official planning agencies are so timid in their leadership. The aspirations of city people are suffocating. Some cities may have illusions of grandeur, others have ambitions for greatness, but false pride obscures their decadence. We can hardly conclude that the ugliness of our environment is due to a complete absence of civic pride, that nerve-wracking congestion and unhealthful overcrowding answer the natural desire for activity and vitality, and that people have become so inured to their surroundings that they prefer mediocrity to an environment of decency and culture regardless of their social or economic station in life.

What is there to stir the citydweller in the prospect of nothing better than more of the same? The people need to see new plans. Civic leadership needs to emerge with standards of urban development that will convince the people it will be worth the cost to restore decency to their cities. Planning implies a goal to be reached. This, in turn, suggests some unity of purpose. Sorely needed progress is frustrated by disunity and unimaginative leadership. Unity of purpose—a conviction about the form and character we desire for our cities—has been absent. Consequently, planning has wandered aimlessly, frequently promising much but delivering little.

Cities have not reached the stage of crowding and congestion that present laws permit, and yet they are already pitifully overcrowded and congested. These legal limits have induced a state of anarchy in city building. Feeble innovations for improvements are not enough. Facelifting will not do the job; it will take a major operation. Our conception of unlimited exploitation in urban property and people will need modification; the relation between the amount of space occupied by buildings and the amount of land about them must be altered. An inspiring projection of the City of Tomorrow by Le Corbusier, a studied group like Rockefeller Center, a well-planned subdivision like River Oaks, and the parkways of New York and Chicago have pointed the way. If we expect our cities to be shaped in their images, however, we must look to the laws that set the standards for that accomplishment.

Cities are breaking down. As they are rebuilt they must conform to standards that ensure they will not break down again. This will require major decisions, and we must be prepared to make them. Unless these decisions are made wisely, it would be far better and more economical to beat a hasty retreat from the congested urban centers and build new communities elsewhere.

We can build better cities when we quit gnawing at the fringe of the urban garment and accept some of the bitter with the sweet. We will replan our cities to provide a rational density of population, and from these plans we will lay a foundation of law that prohibits crowding and congestions of people and buildings. We will plan for such expansion and decentralization as the regions about our cities require, and we will plan for such rebuilding as obsolescence and decay demand. We will go about this as civilized human beings with due consideration for each other, rather than barbarians bent upon destruction or as creatures of greed and deception bent on personal power and profit. We will seek the values in cities Thomas Guthrie described in the early nineteenth century:

> They have been as lamps of life along the pathway of humanity and religion. Within them science has given birth to her noblest discoveries. Behind their walls, freedom has fought her noblest battles. They have stood on the surface of the earth like great breakwaters, rolling back or turning aside the swelling tide of oppression. Cities, indeed, have been the cradles of human liberty.[12]

The tragic impact of the great city on human welfare aroused the search by the new utopians, and their vision may light the way toward a metamorphosis of the city. Statistics, economic analyses, graphs, and charts urge a popular plea that planning must adopt scientific methods for the direction of future urban growth. The facts are essential: there can be no question about the necessity for full and complete information about our cities. But cities are the creatures of the people, built by people for people, and their form is subject to the will of the people. Scientific analysis may indicate trends, but it does not direct action.

Science is an invention, an instrument with which people reach their objectives, the goals they may set for themselves. The force that moves humankind in the selection of these goals is morality, not science; it is a morality rooted deep in their culture and sharpened by their intuitive capacity. People have the power to control their environment: they can mold it to their purposes. They can observe trends, determine their direction, then reverse or shift them to suit their purposes. The course of human events is not some inevitable fate to which the people are destined; it is subject to their will. They can examine the facts and from them they can select their course. This is the power of humans, and it is the purpose of planning. Guided by a high moral sense and acting with freedom, the people can plan their cities of tomorrow. And, in the words of John Ruskin, "let it be as such work that our descendants will thank us for . . . and that men will say, as they look upon the labor and the wrought substance of them, 'See this our fathers did for us.' "

---

12. Thomas Guthrie, "The City, Its Sins and Sorrows," *Sunday Magazine,* Scotland, 1857.

CHAPTER 45

REGIONAL CONCEPTS

Many persons, like Lewis Mumford, have contributed to the understanding of the complexities of the planning process. Few have understood as well as he the essential relationships between local and regional planning and the dependence on national policies in the development of civilized communities.

An ecology of natural and human resources is linked inextricably with the ecology of urban resources in the industrial age. In the final decades of the twentieth century, complicated social, economic, and technological phenomena have extracted the dimensions of urbanization beyond the concentration of traditional cities. It should be the objective of a civilized society to achieve a harmonious, attractive, convenient, and healthy living environment. The extent to which we meet this challenge will be the test of contemporary society. Thus far, the prospects are not encouraging. Creeping urbanization is engulfing entire regions, reducing the significance of political boundaries between cities and counties to a shambles of legal technicalities.

The growing regional agglomerations along the northern Atlantic and southern Pacific coasts are well known, and no viable mechanism of government has been devised to deal with these massive groupings of people and conflicting overlapping public and private institutions. New public policies are required, fashioned at national and state levels of government, to direct the distribution of population, industry, transportation, and the conservation of resources essential to sustain the structure of the national economy.

URBAN ECOLOGY

REGIONAL PLANNING EFFORTS

Like many other important programs for public improvement, regional planning efforts started with a group of dedicated and concerned private citizens. Observing the many areas where public functions overlapped and wastefully duplicated activities, this group of persons, including Charles H. Whitaker, Benton Mac-Kaye, Clarence Stein, Henry Wright, and Lewis Mumford, formed the influential Regional Planning Association of America (RPAA) in 1923, an informal group dedicated to social betterment through planning. At about the same time the RPAA was being formed, another private effort was starting—this one to produce a regional plan for New York and environs. The work was directed by Thomas Adams, a Scot who had worked on Letchworth and Welwyn, garden cities outside London.

The efforts of both groups resulted in the preparation of comprehensive reports citing the virtues of regional planning and are, in fact, the basis for some of the efforts that initiated the development of the New York–New Jersey Port Authority, a regional effort affecting both New York and New Jersey.

In the early days of the New Deal, President Franklin Delano Roosevelt proposed and the Congress created the National Resources Board, a federal agency that later became the National Resources Planning Board. The board produced voluminous reports dealing with every aspect of broad-gauge planning. In the final term of President Roosevelt's administration, Congress, alienated by some of the efforts of the board, cut the appropriations that supported it. The president continued to finance its activities with special funds until the end of his terms.

It is difficult to evaluate the byproducts of this effort. Although the individual recommendations have little or no application today, the overall recognition of the importance of regional planning has affected many parts of the states and the nation. For instance, the army divided the nation into its own form of regions, the Federal Reserve Board created others, and so on.

The one great regional planning effort supported by President Roosevelt and Congress was the Depression-born Tennessee Valley Authority (TVA). This project achieved the goals that had been set for it, including flood control and the development of electric power in an area badly needing it. At about the same time the Port of New York Authority was created. Its function has been to promote commerce and transportation in the New York metropolitan area and, like the TVA, it has affected several states.

A more limited example of regional planning is the Los Angeles County Regional Planning Commission. Created in 1923, it was initially charged with drawing up a master plan for Los Angeles County (some 4,000 square miles). The commission's main objective at that time was to develop a network of major and secondary highways. Programs were also initiated in the Midwest and in Canada.

REGIONAL PLANNING

Regional planning offers a marked advantage for contiguous areas sharing common interests. Such matters as air pollution, unified circulation systems, water distribution, and sewage and solid waste disposal cannot be regulated by an individual community. An overriding authority with the power to enforce decrees is needed to deal with these problems.

Why So Little?

The main reason why so little regional planning has been done is that local political entities fear a loss of their power. Another reason is that a regional agency, if it is to have real authority, must have the power to tax. This alone is enough to frighten local communities into opposition. One more taxing body, one more layer of government, seems to add up to additional expenses for what is seen as a superfluous governmental body.

In the early 1970s California tried to establish planning districts. Meetings were held in various areas of the state to determine the districts that had common economic, social, and cultural interests. The result: the local communities resented the initiative that had been taken by the state; the project was a fiasco.

John Friedman, in his "The Concept of a Planning Region," states:

> Regional planning in the United States has at various times had reference to different types of activity as well as to different types of area. There was a time, roughly 1933 until the end of World War II, when regional planning meant primarily the development of water resources and the adjacent land resources within a given river basin. The basic planning unit was the watershed and the objective, the fullest possible use of all physical resources for the improvement of living levels within the area. The Tennessee Valley Authority has been the outstanding example of this type of planning, but a number of other river basins have followed suit: the Columbia; the Central Valley of California; the Missouri; the Arkansas; and the Red River. The TVA, however, remains the only authority in full charge of a comprehensive development program.[1]

During the past few years in almost every state there has been created one or more coordinating agencies concerned with aspects of regional planning. These councils of government (COG) are usually voluntary associations with little or no power other than to make an effort at coordination of the individual planning going on in the various member communities.

NATIONAL PLANNING

Despite the inability of independent community jurisdictions to cope with air contamination, transportation, sanitation, and water supply, the concept of local control is retained with fanatical fervor. The rule of "divide and conquer" breeds intense rivalry between cities and counties for economic advantage. Competition to capture the maximum tax-productive enterprise justifies irrational land uses, induces the relaxation of development standards to attract business and industry, and favors local politicians bent on perverting the public interest to the benefit of special interests. National planning is needed for the conservation of natural resources, the designation of areas in which the new urbanization would be compatible with related land uses, new industrial and energy development, and transportation by land and air.

The United States

With the possibility for a population increase of 60 million in the United States by 2000 A.D., urban centers will have to accommodate nearly 40 million more people than now occupy the nation's cities, or the equivalent of forty new cities of one million. New forms of urban development will be needed.

Land use planning at state and national levels of government is either faltering or nonexistent. A galaxy of "regulating agencies" struggles within limited and often competing jurisdictions. The annual cost of preparing environmental impact statements by only three of the federal agencies was $16 million and countless

---

1. John Friedman and William Alonzo, eds., *Regional Development and Planning* (Cambridge, Mass.: MIT Press, 1964).

worker hours, with few if any national policies by which to measure the validity of these studies.[2] These costs have increased tremendously in the past decade.

Piecemeal planning in 1992 is a costly undertaking. Consolidation of the fragmented budgets for administration of public resources would provide a tidy sum with which to launch a comprehensive national planning program. It will call for a national commitment to the public interest unprecedented in the nation's history. Some measure of the gap between necessity and realization has been illustrated by the fate of Federal Land Use Planning Legislation[3] in the Congress. After strong support by environmentalists, state governors, and the House Committee on the Interior, as late as 1974 the legislation was sidetracked by adverse political manipulation, in what the *New York Times* referred to as "a perversion of the democratic process" on a "question of immense national importance." No progress is yet visible at a national level, and with the current federal attitudes, little immediate change can be anticipated.

Changing Patterns of Land Settlement: Israel

Rural settlement in Israel can be described as a synthesis of European and traditional/local models imbued with modern social concepts. Two main patterns have evolved: the collective and the cooperative. A third intermediate pattern, combining joint production with individual domestic living, has exerted considerable influence on other settlement forms in spite of its limited numbers. All settlement patterns in Israel adhere to the principle of agglomeration, but without sacrificing farmyard space. Adequate room for farmyard activities has encouraged diversification and facilitated the expansion of production.

The amalgamation of rural settlements into an independent system of regional cooperation is another common feature of the Israeli village. The physical plans reflect the tendency to shift to bigger units in order to achieve economies of scale in supporting services and specific production lines. The resulting returns, both in economic and social areas, have generated new sources of employment for the younger generation, thereby counteracting the universal trend of depopulation that usually follows the modernization of agriculture.[4]

Current Regional Planning in Israel

The regional development bloc was a concept that evolved in Israel during the 1960s where, clusters of cooperative agricultural villages of the three types mentioned above were established near each other with strong regional councils to deal with matters of common social and economic concern. A large urban center served both as an industrial base and marketing outlet as well as the site of hospitals, high schools, theaters, and other facilities designed to serve the entire region.

The most successful bloc was established in the Lachish area of the northern Negev, with a total of twenty-nine villages. At its hub is the town of Kiryat Gat, where the cotton and sugar beets grown in the region are processed, heavy equipment is repaired, and other commercial, administrative, social, and industrial services are provided.

---

2. Estimated cost for environmental impact statements by the Atomic Energy Commission was $6 million; Department of Agriculture, $2 million; Department of the Interior, $8 million. *Traffic Quarterly*, Eno Foundation, January 1974.

3. H.R. 10294.

4. Jacob O. Maos, in *Papers and Proceedings, 35th World Congress, International Federation for Housing and Town Planning*, Jerusalem, 1980.

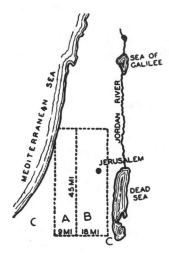

A Lands for City People
B Lands for Priests
C Lands for Princes

Regional planning in ancient times. *While in captivity in the sixth century* B.C., *the Israelites planned their return to Jerusalem. In Ezekiel 25:45 the prophet had described plans desired by God for the allocation and use of the land on their return. An area of 10,000 by 25,000 reeds (18 by 45 miles) was to be set aside for the people of the city. The land on both sides of these areas was reserved as princely lands.*
There was no indication of the precise location of the boundaries. It is probable that Ezekiel understood God's wishes were directed more to the area of land needed for the production and distribution of abundant goods than to the exact location surrounding the city of Jerusalem. Perhaps the amount of land allocated to the people was less than that for the priests because Jerusalem was a crossroads for trade routes; people derived considerable wealth from the resulting commercial enterprise in which they were engaged. The princely lands supported the kings, who maintained residences near the Mediterranean and Dead seas as well as in Jerusalem.

An Israeli plan for the southern area of the country is intended for a population of 900,000 within a total projected population of 5 million by the end of the twentieth century. With the 1990's influx of emigrants from Russia and other central European countries, the prediction is more than realized. The preliminary surveys were completed and the regional scheme is now being implemented. Special attention is devoted to problems of infrastructure. The scheme deals with the siting of urban and rural settlements, improvement of existing settlements, and rural service centers. A special feature is the planning of Bedouin settlements, intended to convert the nomads into settled farmers.

The main water-supply lines have been indicated, as well as the means of storm water interception, and the location of spreading grounds, dams, and other works involved in the water economy. Areas have been indicated for the utilization of natural resources and for basic heavy industries, as well as sites for combined industries, processing raw materials and minerals, major pipelines for conveying crude oil, oil products, natural gas, oil pumping stations, tank farms for oil storage, and sites for plants connected with the processing of oil. Areas have also been sited for national parks and large nature reserves.

After years of intensive study, a route was selected for the Mediterranean–Dead Sea Canal. The canal is more a series of tunnels than an open trench, the usual definition of a canal. The intent of this multipurpose waterway is to bring relatively low-salt water from the Mediterranean Sea to raise the level of the high-salt Dead Sea, or at least to counter the evaporation that has lowered the level of the water in recent years, while at the same time providing for development of electrical energy.

In the course of its meander from the Mediterranean Sea to the Dead Sea the aquaduct passes from sea level some 1312 feet below sea level. In the interim areas, water would be drawn off through adits or towers for agricultural use in the Negev Desert, thus making multiple use of the resource.

STATE PLANNING
Hawaii

National planning requires implementation by the individual states, and state plans are slow to emerge. Hawaii is the first state with such a plan.

Planning was initiated in Hawaii with the creation of a planning commission for Honolulu in 1915, and a zoning law was initiated in 1922. The Territorial Planning Agency established in the late thirties became the State Planning Office when Hawaii became a state in 1957. The State Land Use Law of 1961 defined three basic land use zones for all land in the state: urban, agricultural, and conservation. Regulation of land uses within designated urban zones is administered by the county governments, which also maintain a measure of control within agricultural districts. The conservation zone is administered by the state. Zonal boundaries are defined by the State Land Use Commission.

Both planning and land use zoning are aided by several unique advantages. Overlapping governmental jurisdictions are absent. Each island, with a small number of exceptions, is a county, and each county is surrounded by the permanent "bluebelt" of the Pacific Ocean. Each has a city-type government; there are no independently incorporated cities. Authority for property assessment and taxation is vested in the state government, and taxes are assessed in accordance with land use zoning. The director of state planning and economic development is a member of the governor's cabinet.

Despite this idyllic setting, the people of the island paradise display characteristics similar to those of citizens elsewhere in the nation. Shortly after adoption of the three zoning districts, a fourth zone, rural, was incorporated by the legislature. Within this zone the provision for half-acre lots allows for land exploitation, which the legislation was intended to curb. The rural district was omitted from Oahu, where the declining role of agriculture leads to the pressure for urbanization of agricultural land. This trend is progressing at such a rate that urbanization of the entire island seems imminent.

There is little contemporary evidence that urbanization in Hawaii will be more humane than elsewhere. There have been urban slums in Honolulu for generations, although a benevolent climate somewhat tempers the harshness of typical ghettos. Poverty is a fact of life here, too. It is apparent that the tradition of plantation villages has been forsaken for suburban sprawl, as in other American cities, and the same brutalism is present in the proliferation of ever-taller commercial and residential structures.

The natural beauty of Hawaii has been impaired in the course of accommodating tourists attracted by climate, tropical character, traditions, and the racial blend of the islands' populace. It is not, however, the welcome to brief visitors that presents the major threat. It is the insidious trend toward exploitation of a lovely land for an unlimited increase in permanent population that will inevitably compound the burden of economic support from sources beyond the island shores. How this strong temptation will be controlled is the pressing issue for state and county leadership. In the words of Robert Wenkam, stalwart conservationist: "Treat gently. These are the only Hawaiian Islands we have."[5]

Issues that prompted state planning in Hawaii are even more critical in states on the mainland. The tangled political boundaries between counties and cities, the desperate competition for tax-productive enterprise, and the rivalry between cities to outstrip their neighbors in population statistics all present formidable obstacles to the prospects for rational and essential planning at state and federal levels of government. Yet these same obstacles render the need for planning even more urgent. State planning and broad classifications of land use zoning are as essential to administration of the public business as the general plan and detailed zoning ordinances are at the city and county levels of government.

The annual flood of 300,000 new residents and the 57,000 acres of land converted to urbanization in Florida demand more than measures like the Environmental Land and Water Act, the Water Management Act, and the Land Conservation and Comprehensive Planning Act that the state adopted in 1972; there must be a comprehensive state land use and zoning plan as the basic reference for administration of the state agencies and county or regional authorities. Without such a definition of land use zoning, the ambitious program to evaluate "developments of regional impact" can only drift ineffectually.[6]

Thwarted by political ineptitude and a California state planning department with no plan,[7] a group of enlightened citizens determined to construct a framework for comprehensive planning for the state. Taking into account all aspects of the state's economy, its social structure, and its physical characteristics, the "California Tomorrow Plan"[8] is a guide to state planning. Adopting land use categories similar to Hawaii's, the plan divides the state into four zones: urban, agriculture, conservation, and regional reserves, administered by regional government authorities. This plan was never officially accepted by the state.

Jacob Dash had this to say in 1980:

> There is growing recognition at the national and regional planning levels of the close interdependence of town, region and state resulting from the intensified interconnections and rapid communications which govern modern life in the country. The need is steadily growing for combined planning within one regional framework of rural and urban settlements and of the larger towns. This is essential as a means of assisting the people in finding employment and adequate income from their economic assets, to enable them to receive such services as communications, water supply, sewage, health and educational services, and benefit from gardens, shopping centers and various communal services.
>
> The planners have realized long since the need, when planning a town, of bearing in mind the public, commercial and employment services the town should also supply to the rural areas in its surroundings. Likewise, the planning of a town must

Other States

REGIONALISM ON THE LOCAL LEVEL

---

5. *Hawaii* (Chicago: Rand McNally & Company, 1972).

6. "Developments of regional impact" are equivalent to "environmental impact statements" and are administered under the Comprehensive Planning Act.

7. Alfred Heller observed that after 10 years and an expenditure of $4 million, the State Development Plan Program simply recommended further studies (speech at National Forum on Growth with Environmental Quality, Tulsa, Okla., September 25, 1973).

8. *The California Tomorrow Plan* (Los Altos, Calif.: William Kaufman, 1972).

take into consideration the services, supplies and employment that the town's inhabitants can obtain in the rural areas around it. The lines of communications must be planned so as to meet all these requirements, and the whole combined region must be planned as one organic whole.

Present-day planning trends throughout the world are towards reducing the attraction of metropolitan areas and limiting the growth of large cities.[9]

The City and the Region

Cities are the focal points of intensive economic development within most regions. They are intimately related to the hinterland from which the raw materials are imported. They are also, to a large extent, the purchasers of the finished products. No effective planning can be done without a deep concern for the interrelationships that must be protected and conserved. There can be no waste of resources in this partnership, whether land, water, or energy, without the community structure becoming unbalanced and uneconomic. The social consequences result in both areas losing their viability. Sound planning must take into consideration the total environment that makes the city function as the core for the total economic structure.

Recent efforts at metropolitan area planning take into account the importance of both the urbanized core and the surrounding areas, which in some instances are called the "areas of influence." However, it is important to realize that in most cases the power to control the development of areas surrounding a city lies with the rural government.

REGIONALISM IS IMPERATIVE

In states where urbanization and industrial concentration infringe heavily upon land resources, state zoning and national policies (planning) for industrial allocation and population distribution are imperative. Yet conservation of agriculture, timber, water, and mineral resources is equally vital in the states that thus far have been saved from excess urbanization. The "energy crisis" of the early seventies emphasizes the urgency of this problem.

The necessity for both federal and state financial assistance to support urban functions amply demonstrates that cities and rural areas cannot "go it alone," however attractive the concept of local autonomy may be. Thus far most states rely on reviews by state agencies or on the preparation of environmental impact statements for approval of various types of development in so-called critical areas. The inevitable increase in population can only compound both the number and extent of these critical areas. It would demonstrate appropriate public responsibility to establish land use zoning regulations both to preserve state resources and to set parameters for economic and urban development. Meanwhile, city and county governments struggle at the administrative level and in the courts to maintain some semblance of environmental equilibrium.

Acknowledging the limitations of independent cities in attempting to cope with the full range of urban ills, some forms of regional authorities have already been created. The San Francisco Bay Conservation and Development Commission was created by the state of California in 1965. The Miami Valley Regional Planning Commission has jurisdiction within the metropolitan area around Dayton, Ohio, and the Twin Cities Metropolitan Council encompasses Minneapolis and St. Paul, Minnesota. The Hackensack Meadowlands Development Commission

---

9. Jacob Dash, Speech at the IFHP Conference (International Federation for Housing and Town Planning), Jerusalem, 1980.

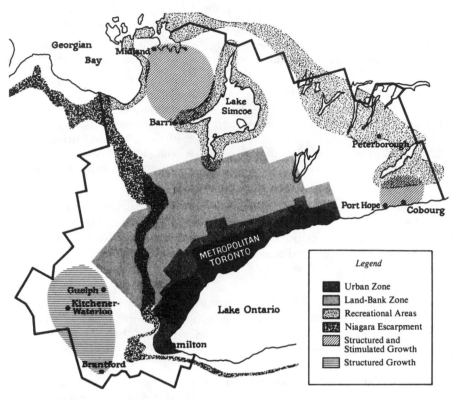

A development concept for the Toronto region. *In 1965 the provincial government of Ontario initiated a program for regional planning and development, centered about the city of Toronto. The program was under the direction of Dr. Richard S. Thoman between 1967 and 1971.*
(Map from Richard Thoman, "A Checklist for California," Cry California, Fall 1974.)

includes fourteen cities and two counties in New Jersey. The regional government of Dade County, Florida, which has jurisdiction over all local communities, is considered highly effective. Councils of government with limited powers have been created in some areas to conform to the federal requirement for a regional clearinghouse for programs involving federal grants.

The California Chapter of the American Planners Association met in March 1990 and recommended many programs of action for consideration by the state legislature and governor. Among these was the need for regional planning and the coordination of all planning and development proposals, as follows:

> *Need.* Although most urban areas of the state are composed of many cities, counties, special districts, and other agencies, there is no requirement that local plans be consistent with one another. Problems of regional significance—transportation, air and water quality, waste disposal, and location of jobs and housing—are exacerbated by local governments making land use decisions in isolation.

> California is too big and diverse for the state to review local plans directly. Yet, existing regional structures have not worked. Councils of Government (COGs) are voluntary and ineffective. Special purpose regional agencies deal with only a single issue such as air quality. Counties have inadequate resources and powers to act as regional planning bodies. There are no means of assuring that the plans of single purpose agencies are consistent with each other, nor that the land use authority exercised by local governments is consistent with regional and statewide goals.

NEED FOR ACTION AND COORDINATION

Regional Planning

Resulting problems include the jobs and housing imbalance, traffic congestion, environmental pollution, and loss of open space.

Goal. Effective regional planning through effective multipurpose regional agencies to assure growth management, environmental protection, and adequate infrastructure.

Recommended Actions. The legislature and governor should enact legislation to define newly elected regional governing bodies. These bodies should have responsibility for both regional planning and growth management and for the functions of the existing special purpose districts within each of the urban and urbanizing areas of California. The boundaries should be large enough to encompass areas likely to urbanize over a 20 year period, and boundaries should be subject to periodic revision. Provisions should be made for subregional agencies within these areas.

The regional agencies should prepare plans for growth and environmental protection of each region which are consistent with the State Growth Management Plan, accommodate the population and employment growth projected for the regions in the State Plan, and are based on the capacity of local areas to accommodate that growth.

The regional agencies should review local general plans for consistency with the regional plan and develop a mediation program to resolve differences. Once approved by the regional agencies, local general plans should be presumed to be adequate under state planning law.

Land Acquisition

Acquisition of land within and around cities has been policy and practice in a number of European countries since the turn of the century. The policy has been implemented in Sweden since 1904; some 200 square miles are now owned by the city of Stockholm, a program that made possible the new towns of Farsta and Vallingby. The development of "land banks" in the United States has been confined to New York, Louisiana, and Puerto Rico. The appropriate responsibility for stewardship of the land has been generally abdicated in favor of private interests in land ownership and development. Partially filling the vacuum, nonprofit "trusts" are acquiring or leasing land to remain as open space. The Nature Conservancy has preserved more than 377,000 acres in various parts of the country, holding the land until public agencies are financially able to acquire it. The Trust for Public Land (TPL) is directly concerned with preservation of a 672-acre ranch for the city of Los Angeles.

It is a gross irony that state legislatures require cities and counties to make plans and enact zoning ordinances in conformance with them, yet reject their own responsibility to create plans and land use zoning for the states. The situation is further aggravated in states that require local communities to plan for open space and conservation; in the absence of funds for the necessary land acquisition, communities are confronted with threats of "inverse condemnation" suits as a result of conforming with state laws.

REGIONAL GREENWAYS

Projects for preserving classic scenic routes of travel and connecting them into a regional network of "greenways" have received new inspiration from the activities of the conservationists in many parts of America. An article in the June 1990 issue of *National Geographic* describes the many successful efforts.[10] The pleasure these pathways afford the walkers, hikers, joggers, and bicyclists make them an

---

10. The list of greenways is based on the map on p. 82, which depicts the grassroots efforts across America. © National Geographic Society, June 1990.

important element in the total scheme of recreation and the conservation of historically important landscape and geographical features.

Some of the most important of these greenways include the Pacific Crest Trail, which runs from San Diego, California, to Seattle, Washington; the Continental Divide Trail, which travels from Mexico to Canada along the Great Divide created by the Rocky Mountains; the North County Trail, which follows the Canadian border from North Dakota to Vermont; the Natchez Trace Trail, from Natchez, Mississippi, to Nashville, Tennessee; the Appalachian Trail, which follows the Appalachian Mountains from Georgia to Maine; and the Potomac Heritage Trail, which serves the Pennsylvania and Maryland areas, including Washington, D.C. The Florida Trail provides for recreational travel from the south of Florida north almost to Alabama on the west.

In addition, there are the specialized large-scale recreational areas, such as the Loxahatchee National Wildlife Refuge; and the Wekiva River Basin, both in Florida; the National Capital Area Greenway serving Washington, D.C.; the Brooklyn-Queens Greenway in New York, and the Olmsted Emerald Necklace in Massachusetts, in 1991 was selected by the American Planners Association as a historical landmark.

The search for money does not stop greenway builders. When city council members at High Point, North Carolina, said the city budget could not afford the entire cost of greenway construction, a citizen group sold "deeds" to foot-long sections of the path. Fifteen hundred miles to the west, trail makers at Pueblo, Colorado, sold bricks inscribed with donors' names and used them for the path's centerline.

Financing the Greenway System

Recognizing a demand for outdoor recreation, more and more states are funneling money from special taxes and user fees to greenways. The National Park Service includes a small division that offers communities technical assistance and advice on greenway acquisition and development.

With its grants from the Land and Water Conservation Fund (LWCF), the federal government has been the single largest funder of recreation corridors. Since its establishment in 1964 as a trust funded by revenue from federal property sales, boat fuel taxes, and oil and gas leases on the continental shelf, the LWCF has generated more than $1 billion for the building of community pathways.

But federal deficits have all but dried up that source. Only $3 million a year is currently dispensed for trails, although legislative efforts to create a federal environmental fund continue.

Deep state and local government pockets are empty, necessitating creative financing. Coalitions of public and private groups are being formed to purchase parklands and greenways, spurring connections over ever-larger areas. New York State, for example, passed legislation in 1988 that called for study of a Hudson River Valley Greenway along 154 miles of the scenic river that is sometimes called America's Rhine.

> "We want to examine every possible opportunity along the corridor—parks, old mansions, preserves, historic sites—and then figure out how to preserve and connect them, so they can be part of an outdoor experience," said Barry Didato, the greenway coordinator for a group called Scenic Hudson, Inc. "With nearly four

million people living in the valley and many more expected by the end of the century, we want to plan open spaces for them to enjoy."

"We're not talking about just one trail or one connection but a network of outdoor experiences," explained Frances Dunwell of New York's Department of Environmental Conservation. "It's more a philosophy of future land use for a whole valley."

Or a nation.[11]

OTHER REGIONAL ACTIVITIES SUBJECT TO PLANNING

The definition of a region varies with the nature of the activities in which the residents are engaged. Thus the air quality control region has only the limits set by nature and the inversions and contaminants released into the atmosphere. The mass transit region is whatever cooperation and coordination can achieve in supplying reasonable service to the multiplicity of communities along the service corridors. The waste disposal region is generally the area where sewers or drainage accommodate waste and control flooding conditions. The educational region generally involves higher education facilities that serve not only the communities in which they are located but, often, the entire world. The criminal activity region spills over all local jurisdictions, creating the need for the cooperation that can only be provided by regional forces, sometimes the county bodies, at other times, state or national organizations. The economic region is produced by many factors and has boundaries of interest that may vary with industrial or commercial activity. For instance, local banking now also involves interstate and international participants. One rarely knows the home base of a local bank. For example, in Los Angeles the Union Bank, formerly local to the region, was acquired by California First Bank a subsidiary of the Bank of Tokyo, Japan. The infrastructure region varies with the nature of the installation, whether it is public or private, and the capacities for service that each element can provide. There are overlaps in many cases where an element of the local infrastructure contracts for services with either unincorporated areas or other municipalities.

CURRENT SIGNIFICANCE OF THE REGIONAL PLAN

Numerous legal cases have called for the community comprehensive plan to be consistent with the regional plan of the subject jurisdiction. Until now it seemed that most, if not all, of the comprehensive plans stopped at a local jurisdictional boundary because of the scarcity of comprehensive regional plans. All this has to change since the courts realized that so many influences on internal problems stemmed from external forces, for instance, transportation, sewerage disposal, air pollution, flooding, access to water, and many other normal, daily impacts on humans.

This raised the question of who will finance the preparation of the regional plans. Will it be the county for the territory within its physical boundaries or will a new level of regional government be created to control the many counties in a geographic area that have common problems that can only be dealt with on a grander scale than that of the individual counties?

Will these new agencies have taxing power? How else can they secure funds to employ the human power to perform their wide-ranging activities? With regional jealousies and competition for economic advantages, how will taxes for this new level of government be generated?

11. "Greenways, Paths to the Future," *National Geographic,* 1990. © National Geographic Society.

As cities and counties face the challenge to their planning efforts, both from the proponents of planning and from those whose proposals are rejected because there is a lack of a frame of reference for adverse decisions for the local actions, the demand for effective regional planning and coordination of policies related to decisions will provide the basis for the designation of regions, the creation of effective administration, and the power to enforce the regional mandates. Survival will depend on cooperation and coordination of previously individual actions and selfish decisions. The nation and state must demand this.

California state law directs cities and counties to refer their proposals for comprehensive plan adoptions and substantial amendments to the Local Agency Formation Commission (LAFCO). The LAFCO has 45 days (from the date the proposal is mailed or delivered) to comment on the project.

LAFCOs are important to the planning process because they have the power to review and approve or disapprove boundary change proposals. These include city incorporations or disincorporation, special district formations or dissolutions, city or special district annexations, detachments or consolidations, or combinations of two or more of these. LAFCOs are responsible for adopting "spheres of influence" that describe "the probable ultimate physical boundaries and service area" of cities and special districts.

As in the case of LAFCOs, state law directs cities and counties to refer proposals for comprehensive plan adoptions and substantial amendments to "any area wide planning agency whose operations may be significantly affected by the proposed action, as determined by the planning agency." Some of these agencies actually carry out their own planning and regulatory activities.

Councils of Governments (COGs) were created under the Joint Exercise of Powers Act. These agencies carry out a range of planning programs affecting land use, housing, transportation, air and water quality, economic development, health systems, and criminal justice. There are both single-county COGs and multicounty COGs. Many are designated as areawide clearinghouses for local grant applications for federal funds.

The weakness of the COGs lies in their dependence on financial support from the cities and counties within their jurisdiction.

FUTURE OF REGIONAL PLANNING

COUNCILS OF GOVERNMENT AND OTHER REGIONAL AGENCIES

Local Agency Formation Commissions

Regional Agencies

Voluntary Councils of Governments

PART 9

METAMORPHOSIS

CHAPTER 46

SYMBOLS OF PURPOSE

Freedom seems to be a natural need of humans. It has been sought and fought for from time immemorial. Transcending the animal's instinct for self-preservation, the human mind makes a person a social entity. The animal's behavior is conditioned by its environment, whereas people have the capacity to mold their environment to their purpose through their intellect. Purpose, then, lies at the vital core of human conduct.

Material progress marks peaks of civilization, but the culture of a people is measured by relative social values and the purpose that directs human progress. The cultivation of human sensibilities, the shaping of intuitive power, and the spiritual content of social institutions elevate a people to the cultural plane. These processes are nurtured in the soil of freedom wherein people share responsibility for society, and individuals are active collaborators with their compatriots in directing mutual affairs.

The city is a laboratory in which the search for freedom is carried on and experiences are tested. The design of the city is the warp and woof of people's lives; the pattern is woven with the toil of mind and hand guided by a purpose. We cannot dissociate purpose from achievement in evaluating affairs or charting a course toward human welfare. We detect symbols of that purpose in city building; symbols of the dominant will of a tyrant or the common weal of free persons, the rigid formality of ruling authority or the plastic form of liberty, the sumptuous pretension of aristocracy or the false symbol of unity: the pyramid.

Forged with the toil of countless slaves, the pyramid is a symbol of the "unity" of uncontested power wielded by autocratic rulers over the lives of people. The emperors of Rome built great fora, a series of huge projects dedicated to the glory of mighty rulers from Rome's past. Each forum was designed about an axis, the arrangement of structures and spaces dictated by symmetry. Like a symbol of undaunted might, the centerline dominated the cities built by emperors, and when their power waned there were no strong citizens to sustain the same social order.

The monarchs of France built avenues and plazas about the symbolic axis of autocratic power. The liberated space of the baroque city was appropriated by rulers rather than the ruled. Louis XIV built his palace and gardens at Versailles. Aloof from the motley crowd of the city, he transferred his court to these magnificent spaces and ordered the streets to focus upon them. *L'état, C'est Moi.* Louis XV built the Place de la Concorde, and in the center of the formal square he placed a statue of himself. The city was a formless mass of slums on which the bloated forms of palaces and gardens, boulevards and plazas, were grafted. The urban population, with no identity as people, became the crowd. Uniform facades lined the avenues as a frame for royalty. The people receded to the borders of the boulevards and took their places as spectators of the stately display rather than as participants.

The city of Hellenic democracy was planned for the people. The houses were designed for the amenities of living, each dwelling arranged as every other dwelling for appropriate orientation and privacy. The agora was the meeting place for people, and the marketplace and center of urban activity designed as an outdoor area for the mingling of citizens. The axis was incidental; it was not a dominant feature. Hellenic builders composed rectilinear forms with subtle refinement, shifted the scene from major to minor squares, and surrounded them with the continuous rhythm of colonnades. Streets did not bisect and obstruct the open space reserved for public assembly, and sculpture adorned the public square about the periphery of the open space. Size itself was not the aim of Greek city builders. The agora was large enough to accommodate the citizen population; its space was commodious, but the urban population was small. A monumental quality in public spaces was obtained through a juxtaposition of small and large spaces, contrast between the shape of forms, and the rhythm of voids and solids. The distinction between space for the movement across and circulation within the simple rectangular forms produced an order of quiet dignity.

Human scale was the measure of design in the Hellenic city, and it likewise guided the builders of the medieval town. Emerging from the Dark Ages and unprotected by the broad reaches of empire, the feudal town huddled within the confines of its encircling walls. The church provided the new common bond for humanity and, in response to the spiritual need of the people, the cathedral dominated the town but was not set apart from its surroundings. Built against other buildings, it formed an integral part of the enclosing walls of the plaza. Town life centered upon this plaza. It was designed for the mingling of people intent upon exchanging the products of their labor and learning the news of their fellow men. The urban facilities were designed for use, and they were arranged accordingly. Roadways traversed the plaza but left open space free for the movement of people. Fountains served the vital function of water supply and they, like buildings and sculpture, were not isolated within the open space of the public squares.

City design is inextricably woven into the social order of people. The design reveals symbols of the dominant economic, social, political, and spiritual patterns of civilization. The city is a melting pot of cultural forces, and its design is the expression.

In the latter part of the eighteenth century and the early nineteenth century social upheaval burst the bonds of monarchical tyranny; the violent tensions of the Industrial Revolution broke the chain of cultural development. A new freedom was unleashed, but uncertainty as to our cultural direction aroused emotional conflicts. An air of overconfidence concealed the indecision of society. The fancy of personal taste was the new right of every individual and it confused critical judgment. Good taste was absent, and ugliness settled upon the city.

ECLECTICISM

Recoiling from the dread monotony of the industrial city, people sought escape from the ugly reality. They cloaked public edifices with an artificial pomposity and found retreat in dwellings that simulated sumptuous surroundings of a glorified ancestry. As though to insulate themselves from aesthetic degradation, the arts donned the mantle of classic pedigree. A cultural veneer obscured the ugly environment of the "brown decades," and eclecticism engulfed society. Artificial taste flavored parlor conversation on the arts. Art became a commodity to be bought, sold, and collected; it moved from the streets of the people into the salon.

The muralist who once adorned the walls of buildings stepped down from his scaffold, retired to his studio, and painted pictures to be framed and hung in galleries. Works of art were no longer integral with the environment of people. The legends in stained glass of the cathedral were replaced by book printing. Sculptured figures draped in Roman togas were fitted into classic pediments of banks and courthouses. Fountains no longer supplied water for the population; they dripped or spouted solely in memory of some event or person.

Civic design reflected the confusion and uncertainty of aesthetics. Scholars studied the cities of old; they observed the assurance and strong centerline of imperialism and the picturesqueness of the Middle Ages. The past was a vast storehouse of historic forms available for reproduction. New buildings, each with its historic prototype, were assembled about a whole complex of axes shooting off in all directions. Plazas were laced with major and minor axes, streets bisected open spaces at diagonals and right angles, avenues focused on pompous structures, and a galaxy of artificial features, statues, fountains, and formal landscape effects were arbitrarily distributed about these spaces. The variety of symmetrical effects interrupted the flow of traffic; both the utility and the scale of open spaces were lost to the people who traversed them.

The grandiose formality of open spaces was awe-inspiring, and the people were impressed. The grand planning of the world's fairs "took." Like the great Mall in Washington, D.C., generous open spaces were admired but did not invite relaxation and rarely served as gathering places for people. Their formal character was like a picture to be observed rather than partaken of. The delightful quality of our capital city lies in the fine old elm trees that grace the residential streets and the quaint Georgian houses of the eighteenth century. Frederick Law Olmsted, the great landscape architect, strove to design open spaces for people rather than as an abstract feature in the grand plan, and Central Park in New

York City is a case in point. While the people might be better served if this huge space had been more adequately distributed, it is nevertheless designed as a natural park for the people to use.

Eclecticism was a masquerade, and a veritable bazaar of planning forms appeared. The face of the city concealed the misshapen bulk behind the masque. Once-functional features occupying a graceful place in the environment of people were now used as decorations on the false face of the city. The shopping street became the main variety show, but there were also special features. Forms of ancient Rome were frozen into civic centers, and plazas were carved out of slums to reveal a railroad station or open a traffic artery. New obstructions were then substituted: interrupting "squares" or "circles" as spots in which to isolate diminutive statues. The entire range of architectural and planning styles from the past was applied to the new city. Tastes were torn asunder in the process of selecting the appropriate garment or applying the right cosmetic. Inspired by the Gothic cathedral, the impressiveness of St. Peter's, the charm of the colonial meeting house, and the dignity of the Georgian mansion, the choice was not an easy one.

SYMMETRY OR FREEDOM?

Democracy in city building is a framework in which the manifold functions of contemporary urban life may be accommodated with freedom of expression. Such freedom in organized society, as we are gradually coming to realize, implies self-discipline and respect for the dignity of all people.

Building laws not only permit but have actually forced an enormous bulk to be loaded on the land. Consequently, the city has been reduced to a network of street pavements lined with facades of unrelated buildings. Architectural banality and chaos are inevitable. The "right" to build as one wishes has approached a degree of license, and the ugliness has frequently provoked the panacea of architectural control.

The proponents of architectural control state that it will not interfere with free expression or democracy. Actually there is little else it can do. By its nature architectural control sets a form, usually in terms of some particular "style of architecture" or its equivalent, and the design is henceforth bound by the capricious taste of a select few.

There are designers who produce a higher order of creative work than those of lesser talent, but should their genius deny the right of self-expression to those of lesser competence? Rare is the genius in the welter of people that can capture the sublime in steel, stone, and space. This is clear when we observe all the buildings of past ages rather than the monuments alone. If talent to produce appropriate and beautiful buildings is limited, it is the task of society to raise the level of competence and widen the cultural horizon, not remove freedom of expression.

The city takes shape over the years through the enterprise of all the people. Moved by their desires, their opportunities, and the evolution of changing conditions, the city is in a continuous state of flux and its plan must accommodate a variety of forms. Eclecticism cultivated the impression that harmony of form is synonymous with symmetry and planning assumed a rigid formality. Symmetry about an axis was assumed to produce a grand unity among the forms of the city. City building did not follow those plans, however, and the result was most discouraging if not a little puzzling: it seemed that planning was a futile enterprise, and indeed the form it had acquired was futile.

There was reason for the failure of "grand" planning: boldly reminiscent of imperial domination over the lives of people, its forms were inimical to the tenets of democracy. Not only is the urge for free expression an integral characteristic of democratic society, it is a distinct right. There can be no "centerline" about which the city of democracy is built; it is a fluid, changing form. The rigid symmetry of formal planning is alien to democracy. An autocrat may decree a great plan and have the power to draft the labor of people to execute it accordingly, but when that power transfers to the people a new concept of urban conduct emerges.

The building of the Piazza of St. Mark's spanned five centuries. In it we find no sterile symmetry. It was an open space in which throngs of people could congregate. The ornate church of St. Mark's was erected in the eleventh century in the flourishing Byzantine style. The Palace of the Doges, built in the fourteenth and fifteenth centuries, was designed in the Gothic style of that period. It was a colorful building, but the facades were simple rectangles facing the sea and forming one side of the Piazzetta. The facade leading from the waterfront was set back to frame a view of the church from the canal. Detached from the church, the Campanile was a powerful accent in the group arrangement. When the Procuriate buildings were built in the late fifteenth and early sixteenth centuries, the Renaissance style was in flower. They were arranged about a long Piazza placed at right angles to the Piazzetta. Located at the intersection of these two plazas, the Campanile was visually linked with the long facades of the Procuriatie Vecchie and Library; the tower was not isolated in space like a centerpiece.

There was variety among the forms, each successive addition to the plaza built in the "style" of its period. The spaces were planned to harmonize these variations: no part was tacked on to complete an "original." The differences in architectural styles enhance the effect of this great plaza; the absence of axial symmetry impresses the observer. The flat facade of the Doges' Palace was not imitated elsewhere to conform to a preconceived "scheme"; the facades of the Procuriate buildings were stretched into an oblong plan at an angle to the Piazzetta, and the contrasts in the forms and space were emphasized by slanting the buildings in plan. The plastic quality of this great plaza is eloquent refutation of the sterile process of symmetrical planning which has been frequently substituted for monumentality in our period of eclecticism.

Forms may be harmoniously integrated by appropriate contrasts—contrasts in plan forms adjusted to accommodate the contrasts in contemporary expression as it evolves in successive periods of culture. Michelangelo sought such a contrast when he selected the location for his sixteenth-century statue of David against the background of the rough-hewn walls of the fourteenth-century Palazzo Vecchio in Florence. Rather than becoming an unrelated centerpiece to which similar features have since degenerated, this statue was treated as an integral part of the design of the Piazza dei Signoria.

CHAPTER 47

EPILOGUE

The legitimate object of government is to do for a community of people whatever they need to have done, but cannot do so well for themselves in separate and individual capacities.

Abraham Lincoln

Any attempt to project into the future of a city, even if only into the short-range future of ten to twenty years, must attempt to define the variables that could, in the intervening years, affect the course of that city's development. But even before this can be done, existing conditions must be evaluated. So far, cities have not developed comprehensive approaches to solving the problems they face. Responses have only been to emergency situations. Band-Aids have been applied, or the problems have been swept under the municipal rug in the hope that they will go away. There must be a new attempt to understand the effects on cities of the multiple impacts of growth, decay, and economic impoverishment, especially when they occur at the same time.

The real crux in predicting the future lies in whether we have a choice in determining that future, and who the "we" are who will make that choice. Depending on attitudes and economic and political policies, it is possible to imagine many alternative scenarios for the shape of future cities.

Scenario 1: Cities will continue in the direction they are going.

Cities will get older, and they will reflect the serious economic problems that face the nation as a whole. The larger the city, the more complex the economic problems will be that relate to the provision of services protecting the health, safety, and general welfare of its inhabitants.

Scenario 2: Cities will improve in response to enlightened leadership.

Massive allocation of funds will be redirected toward the improvement of the physical/social structure of cities, and people's hope for life in the city will be reborn. Redevelopment and revitalization programs will face up to and meet the housing crisis, and there will be new opportunities and assurances for improved economic futures. With abundant open space and clean air, the city will become the refuge that it should be, bringing light, friendliness, and security.

Scenario 3: Terminalitis

The danger of accidental or planned conflict cannot be discounted lightly. The mass destruction of cities, as well as all other places of human habitation, could occur. It matters little if the neutron bomb will only destroy people while leaving structures intact or if the "regular" megaton nuclear bombs destroy both buildings and people indiscriminately. The end result will be the same: cities without people or cities of brutalized people without the essential life supports that make existence possible.

The remains of Ephesus, Mycenae, Knossos, Tyre, Babylon, Athens, Ancient Rome, Luxor, Machu Picchu, Angkor, and the many other cities born in ancient times remind us of the temporal nature of all human handiwork. If the "terminal scenario" is acted out, archaeologists examining the ruins will wonder how a civilization with the wealth and capabilities and the genius of persons such as Ebenezer Howard, Clarence Stein, Henry Wright, Le Corbusier, Frank Lloyd Wright, and other "philosophers" with concepts of better cities could have come to such an end.

URBAN PLANNERS AS SURVIVALISTS

Some Native Americans believed that all life is a circle. In the course of history, city after city has come and gone, sometimes to be replaced in the birth of new and better cities that will survive for quite a long time into the future. Some have disappeared as a result of natural forces: others have disappeared through human corruption, waste, and abuse of resources. Will this be the fate of twentieth-century cities? Is the life of our cities to be part of a great circle? There is no doubt that the serious urban planner, as a survivalist, takes a forward-looking approach based on the nature of the profession.

COMMUNICATIONS REVOLUTION

In this age, where communications between outer space and the earth could bring people in contact with each other to resolve their problems in peace and harmony, we find instead that person-to-person communications are disrupted by clouds of suspicion and fear. With the radio, television, and other means at our disposal it appears that people have been drawn inward by events close to their habitat. Never before in the history of the earth have people been closer to each other yet farther apart—locally, nationally, and internationally. The very means that could open avenues of cultural pleasure are to a great extent exploiting brutality and violence.

WISDOM AND KNOWLEDGE

Many years ago T. S. Eliot asked, "Where is the wisdom we have lost in knowledge? Where is the knowledge we have lost in information?" Since then we have moved farther down the same path and can ask, "Where is the information we have lost in data? Where is the data we have lost in computers?"

The new electronic technologies offer exciting possibilities for handling and processing data, but they do not give us the wisdom required to resolve the great dilemmas that confront our civilization. What we must now do is create a world future network, that is, a system that will link up people and institutions all over the world so that they can communicate effectively with each other. Communication is an essential preliminary to collaboration. If we can use the new technology to share our knowledge, our ideas, our dreams on a global scale, we may be able, little by little, to agree on planetary goals and begin to work harmoniously together.

"Communications and the Future" will be a major step in the creation of the world future network that can provide a basis for global wisdom that we desperately need to manage our planet during this period of convulsive change.[1]

OBSER-VATIONS

The patterns of urbanism are much the same the world over. The texture of the fabric that constitutes an urban complex may vary from one country to another, from one area of a nation to another, but the basic elements do not vary. Urban areas, be they large or small, all need places for residences, places for commerce and industry, places for recreation and open space, and places for transportation and communication systems.

As long as there are cities they will, to a greater or lesser degree, depend on the surrounding rural areas for the many ingredients necessary to sustain and support life. Conversion and distribution of goods and the reinforcing of people's efforts in the rural areas are among the responsibilities of urban areas.

Short of catastrophic destruction, the urban places of the world will, in one form or another, continue to exist. The pattern that urbanism will take should, if the people of the future learn from history, result in better, more civilized environments where people can enjoy freedom from fear and corruption. Cities and other urban places should be dedicated to assuring both internal peace of mind and freedom from the aggressive competition that destroys those human values so essential to the survival of an intelligent society.

To these hopes and ideas, *The Urban Pattern* is dedicated.

---

1. Edward Cornish, president, World Future Society General Assembly and Exposition, Washington, D.C., July 1982.

BIBLIOGRAPHY

PART 1

Amos, William H. *Hawaii, Cradle of Life*. Washington, D.C. National Geographic Society, July, 1990.

Attenborough, David. *Destruction of the Rain Forest*. Portrait of the Earth. Los Angeles: BBC Broadcast via KCET. July 26, 1990.

Boslough, John. *The Enigma of Time*. Washington, D.C.: National Geographic Society, December, 1989.
——. *California, The Next Frontier*. San Francisco: California Tomorrow, Summer, 1982.

Conniff, Richard. *Rain Forest Patrol—Countdown in Ecuador*. Washington, D.C.: Smithsonian Magazine, July 1991.

Cottrell, Leonard. *Lost Worlds*. N.Y.: American Heritage Co., 1962.

Council on Environmental Quality 12th Annual Report. Washington, D.C.: U.S. Government Printing Office, 1981.
Arid and Semi Arid Ecosystems and Desertification
Crop Resources
Environment and Natural Resources
Mineral Resources
National Effort to Protect Air Quality
National Resources Planning Act
Water Resources

Currier, Jim. *The Colorado River—A River Drained Dry*. Washington, D.C.: National Geographic Society, June, 1991.

Ellis, William S. *California's Harvest of Change*. Washington, D.C.: National Geographic Society, February 1990.

Ellis, William S. *Soviet Sea Lies Dying*. Washington, D.C.: National Geographic Society, February, 1991.

Findley, Rowe. *Will We Save Our Endangered Forests?* Washington, D.C.: National Geographic Society, September, 1990.

Fineman, Mark. *India's Gamble on the Holy Naramada*. Wash. D.C.: The Destruction of the Forests & Etc., Smithsonian, Nov., 1990.
——. *Ecology Defined*. Danbury, Connecticut. Encyclopedia Americana, 1948 Edition, Grolier Corporation.

Gibbons, Boyd. *The Plant Hunters*. Washington, D.C. National Geographic Society, August, 1990.
——. *Guideline For Solar Access*. Sacramento, California. California Energy Commission, March, 1980.

Halle', Francis. *A Raft Atop The Rain Forest*. Washington, D.C.: National Geographic Society, October, 1990.

Heller, Alfred & Samuel Wood. *Fuelish Hopes*. San Francisco, CA: The Next Frontier California Tomorrow, Summer, 1982.

Hoffman, Carl. *Tractors Pull Their Own

Weight. Washington, D.C.: Smithsonian Associates, August, 1991.

Housing & Urban Development Department. *Environmental Assessment For Project Level Action*. Washington, D.C.: 1974.

Hutchison, Robert A. *Tree Huggers Of The Himalayas*. Washington, D.C.: Smithsonian Magazine, February, 1988.

———. *Landscape Ecology*. University of California, Davis Extension Catalogue, October, 1990.

Mader, George. *Hazard Planning*. San Francisco: California Planner, California Chapter, APA, March, 1980.

Marks, Wesley. *Disaster Planning*. San Francisco: Cry California, California Tomorrow, Summer, 1978.

Mayer, Jim. *Natural Waste Treatment*. Sacramento: Sacramento Bee. October, 1990.

McLaughlin, Donald A. *Man's Selective Attack On Ores and Minerals*. Man's Role in Changing the Face of the Earth, University of Chicago Press, 1956.

Miller, Peter. *Comeback Of Nuclear Power*. Washington, D.C.: National Geographic Society, August, 1991.

Mumford, Lewis. "The Natural History of Urbanization" In *Man's Role in Changing the Face of the Earth*. Ed. William L. Thomas, Sr. Chicago: University of Chicago Press, 1956.

———. *Need for Economic Planning*. San Francisco: California Tomorrow, Fall/Winter, 1981.

Pac. Gas & Elec. Co. *It Can Be Done*. Rpt. to Stockholder, Oct. 1990.

———. *Planet Earth*. KQED Pittsburgh, in association with National Academy of Science, 1985 (Video).

Parfit, Michael. *You Could See It Coming*. Washington, D.C.: Smithsonian Associates, June, 1989.

Raines, Diana. *Massive Dam Project in Anatolia*. Washington, D.C.: Smithsonian Associates, August, 1990.

Rathje, William L. *Once and Future Landfills,* Washington, D.C.: National Geographic Society, May, 1991.

Reich, Hanns. *The World From Above*. N.Y.: Hill and Wang, 1966.

Rhoades, Robert E. *World Food Supply At Risk*. Washington, D.C.: National Geographic Society, April 1991.

———. *Solar Access, A Guidebook for California Communities*. Sacramento:

California Energy Commission, March, 1980.

Southern Sierran. *The 101st Congress and The Environment*. San Francisco, California: Sierra Club, December, 1990.

Sterling, Dr. Raymond, John Carmady. Gail Efnicky. *Earth Sheltered Community Design*. New York: Van Nostrand Reinhold Co., 1981.

Wagner, Richard H. *Environment and Man*. New York: W.W. Norton, 1971.

———. *Water Planning*. San Francisco. Cry California, edited by Alfred Heller, Fall/Winter, 1981.

Zhu Yuchao. *Tangshan Earthquakes*. China Reconstructs, March, 1986.

PART 2

Adams, Thomas. *Outline of Town and City Planning*. New York: Russell Sage Foundation, 1935.

———. *Ancient Egypt*. Washington, D.C.: National Geographic Society, 1978.

Bannister, Turpin. *Town Planning in New York State*. American Society of Architectural Historians.

Bemis, Albert and John Burchard. *The Evolving House, Vol. I* A History of the Home. Cambridge, Massachusetts: Mit Press 1933–36.

Bosanquet, R. C. *Greek and Roman Towns*. Town Planning Review, October, 1915.

Breasted, James Henry. *Ancient Times*. A History of the Early World. Boston: Ginn & Co., 1914.

Brion, Marcel. *Pompeii and Herculaneum*. New York: Crown Publishers, 1960.

Clark, Kenneth. *Civilization*. New York: Harper and Row, 1969.

Giulio, Gianelli, ed. *World of Ancient Rome*. New York: Putnam, 1967.

Glotz, Gustave. *The Greek City and Its Institutions*. Translated by N. Mallison. London: Routledge & Kega, 1929.

———. *The Aegean Civilization*. New York: Alfred A. Knopf, 1925.

Green, Constance M. *American Cities in the Growth of the Nation*. New York: John de Graff, 1957.

Hammerstrand, Nils. *Cities Old and New*. Journal of the American Institute of Architects, 1926.

Hatt, P. K., and Reiss, A. J., Jr. *Cities and Society*. The Revised Reader in Urban Sociology. Glencoe: Free Press, 1957.

Haverfield, Francis J. *Ancient Town Planning* Oxford: Clarendon Press, 1913.

———. *Town Planning in the Roman World*. Town Planning Conference, Transactions, R.I.B.A., London, 1910.

Hiberseimer, Ludwig. *The New City*. Chicago: Paul Theobald, 1944.

———. *The Nature of Cities: Origin, Growth, and Decline*. Pattern and Form: Planning Problems. Chicago: Paul Theobald, 1955.

Hiorns, Frederick Robert. *Town Building in History*. London: Harrap LTD., 1956.

Korn, Arthur. *History Builds the Town*. London: Lund Humphries, 1953.

Lee, R. H. *The City: Urbanism and Urbanization in Major World Regions*. Philadelphia: J. B. Lippincott, 1955.

Macaulay, Rose, and Roloff, Beny. *Pleasure of Ruins*. Norwich: Thames and Hudson, 1964.

Maiuri, Amedeo. *Pompeii*. Novara, Italy: Instituto Geographico De Agostini, 1960.

Marinatos, Spyridon. *Crete & Mycenae*. New York: Harry N. Abrams, 1961.

Marshall, Sir John. *Mohenjo-daro and the Indus Civilization*. London: Arthur Probsthain, 1931.

Mathioulaks, C. H. R. *Knossos*. Athens: Mathioulakis & Gouvoussis, 1974.

Mayer, Harold H., and Kohn, Clyde F. *Readings in Urban Geography*. Chicago: University of Chicago Press, 1959.

McDonald, William A. *The Political Meeting Places of the Greeks*. Baltimore, Johns Hopkins University Press, 1943.

Moses, Robert. *What Happened to Haussmann*. Architectural Forum, July, 1942.

———. *The Condition of Man*. New York: Harcourt, Brace, 1938.

———. *City Development*. New York: Harcourt, Brace, 1945.

———. *The Natural History of Urbanization.* In International Symposium on Man's Role in Changing the Face of the Earth. Chicago: University of Chicago Press, 1956.

———. *The City in History: Its Origins, Its*

Transformations, and Its Prospects. New York: Harcourt, Brace, 1961.

Mumford, Lewis. "Natural History of Urbanization." In *Man's Role in Changing the Face of the Earth.* Ed. William L. Thomas, Sr. University of Chicago Press, 1956.

Murphy, Raymond E. *The American City: An Urban Geography.* New York: McGraw-Hill, 1966.

National Geographic Society, editors. *Our Continent: A Natural History of North America.* Washington, D.C.: National Geographic Society, 1976.

Nien Ting Chang. *Lu Kaing, An Old Port in Taiwan.* Unpublished paper, U.C.L.A., 1974.

Peets, Elbert. *The Genealogy of L'Enfant's Washington.* Journal of the American Institute of Architects, April–June, 1927.

Pirenne, Henri. *Medieval Cities.* Translated by Frank Halsey. Princeton: Princeton University Press, 1925.

Reich, Hans. *The World From Above.* New York: Hill & Wang, 1966.

Robson, W. A., ed. *Great Cities of the World: Their Government, Politics and Planning.* New York: Macmillan Publishing Co. 1955.

Roseman, Rose. *The Ideal City.* Boston Book & Art Shop, 1959.

Sandstrom, Gosta E. *Man the Builder.* New York: McGraw-Hill, Inc., 1970.

Seminar Research Bureau. *City in Crisis.* Chestnut Hill: Boston College, 1959.

Sitte, Camille. *The Art of Building Cities.* New York: Reinhold Publishing, 1945.

Smithsonian Institution. *Bureau of Ethnology, 8th Annual Report.* Government Printing Office, 1891.

———. *Splendors of the Past, Lost Cities of The Ancient World.* Washington, D.C.: National Geographic Society, 1981.

Stewart, C. A. *Prospect of Cities: Being Studied Towards a History of Town Planning.* London: Longmans, Green & Co., 1952.

Straus and Wegg. Housing Comes of Age. New York: Oxford University Press, 1938.

Thomas, William I., ed., with the collaboration of Carl O. Sauer, Marston Bates, & Lewis Mumford. *Man's Role in Changing the Face of the Earth.* University of Chicago Press, 1956.

———. *The World of the American Indian.* A Compilation of Essays, Washington, D.C.: National Geographic Society, 1974.

Tunnard, C. *The City of Man.* New York: Scribner, 1953.

Wallbank, T. Walter, and Taylor. Alastair M. *Civilian Past and Present.* Chicago: Scott Foresman & Co., 1942.

Williams, Henry Smith. *The Historians, History of the World.* The Outlook Co., 1904.

Wirth, Louis. *Urbanism as a Way of Life.* American Journal of Sociology 44. July, 1938.

Wolfe, M. R. *Locational Factors—Suburban Land Development.* Prepared for the Weyerhaeuser Co. in the College of Agriculture and Urban Planning. Seattle: University of Washington, July, 1961.

Wycherley, R. E. *How the Greeks Built Cities.* New York: Macmillan Publishing Co., 1949.

———. *The World of the American Indian.* Washington, D.C.: National Geographic Society, 1974.

The Yugoslav Review Magazine. *Yugoslav Cities.* Turisheka Stampa Publishers, 1961.

Yutang, Lin. *Imperial Peking.* New York: Crown Publishers, 1961.

PART 3

Abercrombie, Patrick. *Greater London Plan, 1944.* London: His Majesty's Stationery Office, 1945.

Abrams, Charles. *The Future of Housing.* New York: Harper & Brothers, 1946.

Albutt, Dr. Clifford. *The Degraded Environment.* England, 1865.

Alm, Ulla. *Cooperative Housing In Sweden.* Stockholm: The Royal Swedish Commission, 1939.

American Institute of Architects. *Reports of a Committee on Community Planning.* New York: 1924, 1925, 1926, 1927.

ASCORAL. *Les Trois Establissements Humains.* Paris: DeNoel, 1945.

Bartholomew, Harland. *Urban Land Uses.* (Harvard City Planning Series).

Cambridge: Harvard University Press, 1932.

Bauer, Catherine. *Modern Housing.* Boston: Houghton Mifflin Co., 1934.

Bhattacharjee, Professor K. D. *Strategy for Housing Development in India 1980–1990.* IFHP World Conference. Jerusalem, 1980.

Boardman, Philip. *Patrick Geddes: Maker of the Future.* Chapel Hill: University of North Carolina Press, 1944.

Burnham, Daniel H., and Bennett, Edward H. *Plan of Chicago.* Edited by Charles Moore. Chicago: Commercial Club, 1909.

———. *Census of Population, General Characteristics.* U.S. Summary 1980. U.S. Dept. of Commerce Bureau of the Census.

Community Redevelopment Agency of Sacramento. *Blight Defined.* (Brochure). Sacramento: 1984.

Davis, Martha M. *U.S. City Planners in China: Chicago: Urban Planning Update.* APA, Chicago: May, 1980.

DeForest and Veiller. *The Tenement House Proble. Vols. I and II.* New York: Macmillian Publishing Co., 1903.

———. *Economic Management in China.* Modern China Series No. 4, Anglo–Chinese Educational Institute, Beijing, 1976.

Encyclopedia Britannica. *Land, Vol. 14. R. S. Peal Edition.* Chicago: The Werner Co., 1982.

Ford, James. *Slums and Housing.* Cambridge: Harvard University Press, 1936.

Forshaw, J. H., and Abercrombie, Patrick. *County of London Plan.* London: Macmillan & Co., 1943.

Geddes, Patrick. *City of Deterioration and the Need of City Survey.* The Annals of the American Academy of Political and Social Sciences. July, 1909.

———. *Talks From My Outlook Tower.* Survey Graphic. February–April, 1925.

George, Henry. *Progress and Poverty.* Canaan: Phoenix Publishing, 1979.

Gerckens, Laurence C. *American City Planning Since 1900 A.D.* 1976–77 ed. Unpublished syllabus. Columbus: Ohio State University.

Graham, John. *Housing in Scandinavia.* Chapel Hill: University of North Carolina Press, 1940.

Hardy, Charles O., assisted by Kucznzki, Robert R. *The Housing Program of the City of Vienna.* Washington, D.C.: The Brookings Institution, 1934.

Hegemann, Werner. *City Planning: Housing, Vol. I, Historical and Sociological.* New York: Architectural Book Publishing Co., 1936.

———. *City Planning: Housing, Vol. II, Political Economy and Civic Art.* New York: Architectural Book Publishing Co., 1938.

———. *City Planning: Housing, Vol. III, A Graphic Review of Civic Art.* New York: Architectural Book Publishing Co., 1938.

Hoagland, Henry. *Real Estate Principles.* New York: McGraw-Hill, 1940.

Hong Kong 1985. Hong Kong: Hong Kong Government Information Service, 1985.

Hong Kong 1991. *A Review of 1990.* Hong Kong Government Information Service, 1991.

———. *Housing: The Facts.* Hong Kong Government Information Service, 1990.

Housing and Public Health Committee. *London Housing.* London: London County Council, 1937.

Hoyt, Homer. *100 Years of Land Values in Chicago.* Chicago: University of Chicago Press, 1933.

Jahansson, Alf, and Svenson, Waldemar. *Swedish Housing Policy: The Royal Swedish Commission.* Annals of the American Academy of Political and Social Sciences, May, 1938.

Johnson-Marshall, Percey. *Rebuilding Cities.* Chicago: Aldine Publishing Co., 1966.

Justement, Louis. *New Cities for Old.* New York: McGraw-Hill, 1946.

Le Courbusier. *The City of Tomorrow.* London: The Architectural Press, 1929.

———. *La Villa Radieuse.* Boulogne, 1934.

———. *When the Cathedrals Were White.* New York: Reynal & Hitchcock, 1947.

———. *Concerning Town Planning.* Translated by Clive Entwistle. New Haven: Yale University Press, 1948.

Lohmann, Karl B. *Principles of City Planning.* New York: McGraw-Hill, 1931.

McAllister, Gilbert, and Glen, Elizabeth. *Town and County Planning.* London: Faber & Faber, 1941.

McQuade, Walter. *Cities to Live In and How We Can Make Them Happen.* New York: Macmillan, 1971.

McRae, John. *Elderly in the Environment: Northern Europe.* Gainesville: University Press of Florida, 1975.

———. *Metroplan, The Aims.* Hong Kong Government, April, 1988.

Moore, Charles. *Daniel Burnham: Architect, Planner of Cities.* Boston, 1921.

Mumford, Lewis. *The Story of the Utopias.* Magnolia: Peter Smith Publishers, Inc., 1922.

Olmsted, Frederick Law. *Public Parks and the Enlargement of Towns.* New York: Amo, 1980 (reprint of 1870 edition).

———. *New World of Space.* New York: Reynal & Hitchcock, 1948.

Osman, John. *The City as a Sacramental Act.* Architectural Forum, August, 1957.

———. *Population Densities.* London and New York City: American Encyclopedia 1875 Vol. XII, p. 382.

Reps, John W. *The Making of Urban America.* Princeton: Princeton University Press, 1965.

Riis, Jacob. *How the Other Half Lives.* New York: Charles Scribner's Sons, 1934.

Robinson, Joan. *Economic Management in China.* Modern China Series. London: Anglo-Chinese Education Institute, Nov., 1976.

Scott, Mel. *Cities are for People.* Los Angeles: Pacific Southwest Academy, 1942.

Sert, Jose. *Can Our Cities Survive?* Cambridge: Harvard University Press, 1942.

Simon, Sir E. D. *Rebuilding Britain: A Twenty Year Plan.* London: Victor Gollanez, Ltd., 1945.

———. *The Rebuilding of Manchester.* New York: Longmans, Green & Co., 1935.

———. *Statistical Abstracts of the U.S. Census.* Department of Commerce, Bureau of the Census, 1984, 1991.

Steffens, Lincoln. *The Shame of the Cities.* New York: Hill & Wang, 1957.

Stein, Clarence. *The Price of Slum Clearance.* Architectural Forum, February, 1934.

Stern, Sylvia. *Housing for the Elderly.* Unpublished paper. U.C.L.A., 1978.

Stokes, Bruce. *Housing, The Environmental Sleeper.* Sacramento: Sierra Magazine, September-October, 1982.

Straus, Nathan. *The Seven Myths of Housing.* New York: Alfred A. Knopf, 1944.

Town Planning, Hong Kong. *The Facts.* Hong Kong Government Information Services, July, 1991.

Tsing Tai Chow. *Masters Thesis on China.* Los Angeles: University of Southern California, 1950.

United States Department of Commerce Bureau of the Census. *1980 Census of Population. General Population Characteristics. United States Summary.* Washington, D.C.: United States Government Printing Office, 1981.

———. *Statistical Abstracts of the United States.* Washington, D.C.: U.S. Government Printing Office, 1991.

Unwin, Raymond. *Nothing Gained in Overcrowding.* London: Garden Cities an Town Planning Association, 1912.

Weimar, Arthur, and Hoyt, Homer. *Principles of Real Estate.* New York: The Ronald Press Co., 1954.

Wright, Henry. *Rehousing Urban America.* New York: Columbia University Press, 1935.

PART 4

Abrams, Charles. *Revolution in Land.* N.Y.: Harper & Bros. 1939.

Adams, Thomas. *Outline of Town and City Planning.* New York: Russell Sage Foundation, 1935.

Bauer, C. *The Pattern of Urban and Economic Development.* American Academy of Political Science Annals, May, 1956.

———. *City and Regional Papers.* Edited by Arthur C. Comey. Cambridge: Harvard University Press, 1946.

Bogardus, E. S. *Fundamentals of Social Psychology.* New York: D. Appleton-Century Co., 1942.

Bogue, D. J., ed. *Applications of Demography: The Situation in the United States in 1975.* Oxford, Ohio: Scripps Foundation Studies in Population, 1957.

Citizens' Housing and Planning Council of New York. *A Citizen's Guide to Rezoning.* New York: 1959.

Frank, Denise P. and Frank, Michael J. *Planning.* American Society of Planning Officials. p. 340. Chicago: 1978.

Friedmann, John. *The Good Society.* Los Angeles: UCLA, June, 1976.

agman, Donald G. *Urban Planning and Land Development Control Laws*. St. Paul: West Publishing Co., 1975.

———. *Housing and Urban Development Program 1989–1990*. Washington, D.C.: United States Department of Housing and Urban Development.

cRae, John. *Elderly in the Environment— Northern Europe*. Gainesville: University of Florida, 1975.

Moody, W. D. *Wacker's Manual of the Plan of Chicago*. Chicago: Calumet Publishing Co., 1916.

Myers, William, Dorward, Robert, & Kline, David. "Social Ecology and Citizens Boards: A Problem for Planners." *A.I.P. Journal*, April, 1977.

National Municipal League. *The Citizen Association: How to Organize and Run It*. New York: 1958.

———. *The Citizen Association: How to Win Civic Campaigns*, 2nd ed. New York: 1959.

Opportunities for Building Rental Properties. Conference on Local Residential Construction. Washington, D.C.: Chamber of Commerce of the United States, 1937.

Scott, Mel. *Cities Are For People*. Los Angeles: Pacific Southwest Academy, 1942.

Stern, Sylvia. *Housing the Elderly in Europe*. Unpublished paper. Los Angeles: UCLA, 1978.

Walker, Robert Averill. *The Planning Function in Urban Government*. Chicago: University of Chicago Press, 1950.

Webster, Donald H. *Urban Planning and Municipal Public Policy*. New York: Harper and Row, 1958.

Wood, Robert. *1400 Governments*. Cambridge: Harvard University Press, 1961.

PART 5

———. *Aesthetic Control in Historical Areas*. 933 Mass. 773 and 783 (1955).

ASCORAL. *Les Trois Establissement Humains*. Paris: DeNoel, 1945.

Bassett, Edward M. *Zoning*. N.Y.: Russell Sage Foundation. 1940.

Bettman, Alfred. *The Decisions of the Supreme Court of the U.S. in the Euclid Village Zoning Case*. University of Cincinnati Law Review, March, 1957.

———. *City and Regional Papers*. Edited by Arthur C. Comey, Cambridge Harvard University Press, 1946.

———. *Eminent Domain*. Cal Juris Zd, #85 Am. Jur. Zd Eminent Domain #157 seq.

Chase, Stuart. *Zoning Comes to Town*. Readers Digest, Feb., 1957.

Hagman, Donald G. *Urban Planning and Land Development Common Laws*. St. Paul: West Publishing Co., 1975.

Highway Research Board. *Parking Requirements in Zoning Ordinances*. Bulletin 99, Publication 347. Washington, D.C.: 1955.

———. *Zoning for Truck-Loading Facilities*. Bulletin 59, Publication 243. Washington, D.C.: 1952.

Housing and Home Finance Agency. *Suggested Land Subdivision Regulations*. Wash., D.C.: Division of Housing Research, 1952.

Lautner, Harold W. *Subdivision Regulations: An Analysis of Land Subdivision*. Chicago: Public Administration Service, 1941.

———. Lectures on Land Use Law for Planners and Lawyers, American Inst. of Certified Planners Training Service, 1982.

LAWS RELATED TO PLANNING

Federal Constitution, 14th Amendment, (1869)

California Laws Related to Conservation and Planning, Section 65300.

LeCorbusier. *When the Cathedrals Were White*. New York: Reyhal and Hitchcock, 1947.

LEGAL CHALLENGES, EARLY

Berman v. Parker, 348 W.S. 26 75 Supreme Court 98. 99 99 Law Ed. 27 (1954).

Brougher v. Board of Public Works, 205 California 426 (1928).

Camp. V. Board of Supervisors, 123 California Appellate 331, (1981).

Chicago B & R Co. v. Drainage Commissioners 200 U.S. 561, 592.

Ex Parte Lacy, 108 California 326.

Ex Parte Shrader, San Francisco (1867).

Fritts v. City of Ashland, Court of Appeals of Kentucky 348 S. W. Zd. 712, June, 1961, Zoning Digest, ASPO October, 1961.

Golden v. Planning Board, Town of Ramzpo, New York, 1972.

Hadacheck v. Sebastian, 2390. Supreme Court 394 60 Law Ed. 348.

Housing Act of 1949 U.S.

Munn v. Illinois 94 U.S. 113 (1876).

Parker v. Otis (Police Power) 130 California 332.

Passaic v. Patterson, 62A, 267 New Jersey Supreme Ct. (1905).

Racial & Ethnic Restrictions Not Enforceable U.S. Supreme Court (1964).

Smith v. Collison, 119 California Appellate, 180 (931).

Tenement House Act of 1901, (New York)

Village of Euclid, Ohio v. Ambler Realty, 272 U.S. 365 (1926).

Windsor v. Whitney, 95 Connecticut 357, 363.

Wolf, Charles, Packing Co. v. Court of Industrial Relations, State of Kansas, 262 U.S. 522 (1923).

Yick Wo v. Hopkins, San Francisco, 118 U.S. 356 (1895).

LEGAL CHALLENGES, RECENT

Mt. Laurel Ruling. . . . Municipalities Shall Accommodate Their Fair Share of Low and Middle Income Housing. New Jersey Supreme Court, 1975. So. Burlington, NV NAACP v. Township of Mt. Laurel, 67 N.J. 15 336 A. Zd, 713.

Environmental Impact Report and Comprehensive Plan

Twain Hart Homeowners Association v. County of Tuolumne, December, 1982. 138 Cal App 3rd 664, California Court of Appeals.

Growth Control and Comprehensive Plan

Garat v. City of Riverside, August 1, 1989, Riverside County Superior Court Case No. 191567.

Inadequacy of Comprehensive Plan

Concerned Citizens of Calavaras County v. Board of Supervisors of Calavaras County, March 26, 1985. 166 Ca. App 3 90, Third District Court of Appeals.

Keystone Bituminous Coal Association v. DeBenedictus, 107 Supreme Court 1232, 1987.

Mt. Laurel II, *"The ruling of the court required each community to take steps to encourage construction of lower income units."* New Jersey Supreme Court, 1983.

Subdivision Maps

Camp v. Board of Supervisors, California
Court of Appeals, September 1, 1981.
123 Ca App. 3d 331.
Taking—Flood Control
First English Evangelical Lutheran Church
of Glendale, CA. v. County of Los
Angeles, June 9, 1987, 55 USLW 1781,
U.S. Supreme Court.
Taking—Coastal Commission
Nollan v. California Coastal Commission
June 26, 1987 55 USLW, 5154 United
States Supreme Court.
Taking—Coastal Commission v. Superior
Court
California Coastal Commission v. Superior
Court, May 18, 1989 as modified June 9,
1989, 210 Cal App 3d, 1488 Fourth
District Court of Appeals.
Lovelace, Eldridge, and Weismantel, William
L. *"Density Zoning: Organic Zoning of
Planned Residential Developments."* Urban
Land Institute, Technical Bulletin No.
42, July, 1961.
Lynch, Kevin. *The Image of the City*.
Cambridge: Technology Press and
Harvard University Press (Publication of
the Joint Center for Urban Studies),
1960.

McHarg, Ian. *Design with Nature*. New York:
Doubleday, 1971.
McHugh, K. S. Commission. *Local Planning
and Zoning*. State of New York,
Department of Commerce, 1960.
Merriam, Robert E. *The Subdivision of Land:
A Guide for Municipal Officials in the
Regulation of Land Subdivision*. Chicago:
American Society of Planning Officials,
1942.
Metzenbaum, James. *The Law of Zoning*. 3
Vols. and Supplement. New York:
Baker, Voorhis, 1955, 1961.
Moore, Charles Daniel Burnham. *Architect,
Planner of Cities. Boston, 1921*.
———. *"Mr. Ford's Page."* The Dearborn
Independent. Dearborn, Michigan:
1922.

National Housing Agency. *A Checklist for the
Review of Local Subdivision Controls*.
Washington, D.C.: U.S. Government
Printing Office, 1947.

Osborn. F. J. *Nothing Gained by High Density*.
London: Town and County Planning
Association, 1953.
Owings, Nathaniel. *The Spaces in Between:
An Architect's Journey*. New York:
Houghton Mifflin Co., 1973.

Perloff, Harvey S., Ed. *Planning and the Urban
Community*. Pittsburgh: University of
Pittsburgh Press, 1961.
*Planning Policies of American Institute of
Planners*, 1977.

Redman, Albert E. *Steps to Secure Sound
Zoning*. Columbus: National Industrial
Zoning Committee, 1958.

Santa Clara Co. Planning Dept. *Exclusive
Agricultural Zoning*, 1938.
Schulz, E. E. *Performance Standards in Zoning
Ordinances*. Pittsburgh: Air Pollution
Control Association, 1959.
Scott. Mel. *Cities Are for People*. Los Angeles:
Pacific Southwest Academy, 1942.
Siegel, Shirley Adelson. *The Law of Open
Space: Legal Aspects of Acquiring or
Otherwise Preserving Open Space in the
Tri-State New York Metropolitan Region*,
N.Y.: Regional Plan Association, 1960.
Stewart, Lyle A. *"Tax Increment Financing of
Redevelopment."* Unpublished paper,
1983.
Superintendent of Documents. *Suggested Land
Subdivision Regulations*. Washington, D.C.:
U.S. Government Printing Office, 1960.

Tax Reform Act of 1976. Washington, D.C.:
Reprint of Legislation. National Trust
for Historic Preservation, 1984.

United States Chamber of Commerce.
Zoning and Civic Development.
Washington, D.C.: Construction and
Civic Development Department, 1950.
United States Department of Agriculture.
Talks on Rural Zoning. Washington,
D.C.: United States Government
Printing Office, 1960.
———. *To Hold This Soil*. Washington,
D.C.: United States Government
Printing Office, 1938.
———. *The Way and How of Rural Zoning*.
Bulletin No. 196. Washington, D.C.:
United States Government Printing
Office, 1958.

Yokley, E. C. *Zoning Law and Practice, Vols.
1 and 2*. Charlottesville: The Michie Co.,
1958.

PART 6

Abrahamson, Julia. *A Neighborhood Finds
Itself*. New York: Harper & Row 1959.

Abrams, Charles. *Revolution in Land*. N.Y.:
Harper & Bros. 1939.
Adams, Thomas. *Design of Residential Areas*.
Cambridge: Harvard University Press.
1934.
———. *"What Proportion of Public Land and
Private Land Should be Reserved for Open
Space."* American City, June, 1928.
Adams, Frederick J. *Density Standards for
Multi-Family Residential Areas*.
Cambridge: American Institute of
Planners, 1943.
Alterman, Rachelle, and Hill, Morris.
*"Implementation of Urban Land Use
Plans."* Wash., D.C.: A.I.P. Journal,
July, 1978.
American Association of State Highway
Officials. *A Policy of Arterial Highways
Urban Areas*. Washington, D.C.: 1957.
American Automobile Association. *Parking
and Terminal Facilities*. Washington,
D.C.: 1940.
———. *Parking Manual: How to Solve
Community Parking Problems*.
Washington, D.C.: 1946.
———. *Roadside Protection*. Washington,
D.C.: 1951.
American City Planning Institute. *"Control
Land Subdivision and Building
Development."* City Planning, July, 192
American Institute of Planners, California
Chapter. *California Planning Commission
Handbook*. Sacramento: 1954.
American Public Health Association. *Planni
the Neighborhood*. Chicago: Committee
on the Hygiene of Housing, Public
Administration Service, 1960.
American Public Works Association. *Airpor
Location, Design, Financing, Zoning, and
Control*. Chicago: 1954.
American Society of Planning Officials.
*"Preliminary Report of Committee on Park
& Recreation Standards."* In ASPO
Proceedings, 1943.
———. *"A Program for Tax Abandoned
Lands."* Chicago: In American Society
Planning Officials Proceedings, 1942.
———. *"A Model State Subdivision Control
Act."* In American Society of Planning
Officials Proceedings, 1947.
American Society of Planning Officials.
*Exclusive Industrial and Commercial
Zoning*. Planning Advisory Service
Information Report No. 91. Chicago:
1956.
———. *The Restoration of Nonconforming Use
Planning Advisory Service Information
Report No. 94. Chicago: 1957.
Anderson, Nels, and Linderman, E. C. *Urb

Sociology. New York: Alfred A. Knopf, 1928.

nnual Report of the Council for Environmental Quality. *Solving Environmental Problems.* Washington, D.C.: 1990.

rnold, Christopher, and Reitherman, Robert. *Building Configuration and Seismic Design—Architecture of Earthquake Resistance.* Menlo Park: Building Systems Development, Inc., 1981.

aker, Geoffrey, and Funaro, Bruno. *Parking.* New York: Reinhold Publishing, 1958.

artley, Ernest A., and Bair, Frederick H. Jr. *Mobile Home Parks and Comprehensive Community Planning.* Studies in Public Administration #19. Public Administration Clearing Service. Miami: University of Florida, 1960.

asset, Edward M. *Model Laws for the Planning of Cities, Counties and States.* Cambridge: Harvard University Press, 1935.

———. *The Master Plan.* New York: Russell Sage Foundation, 1940.

———. *Zoning.* New York: Russell Sage Foundation, 1940.

Black, H. *"Detroit: A Case Study in Industrial Problems of a Central City."* Land Economics, August, 1958.

Black, Russell Van Nest. *Planning the Small American City.* Chicago: Public Administration Service, 1944.

Blucher, Walter H., Executive Director ASPO. *Planning Part I.* Chicago: 1945.

Blumenfeld, Hans. *"Are Land Use Patterns Predictable?"* A.I.P. Journal, May, 1959.

Breese, G. W. *Industrial Site Selection, Burlington County, N.J.* A Case Study of Existing and Potential Industrial Location. Princeton: Princeton University Press, 1954.

Brown, Thomas II. *"Long Range Aviation Planning in the Northwest."* Westport, Connecticut: Traffic Quarterly. End Foundation for Transportation, January, 1979.

Buckley, James C. *"Comprehensive Transportation and Terminal Planning for Large Urban Centers."* A.I.P. Journal, Winter, 1947.

Bureau of Public Roads. *Toll Roads and Free Roads.* Washington, D.C.: Department of Agriculture, 1939.

Butler, George. *Introduction to Community Recreation.* New York: McGraw-Hill, 1940.

California Division of Highways. *Los Angeles Regional Transportation Study.* Los Angeles: 1960.

California Environmental Quality Guidelines. *Hazardous Waste.* State of California, Office of Planning and Research, Sacramento: 1981.

California State Reconstruction and Reemployment Commission. *Forecasting a City's Future.* Sacramento: 1946.

Central Association of Seattle. *"Planning the Future of Seattle's Central Area."* A report from the Planning Commission. Seattle: 1959.

Chapin, F. Stuart, Jr. *Urban Land Use Planning.* New York: Harper & Row, 1957.

———. *Shopping Centers: Design and Operation.* New York: Reinhold Publishing, 1951.

Churchill, Henry, and Ittleson, Roslyn. *Neighborhood Design and Control.* An Analysis of the Problem of Planned Subdivisions. New York: National Committee on Housing, 1944.

City of Detroit, City Planning Commission. *Proposed Generalized Land Use Plan.* Detroit: 1947.

Claire, William H. *Study of a Truck Terminal Under A Freeway.* Los Angeles: Community Redevelopment Agency, 1952.

Clawson, Marion. *The Dynamics of Park Demand.* New York: Regional Plan Association, 1960.

———. *Methods of Measuring the Demand For and Value of Outdoor Recreation.* Washington, D.C.: Resources for the Future, Inc., 1959.

———. Held, R. Burnell, and Stoddard, Charles II. *Land For The Future.* Baltimore: Johns Hopkins University Press, 1960.

Collison, Peter. *"British Town Planning and the Neighborhood Idea."* Oxford University Housing Center Review: 6.

———. *Computer Revolution.* Urban Transportation Perspective & Prospects, Eno Fnd. for Transportation. Westport, CN: 1982.

———. *Community Builders Handbook.* Executive Edition. Washington, D.C.: Urban Land Institute, 1960.

———. *Community Centers as a Moral Force.* International Journal of Ethics Vol. 30. April, 1920.

Contini, Edgardo. *The Renewal of Downtown U.S. A.* Los Angeles: Victor Gruen & Associates, 1956.

Council on Environmental Quality 12th Annual Report. Washington, D.C.: U.S. Government Printing Office, 1982.

County of Los Angeles Regional Planning Commission. *"Master Plan of Airports."* Los Angeles: 1940.

Crane, Jacob. *Urban Planning—Illusions and Reality.* New York: Viking Press, 1973.

Dahir, James. *The Neighborhood Unit Plan.* New York: Russell Sage Foundation, 1947.

Davis, David I. and Pavlinski, Lawrence A. *Traffic Quarterly.* Westport, Conn.: Eno Foundation for Transportation, July, 1978.

Davis, Harmer E. *How May the Planning, Financing, and Construction of Vehicular and Mass Transit Systems in the Modern Metropolitan Areas Be Integrated?* Part I: A Statement of the General Problem. Berkeley: University of California, 1955.

De Leuw, Cather & Co. *Report on Parking Facilities for the City of Chicago.* Chicago: 1956.

Denby, Elizabeth. *Europe Rehoused.* New York: W. W. Norton, 1938.

Denver Planning Office. *"Lower Downtown Denver."* Denver, Colorado, 1958.

Detroit City Plan Commission. *Neighborhood Conservation.* Detroit: Committee for Neighborhood Conservation and Approved Housing, 1956.

Dobriner, William M. *The Suburban Community.* New York: G. P. Putnam's Sons, 1958.

Dowling, Robert. *"Neighborhood Shopping Centers."* Architectural Forum. October, 1943.

Eckbo, Garrett. *Landscape for Living.* N.Y.: F. W. Dodge Corp., 1950.

Eisner, Simon. *"Freeways for the Region."* County of Los Angeles Regional Planning Commission, 1943.

Eisner, Smith, and Associates. *Palm Springs, CA: Highland Hills Plans.* San Bernardino, 1982.

Englehardt, N. I., Jr. "The School Neighborhood Nucleus." *Architectural Focus.* October, 1943.

Englehardt. N. I. and Engelhardt, F. *Planning School Building Programs.* New York: Columbia University Press. 1930.

Fagin, II, and Wemberg, K. C., eds. *Planning and Community Appearance.* N.Y.: New York Regional Plan Association, 1958.

Fawcett, C. B. *A Residential Unit for Town*

and Country Planning. London: University of London Press, 1943.

Federal Census of the United States. Examples of Types of Statistics. 1980 Census.

Federal Housing Administration. Planning Profitable Neighborhoods. Washington, D.C.: 1938.

Foley, Donald L. "The Daily Movement of Population Into Central Business Districts." Amer. Sociological Review, Oct., 1952.

Ford, George B. Building Height, Bulk and Form. Cambridge: Harvard University Press, 1931.

Ford, Henry. Ford Ideals. A Selection from "Mr. Ford's Page" in the Dearborn Independent. Dearborn: The Dearborn Publishing Company, 1922.

Freilich, Robert H. and Ragsdale, John W., Jr. Development Framework Data Report. St. Paul: Metropolitan Council of the Twin City Area, 1974.

Garrison, William L., and Marts, Marion E. Influence of Highway Improvements on Urban Land: A Graphic Summary. Highway Economic Studies. Seattle: University of Washington, 1958.

Geddes, Normal Bel. Magic Motorways. N.Y.: Random House, 1940.

Goldston, Ell, and Scheur, James II. "Zoning of Planned Residential Developments." Harvard Law Review, Dec., 1959.

Goodman, Percival and Paul. Communitias. Chicago: University of Chicago Press, 1947.

Gruen, Victor. The Heart of Our Cities. New York: Simon and Schuster, 1964.

Gruen, Victor, and Smith, Larry. Shopping Towns U.S.A. New York: Reinhold Publishing Corp., 1960.

Haar, Charles M. Land Use Planning. Boston: Little, Brown & Co., 1959.

Haar, Charles M., and Hering, Barbara. "The Lower Gwynedd Township Case: Too Flexible Zoning or an Inflexible Judiciary?" Harvard Law Review, June, 1961.

Hagman, Donald. "A New Deal: Trading Windfalls for Wipeouts." Planning, September, 1974.

Herrey, Hermann. "Comprehensive Planning for the City: Market and Dwelling Place, Part I, Traffic Design." Pencil Points, April, 1944.

Heyer, Paul. Architects on Architecture. New York: Walker, 1966, p. 195.

Highbee, Edward. The Squeeze: Cities Without Space. New York: William Morrow & Co., 1960.

Highway Research Board. Parking Requirements in Zoning Ordinances. Bulletin 99, Publication 347. Washington, D.C.: 1955.

———. Zoning for Truck-Loading Facilities. Bulletin 59, Publication 243. Washington, D.C.: 1952.

Hjelte, George. The Administration of Public Recreation. New York: Macmillan Publishing Co., 1939.

Horack, F. E. D. Jr., and Nolan, V., Jr. Land Use Controls. St. Paul: West Publishing Co., 1955.

Horwood, Edgar M., and Boyce, Ronald R. Studies of the Central Business District and Urban Freeway Development. Seattle: University of Washington Press, 1959.

———. Housing Act of 1949. Washington, D.C.: Journal of the American Institute of Planners XV, Fall, 1949.

Hong Kong 1991. A Review of 1990, Hong Kong. Hong Kong Government Information Service. 1991.

Housing and Urban Development, Washington, D.C.: "Historic Preservation Plan." Savannah, GA: 1973.

Hoyt, Homer, Urban Land. September, 1961.

Hurd, Fred W. "These Traffic Factors Are Involved in Intersection Design." Traffic Quarterly, 1953.

Huth, Mary Jo and Schneider, Jerry B. "Toward a Multimodel Structure." Traffic Quarterly, ENO Foundation for Transportation, Westport, April, 1983.

Hyde, D. C. "Fringe Parking." Traffic Quarterly, July, 1953.

Ingraham, J. Modern Traffic Control. New York: Funk & Wagnalls, 1954.

Issacs, Reginald R. "Are Neighborhoods Possible?" Journal of Housing, July, 1948.

———. "The 'Neighborhood Unit' Is an Instrument for Segregation." Journal of Housing, August, 1948.

Jurkat, E. H. "Land Use Analysis and Forecasting in Traffic Planning." Traffic Quarterly, April, 1957.

Kaptur, Marcia C. "Neighborhoods and Urban Policy: A View From the White House." Practical Planner, September, 1978.

Kelley, Eugene J. "Shopping Centers: Location Controlled Regional Centers." Traffic Quarterly, 1956.

Kennedy, G. Donald. Modern Highways. Rept. of Conference Committee on

Urban Problems, U.S. Chamber of Commerce, Wash., D.C.: 1944.

Knack, Ruth Eckdish. "Malls 20 Years Later. Washington, D.C.: A. P. A. Planning Magazine, December, 1982.

———. Theory and Principles of Cluster Housing. Washington, D.C.: Planning Magazine of the American Planners Association, September, 1990.

Kostka, Vladimir Joseph. Neighborhood Planning. Winnipeg: University of Manitoba School of Architecture, 1957.

Lang, Laura. Planning and The Computer. Planning, Magazine of American Planners Association.

Lang, Laura. Micro-Computer Application to Support Safety and Traffic Operation. Washington, D.C.: Planning, Magazine American Planners Association, 1990.

League of California Cities. Noise Element Guidelines. Sacramento, CA: Planning Commissioners Handbook, 1984.

———. Planning Residential Subdivisions. Winnipeg: University of Manitoba School of Architecture, 1954.

Lederman, Alfred, and Trachsel, Alfred. Creative Playgrounds and Recreation Centers. New York: Frederick A. Praeger, 1959.

Lewis, David. The Pedestrian in the City. New York: D. Van Nostrand Co., 1966.

Litchfield Park Study, Arizona: Bureau of Educational Research and Services, 1968.

Lohmann, Karl. Principles of City Planning. NY: McGraw-Hill, 1931.

MacElwee, Roy S. Ports and Terminal Facilities. New York: McGraw-Hill, 1926.

Mace, Ruth L., Ed. Guidelines for Business Leaders and City Officials to a New Central Business. Chapel Hill: University of North Carolina, Institute of Government, 1961.

Mahoney, John H. Intermodal Freight Transportation. Eno Foundation for Transportation, Westport, Connecticut: 1985.

Malley, Frank H. Location and Function of Urban Freeways: Post War Patterns of City Growth. New York: American Transit Association, 1946.

Mandelker, Daniel R. Green Belts and Urban Growth. Madison: University of Wisconsin Press, 1962.

Mansfield and Sweet, Inc. Town of West Orange. The Comprehensive Plan and Guide to Orderly Growth. New Jersey Supra.

Marks, Harold. *Subdividing for Traffic Safety."* Unpublished paper. Los Angeles County Road Department, Ninth Annual California Street and Highway Conference, University of California, Berkeley, CA 1957.

Master Plan of Land Use. Regional Planning Commission. County of Los Angeles, California: 1939.

Mayer, Jim. *Making the Most of Waste.* Sacramento Bee, 1991.

McClintock, Miller. *Short Count Traffic Surveys and Their Application to Highway Design.* Chicago: Portland Cement Association, 1935.

McKaye, Benton. *The New Exploration: A Philosophy of Regional Planning.* New York: Harcourt, Brace & Co., 1928.

McKaye, Benton, and Mumford, Lewis. *"Townless Highways for the Motorist."* Harper's, August, 1931.

Mintier, J. Laurence. A.I.C.P. *"Future of Metropolitan Downtown to Accommodate Future Growth."* Planning Consultant. Sacramento, California: 1990.

Mitchell, R. B., and Rapkin, C. *Urban Traffic: A Function of Land Use.* New York: Columbia University Institute, Urban Land Use and Housing Studies, 1954.

Mott, Seward H., and Hayden, Buford. *"Providing for Automotive Services in Urban Land Development."* Traffic Qtrly., 1953.

Mott. Seward H., & Wehrly, Max S. *Shopping Center: An Analysis.* Wash.: Technical Bulletin No. 11, Urban Land Institute, 1949.

Moulton, Harold G. *The American Transportation Problem.* Washington, D.C.: The Brookings Institution, 1933.

———. *Moving People in the Modern City.* New York: American Transit Association, 1944.

Muncy, D. A. *"Land for Industry."* Harvard Bus. Review, Mar., 1954.

Murphy, Raymond E., Vance, J.D., Jr., & Epstein, Bart J. *Central Business District Studies.* Worcester: Clark Univ., 1955.

Nader, Ralph. *"Politics of Land: Report on Land Use in California."* New York: Ralph Nader's Study Group, Robert Z. Fellmuth, Project Director, 1973.

National Assn of Real Estate Boards. *Blueprint for Neighborhood Conservation.* Washington, D.C.: The Build American Better Council, 1943.

National Resources Planning Board. *Human Conservation.* Washington, D.C.: U.S. Government Printing Office, 1938.

———. *Transportation and National Policy.* Washington, D.C.: U.S. Government Printing Office, 1943.

National Committee on Urban Transportation. *Better Transportation for Your City: A Guide to the Factual Development of Urban Transportation Plans.* Chicago: Public Administration Service, 1958.

National Federation of Settlements and Neighborhood Centers. *"Neighborhood Goals in a Rapidly Changing World."* Unpublished paper. Action Research Workshop held at Arden House, Harriman, N.Y., 1958.

National Recreation Association. *"Play Space in New Neighborhoods."* A Committee Report on Standards of Outdoor Recreation Areas in Housing Developments. New York: 1939.

National Resources Board. *"Recreation Use of Land in the United States, Vol. IX."* Report of Land Planning Committee. Washington, D.C.: 1938.

Neff, Edgar R. *Planned Shopping Centers vs. Neighborhood Shopping Areas.* Marketing Series No. 3, Business Research Center. Syracuse: College of Business Administration, Syracuse University, 1955.

Nelson, Richard Lawrence. *The Selection of Retail Location.* New York: F. W. Dodge, 1958.

Nelting, Orin F., and Opperman, Paul. *The Parking Problem in Central Business Districts.* Chicago: Public Administration Service, 1938.

Nez, George. *Park and School Standards.* Denver: Intercounty Regional Planning Commission, Urban Land. May, 1961.

———. *Noise Element Guidelines.* Planning Commissioners Handbook. Sacramento: League of California Cities, 1984.

Office of Planning Research. *Housing Element.* Sacramento: California State Planning Law, 1980.

Owen, Wilfred. *The Accessible City.* Washington, D.C.: The Brookings Institution, 1972.

———. *Cities in the Motor Age.* New York: Viking Press, 1959.

Pennsylvania State University College of Agriculture. *"The Economic and Social Impact of Highways."* A Progress Summary of the Monroeville Case Study. Agricultural Experiment Station, University Park, PA, Progress Report 219, 1960.

Perry, Clarence. *The Neighborhood Unit, Vol. 7: Neighborhood and Community Planning.* New York: Regional Survey of New York and Its Environs, 1929.

Peterson, John Eric. *Airports for Jets.* Chicago: American Society of Planning Officials, 1959.

Pfouts, Ralph W. *The Techniques of Urban Economic Analysis.* West Trenton: Chandler-Davis Publishing Co., 1960.

Prytula, George. *Community Mobility Systems.* Washington, D.C.: Community Builders Handbook. Washington, D.C.: Special Report. Urban Land Institute. 1970.

Pushkarev, Boris and Jeffery Zupan. *Combining Transport and Community Development.* Urban Transportation Perspective and Prospects, Eno Foundation for Transportation, Inc., Westport, Connecticut, 1982.

Rannels, John. *The Core of the City.* A Pilot Study of Changing Land Uses in Central Business District. New York: Columbia University Press. 1956.

Rasmussen, Steen Eiler. *"Neighborhood Planning."* Town Planning Review, January, 1957.

Ratcliff, Richard U. *Urban Land Economics.* New York: McGraw-Hill, 1949.

Reidercorn, John H. and F. R. Hearle. *Community Builders Handbook.* Washington, D.C.: Urban Land Institute, 1968.

Renne, R. I. *Land Economics, Rev. ed.* New York: Harper & Row, 1958.

Roterus, Victor. *"The Economic Background for Local Planning."* In Proceedings, Annual Meeting of American Society of Planning Officials. Chicago: 1946.

Saarinen, Eliel. *The City: Its Growth, Its Decay, Its Future.* New York: Reinhold Publishers, 1943.

Sacramento Energy Commission. *Solar Access.* A Guidebook for California Communities. Sacramento, 1980.

Segoe, Ladislas. *Local Planning Administration, 1st ed.* Chicago: International City Managers' Association, 1941.

Sharp, Thomas. *The Anatomy of the Village.* Harmondsworth, Middlesex, Penguin Books, 1946.

Shoup, Donald C., and Pickrell, Don H. *Free Parking as a Transportation Problem.* Washington: U.S. Department of Transportation Office of University Research, 1980.

Smith, Larry. *"Space for the CBD's Functions." Journal of the American Institute of Planners, February, 1961.*

Smith, Paul E. *Shopping Centers: Planning and Management.* New York: National Retail Dry Goods Association, 1956.

Smith, Wilbur S., & LeCraw, Charles S. *"Parking."* Westport, CN: Traffic Quarterly, Eno Foundation for Transportation, December, 1946.

Snow, William Brewster. *The Highway and the Landscape.* New Brunswick: Rutgers University Press, 1959.

Spengler, Edwin H. *Land Values in New York in Relation to Transit Facilities.* New York: Columbia University Press, 1930.

———. *Statistical Abstracts.* Washington, D.C.: U.S. Bureau of the Census, 1984 and 1991.

———. State of California, Laws Related to Conservation, Planning and Zoning, Sacramento, State Printing Office, 1959.

Stead, Frank. *Preservation of the Biosphere.* Health News, August, 1974.

Stephens, Dr. William F. *Techniques for Improving the Effectiveness of Ride Sharing Programs.* Eno Foundation for Transportation. Westport, Connecticut: 1990.

Stein, Clarence, and Bauer, Catherine. *"Store Buildings and Neighborhood Shopping Centers."* Architectural Record, February, 1934.

Stonrov, Oscar, and Kahn, Louis I. *You and Your Neighborhood.* New York: J. B. Lippencott, 1937.

———. *Strategy for Building a Better America.* American Institute of Architects, 1972.

Sutherland, Robert I., and Woodward, Julian I. *Introductory Sociology.* New York: J. B. Lippencott, 1937.

Technical Committee on Industrial Classification. *Standard Industrial Classification Manual.* Office of Statistical Standards. Superintendent of Documents. U.S. Government Printing Office, Washington, D.C., 1957.

Thompson, Richard Grant. *A Study of Shopping Centers.* Berkeley: Real Estate Research Program. Institute of Business and Economic Research, University of California, 1961.

Tobias, Katheryn, A.I.C.P. *An Encouraging Note.* Brand. Semour and Rohwer, Attorneys, Sacramento, CA: October, 1990.

Transit Research Foundation of Los Angeles,

Inc. *City and Suburban Travel Issue 2N.* Los Angeles: 1960.

Tratman, E. E. R. *"Unification of Railway Passenger Terminals."* Engineering News-Record, February 14, 1927.

Tuner, D. L. *"The Fundamentals of Transit Planning for Cities."* In Proceedings, 14th Nat'l Conference on City Planning, 1922.

Tyerman, Donald. *Timid Planning.* London: Architectural Forum, September, 1944.

———. *United States Census Report.* Washington, D.C.: Department of Commerce, Bureau of the Census, 1980.

United States Bureaus of Public Roads. *Parking Guide for Cities.* Washington, D.C.: 1956.

United States Chamber of Commerce. *The Community Industrial Development Survey,* Dept. of Manufacturer, Washington, D.C., 1959.

United States Congress. *Control of Advertising on Interstate Highways.* Washington, D.C.: Hearings, Senate Committee on Public Works. March 10, 1958.

———. *The Impact of Suburban Shopping Centers on Independent Retailers: A Report.* Senate Select Committee on Small Bus., 86th Congress, Senate Rept. No. 1016, January 5, 1960.

United States Department of Commerce. *Data Sources for Plant Location Analysis.* Business and Defense Services Administration. Office of Area Development, Superintendent of Documents, U.S. Government Printing Office, Washington, D.C., 1959.

United States Department of Commerce. Bureau of Statistics. *Statistical Abstracts of the United States.* Washington, D.C.: United States Government Printing Office, 1984.

———. *Federal Laws, Regulations, and Other Material Relating to Highways.* Bureau of Public Roads, August, 1960.

———. *General Location of National System of Interstate Highways.* Superintendent of Documents, U.S. Government Printing Office, Washington, D.C., 1958.

———. *Highway Transportation Criteria in Zoning Law and Police Power and Planning for Arterial Streets.* Bureau of Public Roads, Washington, D.C., 1958.

———. *National Airport Plan for 1958.* Superintendent of Documents. U.S. Government Printing Office, Washington, D.C., 1958.

———. *Parking Guides for Cities.* Bureau of Public Roads. Superintendent of Documents, U.S. Government Printing Office, Washington, D.C., 1956.

United States Department of Transportation. *Home-to-Work Trips.* Washington, D.C. Nationwide Personal Transportation Study, December, 1980.

United States Federal Aviation Agency. *Small Airports.* Washington, D.C.: January, 1959.

United States Small Business Administration. *Basic Information Sources of Downtown Shopping Districts.* Washington, D.C.: December, 1955.

Urban Land Institute. *Automobile Parking in Central Business Districts.* Technical Bulletin No. 6, Wash., D.C., 1946.

———. *Community Builders Handbook: Executive Edition.* Washington, D.C.: 1960.

———. *Conservation and Rehabilitation of Major Shopping Districts.* Technical Bulletin No. 22. Washington, D.C., 1954.

———. *Industrial Districts Restudied: An Analysis of Characteristics.* Technical Bulletin No. 41. Washington, D.C., 1961.

———. *New Approaches to Residential Land Development.* Technical Bulletin No. 40. Washington, D.C.: 1961.

———. *A Re-Examination of the Shopping Center Market.* Technical Bulletin No. 33. Washington, D.C.: 1958.

———. *Securing Open Space for Urban America.* Technical Bulletin No. 36. Washington, D.C.: 1959.

———. *Shopping Centers Restudied, Part One: Emerging Patterns.* Washington, D.C.: 1957.

Urban Transportation. *Perspectives and Prospects.* Westport, Connecticut: 1982. Eno Foundation for Transportation, Inc., Edited by Herbert S. Levinson and Robert A. Weant.

Vernon, R. *The Changing Economic Function of the Central City.* New York: Committee on Economic Development, 1959.

Villanueva, Marcel. *Planning Neighborhood Shopping Centers.* New York: National Committee on Housing, Inc., 1945.

Voorhees, A. M., ed. *"Land Use and Traffic Models."* Journal of The American Institute of Planners, May, 1959.

Vuchic, Vukan R., and Shinya Kikuchi. *Design of Outlying Rapid Transit Areas.* Urban Transportation, Perspective and

Prospects, Eno Foundation for Transportation, Inc., 1982.

Wagner, Hulse. *The Economic Effects of Bypass Highways on Selected Kansas Communities.* Lawrence: Center for Research in Business, University of Kansas, 1961.

Watson, Charles S., Jr. *The Land Nobody Knows.* San Francisco: Sierra Club Bulletin, September, 1973.

Weir, L. H. Parks: *A Manual of Municipal and County Parks.* New York: A. S. Barnes Co., 1928.

Weiss, Shirley F. *The Central Business District in Transition.* City and Regional Planning Studies Research Paper No. 1, Department of City and Regional Planning, University of North Carolina, 1957.

Welch, Kenneth C. *Regional Shopping Centers.* Grand Rapids: City Planning Commission, 1948.

Wheaton, William L.C. *Adoption of the Housing Act of 1949.* Journal for the American Institute of Planners, Fall, 1949.

Whitten, Robert, and Adams, Thomas. *Neighborhoods of Small Homes: Economic Density of Low-Cost Housing in America and England.* Cambridge: Harvard University Press, 1931.

Wilbur Smith & Associates. "Parking." *Transportation Quarterly.* ENO Foundation for Transportation. Westport: December 1946.

Williams, Richard L. *"When the Earth is Stretched too Far."* Smithsonian Associates, April/July, 1983.

Williams, Wayne R. *Recreation Places.* New York: Reinhold Publishing, 1958.

Wilson, Leonard U. *"Precedent-Setting Swap in Vermont."* Journal for the American Institute of Architects, March, 1974.

Wingo, Lowdon, Jr. *Transportation and Urban Land.* Washington, D.C.: Resources for the Future, Inc., 1961.

Wood, Elizabeth. *A New Look at the Balanced Neighborhood: A Study and Recommendations.* New York: Citizens' Housing and Planning Council of New York City, 1961.

Wythe, William H. *Assessment of Community Character.* New York: New Yorker Magazine, August, 1990.

———. *Zoning Plan.* Chapter 34.

PART 7

Bartholomew, Harland. *Urban Land Uses.* Cambridge, Mass.: Harvard City Planning Series, Harvard University Press, 1921.

———. "California Voters Support Improvement in Transportation." *Planning Magazine.* August, 1986.

Calavita, Nico. "Trust Funds for Meeting Housing Needs." *Planning Magazine.* June, 1990.

———. *El Pueblo.* Los Angeles: Security Trust and Savings Bank, 1948.

———. *Exclusionary Zoning.* Mt. Laurel, N.J.: 336A Zd 713, N.J., 1975.

Creamer, Daniel B. *Is Industry Decentralizing?* Philadelphia: University of Pennsylvania Press, 1935.

Encylcopedia Britannica, American Revision 1893. "Land Tenure." Chicago: The Werner Company, 1893.

Executive Office of the President. *Report of Council on Environmental Quality, Annual Report 1981.* Washington, D.C.: U.S. Government Printing Office, 1981.

———. *Report of Council on Environmental Quality, Annual Report 1990.* Washington, D.C.: U.S. Government Printing Office, 1990.

Freilich, Robert H., and David T. Greis. "Timing and Sequence Development." Unpublished draft, 1974.

Fritts v. City of Ashland. Court of Appeals of Kentucky, 348 S.W. 2d 712, June 16, 1961.

Fulton, William. "Financing Improvements." *Planning Magazine.* July, 1990.

———. "Funding Sewerage Disposal." Report of the Council on Environmental Quality, 1981.

George, Henry. *Progress and Poverty.* 1879.

Havighurst, Walter. "The Land and the People." *Land Policy Review.* June, 1941.

Ho, Christopher. "Redevelopment Funds for Homeless Housing." *Planning Magazine.* June, 1989.

Housing and Home Finance Agency. *Suggested Land Subdivision Regulations.* Washington, D.C.: Division of Housing Research, 1952.

Housing and Urban Development Agency (HUD). *Community Development Block Grants.* Washington, D.C.: HUD, 1979.

Hoyt, Homer. *One Hundred Years of Land Values in Chicago.* Chicago: University of Chicago Press, 1933.

———. *Structure and Growth of Residential Neighborhoods in American Cities.*

Isard, Walter, and Robert E. Coughlin. *Municipal Costs and Revenues Resulting From Community Growth.* Boston: Federal Reserve Bank of Boston & American Institute of Planners, 1957.

Krohe, James Jr. "Neoclassical Method of Financing Infrastructure Improvements." *Planning Magazine.* August, 1986.

Lautner, Harold W. *Subdivision Regulations: An Analysis of Land Subdivision.* Chicago: Public Administration Service, 1941.

Lovelace, Eldridge, and William L. Weismantel. "Density Zoning: Organic Zoning for Planned Residential Developments." *Urban Land Institute, Technical Bulletin No. 42.* July, 1961.

Mader, George. "Impact Studies." *Planning Magazine.* March, 1980.

McHugh, K. S. *"Local Planning and Zoning."* State of New York, Department of Commerce, 1960.

Merriam, Robert E. *The Subdivision of Land: A Guide for Municipal Officials in The Regulation of Land Subdivision.* Chicago: American Society of Planning Officials, 1942.

Metzenbaum, James. *The Law of Zoning.* 3 vols. and supplement. New York: Baker, Voorhis, 1955, 1961.

Mills, Stephanie. "Need for Economic Planning." *California Tomorrow.* Fall–Winter, 1982.

National Housing Agency. *A Checklist for the Review of Local Subdivision Controls.* Washington, D.C.: U.S. Government Printing Office, 1947.

National Trust for Historic Preservation, Educational Service. *Historic Preservation.* Washington, D.C.: The National Trust for Historic Preservation, 1981.

Osborn, F. J. *Nothing Gained by High Density.* London: Town and County Planning Association, 1953.

Owings, Nathaniel. *The Spaces in Between: An Architect's Journey.* New York: Houghton Mifflin Co., 1973.

Perloff, Harvey S., ed. *Planning and the Urban Community*. Pittsburgh: University of Pittsburgh Press, 1961.

Ranes, Herman. *The Impact of Political Decision Making on Planning*. Master's Thesis, The School of Architecture, Columbia University, 1959.

Redman, Albert E. *Steps to Secure Sound Zoning*. Columbus, Ohio: National Industrial Zoning Committee, 1958.

Sanders, S. E., and A. J. Rabuck. *New City Patterns*. New York: Reinhold Publishing, 1946.

Santa Clara County Planning Department. *Exclusive Agricultural Zoning*, 1958.

Schulz, E. E. *Performance Standards in Zoning Ordinances*. Pittsburgh: Air Pollution Control Association, 1959.

Segoe, Ladislas. *Local Planning Administration*. Chicago: International City Managers Association, 1941.

Training Workshop of the American Institute of Certified Planners. *Methods for Determining Impact Fees*. San Francisco: American Institute of Certified Planners, 1980.

Tunnard, C., and H. H. Reed. *American Skyline: The Growth and Form of our Cities and Town*. Boston: Houghton Mifflin, 1955.

United States Chamber of Commerce. *Zoning and Civic Development*. Washington, D.C.: Construction and Civic Development Department, 1950.

United States Department of Agriculture. *Talks on Rural Zoning*. Washington, D.C.: U.S. Government Printing Office, 1960.

————. *To Hold This Soil*. Washington, D.C.: U.S. Government Printing Office, 1938.

————. *The Why and How of Rural Zoning*. Bulletin No. 196. Washington, D.C.: U.S. Government Printing Office, 1958.

————. *We Need Economic Planning. California Tomorrow*. Fall–Winter, 1981.

Willdan & Associates, Planning Consultants, City of Industry, CA. *Elements of A Growth Management Program*, 1990.

PART 8

Akre, Nancy, ed. *Cities*. New York: Cooper Hewitt Museum, 1982.

American Institute of Architects. *A Plan for Urban Growth: Report of the National Policy Task Force*. Washington, D.C.: American Institute of Architects, 1972.

————. *Strategy for Building A Better America*. Washington, D.C.: American Institute of Architects, 1972.

————. *Structure for a National Policy*. Washington, D.C.: American Institute of Architects, 1972.

Broadeur, Mark J. *Urban Design Guidelines*. Planning Magazine. June, 1987.

Bronson, William. *How to Kill a Golden State*. Garden City, N.J.: Doubleday, 1968.

Brook, James. *Another Indian Homeland (Brazil)*. New York: New York Times, December, 1991.

Brown, Nicholas R. "Design Review Boards." APA Dispatch. August, 1990.

Buttenheim, Harold. *The American Standard of Living*. New York: Architectural Forum, 1948.

Cahn, Robert. *Where Do We Grow From Here?* Boston: Christian Science Publishing Society, 1973.

California Roadside Council, Inc. "More Attractive Communities for California." San Francisco: 1960.

Chamber of Commerce of the United States: "Balance Rebuilding of Cities." Statement issued by the Construction and Civic Development Committee, Washington, D.C., 1937.

Chase, Stuart. *The Road We Are Traveling*. New York: The Twentieth Century Fund, 1942.

————. *For This We Fought*. N.Y.: The 20th Century Fund, 1942.

Cheney, Charles. "Architectural Control of Private Property." Proceedings, National Conference on City Planning. Palos Verdes Estates, CA, 1927.

Comarc Design Systems, Inc. *Computer Graphics Planning Information System*. San Francisco: Comarc, Inc., 1978.

Copenhagen Regional Planning Office. *Preliminary Outline Plan for the Copenhagen Metropolitan Region*. August, 1961.

Dash, Jacob. "A Regional Approach to Local Planning." Unpublished paper presented at International Federation for Housing

and Planning Conference, Jerusalem, 1980.

————, and Elisha Efart. *The Israel Physical Master Plan*. Jerusalem: Ministry of the Interior Planning Department, 1964.

Dahinden, Justus. *Urban Structures for the Future*. New York: Praeger Publishers, 1972.

Dickinson, R. E. *City, Region and Regionalism*. New York: Grove Press, 1954.

Directive Committee on Regional Planning. *The Case of Regional Planning with Special Reference to New England*. New Haven: Yale University Press, 1947.

Downs, Roger M., and David Stea. *Image and the Environment*. Chicago: Aldine Publishing, 1973.

Driskell, David C. *Two Centuries of Black American Art*. New York: Alfred K. Knopf, 1976.

Dudar, Helen. *Superstardom of David Hockney*. Washington, D.C.: Smithsonian Associates, 1988.

Duff, A. C. *Britain's New Towns*. London: Pall Mall Press, 1961.

————. "Early Studies in Community Design." Los Angeles: Report, Section 4, Los Angeles County Regional Planning Commission, 1931.

Eisner, Shelley. "Urban Design." Unpublished article, 1991.

Eisner, Simon. *Art in the Economic Life of the City—Locational Planning*. Los Angeles: Council for the Arts, 1979.

Englebert, Ernest A., ed. *The Nature and Control of Urban Dispersal*. California Chapter of the A.I.P., 1960.

Fagin, H., and R. C. Weinberg, eds. *Planning and Community Appearance*. New York: New York Regional Plan Association, 1958.

Faure, George. "Cities Are For People—Or Are They?" *Christian Science Monitor*. June 14, 1972.

Freidrich, Otto. "The Peales, America's First Family of Art." *National Geographic*. December, 1990.

Friedman, John and William Alonza, eds. Cambridge: Regional Development and Planning, M.I.T. Press, 1964.

Gibberd, Frederick. *Town Design, 3rd Ed*. New York: Reinhold Publishing Corp., 1959.

Golany, Gideon. *New Towns*. New York: Cooper Hewitt Museum, 1982.

...ipaios, Peter. *Impact of New Towns on Central London.* New York: Cooper Hewitt Museum, 1982.

...opius, Walter. *Rebuilding Our Communities.* Chicago: Paul Theobald, 1945.

...ruen, Victor. "The Emerging Urban Pattern." *Progressive Architecture.* July, 1959.

...uttenberg, Albert Z. "City Encounter and Desert Encounter: Two Sources of Regional Planning Thought." *AIP Journal.* October, 1978.

...rove, Noel. "Greenways, Paths to the Future." June, 1990.

...amilton, Calvin and staff. "Location of Artists Centers—The Situation in Los Angeles." Los Angeles City Planning Department, 1985.

...awley, Amos H. *The Changing Shape of Metropolitan America: Deconcentration Since 1920.* Glencoe: Free Press, 1956.

...egemann, Werner, and Elbert Peets. *Civic Art: The American Vitruvius.* New York: Architectural Book Publishing Co., 1922.

...eller, Alfred. *The California Tomorrow Plan.* Los Altos, CA: William Kaufmann, Inc., 1972.

...oustoun, Lawrence O., Jr. "Saving Urban Charm." *Planning Magazine.* December, 1974.

...nter-County Regional Planning Commission. Denver Metropolitan Growth Plan, 1970–2000. 1959.
———. *Introduction to Redevelopment.* Compiled by Community Redevelopment Agencies Association.
———. *Introduction to Urban Land Uses.* Cambridge: Harvard City Planning Series, Harvard University Press, 1932.

Issermann, Andres, W. "The Location-quotient Approach to Estimating Regional Economic Impacts." *AIP Journal.* January, 1977.

Knox, Napthali. "Definition of Urban Design." California Planners Roundtable, 1990.

Kuterman, Udo. *New Architecture in the World.* New York: Universe Books, 1965.

Lewis, David, ed. *Pedestrian in the City.* New York: Universe Books, 1965.

Lynch, Kevin. *The Image of the City.* Cambridge: Technology Press and Harvard University Press (Publication of the Joint Center for Urban Studies), 1960.

Maos, Jacob O. *Changing Patterns of Land Settlement—Israel.* Jerusalem: Papers and Proceedings of the 35th World Congress IFHP, 1980.

McHarg, Ian. *Design With Nature.* New York: Doubleday, 1971.

McKaye, Benton. *The New Exploration: A Philosophy of Regional Planning.* New York: Harcourt, Brace, 1928.

McLuhan, T. C. *Touch The Earth: A Self-Portrait of Indian Existence.* New York: Outerbridge and Dienstfrey, 1971.

Meryman, Richard. "The Wyeth Family." *National Geographic.* July, 1991.

Osborn, Frederic J. "Planning Commentary —U.S.A. on the Way to New Town." *Town and Country Planning.* October–November, 1968.

Osman, John. "Ford Foundation For Adult Education." *Architectural Forum.* August, 1957.

Perloff, Harvey S. "The Arts in the Economic Life of the City." National Endowment of the Arts, 1970–80.

Pfeiffer, John E. "Wall Art." Smithsonian Associates. April, 1983.

Planning Commentary. "U.S.A. on the Way to New Towns." London Town and Country Planning. October–November, 1968.

Pooley, Beverly J. *The Evolution of British Planning Legislation.* Ann Arbor, Michigan: University of Michigan Law School, 1960.

Reade, Eric. "Plan for Copenhagen." *Journal of the Land Planning Institute.* 1961–1962.

Regional Survey of New York and Its Environs. New York: Russell Sage Foundation, 1927–1931.

Vol. I.	*Major Economic Factors in Metropolitan Growth and Arrangement.*
Vol. II.	*Population, Land Values and Government.*
Vol. III.	*Highway Traffic.*
Vol. IV.	*Transit and Transportation.*
Vol. V.	*Public Recreation.*
Vol. VI.	*Buildings: Their Uses and the Spaces About Them.*
Vol. VII.	*Neighborhood and Community Planning.*
Vol. VIII.	*Physical Conditions and Public Services.*
Regional Plan, Vol. I.	*The Graphic Plan.*
Regional Plan, Vol. II.	*The Building of the City.*

Report of the Expert Committee on Compensation and Better? London: September, 1942.

Report of the Potomac Planning Task Force. *The Potomac.* Washington, D.C.: U.S. Government Printing Office, 1967.

Rodwin, Lloyd. *The British New Towns.* Cambridge, Massachusetts: Harvard University Press, 1956.

Rouse, James. *Taming the Metropolis—How to Manage an Urbanized World.* New York: Doubleday & Company, Inc., 1967.

Seldis, Henry. *Henry Moore in America.* New York: Praeger Publishers, 1973.

Sharp, Evelyn. "Architects' Preference for Occasional High Block." *Town and Country Planning.* January, 1961.

Soleri, Paolo. Arcology: *The City in the Image of Man.* Cambridge, Massachusetts: M.I.T. Press, 1969.

Stephenson, Gordon. *New Town Policies in Great Britain: A Brief Description.* Liverpool: Department of Civic Planning, Liverpool University, 1948.

Stein, Clarence S. *Toward New Towns for America.* New York: Reinhold Publishing Corp., 1957.

Urban Land Institute. *The Community Builders Handbook.* Washington, D.C.: The Urban Land Institute, 1968.

Weiss, Shirley. *New Town Developments in the United States.* Chapel Hill: University of North Carolina Press, 1973.

White, Sylvia. "Will the 'Real' Region Please Step Up." *Planning Magazine.* December, 1991.

Wolkomir, Richard. "Art Goes Underground in Boston." Smithsonian Associates, Washington, D.C. April, 1987.
———. *Women Artists 1550–1950.* Museum Associates of the Los Angeles County Museum of Art and Alfred A. Knopf, Inc., New York, and The National Foundation for the Arts, 1976.
———. *World of the American Indian.* National Geographic. 1974.

Ziegler, David S. "Lake Tahoe: Making Growth Management and Regionalism

Work." *Planning Magazine*. December, 1991.

PART 9

Aronovici, C. *Community Building: Science, Technique, Art*. Garden City, N.J.: Doubleday, 1956.

Bauer, Catherine. "Cities in Flux." *The American Scholar*. Winter, 1943–1944.

Cornish, Edward. *Wisdom and Knowledge*. Washington, D.C.: World Future Society Assembly and Exposition, 1982.

Crane, Jacob. *Urban Planning—Illusion and Reality*. New York: Vantage Press, 1973.

Eisner, Simon. *The Future of Cities*. Los Angeles: Cooper Hewitt Museum, 1982.

Futterman, Robert A. *The Future of Our Cities*. New York: Doubleday & Co., 1961.

Herrey, Hermann, Erna Herrey, and Constantine Perzoff. "An Organic Theory of City Planning." *Architectural Forum*. April, 1944.

Huxley, Aldous. *On Living in a Revolution*. New York: Harper & Brothers, 1944.

Jacobs, Jane. *The Death and Life of Great American Cities*. New York: Random House, 1961.

Justement, Louis. *New Cities for Old*. New York: McGraw-Hill, 1972.

Macauley, Rose and Rolff Beny. *The Pleasure of Ruins*. London: Thames and Hudson Ltd., 1964.

———. "Our Continent—A Natural History of North America." *National Geographic*, 1976.

———. "Planning Policies." *California Tomorrow*, 1980.

Saarinen, Eliel. *The City: Its Growth, Its Decay, Its Future*. New York: Reinhold Publishing Corp., 1943.

———. "Splendors of the Past." *Lost Cities of the World*. National Geographic Society, 1981.

———. *The Future Metropolis*. New York: George Braziller, Inc., 1961.

Wolf, Peter. *The Future of the City*. New York: Watson–Guptill Publishings, 1973.

Wood, Samuel E., and Alfred F. Heller. "California, Going, Going, Going." *California Tomorrow.*, 1962.

SUPPLEMENTAL BIBLIOGRAPHY
—CHAPTER 7

Assembly Office of Research. *California 2000: Getting Ahead of the Growth Curve—The Future of Local Government in California*. Sacramento, December, 1989.

Association of Bay Area Governments. "Seizing the Growth Initiative— Assessing the Effects of Ballot Box Planning." *Proceedings of the General Assembly*. San Francisco, October 21, 1988.

Bay Area Council. *Making Sense of the Region's Growth*. San Francisco, November, 1988.

Bay Area Economic Forum. *The Bay Area Economy: A Region at Risk*. Report Summary plus Opinion Survey Results: What the Bay Area's Government and Business Leaders Think. San Francisco, March, 1989.

California Association of Realtors. *California's Housing Crisis: The American Dream Deferred*. Policy Recommendations for State and Local Housing Issues. Los Angeles, August, 1989.

California Councils of Governments. *Growth Management in California: A Policy Statement of the California Councils of Governments*. Palm Springs, April, 1990.

California Economic Development Corporation. *Vision: California 2010. A Special Report to the Governor*. Sacramento, March, 1988.

California Economic Development Corporation. *Vision: California 2010 Revisited. A Special Report to the Governor*. Sacramento, August, 1990.

California Planning Foundation. *Bridging the Land Use/Transportation Planning Gap: Suggested Approaches*. Task Force on Transportation Planning convened by California Planning Foundation and California Chapter, American Planning Association. Sacramento, September, 1988.

California Planning Roundtable. *Welcome to California 1990's. Jobs, Housing, and Transportation . . . The Great Balancing Act*. Sacramento, October 1988.

California Planning Roundtable. *Data in Support of "Welcome to California" 1990's Jobs, Housing, and Transportation . . . The Great Balancing Act."* Compiled and edited by Marucia Britto. Sacramento, November, 1988.

Peter Detwiler, Principal Consultant to the California Senate Local Government Committee, Sacramento

Senate Budget and Fiscal Review Committee. *The Proceedings—The 1989 Senate Budget and Fiscal Review Committee Retreat*. University of California, Berkeley, February 2–4, 1989.

Senate Office of Research. *Does California Need a Policy to Manage Urban Growth?* A Report from the Senate Urban Growth Policy Project, pursuant to Senate Resolution 39 of 1988, authored by Senator Robert Presley, D-Riverside. Sacramento, June, 1989.

Senate Select Committee on Planning for California's Growth and the Senate Committee on Local Government. *Joint Interim Hearing on Growth Management: Local Decisions, Regional Needs, and Statewide Goals*. Sacramento, December 13, 1988.

Southern California Association of Governments. *Growth Management and Transportation Task Force Final Report*. Los Angeles, June, 1990.

INDEX

Note: page numbers in *italics* refer to illustrations